Customer Behaviour

A Managerial Perspective

FIRST CANADIAN EDITION

Customer Behaviour

A Managerial Perspective

FIRST CANADIAN EDITION

JAGDISH N. SHETH
Emory University

BANWARI MITTAL
Northern Kentucky University

MICHEL LAROCHE
Concordia University

Australia Canada Mexico Singapore Spain United Kingdom United States

Customer Behaviour: A Managerial Perspective, First Canadian Edition
by Jagdish N. Sheth, Banwari Mittal, Michel Laroche

Associate Vice President, Editorial Director:
Evelyn Veitch

Publisher:
Veronica Visentin

Marketing Manager:
Kathleen McCormick

Senior Developmental Editor:
Joanne Sutherland

Photo Researcher:
Joanne Sutherland

Permissions Coordinator:
Susan Selby

Content Production Manager:
Jamie Larson

Production Service:
GEX Publishing Services

Copy Editor:
GEX Publishing Services

Proofreader:
GEX Publishing Services

Indexer:
GEX Publishing Services

Manufacturing Coordinator:
Joanne McNeil

Design Director:
Ken Phipps

Interior Design:
Dianna Little

Cover Design:
William Bache

Cover and Part Opener Images:
Henry Hanna/Iconica/Getty Images

Compositor:
GEX Publishing Services

Printer:
Edwards Brothers

Printed and bound in the United States of America
1 2 3 4 10 09 08 07

For more information contact Nelson, 1120 Birchmount Road, Toronto, Ontario, M1K 5G4. Or you can visit our Internet site at http://www.nelson.com

Library and Archives Canada Cataloguing in Publication

Sheth, Jagdish N
Customer behaviour : a managerial perspective / Jagdish N. Sheth, Banwari Mittal, Michel Laroche. — 1st Canadian ed.

Include index.
ISBN-13: 978-0-17-640620-2
ISBN-10: 0-17-640620-4

1. Consumer behavior—Textbooks. I. Mittal, Banwari II. Laroche, Michel, 1945 III. Title.

HF5415.32.S54 2007 658.8'342
C2006-906383-4

To my older brothers:
Himatlal N. Sheth and Gulabchand N. Sheth.
— JS

To the memory of my parents.
— BM

To the memory of my mother, my uncles, and aunts who were always on my side.
— ML

About the Authors

JAGDISH N. SHETH

Jagdish N. Sheth is the Charles H. Kellstadt Professor of Marketing at the Goizueta Business School and the founder of the Center for Relationship Marketing (CRM) at Emory University. Prior to his present position, he was the Robert E. Brooker Professor of Marketing at the University of Southern California and the founder of the Center for Telecommunications Management; the Walter H. Stellner Distinguished Professor of Marketing at the University of Illinois, and a member of the faculty of Columbia University and the Massachusetts Institute of Technology. Dr. Sheth is nationally and internationally known for his scholarly contributions in Consumer Behaviour, Marketing, Global Competition, and Strategic Thinking.

Jag has published more than 200 books and research papers in different areas of marketing. His book *The Theory of Buyer Behavior* (1969) with John A. Howard is a classic in the field. He is also a co-author of *Marketing Theory: Evolution and Evaluation* (1988), *Consumption Values and Market Choices* (1991), *Clients for Life* (2000), *ValueSpace: Winning the Battle for Market Leadership* (2001), and *The Rule of Three* (2002).

Jag is an American Psychological Association Fellow and former President of APA's Consumer Psychology Division and Association for Consumer Research (ACR). He was the recipient of the Viktor Mataja Medal from the Austrian Research Society in Vienna (1977) and the 1989 Outstanding Marketing Educator Award from the Academy of Marketing Science. Jag was also awarded the P.D. Converse Award for his outstanding contributions to marketing theory in 1992 by the American Marketing Association. In 1996, Dr. Sheth was selected as the Distinguished Fellow of the Academy of Marketing Science. In November of 1997, he was awarded the Distinguished Fellow Award from the International Engineering Consortium.

Professor Sheth has worked in numerous industries and for numerous companies in the United States, Europe, and Asia, both as an Advisor and as a Seminar Leader. His clients include AT&T, BellSouth, Comstream, Cox Communications, Ford, Motorola, Nortel, 3M, Whirlpool, and many more. He has made more than 6,000 presentations in at least 20 countries.

BANWARI MITTAL

Banwari ('Ban') Mittal holds a Ph.D. in marketing from the University of Pittsburgh, with a specialization in consumer choice process. Currently, he is a member of the management and marketing faculty at Northern Kentucky University, where he teaches consumer behaviour, advertising and promotion, services marketing, marketing management, and e-marketing. He has previously taught at the University of Pittsburgh, the State University of New York at Buffalo, and the University of Miami. His research topics include consumer attitudes, and response to marketing communications and promotions as well as to services marketing programs. His papers have been published in *Journal of Marketing, Journal of Marketing Research, Journal of Economic Psychology, Psychology and Marketing, Journal of Retailing, Journal of Market-Focused Management, Journal of Applied Social Psychology, Journal of Services Marketing, Health Care Marketing,* and *Journal of Consumer Marketing,* among others. He is an Associate Editor of *Journal of Business Research,* and also serves on the editorial boards of

Psychology and Marketing and *the Journal of the Academy of Marketing Science*. Based on research on how *Fortune*'s "most admired companies" create value for the customer, Ban has coauthored *ValueSpace: Winning the Battle for Market Leadership* (McGraw Hill, 2001).

MICHEL LAROCHE

Michel Laroche, Royal Bank Distinguished Professor of Marketing, holds a Diplôme d'ingénieur (École Centrale de Paris), an M.S.E. (Johns Hopkins), an M.Ph. and a Ph.D. (Columbia), and a Doctor of Science *honoris causa* from the University of Guelph. He is a Fellow of the Royal Society of Canada, a Fellow of the American Psychological Association, and a Distinguished Fellow of both the Society for Marketing Advances and the Academy of Marketing Science. He was also named the 2000 Concordia University Research Fellow, and received the 2000 Jacques-Rousseau Medal for the best multidisciplinary researcher in Canada. He is the first recipient of the Royal Bank Distinguished Professorship in Marketing at the John Molson School of Business. In 2001, the Montreal Chapter of the AMA elected him a member of the Academy of Marketing Personalities. In 2002, he received from HEC-Montreal the fifth *Living Legend of Marketing Award*, and in 2003 the Sprott *Leader in Business Research & Practice* Award.

He is the coauthor of 23 major textbooks (all available in French), including *Marketing in Canada* (*Le marketing: fondements et applications*), *Advertising in Canada* (*Gestion de la publicité*), *Consumer Behaviour: A Canadian Perspective* (*Le comportement du consommateur*), *Marketing Research in Canada* (*Les fondements de la recherche commerciale*), and *Canadian Retailing* (*Les commerce de détail: Marketing et gestion*). Most of these are original Canadian texts. He has also coauthored a major annotated bibliography (published by the AMA) and several workbooks and study guides. He has edited several other books and written several invited book chapters.

He has also published more than 105 papers in, among others, *Journal of Consumer Research*, *Journal of Business Research*, *Journal of the Academy of Marketing Science*, *Journal of Retailing*, *Journal of Cross-Cultural Psychology*, *Journal of International Business Studies*, *Journal of Service Research*, *Journal of Public Policy and Marketing*, *International Journal of Research in Marketing*, *Journal of Economic Psychology*, *Canadian Journal of Administrative Sciences*, *Journal of Retailing and Consumer Services*, *Journal of Consumer Marketing*, *International Journal of Advertising*, *Journal of International Consumer Marketing*, *International Journal of Bank Marketing*, *Journal of Psychology*, *Journal of Social Psychology*, *Behavioral Science*, *Marketing Intelligence and Planning*, *Recherche et Applications en Marketing*, and *Business Forum*.

Preface

Customer Behaviour: A Managerial Perspective, First Canadian Edition, is about the behaviour of customers around the world. Customer behaviour is an extremely dynamic field; it exercises an increasingly visible influence on corporations both small and large, domestic and global. There is a huge body of knowledge about customer behaviour, both on theory and practice, often not published before. We have sought to bring together and give form to this knowledge, which has been accumulated through some 30 years of research, consulting, and teaching experience, and conversations with CEOs, senior executives, business and household customers, researchers, teachers, colleagues, and students on many continents.

Our goal has been to make the book comprehensive in its coverage, managerial in its focus, global in its orientation, and innovative in its organization and presentation. It dwells on the traditional issues in the field and then extends them to emerging topics both in theory and practice. The book goes beyond the conventional subject matter of "consumer behaviour" textbooks in four ways:

- It covers the behaviours of customers both in the household market and the business market. The term *customer* is used to apply to both the individual household members as well as business units who buy products and services in the market.
- The person who pays for the product or service is not always the user, nor is the user always the buyer. This book reaches beyond the usual scope of this field by focusing not only on the buyer but also on the role of the user and the payer. The authors recognize that a person may play one or more of the three customer roles: user, payer, and buyer. Each role makes the person a customer.
- The book adopts a managerial, action-oriented approach to the study of customer behaviour. It makes a connection between the principles of customer behaviour and the elements of marketing strategy, allowing students to see how an understanding of customer behaviour is crucial to creating successful marketing programs.
- The book also casts its view beyond packaged consumer goods that dominate in branding mass media advertising and promotion. In illustrations and applications, we constantly draw upon both goods *and* services (both covered under the term *products*), consumers and business customers, and the domestic and international marketplaces. Specifically, we include significant knowledge about online customer behaviour and the impact of the Internet on customer behaviour, especially in business markets.

A NEW ORIENTATION: CUSTOMER VALUES

In this book, we have adopted a new perspective and framework: customer values. From this perspective, all customer behaviour is driven by the market values customers seek. Six values are proposed, two for each of the three roles: user, payer and buyer. For each role, there is a "universal" value category, sought by all customers, and a "personal" value category, sought by customers as individuals. Specifically, for the user, the universal value is performance and the personal value is social/emotional value. For the buyer, the universal value is service value and the personal value is convenience and personalization; and for the payer, the universal value is price value, and personal value is credit and financing. This framework is used throughout the text to explain the significance of all concepts to diverse customers. The practice of marketing is shifting from a transaction focus to a relationship marketing orientation, and the linchpin of this orientation is the long-term customer retention. We believe that the six-values framework offers marketers an avenue to the practice of relationship orientation and, as a result, to achieving customer satisfaction and retention.

CONTENT AND ORGANIZATION

While striving for uniqueness in content and the three-customer-roles framework, the book is organized for easy understanding into four sections:

I. Customer Behaviour: Power, Scope, and Impact
II. Foundations of Customer Behaviour
III. Customer Decisions and Relationships
IV. Building Loyalty and Customer Value

I. Customer Behaviour: Power, Scope, and Impact What is Customer Behaviour? Who is a customer? Why should students of management study this subject? What role does an understanding of customers play in organizational performance? What do customers seek in market exchanges, and how can organizations respond to customer search for value? What factors determine customer behaviour, and in what manner? And, how are customer behaviour and its determinants poised to change in the coming years? These and related questions are addressed in this section.

In Chapter 1, we begin by defining the concepts of customer characteristics, customer behaviour, customer needs and wants, customer value, and customer roles. We advocate that organizations must adopt customer orientation, and we describe the competitive advantages of such a practice. We introduce the reader to a new view of the customer as playing not one role but three roles (user, payer, buyer) and as seeking a set of role-specific market values (performance, price, and service).

In Chapter 2, we explore various aspects of the environment that surrounds the customer—an environment that is economical, political, social, technological, physical, and ecological. We also explore the role of the customer's personal characteristics such as genetics, age, gender, race, and personality. We describe how these environmental and personal factors help determine customer behaviour.

These determinants are not static; by nature, they change. In Chapter 3, we describe the expected changes in these factors—specifically in customer demographics, technology, and public policy—and map out the manner in which these will in turn alter the marketplace and the future behaviour of customers.

II. Foundations of Customer Behaviour Having discussed the nature of customer behaviour and its external environmental determinants, we move in Part II to "internal determinants": factors and processes that form the mindset of the customer. These include the processes of perception, learning, motivation, and attitude. In Chapter 4, under perception, we describe the perceptual process: biases and distortions in how customers view diverse marketplace offerings. And with regard to learning, we cover the various mechanisms of human learning, from conditioning to modelling to cognitive, and apply that data to the way a customer learns about and adopts new products and innovations.

In Chapter 5, we describe customer motives—the basic internal driver of all human behaviour—and explore their nature and diversity, conscious as well as unconscious. These motives take the form of needs and wants, the entities that bring the customer into the marketplace, searching for satisfying products. Next, we discuss customer emotions as valuable motivators and as the outcomes of many consumption experiences. Finally, we describe customer psychographics—values, self-concept, and lifestyle. It is in order to enact core values, fulfill one's self-concept, and build and live one's chosen lifestyle that customers constantly seek out products.

In Chapter 6, we discuss customer attitudes as the sum total thoughts and feelings toward any product, person, and organization. Attitudes are the most direct precursor of behaviour, and, consequently, the target of all marketplace communications. We describe various models of attitude and explain various processes underlying both attitude formation and change.

Based on this theoretical understanding of the mental processes, from perceptions to attitude, we are now ready to observe and measure these processes in real customers. In Chapter 7, we introduce the reader to the value of researching customer behaviour and explain various research methods of uncovering the customer's mindset and overt behaviour.

III. Customer Decisions and Relationships Having covered both external environmental factors and internal mindset processes in the previous section, Part 3 moves to the core of customer behaviour itself: the customer decision process. We explore this process in individual customers in Chapter 8 and in consumers as groups in Chapter 9. In each chapter, we unravel the steps in the decision process, starting with need recognition and ending with the post-purchase consumption experience.

An important question for marketers is how, when faced with so many product alternatives, do customers choose what they buy. To answer this question, we describe elements of human information processing, or how customers take in and use marketplace information. Then we explain various decision and judgment models that help customers eliminate undesirable and less desirable alternatives in order to finally identify the one likely to be most satisfying.

These same intra-individual decision processes become more complicated when customers have to make decisions in groups such as spouses or whole families. In Chapter 9, we study decision making for three broad groups: families, business firms, and government organizations.

While decision-making models and processes focus on individual instances of customer choice decisions, in practice, many customer choices are ongoing replications of prior choice; they are part of a relationship with vendors, brands, and marketers. In Chapter 10, we describe relationship-based buying and identify customer motivations for it. We then explain the importance of trust and commitment, describe how these motivations are engendered and sustained, and elaborate on the imperative of nurturing suppliers. This important chapter serves the valuable purpose of linking the study of customer behaviour to the new paradigm of business, relationship marketing.

IV. Building Loyalty and Customer Value From a focus on marketplace decisions in the preceding section, we now move to post-choice experience of consumption and exchange. The satisfactions derived from consumption and exchange translate into customer loyalty for products, brands, and stores. We describe, in Chapter 11, various motivations for and distractions from customer loyalty. Knowledge of these favourable and unfavourable factors is valuable for marketers seeking to build customer loyalty and achieve stronger brand equity.

While the marketer must try to build loyalty and brand equity, he or she cannot ignore the newest marketplace reality in the physical marketplace as well in cyberspace: the all-pervasive Internet. And customers are increasingly visiting the cyber marketplace to learn about goods and services, and to buy them. In Chapter 12, we describe customer behaviour as it unfolds in cyberspace. We shed light on the customer advantages of Internet shopping and how the cyber marketplace facilitates customer progress through the various decision-making stages; we also describe various types of cyber markets and how they differ from the customer's point of view.

In the final chapter of the book (Chapter 13), we come back full circle to the concept of customer value (i.e., market values customers seek). Having already described the nature and types of customer value in the opening chapter, here we move to a detailed survey of organizational processes and actions needed to deliver specific customer value. We illustrate these value-driven processes by drawing from a study of *Fortune*'s Most Admired Companies.

SPECIAL FEATURES

Customer Behaviour: A Managerial Perspective, First Canadian Edition, goes beyond the conventional subject matter by examining such issues as:

- the notable influence of our physical environment: climate, topography, and ecology
- government buying behaviour
- researching customer behaviour
- customer decisions by intermediaries such as resellers, buying clubs, and membership groups
- relationship-based buying, reverse marketing, and supplier partnering
- strategies for creating customer values
- trends in customer behaviour, such as anticipated developments in demographics, technology, and public policy on a worldwide basis.

The book also provides expanded and innovative treatment of such topics as:

- models of customer loyalty
- intergenerational influence on household buying behaviour
- simulation, virtual reality, and the Internet as research tools
- the emotional basis of customer motivation
- the role of personality in business buying
- the role of culture in business buying
- major international cultures and subcultures
- customer resistance to innovations

- a model of customer store choice
- brand equity from the customer's point of view.

A notable feature of the book is that, in addition to a full chapter (Chapter 12) on customer behaviour in the cyber marketplace, it incorporates Internet applications of that chapter's concepts throughout the book.

ILLUSTRATIONS AND APPLICATIONS IN THE FIRST CANADIAN EDITION

The subject matter in the text is made relevant and practical for the student by describing applications and narrating stories. Each chapter features illustrative boxes called Window on Research and Window on Practice.

Window on Research showcases current research on significant topics covered in the chapter. Examples include:

- the role that marketing will play as a customer consulting function in the network economy (Chapter 1)
- a profile of the green consumer (Chapter 3)
- the PSYTE Canada Advantage cluster of MapInfo, which categorizes every Canadian neighbourhood into 61 clusters (Chapter 7)
- the Zaltman Metaphor technique for customer research (Chapter 7)
- a virtual-reality consumer research project (Chapter 7)
- perceived risk and business buying behaviour: 25 years of research findings (Chapter 9)
- nurturing a buyer-seller relationship (Chapter 10)

Windows on Practice is a unique collection of current practice stories. Examples include:

- Segmentation of South Asian Consumers in Toronto (Chapter 2)
- Beyond Pink and through the Gender Lens: three examples of Canadian companies that have developed gender-intelligent strategies (Chapter 2)
- Amazon.com—Implications for Dynamic Pricing (Chapter 7)
- How Robin Hood Flour has used the online medium to develop and sustain loyalty (Chapter 12)
- Value in Service Delivery at Harry Rosen (Chapter 13)
- Re-engineering at Canada Post (chapter 13)

Global orientation: The book incorporates examples from around the world in every chapter. For example, we discuss:

- vying for the Chinese cellular phone market (Chapter 2)
- the Japan VALS: A Portrait of Japan in Change (Chapter 5)
- building relationships in Russia (Chapter 10)

- segmenting British supermarket shoppers by loyalty (Chapter 11)
- the impact of the Internet in rural India (Chapter 12)

Internet Applications: The text also incorporates Internet examples for all topics throughout the book, such as:

- characteristics of early adopters of the Internet technology for online shopping (Chapter 4)
- motivations for Web usage (Chapter 5)
- customer relationship management on the Web (Chapter 11)

Opening Vignette: Each chapter opens with a vignette, intended to engage the student's interest from the very beginning, with such captivating stories as:

- how consumer-oriented organizations, like the Vancouver Symphony Orchestra and the Toronto Symphony Orchestra, are finding ways to attract new audiences (Chapter 1)
- how the aging of the Baby Boomers is expected to have a significant impact in the market place in Canada (Chapter 3)
- how Tim Hortons has grown into the nation's top food-service chain (Chapter 11)

Each topic, whether traditional or new, is presented with the current body of knowledge. Where knowledge is still emerging or gaps exist in the current literature, we develop new frameworks and concepts, extending the frontiers of knowledge in the field. The textbook is enriched with topics new to the field, and is unprecedented in its comprehensive treatment. In this aspect, the book is unique; it educates the student's mind with well-established knowledge, and then it piques the student's curiosity to question and explore the still-brewing pot of emerging knowledge.

A LEARNING EXPERIENCE

Writing a textbook is as much about learning the subject ourselves as it is about teaching the student. The process of learning about customer behaviour has spanned three decades. In gathering material for the book and in formalizing what we thought we knew, we were impressed to discover the vast amount of knowledge both in the academic writings and among the practitioners. It is our eclectic sourcing of materials, combined with our own endeavour to fill gaps in the current body of knowledge, that made us at once feel both humble and energized. Truly, we have learned a lot. But our learning has just begun. We expect to continue our journey by benefiting from the feedback from readers and adopters like you. We hope you would write, call, question, and advise us as you use this book.

JS
BM
ML

A Complete and Innovative Support Package

INSTRUCTOR'S RESOURCE CD (IRCD)

The Instructor's Resource CD delivers all the traditional instructor support materials in one handy place: a CD. Electronic files are included on the CD for the complete Instructor's Manual, a Test Bank, a computerized Test Bank (ExamView), and chapter-by-chapter PowerPoint presentation files that can be used to enhance in-class lectures.

Instructor's Manual

The Instructor's Manual for the First Canadian Edition of *Customer Behaviour* contains many helpful teaching suggestions and additional student assignments to help instructors incorporate the text materials into their class. Each chapter includes the following materials, designed to meet the instructor's needs:

- Learning goals and teaching suggestions
- Lecture outline
- Answers to review questions from text
- Suggested comprehensive projects
- Guest speaker suggestions
- Term paper suggestions

Test Bank

The Test Bank includes 2,500-plus questions, including multiple-choice questions, true/false questions, and short essays that emphasize the important concepts presented in each chapter. The Test Bank questions vary in levels of difficulty so that each instructor can tailor his or her testing to meet his or her specific needs.

ExamView (Computerized) Test Bank

The Test Bank is also in a computerized format (ExamView), allowing instructors to select problems at random by type or level of difficulty, customize or add test questions, and scramble questions to create up to 99 versions of the same test. This software is available in DOS, Mac or Windows formats.

PowerPoint Presentation Slides

Classroom lectures and discussions come to life with the Microsoft PowerPoint presentation tool. Extremely professor-friendly and organized by chapter, these presentations outline content and use figures, tables, and graphs pulled directly from the text. The eye-appealing and easy-to-read slides match the internal design of the text and make lectures more interesting.

WEBSITE

Visit the text website at **www.customerbehaviour.nelson.com** to find instructor's support materials and study resources that will help students practice and apply the concepts they have learned in class.

Student Resources

- Online quizzes for each chapter are available on the website for those students who would like additional study materials. After each quiz is submitted, automatic feedback tells the students how they scored and gives the correct answers to the questions they missed. Students are then able to e-mail their results directly to their instructor if desired.
- A list of glossary terms and definitions arranged by chapter is available for extra review of key terms found in the text.
- Students can download the PowerPoint presentation slides from the website to use as lecture notes.
- Internet exercises and the direct weblinks needed to complete the exercises are on the Web for extra student practice and/or research.

Instructor Resources

- Downloadable Instructor's Manual files are available in Microsoft Word format and Adobe Acrobat format.
- Downloadable PowerPoint presentation files are available in Microsoft PowerPoint format.

Acknowledgments

A project of this magnitude cannot be completed without the support of many individuals. An important group among them is the colleagues and teachers of consumer behaviour who reviewed the book. As reviewers, they worked hard to (a) ensure the accuracy of facts, (b) improve readability, (c) suggest leads and research references, and (d) in general, serve as a "second opinion." Their valuable contribution is reflected in the significant improvement of the book.

Ed Bruning, University of Manitoba

Mary-Ann Cipriano, Concordia University

Bill Crowe, St. Lawrence College

Peter Dunne, Memorial University

Hany Kirolos, Georgian College

Anne Lavack, University of Regina

Jim Sherritt, University of Northern British Columbia

Ian Skurnik, University of Toronto

Robert Soroka, Dawson College

Padma Vipat, Douglas College

Barry Wallace, George Brown College

Other individuals contributed more directly to the contents of the First Canadian Edition of the book and its accompanying support materials. Isabelle Miodek worked diligently to assist me in producing the Instructor's Manual, First Canadian Edition, as well as in updating the Test Bank and created the content and template designs for the dynamic PowerPoint presentations.

The First Canadian Edition owes much to the hard work of many individuals at Thomson Nelson Publisher. Veronica Visentin was instrumental in keeping me energized as well as focused. She brought to the project invaluable experience and organizational and leadership skills. Joanne Sutherland's contribution as developmental editor is unparalleled: her many thoughtful additions brought clarity and balance to the material. Equally helpful were the other members of the Thomson Nelson team: the copyeditor, Jerry Cowan; the editorial assistant, Mary Stangolis; the content production manager, Jamie Larson; project manager, Gina Dishman; the designer, Dianna Little; and marketing manager, Kathleen McCormick. To all these fine individuals, I express my sincere thanks.

Finally, I would like to thank my colleagues and associates, as well as my wonderful wife, for their help and support.

Michel Laroche

Brief Contents

Contents

PART 2

Foundations of Customer Behaviour 125

PART 3

Customer Decisions and Relationships 277

PART 1

Customer Behaviour: Power, Scope, and Context

CHAPTER 

The Customer: Key to Market Success

LEARNING OBJECTIVES

After reading this chapter you should be able to:

LO 1 Understand the concept of customer orientation

LO 2 Define customer behaviour

LO 3 Identify the three roles of the customer

LO 4 Explain role specialization

LO 5 Define needs and wants, and identify their determinants

LO 6 Describe the classification of market values

LO 7 Describe the characteristics of customer values.

Who Are the Symphony Orchestra's Customers?

Across Canada, all symphony orchestras are faced with a major dilemma: on one hand, their traditional audiences are shrinking and getting older; on the other, the younger audiences have many different tastes in music, have been weaned on MuchMusic, and spend a large part of their discretionary income on popular culture (e.g., CDs, concerts, etc.). Statistics Canada estimated that in 2001, accumulated deficits for orchestras amounted to more than $18 million.

Consumer-oriented organizations, like the Vancouver Symphony Orchestra (VSO) and the Toronto Symphony Orchestra (TSO), are finding ways to attract new audiences. Audiences for the VSO were down 30 percent by 2002, with a deficit of $1.3 million. The VSO is the fourth largest orchestra and the seventh largest performing arts company in Canada. Ticket sales account for 43 percent of revenues, 24 percent coming from fund raising, and the rest from government subsidies. About 20 percent of the $9.1 million budget is spent for marketing activities.

The VSO's research showed that the younger audiences disliked traditional dress codes and wanted to see and interact with the conductor (instead of watching his or her back). New types of events included a mix of eclectic concerts such as Goldie Hawn introducing a musical tribute to the Dalai Lama, a concert by world-renowned cellist Yo-Yo Ma, and afternoon kids' concerts, with kids going up on stage to try out different instruments and compose their own music, which is then played by a musician. Also, Musically Speaking (sponsored by Telus) is a series in which music director Bramwell Tovey talks to the audience about various composers and their music, with interactions, video screens that show close-ups of musicians' performances, and interviews with soloists about their work and their views on music. Musically Speaking is marketed via brochures distributed through restaurants, cafés and community centres, ads in repertory cinemas, and by Telus to its subscribers via a link with the website mytelus.com. These concerts are all sold out and attracting 25–35-year-old audiences, many of them first-time concert-goers who are clearly enjoying the new experience. As a result, subscriptions and ticket sales are up for the 2004 season, and the VSO is expected to make a small surplus.

For the TSO, the key to the solution was to exploit the ethnic diversity of the Greater Toronto Area (GTA), some of whose residents view acquiring a good musical education and going to concerts as part of their traditions. At first the TSO focused on Chinese families because they have a higher musical literacy than the average family in Canada; about 70 percent of their children take music lessons, and their parents strongly believe that it is good for their children's development. In developing a marketing promotional program for the TSO, care was taken to integrate advertising, public relations, the box office, incentives and promotions, and the use of the correct Chinese languages (Mandarin and Cantonese). The TSO is producing brochures in Chinese, has modified its website to include a Chinese section, and advertises regularly in Chinese newspapers and on Chinese radio programs. For example, while the TSO motto is "We're All Yours," a motto was developed in Chinese to mean "Your Orchestra, Your World of Music." A public relations campaign was developed which included: communications with Chinese music schools and community centres; information about the youth training program at the TSO; placing articles about concerts, and about famous performers such as Yo-Yo Ma and Lang Lang, in the Chinese media; kids' concerts; and discount programs (tsoundcheck.com). From targeting the Chinese families, the TSO moved to Italian, Korean, and Russian families.[1]

The above examples show that even for a symphony orchestra, marketing is not easy these days. It requires a customer orientation. This is true of every company in the marketplace, whether it caters to household or business customers. Several companies have failed in the market because their products were too complex or too expensive; in short, because they did not have a customer orientation, and consequently did not offer any value advantage to customers. Understanding customer behaviour is critical for market success.

WHY UNDERSTANDING CUSTOMER BEHAVIOUR IS IMPORTANT

Just as in the case of the Vancouver and Toronto Symphony Orchestras, businesses everywhere are recognizing the importance of understanding customer behaviour as a key to their success. It is the first step toward meeting the challenges of the exciting world of business. Specifically, it helps companies (a) *satisfy customers*, (b) *adopt their marketing concept*, and (c) *gain legitimacy in society*. Let us discuss each in turn.

Satisfying the Customer

Peter F. Drucker believes that the purpose of business is to create and retain a satisfied customer.[2] He argues that making money is a necessity, not just a purpose. Moreover, a business makes money only if it satisfies its customers by catering to their needs. This has led companies to adopt a **customer culture**—a culture that incorporates customer satisfaction as an integral part of the corporate mission and includes an understanding of customer behaviour and its importance to all its marketing plans and decisions. Lands' End, the second-largest catalog clothing retailer in North America, operates with high inventory levels. Its managers would rather carry excess inventory than fail to fill an order and risk losing a customer. "If we don't keep the customer for several years, we don't make money," said the company's CEO at the time, William End. "We need a long-term payback for the

Customer culture
A culture that incorporates customer satisfaction as an integral part of the corporate mission and plans.

expense of coming up with a buyer."[3] As we move from a traditional to an Internet economy, customers become more demanding, more time-driven, more information-intensive, and more individualistic.[4] They will evaluate marketers on the latter's ability to deliver "total customer convenience"—hassle-free product information search (e.g., advertising-on-demand), hassle-free acquisition (e.g., home delivery), hassle-free consumption (e.g., products that are durable, reliable, and easy to use), and hassle-free disposal. A report by Boston Consulting Group (BCG) states that customers who have had a satisfying first-purchase experience online are likely to spend more time and money online; on average, the satisfied first-time purchaser engaged in 12 online transactions and spent $500 during the previous 12 months; the dissatisfied first-time purchaser engaged in only four transactions and spent only $140 on online transactions.[5]

LO 1 Adopting the Marketing Concept

Selling concept
A firm focuses on persuading the customer to buy what it makes and offers.

Marketing concept
A firm focuses on making what the customer wants.

According to Philip Kotler, the *marketing concept* is an improvement over the *selling concept*.[6] In the **selling concept**, the firm's focus is on finding a buyer for its product and somehow "selling" that customer into parting with his or her cash in exchange for that product. In contrast, under the **marketing concept**, the firm's obsession is to make what the customer needs or wants. The marketing concept can bring a firm greater market success because customers will seek out such products, and these products will meet customer needs better.

Also, the marketing concept entails the market-oriented firm focusing on understanding its customers' dynamic needs and wants. That is, instead of pushing a product on the customer, the firm now assumes a consultative role, helping customers identify products that would best meet their needs. The Window on Research box presents the role that marketing will play in the network economy as a customer-consulting function.

Gaining Legitimacy in Society

If making money is the only goal of an organization, that is not a legitimate reason for society to support businesses. Rather, a society supports businesses because they serve its members by catering to their needs and wants. Focusing on the customer leads to better serving the society's needs. Paying attention to customer behaviour and fashioning a business to respond to customer needs, desires, and preferences amounts to business democracy for a nation's citizens, and serves both public and private interests.[7] The changes taking place in Eastern Europe and China demonstrate how economic democracy is taking a foothold in countries around the world, benefiting both businesses and newly liberated (in both political and economic terms) citizens (i.e., "customers").[8]

Customer orientation
Gaining a thorough understanding of customers' needs and wants, and using them as the basis for all of the firm's plans and actions in order to create satisfied customers.

CUSTOMER BEHAVIOUR AND CUSTOMER ORIENTATION

The principles of customer behaviour serve a company best when they are applied to developing and maintaining a customer orientation. **Customer orientation** (also referred to as **market orientation**) is a thorough understanding of customers' needs and wants, the competitive environment, and the nature of the market, all used to formulate the firm's plans and actions in order to create satisfied customers.[9]

WINDOW ON RESEARCH

Marketing as Seller's Agent to Customer's Agent

Ravi S. Achrol and Philip Kotler specify the role of marketing in the network economy. One of the manifestations of this new development is *customer opportunity networks*. These are organized around customer needs and market opportunities, and are designed to search for the best solutions to them. The core competency of the network is knowledge about product technology. Through a global network of offices and information centres, the network matches consumer needs and inquiries, market intelligence, and economic trends with a worldwide directory of product suppliers, with all relevant information. These matches between customer needs and suppliers will be conveyed to the customers; the transaction will be negotiated and then conveyed to the supplier's or the network company's distribution and delivery systems. In this form, the marketing function may reach its highest level of development as a customer-consulting function, making the marketing-consumer relationship dominant over the marketing-producer relationship. Organizing marketing around the consumer offers at least three important opportunities in the network economy.

First is the opportunity to capitalize on information about consumers as a business asset and, on the basis of its market value, realize appropriate economic rents for consumers for the use of this information. *Infomediaries* will emerge who collect information from consumers and make it available to companies willing to pay for the information in the form of price or value benefits for consumers.

At the same time, the infomediaries could also handle concerns about privacy on the Internet. They could offer the consumer secure portals and protective software to facilitate financial transactions so that the consumer could search commercial websites without their personal information being known to the sites. SuperProfile and PrivaSeek are among the first Web-based infomediary start-ups to emerge, and financial services companies with large existing databases such as Citigroup and RBC Financial Services are experimenting with the concept.

Second is the opportunity to provide consumers with content and usage information about products. Consumers would have access to product performance data, repair and warranty histories, customer comments, sale prices, and promotional offers. As the consumer is inundated with choices, the opportunity network would help to minimize the consumer's effort in searching for, evaluating, and negotiating the best value. The network company will screen suppliers, evaluate their products, compare and rate them, and collect information on product performance and consumer complaints. Thus, there will be a *re-intermediation* by consumer opportunity networks, and network companies could actually consolidate consumer needs (e.g., the travel or grocery needs of a network of consumers for a year) and could seek bids from qualified suppliers.

Third is the opportunity to facilitate such interaction by organizing consumers into lifestyle-related virtual communities, such as communities of retirees, sports fans, or outdoor enthusiasts. Hagel and Armstrong state that commercial success in the online arena will belong to businesses that organize electronic communities to meet multiple social and commercial needs. Electronic communities meet four types of consumer needs: *transaction, interest, fantasy,* and *relationship.*

- *Communities of transaction* primarily facilitate the buying and selling of products and deliver information related to those transactions. Examples are Travelocity.ca and webvine.com, services that sell flight bookings and wine respectively.
- *Communities of interest* bring together participants who interact extensively on specific topics. Gardenweb.com is a community of interest where visitors can exchange gardening experiences and tips, share ideas, request seeds, and ask questions.

(continued)

- In *communities of fantasy*, people create new environments, personalities, or stories. On ESPN.com, participants can indulge in their fantasies by creating their own sports teams (using the names of real players), which then compete against teams created by other participants.
- *Communities of relationship* revolve around certain life experiences that are often intense and can lead to the formation of deep personal connections. The Cancer Forum on Compuserve and groups focused on widowhood or divorce are examples of such groups. These communities have mushroomed to become part of the blogging revolution.

A blog is a "frequent, chronological publication of personal thoughts and Web links," and is derived from *weblog* (Marketingterms.com). A blog can be a mixture of what is happening in someone's life and on the Web, a hybrid diary and guide site. People maintained blogs before the term was coined, but the trend grew with the introduction of automated publishing systems (e.g., Blogger at blogger.com).

Companies develop customer communities that are involved with a company because that company's product represents a significant aspect of their lifestyle, and because those communities can enhance their satisfaction by participating in information- and experience-rich exchanges with the company and among themselves. For example, marketers of recreational vehicles (RVs) hold large conventions at which thousands of RV owners congregate to socialize, exchange experiences, and participate in seminars on RV ownership and recreation. Some other strong brand communities are Apple Computers, Harley-Davidson, Shiseido, and Nintendo. In this millennium, opportunity networks integrated with customer communities represent the most dramatic scenario of a change in marketing techniques.

SOURCES: Adapted from Ravi. S. Achrol and Philip Kotler, "Marketing in the Network Economy," *Journal of Marketing*, Vol. 63, Special issue 1999, 146–63. Arthur Armstrong and John Hagel III, "The Real Value of Online Communities," *Harvard Business Review*, May–June 1996, 134–41. Andrew Sullivan, "The Blogging Revolution," *Wired Magazine*, May 2002.

Frederick E. Webster, Jr. has articulated the role of the marketing function and organization in the corporation as follows: "At the corporate level, marketing managers have a critical role to play as *advocates for the customer and for a set of values and beliefs that put the customer first* in the firm's decision making."[10] At this point, we ask you to take the quiz in the Customer Insight box.

Following a customer orientation provides a company with competitive advantages that lead to higher corporate performance, increased profitability, and revenue growth. There are six advantages, three that increase profitability and three that generate revenue growth. The first three advantages are (1) cost efficiencies from repeat customers, (2) price premiums from established customers, and (3) customer loyalty in corporate crises. The three advantages that generate growth are (1) increased word of mouth, (2) one-stop shopping, and (3) new product innovations.[11] Figure 1.1 on page 8 summarizes these six advantages, which contribute to corporate profits. Following a customer orientation also results in internal success for the company, as it produces a work force that takes pride in its job.

Cost Efficiencies from Repeat Customers

The best way for a company to maintain a competitive advantage in a mature market is to retain its customers. These strategies tend to be less costly than those for gaining new customers. According to some estimates, it costs five times more to attract a new customer than to retain an existing one. Repeat customers mean cost efficiencies. The cost of serving established customers is considerably less than the cost of serving new customers. There are several reasons for this.

CUSTOMER **INSIGHT**

How Customer-Oriented Is Your Firm?

If you are employed by a business firm, take the following survey from your business's perspective. If you are a customer, answer this survey for a company you do business with, based on whatever impressions you may have formed about the firm.

Scale:	Not true	Partially true	True
	−1	0	+1

1. In this business unit, we meet with customers at least once a year to find out what products they will need in the future.
2. Individuals from our manufacturing department interact directly with customers.
3. We periodically review the likely effect of changes in our business environment on customers.
4. Marketing personnel in our firm spend time discussing customers' future needs with other departments.
5. Data on customer satisfaction is collected regularly and disseminated at all levels in this business unit on a regular basis.
6. Our business plans are driven more by customer research than by technological advances.
7. Customer complaints never fall on deaf ears in this business unit.
8. When we find out that customers are unhappy with the quality of our services, we take corrective action immediately.
9. According to top management, serving customers is the most important thing our business unit does.
10. Top managers keep telling all employees that they must gear up now to meet customers' future needs.
11. All managers' salaries and bonuses are partly linked to the level of customer satisfaction.
12. At this firm, everything is done with the customer uppermost in mind.
13. The firm welcomes customer comments and complaints, and tries to do whatever it takes to win a customer over.
14. The employees of this firm with direct customer contact treat their customers as if their pay depends directly on customer feedback.
15. Over time, the firm has offered its customers better value than the competitors.

Scoring: The score could range from −15 to +15. If your score is negative, the firm is not customer-oriented. The firm is unlikely to retain its customers for long. For a score in the positive range, the closer to +15 the firm is, the more customer-oriented it is. Customers of this firm are probably very satisfied with its products. If you are a stockholder, you have reason to be happy, for the firm is likely to be profitable in the long term.

SOURCE: Adapted from Ajay K. Kohli and Bernard J. Jaworski, "Market Orientation: The Construct, Research Propositions, and Managerial Implications," *Journal of Marketing* 54 (April 1990), p. 3. The first 10 questions are adapted from Jaworski and Kohli's research. The last five questions, the scoring method, and suggested score range interpretations are based on the authors' intuition and are offered here to advance student understanding of the customer orientation concept.

FIGURE 1.1 Competitive Advantages through Customer Satisfaction

First, there are economies of scale in manufacturing. Accumulated learning and the resulting increased productivity make it less costly to produce the same item for the same customer. Furthermore, for many products, one has to spend time and energy in offering pre-sale and post-sale service, which new customers require much more than do continuing customers. Salespeople servicing new accounts need more time to familiarize themselves with the purchasing procedures.

The second reason is that dissatisfied customers increase the costs of doing business. At a minimum, dissatisfied customers slow down payments and elevate complaints to higher levels of management. Sometimes, the price a company pays for a dissatisfied customer goes beyond simply losing the customer. The costs of dissatisfied customers are staggering: 96 percent of unhappy customers don't complain about rude service people, but 90 percent who are dissatisfied will not buy again or will tell their story to at least nine other people,[12] and 13 percent of those unhappy former customers will tell of their experience to more than 20 people.[13] Dissatisfaction, in short, gets broadcast widely.

It is also evident to marketers that it is impossible to satisfy all customers—some have unique requirements, their locations are too remote to serve them properly, and their user environments may not be conducive to proper product use. Hence, selecting the right customers and retaining them is an important goal for the company, as we saw in the case of the Vancouver Symphony Orchestra. Finally, it is easier to prevent dissatisfaction than to correct it after it is created. It is, therefore, extremely important not to create unrealistic expectations. The higher the expectations a firm creates, the higher the cost of correcting them if customer expectations are not met by their product experience.

"Customer loyalty, measured in repeat purchases and referrals, is the key driver of profitability for online businesses, even more so than for offline companies," according to a study of online customers which covered three online sectors; apparel, grocery, and electronics. It shows that customers spend more money and generate more profits for online retailers when they visit the same site more frequently and stay loyal to the site. For example, at online apparel sites, customers were found to spend 67 percent more overall in the third year of their shopping relationship with the retailer than in the first six months. One-time customers are not profitable for online retailers. The study estimates that an online apparel customer would need to visit a site 4 times in 12 months for the retailer to break even. Hence, online retailers need to develop strategies to keep customers coming back to their site. Loyal customers tend to refer more people to the site, and referrals from online grocery shoppers were found to spend an additional 75 percent of what the original shopper spent at the site. Therefore, providing existing customers with a fabulous shopping experience is a good way to acquire new customers through positive word of mouth.[14]

Premium Prices from Established Customers

Established customers are already satisfied with the firm. Unless there is a strong reason to do so, they are unlikely to switch their current suppliers. There are always some costs in switching, and sometimes these costs can be prohibitive. For example, if one has invested in a computerized ordering system linked directly to the supplier, switching to a new supplier would mean retooling the computer network or installing a new one. Thus, if a competitor wants to capture satisfied customers, it must offer significantly better value in terms of lower price or higher performance.

This was the experience of Airborne and Emery in competing with Federal Express in the overnight-delivery business. This has also been the experience of long-distance telephone companies such as Telus and Rogers as they try to capture the customer base of traditonal telephone companies (Bell, MTS, or SaskTel). It is estimated that a minimum 5 percent price advantage is generated through customer satisfaction. In niche markets and for specialty products, this premium could be as high as 30 percent. The price advantage occurs not only because the established customers are unwilling to go through the hassle of switching for a lower price, but also because a customer-oriented firm is able to offer its customers value from four other avenues: (a) product excellence, (b) service excellence, (c) brand reputation, and (d) a customer-oriented culture in general.

A good example of price advantage through product excellence is provided by the 3M company. 3M has excellent products like Scotch® tape, Post-it® note pads, and 3M floppy disks, which have retained their performance superiority to command higher prices despite competition. On the other hand, IBM has maintained a price advantage in the mainframe business primarily through service excellence.

A third source of price advantage through differentiation is brand reputation. In areas where quality varies significantly across competitors and the customer is unable to judge or control quality consistency, brand reputation becomes a significant price advantage. This is true for McDonald's in the fast-food business, for Marriott in the hospitality business, and for Boeing in the commercial-aircraft business. Branding and trust are more important in the online context because there is a spatial and temporal separation between the customer and the retailer. Research by Erik Brynjolfsson and Michael D. Smith shows that consumers may be willing to pay a premium to the online retailer they trust instead of an unknown online retailer. They found that brick-and-mortar brand names with an online presence are actually able to charge a price premium of 8–9 percent on goods and services compared to pure-play Internet retailers (i.e., retailers without physical stores).[15]

A fourth source of price advantage through differentiation comes from a customer-oriented culture. There are several North American and foreign companies where customer satisfaction is part of the corporate creed and practiced at the highest level of management. Examples include Harry Rosen in the men's-apparel business, Costco in the large-discount-stores business, and Singapore Airlines in the airlines business.

Protection Against Corporate Crisis

The third way a customer orientation enhances profits is by providing insulation against a corporate crisis. Four major sources of crises directly relevant to customer satisfaction are *product tampering*, *unfair competition*, *operational breakdowns*, and *industry restructuring*. When a company uses customer orientation to cultivate more committed customers, those customers will be willing to assist the company to ensure its survival.

Corporate crisis can come from product tampering; for example, when the Tylenol brand of analgesics was tampered with, company loyalty built up over the years prevented an erosion of the company's customer base. Tampering of software programs and planting of "viruses," which can cause a corporate crisis, are also a definite threat in today's times. Loyal customers also will resist unfair and unethical business practices of competitors against a company they really like. Similarly, large and highly visible companies like McDonald's, Coca-Cola, and Procter & Gamble are sometimes targets of rumours and social protests. For example, not too long ago, it was rumoured that McDonald's products contain spider webs, and that Coca-Cola is a narcotic. Loyal customers tend to ignore rumours and calls to boycott products, and continue to patronize the firm.

Another source of corporate crisis is internal operational problems that may be created by breakdowns, strikes, shortages, or sabotage. Again, loyal customers would, to the extent possible, patiently wait or postpone their purchases. UPS's recovery from its labor strike suggests that its customers are loyal. Instead of switching carriers permanently, they returned to UPS in large numbers. In recent years, a common source of corporate crisis has been industry restructuring—the result of either consolidation within the industry or a government mandate. Companies that have maintained a strong customer orientation and, consequently, a loyal customer base, have survived these changes while companies with high levels of customer dissatisfaction have not. For example, in the airline industry, Air Canada, Delta, and United survived, but Jetsgo and Eastern Airlines did not.

Increased Word of Mouth

The best way to grow a business is to gain new customers without significant investment of product, marketing, or sales resources. This can be accomplished through word-of-mouth communication. For many years, the legal and medical professions have relied on a referral system to acquire new customers. A customer orientation produces satisfied customers, who will then be willing to invest their own time to tell others about your company. Word-of-mouth communication is a very powerful form of communication and influence since it is more credible and goes through fewer perceptual filters. Research indicates that satisfied customers talk to three other customers, while dissatisfied customers talk to nine other customers.

Word-of-mouth communication is especially important when the product is risky. Customers will want reassurance from others if there is a performance risk (e.g., What if the machine breaks down?), safety risk (e.g., What if the chemical is unsafe to handle?), economic risk (e.g., Is this a good investment?), or social risk (e.g., Is the style of this suit appropriate for the business interview?). Hospitals, doctors, law firms, business consultants, and local service firms such as car mechanics, plumbers, construction crew suppliers, and recruitment firms gain new customers largely by word of mouth.

One-Stop Shopping

The second source of business growth is the increase in the number of products a satisfied customer buys from the same company. Both household and business customers prefer to do one-stop shopping for several reasons. It is more economical for a customer to do business with the same firm because of volume discounts, favorable terms, better support service, and savings on procurement paperwork. It is also more convenient, since the procedures for ordering, payments, and delivery are standardized. Finally, it eliminates the uncertainty that comes with doing business with a new company. For the company, the competitive advantage of one-stop shopping is the company's ability to expand its product line and generate more growth from the same customer base without significant risk. For example, McDonald's has expanded its product line from hamburgers to include a breakfast menu, chicken, salads, sandwiches, and other products.

The fundamental concept underlying one-stop shopping is **lifetime value**. It represents the net present value of all products a satisfied customer is likely to buy over his or her lifetime. The lifetime value concept has interesting implications. It enhances respect, even for small accounts. Second, there is a significant amount of downstream revenues from value-added services. For example, from selling machinery, one also can sell insurance, financing, maintenance, and repair services. Third, the customer puts trust in the company and, therefore, expects comparable performance in value-added services or other products from the company. Therefore, one-stop shopping will demand a high degree of consistency across diverse products and business units.

Lifetime value
The cumulative revenues a firm can obtain from a customer over his or her lifetime.

New Product Innovations

A third way that a customer orientation generates revenue growth is by facilitating the introduction of new products. Customer input in the early stages of new-product development is one of the major reasons for success of an innovation because it allows the research and development departments to incorporate customers' wishes as they develop new technologies. This process is facilitated by satisfied and loyal customers who are more open to sharing their experiences with the firm.

Customer Orientation Creates Pride in Employees

Customer orientation also has an effect on employee morale in the company. Front-line employees' job satisfaction depends greatly on the extent to which they are able to satisfy their customers. By doing well by the customer, employees feel strong pride in their company. Hal Rosenbluth, in *The Customer Comes Second*, says that companies should put their employees first if they want to offer stellar service. The reason is that satisfied employees create satisfied customers. But the influence flows in the reverse direction as well. Happy customers lead to employee happiness. Grudging, complaining, dissatisfied customers actually take a toll on employee morale. Bad employees drive out good customers, and bad customers drive out good employees. How often have consumers found themselves switching hairdressers or dry cleaners because of mistreatment by an employee? Likewise, it is not uncommon for employees working in retail settings to leave their jobs as a result of harassment by dissatisfied customers.[16]

LO 2 WHAT IS CUSTOMER BEHAVIOUR?

Customer behaviour
Mental and physical activities undertaken by customers that result in decisions and actions to pay for, buy, and use products.

Household markets
A consumption unit of one or more persons, identified by a common location with an address.

Business markets
Customers who buy products for use in the organizations they work for.

Consumer
Another term for "customer," but in a household market.

Now that we know the benefits that a firm can achieve through customer orientation, let us formally define customer behaviour. **Customer behaviour** is the mental and physical activities undertaken by household and business customers that result in decisions and actions to pay for, purchase, and use products. Our definition of *customer behaviour* includes a variety of activities and a number of roles that people can hold. Figure 1.2 illustrates the dimensions of customer behaviour. These dimensions go beyond marketers' more traditional focus on consumer behaviour. Our definition covers the behaviours of customers in both the **household** and the **business markets**. Conventionally, the term **consumer** has referred to household markets, and the corresponding term for the business market has been "customer." We use the term "customer" to refer to both markets.

In a marketplace transaction, a customer can play one or any combination of the following roles: (1) a buyer (i.e., selecting a product), (2) a payer (i.e., paying for a product), or (3) a user/consumer (i.e., using or consuming a product). This book includes the behaviour of buyers and payers. The customer also can play other roles in the buying decision, such as the initiator (a person who suggests the idea of buying the product), influencer (a person whose view or advice influences the decision), decider (a person who decides on any component of the buying decision: when to buy, where to buy, what to buy, or how to buy), approver (a person who approves of the recommendations of the decider after considering the concerns of influencers and users), or gatekeeper (a person who controls access of information to any of the other roles). We concentrate on the three most important roles of the customer, namely, user, payer, and buyer.[17]

Our definition of customer behaviour includes both mental and physical activities. Examples of mental activities are: assessing the suitability of a product brand, making inferences about a product's qualities from advertising information, and evaluating actual experiences with the product. Physical activities include: visiting stores, searching for information on the Net, reading *Consumer Reports* (or accessing it online at consumerreports.org), talking to salespeople, and issuing a purchase order. A customer's mental and physical activities are directed toward some type of product.

Throughout this book, we discuss products that households buy and use regularly, both online and in brick-and-mortar stores, such as automobiles, appliances, shirts, banking, dry cleaning, and insurance. But the discussion also goes beyond these typical household products and includes products that businesses use, such as office supplies, equipment, and bookkeeping services. Figure 1.3 presents the four types of products that constitute the domain of customer behaviour.

FIGURE 1.2 Customers: Types, Roles, and Behaviours

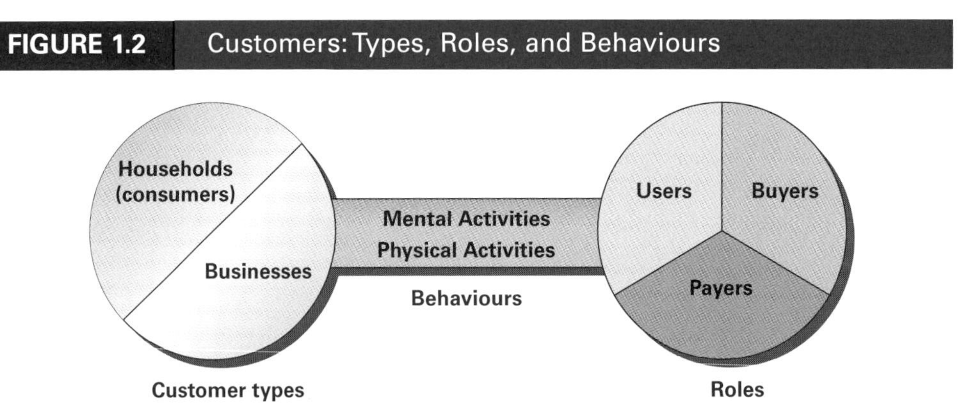

FIGURE 1.3 Customer Behaviour Domain

	HOUSEHOLD	BUSINESS
GOODS	Consumer Goods	Business Goods
SERVICES	Consumer Services	Business Services

In the upper left-hand quadrant are household products targeted exclusively to the household market. Items that are often replenished, such as food and milk, are examples of such products. Other products that are not replenished as often, such as clothing, electric razors, and irons are also listed in this category. Finally, major purchases, such as a home, car, and household appliances are also part of this category.

In the upper right-hand quadrant are business products that are sold exclusively to business firms or to individuals who use them to conduct their business. Examples include machine tools, corporate jets, internal power generators, office supplies, and raw materials.

In the lower left-hand quadrant are consumer services targeted exclusively to the household market. Examples include hair-styling, dental cleaning, baby-sitting, home-cleaning service, and home-appliance repairs.

In the lower right-hand quadrant is the business services sector, targeted to businesses. Examples include management training and consulting services, employee benefit services, janitorial services, and document delivery services.

Of course, some products, like automobiles, are targeted to both household and business markets. Other examples of products used by both household and business customers are cellular phones, fax machines, desktop computers, bottled drinking water, and wall fixtures. In many instances, although the product categories are common, the design specifications might differ for the household and business markets. As with goods, some services are used by both household and business customers. Examples include banking, security of physical premises, telecommunications, and insurance. While the same service company might target both markets, specific features are often tailored to each market segment.

THREE ROLES OF THE CUSTOMER

LO 3

A **customer** is a person or an organizational unit that plays a role in the consummation of a transaction with the marketer or an entity. A customer can play three different roles in a marketplace transaction. The **user** is the person who actually consumes or uses the product or receives the benefits of the service. The **payer** is the person who finances the purchase, and the **buyer** is the person who participates in the procurement of the product from the marketplace.

Customer
A person or an organizational unit that plays a role in the consummation of a transaction with an organization.

Each of these roles may be carried out by the same person or an organizational unit (e.g., a department) or by different persons or departments. For example, many teenagers buy groceries and household items for the entire family because both parents work. Parents pay for the purchases but do not always specify what specific food items to buy and/or which brands to purchase. Or they specify broadly, leaving the final decision to the teenager. Anyone

User
A person who actually consumes or uses the product or receives the benefits of the service.

Payer
A person who pays or finances the purchase.

Buyer
A person who participates in the procurement of the product.

who carries out at least one of these roles—end user, payer, or buyer—meets our definition of a customer.

Successful marketers are aware of the value of each of the above-mentioned customer roles. First and foremost, the user role is important in the design of the product. Its features have to be the ones that the user is seeking and that will best meet the user's needs or wants. The other two roles are equally important. The payer plays a critical role in that if the price or other financial considerations do not satisfy the payer, the user simply cannot buy the product. Without the payer, no sale will ever occur. Finally, the buyer's task is to locate the merchandise and find a way to order or acquire it. If the buyer's access to the product is constrained, the buyer will simply not buy it, and the user would not have the product available for use. Marketers must facilitate the buyer's task by making it convenient to buy and acquire the product. The Internet has played a crucial role in facilitating access to markets and products for the buyer.

LO 4 Role Specialization

Role specialization
Dividing the customer roles (user, payer, and buyer) among individuals or groups.

Dividing the customer roles—user, payer, and buyer—among individuals or groups is called **role specialization.**[18] Regardless of whether the same person is the user, payer, and buyer, each role dictates a different set of values that are sought by the customer. For example, an office worker who is using a personal computer is concerned with the performance of the machine, whereas the purchasing agent for the company who buys the PC is more concerned with the price. Successful marketers are aware of the possible ways in which customers divide their roles among themselves. They adapt their marketing effort to the type of role specialization. Some scenarios of role specialization are discussed below.

User Is Neither Payer Nor Buyer

In some cases, the user is distinct from both the payer and the buyer roles. For example, parents typically pay for and actually buy most of the products their children use. Pet foods and veterinary care are categories where the user is definitely different from a buyer or a payer. Other products can sometimes fall into this category (e.g., a car bought and paid for by parents for their son or daughter or a health insurance policy bought and paid for by the employer, and used by the nonworking members of the household). Likewise, in a business setting, an employee is the user of office furniture, like a desk and chair, but the purchase and payment of these products are made by someone else, such as the purchasing and the accounts-payable departments of the business.

User Is Payer but Not Buyer

In other cases, the user is also a payer, but not a buyer. For example, stockbrokers act as agents for clients who enlist them to buy stocks of various companies. In business markets, an office assistant may purchase office supplies for someone else's use that are paid for by the department budget. Travel services used by different members of the organization are paid for by the organization but bought through an external travel agent.

User Is Buyer but Not Payer

The user may be a buyer but not a payer. A household example is a customer selecting and using a car towing service whose invoice is then reimbursed by an insurance company. Similarly, a business executive might buy a painting or sculpture for his or her office, to be paid for by the firm. Not-for-profit organizations purchase products for their clients using donations obtained from others.

User Is Buyer and Payer

Finally, the user may also be both the buyer and the payer for a product, combining all three roles into a single person or department. Most consumers purchase and pay for products for their personal use, such as clothing, watches, airline tickets, haircuts, and colognes and perfumes. In the business markets, small-business owners often combine all three roles when they acquire office equipment, furniture, and the services of an accountant or a bookkeeper.

Reasons for Role Specialization

When a single customer carries out all the roles, marketers will likely use a different strategy than when different people act as user, payer, and buyer. Thus, it is helpful to be able to identify the conditions under which the various kinds of role specialization occur. In general, users are unlikely to play other customer roles when they lack expertise, time, buying power, or access to the market, or when the product is either unaffordable, subsidized, or free.

Lack of Expertise

Often, the user just does not have adequate knowledge to make an informed choice, and she or he is likely to delegate the buying task to someone else, who then becomes the buyer. For example, patients lack medical expertise and therefore depend on their doctors for their choice of medication. Elderly persons who need a nursing home may not be physically or mentally able to evaluate, choose, and arrange for the nursing home; consequently, they may depend on their family to act as the buyer. In business markets, a firm may hire a consultant to give advice on and execute the buying task for a complex piece of machinery because the firm does not have the in-house expertise related to evaluating alternative suppliers.

The Internet has significantly reduced the risk of making uninformed purchase decisions; in fact, one can even say that it has led to a democratization of information to customers. Online information search is helping customers gather a reasonable level of expertise before they visit a retailer, such as an auto dealer or even their doctor.

Lack of Time

Another reason a user may delegate the purchasing task to someone else is lack of time. For example, executives delegate purchase decisions, such as making airline and hotel reservations or choosing a mail carrier service, to their assistants or secretaries. Likewise, many homemakers are delegating household chores to their spouses, teenage children, or paid shopping consultants because they are too busy themselves. As customers face an information overload on the Internet, they use a new type of search intermediary called the *Infomediary*,[19] which helps them find products that match their personal preferences. DealPilot.com allows customers to search for best deals on books, videos, and CDs from more than 100 Internet retailers. The customer delegates the search task in buying to an intermediary and focuses on use and payment.

Lack of Buying Power

Often users have to delegate the buying task to someone else because they lack the buying power. Corporations often adopt the "centralized procurement" practice to take advantage of economies of scale. Media buying agencies use their clout to negotiate better deals on media placements (mostly TV) on behalf of their clients. According to a report by Access Markets International (AMI) Partners and *Inc. Magazine*, 670,000 small businesses have ventured into the online auction arena, bidding for products. Nearly 1 million small businesses participated in online auctions in 2000, and 1.3 million small businesses are interested in using the Internet to collaborate or pool with other businesses to buy in groups to obtain better prices for products.[20]

Lack of Access

Many times, the consumer is prohibited from buying a product directly from the marketer, either by law, by physical barriers, or simply by industry practice. An example of prohibition by law is the purchase of prescription drugs. Even though patients may know, based on past experience, what medicine works best for them, they cannot make the purchase decision; they need a doctor's prescription. A global supplier often presents a physical barrier. Because of language, distance, or other access barriers, the user has to go through a middleman, a trading or import/export agent, or a bank if it is a financial transaction. In such cases, customers must partner with other firms that have better access to markets. The Internet is fast reducing these physical barriers as customers increasingly rely on the World Wide Web.

Lack of Affordability

When a product is not affordable to the user, the role separation is between the user and the payer. The user may be the primary decider of what to buy, but the payer (who is also a customer by virtue of playing the payer role) may also influence the decision by restricting the choices that would qualify the payer's funds. College tuition is an obvious example: Parents are often the payers, and influence the college their daughter or son chooses. The Internet has opened up options from the point of view of the buyer, who now has access to a wide range of price points for each product.

When the Product Is Subsidized by Payers

In many situations, payers provide partial subsidies. An example is benefit programs offered by a company to its employees for dental services. Another example is corporate cafeterias, where the cost to the employee is only a percentage of the actual cost because of the subsidy paid by the company.

When the Product Is Free

Finally, the user and the other roles of the customer are separated when the product is given free to the user. The user accepts these products because of their free availability. Public parks, free music concerts, public libraries, and free coffee on some interstate highways represent instances of such free products. In these instances, the user of the service is not the same as the purchaser. As a publisher of books, a supplier of coffee, or a construction company engaged in building public parks, the marketer has to deal with city governments in their role as the purchaser and payer, separated from the role of the user. To the city government building the park, the important concerns are cost and ease of dealing with the contractor. In contrast, the residents who use the park will be more concerned with the performance and safety of the swing sets and jungle gyms their children will be playing on.

CUSTOMER NEEDS AND WANTS

LO 5

Because it is the needs and wants of customers that marketers have to satisfy, it is important for businesses to know the needs and wants of users, payers, and buyers in order to be customer oriented.

A **need** is an unsatisfactory condition of the customer that leads him or her to an action that will make the condition better. A **want** is a desire to obtain more satisfaction than is absolutely necessary to improve an unsatisfactory condition. The difference between a need and a want is that need arousal is driven by discomfort with a person's physical and psychological conditions, whereas wants occur when people desire to take their physical and psychological conditions beyond the state of minimal comfort. Thus, food satisfies a need, and gourmet food additionally satisfies a want. Just as any car satisfies a need for transportation from point A to point B, a Miata, Porsche, Lexus, or Mercedes, in addition, satisfies a desire to get the excitement of performance, gain prestige among one's peers, or project the right image to significant others.

Need
An unsatisfactory physical condition of the customer that leads him or her to take action to remedy that condition.

Want
An unsatisfactory psychological/social condition of the customer that leads him or her to take action to remedy that condition.

In the business context, introduction of a new product may lead to a need for increased plant capacity, or a government regulation may lead to a need for improved safety standards. Club memberships for top executives, expensive furniture for the offices, and corporate jets are examples of wants. Only when needs are satisfied do wants surface. As the information revolution takes hold, we see a move toward "desires of a few" becoming "wants of all," and "wants of all" becoming "necessities," especially in the developed countries. Some examples of the latter category are the television remote, power locks, and cell phones.

Determinants of Needs and Wants

Needs and wants also differ in terms of the factors that cause them. Customer needs are determined by the traits of the individual and of the environment. The three personal traits that determine needs are genetics, biogenics, and psychogenics; the three market traits are climate, topography, and ecology. In contrast, customer wants are determined by the individual context and the environmental context. The individual context consists of three dimensions: an individual's personal financial worth, institutions, and culture. The market context also consists of three dimensions: economy, technology, and public policy. These traits and context dimensions are discussed in detail in Chapter 2.

Table 1.1 summarizes how each determinant shapes the needs and wants of customers in the marketplace. Their impact falls into four broad categories.

1. *Needs-driven markets.* When both personal and environmental characteristics are physical, pure needs drive customer behaviour. Examples include climate-relevant clothing, medicine during allergy season, and flood insurance in flood zones.

TABLE 1.1 Matrix of Personal and Environmental Characteristics

		ENVIRONMENTAL CHARACTERISTICS	
		Physical	**Contextual**
Personal Characteristics	**Physical**	Needs-driven markets (e.g., allergy medicine)	Personal needs and environmental wants (e.g., microwavable food)
	Contextual	Personal wants and environmental needs-driven markets (e.g., fur coat)	Wants-driven markets (e.g., theatre attendance)

2. *Personal wants and environmental needs.* When the relevant environmental characteristics are physical, but personal characteristics are contextual, the driver of customer behaviour is a personal want but an environmental need. Examples include product categories that are driven by climate, topography, or ecology but where brand usage reflects one's wealth, social standing, and self-concept (e.g., name-brand warm clothing, a fur coat, a contemporary off-road vehicle).
3. *Personal needs and environmental wants.* When the relevant personal characteristics are physical but environmental characteristics are contextual (economy, technology, and public policy), customers seek something that will satisfy a personal need but an environmental want. Examples include microwavable food, home-shopping network or online shopping, and technological gadgets.
4. *Wants-driven markets.* Finally, when both personal and environmental contexts are salient, customer behaviour is driven by pure wants. Examples include consuming arts and theatre, participating in politics, voting, buying designer clothing, and sporting the grunge look.

LO 6 ›› MARKET VALUES CUSTOMERS SEEK

All customer behaviour is driven by needs and wants, whose satisfaction customers seek and value. Thus, all customer behaviour is driven by the value received through the acquisition and use of a product. The recognition of customers as seekers of solutions to their problems and the resulting value is fundamental to long-term business viability. As argued in the book *Valuespace*, customer value is "the be-all and the end-all of all business activity; the only purpose of all organizations, all business enterprises. It is the only justifiable goal of all reengineering, organizational renewal, entrepreneurship and corporate innovation. And it is the only path for sustained growth, and for winning the battle for market leadership."[21] Indeed, it goes to the very core of how a business defines and views itself.

Marketing myopia A narrow vision wherein a firm views itself in limited, product-centered ways—as makers and sellers of products they produce and sell.

Theodore Levitt has argued that many companies do not know what business they are in. They view themselves too narrowly and, thus, suffer from what Levitt calls "marketing myopia."[22] **Marketing myopia** refers to the narrow vision wherein firms view themselves in limited, product-centered ways—as makers and sellers of products. Consequently, firms that thought they were in the buggy business rather than in the business of providing their customers transportation solutions suffered from marketing myopia and were replaced by the automobile industry. Likewise, in obtaining a life insurance or a health insurance policy, customers are not seeking merely a paper document; rather, they are seeking "peace of mind"—freedom from anxieties about the unknown future. The problem-solving abilities of products are what constitute value to the customer.

A **market value** is the potential of a product to satisfy customers' needs and wants. Value is created only if the product can satisfy a customer's needs and wants. At the same time, since not all customers' needs and wants are identical, a product may be more valuable to one and less valuable to another because it satisfies one customer's needs and wants better than another customer's needs and wants. Furthermore, the customer's context or situation may make a product more or less valuable. For example, a product may be very valuable in one climate but totally valueless in another (e.g., a raincoat is valuable where it often rains).[23] Thus, value is created by the convergence of a product's capability with the context of the consumer. Market value differs among customer segments. For example, a business traveller is willing to pay more to be home by Friday evening than a leisure traveller who doesn't mind flying on the weekend.

Market values
The benefits (tangible or intangible) a customer receives from a product.

CLASSIFICATION OF MARKET VALUES

In general, a product's market values may be universal, personal, or both. **Universal values** are values that satisfy the *needs* of the customer. These pertain to the basic purpose of buying a product or for doing business with the firm. They are termed "universal" because all customers invariably seek them in a product, across nations and cultures.

Universal values
Product or service benefits that satisfy the *needs* of the customer.

Personal values are those product or service benefits that satisfy the *wants* of the customer. Personal values pertain to something beyond the basic or universal reason for buying a product or for doing business with a firm. They are called "personal" because wants are more diverse than needs and differ from person to person. Some personal values, called group-specific, are desired by and offered alike to a group of customers. Other personal values, called individual-specific, are more individualized, more internal, and more related to one's own personal enjoyment or comfort.

Personal values
Those product or service benefits that satisfy the *wants* of the customer.

Each class of values corresponds to a marketing strategy. Universal values are the basis of product differentiation strategies (those that distinguish a product from competition). Group-specific values are the basis of segmentation strategies (those that focus on subsets of the total market), and individual-specific personal values are the basis of one-to-one marketing as well as relationship marketing.

As shown in Figure 1.4, each of the three customer roles seeks a particular category of universal and personal values. For the user, the universal value is performance; the personal value is social at the group level and emotional at the individual level. For the payer, the universal value is price; the personal value is credit at the group level and financing at the individual level. Finally, for the buyer, the universal value is service; the group-related personal value is convenience, and the individualized personal value is personalization. Products deliver bundles of values to the various customer roles. This is true for each basic category of products, from consumer durables to business services.

Market Values Sought by Users

Universal Value: Performance

A product's **performance value** is the quality of physical outcome of using the product, (i.e., it refers to how well a product serves its principal physical function consistently). The performance value resides in and stems from the physical composition of the goods or from the design of the service. When customers buy detergent, for example, they seek such performance values as removal of dirt and stain from clothing and protection against colour fading.

Performance value
The quality of the physical outcome of using a product.

FIGURE 1.4 Matrix of Values and Customer Roles

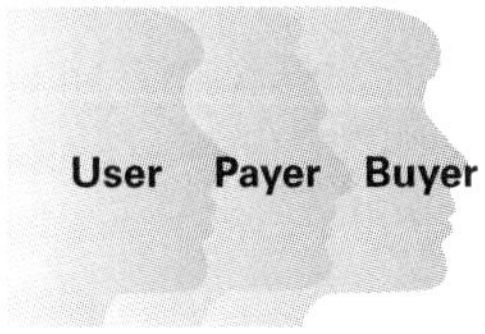

	CUSTOMER ROLES		
	User	Payer	Buyer
UNIVERSAL VALUES	Performance value	Price value	Service value
PERSONAL VALUES Group-specific Individual-specific	 Social value Emotional value	 Credit value Financing value	 Convenience value Personalization value

Consumers with dandruff desire a strong shampoo that eliminates dandruff. For business products, performance consists in how accurately and reliably the products perform. For example, blood testing equipment in a hospital must give correct measurements; a machine tool must cut metallic surfaces within certain tolerance limits; the copier must give good colour reproduction and must not get jammed up. In services, the performance value of a hair salon is simply cutting hair in patterns. The performance value of a travel agent is to find the traveller the most suitable travel plan.

Personal Values: Social and Emotional

Products are bought and consumed not just for their physical function but also for social benefits. For the user, these benefits are termed social and emotional values. These values include sensory enjoyment, attainment of desired mood states, achievement of social goals (e.g., social status or acceptance by one's reference groups), and self-concept fulfillment.

Social value
The benefit of a product directed at satisfying a person's desire to gain social approval or admiration.

Some market choices may be determined primarily by social value. Users driven by **social value** choose products that convey an image congruent with the norms of their friends and associates, or that convey the social image they wish to project. Social value exists when products come to be associated with positively perceived social groups. Users in both household and business settings are often concerned with the social meaning of the product they use (see the Window on Research box to understand the symbolic value attached to the television set in China). Certain types of clothing, for example, are associated with certain groups and are either embraced or avoided, depending on whether that group is desirable or undesirable. As a business person or as a corporate employee, the kind of clothes you wear, the kind of car you drive, and the kind of house you live in can signal to others whether you fit in. Other examples of products connoting social value in a business setting could be membership in country clubs, use of corporate jets, and first-class travel. Highly visible products lend themselves to acquiring positive or negative social value.[24] A Montreal restaurant called Chez la Mère Michèle is fashionable, exclusive, small—and expensive. The same image reigns at Toronto's Bistro 990, Vancouver's Bishop's, and for aficionados of creole cuisine, New Orleans's Emeril. What do customers seek from restaurants? Superb performance value from exotic cuisine, for one; social value from being among the select

WINDOW ON RESEARCH

Symbolic Consumption of Television Sets in China

As the People's Republic of China emerges as a consumer market, certain products are taking on enormous symbolic meaning, and television sets are one such product. China's exposure to television has been brief by Western standards—about 10 years—but penetration is as high as 80 percent, with urban penetration approaching 98 percent of the homes. Due to the symbolic nature of the product, most of these sets are are large (18 or more inches) colour sets. Data on Chinese consumers and their interaction with this symbolic product was obtained from 15 consumers in three focus groups and 40 in-depth interviews in Beijing. Living conditions in China hold the key to understanding the importance of television sets in modern Chinese life. Products such as cars or houses are seldom symbolic in China, unlike in the West. Housing in China is provided by the employer, according to an established set of needs for the individual and his or her family, and the rent is minimal. Consequently, savings rates for the Chinese run as high as 60 percent. Even so, the car remains unaffordable for most Chinese, but a television set has become an affordable indulgence. The average living space in China for a family of three is about 250 square feet, and in this small space, the television set becomes a focal point. Hence, the size of the TV is of paramount importance to Chinese consumers, and they wish to buy the largest television that will fit into their home. The TV set is often accompanied by a DVD for watching movies and family videos, as well as karaoke equipment, since karaoke is very popular in China, even at home.

To the Chinese consumer, the television represents freedom from the past and access to information. It provides education, entertainment, and news programming to those who otherwise would have little access to them. It represents an escape from the crowding, noise, and dirt of everyday life. The choice of the television set plays an important symbolic role in establishing one's financial self-image as well as projecting an aura of personal success. This symbolic importance also explains why the selection and purchase of a television set plays such an important role in a couple's wedding plans and subsequent marital success. Saving for an appropriate make and model is an ordeal for most young adults, and it even influences when the wedding date is set. Moreover, most Chinese prefer a Japanese-made TV set over a Chinese-made one because of the status attached to the former. The television set purchased in China is a representation of self-worth, freedom from oppression, and the wealth and promise of the "new" China.

SOURCE: Adapted from Kathleen Brewer Doran (1997), "Symbolic Consumption in China: The Color Television as a Life Statement," *Advances in Consumer Research*, Vol. 24, pp. 128–131, http://www.acrweb.org.

celebrity circuit, for another.[25] Customers may derive social value by going into a particular store to purchase a product. This value is removed when they buy prestige goods online.

Still other market choices are made primarily because of their potential to arouse and satisfy emotions (see the Window on Research box—Utilitarian versus Expressive Product Appeals). **Emotional value** refers to the enjoyment and emotional satisfaction products offer their users. Many products offer desired emotions (e.g., feelings of attractiveness or enhanced confidence created by wearing a special perfume or attractive clothing). Most experiential consumption offers emotional value. **Experiential consumption** refers to the use of a product where the use itself offers value. Some examples are watching a movie, eating a favorite dessert, savouring a glass of wine, or travelling to an exotic place. In business settings, attending a convention can be, for some, an experiential consumption.[26] This experiential component of purchasing goods in a store where the individual customer is recognized by a salesperson and bonds are forged is something that the customer will have to forego when purchasing goods over the Internet. Older, retired people may welcome the opportunity to purchase goods in retail outlets simply because this gives them the opportunity for social contact.

Emotional value
The enjoyment and emotional satisfaction users obtain from products.

Experiential consumption
The use of a product in which the process of use itself offers value.

WINDOW ON RESEARCH

Utilitarian versus Expressive Product Appeals

Several researchers have argued that two major appeals of products for consumers are utilitarian benefits and value-expressive benefits. These two values are analogous to our performance and socio-emotional user values, respectively. Authors have defined utilitarian appeals as those that stem from the functional features of the product (i.e., what physical job the product does). The value-expressive appeals are designed to create an image of the typical user of the product (i.e., what social image or self-image the product's use will give its user). It draws on the concept of self-concept, personality, and lifestyle research. Various researchers have argued that customers seek products whose functional benefits match their functional needs. Likewise, customers seek those products whose social image fits with their self-concept.

In one study, consumers were given the names of several products and asked to write down the associations they made with these products. Their thoughts were coded by independent judges who did not know what products elicited particular responses. For such utilitarian products as air conditioners and aspirin, the associations were mostly related to the product's attributes and objective benefits; in contrast, for such expressive products as wedding rings and the national flag, the associations were image- and emotion-related. In a follow-up experiment, consumers were shown advertising appeals that centered on functional benefits or, alternatively, on image appeals, each for both types of products.

As expected, consumers found image appeals more persuasive for image products and functional appeals more persuasive for functional products. Furthermore, for such twin user-value products as watches and sunglasses, one type of appeal was more persuasive for one set of consumers, and the other type of appeal was more persuasive for another set of consumers. Further analysis revealed that consumers who were high in self-monitoring (i.e., those who are conscious of the impressions they create in others) found image appeals more persuasive, whereas those low in self-monitoring found functional appeals more persuasive. This shows that consumers who seek performance value in a product find performance benefits more appealing; in contrast, those who seek socio-emotional values look for products that promise these values.

SOURCES: Adapted from P. W. Miniard and J. B. Cohen, "Modeling Personal and Normative Influences on Behaviour," *Journal of Advertising Research* 21 (1983), pp. 37–46; Banwari Mittal, Brian Ratchford, and Paul Prabhakar, "Functional and Expressive Attributes as Determinants of Brand Attitudes," *Research in Marketing* (JAI Press, 1989); J. S. Johar and Joseph M. Sirgy, "Value Expressive Versus Utilitarian Advertising Appeals: When and Why to Use Which Appeal," *Journal of Advertising* 20, No. 3 (September 1991), pp. 23–34; Morris Holbrook and Elizabeth Hirschman, "The Experiential Aspects of Consumption: Consumer Fantasies, Feelings, and Fun," *Journal of Consumer Research* 9 (September 1982), pp. 132–40.

Market Values Sought by Payers

Universal Value: Price

Price value
A fair price and other financial costs incurred when acquiring the product.

For a payer, the universal value is **price value**—the fair prices and other financial costs incurred in acquiring the product (e.g., shipping, maintenance). Catering to this universal value, there are several websites that allow consumers to compare prices among vendors. In business settings, price value is of importance in commodity purchases. A new trend on the Internet is *reverse auctions,* wherein qualified bidders compete on price in an anonymous online auction. This process drastically reduces the prices the company can get from suppliers and increases price value. When payers consider prices and costs, they also consider the payoffs they will receive. Thus, judgments about the reasonableness of price and costs are made in the context of product benefits.[27] Note that the cost of obtaining the benefits that a product gives is more than the purchase price; it includes the operational and maintenance costs. For example, the major cost of an air conditioning unit is not the purchase price but rather the operating cost (i.e., the charges for electricity). So the marketer of an air conditioner or a refrigerator must use the higher operative efficiency of the unit and the installation and maintenance cost advantages of his unit as his selling point. True price value consists in computing the life-cycle costs of owning and using a product[28]—be it a car or a piece of machinery for a business.

Personal Values: Credit and Financing

In their payer role, customers desire the freedom from having to exchange cash at the time of purchase or from becoming liable for immediate payment. They receive this value, called **credit value**, when the seller accepts a credit card issued by a third-party financial institution. Some sellers also issue their own credit cards (e.g., The Bay's credit card, The Brick's credit card, or even a gas station credit card); thus, they offer credit value to customers who may not have been able to obtain bank-issued credit cards. The purpose of the credit value is not so much to offer long-term deferment of payment liability as it is to offer "convenience" to the payer in making the payment. To business customers, their supplier's credit policy is crucial. The usual credit terms are 30 days, net 2 percent. Most businesses will avail themselves of the 2 percent cash discount. In some industries, customers are allowed a "float"—always carrying the credit equivalent to a given number of months' inventory. For example, in the diamond trade, the usual float is six months—if a customer's annual sale is $10 million, that customer is allowed to carry $5 million of outstanding dues.

Credit value
Freedom from having to exchange cash at the time of purchase or from becoming liable for immediate payment.

Payers value affordability as well as convenience. **Financing value** consists of offering the terms of purchase that make the payment more affordable by distributing the liability over an extended period of time. Financing allows and often entails more "customized" payment schedules, designed with customer-specific requirements. The financing value becomes more salient in those choice settings where the price of a product or cost of a service is relatively high. Chrysler Credit Corporation and GMAC Financial Services are now separate profit centres of these automakers. Good sources of profit in their own right, they are also helping the car sales divisions sell more cars by offering the financing value.

Financing value
Offering the terms of payment more affordable by distributing the liability over an extended period of time.

In recent years, leasing has become a very attractive option in automobiles, office equipment, and machinery, as it lowers the entry barrier, often requiring zero or a small amount in down payment. The Internet is significant in that it affords the potential customer far more accessibility to different financing options. According to a study by Brittain Associates, more than 15 million adults state that they have conducted research on mortgage and equity rates online. Approximately one in five of these shoppers has also obtained a mortgage or equity loan following an online search.[29]

Market Values Sought by Buyers

Universal Value: Service

For buyers, the universal value is **service value**—the assistance customers seek in purchasing a product. It has three elements:

Service value
The assistance customers seek in buying a product.

1. Pre-purchase advice and assistance.
2. Post-purchase advice and assistance in maintaining the product's use-worthiness.
3. Freedom from the risk of a mispurchase by being able to refund or exchange the merchandise.

Buyers value pre-purchase assistance because they seek product information. For example, they want to know the technical features and performance information about various models of cellular phones, the itinerary and activity schedule of a cruise trip, or the availability of a vegetarian menu in a restaurant. Product demonstration and service explanations, key aspects of a salesperson's job, are also included in pre-purchase service. Customers of Amazon.com can access media reviews of products and readers' comments, and can get recommendations for gifts, thus aiding the buying process. Sites like epinions.com aim to consolidate buyer feedback and provide customer experiences to aid others in making a purchase decision. The reviewers are actually compensated based on how useful their reviews are rated by readers.

Second, customers seek post-purchase advice and assistance in keeping the product use-worthy. Thus, when they receive delivery of a car, appliance, or (for business-to-business customers) machinery, they look to the salesperson or customer service engineer to explain the maintenance procedures. Furthermore, customers seek prompt and reliable repairs and maintenance service so that the product is always use-worthy. For example, the car should always be in working condition and a substitute car should be available during repairs; the office copying machines should be kept on an effective preventive maintenance schedule. Most software and hardware companies have websites where they "hand-hold" the customer through most post-purchase problems, either by accessing the FAQs or by e-mail interaction.

Third, customers seek freedom from risk of a mispurchase. They seek this value in the form of being able to easily return the purchased merchandise for refund or exchange if they later come to realize that they made a wrong decision or if the merchandise turns out to be defective after some use.

Personal Values: Convenience and Personalization

Acquiring a product requires time and effort. The effort includes the distance the customer has to travel to acquire the product, the hours of operation during which the customer may conduct the exchange transaction, the ease with which the customer can locate the merchandise, and the ease with which the customer can acquire title to (i.e., take ownership of) the product and consummate the exchange. **Convenience value** refers to savings in the time and effort required to acquire the product. Three out of four shoppers in Hong Kong still buy fresh vegetables, fruits, meat, and poultry at their local "wet" market. However, now younger consumers and working women are opting for the convenience, time saving, and cleanliness of the supermarkets that provide these fresh products—all cleaned and packaged in serving sizes.[30]

Convenience value
A saving in the amount of time and effort needed to acquire the product.

Certain retailers specialize in offering convenience value. Convenience stores feature easy-to-reach locations, parking spaces near the door, and limited selection to make shopping fast and easy. Home shopping networks, banking by computer, shopping on the Internet, or home delivery of products such as pizza are examples of easy physical access. ATM machines in grocery stores and 24-hour convenience stores appeal to "convenience shoppers." Besides convenient locations and hours, customers seek convenience value during the exchange transaction itself. They want the acquisition of title on goods and consummation of exchange made easy via short checkout lines, bar-coding of the merchandise so that it can be scanned quickly, and quick credit-check procedures. Note that convenience in buying is different from convenience in use.

For services, customers seek convenience value in the way the service is provided. For example, in the installation of a phone or cable service, there was a time when the local cable company could not tell customers when the repair person would show up for service installation, forcing them to stay home and wait the whole day. Now, many cable and utility companies have improved their operations to give customers a two-hour time window during which the repair person will arrive. This has increased the convenience value for the buyer considerably. See the Window on Research box to understand how all six values are equally applicable for services. For business-to-business customers as well, convenience value plays a significant role. They are increasingly seeking marketers who make it easy for them to do business. Small businesses operating out of homes seek and appreciate (as indeed do employees in corporations) such wide-ranging products as office deliveries of packed lunches and office supplies (for example, Office Depot, a major supplier of office supplies, offers this service), online ordering of office supplies, mail pick-up, delivery of car parts to repair mechanics, and windshield replacement at customers' premises (both homes and offices).

Customization Receiving the product in a manner tailor-made to an individual customer's circumstances.

Buyers also may want to consummate the transaction in a personalized or individualized manner. This personalization value has two aspects: customization and interpersonal interaction. **Customization** refers to receiving the product in a manner tailored to an individual customer's circumstance. Customization is common in business markets where

WINDOW ON RESEARCH

Values Customers Seek in Various Service Purchases

What market values do customers seek in the various services they buy? Are these values equally important for different services? These questions were studied by Banwari Mittal and Walfried Lassar. They measured the extent to which various services offered three attributes: reliability, responsiveness, and personalization. Of these, reliability was measured by testing such statements as "The firm performs the service right the first time;" as such, it may be deemed to be equivalent to performance value. Responsiveness was measured by testing such statements as "Employees of this firm are always willing to help you;" as such, responsiveness can be deemed to be equivalent to the prepurchase and during-purchase assistance component of the service value. Finally, personalization was measured by testing such statements as "Employees are friendly and pleasant" and "They take the time to know you personally." These can be deemed to represent the personalization element of the service value.

Mittal and Lassar studied customer satisfaction for two services: health care and car repair. They pointed out that how well the car was repaired could always be credited to or blamed on the car mechanic, but recovery from illness did not always depend on the quality of the doctor. They argued, therefore, that reliability (i.e., performance value) should be especially influential in customer satisfaction for car repair compared to health-care services. In sharp contrast, personalization should have the opposite influence. Since there was not much opportunity for interpersonal interaction in car-repair services, personalization should not play much role in customer satisfaction for car-repair services. On the other hand, since there were opportunities for extended interaction with health-care personnel, how well customers received the personalization value should have a strong influence on their satisfaction with the health-care service providers.

Their results supported the researchers' expectations. Personalization had a strong influence in satisfying health-care customers, whereas it played no role in car-repair services. For car-repair services, the performance value (reliability) was most influential in satisfying the customers.

SOURCE: Adapted from Banwari Mittal and Walfried Lassar, "The Role of Personalization in Service Encounters," *Journal of Retailing* 72, No. 1, (1996), pp. 95–109.]

schedules of deliveries are matched to the production schedule and delivered as close to the production site as possible. The second aspect of personalization is the desire for the transaction to occur in an environment of pleasant *interpersonal interaction*. Customers seek this value in the form of positive experience in interacting with the sales or customer service employees. Basically, the attitudes and behaviours of employees interacting with the customer determine this value. Some shoppers purposely seek positive interpersonal experience during shopping and were classified as "personalizing shoppers" in a classic study on shopper types.[31]

Several service companies are offering more customized services. For example, if one has an investment account with RBC Investments, one can open a Cash Management Account (CMA). With this account, the account manager will automatically manage the portfolio—transferring funds as needed from cash/chequing to investment accounts, or the reverse—to maximize the total return from the assets. According to a study by IBM and Louis Harris & Associates on consumers in the United States, Germany, and the U.K., online retailers need to provide personalized services to customers and ensure privacy of their personal data to prevail on the Web. Another survey, conducted by Opinion Research for Privacy and American Business, also found that customers were willing to part with preference information in order to receive personalized information tailored to their needs, provided online retailers gave them notice and choice.[32] Internet portals like Amazon.com and Yahoo.com deliver personalization value to their customers by customizing their content based on the customer's tastes and preferences. Yahoo allows customers to develop a page called *My Yahoo*, which the customer can tailor to his or her interests, and Amazon.com greets the customer by name whenever he or she accesses the website and offers recommendations based on the customer's earlier purchases.

The Window on Practice box presents some exemplary descriptions of how customers of selected market-leading companies are receiving extraordinary value.

LO 7 ▸ CHARACTERISTICS OF CUSTOMER VALUES

There are several characteristics of customer values. Values are instrumental, dynamic, and hierarchical. As one moves up the hierarchy of values, they become increasingly diverse. In addition, customer values are synergistic and role-specific, and they vary among customers.

Values Are Instrumental

Instrumentality of market values Products being instrumental in fulfilling needs or wants of customers.

Instrumentality of market values refers to products being instrumental in fulfilling needs or wants of customers. Thus, it is important for marketers not only to create values in their offerings, but also to link or associate these offerings to specific customer needs and wants. A person will perceive a product, object, or idea to be useful only if he or she can establish its instrumentality in achieving his or her goals. If recreation is not a particular customer's goal, then watching sports has no value. If one is thirsty, then water or another kind of drink, rather than a music CD, have value instrumentality. If one opens any business magazine, such as *Canadian Business* or *Fortune*, or even a consumer magazine like *Macleans* or *Time*, one can find an advertisement for one month's free trial of Prodigy, Compuserve, or America Online—interactive information services. Yet only some people take advantage of the free offer. Others do not respond to such free offers simply because they do not see how the free service meets any of their needs or wants; that is, they do not see any instrumentality in the free offer.

WINDOW ON **PRACTICE**

Showcasing Some Customer Values

Social Emotional Value from Fossil Watches

Fossil watches are popular among consumers 17 to 24 years old. While the watches are of solid quality, the watch in and of itself is *not* the principal source of value to its core customers. Certainly, were the watch of inferior quality, it would be hard to find a customer. But what really draws the consumer to Fossil is the brand's unique personality—it has an identity that is reminiscent of the 1950s. To cultivate this personality, the company has surrounded the brand with images and artifacts from that era. These images are everywhere—in the architectural style of its headquarters building, in the artwork that decorates its offices, in the in-store displays, in its point-of-sale materials, and on the company's stationery. The company's executives scout antique shops, flee markets, garage sales, old magazines, and the like for ideas as well as actual objects. Perhaps the most off-beat incarnation of this image is in its packaging. Fondly and simply called the *Tin*, it is a tin box with imprints of the images of the 1950s—about a hundred designs at any time. The customer chooses a watch, and then he or she chooses a tin (which is given free of charge). Once home, it sits on the consumer's desk, dresser, or bookshelf, reminding the user of the brand's unique identity. The '50s style is executed by surrounding the brand with images and facts from that era. Fossil executives explain that "the images are unique and so different. They look like they are from—not just a different era—but a different planet; the artwork looks surreal—depicting people that are happy, people with a little goofy smile. There is a certain casual attitude about life in these characters and in these artifacts. And it has just caught the fascination of young people. It has become an aspirational brand. The target consumer thinks that if they buy this watch, they belong to a certain group of people, that they are part of some surreal culture, and are living a certain experience."

Credit and Financing Value from AutoNation

Perhaps the area of greatest distrust among customers is dealer financing and the perplexing payment amounts customers are charged after they have agreed to buy a car. AutoNation is trying to overcome this distrust with a menu approach. "We present the customer with a menu of services with prices clearly identified for each service. Our pricing for these services is open, honest, and transparent," says CEO Mike Jackson. Basically, the "menu" is a pro forma that offers four preassembled packages of services, such as: the Vehicle Protection Program (which is essentially an extended warranty program); the Vehicle Care Program, which serves as a prepaid routine maintenance service; the Theft Protection Program, based on window engraving; the Lojack Protection Program, which activates a specially installed transmitter in coordination with the local police; and the Guaranteed Auto Protection (GAP), which makes up the gap between what you owe the bank and what your insurance company pays you in the event of a loss. The four preconfigured service packages include these in what the company considers the most desired combinations. And the price of each is clearly mentioned.

How is this different from the traditional practice? Explains Ric Gregson: "Traditionally, what the dealers would do is to give you a single final figure that incorporates the basic financing payment. Let us say you agreed to a 9 percent financing rate, so you will be given, say, a $600 monthly payment, and that payment included all the services and options, and you didn't know why the payment was so high. Then the negotiation process began, where the salesperson would delete a service here and a service there to come to a lower figure, and you still didn't know how much your basic payment would have been." In the menu, a box at the top left corner shows the base payment, which is exactly what you were told and what you agreed to when the credit finance was discussed. Then, in four columns, there are four different payment amounts depending upon which of the four preconfigured packages you desire. In one such demo sheet, the base amount was $425 a month for 54 months. You can buy one of the four protection packages for a combined monthly payment of $460 a month, including the base payment of $425; or you can keep the payment constant at $425 (at the same amount as the basic payment) provided you can accept

(continued)

a 60-month payment period instead of the 54 months, and you still get all the protection. This form also included one other slightly reduced protection option that would cost $445 a month for 54 months but, in fact, cost only $410 a month (less than the basic payment of $425 on a 54-month option) for a 60-month period. Don't like any of the prepackaged options? The next page has a column for a totally customized protection plan, including the two insurance options (appearance protection and credit insurance) that were not included in the four preconfigured packages.

Access Value from Rosenbluth International

Rosenbluth International takes great pride in its customer service, whose quality positions it as a leader in Personalization Valuespace. Certainly, it offers its customers easy access. Many of its travel operations are located on client premises and work seamlessly with client organizations. Its reservation and customer service centres are accessible 24 hours a day, 7 days a week, and state-of-the-art equipment routes the calls to the next available representative anywhere in the world! Customers can also make a travel reservation themselves, using its E-Res® system on their PCs. A more recently launched system also allows customers to access the company online and complete the travel reservation with a few simple mouse clicks. In Europe, to reach Rosenbluth International one calls a local number, and the call is automatically connected to its most recent Intellicentre in Killarney, Ireland. And the associate who answers the call will speak in the caller's native language. Its automated call-routing system sends the call to an associate designated to receive calls from the country where the call originated.

Values Are Dynamic

The market values that customers seek change over time. First, they change because individual customer needs and wants change due to alteration in life stages and resources. Second, they change because of the rising expectations of the entire market. As marketers meet or exceed market expectations, those expectations become the new baseline against which the marketers will be judged. In business, network reliability of services is expected to be nearly 100 percent since many market suppliers have indeed met this level. Business people expect punctuality from the salespeople who call on them; in contrast, punctuality is an exception in third-world countries such as India.

Values Are Hierarchical

Values are arranged in a hierarchy, with the universal values at the foundation. These are the market values a product must offer first. If the universal values are absent, the customer would not even care if the product provided personal values. Once universal values are met, customers look for personal values—first group-specific, then individual-specific. This hierarchy of values is similar to classification of needs, such as Maslow's needs hierarchy (which ranks needs in order from physiological to safety to social status to self-esteem to self-actualization) and Katona's classification of needs (survival to comfort to convenience to spiritual). Need hierarchies will be described in detail in Chapter 5.

Diversity of Customer Values Increases with Hierarchy

A market for any product category will be more homogeneous if it is dictated primarily by universal values, and more diverse if it is dictated by personal values. Commodities (e.g., grain, steel, coal, electricity) and necessities (e.g., medicines, vitamins, food, detergents) serve universal values and, therefore, have limited potential for diversity among market offerings. Of course, even for products sought primarily for performance value, feature variations do exist because of customers' differentiation of needs (e.g., shampoo varieties for dry, oily, thin, thick, damaged, or sensitive hair). Yet, this variety is much greater for products sought for personal (e.g., socio-emotional) values. In business markets, in buying raw materials and components, customers mainly seek universal values; in contrast, when buying personal office furnishings, customers seek socio-emotional values as well.

Values Are Synergistic

Value synergy means that one value enhances the utility of another value. That is, performance value, price value, and service value (the three universal values) are highest when there is no trade-off among them. Likewise, the social or emotional value, convenience or personalization value, and credit or financing value work best without a trade-off among them.

Value synergy Each value enhances the utility of another value.

Best Universal Value = (performance) × (price) × (service value); and

Best Personal Value = (social and emotional) × (convenience and personalization) × (credit and financing)

In other words, the relationship among universal values (and likewise among personal values) is multiplicative instead of additive. The idea is to create a synergistic relationship among the values. For example, performance should not be traded off at the expense of price. The best strategy for the marketer is to keep prices low and increase the performance.

Values Are Role-Specific

The role-specific nature of values means that they differ among the user, payer, and buyer. Because of role specificity, customers may change priorities among diverse values when they change their roles. For example, employees who are paying out of their own pockets may choose differently than when the company pays for travel and restaurants. Similarly, when children have to pay for the purchase of a product themselves, they choose differently than when someone else pays for them.

Values Vary Across Customers

What is valuable in a product to one customer may not be valuable to another. Consequently, a product is more versatile if it is capable of generating multiple values to satisfy different customers. For example, personal computers have a high degree of versatility because they must satisfy different needs: word processing, storage of information, communication with the outside world via e-mail, entertainment and so on. This product has a degree of versatility that allows it to be of value in various applications. Finally, for a company to assess how well it satisfies customer needs and wants, it needs to measure customer perceptions of the values its products offer. The Window on Research box on page 30 provides a methodology for measurement of market values.

CONCEPTUAL FRAMEWORK

In the above section, we have discussed the three roles of the customer (user, payer, buyer), their needs and wants, and the values sought by each of these roles from products. Figure 1.5 on page 32 presents a conceptual framework that identifies the factors influencing these three

WINDOW ON RESEARCH

Measuring Market Values

One way to measure customer perceptions is to ask a representative sample of customers whether specific choices possess any of the specified values. Here, customer choice refers to three levels of customer decisions:

1. Whether to buy a product (e.g., whether to buy a computer).
2. Which brand or make to buy (e.g., should one buy IBM, Apple, Toshiba, Dell, or some other make?).
3. From which supplier to buy it (e.g., from Future Shop, Office Depot, or the Internet).

The values can be assessed at any of the three levels. The first step in generating a measurement scale is to specify the "content" of various values. This is best done by asking customers (buyers, users, and payers), such as in a focus-group setting. The questioning would pertain to each of the values customers take into account while evaluating a set of choice alternatives. Some examples of the questions to be asked would be:

1. When people decide whether or not to buy a _______ (product name), what needs and wants are they expecting to satisfy?
2. When customers are deciding which brand of _______ to buy, what social associations (which brands of _______ would have) would they generally consider?
3. Sometimes people expect certain emotional satisfactions from their use of _______ (product name); what might be the various emotions people might expect to experience in their selection and use of this product?

Note that these are merely examples, and such questions need to be framed for each of the values discussed in this chapter. The next stage would be to elicit from customers a rating of a given brand or supplier (i.e., an alternative) on the "value items" generated in the focus groups. Suppose focus groups generate five social associations from the ownership of a car; then we would list these five associations and ask customers (users, in this case) to check which associations apply for a given brand. For example, people who buy a Saab are: (1) successful, (2) financially prudent, (3) mature, (4) youthful, and (5) outdoorsy. Similarly, one could list various emotions (generated from the focus groups) and ask which emotions are likely to be experienced by the user of a particular brand. For example, when you own and drive a Saab, you are likely to feel: (1) overjoyed, (2) confident, (3) embarrassed, and so on. In the same manner, we could measure performance value by asking the user to score Saab on (1) gas mileage efficiency, (2) maintenance needs, (3) road handling, and so on (the list of performance features based on focus groups).

Likewise, for the payer, the economic/price value can be measured by such items as: (1) this brand or store offers good value for money; (2) this brand at this price is a good bargain; (3) this brand is priced right; and so on. The credit/financing value can be measured by having payers rate the accuracy of statements such as: (1) the company or store offers good credit terms; (2) the installment payment system for this store/brand makes it possible for me to afford this item.

Finally, for the buyer, the service value can be measured by such aspects as: (1) this company makes it easy for me to do business with it; (2) I do get the necessary assistance for purchasing the product at this store or from this firm; (3) it is easy to deal with this firm. The convenience value can be measured as: It is convenient for me to shop at _______ (store name). The personalization value can be measured by rating statements such as: (1) the employees at this store or firm are very polite and friendly; (2) I enjoy talking to sales clerks at this firm or store; (3) employees at this firm or store make shopping a pleasure for me.

These examples give only an introductory outline, but they demonstrate that the various values discussed in this chapter need to be measured, and they show how these measures can be obtained from customers. To fully understand its markets, a firm would need to assess these values for its own brands as well as for competitors' brands. Moreover, these assessments need to be obtained from its customers as well as from the customers of the competing brands. These consumer data would then enable a firm to map its position on a value grid against its competitors. Such grids help identify which customer values the firm satisfies better and which it satisfies worse than its competitors. This, in turn, suggests which values need to be improved.

roles: 1) external determinants and 2) the internal mindset of the consumer. The influence of these factors on the three roles affects customer decision making, not only for individual and household-level customers but also for business and government customers.

This book is organized as follows. Chapter 2 focuses on the determinants of customer behaviour; that is, the external influences on customer behaviour. We examine four sets of external influence factors—personal traits (comprising genetics, race, gender, age, and personality), personal context (comprising culture, reference groups, and personal worth), market traits (comprising climate, topography, and ecology), and market context (comprising economy, government, and technology). Chapter 3 elaborates on the current trends in these determinants of customer behaviour and discusses how these trends are likely to affect marketing strategy. We focus on three factors that are expected to cause the most significant change in future customer behaviour: changes in demographics, advances in technology, and changes in public policy.

Chapters 4, 5, and 6 examine the "mind-set of the customer"—the internal influences on customer behaviour. Chapter 4 explores what it means for customers to be perceivers and learners. It identifies elements of the perception process, customers' biases in the process, and the managerial uses of the perceptual process. The chapter also explains how learning occurs and how customers alter the basic process through simplification and complication. An important aspect of learning is customer response to product innovations, and the chapter examines this topic. Chapter 5 attempts to understand why people behave the way they do—the motivations for behaviour. It identifies three facets of customer motivation—needs, emotions, and psychographics—and examines each facet in detail. Chapter 6 presents the current state of marketing knowledge about customer attitudes—the underlying psychological processes and the various theories that capture these processes. The chapter discusses the three-component view of attitudes and also explains attitude as a global concept. It dwells on the multi-attribute models of attitude formation and also explains the functional theory of attitudes. Knowing what functions an attitude serves helps us understand the deeper motivation of customer attitudes.

Having understood the different internal and external determinants of customer behaviour, Chapter 7 describes how marketers conduct research to understand customer behaviour. Several methods for conducting both qualitative and quantitative research are described in the chapter. The chapter also explores some recent innovations in marketing research—specifically, applications of virtual reality and the collection of data on the Internet.

Chapters 8 and 9 focus on "customer decision making." These chapters examine the choice process of individual customers, households, and business and government customers.

FIGURE 1.5 Conceptual Framework

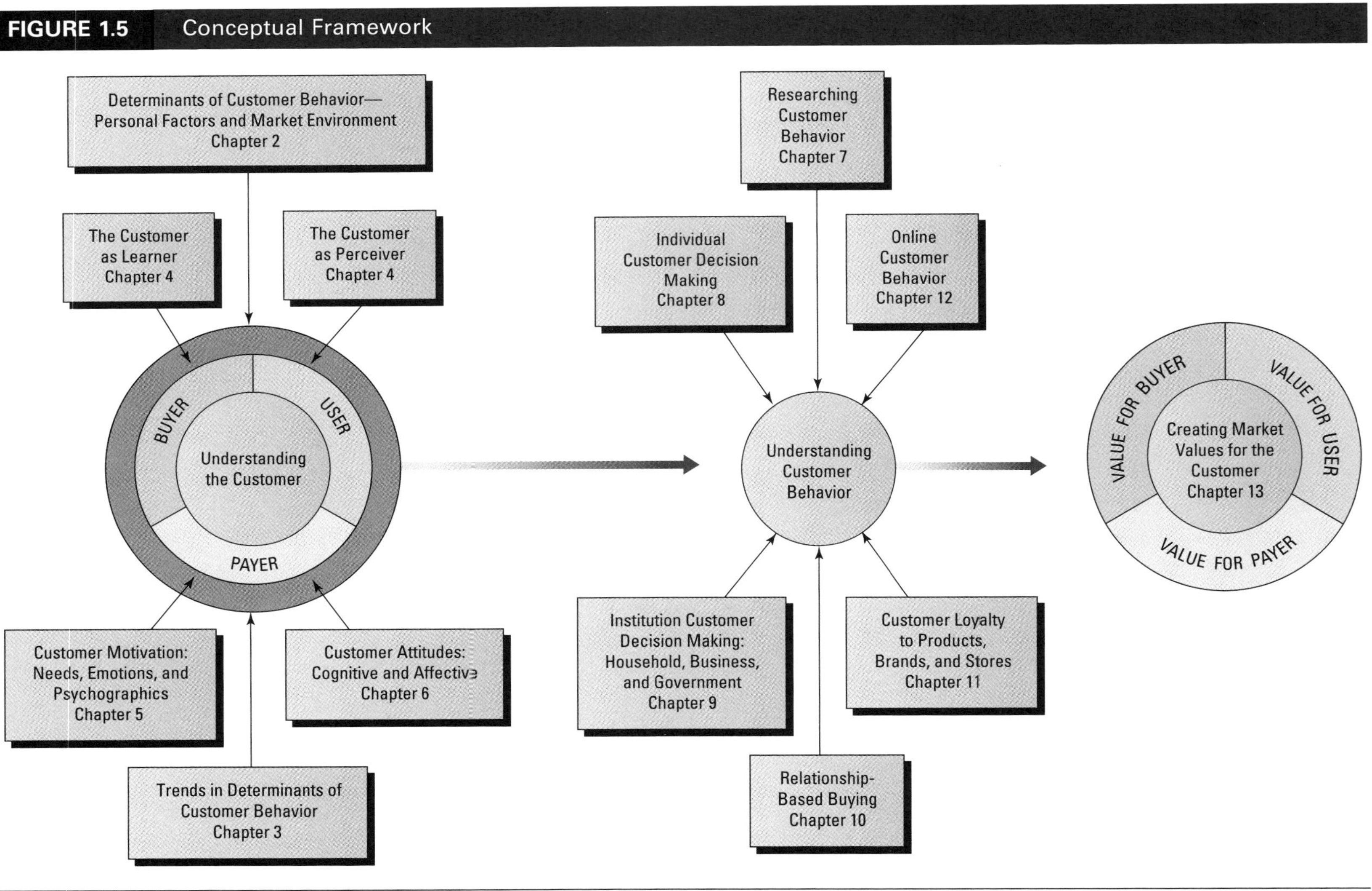

Chapter 8 concerns individual decision making and identifies the steps in the customer's decision process, including the types of decisions relevant to customer behaviour and the ways in which customers gather information. It presents several models for the process of evaluating alternatives and analyzes purchase and post-purchase behaviour as part of the decision process. Chapter 9, on institutional decision making, elaborates on the buying process of households, businesses, and government customers. The household is the basic unit of buying and consumption in a society, and the chapter discusses the influence of family members at various stages of the household buying process. Next, for business customers, the chapter discusses the components of the buying process, including the steps in, influences on, and participants in the process, as well as business customers' conflict resolution techniques. The government is a major customer in every country, and this chapter describes procedures and regulations that characterize government buying, as well as the challenges and rewards of doing business with the government.

Over a period of time, two important manifestations of customer behaviour are relationship-based buying and customer loyalty. We discuss these topics in Chapters 10 and 11. Chapter 10 examines how and why household and business customers engage in relationship-based buying and how marketers need to respond to this behaviour. The model of relationship-based buying in this chapter discusses the antecedents of relationship-based buying (cost-benefit and socio-cultural factors) and its outcomes (customer loyalty to the supplier, increased buying, willingness to pay more, favourable word of mouth, and customer equity or goodwill). The process of relationship buying in business markets is captured in the IMP (Industrial Marketing and Purchasing) model.

Marketers expect that their efforts should result in loyal customers, and Chapter 11 discusses the concepts of brand and store loyalty. The chapter presents a model of brand loyalty that brings together its diverse determinants. It also discusses the concept of brand equity and discusses its significance for marketers. Customers' shopping motives, store choice process, and the underlying factors determining customers' store loyalty are also presented in this chapter.

We have examined the influence of the Internet and the World Wide Web on customer behaviour throughout the book. Chapter 12, on online customer behaviour, looks at this burgeoning area in detail. It discusses the history of the Internet in brief and presents different facets of online customer behaviour across the pre-purchase, purchase, and post-purchase stages of the customer decision-making process. Business-to-business models and e-procurement are also discussed, and, finally, some future trends in e-commerce are presented.

The final chapter, Chapter 13, identifies a set of action strategies for management to deliver each of the specific values sought by the three customer roles. Firms should attempt to differentiate themselves by exceeding on more than one type of customer value. The chapter urges customer-driven companies to constantly listen to the voice of the customer and continually strive to offer better value to their customers.

SUMMARY

In this chapter, you learned that a customer is a person or organizational unit that plays a role in the consummation of a transaction with the marketer or a business entity. You learned why companies need to be customer-driven and what are the managerial implications of taking a customer orientation. First, creating and maintaining satisfied customers is the purpose of business. Second, according to the marketing concept, business should focus its efforts on the customer. Third, it leads to economic democracy by serving the society's needs better.

LO 1, 2 ➡ Following a customer orientation results in a competitive advantage for the firm in the external market and success internally by creating a workforce that feels pride in its job. The competitive advantages in the external market are due to increased profits and revenue growth from satisfied customers. Increased profits come from the reduced costs of doing business with repeat customers, ability to maintain price premiums, and customer loyalty in corporate crisis. Revenue growth comes from increased favourable word of mouth, one-stop shopping, and new product innovations.

LO 3, 4 ➡ Customers play three roles: user (the person who actually consumes or uses the product or receives the benefits of the service), payer (the person who finances the purchase), and buyer (the person who participates in the physical exchange of the product with the marketer). The chapter then built on this role distinction to identify conditions under which the three roles of the customer are likely to be separated (i.e., the buyer and/or payer will be a different person from the user). The conditions include a lack of expertise, lack of time, lack of buying power, lack of access, lack of affordability, and situations where the product is free.

LO 5 ➡ Next, the chapter covered the needs and wants of customers, whether as users, payers or buyers. A need was defined as an unsatisfactory physical condition of the customer that leads him or her to an action that will satisfy or fulfill that condition. A want was defined as an unsatisfactory psychological or social condition of the customer that will lead him or her to an action that will satisfy or fulfill that condition. Needs are determined by the personal traits of the customer and by the physical traits of the environment. The personal traits of a customer are genetics, biogenics, and psychogenics. The physical traits of the environment are climate, topography, and ecology. Wants are determined by the individual context and by the environmental context of the customer. The individual context can be broken down into three areas: culture, institutions and groups, and net worth. The environmental context is shaped by the economy, technology, and public policy.

LO 6 ➡ We then defined values as the potential of a product to satisfy customers' needs and wants. Two broad clusters of values were named: universal values and personal values. Each cluster has three values, one each for the three roles of the customer. The three universal values are performance value for the user, price value for the payer, and service value for the buyer. Analogously, the three personal values are social and emotional for the user, credit and financing for the payer, and convenience and personalization for the buyer. Consumer and business products offer a bundle of values in some or all of these categories.

LO 7 ➡ We identified and described important characteristics of values. Values are instrumental, dynamic, and hierarchical; they work synergistically; they are role specific; they vary among customers; and their diversity increases with hierarchy. We also introduced methods of measuring these values from a customer's viewpoint. This measurement would enable a firm to identify which values the firm needs to improve.

Finally, the last section presented a conceptual framework that shows how the three roles of the customer are influenced by external and internal factors that, in turn, affect customer decision making.

The next chapter will look at the different determinants of customer behaviour and how they affect the three customer roles.

KEY TERMS

Business Markets 12
Buyer 14
Consumer 12
Convenience Value 24
Credit Value 23
Customer 13
Customer Behaviour 12
Customer Culture 3
Customer Orientation 4
Customization 25
Emotional Value 21
Experiential Consumption 21
Financing Value 23
Household Markets 12
Instrumentality of Market Values 26
Lifetime Value 11
Market Orientation 4
Market Value 19
Marketing Concept 4
Marketing Myopia 18
Need 17
Payer 14
Performance Value 19
Personal Values 19
Price Value 22
Role Specialization 14
Selling Concept 4
Service Value 23
Social Value 20
Universal Values 19
User 13
Value Synergy 29
Want 17

DISCUSSION QUESTIONS AND EXERCISES

1. Some consumer groups and consumer rights advocates have accused marketers of unfairly creating needs and wants by offering customers unnecessary and often high-priced items. How would you defend the marketers' point of view that needs and wants cannot be artificially created?
2. You are the new marketing assistant to the vice president of admissions at a large Canadian university. Historically, the marketing program of this university has consisted of sending a team to visit various high schools (CEGEPs in Quebec) around the country. On these visits, the team meets with students during their class periods. This arrangement does not make it feasible for parents to be present, nor has the team considered it necessary. Write your boss a memo explaining why she should consider other kinds of people (rather than merely high school students) as prospective customers and outlining the appeals that would make sense to these other potential customers.
3. Describe the process of measuring values. Design a questionnaire for measuring all customer values for the following products:
   - **a.** Washing machine for household use.
   - **b.** Long-distance phone service in household markets.
   - **c.** Employee recruitment and outsourcing services for business customers.
   - **d.** Babysitting services in hotels for guests from diverse foreign countries where parents' child-rearing goals differ vastly.
4. Find three friends or classmates to interview. Ask each of them about their recent purchases of the following items:
   - **a.** Jeans or slacks;
   - **b.** Athletic shoes;
   - **c.** Jewelry or watch;

Ask them what value(s) they were most concerned with as they chose from different brands, and whether they made trade-offs between values in their decision making.

5. As the director of marketing of a major international hotel chain, you are faced with increasing competition in your home country (the U.K.) as well as in other countries in which you are currently doing business and in those that you wish to enter. Your main concern is that customers be fully satisfied with the diverse customer values they seek from your offerings. Design a hotel management manual (which will also serve as a basis for all staff training) that would enhance your value-delivery potential to diverse groups of guests.
6. Using a toll-free telephone number or the Internet, call or access three international airlines that fly from Canada to Europe, Asia, and Latin America, and get a list of the different types of special meals that can be ordered. Use that information to discuss the importance of taking a customer orientation and how this might influence the prosperity of these airlines.
7. Interview the marketing managers of two companies, one who operates in a very competitive environment and the other in a relatively monopolistic industry. Conduct the customer orientation survey with each manager. Which company's scores are higher? Is your finding consistent with your expectations? Please comment.

NOTES

1 Adapted from Eve Lazarus, "Working the Crowd," *Marketing Magazine*, March 8, 2004, p. 8; Loretta Lam, "Music to Ethnic Ears," *Marketing Magazine*, May 19, 2003, p. 10.

2 Peter F. Drucker, *Management: Tasks, Responsibilities, Practices* (New York: Harper & Row, 1973).

3 Robert Blattberg and John Deighton, "Manage Marketing by the Customer Equity Test," *Harvard Business Review*, July–August 1996, pp. 136–45.

4 Jagdish N. Sheth, Rajendra S. Sisodia, and Arun Sharma, "The Impact of Demographic Shifts and Facilitating Technology Trends on Future Customer Behaviour," *Journal of the Academy of Marketing Science*, Special Issue 1999, http://www.jagsheth.com.

5 David Pecaut, Michael Silverstein, and Peter Stanger, "Winning the Online Consumer: Insights into Online Consumer Behaviour," *BCG report*, 1/1/00, http://www.bcg.com/publications–search type =word and topic =ecommerce.

6 *Chicago Tribune*, January 13, 1994, Section 3, p. 3.

7 This was echoed by Adam Smith, *The Wealth of Nations*. For a discussion of Smith's thinking, see Athol Fitzgibbons, *Adam Smith's System of Liberty, Wealth, and Virtue: The Moral and Political Foundations of The Wealth of Nations* (New York: Oxford University Press, 1995).

8 For a provocative essay on the role of consumers in business democracy, see Roger A. Dickinson and Stanley C. Hollander, "Consumer Votes," *Journal of Business Research* 23 (1991), pp. 9–20.

9 Ajay K. Kohli and Bernard J. Jaworski, "Market Orientation: The Construct, Research Propositions, and Managerial Implications," *Journal of Marketing* 54 (April 1990), p. 3.

10 Frederick E. Webster, Jr., "The Changing Role of Marketing in the Corporation," *Journal of Marketing* 56, No. 4 (October 1992), pp. 1–17.

11 Jagdish Sheth, "Competitive Advantages through Customer Satisfaction," *BMA Review* 2, No. 1 (January–February 1991), pp. 13–25.

12 Robert G. Cooper, "New Products: What Distinguishes the Winners?" *Research-Technology Management* 33 (November/December 1990).

13 Roger L. Desatnick, *Keep the Customer* (Boston: Houghton-Mifflin Co., 1990), p. 4.

14 "Customer Loyalty–Key to E-commerce Profitability," March 30, 2000, http://cyberatlas.internet.com/markets/retailing/article/0,,6061_331431,00.

15 E. Brynjolfsson and M. Smith (1999), "Frictionless Commerce? A Comparison Of Internet And Conventional Retailers," Working paper, January, http://ecommerce.mit.edu/papers/friction/friction.pdf.

16 Hal Rosenbluth with Diane McFerrin Peters, *The Customer Comes Second* (New York: Morrow Publishing Co., 1992).

17 Adapted from Philip Kotler, *Marketing Management, Analysis, Planning, Implementation and Control*, 9th ed., p. 190 (New Jersey: Prentice Hall, 1997), Richard P. Bagozzi, Jose Antonio Rosa, Kirti Sawhney Celly, and Francisco Coronel, *Marketing Management,* p. 252 (New Jersey: Prentice Hall, 1998).

18 Berkman and Gilson (1986) recognize the terms *consumer* and *buyer* but align this distinction with the household versus institutional settings, respectively. Runyon and Stewart (1987) recognize that the buyer may be different from the user, but they use the term *consumer* to include both roles. Likewise, Solomon (1992), while recognizing the separation of the buyer and user roles in some situations, uses the term *consumer* to encompass the processes of buying, having, and being. See Harold W. Berkman and Christopher Gilson, *Consumer Behaviour: Concepts and Strategies* (Boston: Kent Publishing Company, 1986), p. 7; Kenneth E. Runyon and David W. Stewart, *Consumer Behaviour And the Practice of Marketing* (Columbus: Merrill Publishing Company, 1987), p. 5; Michael R. Solomon, *Consumer Behaviour: Buying, Having, and Being* (Boston: Allyn and Bacon, 1992), pp. 4–5.

19 John Hagel III and Marc Singer, *Net Worth* (Boston, Mass.: Harvard Business School Press, 1999).

20 "Small Businesses Buy, But Shy to Sell, Online," May 17, 2000, http://cyberatlas.internet.com/markets/smallbiz/article/0,,10098_365281,00.

21 Banwari Mittal and Jagdish N. Sheth, *ValueSpace, Winning the Battle for the Market Leadership, Lesson from the World's Most Admired Companies* (McGraw Hill, 2001).

22 Theodore Levitt, *Marketing Imagination* (The Free Press, 1985).

23 Vast literature exists on the role of situations in consumer behaviour. For example, see Russell W. Belk, "Situational Variables and Consumer Behaviour," *Journal of Consumer Research* 2 (December 1975), pp. 157–64; Richard J. Lutz, "On Getting Situated: The Role of Situational Factors in Consumer Research," *Advances in Consumer Research* 7 (1980); U. N. Umesh and Joseph A. Cote, "Influence of Situational Variables on Brand Choice Models," *Journal of Business Research* 16 (March 1988), pp. 91–100.

24 Roger S. Mason, *Conspicuous Consumption: A Study of Exceptional Consumer Behaviour* (New York: St. Martin's Press, 1981).

25 Amy Stevens, "Does Monsieur Have a Reservation? Let Me See. . . ," *The Wall Street Journal*, December 6, 1996, pp. B1, B10.

26 Morris B. Holbrook and Elizabeth C. Hirschman, "The Experiential Aspects of Consumption: Consumer Fantasies, Feelings, and Fun," *Journal of Consumer Research* 9 (September 1982), pp. 132–40; Elizabeth C. Hirschman and Morris B. Holbrook, "Hedonic Consumption: Emerging Concepts, Methods, and Propositions," *Journal of Marketing* 46 (Summer 1982), pp. 92–101.

27 Valarie A. Zeithaml, "Consumer Perceptions of Price, Quality, and Value: A Means-End Model and Synthesis of Evidence," *Journal of Marketing* 52 (July 1988), pp. 2–22.

28 Milind M. Lele and Jagdish N. Sheth, *The Customer Is Key* (John Wiley, 1991).

29 Net Used for Financial Research, November 17, 1998, http://cyberatlas.internet.com/markets/finance/article/0,,5961_152971,00.

30 Cecile Leonard, "Hong Kong Supermarkets Woo Wet-Market Clients," *The Wall Street Journal*, November 13, 2000.

31 Edward M.Tauber, "Why Do People Shop?" *Journal of Marketing*, 36 (October) 1972, pp. 46–59.

32 "Consumers Will Provide Information for Personalization," November 10, 1999, http://cyberatlas.internet.com/markets/advertising/article/0,,5941_236141,00.

CHAPTER 2

Determinants of Customer Behaviour: Personal Factors and Market Environment

LEARNING OBJECTIVES

After reading this chapter you should be able to:

LO 1 Explain the three personal traits of customer behaviour.

LO 2 Explain the three personal contexts of customer behaviour.

LO 3 Explain how the market environment affects customer behaviour.

LO 4 Explain the market context as environmental determinants of customer behaviour.

LO 5 Explain how the personal traits, the personal context, the market environment, and the market context influence the three customer roles.

Women Shop, Men Buy

In April 1991, a new magazine for men—*Full-Time Dads*—appeared on the newsstand. It contained stories about the joys and frustrations of child rearing. Utterly familiar to women, these topics were largely new to men. At least until the 1970s, men in much of the Western world didn't spend much time shopping, cooking, or changing diapers. But in the 1980s, and much more so in the 1990s, men started sharing more and more of the homemaking chores, partly because women were increasingly entering the labour force, and partly because of a movement toward equality of the sexes. The old adage *Real men don't*...changed into *Enlightened men do*....

According to a survey by Maritz Marketing Research, only 45 percent of men buy all of their personal items themselves, compared to 82 percent of women who buy or control all of their personal purchases. Retailers generally believe that while women shop, men buy—meaning that men don't enjoy shopping, and that they don't do comparison shopping. Moreover, the want or need that men and women expect their purchase to satisfy differs. As one clothing retailer has put it, "Women shop to look beautiful; men shop not to look stupid." Men are also less likely to be buyers of household products—cleaning supplies, for example. Only 28 percent of men buy these products, as opposed to 77 percent of women. Men have a greater motivation for knowing how things they buy work. Dubbed the "must-know" segment of men (some 25 percent), these men are good at do-it-yourself jobs and influence others about products.

In media, men read more newspapers while women read more magazines and books. Men also read more nonfiction, whereas women read more fiction. On TV, men watch more sports, action, or science programs, whereas women watch more daytime dramas, feature films, game shows, and sitcoms.

In other categories, men are becoming more savvy about household products; women are learning to buy cars, electronics, and power tools. Still, some activities remain mostly the "men thing," like watching sports or drinking beer.[1]

According to the 2001 Census of Canada, the number of single-father households rose 49 percent between 1990 and 2000. The increase in single dads outpaced the growth of single moms, which increased 35 percent in the same 10-year period. As more men join the ranks of full-time dads, household products previously bought mostly by women will increasingly be bought as often by men. The trend indicates that gender as a personal trait will continue to affect customer behaviour in a more profound manner in the twenty-first century.

In order to understand customer behaviour, we examine two groups of key variables, namely personal factors and market environment.

Gender, which was discussed in the vignette, is only one of the personal traits that influence customer values and preferences. Personal traits refer to the characteristics customers possess as individuals. These can be grouped into three broad categories: *genetics*, *biogenics*, and *personality*. Race, gender, and age are the three biogenic personal traits affecting customer behaviour.

The second set of personal factors affecting the customer is the personal context—the social, economic, and cultural environment in which the customer has lived and is living. The dimensions of personal context are culture, groups and institutions, personal worth, and social class.

Apart from the personal factors, two facets of market environment—natural (the market traits) and man-made (the market context)—also affect customer behaviour. Market traits are the physical characteristics of the marketplace. Where customers live, purchase, and use products affects customers' needs and wants in all areas of life (food habits, clothing, tastes, and leisure choices, to name a few). These influences are not merely weather-related, but are related more broadly to customers' habitat, including the climate, topography, and ecology.

In contrast to the three market traits, the economy and other aspects of the marketplace are created by humans as members of an organized society. In this chapter, we explore the influence on customer behaviour of market context, namely the economy, government policy, and technology. We begin with the impact of economy—in particular, financial resources, customer sentiment, and business cycles. We then consider how various types of government policies and technology influence customer wants and behaviour. Figure 2.1 presents the different external determinants, both personal and market-related, that affect the three roles of the customer—user, payer, and buyer.

Finally, we summarize how the dimensions of market environment and personal factors affect these three customer roles. With all this valuable information and statistics, this chapter covers some of the most important aspects that a marketer must realize in understanding customer behaviour.

PERSONAL FACTORS

Personal factors can be divided into two broad classes: personal traits and the personal context. Personal traits refer to the characteristics customers possess as individuals. The personal context refers to the characteristics of the social, economic, and cultural environment in which the customer has lived and is living.

FIGURE 2.1 Framework

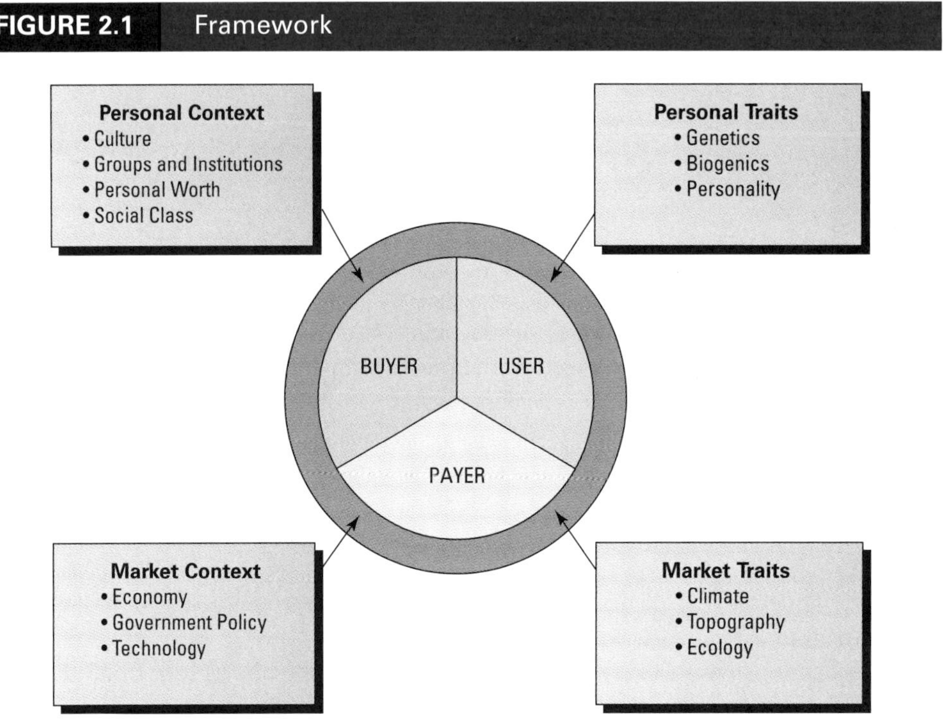

LO 1 PERSONAL TRAITS

Personal traits include the biological and physiological features a person is born with: those that don't change, and those that develop as a person grows. There are two types of personal characteristics: *individual traits* and *group traits*.

Individual traits
Unique biogenic and psychogenic aspects of the individual customer.

Individual traits consist of the unique biogenic and pyschogenic aspects of an individual customer. Biogenic individual traits are called genetics. Psychogenic individual traits are called personality traits. *Genetics* are ascribed (i.e., a human inherits them at conception), while *personality traits* are produced by a combination of genetics, group traits, and a person's external environment.

Group traits
Common biogenic categories such as race, gender, and age.

Group traits consist of common biogenic categories including race, gender, and age. These are considered group traits because they are not unique to an individual; rather, they are shared by, and describe, a group of persons such as "all men 25 years of age." A person is born with these traits and cannot alter them. These group traits allow researchers to analyze customers at a group or segment level to see whether trends or significant differences exist between groups of customers with different traits.

Genetics: The Cards We Are Dealt at Birth

Genetics refers to the biochemical heredity of an organism, specifically to sequences of chemical compounds in DNA. DNA (an acronym for deoxyribonucleic acid) refers to the chemicals in cell nuclei that form the molecular basis of heredity in organisms. Genes, or segments of DNA, synthesize the proteins of which the human body is made. In so doing, the 100,000 or so genes within each human cell provide the code that determines our characteristics. Currently, research is in progress on genetics and DNA, seeking to uncover secrets of the human condition and behaviour. Advances in neurology are uncovering various chemicals that regulate human emotions and behaviour. These discoveries support the idea of **biological determinism**—the belief that human behaviour is determined by biological factors such as genetics and DNA. However, we need to note that other nonbiological factors, such as culture, perception, learning, and individual motivation determine much of adult behaviour as well.

Biological determinism The belief that human behaviour is determined by biological factors such as genetics and DNA.

Genetics affects customer needs and behaviour by establishing the following four factors: (1) *physiological differences*, (2) *diseases and mental disorder*, (3) *circadian rhythm*, and (4) *emotions and behaviour*.

The most direct and vivid effect of genetics is on a person's physical features and *physiological characteristics*—height, weight, skin colour and tone, eye colour, hair colour and texture, and physical reactions to variations in temperature and other environmental changes (e.g., allergies), which are all caused or influenced by genetics.

Genetics and biological makeup immediately affect human susceptibility to certain diseases, such as Huntington's chorea, hemophilia, Alzheimer's disease, and schizophrenia. The effects of genetic makeup cause customers to seek special products, environments, and medical services and treatments to alleviate or cure genetics-produced diseases.

All living creatures, humans included, have a daily cycle of activity, called their *circadian rhythm*. This biological "clock" governs rhythms such as sleep-wake cycles. People's rhythms affect, among other things, when shoppers like to shop, and research is also examining whether consumers might process advertisements differently at different times of the day according to their circadian rhythms. Finally, many emotions or emotional disorders and behaviours are rooted in biological factors.[2]

An interesting debate concerns whether human behaviour is determined by **nature** (biological factors) or **nurture** (the familial and social environment). Those who favour nurture argue that behaviour is determined by a person's upbringing, family life, parental values, peer group influences, school, and other social groups. The nature argument credits a person's genetic makeup for much of human behaviour: our emotions, sexual preference, tribalism, love of status, notions of beauty, sociability, creativity, and morality. Adherents to the nurture-based argument insist that we learn these behaviours by observing how we and others are treated. On the nature side of the debate, one particular factor that researchers have studied is the birth order of children born of the same mother. Frank Sulloway has studied thousands of famous people of the last five centuries and has concluded that birth order matters. Specifically, older children are control freaks—aspiring, ambitious, and driven. Having no younger siblings in their family during the initial years, they identify with adults and learn to act responsibly and to maintain and enforce law and order. Younger siblings, in contrast, take themselves much less seriously and are more sociable, less judgmental, more risk taking, and more open to new things and to change.

Nature Biological factors; the premise that a person's genetic makeup determines human behaviour, such as emotions, sexual preference, tribalism, love of status, notions of beauty, sociability, creativity, and morality.

Nurture The familial and social environment; the premise that behaviour is determined by a person's upbringing, family life, parental values, peer group influences, school, and religious group.

Race

Race refers to a person's genetic heritage group. A related concept is *ethnic identity*, which refers to one's ethnic heritage. Canada is one of the most ethnically diverse countries in the world. Canadians listed more than 200 ethnic groups in answering the 2001 Census question on ethnic ancestry. Canada's ethnic mix has changed over the years—a reflection of many factors, such as ethnic intermarriage and immigration patterns. Half a century ago, most immigrants came from Europe. Now most newcomers are from Asia. As a result, the number of visible minorities in Canada is growing. In 2001, 13 percent of the population identified themselves as belonging to a visible minority group as defined in the *Employment Equity Act*.[3] By 2017, it is projected that roughly one out of every five people in Canada could be a member of a visible minority. Figure 2.2 illustrates the ethnic origin of Canadian immigrants who contributed to Canada's cultural mosaic prior to 1961, and then between 1991 and 2001. Figure 2.3 shows the percentage of visible minorities in the ten Census Metropolitan Areas (CMA's) with the largest number of visible minority in 2001 with projections for 2017.

Figure 2.2 shows the top ethnic origins in Canada as per the 2001 Census. Descendants of the two founding cultures, i.e., the British and the French, constitute in numbers the most important markets. However, due to intermarriage, a vast number of people are reporting more than one ethnic ancestry. In 2001, 11.3 million people, or 38 percent of the population, reported multiple ethnic origins. People more likely to report multiple origins included those from European backgrounds whose ancestors have lived in Canada for several generations. In general, groups with a more recent history in Canada were more likely to report single responses. Of the 11.7 million Canadians who responded Canadian, either alone or in combination with other origins, English or French was the mother tongue of most, and most were born in Canada, as were both parents of most of them. The following is a brief overview of the largest cultural groups in Canada in terms of ethnic origin or visible minority identification.

English-Canadians. According to the 2001 Census, English-Canadians represent the largest group in Canada with more than 14 million people (excluding those who responded "Canadian" as their ethnic origin). They are present in all major markets in Canada, although they are not a homogeneous group, with regional differences among those of English descent (42 percent), Scottish descent (29 percent), and Irish descent (27 percent). However, as a group, English-Canadians exhibit consumption and shopping behaviour that is different from that of other groups. For example, compared to French-Canadians, they consume more frozen vegetables and hard liquor, but less beer and wine.

French-Canadians. French-Canadians represent the second-largest market in Canada, with over 4.7 million people, or 16 percent of the total Canadian population. However, this figure excludes those who responded "Canadian" as their ethnic origin in the 2001 Census.

FIGURE 2.2 Birthplaces of Canadian Immigrants

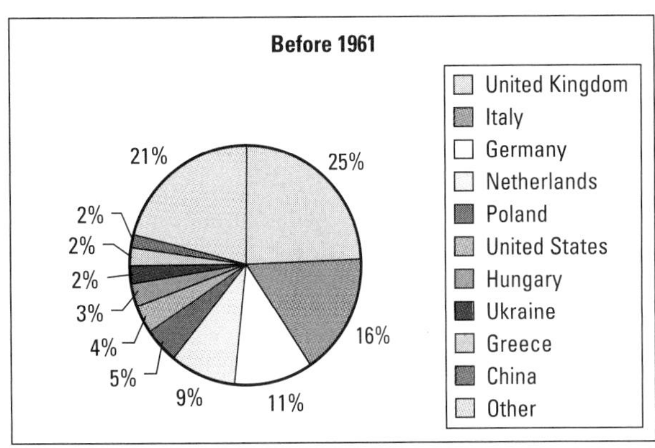

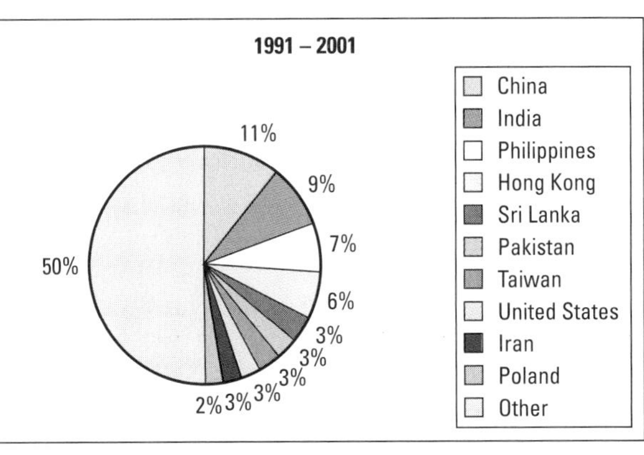

SOURCE: Adapted from Statistics Canada. *Immigrant Status and Period of Immigration (10A) and Place of Birth of Respondent (260) for Immigrants and Non-permanent Residents, for Canada, Provinces, Territories, Census Metropolitan Areas and Census Agglomerations, 2001 Census – 20% Sample Data, Cat. 97F009XCB2001002.*

FIGURE 2.3 Percentage of Visible Minorities in Selected Census Metropolitan Areas (CMA's), 2001 Census and 2017 Projections

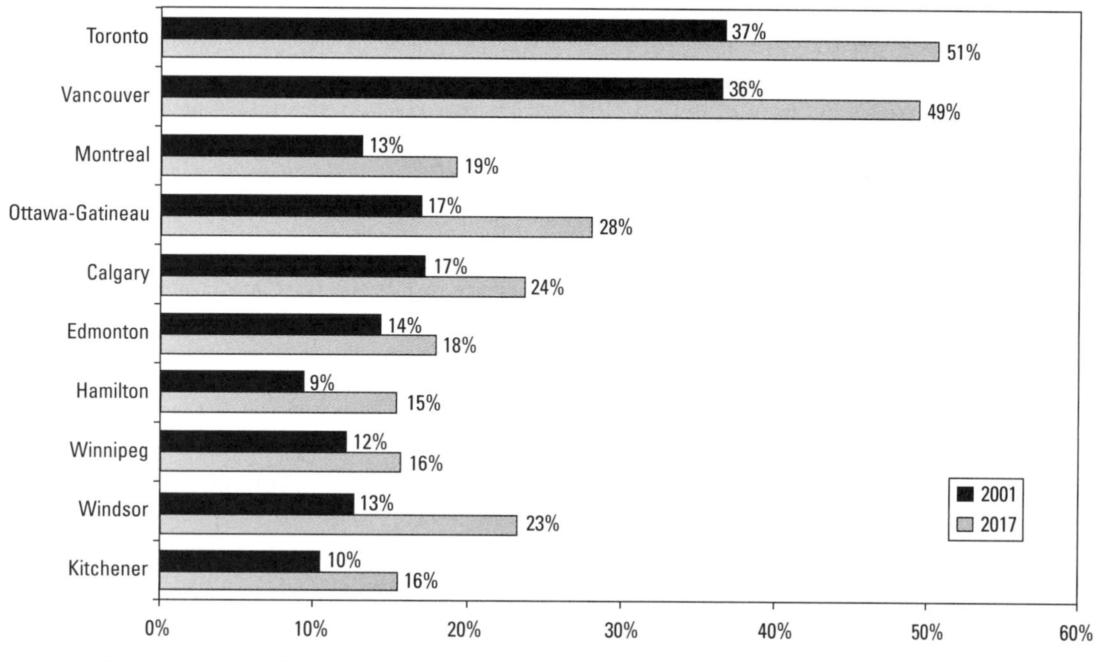

SOURCE: Adapted from Statistics Canada, *Population projections of visible minority groups, Canada, provinces and regions*, p. 29, 2001–2017, Cat. No. 91-541-XIE.

Based on French as the mother tongue, this market would comprise 5.8 million in Quebec, 496,560 in Ontario, and 238,940 in New Brunswick for a total of approximately 6.6 million, or 22 percent of the total Canadian population. Compared to English-Canadians, French-Canadians are more introspective, more humanistic, more emotional, less materialistic, and less pragmatic. In many ways, Quebeckers exhibit different consumption behaviour from the rest of the country; for example, Quebeckers' need for instant gratification creates problems for retailers trying to establish loyalty programs in the province. A recent study by Leger Marketing revealed that fewer Quebeckers (54 percent) participate in loyalty programs than people living in other provinces (64 percent).[4] Surveys conducted by Visa and the Bank of Nova Scotia during the 2005 Christmas shopping season revealed that Quebeckers tend to spend less on Christmas gifts and are less likely to give gifts outside their families than Canadians in general[5,6] but they take more time off during the season,[5] a behaviour reflecting the fact that they value quality of life and relationships more than materialism.

German-Canadians. German-Canadians number about 2.7 million and are mostly concentrated west of Ontario, comprising 23 percent of the population of Kitchener, 32 percent of Regina, and 29 percent of Saskatoon. Although they maintain their ethnicity through celebrations and rituals, German is the mother tongue of only 16 percent, and only 8 percent speak German at home. The four major values of this group are a strong sense of family, the work ethic, a drive for education, and a sense of justice. The German immigrants, most of whom arrived at least 36 years ago, have acculturated or assimilated to a much higher degree than the Chinese immigrants, who have only recently arrived.[7] Inter-marriage has also contributed to their assimilation into the mainstream culture.

Italian-Canadians. Italian-Canadians number 1.3 million and are concentrated in the metropolitan areas of Quebec and Ontario. They represent 9 percent of the population of Toronto, 12 percent of St. Catharines-Niagara, 13 percent of Thunder Bay, 10 percent of Windsor, and 7 percent of Montreal. Italian-Canadians have maintained a strong culture by developing a community with its own stores, cinemas, newspapers, radio stations, and TV programs. Italian is the mother tongue of about 37 percent, and 29 percent speak it at home. They have a very distinct consumption pattern. Their primary relations are with people of their own background, and as their level of affluence increases, they become more status-conscious, and want to own their homes, buy new cars, and send their children to university.

Chinese-Canadians. Starting in the 1970s, waves of Chinese immigrants, mainly from Hong Kong and the People's Republic of China, have made Chinese one of Canada's fastest-growing visible minority populations. According to the 2001 Census, 1,029,000 individuals identified themselves as Chinese, and they accounted for 26-percent of the visible minority population. Thirty-four percent of Canada's Chinese population lives in Vancouver, accounting for 18 percent of the city's population; 42 percent live in Toronto, where they represent about 9 percent of the city's population. Immigrants from Taiwan and China speak Mandarin, while those from Hong Kong speak Cantonese. About four-fifths of them speak their mother tongue at home. They have their own Chinese radio stations, TV channels, and Chinese newspapers. Confucianism has a big influence on many Chinese. This system of beliefs values hard work, long-term reciprocal relationships, respect for authority (especially teachers and parents), harmony in all things, discipline, and delayed gratification. Asian-Canadians have unique behavioural patterns and needs, and present interesting opportunities for marketers. The Chinese population is upwardly mobile and has become one of the most important and distinct consumer groups in Canada. The affluent Chinese-Canadian population offers interesting market opportunities; for instance, Chinese-speaking consumers spend more than $1 billion in groceries and restaurants, more than $300 million on clothing, and nearly $400 million on recreation.[8] The Window on Practice shows examples of marketing campaigns targeting the Chinese market.

Aboriginals. The Aboriginal population of Canada represents about 1 million, and it is much younger than the total Canadian population: half of the people of aboriginal descent are under 30, and their total number is expected to double in 15 years. About 65 percent of this group identify themselves as North American Indian, 30 percent Métis, and 5 percent Inuit. Ontario is home to the largest number of Aboriginal people, with 188,315. British Columbia ranks second with 170,025, followed by Alberta, Manitoba, and Saskatchewan. Aboriginal people form a much higher proportion of the population in the North and much of the West: 85 percent in Nunavut, 51 percent in the Northwest Territories, 23 percent in the Yukon, and 14 percent in both Manitoba and Saskatchewan. It is a group whose annual incomes, although low on average, are rising, and whose education levels are increasing. Data on aboriginal consumer behaviour is limited, but some companies, such as Tim Horton's, have directed some advertising at this ethnic group through the Aboriginal Peoples Television network.[9]

Ukrainians. This ethnic group numbers about 1 million. They are mostly concentrated west of Ontario, where they represent 16 percent of the population of Winnipeg, 15 percent of

WINDOW ON **PRACTICE**

Vying for the Chinese Cellular Phone Market

In the highly competitively wireless communication market, two of the companies that have targeted the Chinese market are Fido and Telus. Chinese consumers are typically early adopters of technology. The average Chinese-Canadian household has two or three cell phones, and many Chinese business owners carry multiple phones with them at one time. This market also has a great appreciation for high-end phones with innovative features, and frequently switches to the newest phone model each year. The Chinese market differs from the mainstream market in that their usage of cell phones is more socially intensive. The two-week Chinese New Year festival, during which Chinese people get together and give gifts and greetings of good luck, and symbols of luck and prosperity abound, is the most important festival to the Chinese community. It represents an excellent marketing opportunity.

1. To penetrate this market, Fido understood the need to speak to the community in its own language and with creative imagery to which its members could relate, Fido created the Chinese brand name Fi-Dat, which conveys the meaning of speed. The brand name also has the same phonetic sound as "prosperity," which is culturally very important to Chinese consumers and is easy to remember. Fido launched a fully integrated marketing campaign, using well-known Chinese media celebrities, and sponsored Chinese cultural festivities. In 2003's New Year campaign, Fido created a "Fortune Dog," playing on the image of the popular "Fortune Cat." The company further supported these events with special "Chinese New Year" offers and Chinese lucky phone numbers such as 888 to reap successful acquisitions.
2. To reach out to the Chinese community, Telus also developed a Chinese version of its company name, which translates into "explore, research, and develop technology." Also, the company offered support to Chinese clients in Mandarin and Cantonese. The Chinese New Year's promotion became one important aspect of the overall niche strategy. Each year, Telus Mobility's promotion is supported through an extensive ad campaign that includes culturally significant gifts intended to appeal to the high-end clients. For example, in honour of Year of the Rooster, Swarovski crystal chickens were offered to selected clients.

The above examples highlight the importance of understanding the culture, and the purchasing and product usage behaviour of a targeted ethnic group for a successful marketing campaign.

SOURCES: Lee, Aline. "Luck and Prosperity." *Marketing*, Feb. 14, 2005; Khan, Sharifa, "Fido Dials Chinese," *Marketing*, May 19, 2003.

Saskatoon, and 14 percent of both Edmonton and Thunder Bay. Ukrainian is the mother tongue of only 15 percent, and 7 percent speak it at home. A study of the Ukrainian community in rural Saskatchewan revealed that this group has unique customs in terms of food, handcrafts, clothing, building construction techniques, home decoration, and leisure activities. However, these particularities have become less important for the third generation of Ukrainians.[10] Like the Germans, this group exhibits a large degree of multiple ethnic origins.

South Asians. This group numbers about 917,000, and they are the second-largest visible minority population, accounting for 23 percent of the visible minority population. South Asians account for 28 percent of all Toronto's visible minorities and they represent 10 percent of Toronto's total population. Toronto is home to more than one half (52 percent) of all South

Asians in the country. South Asians in Vancouver represent 8 percent of its total population. This group includes people with Bangladeshi, Bengali, East Indian, Goan, Gujarati, South Asian, Sri Lankan, and Tamil ancestry.

One of the most remarkable traits of this ethnic group is a faith in the Hindu philosophy of Karma. Karma, a gospel from the Hindu lord Krishna, emphasizes two seemingly contradictory dictums: (1) a person is predestined to get and achieve whatever is his or her due, based on his or her deeds in a previous life, or whatever God has willed for him or her; and (2) at the same time, it is a person's duty to do his or her work diligently since the work, too, is willed by God. Karma does not imply fatalism; it urges people not to shirk effort but to make peace with whatever is the outcome of their effort.

Asian Indians value their families, are deeply religious, and like to maintain their traditions and customs, such as holidays and celebrations, food, clothing, and art. They are also hardworking and ambitious. Among Asians in general, humility and self-denial for the sake of the group are valued. Many Asian Indians are vegetarians. But even among those who are not, Hindus will not eat beef. Many Indians prefer Pizza Hut to McDonald's. Telus is well known for the colourful use of animals in its advertising, but finding fauna that resonated with the South Asian population wasn't easy. Hummingbirds and rainbow-coloured fish were found to fit in its campaign targeting South Asians.[11] The Window on Practice presents a segmentation of South Asian consumers in Toronto.

WINDOW ON PRACTICE

Segmentation of South Asian Consumers in Toronto

The following five lifestyle clusters were developed by Omni Television (part of Rogers Broadcasting):

1. *Well Established*: about 28 percent of households, or 154,000 people. Families are large and average household income is $84,000. They own large homes; they are professionals; they like to travel; and they are interested in sports, fashion, business, and news.
2. *Family and Home*: about 21 percent of households, or 113,000 people. Families include fathers in the 25–44 age group, with children under 6, and with average household income between $62,000 and $74,000. They work in business, finance, middle management, and technology, are preoccupied with renovating the home, paying down the mortgage, and obtaining an education for their children.
3. *New Immigrants*: about 21 percent of households, or 112,000 people. Families include fathers in the 25–34 age group, with young children and older relatives, and with average household income in the $40,000 range. Most rent apartments, use mass transit, and rent cars if needed. They are well educated, read, and spend more than average on education and training.
4. *Road Trippers*: about 4 percent of households or 21,000 people. Families are mostly blue collar, renting apartments, with average household incomes of about $30,000.
5. *High-Tech Oriented*: about 3 percent of households or 14,000. They are well-educated professionals who spend above average amounts on education and child care, and want to acquire the latest high-technology items. Household incomes are above $95,000.

SOURCE: Adapted from Lazarus, Eve. "South Asian Consumers in Toronto." *Marketing,* October 24, 2005.

Blacks. This third-largest visible minority comprises 662,200 individuals, representing 2.2 percent of the total population and 17 percent of the visible minority population. Forty-seven percent (310,500) of Blacks live in Toronto, where they represent 18 percent of the city's population. About 139,300 reside in Montreal, representing 30 percent of all visible minorities living there. Projections show that the Black population will remain the third-largest visible minority, and could reach around 1 million in 2017. It is a heterogeneous group, with diverse ethnic origins; its customs, consumption behaviour, and lifestyles are influenced by the Caribbean, African, and North American Black cultures, and by its mother tongues, English and French among them.

Polish. There are 817,085 individuals of Polish ancestry in Canada. The largest concentration of Poles is in Ontario (Toronto) and in the Prairies and Alberta. Polish is the mother tongue of 25.5 percent of them, and 20 percent speak it at home. Polish families are characterized by mutual respect, support and cooperation, spiritual and financial aid, togetherness, and sacrifice.

Other Groups. Other significant ethnic groups include the Portuguese (357,690), the Jewish (348,605), the Russians (337,960), and the Philippinos (327,545).

Language[12]

Language is obviously a key factor in targeting ethnic customers. Marketing communications need to be in the language with which minorities feel the most comfortable. But targeting ethnic groups goes beyond a simple language translation, as communications should also reflect the particular minorities' cultural values and marketplace norms.

In all provinces, with the exception of Quebec, English is the dominant mother tongue, whereas it is only the mother tongue of 8 percent of Quebeckers. French constitutes the mother tongue of 82 percent of Quebeckers and 33 percent of the New Brunswick population (i.e., Acadians). Manitoba has the highest number of individuals with German (5.8 percent) and Ukrainian (2.4 percent)as the mother tongue. In Ontario, Italian is the mother tongue of 2.7 percent of the population, whereas in British Columbia, 8.2 percent of the population have Chinese and 3.2 percent have Punjabi as the mother tongue. Aboriginal mother tongues are found mainly in the Northwest Territories, Nunavut, Manitoba, and Saskatchewan.

Gender

Gender is a biogenic group trait that divides customers into two groups: males and females. This group trait remains constant throughout a person's life, and it influences customer values and preferences. Concerning food, gender differences exist in health-oriented perceptions of foods and beverages. Women tend to buy fresh vegetables, low-calorie foods, and diet drinks more than men do. In clothing, male–female differences exist with respect to colour, fabric, and style. Certain fabrics, like chiffon or silk, are predominantly used in women's clothing. Bright, full-spectrum colours are usually used for women, whereas men are mostly clothed in white, blue, black, brown, and gray.

Male–female differences in shelter preferences also are well known. In the purchase of a house, women are generally more concerned with functional features such as the amount of closet space in bedrooms, the size and shape of the kitchen, and the proximity of the house to a playground. Men, on the other hand, have historically been more concerned about the heating, cooling, and electrical systems and the kind of building material used. Marketers should, however, be watchful for changes in gender-based preferences since many of the traditional gender roles are changing. Today, a large number of men are buying groceries, and women are buying cars. It is estimated that women purchase about 55 percent of all new cars sold in Canada, and they directly influence at least 80 percent of all other vehicle purchases.[13] So carmakers need to pay attention to women's needs in terms of design and customer relations. The Window on Practice provides three examples of companies that have developed gender-intelligent strategies.

In businesses, male–female differences are also relevant to career paths, benefits, and support services. Male–female differences are moderated by life cycle, education, and income. Sex differences between pre-puberty children are very minimal, but they begin to materialize significantly as a child moves into the teenage years, and even more significantly as the person becomes a young adult and then a parent. However, as a person moves into retirement and the

WINDOW ON **PRACTICE**

Beyond Pink and through the Gender Lens

Women control 80 percent of the consumer dollars spent in North America. Women's buying clout and influence are enormous, and as the number of working women continues to rise, so does their discretionary income. In Canada, 74 percent of women aged 25 to 44 and 71 percent aged 45 to 54 worked outside the home. Yet research has shown that women perceive a lack of understanding of gender differences in consumer behaviour. According to the Television Bureau of Canada, 70 percent of advertisements directed at women are virtually ignored. In a survey conducted in 2002 by The Thomas Yaccato Group and Thompson Lightstone & Company, the majority of women said they are the primary influence in household consumer purchases, but half of them felt that most companies did not recognize that fact. Thus, according to Joanne Thomas Yaccato, marketers should look through the gender lens and develop a gender-intelligent strategy to successfully target women consumers. Here are some examples of companies that have benefited from her approach:

- In the mid-1990s, the RBC Financial Group embarked on an ambitious project to help the bank create a "gender-intelligent sales force." In a period of four years, around 1,500 account managers were trained on the importance of the women's market and about gender communication. After one year, RBC's market share of women entrepreneurs rose 10 points and the bank experienced a 29 percent increase in customer satisfaction levels of women entrepreneurs with their account managers.
- The Holiday Inn on King Street in Toronto created a program for women business travellers called Stay Assured. It focused on gender-intelligent benefits such as safety (a major concern for women travellers) including separate express check-in/out in a private priority club, security escort to and from the garage or room, valet parking, and assigning women travellers rooms closest to the elevator. Other specific features tailored to their specific needs were also included. As a result, the hotel witnessed a 400 percent increase in reservations by women.
- Toyota Canada created a whole new sales process called Access to meet the needs of women consumers. After implementation, Toyota Canada's market share and customer satisfaction numbers increased substantially.

SOURCES: Yaccato, Joanne Thomas, and Yaeger, Judy. *The 80% Minority: Reaching the Real World of Women Consumers.* Toronto: Penguin Books, 2003; Yaccato, Joanne Thomas. "Through the Gender Lens," *Marketing,* June 30–July 7, 2003, 14; Peacock, Peggi. "Women Rule. And They Want What They Want, When They Want It, Where They Want I, How They Want It." *BC Business,* Sept. 01, 2001, 32–37; Wood, Betty. "A Royal Reward: A Smart and Aggressive Program Targeting Female Entrepreneurs Is Paying Off Big for Royal Bank," *Marketing,* July 17, 2000, 11.

pressures to conform to societal norms become less important, the differences become less acute. Education also moderates gender differences so that the role differences between men and women tend to be less pronounced. Finally, income also may mediate gender differences. Higher-income groups (with better education and occupation) are likely to show reduced men–women differences.[14]

Internet usage appears to be gender-balanced. In Canada, approximately 50 percent of women use the Internet, versus 56 percent of men.[15] However, surveys show that "women are 'seekers' online, meaning they go online for a specific reason, while men tend to be surfers or browsers." It follows that men tend to spend more time online while women visit fewer sites for shorter periods of time, and are loyal to these sites. Portal sites like *iVillage.com*, *Women.com*, and *Oxygen.com* provide information on all issues that women are interested in. Studies show that health-care sites such as *OnHealth.com*, *Allhealth.com* (an iVillage site), and *ThriveOnline.com* (owned by Oxygen Media) target women with health-related information.[16]

Age

A person's age, like the preceding two biogenic group traits, has monumental influence on customer behaviour. In this context, we are discussing chronological age, which is different from psychological age (how young a person feels) or mental age. Age is perhaps the most pervasive influence on customer behaviour. It is an important personal determinant to study for three reasons.

First, both needs and wants vary immensely by age. Young people's needs and preferences in clothing, food, and automobiles differ significantly from those of older adults. Second, age helps determine the potential lifetime revenue from a customer. **Lifetime value** is the estimated value a firm may expect to receive from a customer over the customer's lifetime. For example, in the insurance industry, a firm makes money on a policy only after the policy has been in effect for seven years. In such instances, the lifetime value from a customer, rather than the initial sale, becomes the key consideration. The estimation of lifetime value obviously depends on a customer's age. The final reason for studying age is that changes in a population's age composition imply massive shifts in markets and in the values and demands of consumers in the aggregate. In particular, the aging of the Canadian population is creating great age diversity, with corresponding diversity in the kinds of products the market demands, and this diversity is likely to pervade in cybermarkets as well. A recent Annual Internet Study by Media Metrix Canada found that the online buyer age profile showed a positive skew among teenagers and the 18–24 age group (more so in English Canada compared to French Canada), and a negative skew for women (more pronounced in French Canada).[17]

Lifetime value
The estimated value a firm may expect to receive from a customer over the customer's lifetime.

Older Canadians are much less likely to access the Internet: 22 percent of households headed by seniors reported access in 2002, compared to 75 percent of households headed by individuals younger than 35 years old. Age is often a barrier to adoption of new technologies. Survey results indicate that while 77 percent of Canadians aged 18 to 34 would be likely to shop in stores that offer self-service technologies, the acceptance level falls to only 45 percent among those 55 years of age or older.[18]

Identifying the Age Groups

There are three ways to classify consumers by age groups. The first and most direct measure of age is to anchor the counting to the birth year, i.e, chronological age-based grouping. David Foot has developed a descriptive breakdown of the population's age structure; see Table 2.1. From his analysis, he coined new names for the various age cohorts; these names are now commonly used in the media and academic literature.

TABLE 2.1 Common Terminology for Age Cohorts

	Year of Birth	Age in 2001	Proportion* of Total Population in 2001 (Percent)	1981–2001 Growth of Corresponding Age Segment (Percent)
Seniors	1936 and before	65 and older	13	65
Pre-Boom	1937–46	55–64	9	34
Baby Boomers	1947–66	35–54	32	–76
Baby Bust	1967–79	22–34	18	–4
Echo (Gen Y)	1980–95	6–21	22	–1
Kids	1996–	5 and under	7	–1

* Proportions are affected by the number of birth years within each cohort (for example, 13 years for baby busters between 1967 and 1979, and 20 years for baby boomers between 1947 and 1966).

SOURCES: Based on Foot, David K. *Boom, Bust and Echo*. Toronto: Macfarlane Walter & Ross, 1996; Statistics Canada, *CANSIM, table 051-0001*. The Consumer Trend Report, Office of Consumer Affairs, chapter 2.3 (http://strategis.ic.gc.ca/epic/internet/inoca-bc.nsf/en/ca02088e.html).

The *Seniors* category could be split between those born between 1901 and 1936 (pre-war seniors) and those born between 1937 and 1946 (pre-boom seniors). The first generation lived through the Great Depression of the 1930s and World War II. Because Canadian women, on average, live five years longer than men (in 2003, life expectancy at birth was 82.4 years for women versus 77.4 for men), there are more women than men in this age group.[19] The greatest needs for this group are appropriate housing and good health care. *Pre-boom* seniors (born between 1937 and 1946) faced the crises of World War II during their youth. They believed in the success of the system rather than in individual enterprise, seeking secure careers in big corporations. This generation has enjoyed a life of prosperity and the lowest rate of any sociological evils (e.g., crime), all with minimum initiatives.

The *Baby Boomers* are the most self-absorbed of all generations. They desire anti-aging and anti-fat products, cosmetics, body shapers, and so on. As a group, they are more educated and affluent; their household income is higher than the average household income. The younger boomers are in the parenting trap with children under 18, the middle-age boomers have adult children, and the older boomers are getting close to retirement. Employment rates among baby boomers are still high among both sexes, and time is a major constraint, increasing the demand for convenience and time-saving devices.

The Baby Bust, also known as *Generation X,* is so named because of their negation of most Boomer values. As of 2006, the early cohorts are adults (ages 33 to 39) while the latter cohorts are young adults (ages 27 to 32). Their music is not rock 'n' roll or classic rock or retro; it is rap, urban rhythm and blues, and industrial dance music. They are serious about education and enhancing their job prospects. They are more accepting of diversity in race, ethnicity, religion, language, and lifestyles. They support social issues, dislike hype in advertising, and reject conspicuous consumption.

The next age group includes those aged 11–26, known as the *Echo Generation* or *Generation Y,* and deserves special attention. Today's teenagers are about 2.9 million in number in Canada. They spent an estimated $75 to $95 a week.[20] Part of the financial power of members of the Echo Generation comes from what they buy with their own income, which is almost entirely disposable income, since parents provide the essentials. According to YTV's *Kid and Tween Report 2005*, Canada's 2.5 million tweens (9 to 14 years of age) spend some $2.9 billion annually, thanks to the generosity of their Baby Boomer parents.[21] The age group with the most Internet users is the 15–19-year-olds; 90 percent of these teens report using the Internet. Young people aged 15–17 in "connected" homes averaged 9 hours a week, and about 70 percent of them used the Internet to search for information on goods or services.[22] A survey commissioned by Media Awareness Network in 2005 among grade 4–11 students (ages 9 to 17 years old) revealed that among this population, 94 percent of respondents now have Internet in the home; that 15 percent (grade 4) to 40 percent (grade 11) of them shop or get product information online on a regular basis; and that on an "average school day" students spend about 30 minutes shopping or getting product information online.

The top three most popular sites among this population are *addictivegames.com*, *miniclip.com*, and *neopets.com*. Almost all (94 percent) of the students' top 50 sites include marketing material.[23] Teens' favourite sites deliver fun and entertainment, and many offer various features such as chat, e-mail, fashion sports, entertainment, e-commerce, and more. A product's "cool image" tends to draw teens to sites, and they share this information with their peers, thereby bringing referrals to sites. An important problem with teen e-commerce is lack of payment options. Some sites enable parents to create online accounts for their children, so that teens without credit cards can still purchase goods. Teens have also been known to research products online and purchase offline because of a lack of credit cards. Hence, marketers need to focus on making the Web a branding and information vehicle for teen products. Savvy marketers recognize the potential that teens represent, and have made special efforts to respond to their needs and offer them the market values they seek.[23] Generation Y is extremely Internet-savvy. The Window on Practice on pages 52–53 presents a profile of Generation Y.

CUSTOMER **INSIGHT**

How Mature Adults Differ from Young Adults

According to David B. Wolfe, the author of *Serving the Ageless Market*, as a person matures, his or her modes of thinking change. In early childhood, the cues to his or her thinking come from within. During adulthood, the person is more oriented to cues from the external world. During the mature years, the person tends to turn again toward internal cues, combining the external information with the internal cues from one's experiences.

Based on his research, David Wolfe believes that mature persons hold five key values:

- Autonomy and self-sufficiency
- Social and spiritual connectedness
- Altruism
- Personal growth
- Revitalization

(continued)

Thus, to mature adults, the direct benefits of a product (e.g., clean hair) are less appealing than the product's role in fulfilling these values. Some examples illustrate this distinction:

1. Kimberly-Clark's promotion of Depend undergarments was hugely successful. It showed an actress playing golf and going about her active life; in contrast, competitors promoted the product's functional features, such as absorbency, and were not as successful.
2. Freedom Group of Florida developed a senior housing community and recruited residents by having a mortgage-burning party, signifying self-sufficiency and autonomy.
3. Mature adults tend to patronize mom-and-pop stores to a greater degree because their owners are able to offer them personalized service and social connectedness.
4. Thrifty Car Rental Co. found that a donation to a social project was more appealing to seniors than a direct discount.
5. Elderhostel offers mature adults travel programs in conjunction with educational programs at universities worldwide; close to 300,000 adults participate annually in this opportunity for personal growth and revitalization.

These examples show that marketers can benefit greatly by being aware of these values. Each communication and advertising campaign and each product offering should be pre-assessed on how well it reflects the values mature adults hold.

SOURCES: Adapted from Wolfe, David B. *Serving the Ageless Market.* Toronto: McGraw Hill, 1990; Wolfe, David B. "Targeting the Mature Adults." *American Demographics,* March 1994, 32–36.

WINDOW ON **PRACTICE**

Generation Y

Generation Y, those born between 1980 to 1995, is the largest population sector in Canada since the baby-boomer era. Also known as the Echo Boomers, the Digital Generation, and the Millenniums, they account for 22 percent of the Canadian population.

"This generation is destined to eat, breathe, and sleep online." According to a survey by the Fortino Group, Generation Y kids (aged 11 to 18) have been familiar with the Internet most of their lives. The adult cohort of Generation Y (young adults aged 19 to 26) is adept at using the Internet for information search and e-commerce. As Bob Reiner, unit manager of Enterprise Internet Services, puts it: "This is the first generation to truly internalize the Internet, as opposed to other generations that have adopted it."

Marketers are cognizant of this characteristic when they deal with Generation Y members. More and more companies are using the Internet as a marketing tool to target young people. Given the sophisticated nature of the digital media that they are exposed to, they are more tuned to merchandise concepts that involve "exploring the unknown" or focus on "co-production" in terms of developing their own products. In terms of their Internet usage, Generation Y and Generation X customers are quite similar. Brand loyalty is important to Generation Y, and they prefer ordering online to ordering by phone. However, Generation Y customers are "harder to please" and account for higher product returns compared to older customers. Most of the Generation Y consumers have Internet access, and convenience is a key motivation for shopping on the Internet. More than 33 percent are satisfied with their online shopping experience.

A Saatchi & Saatchi study found today's youth to be "confident, self-reliant, optimistic, and positive." Despite being the "cool" generation, they retain family values—they want to marry, have children, and own a home. They admire attributes such as honesty and caring for others as opposed to ambition or fashionability, and they pride themselves on their determination. They are looking for strong, successful careers and want to play a meaningful role in the companies that they work in. They are very strong on the concept of work/life balance.

Market researchers studying Generation Y need to take a rather indirect approach. Projective techniques could be used to gather information about Generation Y peers, and focus groups could be conducted with groups of friends where the generation normally hangs out, e.g., in their homes, in malls or clubs, or at music festivals. It might be worthwhile for marketers to look for Generation Y opinion leaders and interview them to get an idea of trends. As John Almash, president of Stratcom, a marketing consultancy, puts it: "Marketing campaigns to Generation Y would be best low-key and sincere, as this group does not want to be controlled—they would like to be addressed as people who can figure out things for themselves."

SOURCES: Adapted from "Generation Y Web Shoppers Emerge as Mini-Baby Boomers." *Business Wire*, May 9, 2000; Farren, Caela, "Gen Y: A New Breed of Values and Desires." *Philippine Daily Inquirer*, February 21, 2001, 10; Chordas, Lori, "A New Generation in the Cross Hairs." *Best's Review*, February 1, 2001, 49; MacIver, Kenny. "Connectivity from a Lifetime of Clicks." *The Times of London*, November 22, 1999, 19; "Generation X and Y Reveal the Future of Home Improvement and Repair." *PR Newswire*, September 16, 1999; "Landmark Study Identifies Generation Y Preferences." *Children's Business*, March 1, 1999; "Key to Marketing Successfully to Gen X And Y? Break All Your Rules." *Card News*, February 9, 2000.

Another approach to classifying age is based on a person's school year. Categories include preschoolers (under 6 years of age), primary and secondary schoolers (6 to 18 years old), college students (19 to 25 years old), adults (26 to 45 and 46 to 65), and mature adults (over 65). This approach to classifying age is a good one if one is interested in measuring the impact of outside influences (as well as continuing family influences) on a person's development.

The third approach is the **family life cycle concept.** This concept captures the movement of individuals and families as they go through major life events (e.g., marriage, divorce, birth of a baby, death, and so on) and stages (e.g., single persons, families with young children, and empty nesters whose children are living on their own). Each of these and other stages characterize the commonalities that exist among the families in that stage. For example, a young single person is characterized by having relatively low earnings and, therefore, very little discretionary income. Newly married couples are more financially well-off if both spouses work, and they buy products such as automobiles, clothing, and vacations. However, married couples with very young children tend to experience tremendous time pressures (particularly if both spouses are working) and consequently seek time-saving products. Empty nesters tend to spend a greater part of their discretionary income on vacations and recreation, and also become more health-oriented. Thus, the classification of age based on the family life cycle offers marketers valuable insights into the consumption patterns of customers as they move from one age group to the next.

Family life cycle concept
The different stages a family goes through—from the time a person is young and single, to the time when he or she becomes a single solitary survivor.

Intergenerational Differences in Household and Business Markets

The intergenerational differences among the age groups affect their customer behaviour with regard to basic consumer goods—food, clothing, and shelter. There has been a significant change over the last 80 years with respect to what customers value. In regard to the universal values that customers seek, there has been a general shift from a functional and economic orientation among the pre-war Seniors segment to a preoccupation with personal values by successive generations. With respect to food, the universal value of product quality is a driving force for all segments, except that the value of convenient use is also very important for the Baby Boomers and Generation X segments. The ability to use a credit card at the supermarket is a value sought by the Baby Boomers and Generation X segments, in contrast to the two older segments. With regard to clothing, the pre-war segment is more concerned with performance values such as durability, quality, and universal price/economic value, whereas the younger segments, while not ignoring the universal values, tend to place greater importance on the nonfunctional personal value of social image associated with various items and styles of clothing. Among services, insurance is a good example of an industry where age plays a significant role in shaping customer desire for diverse market values. Customers from the Seniors segment have little need for life insurance because their dependents have already grown up. However, the Baby Boomer segment places much greater emphasis on the universal value of financial coverage as well as the personal value of security for their loved ones.

In business markets, age has an influence on a service such as payroll benefits, since employees look for different benefits from a company as they grow older. For example, a Generation X employee will want to start building a pension; in contrast, a younger employee, such as a Generation Y member, would be more concerned with dental insurance and disability insurance.

Customer Personality

As mentioned earlier, personality is a psychogenic trait that affects customer behaviour. *Personality* refers to the consistent ways in which a person responds to his or her environment. Everyday descriptions of people as innovative or tradition-bound, dogmatic or open-minded, sociable or aloof, aggressive or meek, are all references to personality. Humans develop personality because it is efficient to build a standard repertoire of responses to one's environment, as opposed to developing a new response every time a situation arises. Some of these standard responses will apply to a person's behaviour as a customer.

How Is Personality Developed?

Customer personality is a function of two factors: genetic makeup and environmental conditioning.

Personality = Genetics × Environment

These two factors have emerged from separate streams of research: environmental determination and genetic determination. The leading proponent of environmental determination was B. F. Skinner, and the leading proponent of genetic determination was Hans Eysenck. Skinner's theory, known as **behaviourism theory,** is that a person develops a pattern of behavioural responses because of the rewards and punishments offered by the environment. Therefore, personality—a consistent pattern of behavioural responses—is formed and can be molded by a society by means of environmental shaping. Eysenck, on the other hand, considered biogenetic factors as the more important causes of individual differences. As an illustration of the genetic origins of personality, consider the trait of introversion/extroversion. Eysenck demonstrated that a person's relative introversion/extroversion depends highly upon arousal of the brain as mediated by the body systems. Introverts exhibit a more intense state of arousal than extraverts. With intrinsically lower levels of stimulation, extroverts tend to seek it in their external environment, "whereas introverts tend to avoid additional stimulation because

Behaviourism theory
The theory that a person develops a pattern of behavioural responses because of the rewards and punishments offered by his or her environment.

their internal mechanisms are chronically switched to a 'high-gain' position."[24] For an example of research behind these views, see the Window on Research box.

In the psychology literature, two of the dominant theories for explaining the concept of personality are the Freudian *theory of personality* and the *personality trait theory*.

Sigmund Freud, the founder of psychoanalysis, was the first to argue that the human personality is driven by both conscious and unconscious motives (i.e., desires). He proposed three divisions of the human psyche: **id, ego,** and **superego.** The *id* is the basic source of inner energy, directed at avoiding pain and obtaining pleasure, and represents unconscious drives and urges. The *superego* is the moral side of the psyche and reflects societal ideals. The *ego* is the conscious mediator between the id and the superego; that is, between the unconscious and impulsive desires of the id and the societal ideals internalized by the superego. The ego helps a person respond to the world in societally acceptable ways, and such behaviours are called "defense mechanisms." For example, the id may want to own an expensive car, but the superego would remind the ego that, given the person's financial means, it would be unwise to buy an expensive car. To resolve this anxiety, the person saves his or her ego (sense of self) by arguing, for example, that an expensive car is a status symbol, used by people with not enough confidence in their inherent ability or talent. This argument, made to others or to oneself, is an example of a defense mechanism.

Id
A division of the human psyche that refers to the basic source of inner energy directed at avoiding pain and obtaining pleasure; it represents the unconscious drives and urges.

Ego
The conscious mediator between the id and the superego.

Superego
The moral side of the psyche, which reflects societal ideals.

WINDOW ON RESEARCH

Genetics and Personality Traits

Why are some people thrill seekers while others lead a more subdued life? The answer lies in chromosome 11. Thrill-seeking behaviour is affected, according to a recent discovery, by how brain cells process a neural messenger chemical called dopamine. The transmission of that chemical message is determined by a gene called D4DR. Individuals who have a certain kind of extra-long DNA sequence on part of chromosome 11 also score much higher on psychological tests measuring a personality trait called "novelty seeking."

This is the finding of two independent researchers. Richard P. Ebstein and his colleagues tested 124 unrelated Israeli subjects, measuring four personality dimensions—novelty seeking, harm avoidance, reward dependence, and persistence. They took blood samples from each subject for genetic analysis. They found that the subjects who scored the highest on novelty seeking, and were therefore characterized as impulsive, exploratory, fickle, excitable, quick-tempered, and extravagant, were much more likely to have the long seven-segment component of D4DR. In contrast, subjects with the shorter component scored significantly lower and tended to be reflective, rigid, loyal, stoic, slow-tempered, and frugal. This study does not indicate that novelty seeking is controlled by a single gene or a number of genes. Upbringing, life experience, and numerous environmental factors clearly play a major role in complex human behaviours. Indeed, the researchers note that the genetic factor had a relatively minor impact, accounting for some 10 percent of the variance in the novelty-seeking behaviour.

In another study of nearly 2,300 twins, Kathleen McAuliffe found that on a rating scale for happiness, genetically identical twins scored more similarly than even fraternal twins. A person's proclivity for being happy is explained, according to psychologists, only 3 percent by such factors as level of education, family income, marital status, and religious belief; in comparison, it is explained as much as 50 percent by our genetics.

SOURCES: Adapted from Suplee, Curt. "Researchers Find Personality Gene: Chromosome Pattern Markes People Seek Thrills." *International Herald Tribune*, January 3, 1996; McAuliffe, Kathleen., "Born to Be Happy." *Self*, December 1996, 33.

To prevent anxiety and keep the unacceptable id impulses or other threatening material from reaching consciousness, the ego employs a variety of unconscious tactics:

- *Aggression*—To display anger or inflict pain on someone out of frustration and without justification. For example, a customer who suspects the retailer of taking advantage of a market shortage spoils merchandise in the store.
- *Rationalization*—To explain some action by a motive that is more acceptable than the actual motive, which is suppressed from consciousness. The use of corporate jets and country club memberships are rationalized as needed for business efficacy although the real motive and reason in many cases is prestige and a personal sense of vanity.
- *Projection*—To blame others for a person's own shortcomings or to attribute personal feelings to others. For example, a customer breaks an appliance by wrongful use and then blames the manufacturer or the workmanship.
- *Repression*—To devote a great deal of energy to keeping a particular thought or feeling at the unconscious level. Examples of repression include situations in which consumers avoid products that are associated with unattractive situations and, at the same time, deny that association to be the reason for their choice. For example, products associated with a person's ex-spouse may be avoided.
- *Withdrawal*—To simply withdraw from a situation in which one is not successful. Thus, both household and business customers literally withdraw from associations, conferences, book clubs, and so on, if they believe they are not respected in those gatherings.
- *Regression*—To regress, or revert, to childhood behaviours. At special sale events in stores where supplies are limited, many adults resort to fighting like children to get to the merchandise.

Trait theory of personality
The view of a person as a composite of several personality traits.

Personality trait
A consistent, characteristic way of behaving.

Compliant
A personality trait with which a person acts in an agreeable manner to earn the acceptance and friendship of others.

Aggressive
A personality with which a person values personal accomplishment over friendship and seeks power and admiration from others.

Detached
A personality with which a person is independent minded, entertains no obligations, and admits little social influence on personal choices.

In the **trait theory of personality,** a person is viewed as a composite of several personality traits. A **personality trait** is a consistent, characteristic way of behaving.[25] Thus, compulsive people consistently and characteristically act compulsively; people with the personality trait of dogmatism consistently hold on to their beliefs; and variety-seeking individuals are constantly changing their preferences. Catell identified 16 fundamental traits that account for a person's behaviour.[26] He termed these "source traits" since, in his view, these were the source of other "surface traits" or overt behaviour.

In another classification, Karen Horney grouped people into three categories based on social affiliation: compliant, aggressive, and detached (CAD). The **compliant** type seeks the friendship, acceptance, appreciation, and love of others, and tries to be likable and agreeable. The **aggressive** type, on the other hand, values personal accomplishment over friendship and seeks power and admiration from others. Finally, the **detached** person is independent-minded, entertains no obligations, and admits little social influence on personal choices.

The first reported study of personality traits in marketing was conducted by Franklin B. Evans in 1959. Evans used the EPPS measures to examine whether Ford and Chevy owners differed in their personality traits, but he failed to find any personality differences. Another researcher, Joel B. Cohen, used Horney's CAD typology to check for product purchase and consumption differences across the three personality types. Though differences were found for just 7 of the 15 categories used in the study, the study did reveal some interesting findings. For example, mouthwash and Dial soap were used substantially more often by compliants than by the detached group. Old Spice was the favorite deodorant of the aggressive type, whereas the leading brand, Right Guard, was the choice of the other two types. Aggressives used colognes more and preferred Coors beer, whereas the detached types drank tea more than the other groups. Some researchers studied the trait of *tolerance for ambiguity*, which refers to how comfortable a person deals with uncertainty and lack of complete information. Charles M. Schaninger and Donald Sciglimpaglia found that consumers with low tolerance for ambiguity and higher self-esteem tended to use more product information in their brand-choice decision.[27]

Personality research in earlier years has suffered from (1) a lack of personality scales specifically developed for consumer behaviour and (2) a lack of understanding on which personality traits should matter for which consumer choices.[29] Today, trait-oriented personality research has fallen out of favour with consumer researchers, who increasingly use a lifestyles view of personality.

Personality of the Business Customer

In business organizations, people are not simply employees, co-workers, managers, or subordinates. In addition to their job titles and job responsibility, they have a personality that they bring to the work they do and, for our purposes, to how they play their customer role. They could be aggressive or subdued, fast or slow in their speech and movement, emotional or unemotional, and task-oriented or relationship-oriented. One apt personality typology for business customers is the "social styles" classification, proposed by David W. Merill.[30] This classification uses two personality traits:

1. *Assertiveness*—the aspect of behaviour that measures whether a person tends to tell or ask, and the degree to which others see that person as trying to influence their decisions. Assertive people take a stand and make their position clear to others. They are demanding, aggressive, and forceful. In social situations, they are likely to initiate conversation and display a take-charge attitude. In contrast, unassertive people are unassuming, contented, quiet, and easygoing. They tend not to express their ideas or beliefs, but instead to listen to others and to be supportive of others' ideas. The "telling" kind of individuals, when placed in an uneasy social situation, tend to "fight" or confront the situation. The "asking" kind prefer "flight," or avoiding the situation.
2. *Responsiveness*—a person's tendency to emote rather than control feelings, and the extent to which others see that person as an individual who displays feelings or emotions openly in social situations. A more responsive individual readily expresses anger, joy, or hurt feelings and tends to be warm, emotional, or lighthearted. The unresponsive, or the controlling types, tend to be reserved, cautious, and serious; to be independent of or indifferent to others' feelings; and to use reason or logic more in making decisions. An unresponsive person is more task-oriented rather than relationship-oriented, and the reverse is the case with the responsive person.

By combining these two traits—*assertiveness* and *responsiveness*—we can identify the four social styles shown in Figure 2.4: *driving, expressive, amiable*, and *analytical*. The driving types want to dominate in interpersonal situations, want their opinions to prevail, demand compliance with their wishes, and do so in a "cold" manner, without any regard for the feelings of others. The expressive types are also opinionated and demanding of compliance with their requests, but they do so by dealing with emotions, using persuasion rather than authority. The amiable types are unassertive, undemanding, and easygoing, but they also are warm, show their feelings openly, and desire to establish personal relationships with those they deal with. Finally, the analytical types are neither demanding and assertive nor emotional.

They tend to ask questions, collect information, and study the data carefully before forming an opinion. This classification has been used in employee selection and in employee training to increase effectiveness in working with co-workers, subordinates, and superiors.

The following four social types display distinct behaviours, both verbal and nonverbal, that can be used to identify the social style of a customer in business negotiations.

FIGURE 2.4 Classification of Personality into Social Styles

Low Responsiveness

	ANALYTICAL	DRIVING	
	Slow reaction Maximum effort to organize Minimum concern for relationships Historical time frame Cautious action Tends to reject involvement	Swift reaction Maximum effort to control Minimum concern for caution in relationships Present time frame Direct action Tends to reject inaction	
Low Assertiveness			**High Assertiveness**
	AMIABLE	**EXPRESSIVE**	
	Unhurried reaction Maximum effort to relate Minimum concern for effecting change Present time frame Supportive action Tends to reject conflict	Rapid reaction Maximum effort to involve Minimum concern for routine Future time frame Impulsive action Tends to reject isolation	

High Responsiveness

SOURCE: Adapted from Merrill, David W., and Reid, Roger H.. *Personal Styles and Effective Performance: Make Your Style Work for You.* Radnor, PA: Chilton Book Company, 1981.

LO 2 PERSONAL CONTEXT

Our personal context—the characteristics of the socio-economic/cultural environment in which we have lived and are living—has intimately influenced our resources, tastes, and preferences. It therefore affects our behaviour as customers by helping to define what we can and want to use and buy. Personal context has four dimensions that affect customer behaviour: *culture*, *institutions and groups*, *personal worth*, and *social class*. Of these, culture and reference groups influence customers' tastes and preferences, and personal worth influences resources. This quartet of contextual factors forms the conduit through which all customer behaviour is channelled. Without an understanding of these contextual factors, it is nearly impossible to understand why customers from different countries, subcultures, economic means, religions, families, and other institutions seek different values from the marketplace.

Culture

Webster's New Collegiate Dictionary defines culture as "the integrated pattern of human behaviour that includes thought, speech, action, and artifacts and depends on man's capacity for learning and transmitting knowledge to succeeding generations." Thus, culture is everything a person learns and shares with members of a society, including ideas, norms, morals, values, knowledge, skills, technology, tools, material objects, and behaviour. Culture excludes genetically inherited instincts, since these are not learned, as well as those individual behaviours, norms, knowledge, and so on, that are not shared with other members of society.

We learn our culture by the processes of enculturation and acculturation. **Enculturation** is the process of learning one's own culture. **Acculturation** is the process of learning a new culture. Learning a culture entails becoming knowledgeable about its various elements.

Enculturation The process of learning one's own culture.

Acculturation The process of learning a new culture.

- *Values*—Values are conceptions of what is good and desirable versus what is bad and undesirable.
- *Norms*—Norms are rules of behaviour. They are a guide of do's and don'ts. Norms are more specific than values and dictate acceptable and unacceptable behaviour.
- *Rituals*—Rituals are a set of symbolic behaviours that occur in a fixed sequence and tend to be repeated periodically. Being symbolic behaviour, they have a meaning in culture.
- *Myths*—Myths are stories that express some key values of society. For example, the story of Santa Claus is a myth in much of the Christian world.

National culture refers to the culture prevalent in a nation. It comprises the norms, rituals, and values common to everyone in that nation, regardless of the subgroup affiliation. A related concept is that of popular culture. **Popular culture** is the culture of the masses, with norms, rituals, and values that have a mass appeal. For example, Hollywood and the movie industry have influenced popular culture all over the world. **Subculture** is the culture of a group within the larger society. The group may be based on any common characteristics (such as nationality of origin, race, region, age, religion, gender, social class, or profession) identifying that group as distinct from other groups or from the society at large.

National culture The culture prevalent in a nation.

Popular culture The culture of the masses in a nation, with norms, rituals, and values that have a mass appeal.

Subculture The culture of a group within the larger society.

Corporations have culture, too,[31] and it is reflected in a company's rituals and customs, and even in corporate myths and celebration of its heroes. Values such as "People are important," "Merit matters," and "Prosper through diversity" define what success means in the corporation. Cultural heroes, such as Henry Ford at Ford Motor, Thomas Watson at IBM, Jack Welsh at GE, Richard Bronson at Virginia Atlantic, Larry Page and Sergey Brin at Google, and Steve Jobs at Apple, personify the culture's values and provide tangible role models for others.

Characteristics of Culture. The concept of culture has the following six characteristics.

1. *Culture is learned.* We are not born with it. Instinctive behaviour, which we possess since birth, is not culture. The act of crying is not culture; however, knowing when it is proper to cry in public is culture, since that is something we have to learn.
2. *Culture regulates society.* It does so by offering norms and standards of behaviour, and by sanctioning deviations from that behaviour. Everyone in a culture knows the rules to live by.
3. *Culture makes living more efficient.* Because culture is shared, we don't have to learn things anew as we encounter new people and new situations within the same culture.

4. *Culture is adaptive.* Culture is a human response to the environment. As the environment changes, culture is likely to adapt to the new environmental demands. Survival makes adaptation imperative. A Canadian firm doing business in Mexico, for example, would have to adapt its ways of dealing with customers from a Latin culture or else face failure.
5. *Culture is environmental.* It envelops everyone's life alike and at all times. Like environment, we take culture for granted until something unexpected happens. That is, if a cultural norm is broken, only then is our attention drawn to the quiet presence of culture.
6. *Multiple cultures are nested hierarchically.* The culture of a larger group constrains and shapes the culture of the smaller groups within it. For example, the culture of a middle-income Asian family in Canada is actually the culture of the middle class, nested inside the culture of the Asians, in turn nested in the national culture.

Dimensions of Cross-Cultural Values

Although culture includes a host of shared beliefs and behaviours, the bedrock of culture is values. Cultural values may apply to things, ideas, goals, and behaviours. Based on research in a number of countries, Geert Hofstede has developed a classification of value orientations with the following five dimensions: individualism/collectivism, power distance, uncertainty avoidance, masculinity/femininity, and abstract or associative thinking.[32]

Individualism versus collectivism concerns the value individuals place on their own advancement and benefits versus the good of the groups and institutions of which they are members. Cultures marked with individualism exhibit loose ties among individuals, self-interest over the group interest, a large amount of personal freedom, and survival of the fittest. Contrarily, cultures of collectivism exhibit close ties between individuals, group interest over self-interest, a limited amount of personal freedom, and group protection. The United States is an example of a culture of individualism, whereas Asian societies value collectivism.

One implication of this cultural value is the kinds of emotional appeals that will influence consumers in these two types of society. Emotional appeals can be ego-focused—associated with an internal state such as pride, happiness, anger, or frustration. Or emotional appeals can be other-focused—associated with others in a social context and including such emotions as empathy, peacefulness, indebtedness, and shame. In collectivist cultures (e.g., China, Japan, Taiwan), the self is considered to be inseparable from others and the social context. Hence, in an emotional experience, members of a collectivist culture would be expected to focus on interpersonal aspects of the experience, weaving the individual with interpretations of what other people notice, think, and feel about the experience.

Consequently, in the collectivist cultures, other-focused emotional appeals would be expected to be more persuasive than ego-focused appeals; the converse would be expected for individualistic cultures. However, at least one research study found this not to be true. Jennifer Aaker and Patti Williams examined the persuasive effect of emotional appeals on members of a collectivist culture (China) versus an individualistic culture (the United States). They found that ego-focused emotional appeals led to more favourable attitudes for the members of the collectivist culture than other-focused emotional appeals. In this study, when the Chinese participants from the collectivist culture encountered the ego-focused emotional appeal (on a one-to-one basis, as a form of a print advertisement rather than in the presence of others), it actually prompted them to access several parts of their independent self, thus leading to an increase in individual thoughts. Hence, the ego-focused appeal led to more favorable attitudes than the other-focused appeal. The reverse was true of the U.S. participants in the study.[33] Obviously, the way in which the individualistic and collectivist values play out depends on a number of other factors.

Power distance refers to the extent of social inequality and the extent of submissive relationship with authority. In cultures with large power distance, there is greater authoritarianism among persons of different strata in the larger population, among members of the family, and among managerial hierarchy in organizations. In cultures with small power distance, on the other hand, there is greater egalitarianism among those same groups. Consequently, decision making is more participative. Power distance also refers to the extent to which personal relationships are allowed to be formed between members holding different levels of power and authority. In societies with large power distance, subordinates are required to maintain a distance from their superiors and always act in a subservient way. In societies with small power distance, relations between members at different vertical ranks are not as formal. Some countries with large power distance are Egypt, Guatemala, India, Iraq, and Malaysia. Some countries with small power distance are Canada, the United States, Germany, Great Britain, Israel, and Switzerland.

Uncertainty avoidance is defined as the extent to which people in a society feel the need to avoid ambiguous situations. They try to manage these situations by providing or requesting explicit and formal rules and regulations, rejecting novel ideas, and accepting the existence of absolute truths and superordinate goals in the context of work organization. Uncertainty avoidance is directly related to the importance of quality assurance and service guarantees. People who cannot tolerate uncertainty would be expected to seek greater dependability, reliability, and guarantees when buying products.

Masculinity versus femininity refers to the extent to which male and female roles are segregated, and the degree to which masculine roles are considered superior (masculine culture) or inferior (feminine culture). Canada gets a medium score on the masculinity dimension because of greater equality between the genders. In contrast, Asian societies are highly masculine. In a masculine society, dominant values are money, success, and material things. A feminine society more strongly values improving quality of life, preserving the environment, helping others, putting relationships before money and achievement, and thinking "Small is beautiful."

The fifth dimension is *abstract versus associative thinking*. Thinking cultures also differ in terms of the thinking associated with the creation of values in products; that is, whether values are engineered into them or added by associative processes, such as celebrity endorsement of products. In abstract cultures, cause-and-effect relationships and logical thinking are dominant. Abstract cultures emphasize the use of the cause-and-effect relationships, face-to-face communication, logical thinking and eagerness to change and innovate. In associative cultures, people make associations among events that may not have much logical basis. For example, associative cultures tend to link events to the influence of gods or the supernatural, or to link a personality (e.g., Wayne Gretsky) to a product.

Johnston and Johal map the Internet culture on four of Hofstede's cultural dimensions. On the dimension of power distance, the Internet culture leans toward low power distance since it is informal in nature, promotes interaction, treats every user as equal in status and power, and has no differential barriers for access to information. On the individualism-versus-collectivism front, the Internet is slowly moving from having a collective nature (with cooperation, sharing, and free information to all) to having an individualistic nature that is more commercial. As to uncertainty avoidance, the Internet culture scores low on this dimension, as it is innovative, it changes constantly with the introduction of new technology and tools, and it encourages interaction rather than acceptance. The final dimension against which the Internet is matched is that of masculinity/femininity. Johnston and Johal find it difficult to brand the Internet as one or the other since it reflects characteristics of both. The aggressive, competitive masculine nature is certainly present on the Internet, as illustrated in e-commerce activity, and, at the same time, communities on the Net also exhibit the feminine characteristics of caring for and nurturing its members.[34]

Institutions and Groups

Groups
Two or more persons sharing a common purpose.

Institutions
Relatively permanent groups with a pervasive and universal presence in a society, such as schools, religions, and the family.

Besides being part of a culture, customers are members of various institutions and groups, which form the second part of the customer's personal context. **Groups** can be defined as two or more persons sharing a common purpose. **Institutions** are more permanent groups with pervasive and universal presence in society, such as schools, religions, and the family. Since institutions and groups influence individual behaviour by serving as points of reference, and as sources of norm, value, and conduct, they are also called reference groups. Reference groups are persons, groups, and institutions that individuals look to for guidance regarding their own behaviour and values, and whose opinion they respect.

Types of Groups

Groups have been classified in many ways. The common classifications divide groups according to frequency of contact, nature of membership, formality, and group members' ability to choose whether they belong.

Within the category of *frequency of contact*, there are two divisions: primary groups and secondary groups. Primary groups are those a person interacts with frequently (not necessarily face to face) and whose opinions or norms are considered important to follow. In secondary groups, the contact is infrequent, and the norms of the group are considered less binding or obligatory. Examples of primary groups are family, work organization, church groups, business cartels, and so on. Examples of secondary groups are distant relatives and occupational groups such as doctors, lawyers, musicians, and theater artists.

A second dimension is *the nature of the membership*, i.e., whether the membership is real or symbolic. Membership groups are the ones in which an individual claiming to be a member is recognized as such by the head or leader or the key members of the group. In symbolic groups, on the other hand, there is no provision or procedure for granting membership, and the group leader or key members may even deny membership. However, the individual regards himself or herself to be a member, voluntarily and unobtrusively adopts the group's norms and values, and identifies with the group. Examples of membership groups are family, the YMCA, and warehouse clubs, while celebrities and heroes as sources of inspiration may be symbolic groups to customers who emulate the norms, values, and behaviour of their heroes. As shown in Table 2.2, these two bases for classifying groups—frequency of contact and the nature of membership—can be combined to describe many groups.

TABLE 2.2 Types of Groups

	Primary	Secondary
Membership	• Family • Work organizations • Church groups • Fraternities/sororities • Personal role model	• Professional associations • Credit unions • Political campaign volunteers • YMCA • Celebrities
Symbolic	• A significant other • The person one "secretly admires"	• Fortune 500 companies • Other artists (for an artist)

Groups differ in the other two ways to classify groups: the degree of *formality* and whether or not the person has the *freedom to choose the group*. In formal groups, conduct and behaviour tend to be highly codified. Informal groups, in contrast, have few explicit rules about group behaviour. A choice group, as the name implies, is a group a person voluntarily chooses to join. An ascribed or assigned group is one in which membership is automatic for someone who has the characteristics that define the group. Together, these two dimensions lead to four types of groups as depicted in Table 2.3.

Choice-based informal groups include neighbourhood, community, social, and volunteer groups; formal choice-based groups include school, workplace, fraternities, and sororities. Membership in the assigned or ascribed group is usually by birth (family, relatives, or a tribe) or by some formal process, such as becoming a prisoner or being declared a minority for receiving government benefits. Since most people stay in their religion of birth, we consider religious groups as well as families as ascribed groups—the family being an informal institution, and the religious group being a formal institution.

This typology of groups applies to business customers (as opposed to companies offering goods or services) as well. Informal but choice-based groups are "best in class" companies with which a business-customer firm may consider itself to be affiliated. Committees and task forces are two examples of informal ascribed groups. Examples of choice-based formal groups are professional associations, such as the Canadian Manufacturers'Association (CMA), the Retail Council of Canada, and corporate country clubs. An example of a formal but ascribed group in a business setting is a business that is identified as a small business and then being accorded all the privileges and responsibilities of small businesses as a group.

TABLE 2.3 Classification of Groups for Household Customers

	TYPE OF INSTITUTIONS/GROUPS	
	Informal	**Formal**
Choice	• Volunteer groups • Community • Friendship groups • Cultural heroes	• School • Workplace • Fraternities/sororities
Type of Membership		
Ascribed or Assigned	• Family • Relatives • Tribes	• Religion • Prison

Family and Religion as Reference Groups

The family is an ascribed informal group and a primary membership group. It is the most influential reference group for any individual customer. Family can be defined as a group of people related by marriage and biology. Family is the institution in which children, the future adults, receive their precepts and guidance. In families, members interact continually in intense face-to-face communications, and member preferences and desires get constant feedback and are channelled and shaped by reinforcement or sanctions from other members. Families are important and influence customer behaviour across cultures. The influence of family members on one another's buying-decision process is discussed in a later chapter.

Like family, religion is a reference group that may exercise some influence on customers' values, customs, and habits. Religion refers to a system of beliefs about the supernatural and spiritual world, about God, and about how humans, as God's creatures, should behave. Religious affiliation affects customer behaviour principally by influencing the customer's personality structure—his or her beliefs, values, and behavioral tendencies. These personality structures, in turn, affect customers' marketplace behaviours.

Conditions for Reference Group Influence

Francis S. Bourne addressed the question, "When or under what conditions does reference group influence occur?" He proposed that a product's conspicuousness is the principal factor that affects whether or not users of that product will be susceptible to reference group influence.[35] Bourne proposed that there are two dimensions of conspicuousness: exclusivity and public visibility. If everyone owns and uses a product, then the ownership and use of that product has no exclusivity. Hence, there is no basis for being concerned about others' opinions of it. The second dimension, visibility, is critical because a product has to be visible and identifiable in order for reference group members to approve or disapprove it.

Based on Bourne's ideas, William O. Bearden and Michael J. Etzel have suggested that the reference group influence may occur for the ownership of the product per se, for the choice of a specific brand, or for both. This will depend on whether a product is a luxury or a necessity (capturing the "exclusivity" dimension in Bourne's proposal) and whether the product is used in private or in public (capturing the "visibility" dimension of conspicuousness). The following four combinations are presented in Figure 2.5.[36]

1. *Publicly consumed luxuries*—In this case, reference groups will influence both whether the product will be owned and which brand will be purchased.
2. *Privately consumed luxuries*—Here, reference group influence will be strong for the ownership of the product (because it is a luxury) but weak for the brand choice (since it will be used in private, out of public visibility).
3. *Publicly consumed necessities*—In this case, product ownership influence will be absent or weak since everyone owns it, but brand-level influence will be strong due to public visibility.
4. *Privately consumed necessities*—Finally, for products that are necessities and, in addition, are consumed privately, neither product ownership nor the choice of specific brands is likely to be influenced by reference groups.

FIGURE 2.5 Private-Public, Luxury-Necessity, Product-Brand Influences

Public

	Product / Brand	Weak Reference Group Influence (−)	Strong Reference Group Influence (+)	
Necessity	Strong reference group influence (+)	**PUBLIC NECESSITIES** • Influence: Weak product and strong brand • Examples: Wristwatch, automobile, man's suit	**PUBLIC LUXURIES** • Influence: Strong product and brand • Examples: Golf clubs, snow skis, sailboat	**Luxury**
	Weak reference group influence (−)	**PRIVATE NECESSITIES** • Influence: Weak product and brand • Examples: Mattress, floor lamp, refrigerator	**PRIVATE LUXURIES** • Influence: Strong product and weak brand • Examples: TV game, trash compactor, icemaker	

Private

SOURCE: Bearden, William O., and Etzel, Michael J. "Reference Group Influence on Product and Brand Purchase Decisions." *Journal of Consumer Research* 9 (1982): 183–94. Reprinted with permission of the University of Chicago Press.

Types of Reference Group Influence

Whether the reference group influences decisions about a brand or a product category, the influence may operate through several types of power. The nature of influence power exercised by reference group members may be of three types: expertise, reward and sanction, and attractiveness. Corresponding to each type of power is a type of reference group influence: informational, normative, and identificational, respectively.[37]

Informational influence occurs when a consumer seeks and accepts advice from someone else because of the latter's expertise on the performance characteristics of the product being bought. Professional advisors such as doctors, lawyers, or product enthusiasts among your informal groups are examples of informational reference groups. Business customers also seek and accept informational influence from legal, technical, and management consultants.

Normative influence occurs when a consumer's decision is influenced by his or her desire to conform with the expectations of someone else. This influence stems from the reference group's power to reward or sanction the consumption behaviour of others. Family members exercise normative influence on our behaviours as customers, and businesses are subject to normative influence from the government.

Identificational influence occurs when a consumer buys something because it helps him or her to be like someone else. Many people have role models; the consumer emulates, to the extent possible, the lifestyle of people he or she admires, buying products associated with, used by, or endorsed by these admired people. Celebrities from the worlds of entertainment, sports, and politics serve as reference groups for multitudes of consumers. In business markets, identificational influences are at work when companies look to other corporations as "best in class," or the most admired companies, and emulate these companies to gain their advantages.

Personal Worth

Along with culture and reference groups, the customer context that influences the market values a customer seeks includes **personal worth.** Personal worth is equivalent to the financial worth of a person.

Measurement of Personal Worth. Personal worth has three components: *income*, *wealth*, and *borrowing power*.

A person's income is the amount of monetary earnings he or she receives periodically on a more or less regular basis. Although no two families spend their money in exactly the same way, there is, on average, quite a consistent pattern of how income is allocated over expense categories. Statistical analyses of data from families from diverse income groups show that poor families spend their income largely on food, housing, and basic clothing. As income increases, people tend to eat more food, and less of their food is staple, but the proportion of income spent on food declines. Proportion of income spent on housing rises with income in the very low income range, but then it remains fairly constant. Expenditures on clothing, automobiles, and luxury goods rise sharply with income until a very high upper limit is reached. Finally, savings rise dramatically with income within every income category. Similarly, in business markets, cash flows influence what will or will not be bought. Many small business failures can be traced directly to cash-flow problems. On the other hand, rapid growth also can create cash-flow problems from corporate acquisitions. For example, General Foods was built on buying out small local or regional brands and making them national brands, including Yuban, Maxwell House and Sanka coffees, and Bird's Eye frozen vegetables.

The second component and measure of personal worth is wealth. In household markets, wealth is assessed as the net worth of the individual. Net worth of an individual is defined as the current monetary value of all assets owned minus the current monetary value of all liabilities. Wealth can be created by five means:

1. inheritance;
2. income accumulation (savings), including "passive income" from investment of one's wealth;
3. employee stock option plans and RRSP savings;
4. accumulation of nonmonetary wealth such as equity in home ownership, jewelry, or art;
5. lottery winnings.

The counterpart of net worth for a business market is the concept of shareholder equity. Net worth is the book value of the business and may or may not be commensurate with the business's market value as captured in shareholders' equity.

Borrowing power
The anticipated level of income of a person (lifetime disposable income and asset accumulated through savings); a primary indicator, in addition to income and wealth, of a customer's economic condition.

Borrowing power is the final indicator of a customer's economic condition. In consumer markets, borrowing power is the anticipated level of income of the person (lifetime disposable income and asset accumulation through savings). Consumer credit cards, home mortgages, and automobile financing are based on an accounting of the customer's borrowing power. The business market equivalent is the firm's ability to repay debt in the future, and is measured by the creditworthiness of the organization based on ratings by companies such as Standard & Poor's and Dominion Bond Rating Service.

Customers can be divided into segments on the basis of their personal worth: poor, middle class, and affluent, and customer behaviour differs widely across these groups.

For example, in 2000, the bottom 10 percent of families in Canada had incomes below $18,990. The combined income of these families accounted for less than 2 percent of total Canadian family income. In the year 2000, there were 4,720,490 individuals (or 16 percent of the total population) living on low incomes according to Statistics Canada's definition.[38] Forty-five percent of single-parent families with young children were low-income families. Studies show that the poor do not follow wise purchasing strategies and actually pay more for goods and services than do the rest of society. This occurs because poor consumers do not have the skills and transportation to shop for bargains, and because merchants exploit their weaknesses. At the other end of the scale, in 2000 the top 10 percent of families had incomes above $117,850. The combined income of these families accounted for 28 percent of the total income of all Canadian families.[39] Affluent families account for higher consumption of airline travel, new car sales, and luxury goods. There is no single definition of "middle income." One conventional grouping deems household levels of less than $24,000 as low income, from $24,001 to $64,500 as intermediate or middle income, and greater than $64,500 as high income.[40]

The income distribution of Internet users is slowly reflecting the economically privileged and unprivileged classes. Though research on the Internet population has found that Internet users have higher household earnings than the general public, this econo-digital divide seems to be closing. In 2003, nearly 45 percent (1.3 million) of the households with income between $24,000 and $44,000 had someone who used the Internet, up 13 percent from 2002. Eighty-two percent of households in the top 25 percent income group had a member who used the Internet. Non-Internet users earned below average household income, with 49 percent of non-users in the lowest 25 percent income group.[41] Higher-income groups are more attuned to purchasing via the Internet. However, as PC costs decrease, penetration of the Internet will increase in lower-income households, and online purchasing also will become prevalent in the lower-income groups.

Social Class

Many sociologists, economists, and consumer researchers consider social class, rather than personal worth, to be a more meaningful characteristic for understanding and predicting customer behaviour. Income is an important factor in deciding a person's social class, but it is not the only determinant. Social class also depends on one's education and occupation, so that, despite relatively low income, a highly educated person or someone in a more prestigious occupation could be accorded a higher social class, and vice versa. **Social class** is the relative standing of members of a society so that a higher position implies a higher status than those in the lower social class.

Social Class Characteristics. Some characteristics of social class are:

1. *Rank ordering*—Social classes are ranked in terms of social prestige.
2. *Relative permanence*—Social classes is a relatively permanent characteristic of the family. A person's social class does not normally change from day to day or year to year.
3. *Intergenerational class mobility*—It is possible for a person to move out of the social class of his or her birth and into a higher or lower class by acquiring the values, resources, and behaviours of the new class.
4. *Internal homogeneity*—Classes are homogenous within each strata. Persons belonging to the same social class tend to be similar in terms of the types of occupations, the kinds of neighbourhoods they live in, their food habits, socializing habits, and so on.

5. *Distinct from income*—Though income is an important determinant of social class, there is no one-to-one correspondence between the two. Since social class depends as much on other factors, such as education, occupation, and personal tastes, it is not uncommon for a person of relatively middle income to be in the upper social class and vice versa. For example, priests, politicians (when in power), and educators command prestige and status significantly disproportionate with their income earnings.

Social Class in Canada: A Brief Profile. A number of different social-stratification schemes or hierarchies have been developed by North American sociologists. There is no universal system of stratifying a given population into precisely defined social classes. Whatever the classification scheme, each social class is no more than a *conceptual category* in a hierarchy based on status and prestige. Though not a completely reliable predictor of class membership, a person's occupation is usually the best *single* indicator available. In Figure 2.6, 16 occupational groups are ranked from top to bottom in order of decreasing prestige, as per the Pineo-Porter-McRoberts socioeconomic classification of occupations. These occupational groups have been clustered into four major social-class divisions labelled the upper classes, the middle class, the working class, and the lower classes. The upper and lower classes can be further divided into two or more subclasses.[42]

FIGURE 2.6 Subdivisions of the Four Major Social Classes

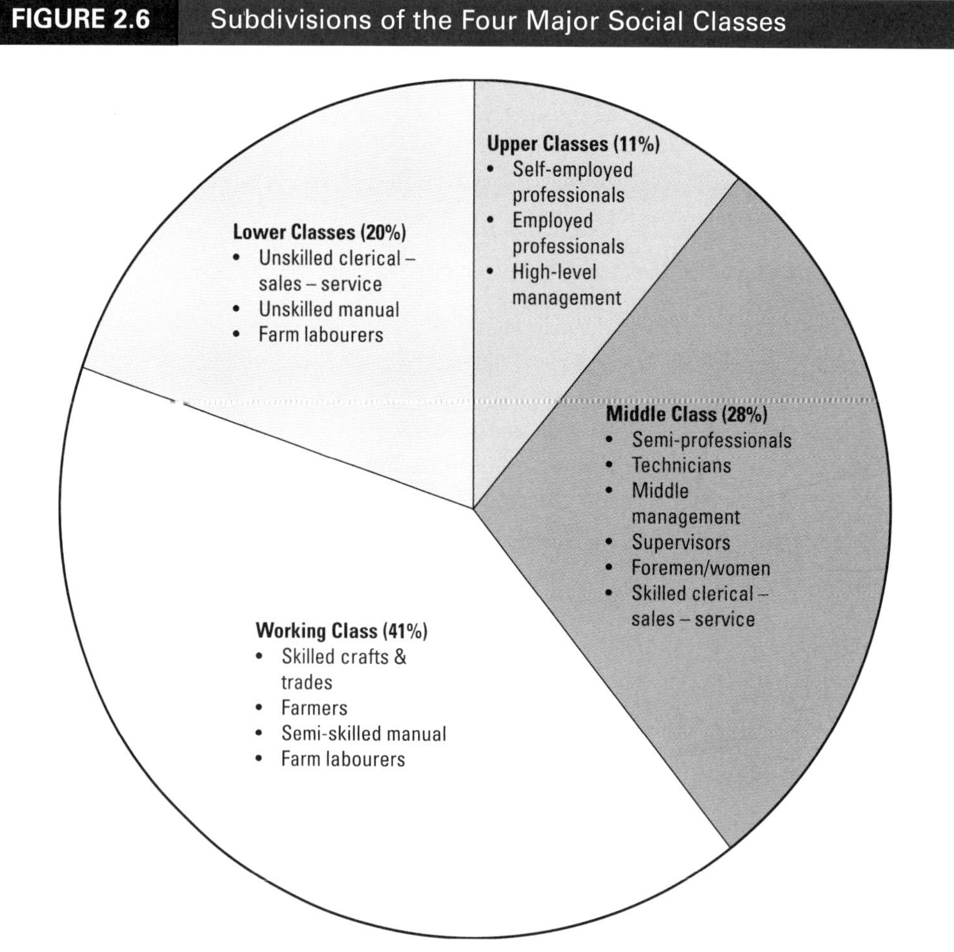

This look at the class structure in Canada is certainly not definitive, but it gives the reader some idea of the proportion of Canadians belonging in each social class. Members of the upper classes are, as a whole, concerned with buying quality merchandise, favouring prestige brands, and spending with good taste. Members of the middle class are most concerned with wanting to "do the right thing" and buying what is popular. They are inclined to buy products that they imagine will validate their status and confer prestige. The horizon of the working class is oriented toward the present rather than the future. They like to see the immediate results of their labours, and they often spend as quickly as they earn—not necessarily frivolously, but on tangible things such as labour-saving household appliances, modern, up-to-date gadgets, elaborate colour TVs, video games, high-tech cameras and watches, or power tools for the home workshop. The lower class is made up of people who participate in the marginal sector of the labour market and those on welfare. In general, the lower-class consumers are considerably less competent and confident in shopping skills and purchase decisions than the middle-class consumers.[43]

MARKET ENVIRONMENT

LO 3

In addition to personal factors, the market environment presents the second group of determinants that affect customer behaviour. We divide market environment into two broad classes: market traits and market context. Market traits refer to the physical characteristics of the surroundings in which consumers select, use, and pay for products in both household and business markets. There are three physical characteristics of a place: *climate*, *topography*, and *ecology*. Market context refers to the man-made forces (as opposed to the natural forces) of the market as a physical place that affects customer wants and needs. It has three components: *economy*, *government policy*, and *technology*.

Market Traits

The market traits—climate, topography, and ecology—influence customers' needs as opposed to wants.

Climate

Climate is the first major component of the geophysical market environment. It consists of temperature, wind, humidity, and rainfall in the area. The patterns of these four elements vary in different locations of the Earth. Research in the area of homeostasis (a process by which the body seeks to regulate its internal environment) reveals that certain behaviours, such as mood and expressed affect, are influenced by variations in the intensity and duration of sunlight and temperatures across climates and seasons. Several other behaviours, such as stimulation and sensation seeking, novelty and variety seeking, risk taking, and impulsivity, are related to the optimal stimulation level of an individual. The optimal stimulation level is a function of the interaction of three neurotransmitters in the brain whose release and synthesis is caused by different levels of sunlight and temperature (heat) in our atmosphere.[44]

Climate
A component of the geophysical market environment, consisting of temperature, wind, humidity, and rainfall in an area that affects consumers' needs for food, clothing, and shelter.

In an attempt to maintain a thermoregulatory balance (an internal core body temperature of about 37°C), humans learn to cope with climate and climate-dependent availability of food, plants, animals, and building materials. This, in turn, intimately influences people's consumption of food, use of clothing, housing patterns, and the geographical distribution of population itself. Food consumption patterns differ dramatically between the tropical and arctic countries. Colder arctic countries rely heavily on animals for food as well as for clothing. Northern Europeans eat more red meat and fewer fruits and vegetables than do southern Europeans. Striking differences in clothing are apparent across different climates with respect to materials, design, and style. People living in colder climates rely on wool and leather, while those living in warmer climates rely on cotton, silk, and other lighter fabrics. Differences are found in customer needs for shelter. Colder countries utilize wood and stone as materials, compared to warmer countries that use clay and brick.

Climate also affects business customers' needs and purchases. All industrial machinery and equipment must be designed to withstand the climatic conditions in which the customer is located. For example, heat, humidity, and dust affect the performance of trucks, tractors, and farm equipment. Computers and other machinery often need climate-controlled environments to perform. In addition to climatic changes from one location to another, climate in any one place also varies throughout the year, causing the annual cycle of seasonality. Business sales vary from month to month in a calendar year. This seasonal variation is caused by three factors: (1) annual climate changes; (2) calendar events such as school year, football season, and so on; and (3) holidays and festivities. To a degree, the last two factors are themselves related to or influenced by the first factor.

The effects of annual climate changes on customer purchases are obvious. Customers need and buy warm clothing for winter and cool clothing for summer. Around the world, coffee, tea, and other hot beverages are purchased more during cold months, and soft drinks and ice creams are bought more during warm months.

Calendar-year events impel other purchases. Some examples of purchases for a typical calendar year in a North American family with children are cold remedies during the January–February flu season, and allergy medications during March, the start of allergy season, when pollen counts start. May begins the four-month-long summer season, where customers embark on outdoor activities, such as bicycling, gardening, swimming, and sports. Accordingly, they buy products related to these activities throughout these four months. June is peak season for weddings and graduations, both inducing purchases of party goods and other celebration merchandise. July and August are peak months for family travel, both vacationing and moving. August is back-to-school month, and sales of school supplies and children's clothing peak. November begins the early holiday shopping season, and December peaks the purchase of all kinds of retail items, including clothing, toys, books, shoes, and gifts. According to a survey by Ipsos-Reid, during the 2004 holiday season, more than 3.5 million Canadian adults bought at least one gift online, up from 2.2 million in 2003. Convenience (avoiding crowds), easier price comparison, wider product selection, and lower prices online are some of the reasons for this boom in online spending in the holiday season.[45]

Topography

Topography
The terrain, altitude, and soil conditions of a location on Earth where customers buy and use a product or service.

Another major component of the geophysical environment is **topography**—the terrain, altitude, and soil conditions of the market where customers buy and use a product. In addition to differences in food, shelter, and clothing across topographical regions, a number of other products also are needed principally due to topographical conditions. These include flood insurance, erosion-resistant foundations for homes, special water treatment plants, and different means of transportation based on terrain.

Consumption varies across different regions of the world, and indeed within a single country. Regional consumption differences are due to two factors: (1) geophysical conditions comprising climate, topography, and ecology and (2) cultural and/or ethnic heritage. To capture regional preference differences, it is illuminating to draw and study maps of regional variations in product consumption. These maps show **geographical variation**—different patterns of consumption in different regions, such as the number of bicycles per household. These differences may occur due to variations in climate, topography, and facilitative infrastructure such as bike lanes on city roads.[46] As against topography, cultural and ethnic heritage plays a major role in the variation in wine consumption in Canada. Annual sales per capita of wine are the highest in Quebec ($231) thanks to its French heritage, although wine production in that province is insignificant. One the other hand, wine-producing regions like Ontario and British Columbia record lower per-capita sales of wines than Quebec.[47]

Geographical variation Different patterns of consumption in different regions.

To address such differences, marketers may use a strategy of **regional marketing**—the practice of adapting marketing programs according to segmentation based on geographic differences among customers. The marketer recognizes customer diversity from one region to another and tailors the entire marketing mix to each region.

Regional marketing The practice of adapting the marketing program according to customer diversity from one region to another.

Ecology

The third market characteristic, **ecology,** refers to the natural resources and the delicate balance and interdependence among vegetation, animals, and humans. It also includes concepts related to the food chain. One of the recent concerns in Canada is what has been referred to as the greenhouse effect and global warming. **Global warming** is the theory that Earth's climate is becoming warmer due to increases in hydrocarbons in the atmosphere, which are released with increased industrialization.

Ecology Natural resources and the balance and interdependence among vegetation, animals, and humans.

Ecology affects customer behaviour by making certain market options less convenient or attractive, and by causing customers to exercise their environmental values, which then bear upon their market choices. Market choices become less attractive, in turn, by two mechanisms: (1) the deteriorating ecology makes certain modes of consumption less convenient or satisfying, and (2) government disincentives make ecologically undesirable behaviours personally more costly. As an example of the ecology itself hindering certain behaviours, consider pollution. To avoid polluting the air, many consumers will reduce the amount of driving they do. On the other hand, as an example of the second mechanism of government disincentives, the government could impose a higher tax on fuel or require certain pollution-reducing equipment to control pollution. Apart from these two options, customers' own environmental values affect customer choices in that they voluntarily seek ecologically friendly options.

Global warming The progressive warming of Earth's climate due to an increase in hydrocarbons in the atmosphere resulting from increased industrialization.

Ecology: Consumers Who Want to Save Nature

Green consumer A customer concerned about the deteriorating environment and willing to modify his or her customer behaviour to save the environment

The **green consumer** is the consumer who is concerned about the deteriorating environment and is willing to take action to help save it, including reducing personal consumption. In a 2002 survey conducted by the firm PWC Consulting, 56 percent of Canadians said that the overall quality of the environment in the country had worsened over the previous five years, and that pollution was likely to affect their health.[48] People who show some commitment to the environment in their marketplace choices are termed **environmentally conscious consumers,** defined as "those who actively seek out products perceived as having relatively minimal impact

Environmentally conscious consumers Customers who actively seek out products with minimal impact on the environment.

on the environment."[49] The different types of green consumer are defined in Table 2.4. The Window on Research box presents a profile of the green consumer. Although the Roper segmentation criteria are based on an American sample, their basic premises can be generalized to the Canadian markets.

The Envirolink network (**http://www.envirolink.netforchange.com**) is an online community forum that provides comprehensive resources for individuals, organizations, and businesses working for social and environmental change. These resources include website and

TABLE 2.4 Environmental Segments

1. True-Blue Greens (9 percent)—The most deeply committed to environment, they are in the forefront of the green movement in Canada, and they express their concern both by advocacy and by pro-environmental consumption behaviour, such as recycling and buying products made from recycled materials.
2. Greenback Greens (6 percent)—This group backs its commitment to environment by showing willingness to pay more for environmentally friendly products.
3. Sprouts (31 percent)—This group shows a moderate level of commitment to environmental issues with a limited amount of pro-environmental behaviour.
4. Grousers (19 percent)—They display a lack of pro-environmental attitudes and behaviour and rationalize their inaction by blaming others.
5. Basic Browns (33 percent)—The environment is not a concern to them, and they do not want to be bothered with environmental issues. The majority of them are poor, and are more preoccupied with just making ends meet.

SOURCE: *The Environment: Public Attitudes and Behaviour*, a report by RoperASW and S.C. Johnson & Sons, Inc. (New York, June 2002).

WINDOW ON **RESEARCH**

Profile of the Green Consumer

What is the profile of green consumers? Demographically, according to various sources, the typical green consumer is a woman, likely 30 to 49 years of age. She has children six years or older; is educated, affluent, politically liberal; and lives in a suburb. Pyschographically, green consumers are very interested in news and politics, and are active in their communities. They think pollution is a serious threat to people's health and are willing to reduce their standard of living in an effort to tighten pollution standards. They do believe that the individual can make a difference in making the environment healthier, and they are even willing to pay more for environmentally friendly products. An intercept sample survey of 704 shoppers in Hong Kong shows that the demographic profile of the green consumer in Hong Kong is very similar to that of the green consumer in the West. They were more likely to have a higher education and higher household income. Heavy green consumers perceive influence from other persons, the government, and other green groups; possess a strong self-identity; and use the mass media for environmental news.

SOURCES: Adapted from Cleveland, Mark, Kalamas, Maria, and Laroche, Michel. "Shades of Green: Linking Environmental Locus of Control and Pro-environmental Behavior." *Journal of Consumer Marketing*, Vol. 22, No. 4 (Summer–Fall 2005), 198–212; Laroche, Michel, Bergeron, Jasmin, and Barbaro-Forleo, Guido. "Targeting Consumers Who Are Willing to Pay More for Environmentally Friendly Products." *Journal of Consumer Marketing*, Vol. 18, No. 6 (2001), 503–520; Chan, Kara. "Market Segmentation of Green Consumers in Hong Kong," *Journal of International Consumer Marketing*, 12 (2), 1999, 7–24.

domain name hosting for environmental and animal rights organizations, discussion forums, and educational and government resources. Despite consumer interest in the environment, environmental products remain a small fraction of the retail market, mainly because shopping for green products is not easy. Reading *Consumer Reports* and other literature to find the most energy-efficient appliance is laborious and impractical for day-to-day shopping. Moreover, studies have found that consumers are skeptical of claims made on the labels of green products. With the growth of e-commerce, online shops will be able to empower consumers by providing them with fast and easily available information and access to green goods. E-tailers like *EcoMall.com* and *GreenMarketplace.com* have seized the business opportunity provided by green consumers to set up sites that offer a wide array of environment-friendly products to customers on the Net. The next generation of sites will rely on sophisticated search engines—or "green bots"—to scan and screen for environmental features of products. Brokers, agents, and buyers' clubs could use these search engines to ferret out the best products for their clients and members. Some search criteria that could be used are published energy and water efficiency ratings of appliances, toxic chemicals used as product ingredients, publicly available information on chemical releases or accidents at manufacturing facilities, and products that use tropical hardwoods or other scarce resources.[50]

Business Response to Environmentalism. In their effort to respond to the consumer demand for a healthier environment, marketers engage in **environmental marketing,** which refers to the marketing of products in a manner that attempts to minimize the damage to the environment. This might entail conservation of scarce resources such as trees and energy; prudent use of pesticides in agricultural production; use of recycled, recyclable, or biodegradable materials in the production of the product as well as in its packaging; product design changes to reduce air or water pollution due to product use; and the adaptation of manufacturing processes that would minimize air or water pollution. For example, Britain's BP has accepted voluntary targets for reduction of carbon-dioxide emissions through the use of an innovative emissions-trading scheme among its dozens of divisions worldwide. The board of directors at Royal Dutch/Shell, an Anglo-Dutch energy giant, now require that all big projects must not only meet the company's required internal rate of return, but also consider the future cost of carbon emissions. This cost will be $5 per ton of carbon dioxide in 2005–2009, rising to $20 per ton from 2010.[51]

Environmental marketing
Marketing of products in a manner that attempts to minimize the damage to the environment.

Market Context

LO 4

The market context—economy, government policy, and technology—are the three other environmental determinants of customer behaviour. In contrast to the market characteristics, these aspects of the market context are created by humans as members of an organized society. The economic conditions in your own country, province, or city affect your purchase behaviour—stimulating it in prosperous times and dampening it during economic downturns. Government policy can create or collapse markets and their competitive structures with the stroke of a pen. Finally, technology can revolutionize both what and how customers buy. If you could visit your mom, for example, on a videophone, or if you could confer with your business associates via a videoconference, you would be less likely to give much business to the airlines.

Economy

Economy
The state of a nation with respect to levels of employment, wages, inflation, interest rates, currency exchange rates, and aggregate household savings and disposable income.

As a component of the market context, we discuss the aspects of the national **economy** that affect the market: levels of employment, wages, inflation, interest rates, currency exchange rates, aggregate household savings, and disposable income. The economic climate affects customer behaviour by three mechanisms:

1. By directly expanding or shrinking the financial resources of a household, or the buying power of these resources, the national economy encourages or constrains customer purchases at the individual household level as well as for business customers. Take the case of the slump in the IT industry in 2001–2002. Companies have been downsizing, and as customers lose jobs, the financial resources in their households shrink drastically.
2. By influencing customer sentiment—optimism or pessimism about the future—the economic climate encourages or dampens consumer spending.
3. By driving business cycles, the economy influences a customer's spending and saving behaviour.

Necessary expenditures
The purchase of goods and services needed for minimal sustenance.

Discretionary expenditures
The purchase of goods and services to make life physically or psychologically more comfortable beyond sustenance.

Customer expectations
Customers' economic outlook about the near future; this outlook shapes their spending.

Speaking of financial resources, George Katona classified all household expenditures as either necessary or discretionary. **Necessary expenditures** entail the purchase of goods and services needed for minimal sustenance, while **discretionary expenditures** entail the purchase of goods and services to make life physically or psychologically more comfortable beyond sustenance. In hard economic times, consumers would cut down on what they consider to be discretionary purchases, limiting their purchases to necessary items.[52]

The effect of the national economy on household purchase behaviour occurs through **customer expectations.** The customer's economic outlook can be optimistic or pessimistic, which will either spur or curb household spending. The economic optimism/pessimism of consumers has been tracked by the Conference Board of Canada. The Index of Consumer Confidence is constructed from responses to four attitudinal questions posed to a random sample of Canadian households. Those surveyed are asked to give their views about their households' current and expected financial positions and the short-term employment outlook. They are also asked to assess whether now is a good or a bad time to make a major purchase such as a house, car, or other big-ticket items. The Index is based on responses to the following four questions:

1. Considering everything, would you say that your family is better off or worse off financially than six months ago?
2. Again, considering everything, do you think that your family will be better off, the same or worse off financially six months from now?
3. How do you feel the job situation and overall employment will be in this community six months from now?
4. Do you think that right now is a good or bad time for the average person to make a major outlay for items such as a home, car, or other major item?

For each of the four questions above, there are three response options: positive, negative, and neutral. For each question, the percentage of respondents who state positive and negative opinions is calculated for each of the socioeconomic and regional classifications as well as for the national aggregated. Each Index of Consumer Confidence is derived by adding the percentage of positive responses, subtracting the percentage of negative responses, adding a scalar equal to 400, and indexing the resulting series to a base year of 1991. The scalar is introduced to force the value of the Index to zero if all responses are negative.[53]

One measure of business performance is the total retail sales of all goods and services in the economy. When total retail sales are rising, the economy is said to be in a boom; with declining sales, the economy is said to be in recession. Often a nation's business goes through a cycle of boom and recession; this is called a **business cycle.** The business cycle works like this: When the economy is doing well and is growing, the unemployment rate is low, and total production is high. Consumer spending is on the rise, causing high demand. Due to rising demand as well as rising wages (which raise the cost of production), consumer prices increase, resulting in inflation. With inflation, interest rates go up, which makes consumers want to save more and reduce spending. Reduced spending leads to a manufacturer inventory buildup, which in turn leads to manufacturers cutting back on production and laying off workers. Consequently, unemployment rises, and consumer spending is further reduced, leading to recession. Eventually, piled-up inventories begin to deplete, and manufacturers begin to return to prerecession levels of production, giving the economy its recovery, and later a boom. Thus, the business cycle is completed.[54]

Business cycle
A cycle of boom and recession experienced by the business world and caused by fluctuations in the economic environment.

Government Policy

Another market context factor—**government policy**—comprises *monetary policy*, *fiscal policy*, and *public policy*. Monetary policy includes decisions on interest rates, the money supply, regulating financial institutions, and so on. Fiscal policy deals with government trade practices, procurement, spending, borrowing, taxing, and the like. Finally, public policy comprises government acts such as economic regulation, environmental regulation, product safety, mergers and acquisitions, and other government policies. Internet marketers are still relatively free of customary and legal restrictions, but new global commercial instruments and laws will evolve to support the global cyberspace market.

Government policy
A market context factor comprising monetary/fiscal policy and public policy.

Monetary and Fiscal Policy. Government influences market behaviour by managing the national economy through adjustments to interest rates, money supply, taxation, and other instruments of monetary and fiscal policy. The Bank of Canada (the nation's central bank) may raise its prime lending rate (the rate at which it loans funds to other commercial banks), which discourages borrowing (e.g., home-buying market slows because interest rate hikes cause higher mortgage rates, making home purchasing less affordable for consumers). A hike in interest rate also causes customers to reduce their overall spending. This happens for several reasons. First, an increase in interest rate translates to higher mortgage payments, which reduces money that the customer will have available for other spending. Second, the higher rates also cause customers to reduce their use of credit cards, which again reduces their purchasing power. Finally, some customers may choose to save their money in order to take advantage of interest rates.

The effect of the Bank of Canada's policy on business customers is just the opposite. Because of lowered consumer demand caused by a decline in cash available to the consumer, businesses cannot command the price they require to keep up with the rising costs. They must rely on cost reduction via productivity gains, so they need to invest in new equipment that may improve productivity. This may result in capital outlays despite the high interest rates for borrowing.

A change in the income tax or sales tax similarly causes shifts in customer purchases. Depending on the nature of tax changes and their expected permanence, customers would postpone or advance their purchases.

Public Policy. Governments at the federal, provincial, and municipal levels enact various laws that influence both business and customer behaviour. These laws establish public policy that influences customer behaviour in four ways: (1) by constraining choices, (2) by mandating certain products, (3) by protecting the consumer in his or her purchases, and (4) by setting up facilitative infrastructure.

Negligent consumer behaviour Customer behaviour that puts oneself or others at risk, or that would, in the long run, impose heavy costs on society.

Constraining Choices. When constraining choices, the government creates regulations that monitor **negligent consumer behaviour.** Negligent behaviour puts the negligent person, or others, at risk, and imposes heavy costs on society or otherwise deteriorates quality of life in the long run. At an individual level, negligent consumer behaviour includes driving under the influence of alcohol, smoking, using steroids or other drugs, and littering along highways. For businesses, such behaviour includes environmental pollution, sale of unsafe products, and the use of harmful ingredients or processes in manufacturing. Government bans or controls the sale and use of what it considers to be harmful products, such as drugs, alcohol, tobacco, and firearms. Government also controls what products may be consumed in public places, for example, by prohibiting smoking, drinking, and gambling in schools.

Compliance Steering customer behaviour by government regulation.

Mandating Choices. Though the government forbids some choices, it mandates others. **Compliance** refers to the government mandate that customers obey certain defined rules and regulations with respect to purchase, payment, and, more important, product usage, including disposal. To obtain customer compliance with these mandates, governments pass laws and issue regulations with penalties for failure to comply. For example, in Canada, the federal and provincial governments require the use of certain products, such as helmets by motorcycle riders and seat belts by drivers and passengers of automobiles.

Protecting the Consumer. The government also can play an important role in enacting and enforcing laws to protect consumers against personal injury or fraud. In effect, all elements of the marketing mix (product, promotion, price, and place) are covered by various laws meant to protect the consumer.

Under Canada's Constitution, the federal and provincial/territorial governments share responsibility for the protection of consumers. The federal government is responsible for national marketplace standards and for ensuring a fair, efficient, and competitive marketplace for producers, traders, and consumers. In keeping with this responsibility, current federal consumer statutes cover product safety (except in electrical equipment), competition, labelling, and weights and measures. The federal government also has exclusive authority to legislate in relation to the banking and the telecommunications industries. Table 2.5 gives a summary of several laws introduced by the federal government to protect consumers.[55]

Provincial and territorial statutes cover matters such as the conditions of sale, warranties, and licensing. Generally speaking, most consumer services are regulated by the provinces and territories, including most non-bank financial services. Most provinces have statutes to control unfair business practices. These statutes vary from province to province; however, the substantive protection given to consumers is broadly similar across the country. Provincial and territorial governments are responsible for contractual matters and most issues related to specific types of businesses or services, such as automotive repairs, door-to-door sales, consumer credit reporting, debt collection practices, and cost of credit disclosure.

Consumers also have recourse to Small Claims Courts, which can be an informal and relatively inexpensive method of resolving disputes in which the amount claimed is less than $3,000, or less than $15,000, depending on the province, and Class Proceedings. Class proceedings legislation is in place in British Columbia, Ontario, and Quebec; it allows individuals

TABLE 2.5	Major Federal Legislation Protecting Consumers

Food and Drugs Act: Establishes standards and requirements relating to food, drugs, cosmetics, and medical devices produced for consumption.

Hazardous Products Act: Provides for nationwide safety standards for a wide variety of consumer products, ranging from child restraint systems for automobiles to hockey helmets.

Motor Vehicle Safety Act: Requires automobile manufacturers to adhere to safety standards in manufacturing their products.

Trademark Act: Governs the creation of trademarks, protecting owners from duplication, and consumers from confusion.

Consumer Packaging and Labelling Act: Presents the law that allows consumers to make informed product choices by providing a uniform method of labelling and packaging of prepackaged consumer goods (products sold at retail).

The Textile Labelling Act: Managed by Industry Canada, the act establishes a standard for labelling textile products in order to inform consumers of the fibre content and other relevant information about the product.

Weights and Measures Act: Provides standards for weighing and measuring products for trade and sale.

Precious Metals Mark Act: Provides information about the law that establishes marking standards to inform customers about the quality and authenticity of precious metals.

Competition Act: Covers consumer issues such as misleading advertising, deceptive telemarketing, and multi-level marketing and pyramid schemes, as well as competition issues such as price discrimination and predatory pricing.

Personal Information Protection and Electronic Documents Act: Allows consumers to know what information is being collected about them by regulated businesses, to opt out of businesses' information collection practices, and to correct inaccurate information.

Quebec's *Act Respecting the protection of personal information in the private sector* governs the information practices of businesses in that province.

SOURCE: Government of Canada, Canadian Consumer Information Gateway website http://consumerinformation.ca/ app/oca/ccig/main .do?language=eng#. Reproduced with the permission of the Minister of Public Works and Government Services, 2006.

sharing a common issue to come together as plaintiffs in a single lawsuit (class action suit). The efficiency of grouping claims in this way may make class proceedings particularly amenable to consumers with a common complaint against a merchant or manufacturer.

Internet shoppers are protected in Canada by a number of laws. The Uniform Electronic Commerce Act applies to all federally regulated industries. The act confirms the validity of electronic documents, signatures, and contracts. It makes companies disclose specific information to consumers and allows for the reversal of credit card charges under certain circumstances. The act says that for online contracts, the "I agree" button is binding once the individual clicks on it, but consumers must first be allowed to review the terms of their contracts. The Personal Information Protection and Electronic Documents Act, revised in January 2004, regulates how personal information—including that collected in Internet transactions—can be used.[56]

Commercial websites collect personal information explicitly through a variety of means, including registration pages, user surveys, online contests, application forms, and order forms. Websites also collect personal information through means that are not obvious to consumers, such as "cookies." Surveys show that "privacy" of personal information submitted is a major concern for consumers who participate in the electronic marketplace. The *Canadian Code of Practice for Consumer Protection in Electronic Commerce,* endorsed in 2004 by federal, provincial, and territorial ministers responsible for consumer affairs, provides a voluntary code so that business can better serve online consumers. Ten principles form the basis for the Model Code for the Protection of Personal Information:

- Accountability
- Identifying Purposes
- Consent
- Limiting Collection
- Limiting Use
- Disclosure and Retention
- Accuracy
- Safeguards
- Openness
- Individual Access
- Challenging Compliance

These 10 principles establish benchmarks for good business practice for merchants conducting commercial activities with consumers online (http://cmcweb.ca).

Federal legislation affecting advertising also includes sections of the Broadcasting Act, the Canadian Human Rights Act, the Criminal Code, the Department of National Revenue, the Income Tax Act, and the Official Languages Act. Bill C-15A became law in July 2002. It deals specifically with child pornography and exploitation on the Internet, and specifically bans cyber-luring (using the Internet to communicate with children for sex).[57]

In addition, the Canadian Advertising Foundation's Broadcast Code for Advertising to Children provides industry guidelines in areas such as product claims, sales pressure techniques, endorsements by program characters, scheduling, safety, and social values.

Environment. The Canadian Environmental Protection Act gives ministers of the Environment and Health the responsibility to investigate substances that may harm the environment or people's health. A list specifying toxic and non-toxic substances is compiled and reviewed by these authorities.

Facilitative Infrastructure. The final mechanism by which government policy shapes customer behaviour is the development of infrastructure. One example is the government's ParticipACTION program, whose mission is to be a leading catalyst and provider of information and social supports to encourage a healthy, active lifestyle for all Canadians. Over three decades of government efforts, including those of corporate sponsors and volunteers, were directed to motivate, educate, and mobilize Canadians around a physical activity initiative.[58] Similarly, in terms of automobile inspection and maintenance, certain jurisdictions in Canada have mandated periodic emissions testing. For example, Air Care covers the greater Vancouver area, and Drive Clean covers Southern Ontario.

Under the Canadian constitution, labour legislation is primarily a provincial responsibility. The federal government, however, administers labour affairs in some sectors. The Canadian Centre for Occupational Health and Safety Act promotes the right to a healthy and safe working environment.[59] Newly phased-in regulations under the Canadian Environmental

Protection Act have been approved to align vehicle emission standards with those of the United States Environmental Protection Agency.

The city of Singapore illustrates how government affects customer behaviour through facilitative infrastructure. Its government has allocated millions of dollars to build a technology infrastructure. Its aim is to convert Singapore from an economy built on trade and services to one built on information technology. Singapore officials have launched a host of new electronic services that make the government more efficient. Central databases allow bureaucrats to track everything from immigrant work permits to detailed information on the population. The education, hospital, and legal systems are seeing changes, and online training courses are being held for government officials. The infrastructure is being set up to prepare Singaporeans for a Web life so that they become the netizens of tomorrow—super-connected, technologically savvy, civic-minded, and knowledgeable.[60]

Technology

In terms of customer behaviour, **technology** is the dimension of market context that consists of the applications of new technology to the development, distribution, and consumption of products that increase the quality of life for all customers. Technological breakthroughs can significantly change market behaviours and customer expectations, affecting customer behaviour through several avenues:

Technology The use of machines and devices to facilitate a practical task.

- By altering the flow of and access to information about marketplace alternatives
- By making newer generations of products available
- By automating processes that give customers greater flexibility and control as well as improving productivity
- By making customized products economically feasible

Increased Access to Information. Technology brings new mass media into being, media that offers consumers information about the marketplace. Before the advent of newspapers, the only sources of market information were town criers, billboards, and word of mouth, and the first two were out-of-home media. With newspapers, radio, and television, advertising has come into consumers' homes, thus increasing consumer access to market information.

The role of conventional mass media in bringing market information to customers has been remarkable, but it pales in comparison to the implications of the most recent advancement in technology—namely, the Internet and the so-called information superhighway. You can buy a car on the Internet today; business travellers can find deals on airlines and hotels worldwide, and students can learn about various colleges and universities. An estimated 7.9 million (64 percent) of the 12.3 million Canadian households had at least one member who used the Internet regularly in 2003. That same year, an estimated 4.9 million households had at least one member who used the Internet to support purchasing decisions, either by window shopping or by placing online orders. Of these 4.9 million households, an estimated 3.2 million, or 65 percent, went beyond window shopping and placed orders online. About 30 percent of e-commerce households reported purchasing reading materials, 22 percent reported making travel arrangements over the Internet, 86 percent reported purchasing commodities, and almost 20 percent bought digital products. Window shopping was greatest for health, beauty items, vitamins, consumer electronics, clothing, jewellery and accessories, and housewares and appliances.[61] Thus, the first area of impact by technological advances on customer behaviour is increasing customer access to marketplace information.

Product Innovation: New Options. The second way that technology affects customer choices is via the availability of new products based on advances in technology. Consider the advent of cable TV, with its multichannel offerings such as pay-per-view and video on demand. Now, customers can order a movie on their television, without leaving home. Obviously, this cuts into sales at movie theatres and video rental stores. For business people computerized reservation systems, online information services, electronic libraries, database marketing, and cable shopping are changing the way they do business with their customers, as well as with suppliers.

More Flexibility and Control. Technology also affects customer behaviour by delivering freedom from the confines of space and time. That is, you can do business *anytime, anywhere*. You can bank at an ATM (automated teller machine) 24 hours a day, or access your account online, or via telephone numbers from anywhere and at any time. You can order flowers online rather than going to the neighbourhood store, and you can receive a college degree without leaving home.

Among business-to-business customers, one noteworthy use of computer technology has been **electronic data interchange (EDI),** a computer link between a supplier and its business customer that transmits customer inventory data to the supplier as it is being used and depleted, which sets into motion an automatic reorder and shipping of the depleted product. Wal-Mart and its supplier, Procter & Gamble, have an EDI system; the use of the system results in lowered costs of ordering and order filling, as well as eliminating costly stock outages on the Wal-Mart shelves.[62] Several automobile manufacturers have similar systems with their suppliers. The EDI technology frees the business customer from the effort of monitoring inventory and reordering, and thus lowers costs.

Electronic data interchange (EDI)
A computer-based link between a supplier and its business customer that transmits customer inventory data to the supplier and automates the reordering and shipping of the depleted product.

Customized Products. One of the most exciting technological developments in recent years is in the manufacturing arena, namely, flexible manufacturing (which allows to custom produce a product). The marketing benefit of this new technology is **mass customization**—producing a product after the customer order is received and tailoring the product to the customer's specific needs without sacrificing the speed or cost efficiencies of conventional mass production methods.

Mass customization
Tailoring the product to the customer's specific needs, without sacrificing the speed or cost efficiencies of conventional mass production methods.

Many companies have capitalized on the use of mass customization. Here are some selected examples.

- Hallmark uses computer technology to offer custom-made cards. By using simple on-screen instructions, you can choose from a selection of graphics, write your own message, and instantly print the card, all for about the same price as an off-the-rack card.
- The John Deere Harvester Works manufacturing plant in Moline, Illinois, is a good example of customization for business customers. The company sells a wide variety of crop planters priced at more than $100,000. The company has revamped its mass-production manufacturing process to respond to customized orders, and it now keeps only about 20 planters in finished goods inventory. Thus, customers can now choose from hundreds of options and purchase a crop planter that matches their individual needs more closely than ever before.[63]

- Companies such as IMIXrecords (**http://www.imixrecords.com**) allow users to customize music CDs and DVDs over the Internet and then have the product shipped directly from the company. Customers are presented with a list of choices and can pick and choose by title, album, artist, or genre.

Technophilia versus Technophobia. Customers differ in their attitude toward technology. While many customers benefit from and welcome new technology, a sizable proportion show a distaste for it. This is explained by:

- *Preference for human interaction*—Some consumers desire the "human touch" rather than high tech.
- *A lack of aptitude for technology*—Some consumers simply find themselves ill-equipped to handle new technology and, indeed, feel a degree of technophobia.

Technophiles Customers who are deeply interested in technology.

Technophobes Customers who fear new technology.

Technophiles, or "**techthusiasts,**" are people who get excited about technology; love to buy new technological innovations as soon as they appear on the market; have early knowledge about technology; and invest substantial time and energy in learning about, acquiring, and using new technological gadgets. **Technophobes,** on the other hand, are the exact opposite. They hate new technology, feel overwhelmed and confused by it, and find themselves ill-equipped to operate even common household and marketplace gadgets. Technophiles are younger, more affluent, and somewhat better educated than the average Canadian. They act as advisors, shopping pals, and decision makers for their colleagues, friends, and relatives. Many technophobes have never used a computer or programmed a VCR. To appeal to this segment, technological products ought to be user-friendly and very simple to operate.

In business-to-business markets, too, adopting a new technology requires a new investment from customers as well as a degree of comfort with the new and the unfamiliar. Consider the new technology that Eastman Kodak can offer its customers for their printing needs. Eastman Kodak's Professional & Printing Image Division (which has been sold to Danka) has advanced beyond the traditional photographic imaging using silver-halide film to employing digital systems for more speed and creative flexibility. Yet, the reason that Kodak and other companies are holding onto the silver-halide technology is because not all customers are ready to switch completely to the newer technology. There is an important customer behaviour lesson here: breakthrough technology that runs ahead of its customers' ability to invest in it or their aptitude for using it will never work from a marketing standpoint.

THE INFLUENCE OF THE DETERMINANTS OF CUSTOMER BEHAVIOUR ON THE THREE CUSTOMER ROLES

LO 5

Table 2.6 (p. 93) summarizes the effect of each of the determinants on the three customer roles.

Personal Traits

The five personal traits influence the three roles in distinct ways.

Influence of Genetics

A person's genetic makeup determines biological needs as well as physical constitution and, hence, the need for products that will satisfy those biological needs or will serve that special physiological constitution. Beyond performance, genetics also affect a person's emotional state and personality, and this, in turn, affects a person's desire for emotion-producing experiential or hedonic products. The payer role is not much affected by genetics directly, but the buyer role is affected, in that certain genetic disorders might incapacitate customers from going to the market, making convenience a more dominant value.

Influence of Race

Some of the effects of race and genetics are similar, while others differ. Due to related genetic differences, race affects skin colour and hair type and texture. Therefore, customers from different races need personal care items with specific performance characteristics. Beyond physiology, a customer's race also implies differences in values, lifestyle, and tastes. Then, race influences the payer role in several ways. First, economic conditions are distributed differently across races due to (1) historical differences in access to opportunities and (2) race-based cultural differences in individual-achievement motivation and belief in upward mobility. Second, there has historically been a systematic bias against certain ethnic minorities in credit approval. Both of these limit the buying power of some ethnic minorities.

The buyer role is also affected by race in at least two ways. First, many ethnic groups prefer to patronize vendors, store owners, and service agents (e.g., insurance agency representatives, real estate agents) of their own race and ethnic background. Second, as buyers, ethnic groups differ in the kind of interaction they seek from suppliers and from store operators. Some races expect mere politeness in commercial transactions and, hence, behave accordingly, while others may expect personal warmth.

Influence of Gender

Gender, too, has a pervasive effect on customer roles. For the user, gender implies the purchase of some gender-specific products, based either on some biological or physiological needs or on culture-generated gender-specific customs and tastes. Many performance-related values differ between men and women, such as the ergonomics of the design of the driver seats in cars or the extra security needs in hotel rooms for women business travellers. But male–female differences also spill over to social and emotional values in the purchase of products to satisfy these values. The payer role is affected only insofar as there exists, in a given society or family unit, gender-based bias in the allocation of the payer role. In contrast, the buyer role is affected by gender, both in allocation of the responsibility and in gender differences in the specific values the customer seeks as a buyer.

Regarding role allocation, again, there are norms about who should be the buyer, which differ across families and cultures. In traditional societies, women do the shopping for routine household items, while men do the shopping for major purchases. In modern societies and families, the sex roles are more egalitarian, so both sexes assume an equal share of purchasing. Because they are strapped for time, women seek more convenience and time-saving means of shopping, and men are learning some necessary purchasing skills as they are being forced to assume more of that role.

Influence of Age

The categories of product needs and wants among users obviously differ across different age groups. As users in business markets, older workers are less likely to be able to use heavy equipment or parts, and, thus, seek different performance value from raw material, parts, and equipment. Moreover, social and emotional values are likely to be more important to younger customers than to the elderly and middle-aged. As payers, customers are affected by age because age influences their station in their career and, accordingly, their financial resources. Age also affects the separation of the payer and the user role. Generally, these two roles are separated for the young and for many elderly, who may depend on younger family members to assist with shopping. Finally, age influences the buyer role. Because they need and seek more service and more convenience, elderly purchasers build relationships with sellers. Word-of-mouth communication about shopping is highest among the young.

Influence of Personality

The role of personality is overarching, affecting all domains of customer behaviour. Outgoing persons participate in outdoor and social activities more and, therefore, consume products relevant to these recreational activities. Similarly, pleasure-seeking individuals would like experiential products more. As payers, some customers are extravagant, while others are very frugal and conservative. Some like to live on credit; others stay well within their current cash resources.

Customer personality also affects the buyer role. Brand loyalty and, likewise, store loyalty vary from person to person. These individual differences in brand and store loyalty are basically personality differences. Some individuals like to stick with the tried and tested; others like to explore new options. Another manifestation of personality is in the shopping style—some are browsers, while some are focused shoppers. The personality of the business customer is influential across the three customer roles. The choice of office decor, airline, and hotel during business trips, performance features such as speed versus memory in a computer (impatient users want more speed), and safety factors in design specifications are dependent on the personality of the user. As payers, the long- versus short-term perspective definitely affects the business customer's choice between options or allocation of funds to a business activity or service. Finally, the four social styles—driving, expressive, amiable, and analytical—directly bear on the kind of interactions buyers would seek with sellers and business negotiators.

TABLE 2.6 Personal Characteristics and the Three Customer Roles

	CUSTOMER ROLE		
Characteristic	**User**	**Payer**	**Buyer**
		PERSONAL TRAITS	
Genetics	• Customers' genetic makeup determines biological needs and the specific performance features sought		• Certain genetic disorders might incapacitate customers from making shopping trips, so value is more desirable
	• Genetics determines personality and emotional makeup to influence specific social and emotional values sought		

(continued)

Race	• For personal-care items, customers seek products that are compatible with their skin and hair needs • Ethnic tastes in food, clothing, and homes differ • Some minority groups seek social values as compensation	• Economic means are unevenly distributed across races and ethnic groups • Race-based discrimination in credit limits affordability for some customers	• Many customers prefer ethnic stores and suppliers • Race and ethnic group influence the preferred modes of interaction with vendors
Gender	• Many products are gender specific, due to either physiology or culture • In some cultures, women might use emotional products more	• Sex roles may be the basis for allocating the payer role	• Sex roles may be the basis for allocating the buyer role • Where sex roles include women in the workforce, they might seek convenience and time saving in shopping • In some cultures, men are still learning shopping skills
Age	• Product usage in many categories is contingent on age • Social and emotional values are more important for youth • Product/service needs are influenced by physical limitations related to aging (such as inability to lift heavy weights or read fine print)	• Age influences the amount of financial resources • The payer's role is more separate from the user's among youth (dependent on parents) and the elderly (dependent on government for income)	• Elderly buyers need more service and convenience • Word-of-mouth communication about shopping is highest among youth • Older buyers (in both businesses and households) prefer to buy based on a relationship with the seller
Personality	• At onset of need, some personality types may either delay or rush use of the product or service • Some personalities will be more open to cross-gender product use • Some personalities will have more need for mood and emotional products	• Some personalities will be frugal; others extravagant • Some personalities (of business and household payers) will focus on long-term investment; others on immediate price	• Personality types will differ in their loyalty to brands and stores • Some personalities enjoy browsing; others focus on obtaining target merchandise • Some personalities focus more on seeking relationships with sellers

(continued)

	PERSONAL CONTEXT		
Culture	• Cultures differ in their insistence on flawless performance	• Cultures vary significantly in sanctioning borrowing and in living in debt	• Cultures assign the buyer role according to their sex-role norms
	• Conspicuous consumption is frowned upon in some cultures	• Cultures allocate the payer role to specific members of the household	• Negotiations and bargaining practices are governed by cultural norms
	• Different cultures permit emotional expressiveness to different degrees		
	• Corporate culture constrains what people wear and drive		
Institutions and groups	• Families differ on seeking materialism emphasis on performance versus social and emotional values	• Families differ in using credit and in individual versus joint responsibility for managing financial matters	• Families differ in blending versus separating the buyer role from the user and/or payer roles
	• Religion prohibits consumption of certain products	• Islam prohibits borrowing	• Some religions disallow women to go shopping
	• Employers and work groups exercise norms on clothing, cars, and business travel options	• Employers affect the payer by assuming partial or full financial burden	• Employers' purchasing policies constrain the purchaser
Personal worth	• Economic classes have distinct cultures of consumption	• By enabling or limiting the resources, economic conditions affect the payer role most directly	• Greater personal worth supports a more confident approach to vendors
			• Economic means may limit access to vendors
			• Higher economic condition leads customers to seek more convenience and personal shopping experience
	MARKET TRAITS		
Climate	• Certain types of food, clothing, and shelter are needed	• Out-of-place products cost more	• Climate-appropriate storage facilities affect accelerated buying
	• Weather-related products are needed	• Out-of-season products cost more	• Bad weather may require postponement of purchase
	• Suitable packaging is required		• Pickup/delivery services may be needed in bad weather

(continued)

Topography	• Products adapted to local conditions (e g , flood insurance, bottled water) are needed • Available means of transportation may be limited	• Special-needs products must be budgeted for	• Transportation difficulties may require minimizing trips, buying in bulk, or delegating purchase to others
Ecology	• Pollution control products are needed • Environmentally friendly products are needed	• Ecologically friendly products may cost more	• Ecologically friendly products may require special search effort
		MARKET CONTEXT	
Economy	• Financial resources affect definition of necessities as opposed to luxuries	• Poor economy requires postponement of major purchases	• Demand and supply imbalances affect choice options • Interest rates influence desirability of borrowing decisions, such as home refinancing
Government	• Government incentives and disincentives influence choice • Use of some products is forbidden or mandated	• Tax laws affect net price	• Government protection and laws of commerce (e. g., blue-sky laws) make purchasing secure • Laws provide protection against a deceptive or unfair price
Technology	• New products are available • Products may be more customized to the user	• New payment options such as credit card infrastructure or payment via Internet may be available	• Purchaser may have access to "anytime, anywhere" shopping • Market information may be more readily available, for example, on the Internet

Personal Context

Let us see how the personal context factors influence the various market values customers seek in their user, payer, and buyer roles.

Culture

The influence of culture on the market values that users seek (performance, social, and emotional) is pervasive and immense. Cultures vary in their insistence on performance and quality. Social value is also interpreted differently in different cultures. Conspicuous consumption is frowned upon in some cultures, such as in more egalitarian societies. Likewise, cultures differ in whether emotional expressiveness is considered proper and natural. Corporate culture constrains the kinds of clothes we wear and the kinds of cars we drive.

Culture influences the payer role in at least two ways. First, it helps determine who plays the payer role. In some cultures, it is the female head of the household; in others, it is the male head. Second, cultures influence the payer role in that they differ significantly in their prescription for borrowing money. In non-Western cultures, for example, borrowing is a sign of being poor; the well-to-do don't borrow money. In Western cultures, in contrast, even millionaires may borrow money, since borrowing is simply a sign of managing money (e.g., in investment portfolios) rather than a sign of not having money.

Finally, culture influences the buyer role, both in terms of who plays the buyer role and what specific values the buyer may tend to seek. In many cultures, there is a clearer allocation of gender roles, including a norm as to what kinds of products will be shopped for mainly by the female members of the household, and what kinds by the male members. In addition, expectations about personal service and convenience differ across cultures. Cultures also vary in negotiating tactics and in allowing the practice of bargaining. Similarly, in business negotiations, the level of direct confrontation that is considered prudent differs across cultures. These cultural nuances make playing the buyer role an art form in many societies.

Institutions and Reference Groups

The larger culture of a society or country shapes all families in it, but each family also has its own culture, norms, and practices. Thus, different families differ in the value they place on materialism and on simplicity versus indulgence, in how much debt they allow themselves to carry, and in the extent to which the user, payer, and buyer roles are blended or separated.

Religion certainly influences what people may or may not consume (e.g., kosher food for Jews). Religion also affects the payer role by sanctioning the practice of borrowing. Islam, for example, forbids the practice of borrowing and lending, since usury is considered a sin. Certain religions prohibit women from going to the market, so the buyer role becomes the exclusive prerogative of men.

Employers and work groups influence all three roles. Beyond a norm about clothes and cars, employers also influence other user decisions, such as what kind of personal computer you can buy for your office desk, what airlines and which fare class you may fly, which hotels you may stay at, and whether you may take your spouse on business trips. Employers affect the payer role in whether they let employees manage their own budgets, in terms of allowing certain business expenses (e.g., entertainment, social club membership), and in the extent to which they partially or fully assume the financial burden for the things one buys as an employee and as a consumer (e.g., extended-benefit health insurance, company car, housing rent subsidy, home phone, paid annual vacation). Finally, purchasing practice is dictated by employers—some allow individual employees to do their own purchasing, while others mandate centralized purchasing (e.g., using your own travel agent versus using the corporate travel agency).

Personal Worth

Personal worth influences customers' behaviour primarily by constraining their resources. Its influence is greatest, therefore, on the payer role. Not only is the amount of money (whether equity or credit) available for market transactions relatively abundant or scarce, but it also affects the extent to which money is tightly controlled among the user, buyer, and payer roles.

Personal worth affects the other two customer roles as well. Economic classes acquire their own consumption cultures, so there is the consumption culture of the poor, of the middle class, and of the rich. As to the buyer role, personal worth affects both the broad mindset of customers and their specific purchase strategies. In broad terms, it influences the confidence versus timidness with which buyers approach their suppliers and vendors, and it influences their choice of vendors as well. In general, then, low personal worth focuses customer attention on universal values in each of the three roles. Only when economic conditions are better does the consumer move up to seeking individual values, whether as a user, a payer, or a buyer.

Market Traits

The three market traits affect all three customer roles. Climate affects the user's need for food, clothing, and shelter. Topography affects the need for particular means of transportation (e.g., the camel in the deserts of Saudi Arabia) and insurance against topography-based mishaps (e.g., floods or hurricanes). Ecology makes ecology-unfriendly products nonviable and channels customer needs toward environmentally friendly products. For the payer role, some physical environmental factors imply greater expense—buying warm clothing in a tropical country is going to be more expensive because of the specialty nature of the products. Similarly, out-of-season merchandise costs more, and ecology-friendly products also are more expensive. The buyer role is also affected by the physical market characteristics. If you live in a very hot climate, either you have a good cold-storage facility or else you buy products in smaller quantities sufficient for immediate consumption. Accelerated buying to take advantage of price and promotional deals becomes infeasible if storage facilities are inadequate. Bad weather also leads purchasers to postpone a shopping trip and order home delivery rather than make in-store acquisitions.

Market Context

In this section, we pull together the diverse effects of the three market context factors on the three customer roles. For the user, the economy affects the purchase of discretionary products and luxuries (wants). Government incentives and disincentives (including mandatory prohibition against certain products) influence customer choice. Technology makes new products available and, thus, influences desire for them. It also enables more customized products, and, consequently, it promotes a desire for more individualized products. For the payer, poor economic climate induces postponement of major purchases. Interest rates influence home buying decisions. Government influences the payer role by means of taxation and protective laws. Laws against deceptive and discriminatory pricing practices serve as assurance to payers that their money will not be taken fraudulently. Technology enables credit card infrastructure, such as the widespread use of technology by merchants across a nation to seek instant credit authorization from credit card vendors. For the buyer, the economy affects the supply and demand, which, in turn, affects the choices available for consideration and the ease or difficulty of acquiring products. Government laws affect the buyer, the user, and the payer by making the purchase activity secure. Finally, technology affects the buyer role by enabling shopping "anytime, anywhere." Technology also has empowered the buyer by making more information more conveniently available, for example, on the Internet, so that the buyer can make more informed decisions.

SUMMARY

This chapter focused on the influence of the external determinants—namely, personal and market factors—on customer behaviour.

LO 1

There are two facets of the personal factors affecting customer behaviour—personal traits and personal context. We first discussed personal traits, and showed how they affect customer behaviour, and the three roles of the customer—user, payer, and buyer. These traits are genetics, the three biogenic features of race, age, and gender, and personality, which is a function of genetics, biogenics, and the environment. The influence of genetics is through its determining role in the physiology of the individual, the diseases to which a person is made susceptible, circadian rhythms, and moods and emotions. Race and ethnic background influence customers' needs for skin-specific personal care items, taste, and differences in food and clothing. We discussed the profiles of major ethnic groups in Canada, such as the Germans, Italians, Chinese, and Ukrainians. We then discussed customer behaviour differences between the two genders with respect to consumption of clothing and personal items. We discussed the diverse categories of age: the Seniors Generation, the Pre-Boom Generation, Baby Boomers, Generation X (Baby Bust), Generation Y, and children. These customers need and want different products because their physical characteristics are different and their tastes are different according to the age of their subculture. Finally, we explained what personality is and how it is formed. The Freudian theory illuminates the nature of personality as a set of conscious and subconscious motives and urges. Trait theory views personality as a pattern of behaviour. Defense mechanisms were described as the ego's attempt to manage anxiety and to protect the self from being slighted. For a business customer, we introduced a specific personality typology—social styles—and we showed the relevance of this typology to customer behaviour in business interactions.

LO 2

We then discussed the second facet of the personal factors—personal context. The personal context is the cultural, social, and economic environment that a customer is a member of and in which the customer resides. We described three context factors—culture, institutions and groups, and personal worth. We defined what culture is, and discussed its characteristics and components. We described national and popular culture. On the business side, we said that corporate culture also has a significant bearing on the behaviours of individuals or departments. We identified five dimensions of cross-cultural value orientations. Institutions and groups, the second context factor, act as reference groups for individuals. Depending on frequency of contact, groups can be primary or secondary, membership or symbolic, choice or ascribed. The influence of groups depends on the conspicuousness of consumption, and as such, it can occur at the product or brand-choice level. The last context is the economic condition surrounding the consumer. Its components are income, wealth, and borrowing power. The concept of social class was discussed. It was argued that social classes are motivational in that they motivate customer behaviour toward certain activities and possessions. The three major social classes (lower, middle, and upper) were contrasted in regard to their consumption behaviour.

LO 3

The first dimension of the market environment is market traits (i.e., the characteristics of the market as a physical place). You learned that there are three geophysical characteristics—climate, topography, and ecology. Climate plays an important role in shaping the market values customers seek, and it affects the three basic necessities of life: food, shelter, and clothing. Businesses are also affected by climate, including the different types of packaging required for warm and cold climates, and the fact that there is a seasonality for products. Topography, the second market trait, refers to the terrain, altitude, and soil conditions where customers use products. Topography also affects choices that households and businesses make with respect to food, clothing, and shelter. Ecology is the final market trait, and it refers to the natural resources and the balance that exist among humans, animals, and vegetation. You learned that ecological changes, such as global warming, air and water pollution, and ozone layer depletion are affecting household and business customers. As an outcome, there are activist movements around the world to save the environment, and marketers are responding to their demands.

LO 5 The second dimension of the market environment is the market context, which refers to the context created by humans—namely, economy, government policy, and technology. You learned that the general state of a country's economy impacts customer behaviour through the sense of optimism that is measured by the spending patterns of businesses and households. Businesses also follow business cycles, and these have a dramatic impact on the behaviour of customers. Government policy affects customers through the monetary and fiscal policies that are enacted, and through the public policies that are passed. You learned that through government policies, customer choice is sometimes constrained, mandated, or protected. A brief overview was given of various governmental agencies that play a role in either constraining, mandating, or protecting the user, payer, and buyer in the marketplace. The last determinant of the market context is technology. We discussed how technological breakthroughs significantly change market behaviours and shape customer expectations. You also learned that businesses also are affected by technology.

These external determinants, both personal and market-based, shape a person's psychological makeup—his or her motives, emotions, and lifestyles.

KEY TERMS

Acculturation 59
Aggressive 56
Behaviourism Theory 54
Biological Determinism 41
Borrowing Power 66
Business Cycle 75
Climate 69
Compliance 76
Compliant 56
Customer Expectations 74
Detached 56
Discretionary Expenditures 74
Ecology 71
Economy 74
Ego 55
Electronic Data Interchange (EDI) 50
Enculturation 59
Environmental Marketing 73
Environmentally Conscious Consumers 71
Family Life Cycle Concept 53
Geographical Variation 71
Global Warming 71
Government Policy 75
Green Consumer 71
Group Traits 40
Groups 62
Id 55
The Index of Consumer Confidence 74
Individual Traits 40
Institutions 62
Lifetime Value 49
Mass Customization 80
National Culture 59
Nature 41
Necessary Expenditures 74
Negligent Consumer Behaviour 76
Nurture 41
Personality Trait 56

Popular Culture 59
Regional Marketing 71
Social Class 67
Subculture 59
Superego 55
Technology 79
Technophiles (or Techthusiasts) 81
Technophobes 81
Topography 70
Trait Theory of Personality 56

DISCUSSION QUESTIONS AND EXERCISES

1. Cosmetic companies have product lines targeted specifically to gay and lesbian consumers. Benetton has been using ads that appear to be culturally insensitive (e..g, one shows a priest and a nun kissing). Do companies have the right to use a subculture's unique characteristics to increase the sales of their products? Or, are they simply following the marketing concept, which states that companies should design products to meet the needs of specific market segments? What are the ethical issues involved in subcultural market segmentation?
2. Describe some of the general gender differences that affect consumers in both household and business markets. What have marketers done to handle these differences? For example, companies like Calvin Klein have tried to minimize gender differences in their advertising. Do you think this strategy is a good idea?
3. How can marketers use the information in this chapter to develop promotional campaigns designed to increase market share among Chinese-Canadian, French-Canadian, and German-Canadian consumers for the following products:
   - Wines and spirits
   - Ready-to-eat cereals
   - Fragrances (perfume or cologne)
4. Interview five consumers from different national cultures. Ask them to identify how their customer behaviours are different in each of the three roles. How much can these differences be attributed to differences in their national cultures?
5. Select two households featured in two TV series with a different social setting. (Sitcoms may be the best source.) First, classify each household into one of the social classes discussed in the chapter. Then, analyze each household's lifestyle and consumption behaviour and compare them in terms of social classes.
6. As the Director of Product Development for a medium-sized international producer of soap, lotion, and detergent, you are fundamentally concerned with the worldwide movement toward protecting and preserving the environment. In many countries, specific raw materials have been banned, and certain packaging materials have been discontinued. In addition to consumer and government pressure to become a "green" marketer, your major competitor, The Body Shop, has exhibited its commitment to the environment in several meaningful ways. How will you move your company toward being more environmentally friendly, and how will you communicate this to your customers?
7. Interview five consumers to rate them on how "environmentally conscious" they are. Then ask them about how their environmental consciousness affects the products they have bought within the past year. Verify whether "environmental consciousness" relates to customers' purchasing behaviour.

8. Assume you are an entrepreneur and you are about to introduce to the market a revolutionary new product—an interactive kiosk—that enables easy, convenient Internet access, and offers a host of value-added services for business travellers. In general, your target group will be fairly computer-savvy, and will be familiar with most office equipment, such as faxes, e-mail, and voice-mail systems. What specific customer values will this new technology product satisfy? How will you introduce your new technology, given the barrage of new innovations in the marketplace? How will you show that your product will appeal to both technophiles and technophobes?

NOTES

1 Quoted in Bill Saporito, "Unsuit Yourself," *Fortune*, September 20, 1993, 118–20; Diane Crispell, "The Brave New World of Men," *American Demographics*, 14, no. 1 (January 1992), 38–43.

2 Statistics Canada, *Canada's Ethnocultural Portrait: The Changing Mosaic,* catalogue 96F0030XIE2001008; Statistics Canada, *Ethno-Cultural Portrait of Canada,* Table 1, Selected Ethnic Origins, for Canada, Provinces and Territories – 20% Sample Data; Statistics Canada, *Population Projection of Visible Minority Groups, Canada, Provinces and Regions, 2001–2017,* Catalogue 91-541-XIE. (91-547-XIE); *Population By Mother Tongue, By Provinces And Territories* (2001 Census). All documents accessed at the Statistics Canada website http://www.statscan.ca.

3 Under the *Employment Equity Act,* members of visible minorities are "persons, other than Aboriginal persons, who are non-Caucasian in race or non-white colour."

4 Tracy Ariel, "Crazy For Coupons: Quebecers Love The Instant Gratification Of Coupons, But Marketers Want The Valuable Customer Data They Can Only Get Through Loyalty Programs." *Marketing,* September 16, 2002, vol. 107, Iss. 37, 14.

5 "The Right Spirit," *The Gazette,* December 7, 2005, A30.

6 Tavia Grant, "Cost of Holiday Season: $900," *Globe and Mail,* December 15, 2005, http://www.theglobeandmail.com/servlet/story/RTGAM.20051216.wspending1216/BNStory/Business/ (accessed December 15, 2005).

7 Sylvia Criger, "Big Enough To Target: How To Decide Whether An Ethnic Group's Size Justifies Directing A Campaign To It," *Marketing,* September 14, 1998, 22.

8 John Gray, "Tailoring the Message," *Canadian Business,* Mar. 29–Apr. 11, 2004, 65.

9 Judy Waytiuk, "The New Native Niche; The West's Aboriginal Market Is Growing And Growing More Wealthy," *Marketing,* May 22, 2000, 13.

10 A. Anderson, "Ukranian ethnicity," in *Two Nations, Many Cultures,* ed. J.L. Elliott, 250–269 (Toronto: Prentice-Hall, 1979).

11 Eve Lazarus, "The New Mainstream," *Marketing,* October 24, 2005, 11.

12 Statistics Canada, *Population by Mother Tongue, by Provinces And Territories* (2001 Census), http://www40.statcan.ca/101/cst01/demo11a.html.

13 "A Market Driven by Women: It Is Estimated Women Purchase About 55% of All New Cars Sold in Canada and Directly Influence At Least 80% of All Other Vehicle Purchases," *National Post,* September 7, 2001, F10.

14 Bernd H. Schmitt, France Leclerc, and Laurette Dubé-Rioux, "Sex Typing and Consumer Behaviour: A Test of Gender Schema Theory," *Journal of Consumer Research* 15 (June 1988), 122–28; Barbara B. Stern, "Sex Role, Self-Concept Measures and Marketing: A Research Note," *Psychology and Marketing* 5 (Spring 1988), 85; Janeen Arnold Costa, ed., *Gender Issues and Consumer Behaviour* (Thousand Oaks, CA: Sage, 1994).

15 Statistics Canada, *Changing our Ways: Why and How Canadians Use the Internet,* "2000 General Social Survey Data, 2000. Catalogue No. 56F0006XIE.

16 e-Demographics Report, http://www.emarketer.com, 2000; http://www.digitrends.net.

17 *Media Digest 2005–2006,* 58–59.

18 *The Consumer Trend Report,* Office of Consumer Affairs, chapter 2.3, chapter 2.2 (Ipsos-Reid2002a), http://strategis.ic.gc.ca/epic/internet/inoca-bc.nsf/en/ca02088e.html.

19 Deaths, 2003, *The Daily,* December 21, 2005, Statistics Canada.

20 "Tweens' Pocket Money Climbs to $1.8 Billion, Says Latest YTV Survey," *Canada NewsWire,* November 16, 2000, 1.

21 "Changing Our Ways: Why and How Canadians Use the Internet, 2000," Statistics Canada Catalogue No. 56F0006XIE.

22 Rothermann, Michelle, "Wired Young Canadians," *Canadian Social Trends,* Winter 2001, Cat. 11-008-XPF, Statistics Canada.

23 "Young Canadians in a Wired World, 2005," *Media Awareness Networks,* http://www.media-awareness.ca.

24 Teens Online, www.emarketer.com, 2000; Michael Pastore, *New Payment Options Will Open E-commerce to Teens,* September 7, 2001, http://cyberatlas.internet.com/markets/retailing/article/0,,6061_880271,00.

25 Hans J. Eysenck, *The Biological Basis of Personality* (Springfield, IL: C. C. Thomas, 1967); *The Structure of Human Personality* (London: Metheun, 1970); Hans J. Eysenck, *Personality, Genetics, and Behaviour: Selected Papers* (New York: Praeger Publishers, 1982).

26 Walter Mischel, "On the Future of Personality Measurement," *American Psychologist,* 32 (April 1977), 2.

27 R.B. Cattell, H.W. Eber, and M.M. Tatsuoka, *Handbook for the Sixteen Personality Factor Questionnaire* (Champaign, IL: Institute for Personality and Ability Testing, 1970).

28 Charles M. Schaninger and Donald Sciglimpaglia, "The Influence of Cognitive Personality Traits and Demographics on Consumer Information Acquisition," *Journal of Consumer Research* 8 (September 1981), 208–16. For a review of personality studies, see Girish N. Punj and David W. Stewart, "An Interaction Framework of Consumer Decision Making," *Journal of Consumer Research* 10 (September 1983), 181–96.

29 Harold H. Kassarjian, "Personality and Consumer Behaviour: A Review," *Journal of Marketing Research* 8 (November 1971), 409–19.

30 David W. Merrill and Roger H. Reid, *Personal Styles and Effective Performance: Make Your Style Work for You* (Radnor, PA: Chilton Book Company, 1981).

31 Parts of this section are adapted from Terrence E. Deal and Allan A. Kennedy, *Corporate Cultures: The Rites and Rituals of Corporate Life* (Reading, MA: Addison-Wesley Publishing Co., 1982).

32 Geert Hofstede, *Cultural Consequences: International Differences in Work-Related Value* (Thousand Oaks, CA: Sage, 1980); Geert Hofstede and Michael H. Bond, "Hofstede's Culture Dimensions: An Independent Validation Using Rokeach's Value Survey," *Journal of Cross-Cultural Psychology,* 15 (December 1984), 417–33.

33 Jennifer L. Aaker and Patti Williams, "Empathy versus Pride: The Influence of Emotional Appeals across Cultures," *Journal of Consumer Research,* 25 (December 1998), 241–61.

34 Kevin Johnston and Parminder Johal, "The Internet As A 'Virtual Cultural Region': Are Extant Cultural Classification Schemes Appropriate?," *Internet Research: Electronic Networking Applications and Policy,* Vol 9, Issue 3, 1999, http://www.emerald-library.com.

35 Francis S. Bourne, "Group Influence in Marketing and Public Relations," in *Some Applications of Behavioral Research,* eds. R. Likert and S.P. Hayes (Basil, Switzerland: UNESCO, 1957).

36 William O. Bearden and Michael J. Etzel, "Reference Group Influence on Product and Brand Purchase Decisions," *Journal of Consumer Research* 9 (1982), 183–94.

37 C. Whan Park and V. Parker Lessig, "Students and Housewives: Differences in Susceptibility to Reference Group Influence," *Journal of Consumer Research* 4, no. 2 (1977), 102–10; Robert E. Burnkrant and Alain Cousineau, "Informational and Normative Social Influence in Buyer Behaviour," *Journal of Consumer Research* 2 (December 1975), 206–15.

38 In general, poverty is a level of personal wealth at which a household cannot even pay for all its basic needs, such as food, clothing, and shelter. Statistics Canada does not measure income but provides low-income cutoffs. A person at low income is someone whose family income falls below Statistics Canada's low-income cutoffs (LICOs). The cutoffs reflect an income level at which a family is likely to spend significantly more of its income on food, shelter, and clothing than the average family. In 2000, a family of four living in a city with a population of half a million or more would be counted as low income if the total of the after-tax income for all family members fell below the cutoff of $34,572. For the same family living in a rural area, the cutoff was $23,892.

39 Statistics Canada, *Analysis of Income in Canada, 2002*, Cat. 75-203-XIE; Statistics Canada, *Income of Canadian Families, 2001 Census,* Cat. 96F0030XIE2001014.

40 "Federal Personal Income Tax: Slicing the Pie," by Patrice Martineau, April, 2005, Catalogue No: 11-621-MIE2005024.

41 Statistics Canada, "Household Internet Use Survey," *The Daily,* July 8, 2004.

42 P.C. Pineo, John Porter, and Hugh A. McRoberts, "The 1971 Census and the Socioeconomic Classification of Occupations," *Canadian Review of Sociology and Anthropology,* 14, no. 1 (February 1977), 91–102; P.C. Pineo, "Revisions of the Pineo-Porter-McRoberts Socioeconomic Classification of Occupations for the 1981 Census," *QSEP Research Report*, No. 125; Statistics Canada, *Labour Force Activity, 1981 Census of Canada,* cat. 92-915; *Statistics Canada, Standard Occupational Classification 1980,* Cat. 12-565E.

43 Gurprit S. Kindra, Michel Laroche, and Thomas E. Muller, Chapter 10, Social Classes in *Consumer Behaviour in Canada* (Toronto: Nelson Canada, 1994).

44 Philip M. Parker and Nader T. Tavassoli, "Homeostasis and Consumer Behaviour Across Cultures," *International Journal of Research in Marketing,* 17 (2000), 33–53.

45 Susan Schwatrz, "Shopping with Your Mouse," *The Montreal Gazette,* December 5, 2005, D1; Michel Laroche, Mark Cleveland, and Elizabeth Browne, "Exploring Age Related Differences in Information Acquisition for a Gift Purchase," *Journal of Economic Psychology,* Vol. 25 (2004), 61–95.

46 Michel Laroche, Nicolas Papadopoulos, Louise A. Heslop, and Mehdi Mourali, "The Influence of Country Image Structure on Consumer Evaluations of Foreign Products," *International Marketing Review,* Vol. 22, No. 1 (2005), 96–115.

47 Statistics Canada, "Control and sales of alcooholic beverages," *The Daily,* September 8, 2005.

48 "56% of Canadians say the overall quality of the Country's environment is getting worse, affecting health," *Canada Newswire,* March 25, 2002, 1.

49 Larry Carpenter, "How to Market to Regions," *American Demographics,* November 1987, 44–48.

50 Nevin Cohen, "eGreen: Efficient Web Shopping for Environmentally-Safe Products," *eMarketer,* April 21, 2000, http://www.emarketer.com/analysis/ecommerce_b2c/042400_green.

51 "Big business bows to global warming; Energy firms and global warming," *The Economist* (US), December 2, 2000, 4.

52 George Katona, "Consumer Saving Pattern," *Journal of Consumer Research* 1, June 1974, 1–12.

53 The Conference Board of Canada, http://www.conferenceboard.ca/weblinx/ica/Default.htm.

54 Alf Lindquist, "A Note on Determinants of Household Saving Behaviour," *Journal of Economic Psychology* 1 (March 1981), pp. 39–57.

55 H. Robert Wientzen, "What Is the Internet's Impact on Direct Marketing Today and Tomorrow?," *Journal of Interactive Marketing,* 14 (3), Summer 2000, 74–78.

56 http://www.cbc.ca/news/background/internet/ecommerce.html.

57 canada.justice.gc.ca/en/news/nr/2002/doc_30531.html.

58 http://www.usask.ca/archives/participaction/english/structure/people.html.

59 http://www.hrsdc.gc.ca/asp/gateway.asp?hr=/en/lp/spila/clli/ohslc/02jurisdiction_federal_government_and_provinces.shtml&hs=oxs.

http//laws.justice.gc.ca/en/C-13/28729.html.

http://consumerinformation.ca/app/oca/ccig/main.do?language=eng.

60 Michelle Levander, "New Economy in Asia: Singapore Is Pushing Populace to the Internet," *The Wall Street Journal Europe,* October 28, 1999.

61 Statistics Canada, "Household Internet Survey," *The Daily,* July 8, 2004; Statistics Canada, "E-Commerce household shopping in the Internet," *The Daily,* September 23, 2004.

62 "Chain Store Age Executive with Shopping Center Age," *Going beyond EDI* 69, no. 3 (March 1993), 150–51.

63 Jeff Moad, "Let Customers Have It Their Way," *Datamation* (April 1, 1995), 34–37.

CHAPTER 3

Trends in Determinants of Customer Behaviour

LEARNING OBJECTIVES

After reading this chapter you should be able to:

LO 1 Explain the main demographic trends in customer behaviour.

LO 2 Explain the main technological trends in customer behaviour.

LO 3 Identify the major trends in public policy.

LO 4 Explain the implications of these trends on the three consumer roles.

The Aging of the Baby Boomers

The change in the *relative proportions* of age groups in Canada is expected to have an important impact in the marketplace. The aging of baby boomers—that is, their transformation into the new senior group—is the greatest determinant of Canada's current and future age structure. Indeed, with improvements in life expectancy, the senior population has already grown significantly.

Healthier, wealthier, more active, and living longer, 50-plus consumers are driving growth across numerous industries. By their sheer numbers, they are a dominant force in the market. According to Statistics Canada, the over-50 crowd went from 5.4 million in 1991 to nearly 7.3 million in 2001. By 2013, it will reach 9.5 million, or one-third of all Canadians. The proportion of people aged 65 and over will start to increase rapidly by 2012, when the oldest baby boomers will reach 65. At the same time, the proportion of the population ages 20 to 64 will start to decline.

People over 50 are deemed responsible for more expenditures than any other group in Canada, at the rate of some $35 billion a year. Unlike previous generations who typically moved into smaller homes or apartments, the 50-plus boomers are upgrading to more expensive properties. Luxury condominiums, gold and adult lifestyle communities, and secondary residences are all trends fuelled by boomers. In the automotive world, boomers are trading up their minivans for SUVs and luxury four-door sedans. In the food industry, boomers are demanding quality, natural foods, with no additives.

Throughout history, the baby-boom generation has transformed housing, schools, and health care; now they are rewriting the book on retirement. The findings of an Ipsos Reid/BMO online survey conducted from October 21 to October 27, 2005, among a randomly selected sample of 5,325 Canadian financial decision-makers aged 45 and over revealed that one in four expect to continue working at least part time after retirement, primarily in order to stay mentally active and keep in touch with people, and also to continue to maintain their lifestyles. When asked ideally how they would like to spend time in retirement, travelling (58 percent) and hobbies and crafts (48 percent) were ranked the highest.

As boomers advance in age, there will be a greater need for products such as assisted-living and full-care residences, home care, home medical supplies, home renovations to promote independence (e.g., ramps, lifts, etc.), wheelchairs, and scooters. Furthermore, there will be a greater demand for enhanced consumer products such as hi-rise washers and dryers, large-button telephones, and enhanced services such as grocery home delivery and tourism-related operations with senior-friendly special facilities. However, to successfully target baby boomers, marketers will have to segment this market by looking at lifestyle, family situations, and psychographics.[1]

Predicting future customer behaviour requires predicting the factors that influence customer behaviour. Almost any of the diverse factors discussed in Chapter 2 is capable of changing customer behaviour. In this chapter, we focus on the three factors that are expected to cause the most significant change in future customer behaviour: (1) changes in demographics, (2) advances in technology, and (3) changes in public policy (see Figure 3.1). Changes in other customer factors are likely as well, but less discernible and perhaps less dramatic. This chapter elaborates on each of these trends and how they affect customer behaviour. It closes with a discussion of how these trends are likely to affect marketing strategy.

FIGURE 3.1 Conceptual Framework

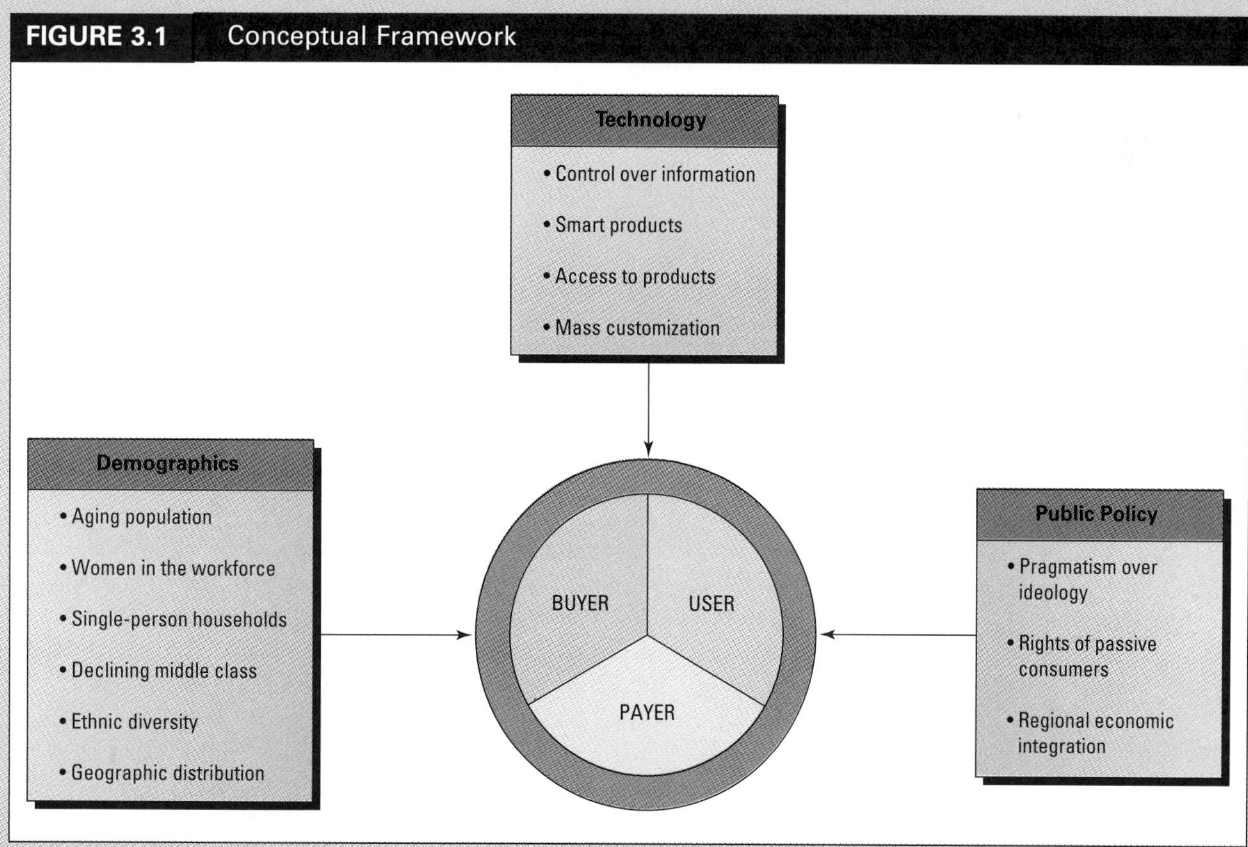

BENEFITS OF ANTICIPATING TRENDS IN CUSTOMER BEHAVIOUR

Anticipating trends in customer behaviour can give companies a key strategic advantage. Foreseeing the coming trends in customers' needs and wants offers companies several advantages. First, if you are the first to spot a market need, you can be the first to start working to meet that need. Consequently, the fulfillment time for that need is reduced, making the economic payback a lot quicker. For example, Sony anticipated the Walkman phenomenon, and, similarly, Netscape anticipated the impact of the Internet. Both companies were the first to come out with their respective products.

Second, by sighting a trend, the industry can create a market by channelling a latent need. One example is the cellular phone industry. Being able to communicate without being grounded in one location (i.e., wireless communication) is certainly on many people's wish list, but not everyone can afford the high initial equipment costs. The industry responded by offering a free phone with a service contract, and the market for cell phones skyrocketed.

Third, anticipating trends in customer needs and wants, and responding to them, creates positive public opinion for the company and the industry, portraying them as responsive. Examples include smoke-free facilities such as airports, airplanes, and restaurants, and environmentally friendly product, such as organically grown foods, recyclable paper products, and cosmetics developed without animal testing.

LO 1 DEMOGRAPHIC TRENDS

Changing demographics Change in characteristics such as age, income, and geographic location of customers in a given market.

Changing demographics of the customer serve as a good indicator of the future marketplace. As explained in Chapter 2, demographic characteristics of a customer such as age, income, race and ethnicity, and geographic location intimately influence his or her customer behaviour. Studying projections or trends in the demographic makeup of a population can, therefore, help marketers anticipate the needs and wants of their customers. Six demographic trends have already begun to transform the marketplace:

1. Aging of the population
2. Rise in number of working women
3. Increase in single-person households
4. Decline of the middle class
5. Increase in ethnic diversity
6. Geographic redistribution

Aging of the Population

In all of the advanced countries of the world, the population is aging. In 2000, Sweden had the oldest population in the world, with 17.2 percent of its people being 65 years of age or older. In comparison, 13.0 percent of the Canadian, 12.6 percent of the American, and 17 percent of the Japanese people were 65 years of age or older. However, by the year 2025, the Japanese are likely to become the oldest, with 27.5 percent of the population being 65 years of age or older.

Populations age for two key reasons: (1) their birthrate declines and (2) their life expectancy rises. In the 1850s, the fertility rate in Canada was about 7 births per woman. At that time, the Canadian economy was driven by farming, and children could be put to work on the farm and were therefore an economic asset. However, in industrial society, children became more of an economic burden. In fact, the current estimates are that the net present value of all the future costs of having and raising a child to age 18 amounted to approximately $167,000 in 2004![2] Consequently, by the 1950s, the Canadian fertility rate had dropped to about 4 children per woman. In 2001, the fertility rate in Canada stood at 1.5 births per woman.[2] As the birthrate declines, the average age of the population goes up.

The second, and more significant, factor behind the aging of the population is the rising life expectancy. A good indicator of the aging of the population is the rise in the number of people 65 or more years old. In 1961, 8 percent of all Canadians were aged 65 or older. By 2002, this proportion had risen to 13 percent. This figure is projected to reach 21 percent, for a total of roughly 7.8 million Canadian senior citizens in 2026.[3] The two fastest-growing segments in the Canadian population are centenarians and people 85+ years of age, further adding to the average age in Canada. Similarly, almost all of the European countries are aging as the proportion of young people is decreasing, with the exception of Ireland, which has a considerably larger population of young people.[4]

These two factors are also behind most of the aging of the Japanese population. In Japan, the life expectancy in the year 2025 will be 82.8 years, compared with 82.4 in Sweden and Canada, and 80.5 in the United States. At the same time, the annual growth rate of Japan is expected to be –0.6 in the year 2025, compared with rates of 0.1 in Sweden, 0.6 in Canada, and 0.8 in the United States.[5] These two factors imply that Japan will have the oldest population in the next few decades.

The aging of the population is creating new needs and wants. In particular, an aging population is relatively concerned about wellness, financial well-being, safety and security, and recreation. Today, seniors often use the Internet to address these concerns. Adults 55 and older represent the fastest-growing group of Internet users in North America, according to International Data Corp. (IDC). It found that the number of seniors will more than triple from 11.1 million in 1999 to 34.1 million in 2004, and that they will account for 20 percent of all new Internet users. However, in Canada, in 2005 only 10 percent of adults aged 55 and over used the Internet.[6]

McMellon and Schiffman conducted a study with online members of SeniorNet—a group of older adults on America Online—and with Retirement+ and AARP—two groups accessible through CompuServe. They suggest that there may be a relationship between the limited out-of-home mobility of seniors and the amount of time they spend on the Internet. Seniors might be using the Internet to keep in touch with their social circle and to keep themselves informed, thus compensating for their limited out-of-home mobility.[7] In confirmation of this study, Greenfield Online found that seniors are getting on the e-commerce bandwagon. Of the 1,265 Web users aged 55 and above, 92 percent have used the Internet for window shopping and 78 percent have made a purchase online. Seniors use e-mail to stay in touch with family and friends, including the exchange of digital photos of children and grandchildren. Surprisingly, they buy more books and software over the Internet than drugstore items. Marketers need to personalize the shopping experience for this segment, which has high purchasing power and plenty of time to spend on the Internet. They are faced with the challenge of converting the seniors' recreational and informational usage of the Internet into profits for their sites, keeping in mind the simple fact that seniors may be looking for a compelling retail experience online to substitute for their limited out-of-home mobility.[8]

Wellness

One of the most important implications of an aging society is a rise in the costs of health care. In Canada, health-care costs made up 7.0 percent of the gross domestic product in 1975. By 2005, the share had increased to 10.2 percent, and it is expected to continue to increase as the population ages. The United States spent the most per capita (US$5,635) in 2003, the latest year for which data are available. Norway, Switzerland, and Canada followed with per capita spending of US$3,807, US$3,781, and US$3,001, respectively.[9]

Inevitably, then, cost containment will be a priority. Health-care programs will need to emphasize not only caring for the ill but also prevention and health-promotion programs. As more people age and live longer, their need for physical well-being will significantly increase demand in the nutrition, drug, and physical fitness industries. Marketers will need to respond to customer needs in these three product areas as well as to educate customers about their importance and proper usage. Already, the concern over health has changed people's food habits and smoking behaviour dramatically. Internet sites such as http://WebMD.com provide customers with complete health-care information and education: health news, a directory of physicians, question-answer sessions with specialists, and provisions for chatting on message boards with regard to specific health interests.

All three customer roles will be involved in these wellness needs of the elderly. For the user, the most important value will be performance value. Food products will have to offer nutritional and dietary value, and drugs will need to offer efficacy as a value in addition to cure and prevention. The personal value of social and emotional needs will also be relevant to some degree. Marketing communications will have to present these foods and nutrients as part of a healthy and active lifestyle that should be supplemented by physical fitness programs tailored to the elderly.

The payer role is affected as the costs of medicine and health supplements increase. In their payer role, end-user customers will be concerned with the price value, even if they pay only a part of the cost. But government and health-insurance agencies will be concerned primarily as a payer. Already, provincial governments are demanding from physicians and hospitals that they use generic or less expensive substitutes for brand-name or more expensive drugs.

Finally, the convenient availability of drugs, food products, and fitness programs will be a concern of the elderly in their buyer role. Buyers will want service (e.g., advice on ingredients) as well as convenience (e.g., locations close to home or work and open longer hours). Some pharmacies in Canada, such as Pharmaprix, now offer home drop-off of prescription drugs at some locations, creating precisely the value elderly buyers will seek even more.

Financial Well-Being

Financial well-being
Financial products such as financial planning, wills and trusts, mutual funds and stocks, etc., acquire new significance in the lives of aging customers.

As people grow older, their concerns also centre around **financial well-being**. Products such as financial planning, wills and trusts, and mutual funds and stocks acquire new significance in the lives of aging customers. The elderly begin to draw on their wealth; wealth, rather than income, therefore, becomes the source of financial resources that elderly customers use to buy and pay for goods and services. A McKinsey study predicts that the global wealth of several advanced economies will be reduced by the combination of older people drawing down their savings and the low saving rates of younger people.[10]

Safety and Security

As people grow older, they become increasingly concerned about physical safety at home, in the workplace, and on the street. Concern also grows about the security of possessions. **Personal safety** has been the concern of many Canadians. The use of antitheft security devices in cars, houses, and even neighbourhoods has increased dramatically. As nations age, antitheft devices, security alarm systems in cars and homes, cell phones for emergencies on the road, and even self-defence classes will increase in popularity.

Personal safety
The safety of one's own person from crime or harmful consumption.

Recent surveys have shown that concerns about safety on the Internet are quite similar between the older and younger population. Safety was defined in the studies as the possibility of other people reading personal e-mail or tracking visits to websites and so on. It does not look like the older population is unduly concerned about safety on the Internet and hence, it cannot be used as a differentiator between the two segments. Seniors are however, more concerned about e-commerce security in relation to banking or making purchases over the Net than the 25–50 age group.

Recreational Needs

With homes paid for and children's university education completed, the elderly find more discretionary income available for travel, eating out, and other recreational activities. As their **recreational needs** increase, they will fuel growth in the travel and restaurant industries. Other beneficiaries will be the businesses involved in manufacturing and marketing bicycles, athletic shoes, and other sporting and recreational equipment.

Recreational needs
A person's need for entertainment and recreation.

With the aging population, recreation also will shift from active to passive. Examples are (1) replacing team contact sports with individualized sports and (2) going out less and staying at home more to watch TV or listen to the radio. This causes a demand for sporting goods for individualized sports and a change in TV and radio programming to include more reality-based programs and programs of interest to the elderly at times that they are most likely to watch.

Women in the Workforce

A second demographic shift is the increasing number of households with women who are part of the paid workforce. The number of women employed has risen steadily over the past several decades. In 1976, 42 percent (or 3.63 million) of women aged 15 and over were employed, and they comprised 37 percent of total employment. By 2003, 57.2 percent (7.34 million) were employed, and they represented 46.6 percent of total employment. In contrast, the proportion of men who were employed in 2003 (68 percent) was well below the figure recorded in 1976 (73 percent).[11]

The increase in the number of working women has resulted in a significant change in the resources of a household, specifically the time resource. There are two effects on time as a resource: time shortage and time shift. **Time shortage** refers to lack of free time; **time shift** refers to the time when nonwork-related activities may be pursued. Because dual-income families are spending close to 60 hours per week in work-related activities on average, adults tend to have discretionary time left only in the evenings and on weekends. This time shift has made it more difficult for businesses to service this segment. For example, automobile repair, store hours, delivery of packages, or even having repairs and maintenance done to the home has

Time shortage
The lack of free time.

Time shift
A period when nonwork-related activities may be pursued.

been made more difficult for many businesses. This makes weekends and evenings a more desirable time for businesses to cater to their customers.

Another effect of the working-women trend is the change in the lifestyle of families. With both spouses working, households have turned into **roommate families,** where parents and children are reluctant to share anything, including food served at mealtime, television shows, and other activities that take place in the household. There is a movement toward highly individualized preferences, especially when it comes to food and television.

Roommate families
Families whose members structure their time, location, and activities independently of one another and with minimal sharing.

Finally, time shortage is resulting in the outsourcing of a typical homemaker's duties—namely, cooking, cleaning, and child care. As a result of more women working outside the home, consumption patterns are changing dramatically. People are eating out more, estimated at two meals a day among adults. In addition, 50 percent of the time, the one meal eaten at home is prepared by someone other than the woman in the household. This has resulted in dramatic changes in the layout of kitchens. Telephones, cable television, security systems, and even personal computers are finding their ways into the kitchens of households today. As the kitchen becomes the family activity centre, customers are demanding larger kitchens. As women work outside the house during the day, housecleaning is being **outsourced,** that is, provided by contractors. Child care is another industry that is booming in response to the need to care for children whose parents are not able to stay home.

Outsourcing
Procuring products that were once produced by the customer him or herself.

Other new patterns include a growth in home-based work and independent contracting for women, flexible schedules, back-to-back shifts among parents, and "sequencing," or moving in and out of the workforce. This shift is not seen statistically yet, but parents are increasingly considering options such as part-time work or one parent quitting work so that he or she gets to spend more time with the children.[12] Some parents prefer one parent to be around when the child is young, while others feel that more support and guidance is needed during a child's teen years and, hence, they need to cut back on work at that time.

Single-Person Households

Living alone by choice represents a shift in the family unit. A number of factors are responsible for this trend. First, as people delay marriage, it forces them to live alone. Second, a significant part of the adult population is in transition. They are between marriages due to situations such as divorce or separation. Third, dual careers split homes. Career opportunities often require the physical separation of spouses. Fourth, as we age, more people will be living alone in old age. Finally, as both men and women have more economic independence, they may prefer to live alone in order to enjoy personal lifestyles and freedom.

An increase in single-person households is not limited to North America. In Europe, too, household sizes are decreasing as the countries age, resulting in fewer children being born, young people leaving home, and older people staying single after becoming divorced or widowed. The average household size in the European Union is now 2.7 people. The smallest household sizes can be found in Denmark (2.0 on average), and the largest in Spain (3.7). This shift has increased demand for more appliances, telecommunication equipment such as telephones, and electronics goods.[13]

Nuclear family unit
A family comprising a married couple with children.

Atomistic family unit
A person living alone.

Living alone shifts the society from a **nuclear family unit** (households of parents plus children) to an **atomistic family unit** (households of individuals). The unit of analysis will become the individual and not the household. People will share less and personalize more. More specifically, the implications of the living-alone trend include loneliness, self-respect and autonomy, cocooning, and increased impulse buying.

Loneliness

One of the potential consequences of living alone is loneliness. This fast-growing disease is generating a significant need for a feeling of belonging. Institutions and objects will become methods and symbols of belonging, replacing the kinship methods of belonging. Not having family members available in day-to-day life, people will identify increasingly with the workplace, homes, pets, automobiles, and membership clubs. Drug and alcohol abuse or suicide could be considered an escape from loneliness. On the positive side, people also will join social causes and contribute their time to volunteer organizations in order to escape loneliness.

The marketplace will feel the impact of this trend with a shifting emphasis on products that will be sold more on the basis of symbolism and social group values rather than merely on their functional or performance values.

Self-Respect and Autonomy

As people live alone and are financially self-sufficient, they will demand more **autonomy** (power to control their own lives) and self-respect from others. They want to be treated correctly as customers, workers, and citizens. To the user, this trend will result in products that are customized to be more appealing. To the buyers in the household, businesses will have to be careful to offer them the best service value possible. Bored at home, many will visit stores for socializing. They will value retail stores where friendly personnel engage them in small talk. Customers also will prefer stores and service establishments (e.g., hair salons, restaurants) where sales staff or service employees are similar to them in demographics and lifestyle.

Autonomy
One's power to control his or her own life.

Cocooning

In contrast to the trend for single people to leave their homes to socialize, there is a demand for new products to be available at home. **Cocooning** is the habit of staying at home rather than going out. Businesses are increasingly providing services and activities in customers' homes to meet the convenience value of the customer. Suppliers of products will have to be as physically close to the customer as possible, offering conveniences such as direct marketing, one-stop shopping, neighbourhood shopping centres, and home delivery. A study by the Peppers and Rogers Group and the Institute for the Future states that the Consumer Direct channel will account for 12 percent of all retail sales by 2010. The study shows that consumers are already using this channel extensively, with 83 percent of consumers making a purchase through direct-to-home channels. Twenty-five percent of these consumers used the Internet to buy products, and the online channel is expected to account for a large portion of consumer direct sales by 2010.[14] Consumers will use the Internet to buy products in all categories.

Cocooning
The habit of staying at home rather than going out.

Impulse Behaviour

As people live alone, they tend to make choices more impulsively. This occurs because there is no social norm or control to slow down the urge or desire. Consequently, they will have greater desire for **instant gratification,** or immediate satisfaction of their wants and needs. For example, as customers do their food shopping, they will be attracted to the performance value of prepared foods.

Instant gratification
The desire for an immediate satisfaction of a need or want.

The Declining Middle Class

During the last 30 years, the middle class has shrunk as a percentage of North American households, even though it has grown in total numbers. The most oft-cited reason for the decline of the middle class is stagnant wages. The stagnation in real wages has hit the middle class the hardest since they (in contrast to the upper class) rely on their wages to pay the bills.[15]

The same compression of the middle class is occurring in other advanced economies as well. However, the middle class is growing in Asia due to the recent and continuing business boom there. For example, in India, the demand from the rapidly expanding middle class is fueling its economy. These middle-class citizens have increasingly higher aspirations and more disposable income and purchasing power. The largest middle class is found in China, with 300 million middle-class citizens fueling industrial growth in that country by 10 percent a year.[16]

In advanced nations such as Canada, the United States, and the nations of Western Europe, the declining middle class has transformed the economics of survival. This trend has four key implications: an increasing range in prices of products, more customer militancy, affordability, and the Neo-rich.

Increasing Range of Prices of Products

One major consequence is that the price range for the same product category, across a range of different brand names, will begin to increase. Generally, when there is a very tight, homogeneous, large middle class, the maximum-to-minimum price ratio is no greater than five. However, with the decline in the middle class and the corresponding growth at the extremes of the income range, the price range becomes much larger, to fit with a diverse range of customer resources, increasing up to 20 to 25 times. For example, the price of the fresh fruits and vegetables being sold in supermarkets today ranges widely, from low-cost vegetables like lettuce and carrots to very fancy vegetation from far-flung parts of the world. The same is true for automobiles, where there are mass-produced cars priced as low as $16,000 to $18,000, to special super-premium cars like the Bentley, priced at over $300,000.

More Customer Militancy

Customer militancy The behaviour of frustrated and dissatisfied customers entailing the taking of the law into their own hands.

A second major consequence of the decline of the middle class is the rise in **customer militancy**—vocal and physical protest if expectations are not met. One cause of customer militancy is the frustration of the lower socioeconomic classes, who are finding it almost impossible to survive. There is an increase in marketplace violence because people are unhappy about the income gap that exists.

Customer militancy can also be attributed to a sense of hopelessness as people see their bills climbing, incomes stagnating, and future prospects for paying their children's educational bills worsening. A lack of control can ultimately lead to a sense of unhappiness, which influences customer behaviour. Buyers of products will seek service-oriented businesses that are receptive to their mood. Unhappy customers will seek stores that have uplifting environments, ones that give them a reason to get out of the house to go shopping.

Affordability

Affordability The possession of adequate economic resources needed to buy and use a product.

A shrinking middle class implies a growth of the low-income class. A large segment of the society will be unable to afford what is considered to be an acceptable middle-class lifestyle—owning a home, raising children, and planning for retirement. This **affordability** issue will become extremely important in the marketplace; it will require marketers to generate creative financing, not only for durables such as automobiles and appliances, but even for consumables. It also will require marketers to bring in low-cost, high-quality products, even if it means offshore manufacturing and procurement. Finally, this trend also implies increased problems with bad debts, shoplifting, and customer fraud in general. Income has been shown to be one of the most important reasons for the "digital divide" among households in Internet access and use. However, recent studies show that computer and Internet access is increasing for Canadian households at all income levels due to the drop in the price of computers and of Internet access.

The Neo-Rich

As the affluent class grows, the wealthy (or what some have referred to as **Neo-rich**) will abandon old symbols of affluence and will patronize new symbols of conspicuous consumption. The lifestyle of the rich and famous will become more and more unique through customized behaviour. In the marketplace, customized (totally unique, not duplicated) products will rise significantly in homes, property, vacations, and so on.

Neo-rich
Persons who have recently become affluent.

Ethnic Diversity

Canada has historically been ethnically diverse, and that trend is on the rise, as mentioned in Chapter 2. Ethnic groups are no longer coming only from Europe, but from Asia, Latin America, Africa, and the Caribbean Islands, bringing to Canada a greater number and wider diversity of people from all over the world. It is estimated that by the year 2017, one of every five people in Canada might be a member of a visible minority. The Chinese, South Asians, and Blacks will continue to be the largest ethnic groups, and it is expected that the West Asian, Korean, and Arab groups will exhibit a fast growth. In addition, ethno-cultural diversity is likely to remain concentrated in a number of urban areas. As was the case in 2001, almost three-quarters of visible minorities in 2017 would be living in one of Canada's three largest metropolitan areas: Toronto, Vancouver, and Montreal. About one-half of the population in Toronto and Vancouver could belong to a visible minority. Increasing globalization of the economy, job opportunities, and sustained immigration are some of the factors accounting for this diversity.[17]

Segmented Markets

In a more diverse population, markets will require more careful segmentation to serve each distinct ethnic group. More choices will be available for food, shelter, and clothing through the mainstream retail institutions. For example, restaurants and supermarkets will carry a wide range of ethnic foods. Department stores will carry ethnic merchandise. Of course, in order to cater to diverse segments, marketers would have to study their customers closely.

Cultural Diversity

With ethnic diversity comes cultural diversity, bringing with it changes in products and marketing communications. For example, it is not uncommon to see advertisements addressed to the Chinese market written in Mandarin or Cantonese. As the proportion of ethnic customers increases in the marketplace, so will the marketer's sensitivity toward incorporating the language and cultural differences of these segments. The Internet is said to be the ultimate vehicle for globalization of business, and has broken all geographical barriers that bind business locally. Yet, in order to truly harness the full potential of the Internet, the issue of language is important and must be tackled. With more than 60 percent of Internet users speaking a language other than English in 2005 (as estimated by the website http://www.computereconomics.com), businesses operating in different countries will need to mirror their sites in different languages and customize them with local content to make them interesting.[18] Table 3.1 gives statistics on Web pages by language. In 2000, English pages accounted for 68.3 percent of total Web pages on the Internet, followed by Japanese at 5.85 percent, German at 5.77 percent, and Chinese at 3.87 percent. However, Chinese pages are slated to be second only to English on the Web in a few years as the number of Internet users in China increases, and more and more of the English content is being translated into a Chinese language.

Geographic Redistribution

In the future, marketers also can expect geographic redistribution, or shifts in population density from one region of a nation or world to another. For example, currently, the western provinces are experiencing higher economic growths that may attract Canadians from other provinces, as well as more immigrants. Other factors can also cause shifts in the geographical distribution of the population:

- As more people come from Asia, they prefer to settle in large metropolitan areas, such as Toronto and Vancouver.
- As Canada continues to move toward a service economy and to become less dependent on natural resources, this means that new businesses can be located in all areas of the country.
- Geographic boundaries are less relevant because information technologies overcome or reduce space and time barriers.
- The **quality of life** in big cities, as measured by crime, traffic, pollution, and education, is very poor. This has resulted in an exodus out of big cities to nearby towns.
- Corporations are relocating in remote locations due to the economic incentives available there, many offered by municipal and provincial governments trying to attract new businesses into their territory.
- As both the federal and provincial governments invest in infrastructures such as highways, utilities, and other public services, they are bridging the gap between big cities and small towns.

Quality of life
A person's living condition, measured by the absence of crime, traffic congestion, and pollution, and the opportunity for education, recreation, and general well-being.

Geographical redistribution affects families directly in that it separates different generations in different space and time zones. This will increase gaps both within generations (i.e., between siblings) and between generations (i.e., between grandparents, parents, and children) as people living in different areas of the country reflect different values, lifestyles, and attitudes. Since families will be split both between generations and within generations, there will be a trend toward fractured families, or a decline in the number of extended families. There also will be less intergenerational influence. No longer will customers buy and use a brand simply because their parents used it. Finally, there will be greater heterogeneity within each region. Every region will have a greater mix of people born elsewhere.

TABLE 3.1 Web Pages by Language

Language	Number of Web Pages	Percent of Total
English	214,250,996	68.39
Japanese	18,335,739	5.85
German	18,069,744	5.77
Chinese	12,113,803	3.87
French	9,262,663	2.96
Spanish	7,573,064	2.42
Russian	5,900,956	1.88
Italian	4,883,497	1.56
Portuguese	4,291,237	1.37
Korean	4,046,530	1.29
Dutch	3,161,844	1.01
Sweden	2,929,241	0.93
Danish	1,374,886	0.44
Norwegian	1,259,189	0.40
Finnish	1,198,956	0.38
Czech	991,075	0.32
Polish	848,672	0.27
Hungarian	498,625	0.16
Catalan	443,301	0.14
Turkish	430,996	0.14
Greek	287,980	0.09
Hebrew	198,030	0.06
Estonian	173,265	0.06
Romanian	141,587	0.05
Icelandic	136,788	0.04
Slovenian	134,454	0.04
Arabic	127,565	0.04
Lithuanian	82,829	0.03
Latvian	60,959	0.02
Bulgarian	51,336	0.02
Basque	36,321	0.01

SOURCES: Vilaweb; "Web Pages by Language," *The Big Picture—Demographics*, July 5, 2000. http://cyberatlas.internet.com/ big_picture/demographics/article/ 0,1323,5901_408521,00.

Regional marketing both responds to and feeds these differences by exposing newly arrived residents to regional tastes. Consequently, procurement and consumption patterns are likely to become more divergent in different regions of the country. National manufacturers and national store chains will have to adapt to the regional differences. Therefore, regional marketing will acquire increasing significance.

LO 2 TECHNOLOGICAL TRENDS

A second force shaping future customer values is technology. As discussed in Chapter 2, advances in technology have already given customers increased access to information, newer generations of products, automation of transaction processes to provide customers with greater flexibility and control, and access to some customized products. Future developments will further change products and the very nature of customer behaviour.

New Technologies

In particular, technological advances are expected to include products that give customers more control over information and information, access-smart products, the automation of processes that liberate customers from operations-driven processes, and products that enable customized lifestyles.

Increased Control Over Information

The information age is already upon us. The computer storage of information has made widespread distribution and access to marketplace information a reality. And yet, the information infrastructure is still evolving, and what we see today is barely the tip of the iceberg. What will the full-blown information age be like? According to Jagdish N. Sheth and Rajendra S. Sisodia:

> The vision of the future information infrastructure is that there will be an interactive broadband digital highway terminating in very high resolution multimedia display terminals in consumer homes and workplaces. . . . Today's World Wide Web represents a crude approximation of the capabilities and functionality that are expected to be widely deployed by the middle of the next decade. It is serving as a very large test bed for companies and as a training platform for consumers to learn new modalities of interaction and consumption.[19]

This prophesy is already unfolding. The appendix in this chapter gives us the status of the Internet information infrastructure across different regions and countries.

The equipment that gives you the combined capabilities of TV and computer is already available, such as WebTV or network computers. In the future, these will become more powerful, sophisticated, portable, easy to use, and affordable (i.e., smarter, easier, smaller, and cheaper). Already currently available handheld computers, such as the latest gizmo, the palmOne LifeDrive™ Mobile Manager, combine phone, digital camera, and PDA (Personnel Digital Assistant) and cost around $500.[20] These smart terminals, along with the much broadened bandwidth and multimedia experience capabilities, will enable consumers to select the information they want, when they want it. Advertising messages will not be broadcast anymore; rather, they will have to be narrowcast (targeted to a narrow group of customers) or even monocast or pointcast (targeted to a single customer). Information will be stored in digital video servers to be viewed or downloaded *on demand*. The viewer will be in control of content, scheduling, and selection. The customer will view, hear, and attend to the market communications of his or her choosing, at a time and place of his or her choosing. In such an environment, information invitations may become a common practice. Companies would have to seek permission to present their case to customers—a far cry from the uninvited barrage of advertising messages cluttering the mass media today.

Smart Products

The newer generation of products will increasingly become **smart products**—products that can communicate their functioning status to an outside agent, or receive communication from an outside agent to adapt their function within predefined limits. Thus, they contain elements of both artificial intelligence and built-in adaptability. For example, smart copiers that communicate impending breakdown to a remote repair agency are already available; the repair person comes and fixes the machine even without the customer making the repair request. Moreover, beyond just communicating their operation status and impending breakdown, such machines could receive instructions from the remote site and recycle the set-up procedures to correct their software-related problems.

Smart products
Products that can communicate their "functioning status" to an outside agent or receive communication from an outside agent in order to adapt their function within predefined limits.

Smart products also are being developed with voice-recognition capabilities. Voice-recognition technology, when incorporated into smart products, offers customers ease of use and assurance against theft or fraud, since voice is an individual's least reproducible characteristic, and therefore best for identification. For example, automated teller machines will be able to receive voice instructions from the customer, making them very user-friendly.

Smart products are being designed to store the selected preferences of their owners and users; in other words, they will have memory. Thus, if you sat in a car or chair once, it might store your ergonomic profile in its memory so that the next time you sit in the same seat, it will, based on a voice code, or, better still, based on a tactile code, automatically shape itself to that ergonomic profile. This profile will, of course, be more customized than the current versions of memorized seat positions available in many automobiles. Such technology is already in use in Mercedes's new line of S-Class cars, which features a front passenger seat that automatically recognizes when a child safety seat is being used and reduces the car's air bag power. The line also features a chip-card key equipped with a profile of the driver. Smart products will also adapt to the intended usage by incorporating a feedback loop. Consider, for example, the water temperature you prefer in the shower. A smart shower will set itself to give you the temperature consistency on the second and later usages. Moreover, it also will adapt the water temperature according to the room temperature. Motorola, the world's leading producer of embedded semi-conductor solutions, has donated $5 million to establish the Motorola DigitalDNA Laboratory at the MIT Media Lab in Cambridge by 2003. The Motorola DigitalDNA Laboratory focuses on linking several smart products, such as set-top TV boxes, automobiles, household appliances, personal digital assistants, and wireless communications systems, thus integrating several independent gadgets into one intelligent mechanism.[21]

Access to Products Anytime, Anywhere

In the industrial age, the customer became a hostage to the marketer and was forced to buy the mass-produced goods at a time and place chosen by the marketer. If the stores were open only from 10 a.m. to 5 p.m., or if the car repair facility was open only on the weekdays, then that was when the customer could buy store products or take the car for repairs. Technology has liberated this hostage customer. Now the customer can buy anytime and anywhere. Moreover, due to mass customization, the customer can better fit the products to his or her needs. Thus, *whatever*, *wherever*, and *whenever* will be the new tenets of customer behaviour. Anytime, anywhere purchasing and consumption will become commonplace. One consequence of this will be that customer desire for instant gratification will increase.

Consumers will engage in a new way of shopping, mainly mobile shopping. A study from Strategy Analytics estimates the mobile e-commerce (m-commerce) market at $200 million in 2004. The study expects radical shifts in consumer behaviour as transactions using mobile phones increase dramatically in the coming years. Mobile phones are expected to be used to purchase goods from vending machines, buy cinema and train tickets, and shop on the Internet.[22] The wireless boom in Japan has already made this scenario a reality by 2002 as services such as *I-mode* (http://www.nttdocomo.com) allow consumers to reserve airline and concert tickets, find restaurants, check bank balances, read the news, check train schedules, send e-mail, and access the Internet from their mobile phones. Technology is a major facilitator for anytime, anywhere m-commerce.

Mass Customization

Mass customization will expand exponentially. With technology, houses, shoes and clothing, and food could all be customized and delivered almost at the speed and cost of mass-produced products. Moreover, customization will diffuse to services. Imagine that the hairstyle you were given the last time you visited the salon can be stored in computer memory, and a visual image can be recalled on a computer screen on your next visit. You could even carry this image with you on a disk. Even more dramatically, using a virtual reality platform, you could see yourself with simulated hairstyle options and choose or create your own style. Your preferences when you visit a restaurant or hotel can be recorded and stored. When you return for another visit, the same amenities and services would be available to you, with the option of making modifications.

Customer Responses to New Technology

Technological developments will, in turn, stimulate changes in customer behaviour. Customers will increasingly take on the role of coproducers. In addition, they will engage in disintermediation, outsourcing, and automation of consumption.

Customers as Coproducers

Because of flexible manufacturing technology in the production stage and computer capabilities in managing customer-specific preferences, it will be possible to mass-customize products. Customers will be able to routinely offer direct input into the making of the product, called **coproduction**. But this is barely the beginning of customer input. The real customer participation will come with virtual reality.

Coproduction
A situation wherein customers routinely provide direct input into the making of a product.

Imagine an architect sitting down with you and, based on your initial specifications, drawing a picture of the house you want to build. Now, you can walk into this building, feel the materials being used, and sense the light variations as you move from one room to another. As you suggest changes, the architect can modify the building, and you can walk into it again. You can repeat this process until you eventually have designed the house of your dreams. All this is possible with virtual reality. Virtual reality will enable you to coproduce the design for your home. Likewise, you would be able to install appliances, put together modular equipment, and repair machines, all guided by realistic graphics beamed from a remote location. Similarly, telemedicine will allow you to consult with a distant doctor, show your physical condition, transmit information about your vital signs (e.g., heart rate and temperature), and follow the physician's advice to medicate yourself.

Thus, for a variety of products, by linking directly into production systems, customers will engage in self-service, self-design, and self-ordering and provisioning. Learning from the problems faced by e-tailers in the previous holiday shopping season, FedEx revamped its Internet-based package return systems in 2000 to involve the customer. Ease of returns to an online retailer has been identified as an important aspect of defining the customer's shopping experience with the online retailer. In 2000, FedEx's NetReturn upgrade allowed customers to print package return labels from their personal computers, and also specified a list of drop-off locations for depositing the packages, which would speed up the crediting procedures for the returned merchandise. This makes the customer a coproducer in the returns process, and at the same time increases the efficiency of the online retailer since he or she is able to track returns online.[23]

Disintermediation

Because information technology will allow you to communicate directly with the factory, you would be able to deal with manufacturers without any intermediaries. Since the enhanced graphics capability of home computers/TV terminals and video transfer of product information will allow you to get a realistic view of the product, you would not have to visit a store. Since advances in distribution technology will allow producers to ship the product to individual customers directly without much loss of speed and economy, there will be no need for intermediaries who maintain inventory closer to where customers live. In other words, customers would make their purchases without intermediaries. This manner of direct transactions between the producers and customers is called **disintermediation.** Disintermediation also provides greater control by customers and coproduction. ATMs are a familiar example; another noteworthy example is FedEx Ship, a software program that customers can run on their PC. Using this software, business customers of FedEx can now self-ship, self-track, and self-invoice the shipping of time-sensitive documents. FedEx Ship is an example of both disintermediation and coproduction of service.

Disintermediation
A practice in which the customer is able to transact directly with a firm without any intermediaries.

Customer Outsourcing

Technology will make it increasingly possible for household customers to cope with rising time pressures by outsourcing what was previously produced in the home. Because customers will be able to order products from anywhere around the country or even from around the globe, outsourcing will not have to depend on whether the suppliers are available nearby. More and more cooked food will be outsourced, for example. Instead of cooking at home, customers will order, using their computer terminals, largely precooked food that merely needs reheating or defrosting. And this ordering will be automated with a prespecified weekly menu, with provision for spur-of-the-moment alterations.

Home-based businesses will continue to grow because technology enables operations to be set up on a small scale, and more people will find it convenient to telecommute. Telecommuting, or the more appropriate term, *teleworking*, blurs the boundaries between home and office so that, for example, office suppliers will have to deliver increasingly to workers' homes. Pizza-style delivery will spread to a wide range of home-office products as well as household-related products. Conversely, to attract and retain qualified workers, offices will be more like homes. Many products not traditionally considered part of an office setting will be delivered to and consumed at the office. For example, more offices will have child care, health and fitness facilities, cooking facilities, and carry-out foods for their employees.

Automated Consumption

Thanks to new technology, time-pressed customers also will be able to benefit from an increasing degree of automation of product purchasing processes. Just as electronic data interchange (EDI) automates the ordering process in business markets, so, too, household customers will be able to automate their order processing. The home pantry will be similar to a store shelf in terms of stock replenishment, equipped with a small home computer. Every time an item is consumed, the user scans it to record stock depletion. When the stock falls to a prespecified level, the computer automatically locates the store with the best price and orders the product, getting the best deal!

In sum, future customers, emboldened by what technology will make feasible, will demand hassle-free product information (e.g., advertising on demand), hassle-free product acquisition (e.g., home delivery), hassle-free consumption (e.g., self-correcting smart products), and also hassle-free disposal. They will seek greater value in terms of (a) better fit of products with their needs and (b) greater savings in time, effort, and money. Armed with user-friendly access to marketplace information, future customers will no longer be the *targets* of marketing activity. Rather, they will be knowledgeable and demanding *drivers* of it.

Technological revolution in all spheres of life will undoubtedly unleash customer behaviour that is more liberated as well as more demanding. As people start to change the way they work, communicate, and spend their leisure time, they will demand a change in the way companies do business with them. They will resent the high costs (both in time and effort) of acquiring the products they seek and will shun marketers who cannot meet their preferences. They will be more demanding, more information-driven, and more individualistic.[24]

There is a flip side to technology and the customer's response to it. A study conducted by the Stanford Institute for the Quantitative Study of Society (SIQSS) of 4,113 adults in 2,689 households, including both Internet users and non-users, points out that "the more hours people use the Internet, the less time they spend in contact with real human beings." The Internet could be the "ultimate isolating technology" as it draws people away from social interaction.[25] Research at Carnegie Mellon University examined the social and psychological impact of the Internet on 169 people in 73 households during their first one to two years online. Longitudinal data was used to examine the effects of the Internet on social involvement and psychological well-being. In this sample, the Internet was used extensively for communication. Nonetheless, greater use of the Internet was associated with declines in participants' communication with family members in the household, declines in the size of their social circles, and increases in their levels of depression and loneliness.[26]

LO 3 TRENDS IN PUBLIC POLICY

Passive consumers Persons who are not consuming the product themselves but who, as bystanders, are being negatively affected by the consumption of others.

Several projected trends in public policy are relevant to a study of customer behaviour. First, economic pragmatism is prevailing over ideology. In addition, many governments are concerned with protection of passive consumers. **Passive consumers** are those who are not consuming a product themselves, but are merely bystanders, consuming the product secondhand, or otherwise being negatively affected by the action of those who consume. Finally, governments on an international level are pursuing **regional economic integration,** the realignment of nations into region-based economic blocs.

Economic Pragmatism Over Ideology

Regional economic integration
The realignment of nations into region-based economic blocs, such as the European Free Trade Association (EFTA).

Many governments are altering their view of the government's role in the national economy. When it comes to business, ideology is giving way to economic pragmatism in country after country. Governments are recognizing, in increasing degrees, the inherent power of free markets and the market economy, and they are getting out of its way, shunning their long-cherished ideologies. This is not to say that economic goals are the only goals with which societies should be concerned or that values other than consumerism are not valid. Instead, freeing economic systems to function will, over the long run, provide benefits such as increased productivity, better allocation of resources, and higher standards of living.

Historically, three ideologies—political, religious, and central planning—have shaped government's role in national economic affairs. Each has favoured other goals over economic progress, but each is being abandoned in favor of economic pragmatism. Figure 3.2 summarizes the implications of these two approaches.

Political Ideology

The former communist bloc countries, such as the USSR, China, and the communist countries of Eastern Europe, have realized that their central control of economy and commerce choked their economy rather than promoted it. The ideological divide between Eastern Europe and the West during the Cold War era was matched by the economic divide: the Western economies flourished while the centrally controlled communist economies suffered. This was a glaring lesson in the power of free-market economies. These once-communist countries are now welcoming foreign investments with open arms, and state control is being replaced with entrepreneurial initiative. This trend toward greater economic freedom will continue.

FIGURE 3.2 Implications of Ideology versus Economic Pragmatism

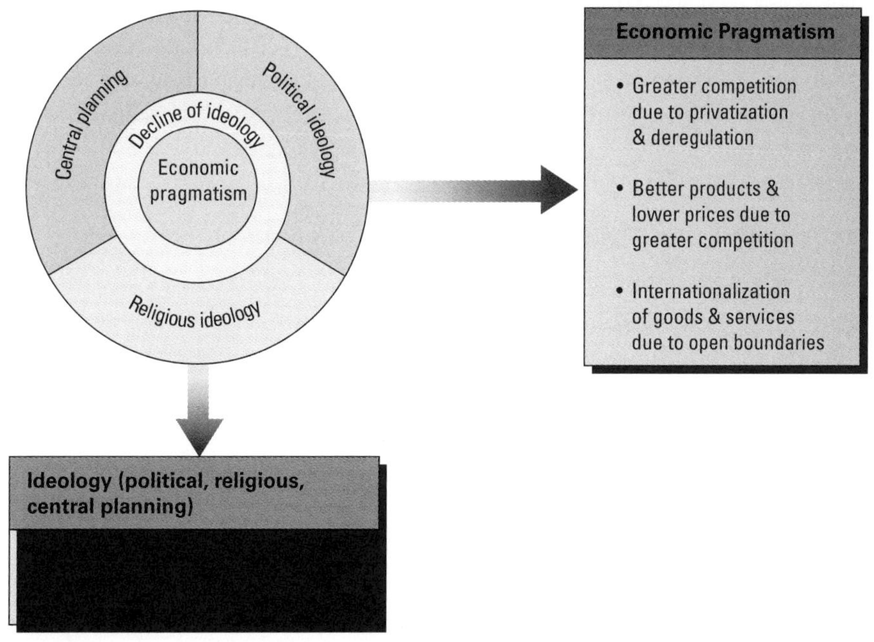

Religious Ideology

Some countries are secular, upholding a separation between government and religion. In many other countries, the government follows a religious ideology. Religious ideology has proven to be a hindrance to modernization and economic development. For instance, Arab countries have historically boycotted doing business with Israel. Muslim countries with nonsecular governments also have looked at foreign investment from non-Muslim nations as undesirable. The Israeli airline has been under a government-imposed prohibition of refraining from business on Saturday (Sabbath), a burden on its ability to compete with other international airlines. Now these governments are realizing the dysfunctional role of allowing religious ideology to dictate to the business world and are loosening their religious-ideological grip.

The Ideology of Central Planning

The third ideology is that of centrally planned economies like India, or, until recently, the United Kingdom. Under this ideology, sectors of the economy considered crucial to public well-being were either government-owned or heavily regulated. Thus, in India, for example, all the infrastructure (railroads, airlines, utility, postal service, insurance, and so on) and basic industries (steel, coal, and defense production) have been either exclusively or dominantly in the public sector. India's state-run banking industry has almost been bankrupt, now barely surviving with constant government bailouts. But the tide is changing; the domestic airline industry has been opened up to private competition. The most dramatic test case of privatization is Britain, where in the 1990s Margaret Thatcher's government rescued a crippled economy by giving up state control of industry after industry: airlines, utilities, and telecommunications. The privatized British Telecom has now become a very competitive communications network, even offering cable TV to its phone subscribers. And even Heathrow Airport in London was privatized in 1987, a first in the aviation industry anywhere in the world, and Lester B. Pearson Airport in Toronto was privatized in 1996.

This trend toward privatization and deregulation will continue. A related development will be the decreasing role of government as a welfare state. Market-based insurance and public assistance programs will replace the straight dole-out welfare programs of today. In North America and Western Europe, government welfare is already being reduced.

Implications for Customer Behaviour

In effect, then, all three ideologies are giving way to market control of economies. This trend has several implications for customer behaviour:

- There will be greater competition. In order to compete, it will become increasingly important for firms to become customer-oriented.
- Competition generally results in better products at lower prices; moreover, with increased competition, firms will have to make it easier to do business with them. Thus, all three customer roles will benefit: the payer by lower prices, the user by better products, and the buyer by ease of doing business.
- Because of more international flow of capital and products, there will be greater internationalization of products. A product available in one corner of the world will also be available in other corners. Due to global markets, there will be more standardization.

Thus, for business and household customers alike, there simply will be more choices, without barriers of distance and time. In consumption terms, we will become what Marshall McLuhan called a global village. Consumers everywhere will be able to have access to the same products, facilitated both by changing public policy and more empowering information technology. Government will use technology like the Internet to make consumers aware of public policy. In the United States, former president Bill Clinton launched a World Wide website called FirstGov (http://firstgov.gov) on September 20, 2000, that gives citizens access to government information and services 24 hours a day, 7 days a week, 365 days a year. "FirstGov allows users to browse a wealth of information—everything from researching at the Library of Congress to tracking a NASA mission. It also enables users to conduct important business online, such as applying for student loans, tracking Social Security benefits, comparing Medicare options, and even administering government grants and contracts."[27] On the other hand, the governments of some countries, such as Saudi Arabia, Qatar, Bahrain, Oman, Kuwait, and China, have censored the Internet. This has obvious implications in terms of unexploited purchasing power and propensity to buy. Saudis obtained access to the Internet in 1999, and the total number of Internet users was estimated to be 300,000 by 2000. Some forbidden topics for Saudis on the Internet are offensive rap music and discussions of opposition to the royal family. The 200 Internet cafés in the kingdom are the primary means for consumers to access the Internet. In Syria, only 5,000 of the country's 17.5 million people have Internet access, and the only ISP in the United Arab Emirates filters certain websites. The Chinese government has rules to prevent "subversive" content entering China via the Internet.[28] The Chinese government came under fire from media freedom groups for blocking access to the popular search engine Google for 10 days; since then, Baidu (nicknamed the Chinese Google) went public in August 2005 and did very well on the NASDAQ.[29]

Rights of Passive Consumers

Even in free-market economies, where governments have given free rein to businesses, they have not given up their role in protecting the public. Consumer protection from unfair business practices and the public's well-being have become a concern of most democratic governments.

While government's direct control of businesses will decline, its protectionist role will increase to protect the innocent victims of reckless consumption. Governments will increasingly come to the rescue of passive consumers. One of these bystander victims is, of course, the physical environment. Damage to the environment, in turn, affects consumers, whether or not they caused the damage in the first place.

As Western economies shift from a production orientation to a consumption orientation, governments have to step in and monitor consumption. Therefore, governments' role in protecting the environment and protecting passive consumers will intensify.

Governments can protect and promote the interests of passive consumers and the general public by three means:

1. *New laws and stricter enforcement.* Governments will resort to making more new laws in the area of protection of the public interest from reckless consumption, and they will enforce stricter compliance. An example is the V-chip on television sets (which allows a display of program ratings to protect children from exposure to unsuitable programs) and the monitoring of indecent content on the Internet.

2. *Financial disincentives.* To discourage consumption deemed not to be in the public interest, fines of ever-increasing amounts will be imposed both on the offending consumers (e.g., an adult carrying a child in a car without a child restraint) and on the businesses that facilitate that consumption (e.g., tobacco and cigarette companies).
3. *Consumer education.* More and more public money is likely to be expended on educating the consumer (e.g., promotion of antidrug education programs in schools).

Concerns have been raised with regard to the content on the Web and the privacy of personal information collected by commercial websites explicitly through a variety of means, including registration pages, user surveys, online contests, application forms, order forms, and cookies. In most countries, the government has no direct restrictions on the content; it is up to the individuals to monitor the sites visited by their children.

Regional Economic Integration

More and more national governments are embracing regional economic integration. In 1992, 12 European nations formed a common market, called the European Union (EU). Its member nations are Belgium, Denmark, France, Germany, Greece, Ireland, Italy, Luxembourg, the Netherlands, Portugal, Spain, and the United Kingdom. By uniting these megaeconomies of Europe into a single supranational entity, the EU is becoming a major world market, with substantial cross-border investment and trade. Similarly, under the European Free Trade Association (EFTA), Austria, Finland, Iceland, Norway, Sweden, and Switzerland have formed a single trading bloc. With the collapse of the communist regime in the USSR, Eastern European countries such as Hungary, the Czech Republic, Slovakia, Poland, Romania, Bulgaria, Bosnia, and Croatia are opening up to Western-style economies. With the reunification of Western and Eastern Germany, Europeans are projecting a future when the countries of Eastern and Western Europe will be marching toward a common economic destiny.

Similarly, in the Western Hemisphere, the United States, Canada, and Mexico are now a single trading bloc, uniting under the North American Free Trade Agreement (NAFTA). By 2015, all of the countries in South America, Central America, and the Caribbean are expected to join this alliance. But even without such a formal alliance, the countries of South America are already wide open to North American trade. In Brazil, for example, North American fast-food franchises and direct-selling companies such as Amway and Tupperware are a popular presence.

Yet another notable alliance is the Association of South East Asian Nations (ASEAN), incorporating such countries as Malaysia, Indonesia, Singapore, Brunei, Thailand, and the Philippines. While Japan is not a formal partner, it is moving toward integrating its economy (e.g., permanently locating some of its manufacturing facilities in these low-cost countries) with the ASEAN bloc. Eventually, Australia and China are likely to join this alliance.

Across continents, then, the trading partnerships are shifting from the East–West axis to the North–South axis; that is, trade among the countries involved was limited to those above the equator and likewise to those below the equator, but there is now a trend toward trading with countries *above and below* the equator (e.g., North American and South American countries within the same bloc). And, the new alliances are more than trading partnerships. Production facilities are being integrated, producing something for the entire bloc wherever it is most economical or feasible to produce; the tariff barriers are being pulled down; and even currencies are being integrated (e.g., the euro). Each bloc is increasingly acting as a single producing and consuming unit. And this phenomenon will continue. Regional economic integration is going to become more widespread, occurring across cultural and climatic boundaries.

Impact on Customer Behaviour

Because of the shift along the North–South axis, climatic boundaries are going to be blended within economic blocs. As a result, products are now available year-round. Seasonality (in the availability of products) is vanishing. Consumers are able to enjoy all goods in all seasons. Furthermore, because production facilities are located where it is most economical, with free trade within regions, consumers are able to obtain better price value. As international trade is liberalized, more and more products will be available from all over the world to consumers anywhere in the world. The user will have more choices, and the buyer will be able to buy conveniently from a vendor at hand.

For business customers, also, regional economic integration will have far-reaching implications. Free trade will allow faster, cheaper, and better sourcing, and sourcing of parts, materials, and components will be global. Within-region sourcing flexibility will increase. Businesses will be able to relocate their manufacturing, procurement, and marketing functions on a distributed basis. Global infrastructure will speed up logistics for things such as transport, payment, and insurance, further enabling global sourcing.

This third customer benefit—global choices to consumers anywhere—is going to further feed into a trend already mentioned, the globalization of the consumer. More and more, the world is becoming a global village. This will give rise to an interesting related phenomenon: local diversity will increase. No longer will there be homogeneous communities, uniform within but different from others. Rather, each nation, each community, each local population group will become more heterogeneous within itself, but as a unit will more and more resemble similarly heterogeneous communities. National, geophysical, climatic, and cultural boundaries are going to exist merely as administrative units but will collapse when it comes to consumption.

In this global village, retailers will buy their merchandise from all over the world. A visit to any Pier 1 Imports store in Canada (whose eclectic home-furnishing merchandise comes from craftsmen in developing countries) or to http://epicureal.com (which offers gourmet products from all over the world) is merely a window on the markets of the future. An industrial tools manufacturer will be able to buy spare parts from countries historically isolated by time, distance, political system, or cultural barriers. Franchise businesses will open new stores in new countries. A household in a tribal town of Africa will be able to get television shows such as MTV and Home Shopping Network. A custom tailor in a village in Romania is likely to have merchandise from the fashion streets of Milan and Paris. A traditional Brahmin family in Madras, India, will be able to savor a Japanese dish.

In such multicultural global consumption villages, who will be the opinion leaders for new-product adoption? What kind of influence will institutions such as the family, school, and religious institutions exercise on consumers? What gender roles will prevail? Who will be whose reference group? Indeed, each community is going to be a laboratory for the observation of consumption. The future is going to be a fascinating time for the study of customer behaviour worldwide!

IMPLICATIONS OF THE TRENDS FOR THE THREE CUSTOMER ROLES

LO 4

The foregoing trends in demographics, technology, and public policy will influence all three customer roles. These influences are briefly outlined in Table 3.2.

Implications of Demographic Trends

The projected demographic changes will influence the needs and wants as well as the resources (time, physical energy, and money) of future customers, and they will do so with respect to all three customer roles. As users, the aging population will need and want increased and improved health care and security (financial and physical) as well as recreational products suitable for their ages and bodies. Cost containment for escalating health-care needs will become a heightened concern for payers (e.g., government, employers, and insurance agencies). Finally, as buyers, the aging population will want more home delivery of products and will seek greater service and convenience value in the buying process.

The impact of women in the workforce will be on time availability, thus creating a demand for time-saving products; as examples, cooking, cleaning, and baby-care services will be increasingly outsourced. As payers, affordability will improve somewhat, especially where both spouses work, enabling them to buy the products they want and value. As buyers, the traditional male–female role specialization (e.g., men buying tools, women buying groceries) will be further diluted so that marketers must cater to either gender's service and convenience needs.

TABLE 3.2 Influence of Major Trends in Demographics, Technology, and Public Policy and Their Influence on the Three Customer Roles

	User	Payer	Buyer
Demographics			
Aging population	• Increased health, security, and recreational needs	• Cost containment for health-care needs a high concern	• Home delivery and convenience in buying important
Working women	• Time-saving appliances; cooking, cleaning, child care outsourced	• Affordability somewhat improved	• Male–female role specialization in buying further diluted
Single-person households	• Social and emotional values in products acquire prominence	• Better affordability	• More impulse and experiential buying
Declining middle class	• Demand for extreme upscale and downscale merchandise	• Financing progressively more important	• More diligent buying effort among the expanded downscale customer groups
Increasing ethnic diversity	• Greater ethnic in customer tastes	• Cross-ethnic differences in affordability	• Expected customer service levels differ across ethnic groups
Geographic redistribution	• Greater regional diversity in customer tastes		
Technology			
Access to information	• More customized products	• Better information on competitor prices	• Product search on the Internet • Product information on demand
Smart products	• Smart products with memory for users preferences	• New methods of identity verification ensure security against frauds	• Automated purchase • Buying direct from the factory
Liberated customer behaviour			• Buyers will need to be technology-savvy
Mass customized lifestyles			

Public Policy			
Economic pragmatism	• Better products due to open-market economy	• Better prices due to competitive economy	• Easier access to global products • Easier to do business with companies
Rights of passive consumers	• Consumers assured protection against passive consumption	• Financial penalties for offensive consumption	• Access to societally harmful products made more difficult
Regional economic integration	• Seasonal products available for year-round consumption • Exposure to diverse consumption cultures	• More economically produced and more economically priced products	• Easier to acquire products from diverse consumption cultures • Local availability of global products

Next, the trend toward more single-person households implies greater demand for social and emotional value in products users seek and in the kind of market transaction the buyers will prefer. For the payer, the single-person trend implies greater affordability as household and per-capita income become one and the same thing. In search of social interaction and self-reward, single individuals also will engage, as buyers, in impulse and experiential buying.

A declining middle-class trend implies, in contrast, a bipolar status in affordability—easy for payers in the expanding affluent class, but more difficult among the expanding poor classes. For the latter, financing will become increasingly important. As users, these bipolar groups separately will demand more upscale and more downscale products. The expanding poorer class of customers also will engage, in their buyer roles, in a more diligent buying process.

The two remaining demographic trends, geographic redistribution and increased ethnic diversity, are interrelated in their impact on customer roles. To users, the two trends will bring greater exposure to regional and ethnic diversity in consumer tastes. As payers, within each market territory, customers will experience greater cross-ethnic differences in affordability. Finally, as buyers, diverse ethnic and geographic customers will bring divergent expectations regarding the desirable level of service and convenience.

Implications of Technological Trends

As described earlier, advances in technology will bring forth new capabilities to customers with respect to all three of their roles. (See the Window on Research box for more examples.) We described four customer behaviour-related technological advances: increased access to information, smart products, liberated customer behaviour, and mass-customized lifestyles. These advances imply, for the user, a desire for, and the availability of, more customized and smart products that memorize the user's preferences on the previous-use occasions and adapt their performance accordingly for the next-use occasion.

For the payer, technology will make available better information about price levels in the market, and credit payment methods will become more secure. For the buyer, marketplace information will be more customized and will be available for perusal on customers' terms (at the time and place of customers' choosing). Technology will make intermediaries redundant, and buyers will be able to convey their product specifications directly to the factory and receive direct delivery. Items of daily consumption will be reordered by an automated purchase system installed in customers' homes. Of course, these technology-based market transactions also would imply that customers will need to become more technology-savvy and learn the skills for technology-mediated commerce.

Implications of Trends in Public Policy

Three trends for public policy are economic pragmatism, rights of passive consumers, and regional economic integration. Each will affect each of the three customer roles. Economic pragmatism will bring forth an open-market economy, which, in turn, will bring better products to users. Due to open-market competition, payers will also benefit by receiving better prices. The same competition also will imply better customer service, which means that buyers will find it easy to do business with companies. Greater public policy attention to the rights of passive consumers will offer value to users by giving them increased protection against harmful and undesired consumption of other customers. Payers will incur heightened costs should they or the users whose consumption they fund choose not to curb their use of societally harmful products. And buyer access to harmful products will become more difficult.

WINDOW ON RESEARCH

High-Tech Forecast

Stephen Millett and William Koop are two of today's most visionary product experts and forecasters; they are associated with the Battelle Technology Intelligence Program. For *The Futurist* magazine, they forecasted the top 10 innovative products in the year 2008. Here is a brief introduction to three we consider most relevant to customer behaviour:

Personalized computers. The personal computer we all know today will become a powerful personalized computer. It will be versatile and mobile, sending and receiving data from wireless remote sites. It will recognize your voice commands, include advanced security features, and be equipped with intelligent agents. These agents will automatically show information that is of interest to you; ask you questions about your needs; remind you of things you need to do and buy; automatically shop for needed items, find the best deals, and order those items; and electronically transfer money from your bank account.

Home health monitors. An electronic medical team will "live" with you in your home, complete with a chemical analysis laboratory. The machines will analyze your urine or blood, for example, and advise you about the status of various physical functions (e.g., liver, heart). They will be nonintrusive, bothering you only when they need to serve you a health alert. Eventually, they will also be able to recommend changes in your diet, exercise, and lifestyle.

Never-owned products. Within the next 10 years, we will begin to lease most household appliances, computers, and durable goods. We will buy the function rather than the item. Manufacturers and distributors will retain ownership and responsibility for repairs as well as for eventual disposal and recycling. Leasing practice will grow exponentially, and the leases themselves will be customized packages of equipment and related service. For example, from a utility company, you will be able to lease a home-environment package, customized to provide the temperature settings in different rooms of the house according to your personal preferences.

According to Millett and Koop, these products will be ready for commercial use by the year 2008, although not everyone will find them of value immediately.

SOURCE: Adapted from Stephen Millett and William Koop, "The Top 10 Innovative Products for 2006: Technology with a Human Touch," *The Futurist*, July–August 1996, pp. 16–20. Additional information available at http://www.battelle.org.

Finally, regional economic integration will give to users products both in and out of season. Users also will be exposed to diverse consumption cultures as the marketplace will carry products from local and foreign cultures alike. Within the broadened and integrated region, production facilities will be located to yield the lowest costs of production, and as a result, payers will find products more economically priced. Buyers, seeking to meet users' broadened and more culturally diverse needs and wants, will find easier access to products from far and wide, all in the nearby local market. In overall terms, both regional economic integration and the changing government policy of economic pragmatism will assure increased local availability of global products. That, in turn, will fundamentally enhance the market values sought by both the user and buyer.

Overall Implications for Marketers

Anticipation of the changes outlined in this chapter will bring about significant shifts in marketing strategies and practices. Continuing the current trend, the economy will become much more service-oriented; this will occur not only because the current service sectors will grow, but also because customers' need for anytime, anywhere purchasing and consumption will add a significant component of service to the marketing of physical products. This shift from a product orientation to a service orientation will require companies to make significant changes: from supply-driven to demand-driven operations, from centralized operations to more widely distributed locations, and from customer-isolated to customer-participative production (i.e., coproduction). Marketers will have to learn to measure customer value of products in terms of time as well as money, as customers continue to make trade-offs that save them time.

In terms of marketing practices, safety, quality, courtesy, and efficiency will become integral parts of the service offered by all companies. One-stop shopping is certainly the trend of the future, generating the growth of superstores. However, the current dominant avenue of one-stop shopping—the regional shopping mall miles from home—will no longer be perceived as convenient. Instead, neighbourhood mini-malls and shopping via catalogues and the Internet are the waves of the future.

More and more firms will have to adopt mass customization to respond to the market discontinuities described in this chapter. A good example of the mass-customization strategy is the concept of the franchise, such as the McDonald's fast-food chain. McDonald's, found today around the globe, became a success because it was the first fast-food chain to standardize its business processes on such a large scale while adapting the menu to local tastes. Although the quality of the product at McDonald's is virtually identical worldwide, the menu is somewhat customized to accommodate regional differences—even different neighbourhoods in the same metropolitan area address ethnic differences. Such franchise-based mass customization will spread to a diverse set of industries.

The time-starved customer will be highly stressed and will demand that services be carried out dependably. Without the time to supervise or adjust schedules, service personnel will have to deliver service reliably without the customer being physically present to scrutinize the quality (e.g., landscaping while the customer is not at home) and in a manner that engenders customer trust. Security will also be a desirable attribute, as customers would have to leave their homes unattended for service personnel to come in and make the repairs (e.g., cable TV installation or service) while the homeowner is away.

The delivery of products to the home and place of business will become increasingly more prevalent. Customers will want all kinds of services delivered to their doorsteps, including health care, accounting, and other professional services. The winning marketing

Instant marketing Being ready to offer without delay a product when the customer wants it.

position will be **instant marketing**—being ready when the customer is. All services must be organized around the concept of no delay (e.g., instant reservations, 24-hour shopping, cash and carry, in-and-out, etc.). Products will have to be designed for hyperspeed: convenient packaging and ease of consumption also will become valuable attributes.

Since the customers of tomorrow will be time- and stress-driven, they will want not only hassle-free service but also empathy. Consequently, the psychological supports of empathy and courtesy will be important market values. Marketers must, then, address the customer from the attitude of "I understand who you are, and I understand your problem."

SUMMARY

LO 1 In this chapter, we have demonstrated how customer needs and wants change over time as a consequence of changing demographics, advances in technology, and the applications of public policy. We described six important demographic changes taking place in Canada today and the implications to the customer in the marketplace as a result of these changes. The six changes include aging of the population, more working women, more single-person households, a declining middle class, geographic redistribution, and increasing ethnic diversity.

LO 2 Advances in technology will also alter the customer-behaviour landscape. We described how four trends in technology, already on the horizon, will further alter customer behaviour in the future. These trends were described as a shift from mere increased customer access to information toward greater customer control over the information, from newer products to smarter products, from operations-driven processes to anytime/anywhere purchasing, and from merely offering customized products to offering customized lifestyles. As an example of the last trend, consider the forecast made by some technology futurists that the consumer of the future will rent, rather than own, most of the durable goods.

LO 3 Finally, changes taking place in public policy were identified. These were a shift in government's economic policy from ideology to market economy, increased protection of passive consumers, and greater regional economic integration. These pro-market trends in public policy, combined with the advances in technology, will enable consumers to satisfy their new set of needs and wants, altered and shaped by changing demographics.

KEY TERMS

Affordability 104
Atomistic Family Unit 102
Autonomy 103
Changing Demographics 98
Cocooning 103
Coproduction 110
Customer Militancy 104
Disintermediation 111
Financial Well-Being 100
Geographic Redistribution 98
Instant Gratification 103
Instant Marketing 122
Neo-Rich 105
Nuclear Family Unit 102
Outsourcing 102
Passive Consumers 112
Personal Safety 101
Quality of Life 106
Recreational Needs 101
Regional Economic Integration 113
Roommate Families 102
Smart Products 109
Time Shift 101
Time Shortage 101

DISCUSSION QUESTIONS AND EXERCISES

1. Review Table 3.1 about the relevance of the trends to the three customer roles. Add at least one example in each of the cells in this table, thus exhibiting your understanding of these concepts.
2. What implications will changes in demographics, changes in technology, and changes in public policy have on market values discussed in Chapter 1? In other words, what is the link between these emerging customer behaviour trends and the market values customers seek?
3. Visualize how technology will have changed the market place in the year 2015. Now, in this marketplace, visualize yourself as a consumer. Describe whether your experience in this marketplace will be one of a happy or a confused consumer. Explain your answer.
4. As a marketing director of home furniture, you have just read about how technology will enable customers to be coproducers. You realize, of course, that this does not mean you will be able to save on labour costs by transferring some of your production labour to customers. How exactly would it affect your company? How can you take advantage of this trend?
5. With the advent of the Internet as a mode of shopping, customers are now realizing the impact that this new technology has on their marketplace behaviour. Describe the pros and cons of Internet shopping from the perspective of a marketer of greeting cards and gifts and for the customers for these products.

NOTES

1 BMO Retirement Trend Study, http://www.bmonesbittburns.com/personalinvest/About/News/20051207_retirement_your_way.asp; Bill Steinburg, "10 Questions," *Canadian Grocer*, Sept. 2003, vol. 117, No. 7, 29; Rebecca Harris, "The Boomers' Golden Age," *Marketing*, July 12–19, 2004, vol. 109, No. 24, 14; The Consumer's Trend Report, Ch. 3, Consumer Demographics, http://strategis.ic.gc.ca/epic/internet/inoca-bc.nsf/en/ca02099e.html#a31.

2 http://www.ccsd.ca/factsheets/family; The Canada e-Book 11-404-XIE.

3 *Ibid.* See also, Jagdish N. Sheth, "Changing Demographics and the Future of Graduate Management Education," *Selections: The Magazine of the Graduate Management Admissions Council*, Spring 1988, 22.

4 S. H. Peter Leeflang and W. Fred van Raaij, "The Changing Consumer in the European Union: A Meta-Analysis," *International Journal of Research in Marketing* 12 (1995), 373–87.

5 U.S. Census Bureau, *IDB Summary Demographic Data*, updated May 10, 2000 (http://www.census.gov/cgi-bin/ipc/www/idbsum.html).

6 "Demographics of the Net Getting Older," August 29, 2000 (http://cyberatlas.internet.com/big_picture/demographics/article/0,1323,5901_448131,00.html); *Media Digest* 05/06, 59.

7 Charles A. McMellon and Leon G. Schiffman, "Cybersenior Mobility: Why Some Older Consumers May Be Adopting the Internet," *Advances in Consumer Research*, Volume 27, 2000, 139–44.

8 "Seniors Use Internet for Shopping," August 31, 1999 (http://cyberatlas.internet.com/big_picture/demographics/article/0,,5901_192461,00.html).

9 Canadian Institute for Health Information (CIHI), Annual report on health care spending in Canada, *National Health Expenditure Trends 1975–2005.*

10 Diana Farrell, Sacha Ghai, and Tim Shavers, "The Demographic Deficit: How Aging Will Reduce Global Wealth," *McKinseyQuaterly*, March 2005 (http://mckinseyquarterly.com).

11 Statistics Canada, Women in the Workplace, Cat. 89F0133XIE, March 2004.

12 Sue Shellenbarger, "Work and Family: The Heralded Return of Traditional Families Is Not What It Seems," *The Wall Street Journal*, May 31, 2000.

13 S. H. Peter Leeflang and W. Fred van Raaij, "The Changing Consumer in the European Union: A Meta-Analysis," *International Journal of Research in Marketing* 12 (1995), 373–87.

14 "Direct-to-Consumer Sales Seen Increasing," June 28, 2000 (http://cyberatlas.internet.com/markets/retailing/article/0,,6061_404851,00); "Net Trends from Web Business" (http://www2.cio.com/webbusiness/metrics/).

15 U.S. Bureau of the Census, *Statistical Abstract of the United States* (http://www.census.gov/prod/; http://www/statistical-abstract-us.html), data revised July 27, 1999, 474.

16 Ravi Marphatia, "Painting Consumers Fuel Industry Boom; Capacity Plays Catch-Up," *Chemical Week* 158, No. 34 (September 11, 1996), 49–51.

17 Study: Canada's visible minority in 2017, The Daily, March 22, 2005, Statistics Canada; Population projections of visible minority groups, Canada, provinces and regions, 2001–1017, Cat. 91-541-XIE, Statistics Canada.

18 Nevin Cohen, "Eurobabel: Language and the Web," May 28, 2000 (http://www.emarketer.com/etopics/articles/052900_eurobabel).

19 Jagdish N. Sheth and Rajendra S. Sisodia, "Consumer Behaviour in the Future," in Robert A. Peterson, ed., *Electronic Marketing and the Consumer* (Sage Publications, 1997), 17–37.

20 http://www.Softmagic.ca.

21 Erica Noonan, "Making Smart Tech Mainstream," *The Associated Press*, March 15, 1999 (http://www.abcnews.go.com/sections/tech/DailyNews/smarttech990315); "Motorola Donates $5 Million to Create Motorola DigitalDNA Laboratory at MIT," *MIT News*, March 15, 1999 (http://web.mit.edu/newsoffice/nr/1999/motorola).

22 "Mobile Ecommerce to Revolutionize Shopping," January 13, 2000 (http://www.nua.ie/surveys/index.cgi?f=VS&art_id=905355523&rel=true).

23 Clare Saliba, "FedEx Revamps Online Return System," October 10, 2000 (http://www.ecommercetimes.com/news/articles2000/001010-2).

24 A significant part of the material in this section is adapted from Sheth and Sisodia 1997; also see Jagdish N. Sheth, "Call It Anytime, Anywhere Future: Telecommunications in the Next 10 Years," *BellSouth Magazine* 7, No. 1 (January–February 1994), 3–5; Jagdish N. Sheth and Rajendra S. Sisodia, "The Information Mall," *Telecommunications Policy*, July 1993, 376–88; Ripley Hotch, "Communications Revolution," *Nation's Business*, May 1993, 20–32.

25 Norman Nie and Lutz Erbring, "How Internet Is Changing Daily Life—Social Aspects of Web Usage," April 2000, http://www.stanford.edu/group/siqss/.

26 Robert Kraut et al, "A Social Technology That Reduces Social Involvement and Psychological Well-Being?" *American Psychologist*, selected article at http://www.apa.org/journals/amp/amp5391017.

27 William Peters and Charlene Porter, "E-Government: No Walls, No Clocks, No Doors," *Global Issues, An Electronic Journal of the U.S. Department of State*, November 2000, Volume 5, No. 3 (http://www.usinfo.state.gov/journals/ itgic/1100/ijge/ijge1100).

28 Tom Sanders, "Chinese Google Rocks Stock Market," http://vnunet.com (accessed August 8, 2005).

29 "Internet Still Censored in Saudi Arabia," September 28, 2000 (http://www.nua.ie/surveys/index.cgi?f=VS&art_id=905356072&rel=true); "Increased Regulation for Chinese Internet Use," October 9, 2000 (http://www.nua.ie/surveys/index.cgi?f=VS&art_id=905356091&rel=true).

PART 2

Foundations of Customer Behaviour

CHAPTER 

The Customer as a Perceiver and Learner

LEARNING OBJECTIVES

After reading this chapter you should be able to:

LO 1 Understand the factors that shape perceptions.

LO 2 Explain biases in the perceptual process and perceptual threshold.

LO 3 Explain the mechanics of learning and the psychology of simplification and complication.

LO 4 Describe the adoption process and the categories of adopters.

LO 5 Describe the characteristics of innovations and explain innovation resistance.

LO 6 Explain how the perceptual and learning processes impact on the three customer roles.

Long Life Perceptions

Milk. You find it in the refrigerator section of the supermarket, and you store it in your refrigerator, not in your pantry. Right? Not necessarily. Parmalat, the world's largest milk producer, markets a type of milk, called *Long Life*, which is specially processed without any preservatives. But ultra-high temperature (UHT) milk has been for sale in Canada since the early 1970s under various brand names (the first of which was *Grand Pré*). The processing technology to produce this milk neutralizes bacteria and thus prevents spoilage. This milk is then packaged in aseptic cartons that are designed to prevent air and light from entering the carton. It does require refrigeration after opening. But until then, it can be stored on dry-goods shelves for up to six months. The advantages of this technology to customers are substantial. It saves refrigerator space, which, in most households, is scarce. Customers can stock extra milk in their pantry so that they don't have to run to the store at midnight because they just discovered they are out of milk. However, Canadians have been reluctant to embrace this innovation. Market share of UHT milk has been pretty static at 10 percent for the last 4 years (based on 2004 retail prices),[1] while consumers in Western Europe drink more UHT milk than ever. With a 100 percent increase in sales of this type of milk over 30 years, long-life milk now accounts for half of all milk sales in the West European market.[2] The product concept sounded great in theory but, somehow, Canadians customers just cannot fathom the concept of fresh milk in a dry-goods can or box. This is one innovation where customers' preexisting perceptions and learning are at odds with the new product concept.

This example of conflict between preexisting perceptions and learning is not an isolated case. Individuals and businesses face such situations regularly as customers. Take the case of the "beef flavour in french fries at McDonald's." Vegetarian customers who consumed the fries perceived that if the french fries were made in pure vegetable oil, they had to be completely vegetarian. However, when the company confirmed that beef extract is used as a natural flavouring in the fries, these customers filed a lawsuit against the company for misleading them. Likewise, a business customer expects accountants from his audit firm to be in business suits; if they show up in jeans, he would suspect their professional qualifications. This is because this reality is at odds with preexisting perceptions.

When we buy, use, or pay for a product, it is not our first exposure and response to the marketplace. Rather, it is one in a sequence of other marketplace decisions we have made in the past. As customers, we bring to each decision a lifetime of learning about the world in general and about the marketplace in particular. This stock of knowledge guides how we respond to new information in the marketplace, as in the case of *Long Life* milk in the above example, and it deeply affects what we learn about various products. These activities characterize the customer's tasks of perceiving and learning.

This chapter explores what it means for customers to be perceivers and learners—the internal influences on customer behaviour (Figure 4.1). It defines perception and identifies elements of the perception process. We then describe how customers perceive, including common distortions of information. Next, we define what it means for customers to be learners. We explain how learning occurs and how customers alter the basic process through simplification and complication. Finally, we discuss an aspect of learning that is crucially important to marketers: customer response to product innovations.

FIGURE 4.1 Perception and Learning

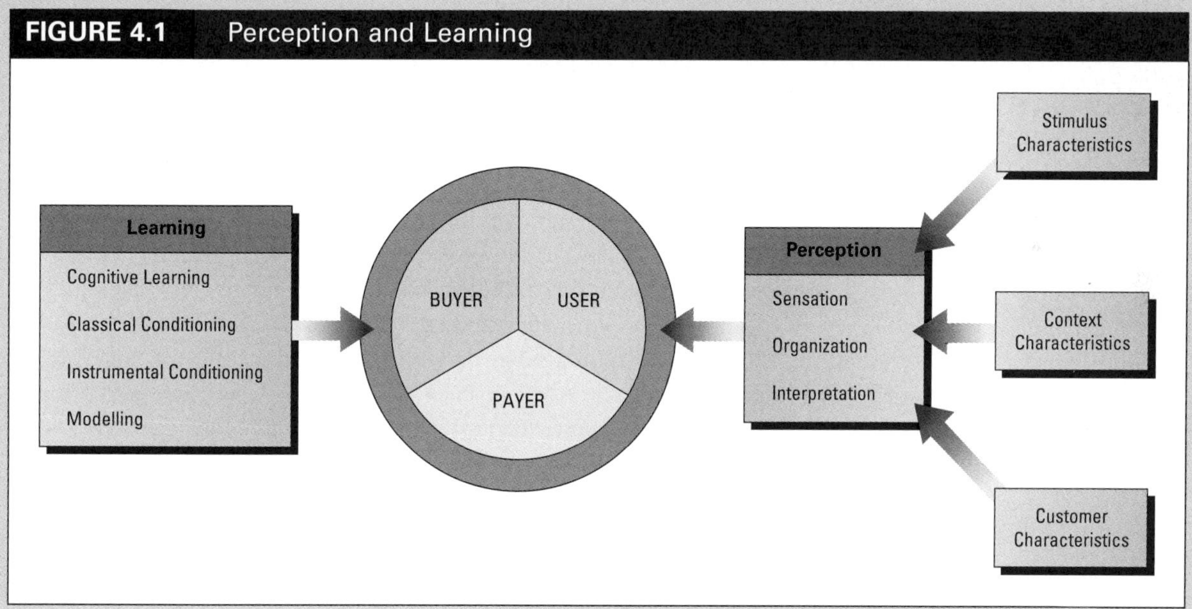

THE CUSTOMER AS A PERCEIVER

LO 1

The objective reality of a product matters little; what matters is the customer's perception of a product or a brand. **Perception** is the process by which an individual selects, organizes, and interprets information received from his or her environment. For example, cereal boxes are made in darker colours to make them look more masculine. Similarly, mouthwashes are coloured green or blue to connote a clean, fresh feeling. One brand, Plax, makes its mouthwash red to distinguish it from competing brands but also to create the impression that it is

Perception
The process by which an individual selects, organizes, and interprets the information received from his or her environment.

medicinal and, therefore, more effective. Similarly, in the business context, colours, shapes, and corporate logos are used to aid customer perception. For example, the TD Bank Financial Group relies on green, the RBC Financial Group on blue, and the CIBC on dark red to register themselves immediately to the customer. The colour and shape of the iMAC Apple computer is designed to appeal to the creative user. The process of perception has three steps:

Sensation
A step in the perception process in which the person attends to an object or an event in his or her environment with one or more of the five senses.

Stimulus
Any object or event that a person perceives in his or her environment.

Organization
A process of stimulus categorization in which the sensed stimulus is matched with similar object categories in one's memory.

Interpretation
A step in the perception process in which meaning is attached to the stimulus.

1. **Sensation**—Attending to an object or an event in the environment with one or more of the five senses: sight, hearing, smell, touch, and taste. Examples include the sensation of an aircraft taking off, or the texture and taste of a hot, juicy hamburger at a particular restaurant. The object or event in an environment is technically called a **stimulus**. Engendering rich sensation is comparatively difficult for Internet sites to achieve, but e-tailers are identifying this as a potential source of differentiation. As a result, a site such as http://Indulge.com has created an ambience reminiscent of the beauty store that it is meant to represent. It creates a soothing ambience with a background in different shades of blue, and customers can use a 1-800 number or live-chat to chat with a customer representative as they would in an off-line store.[3]
2. **Organization**—Categorizing by matching the sensed stimulus with similar object categories in one's memory. In the example of eating a hamburger, organization occurs as the consumer identifies all the ingredients and classifies it as a specific type similar to or different from the ones he or she has eaten before.
3. **Interpretation**—Attaching meaning to the stimulus, forming a "ruling" as to whether it is an object you like and of what value it would be to you, the perceiver.[4] In the hamburger example, interpretation occurs when the consumer judges whether the hamburger tastes good and whether he or she likes it more or less than those eaten before.

To further clarify these perceptual processes, consider an example from everyday life. When you see two parallel headlight beams coming at you in the dark, you subconsciously fill in the rest of the detail and "organize" these two discrete pieces of information (namely, two light beams) as parts of an oncoming car rather than two motorcycles. A little later, judging from its speed—depending on whether it is controlled and slowing down as it approaches you, or astray, uncontrolled, and approaching you with accelerated speed—you "interpret" it to be a friendly or threatening vehicle. At a customer-service centre, when there is a customer call, the operator first asks the consumer to classify his or her problem among several categories of problems available and then, depending on the problem's details, interprets the information, and provides a solution.

FACTORS THAT SHAPE PERCEPTION

Three factors shape customer perceptions:

1. *Stimulus characteristics*—The nature of information from the environment (objects, brands, stores, marketers, friends, government, and so forth).
2. *Context characteristics*—The setting in which the information is received; this includes social, cultural, and organizational contexts.
3. *Customer characteristics*—Personal knowledge and experiences, including the customer's expertise on the relevant topic and prior experience with similar stimuli.

Stimulus Characteristics

People perceive a stimulus differently according to its characteristics, and marketers need to consider both the sensory characteristics and the information content of a stimulus.

A characteristic is **sensory** if it stimulates any of the five senses. For example, strong sensory characteristics include bright colours, loud noises, spicy foods, and strong aromas. Such strong characteristics tend to attract more attention and are perceived more than weak sensory characteristics.

Sensory
A stimulus characteristic that stimulates any of the five senses.

Getting more attention is important because most customers face a flood of stimuli in today's world. For example, a typical customer faces more than 4,000 advertisements in a week.[5] Marketers strive to break through this clutter with stimulus novelty: incorporating new elements into advertisements such as visually distinctive polar bears in the Coca-Cola campaign, handwritten copy in a print advertisement, or a likable celebrity. Supermarkets address the problem of clutter on a supermarket shelf with attractive package designs, point-of-purchase display materials, and eye-level shelf displays.

The aesthetic responses to a product also have an important influence on product preferences. Sensory elements like unity of the product design (congruity among elements of the design such that they look as though they belong together)[6] and prototypicality of the design (the degree to which an object is representative of a category)[7] are important in determining a customer's aesthetic responses to the product.[8] Communicating sensory characteristics is difficult for services (such as electricity, phone, and insurance), and a recommended solution is the use of accompanying tangible facilities to create an identity for the service.[9] For example, financial institutions such as the RBC Financial Group and the ING Group use the trademark of a lion to connote financial strength, Travellers Insurance Company uses the trademark of an umbrella to connote coverage and protection, and Merrill Lynch uses a bull as a trademark to connote its aggressive investment strategy. Similarly, with more and more business being carried out on the Internet, it is also important for marketers to design websites so that customers are not bogged down by unwieldy graphics and big blocks of text that make navigation difficult. Audio and video links that enhance perceptions need to be used with care so that they do not hinder the overall purpose and objective of the site. Web advertising, like TV, radio, or print advertising, has also come into its own, and interactive banner ads and sponsorships help to draw customers to the respective corporate sites.

The other characteristic of a stimulus that shapes perception is its **information content.** After an advertisement has achieved sense perception, by its sense characteristics, informational content moves the perceptual process beyond sensation or stimulus selection toward organization and interpretation. For example, information about an automobile engine's horsepower, acceleration, and style enables one to classify (i.e., organize) it as a performance car or a family sedan; information about the car's country of origin, manufacturer, and price allows inferences about its quality. Research by Cyber Dialogue shows that factors such as site navigation, personalization features, responsiveness to inquiries, user education features, and the ability to compare other consumer opinions are important in shaping customers' perceptions of online financial service brands. In fact, the study states that Internet-based information searching has not only influenced customers' opinions about financial service providers, but in some cases it has been instrumental in the customer's switch between providers.[10] Information content has been identified as one of the key elements by which business-to-business (B2B) e-marketplaces

Information content
The information contained in the stimulus that moves the perceptual process beyond sensation or stimulus selection toward organization and interpretation.

can differentiate themselves and create loyal buyers and sellers. Since most B2B e-marketplaces will be able to facilitate transactions between buyers and sellers, value-added content relating to the transaction, the industry, and all other services related to the transaction will be a major plus for the site.[11]

Context

In perceiving a stimulus with a given set of characteristics, customers also will be influenced by the context of the stimulus.[12] The clearest illustrations of the context effect on the perceptions of marketing stimuli are blind taste-test studies (for example, studies of beer taste). In these tests, customers pick the brand they think is their usual or favourite brand, even when the brand names have been switched. The taste perceptions are influenced by the context the brand name provides.

Customer Characteristics

Expectations Prior beliefs about what something will possess or offer.

Finally, perceptions are influenced by customer characteristics, notably what customers already know and feel about the stimuli. Such prior knowledge and feelings become **expectations**—prior beliefs about what something will possess or offer. Expectations influence perceptions in that we often end up seeing what we expect to see. Students who come to a course having heard good things about it or about the instructor end up liking the course much more than those who enroll having heard criticism of it. The principle underlying this phenomenon is that expectations bias the perception of reality. This principle was tested in a study that showed that customers who were led to have positive expectations about the service level at a hotel actually perceived the service as better (after having a simulated service experience in an experimental condition) than those who had been led to expect a lower level of service.[13] The dominant influence of prior expectations on perceptions occurs within specific conditions: (1) when the stimulus is vague and open to interpretation, and (2) when the perceiver does not have the expertise to evaluate the stimulus objectively. Thus, if the hotel's service levels were very different from expectations, then vivid reality (rather than prior expectations) would drive perception, and the hotel would be perceived unfavourably despite prior expectations. Similarly, a doctor's prior reputation influences a patient's perceptions of his or her skills only when the patient is not knowledgeable about the diagnosis and treatment of disease.

Since customer expectations colour the perception of reality, users, payers, and buyers are also likely to see a product differently Consider a mother shopping with her 19-year-old son to decide which car to buy for him. The son (who will be the user) is delighted about a sports car, which, for him, symbolizes fun and excitement. Mom, the buyer, sees it as an unsafe car. She is also mindful of Dad, who has promised to pay for the insurance, and from his standpoint, a sports car would mean big insurance payments.

Researchers Coupey and Sandgathe state that the Internet as a medium is different from the traditional media such as print, radio, and television, in terms of its increased media richness (media with more cues for developing meaning), interactivity, and selectivity. The interactive and selective nature of the Internet allows a customer to choose the format for information received via the Internet, both in terms of the content and in terms of information needed for decision making. Hence, they suggest that *consumer factors* should be more important than *task/stimulus factors* (communication modalities and media features) and *context factors* (message characteristics) on the Internet. With respect to traditional media, in order to understand how this information will be used by the consumer in the alternative evaluation and purchase stages of the decision-making process, one must understand how modality of communication interacts with messages to influence information search and attention. However, in the Internet environment, search for information is a result of the consumer's active interest, and this ensures exposure and attention to the message. Thus, the focus shifts from information search to information use and the outcomes in terms of decision making. Consumers will use the modality that best balances effort and achieves the accuracy of their goals. Their *own level of knowledge* will determine which mode of communication—plain text, audio, or audio-visual—will be best suited for their decision-making process. The authors state that Internet-based marketers must keep their marketing objectives (such as brand awareness, persuasion, purchase, and knowledge enhancement) in mind while creating information displays, and, while designing features on websites, must also be cognizant of the customer's expected effort/accuracy tradeoffs.[14]

BIASES IN THE PERCEPTUAL PROCESS

LO 2

To cope with the barrage of marketing information (and other information in everyday life), customers become "selective." They ignore some stimuli and some possible interpretations of stimuli, thus biasing their perceptions of incoming information through three processes: *selective exposure, selective attention,* and *selective interpretation.*

Selective Exposure

Of the more than 4,000 promotional or advertising stimuli to which a typical customer is potentially exposed during a typical week,[15] only a small number achieve actual exposure, depending on the customer's needs and interests. Customers seek out some advertisements, some shelf displays, some salespersons, or other sources of information if they are contemplating a purchase. On the other hand, customers not planning a trip may skip the travel section of a newspaper altogether; those not contemplating a computer purchase will skip an entire special advertisement section on computers in a magazine. This selective exposure (also called gatekeeping) is practiced by customers in any of the three roles. For example, a store selling costumes for Halloween (a festivity celebrated yearly in North America on October 31, when everyone wears a mask or scary costume) advertises its special promotions on the radio; however, the customer playing the buyer role tunes out the ad because he or she knows the store location is too far and there is no chance to go there. In contrast, the child user may have gone out of the way to seek information from classmates about the store where a particular kind of costume might be available. Likewise, a customer who, in her payer role, judges a particular store to be too expensive would not enter the store even if it has big signs screaming merchandise clearance savings and even though she happens to pass it while strolling in the mall. Online advertising in Canada has been growing at a fast pace, from $2 million in 1996 to an estimated $510 million in 2005, or 43 percent more than in 2004. At the 2004 level of $364 million, online advertising represented 4 percent of the total advertising dollars spent in Canada.[16] Likewise, in the United States, online advertising has been increasing rapidly, from US$650 million in 1997 to about US$10 billion in 2004. Though advertising spending is increasing, click-though rates (rates for advertising on the Web, which is a measure of "how many people who saw the banner ad or hyperlink, actually clicked on it") have dropped from 1.35 percent in May 1997 to 0.56 percent in the first quarter of 2004. Customers are becoming more selective as ad clutter increases and as they become more savvy in searching the Web for their particular needs and wants.[17]

Selective Attention

Even if an advertisement or product display manages to come face to face with a customer, the customer may still choose to ignore it if it does not relate to his or her interests. A person's attention may be initially impelled by stimulus characteristics such as contrast or vividness, but beyond the initial attention, a person's further processing of a stimulus advertisement or display depends on some personal interest that the featured product arouses. Thus, tennis enthusiasts will read through or continue to watch or listen to an entire advertisement on tennis equipment, while a business customer considering purchasing a computer will fully process the computer advertisement. On the Internet, advertisers are placing customer-specific ad-banners on related websites. For instance, data from media research firms Media Matrix and AdRelevance shows that marketers of pet supplies, personal care products, and home and garden products are targeting their core audience of women by advertising heavily on sites that are specifically geared towards women. It benefits both the marketers and the sites as it increases click-through for marketers and advertising revenues for the sites.[18]

Selective Interpretation

Perceptual distortion In interpreting a stimulus, a person's prior beliefs interfere and distort the meaning to conform to those beliefs.

Customers also interpret the content and message of marketing communications selectively. People generally view a political message or a political candidate, for example, positively or negatively, based on their political affiliation. Similarly, after an important purchase, customers seek communication that will reassure them about the wisdom of their selection. Customers also distort negative information that might threaten their ego. This phenomenon, called **perceptual distortion**, is the encoding of information by a person in a manner that makes it more congruent with his or her prior beliefs than it objectively is. Customers learn certain tricks, so to speak, to cope with the barrage of information available every day, and to more easily solve the purchase-decision problem. Perceptual distortion is one such trick or tactic wherein people distort, whether intentionally or inadvertently, the incoming information to quickly encode it for immediate use or to file it away for later use.

PERCEPTUAL THRESHOLD

Perceptual threshold The minimum level or magnitude at which a stimulus begins to be sensed.

Just noticeable difference (j.n.d.) The magnitude of change necessary for the change to be noticed.

Of the three steps of the perception process (sensation, organization, and interpretation), sensation is the most important since the marketing stimulus is rendered inconsequential if it fails. But not every stimulus is sensed. Consider sitting in a classroom for every week in a semester and taking a look around the room. Are the lights today somewhat dimmer than before? No? Are you absolutely sure? What if the university authorities were to lower the lights just a tad in all the campus buildings? The small decrease in illumination would save them a bundle, and you wouldn't even notice it. You did not notice the change because it was below your **perceptual threshold**, the minimum level or magnitude at which a stimulus begins to be sensed. A related concept is the **just noticeable difference (j.n.d.)**, the magnitude of change necessary for the change to be noticed. Marketers use this principle to marginally reduce product quantity or size in order to keep the prices constant in the wake of rising costs. Some years ago, M&M/Mars did not suffer lower sales when it reduced the size of its candy bars because the size change was slight.

The magnitude of change needed for it to be noticed depends on the base quantity. The larger the base quantity, the larger the magnitude of change needed for the change to be noticed. This is known as **Weber's Law**, named after the German scientist Ernst Weber.[19] For example, a one-half-inch reduction in the size of a five-inch candy bar perhaps will not be noticed, but the same reduction in a two-inch-long stick of chewing gum is likely to be noticed.

Weber's Law
Named after the German scientist Ernst Weber, the law states that the larger the base quantity, the larger the magnitude of change needed for change to be noticed.

MANAGERIAL USES OF THE PERCEPTUAL PROCESS

Customers' perceptual processes are relevant to all aspects of marketing communications—product design, brand names, packages, in-store displays, and mass-media advertisements.

Three special areas of managerial concern where customer perceptual processes are complex and highly consequential are:

1. The psychophysics of customer price perceptions.
2. Country-of-origin effects.
3. Perceived corporate image.

Psychophysics of Price Perceptions

The psychophysics of price refers to how customers psychologically perceive prices. Noteworthy aspects of the psychophysics of price are reference price, assimilation and contrast, and price as a quality cue. **Reference price** is the price that consumers expect to pay.[20] If the actual price is lower than the reference price, it is perceived as good economic value. When a customer walks into a store accidentally, his or her reference price for a given product is the full price; in contrast, the customer who has seen advertisements of "huge savings" has a much lower reference price and is, therefore, disappointed.

Reference price
The price customers expect to pay for a product.

Another important perceptual construct is **assimilation** versus **contrast**. This principle states that customers have a latitude of acceptance and a latitude of rejection, so prices (or other information) that fall within the acceptance latitude are assimilated, and those that fall within the rejection latitude are contrasted and, hence, rejected. For example, a customer who is willing to spend up to $10 to purchase a gift might assimilate a price of $9 or $11, but will reject other prices as either too low or too high. Another way this principle works is that customers have certain cut-off levels for accepting a price, and prices below that level are viewed as acceptable, while those above it are rejected, though the latter may exceed the former by just two cents. That is why marketers adopt the **odd pricing** method, a practice whereby prices are set just below the next round number. For example, a price of $9.99 falls below the $10 range and is acceptable, while a price of $10.01 might not be. Customers often use price as a **quality cue**—as a basis for making inferences about the quality of the product. Such use of price is particularly likely where quality cannot be independently judged.[21] In a review of literature of this topic, Monroe and Krishnan concluded that "a positive price perceived quality relationship does appear to exist."[22] Again, this is especially the case when other clues for inferring quality are unavailable.

Assimilation and contrast
Information within the acceptance range is assimilated and accepted; information outside of this range is contrasted and rejected.

Odd pricing
The setting of prices just below the next round number.

Quality cue
A piece of information that can be used for making inferences about the quality of a product.

Country-of-Origin Effects

Country-of-origin effects
Bias in customer perceptions of products due to the country in which they are made.

Country-of-origin effects refer to the bias in customer perceptions of products based on the country in which these products are made. For example, customers who would be happy to purchase a DVD player from Japan, a fashionable suit from Italy, a machine tool from Germany, or management consulting from a U.S. firm are driven by "country-of-origin" image.[23] Today, Korean companies face a negative country-of-origin effect for their automobiles (e.g., Hyundai) and electronic products (e.g., Goldstar TV). While countries with a poor overall image suffer from this bias, those with a good image benefit from it. The Window on Research shows how this perception of country-of-origin can vary across cultures and across processing conditions.

WINDOW ON RESEARCH

Country-of-Origin Effects

In two studies, Gurhan-Canli and Maheswaran show that perceptions of country of origin are not uniform across cultures and across processing conditions.

Their first study shows that country-of-origin perceptions vary across countries, and these variations can be attributed to culture-specific factors. Customers in an individualistic culture, the United States, and a collectivist culture, Japan, were given attribute information about a mountain bike made either in Japan or the United States. The target product was described as being either inferior or superior to the competition. They found that U.S. customers (individualists) evaluated the home-country product more favourably only when it was superior to the competition. In contrast, Japanese customers (collectivists) evaluated the home-country product more favourably regardless of its superiority. Thus, the cultural dimension of individualism-collectivism is an important dimension in accounting for country-of-origin differences between the United States and Japan. Marketers must know that in collectivist cultures, an advertising strategy based on country of origin is likely to benefit home products while in individualistic cultures, this would be true only if the home product is superior to competition. North American consumers tend to prefer home or foreign products based on the perceived quality differences, and a simple appeal to "buy national products" may not be very effective.

In a second study, they determine the factors that influence customers' country-of-origin perceptions, and show that motivation, processing goals, and the type of information presented affect country-of-origin evaluations. The study shows that customers use country of origin in making judgments only when the motivation for making such judgments is low, or when their processing goal is to evaluate the country of origin itself. Under these conditions, customers direct their attention to country of origin when the information is dispersed across several products manufactured in a country. If unfavourable country-of-origin information is present in only a few products, then customers tend to think of these products as exceptions, and do not consider this information in making a judgment about products made in that country in general. However, if such information is present in every product manufactured from the country, it is used in making judgments. Thus, the type of information presented also affects how the country-of-origin information is used in making judgments. Under high motivation conditions, or when the customer's attention is drawn away from the country-of-origin information, customers do not use the country-of-origin information in making judgments. The study provides pointers to marketers about conditions that foster a focus on country-of-origin information. If marketers want the consumer to use the country-of-origin information in making a judgment, they need to draw attention to the same in advertising.

SOURCES: Adapted from Gurhan-Canli, Zeynep, and Durairaj Maheswaran. "Cultural Variations in Country of Origin Effects." *Journal of Marketing Research*, 37, no. 3 (August 2000): 309–317; Gurhan-Canli, Zeynep, and Durairaj Maheswaran. "Determinants of Country-of-Origin Evaluations," *Journal of Consumer Research*, 27, no. 1 (June 2000): 96–108.

Perceived Corporate Image

Corporate image refers to the public perception of a corporation as a whole.[24] Customer perceptions of corporate image affect everything a firm does. Thus, companies are known to be producers of high- or low-quality products or healthy products, users of high-pressure tactics or of soft-selling approaches, and socially conscious or utterly selfish merchants. The Window on Research shows that cultural differences and differences in processing of linguistic information can lead to differential perceptions of brand image and corporate image for Asian and Western consumers.

Corporate image The public perception of a corporation as a whole.

Sometimes a company's image concerns not the main product the company produces but, rather, some other business actions. To many, Benetton, an Italian clothing company, stands for young and trendy clothing with vibrant colours; but to others, the first image that comes to mind is Benetton's ad campaign, which seems to address controversial contemporary social issues, such as racial prejudice and AIDS. Some companies indulge in deceptive advertising or selling techniques; this is true especially in selected industries where the customer may be more vulnerable, either due to a lack of expertise or of time to understand the nuances of marketers' claims. The home renovations and insurance industries are often cited as examples, where elderly customers are sometimes taken advantage of by unscrupulous marketers engaged in deceptive practices.

THE CUSTOMER AS A LEARNER

LO 3

Consider the following customers and their behaviours:

- As you exit the Service Merchandise store, you run into your friend Mary-Ann walking out with her purchase—a high definition (HD) television set. She bought a Hitachi HD plasma set. What is HD? What is "plasma"? How do these features improve television viewing? Besides, how did Mary-Ann know all this? How did she learn it?
- You present an expensive cologne, Polo, to your friend Ralph on his birthday. He tells you that he uses Woods. Polo is a little loud and stuffy, he tells you, like flaunting your riches. Woods is subtle. How can he say that? You are actually wearing Polo yourself, but he has never been able to tell! Where did he learn this notion about Polo anyway?
- Your friend Lisa always flies with Air Canada. Once, she had to take a flight to Paris at 10:00 p.m. even though Air France had a more convenient 7:00 p.m. flight available. She explains that she is trying to collect a free travel certificate on Aeroplan. How does Air Canada get her to show such loyalty?
- Your neighbour's son, Paul, is in high school, and he wears oversized flannel shirts, baggy pants, baseball hats turned backwards, beads, headbands, and earrings. So do his friends. Where did they learn to dress this way?

Each of these customers is typical of many others, and their behaviours represent instances of learning. None was born with the knowledge, attitude, or behaviour depicted in these examples. Each learned these things as a customer.

WINDOW ON **RESEARCH**

Differences in Corporate and Brand Perceptions between Asian and Western Consumers

Research on Asian consumers shows that they respond to brand names, logos, corporate advertising, and branding communications differently than consumers in the West. Three factors contribute to these differences.

1. *Differences in the processing of linguistic information due to the structures of languages used in the West and in Asia.* Corporate and brand names are linguistic labels for a company and its products. Asian languages—Chinese, Japanese (Kanji), Korean, and Vietnamese—are ideographic in origin (although some phonetic alphabets are also used by Koreans and Japanese, i.e, the "kanas"). That is, they are largely based on Chinese characters (called idiograms), which are sign symbols composed of strokes. Idiograms are visual in nature, and, hence, visual processing would be the primary mode of remembering information in this system. It follows that Asian consumers pay close attention to the writing/spelling of the name and are strongly affected by the writing system in which a name appears.
2. *Differences in how corporate and branding information is categorized.* It is argued that Asian consumers might not evaluate brand extensions on the basis of category fit in terms of attributes or concepts (between parent and extension brands) as in the Western context. They are more likely to use a very simple process in evaluation of extensions: use of the company image as a heuristic. This is likely because of the differences between Asians and Westerners in the perceived abstraction between company name and brand name.
3. *Differences in value structures resulting from broader socio-cultural characteristics.* Several explanatory concepts such as individualism vs. collectivism, attitudes toward risk taking, gender roles, and time perceptions lead to differences between consumers in the West and in Asia. However, in the case of brands, two other differences lie in the concepts of aesthetic values of Asian consumers and mystical beliefs. Confucian ideals and religious backgrounds seem to have developed a far greater aesthetic of naturalism in Asian consumers than is seen in the West, and this affects the way they respond to brand and corporate communications. Further, corporate and brand names are also judged by Asians in terms of whether they are "lucky names." This concept of luck has been applied to colours, numbers (8 is lucky), geometric positions (Feng Shui), and names.

SOURCE: Adapted from Bernd H. Schmitt. "Corporate and Brand Identities in the Asia-Pacific Region: Theoretical and Applied Perspectives." *Asia Pacific Advances in Consumer Research*, 1 (1994): 1–3. http://www.acrweb.org.

Learning
Any change in the content of long-term memory.

Learning is a change in the content of long-term memory. As humans, we learn because what we learn helps us respond better to our environment. Thus, a child who accidentally puts his hand on a hot electric bulb learns never again to touch anything resembling that object. A business learns not to hire a consultant again after finding out the consultant was trading the firm's secrets with competitors. Thus, human learning is directed at acquiring a potential for future adaptive behaviour. In the context of consumer navigation behaviour in an online environment, Hoffman and Novak define "flow" "as a cognitive state occurring during network navigation (1) characterized by a seamless sequence of responses facilitated by machine interactivity, (2) intrinsically enjoyable, (3) accompanied by a loss of self-consciousness, and (4) self-reinforcing." One of the key consequences of flow is increased learning. When the customer is surfing the net without a purposive goal (experiential activity), flow produces latent learning. As a part of latent learning, the consumer learns about the Internet environment in general—sources of information, products, prices, and so on. This translates into higher recall and word-of-mouth activities. However, when the customer surfs the Net to complete a particular task (goal-directed activity), flow leads to more informed decisions.[25]

MECHANISMS OF LEARNING

As customers, we face a marketplace environment of a multitude of product choices; we learn to adapt and respond to this environment. In the scenarios on page 135, Mary-Ann, Ralph, Lisa, and Paul represent four different mechanisms of learning: cognitive learning, classical conditioning, instrumental conditioning, and modelling.

Cognitive Learning

When people talk about learning, they are often thinking of **cognitive learning**, or acquiring new information from written or oral communication. When we acquire information about something, whether incidentally and passively or deliberately and actively, we learn. Cognitive learning occurs on two levels: rote memorization and problem solving. With **rote memorization**, we rehearse the information until it gets firmly lodged in our long-term memory. Rote memorization can result from active rehearsal (as in rehearsing a phone number) or from passive, repeated exposure to the information. A great deal of advertising aims simply to create a rote memory of the brand name by repeated presentation. Top-of-the-mind brand awareness helps customers efficiently make everyday purchase decisions. **Problem solving** is a type of cognitive learning that occurs when the customer is actively processing information (weighing it, discounting some, combining and integrating disparate pieces of information) to reach a certain judgment.

Cognitive learning The acquisition of new information from written or oral communication.

Rote memorization The rehearsal of information until it gets firmly lodged in the long-term memory.

Problem solving A rational approach to conflict resolution wherein participants search for more information, and deliberate on the new information.

Classical Conditioning

Almost everyone has heard about Pavlov's dog. Ivan Petrovich Pavlov was a Russian psychologist interested in understanding the learning process in humans and animals. A Nobel Prize winner in physiology, Pavlov studied human learning processes by experimenting on animals. In his experiments, Pavlov harnessed a dog, gave him some meat powder, and observed that the dog salivated. This salivation is an inherent reflex. Next, he rang a bell just before giving the meat powder, repeating this sequence several times. Then, he merely rang the bell without giving any meat powder. The dog, however, still salivated. The dog was said to have been conditioned to salivate to the bell ringing. Note that the salivating response to the meat powder itself did not have to be learned since it already existed as an instinctual response. Rather, the transfer (i.e., conditioning) of this response to a previously neutral bell stimulus is what constitutes "learning." In this experiment, the meat powder is called an unconditioned stimulus, and the bell is called the conditioned stimulus. **Unconditioned stimulus (UCS)** is a stimulus toward which a customer already has a preexisting specific response, so the response to it does not have to be conditioned. **Conditioned stimulus (CS)** is a stimulus to which the customer either does not have a response or has a preexisting response that needs modification, so a new response needs to be conditioned.[26] In the Pavlov experiment, the sound of the bell is not inherently appealing for the dog, and the dog had never before salivated on hearing it. But the

Unconditioned stimulus (UCS) A stimulus toward which a person already has a pre-existing specific response.

Conditioned stimulus (CS) A stimulus to which a new response needs to be conditioned.

Classical conditioning The process in which a person learns an association between two stimuli due to their constant appearance as a pair.

dog's involuntary reflexive new reaction now is to salivate. This is classical conditioning at work. **Classical conditioning** is the process in which a person learns an association between two stimuli due to their constant appearance as a pair. Because of this constant contiguity (pairing), customers tend to attribute to the previously unknown stimulus whatever they think or feel about the paired other stimulus.

Classical conditioning is pervasive in our everyday lives. It has been proved in marketing in a number of laboratory experiments. Gerald Gorn demonstrated that the classical conditioning principle works in advertising. In this experiment, Gorn selected two musical tunes, one from the movie *Grease* (which customers in his experiment liked) and the other from classical East Indian music (which the same customers disliked). Then he showed slides of two pens that were identical except for their colours, which were pretested to ensure that the chosen colours were preferred equally. The slide for one pen advertisement was paired with the music from *Grease*, while the other was paired with the Indian music. The pen paired with the liked music was preferred by more customers than the other pen. Thus, pairing liked and disliked musical stimuli with two virtually identical pens conditioned customers to prefer the pen that was shown in conjunction with the liked music.[27] In another experiment at a supermarket, the music pace was varied on different days from slow to fast. On the slow-music days, shoppers spent more time in the store and bought more products than on faster-music days.[28] (See Window on Research box for yet another example).

WINDOW ON **RESEARCH**

Seeking Evidence that Classical Conditioning Really Works!

Shimp, Engle, and Stuart performed a series of 21 experiments demonstrating classical conditioning effect in the context of the marketplace.

They used four unknown brands of colas (Cragmont, Elf, My-te-Fine, and Tiger) that were not sold in the region where the experiment was conducted, two moderately known brands (Royal Crown [RC] and Shasta), and two well-known brands (Pepsi and Coke). Each of these served as the CS. For the UCS, the researchers employed four attractive water scenes: a mountain waterfall, a sunset over water, a boat mast against the sky, and a lavender-hued island. An important consideration in classical conditioning experiments is that the UCS have at least some degree of relevance to the CS. Here, water scenes do have relevance to colas because both have a refreshing mood effect.

Subjects were randomly assigned to either an experimental or a control group. The experimental group was shown slides of the cola product and of the water scenes in tandem. Specifically, one cola slide was shown for 7.5 seconds, followed immediately by a scene slide for 7.5 seconds, and then a two-second blank screen. This 17-second showing was termed a "trial." Each subject was shown a total of 80 such trials. Of these, 20 were conditioning trials, in which a cola slide featuring a specific cola brand was followed by a specific water-scene slide; the other 60 were nonconditioning trials that paired a cola slide (other than the cola brand that had been paired with the water-scene slide) with the slide of a neutral stimulus (e.g., license plate, landscape, etc.). The control group was shown all the cola slides and all the scene slides at random; none were paired. Afterward, subjects answered questions pertaining to the evaluation of the brand under study (i.e., the brand paired with the water scene). When the colas were paired consistently with the water scenes, the rating of colas was more favourable than when the colas were accompanied by water or neutral scenes in random fashion. This effect occurred most often for completely unknown brands and least often for previously well-known brands. For moderately known brands, the effect was in between.

Since, in the real world, brands are exposed along with other competing brands, the experiment also used a design in which the 20 slides of the same focal brand (paired with a water scene) were interspersed with 60 slides of the other cola brands (which were paired with neutral scenes). These other colas served as the surrounding context for the focal brand. The favourable rating of the focal brand was always higher when the surrounding context was made up of unknown colas rather than known colas.

This research (comprising 21 separate experiments) was significant both from theory and practice standpoints. In terms of theory, although classical conditioning effects have been demonstrated before, none of the previous research had used a surrounding context (which in this case consisted of competing brands). Thus, it captured the real marketplace conditions better. Moreover, the experiments compared the conditioning effect for well-known, moderately known, and previously unknown brands.

In terms of practice, the research implications are that (1) pairing an unknown brand with a likable audio or visual scene or person can indeed help develop consumer liking for the brand; (2) once the brand is already well known, the brand stands on its own, and pairing it with new likable scenes or persons does not do much for its already favourable rating; and (3) for a relatively unknown brand, it is easier to take advantage of the classical conditioning effect when competitive brands are not being advertised heavily than when intense competitive advertising is occurring. The classical conditioning effects obtained here are with relatively pallid unconditioned stimuli (UCS) of water scenes. In the real world, much more powerful UCS are typically employed; brands are paired with intense, emotionally arousing, alluring audiovisuals, and with highly attractive models with a fan-like following.

SOURCE: Adapted from Shimp, Terence A., Elnora W. Stuart, and Randall W. Engle. "A Program of Classical Conditioning Experiments Testing Variations in the Conditioned Stimulus and Context." *Journal of Consumer Research* 18, no. 1 (June 1991): 1–12. http://www.usc.edu. Reprinted with permission of the University of Chicago Press.

Marketers put this principle to use when they pair their brand with a likable celebrity. The celebrity's personality, by classical conditioning, rubs onto the product itself. Similarly, products are packaged to look expensive or more basic, natural or fancy, healthier or indulgent, special or everyday, environmentally friendly or not, and always, aesthetically appealing. Manufacturing firms exploit the prestige of the distributors and retailers who agree to carry their products. Companies try to associate themselves with other programs with certain public appeal. Some firms even boast about their major clients, hoping that such name-dropping will boost their own public image. The practice of using their association with famous clients is common among advertising agencies and consultants, and among many business-to-business marketers. In a field like medicine, classical conditioning is at work during the residency training period for doctors when they are trained to prescribe drugs for specific symptoms and conditions.

Instrumental Conditioning

The third learning mechanism is **instrumental conditioning**, whereby we learn to respond in certain ways because they are rewarding; that is, a response is instrumental to obtaining a reward. For example, we frequent a particular restaurant because we find its food satisfying. We visit the same barber because the haircut is always perfect. We eat our vegetables, even if not always to our taste, because they are "good for you."

Instrumental conditioning
The learning of a response because it is instrumental to obtaining some reward.

No lesson about instrumental learning is complete without at least a brief glimpse into the work of B. F. Skinner, a famous American psychologist. In 1931, he began experiments to understand the causes of human behaviour. He was uncomfortable with the prevailing explanation that human behaviour was caused by unobservable "inner forces," such as desires and motives. He felt that since these inner forces could not be observed, they could not be scientifically verified. Instead he proposed a simpler theory, verifiable by direct observation: Behaviour occurs because it is reinforced or rewarded. This theory has been called behaviourism, and Skinner is known as the "father of behaviourism."

In a typical experiment with pigeons, Skinner would place a pigeon in a box (now referred to as a "Skinner box") equipped with a key or switch wired to a data recorder as well as a food dispenser. Every time the bird pecked the switch, a premeasured quantity of food was dispensed. Once the pigeons discovered this contingency, they would consistently display this pecking behaviour every time they needed more food. Skinner argued that the pecking behaviour of pigeons can be explained by "external" reinforcements or rewards, and that there was no need to invoke "internal drivers and states." Likewise, he argued that human behaviour can be shaped or modified by rewarding that behaviour. In other words, humans can be made to learn a behaviour by reinforcements or rewards.

How do marketers use this learning mechanism? First, they use instrumental conditioning naturally, and most effectively, when they make the product its own intrinsic reward. But when a brand becomes a parity brand with no intrinsically superior rewards compared to its competing brands, marketers offer extrinsic rewards to attract customer patronage. Examples are coupons, sweepstakes, and rebates. The best examples of instrumental learning are the frequent-flier programs that accumulate mileage toward future free flights.

Modelling

Modelling
The learning of a response by observing others.

Imitative behaviour
The adoption of the behaviour of those whom a person admires or considers successful.

The fourth mechanism of learning is **modelling**, whereby we learn by observing others. Children learn much of their social behaviour by observing the elders around them. We also learn from teachers and other people we admire or who we believe are experts. Neal E. Miller and John Dollard called this type of learning **imitation** or **imitative behaviour**. They explain that we imitate the behaviour of those whom we see rewarded, because we expect to be rewarded ourselves by adopting that behaviour, either by the person we model or by others who admire that person. Based on their studies of imitation, Miller and Dollard identified four classes of people likely to be imitated by others: (1) persons superior in age-grade hierarchy, (2) persons superior in social status, (3) persons superior in intelligence ranking system, and (4) superior technicians in any field.[29]

The choice of models varies from culture to culture. The age hierarchy works more in Eastern countries like Japan, India, and most of the Arab countries, where elders are always respected and emulated. In the Western cultures, grade hierarchy is influential; for example, sixth graders emulate the tenth graders in school. Similarly, in most societies, the more educated are imitated by the less educated, superior technicians are imitated by less-skilled technicians, and people often imitate those higher in social status. So middle-class consumers aspire to the lifestyles of the upper class. The modelling phenomenon works in a similar fashion for businesses. Small companies will adopt new leading edge production machinery after the larger companies have adopted them. The whole management practice of benchmarking dramatically exemplifies organizational imitation or modelling.

THE PSYCHOLOGY OF SIMPLIFICATION AND COMPLICATION

In practice, customers do not always follow a standard path in the learning process. For various reasons shown in Table 4.1, they may engage in simplification or complication.

Simplification

As a lifetime learner of market-related information from diverse sources (marketers, media, and one's own experience), the customer develops a *psychology of simplification*, the customer strategy of simplifying the task. Customers do this by avoiding further information-gathering effort and by relying primarily on what is already learned. Cumulative learning from past experiences helps a customer solve problems more efficiently. When encountered repeatedly, problems are "routinized" with respect to their solution. **Problem routinization** refers to defining a decision problem so that no new decisions need to be made. As customers recall previously made decisions from memory, they simply purchase the same brand as before, a buying strategy termed **habitual purchasing**. Thus, one underlying cause of brand-loyalty is habit formation, and customers adopt the procedure of buying the same brand because it simplifies life; it is the psychology of simplification at work.[30] Customers' natural calling is habituation, routinization, simplification, and inertia. With some exceptions (to be discussed), customers want to reduce the number of choices they need to make, not increase it. This is needed to navigate the marketplace of the twenty-first century, which proliferates with choices.[31] Customers are fundamentally creatures of habit; incentives to switch come from dissatisfaction with current brand, lack of distinction among brands, and offers of distinctly superior value from competing brands or firms.

Problem routinization
Defining a decision problem so that no new decisions need to be made.

Habitual purchasing
Simply repeating previous purchases.

Complication

The **psychology of complication**, or customer desire to redefine a problem so decisions have to be made anew, occurs due to three factors: (1) boredom, which causes exploratory or diversive activities; (2) life status changes and maturation; and (3) the forced irrelevance of current solutions.

Psychology of complication
The customer desire to redefine a problem so that decisions have to be made anew.

TABLE 4.1 Conditions Leading to the Psychology of Simplification and Complication

Psychology of Simplification	Psychology of Complication
Problem routinization	Boredom
Habitual purchasing	Maturation
Desire to limit decision problems	Forced irrelevance of current alternatives

Boredom. Desire for variety is an inherent motivation for humans. As boredom sets in from repeated experience with the same stimulus (product or brand) and its utility declines, customers indulge in variety seeking or novelty seeking.[32] The desire for variety is sought principally from products with social/emotional value rather than mainly performance value. Thus, one doesn't get bored using the same vacuum cleaner daily, but one seeks variety in foods (sensory/emotional value), clothing, perfume/cologne, and other recreational products. Companies satisfy this desire by building variety into their offerings. Thus, Campbell's soup comes in different flavours, and airlines increase the satisfaction of their frequent travellers by varying some part of the service experience (e.g., meals, movies, décor).

Maturation
A self-perceived obsolescence of prior preferences.

Life status change
Major events in a customer's life that change his or her status or personal context.

Maturation. Sometimes, customers outgrow old tastes, such as in music, art, or wine. In formal terms, we call this **maturation**, meaning a self-perceived obsolescence of prior preferences. Maturation is not so much a case of getting bored with the old; rather, it is a feeling that past tastes were poor choices, and that they are no longer appropriate. Change in life-status is one source of maturation. **Life-status change** refers to a major event in a customer's life that changes his or her status—events such as a change in location (e.g., moving to a new city), family composition (e.g., a marriage, divorce, death, birth), resources (e.g., getting a job or a degree), or position (e.g., a promotion, an appointment). These changes bring forth two kinds of needs: (1) a need for products not previously needed, like a bridal gown or baby furniture, and (2) a need to modify the prior solutions to the same need. For example, a promotion to an executive position might require a fundamental change in your wardrobe.

Maturation also results from a change in a person's self-concept, which usually stems from the acquisition of new reference groups. An example is a teenager who may suddenly dissociate himself from the "grunge-clothing type," or a middle-aged person attempting to redefine his or her identity in the face of a midlife crisis. The third source of maturation is the phenomenon of rising expectations. Customers hold all market offerings up to certain expectations, and as these expectations are met, new expectations arise. New expectations make the previous solutions look unsatisfactory, and they search for better products.

Forced irrelevance
An external environmental factor that renders prior solutions irrelevant.

Forced Irrelevance of Current Solutions. While boredom and maturation are internal sources of the psychology of complication, **forced irrelevance** refers to an external environment source that renders prior solutions irrelevant. Three environmental sources that can force people to give up current solutions and look for alternatives are the marketer, business organizations, and the government.

Marketers can rekindle new choices by phasing out certain products, by going out of stock of the regular brand that the customer purchases, or by actually closing the business down, forcing the customer to look for other choices. Businesses also alter available choices. For example, an employer changes its health insurance agency, which forces employees to choose their provider anew. Schools may ban certain clothing styles, necessitating new purchases. Government enacts new regulations that make prior solutions irrelevant and force new decisions for the same customer need. By banning smoking on airplanes and in restaurants, government has forced customers to seek alternatives like the nicotine patch or nicotine gum. Similarly, a ban on the import of certain brands makes purchase of those brands infeasible.

CUSTOMER ACCEPTANCE OF CHANGE: THE ULTIMATE LEARNING EXPERIENCE

LO 4

Innovation
A product or idea that a customer perceives as new.

Some products are entirely new to the world. Such a product is called an **innovation**—a product or idea that a customer perceives to be new. Computers, compact disc players, DVDs, electronic toothbrushes, digital cameras, nicotine patches for smokers, and laser surgery were all innovations when they were first introduced. Among the products that are still innovations today are hair transplants, laser keratotomy (an eye surgery operation), male birth control pills, and hybrid cars. Customers do not rush to purchase these products, no matter how promising they look. Rather, they adopt an extensive process of deliberation, sometimes actively resisting the new product. Customer response to these new products is referred to as *innovation adoption*. For example, the Internet has grown much faster than previous media innovations like the telephone, television, radio, and cable. Morgan Stanley Dean Witter Technical Research states that it has taken radio 38 years to reach 50 million users; television, 13 years; cable, 10 years; and the Internet just 5 years.[33]

Innovation

A product is an innovation if it is new in some sense. "Newness" has two dimensions: (1) uniqueness—how different it is from existing products, and (2) age—how long it has existed in the marketplace. For uniqueness, what matters more than the absolute newness is whether the customer perceives it as unique. Likewise, what matters more than the product's chronological age is when the customer was first exposed to it. Thus, a product that has existed for a long time is still an innovation to a group of people if it was introduced to that subculture or group only recently.[34] Some examples of innovations are computers, televisions, and cell phones in developing countries.

Uniqueness is also a matter of degree. Some products are marginally dissimilar from their existing forms, while others are substantially dissimilar. Based on the degree to which they are unique, marketers classify innovations as *continuous, dynamically continuous,* and *discontinuous*. Both for business and individual customers, where the innovation falls in the continuum depends on prior exposure to it, and on experience with the forerunners of specific innovations. Thus, to a computer-savvy user, a new computer software application service, such as banking by computer, may appear to be a continuous innovation, in contrast to a consumer, totally unaccustomed to computers, who may perceive it as a discontinuous innovation. Hence, marketers must define as their initial target markets those customers who would perceive an innovation as continuous. In addition to the user role, marketers introduce innovations for the buyer and payer roles as well. For example, debit cards (which have a cash reserve against which a merchant draws the amount for the current purchase) or prepaid phone cards are innovations for the payer role. Shopping on the Internet or by computer are innovations for the buyer role.

The Internet itself can be categorized as a discontinuous/radical innovation and a process innovation since it alters the internal operations of a firm, changes their mode of transaction with the various stakeholders (customers and suppliers) and modifies their responses to the market forces (industry and competition).[35]

Categories of Adopters

Diffusion process
The spreading of an innovation's acceptance and use throughout a population.

Innovators
Customers who are the first ones to adopt an innovation.

Imitators
Those who adopt an innovation after observing others who have adopted it.

Opinion leadership
The giving of information and advice that is accepted by the recipient of the opinion.

Expertise
Possessing knowledge about the innovation that is not yet common knowledge.

Trustworthiness
The perceived benevolence and dependability of the opinion giver.

There are various categories of adopters among customers. The categories are defined through the diffusion of an innovation across a population. The **diffusion process** refers to the spreading of an innovation's acceptance and use throughout a population. If one plots all the acceptors of an innovation over time, the diffusion follows a bell curve (see Figure 4.2).

On this curve, the first adopters are called **innovators**, and normally constitute 2.5 percent of the population. They adopt independently of other people. Those who adopt later are **imitators**; namely, early adopters, early majority, late majority, and laggards, in that order. The innovators and early adopters are considered risk takers because they are the first groups to adopt. Those who adopt later are considered risk avoiders, and they wait to see if the risk takers' experience has been satisfactory. Thus, communication between the early groups of adopters and the later adopters is central to the diffusion of innovations.

Innovators and Opinion Leaders

Innovators and early adopters may be opinion leaders. **Opinion leadership** is the giving of information and advice, leading to acceptance of the opinion by the recipient of the opinion. This definition has two implications. First, not only must information be given, but it must be accepted frequently or by a majority of those who receive the opinion. Second, the information given by the opinion leader must pertain to a recommended action, and the recipients of the opinion must act on the recommendation.

Opinion leaders have two qualities, both necessary for their success: expertise and trustworthiness. **Expertise** is possessing knowledge about the innovation that is not yet common knowledge. Since a person cannot be an expert on everything, opinion leadership is by necessity interest-area specific. **Trustworthiness** refers to the perceived benevolence and dependability of the opinion giver. It is founded on the requirement that the opinion giver has no vested interest in promoting a position.[36]

What are the characteristics of innovators and opinion leaders? According to research in the field, these are the characteristics of innovators:[37]

- Risk takers
- Variety seekers
- Upper socioeconomic status

FIGURE 4.2 Adopter Categories: Some Customers Are Quick to Adopt; Some Are Very Slow

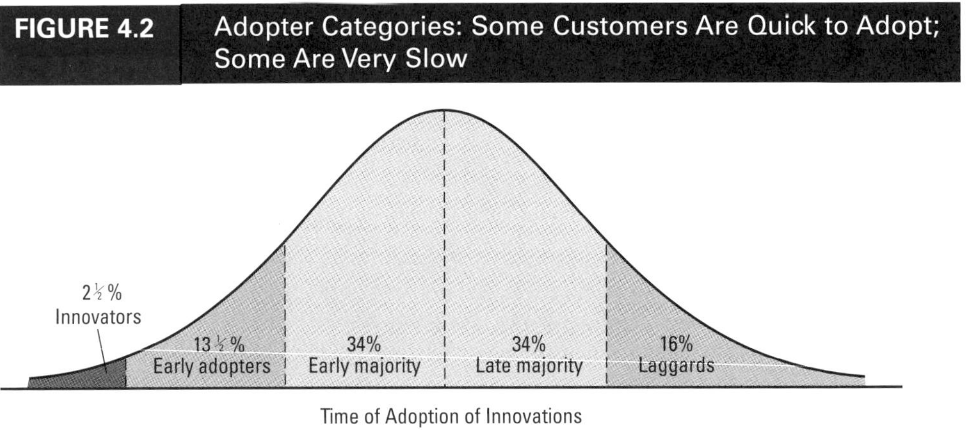

- Product interest
- Less well integrated with other members of the society
- More individualistic and independent in their thinking

Opinion leaders have the following characteristics:

- High product involvement
- Recognized as leaders
- Socially well integrated
- More exposed to a variety of media sources, especially news and information media programs (rather than merely entertainment-oriented media)
- Leaders and formal office holders in social, political, and community organizations.

Figure 4.3 presents some illustrative measures that researchers recommend for measuring opinion leadership and innovativeness. The Window on Practice outlines some characteristics of the early adopters of Internet technology for online shopping.

FIGURE 4.3 Illustrative Measures of Opinion Leadership and Innovativeness

Opinion Leadership

Q. Compared to your friends, are you more likely to be asked, less likely to be asked, or about as likely to be asked about ________?

Q. During the past six months, how many people have you told about ________?
a) Told no one.
b) Told a number of them.

Q. In your discussions with your friends and neighbours about ________, are you more likely to
a) give information/receive information?
b) be used as a source of advice/not be used as a source of advice?

Q. My friends and neighbours often ask my advice about ________ (agree/disagree).

Q. I influence the types of ________ my friends buy (never/sometimes/often).

Q. I look to my friends for advice on ________.

Innovativeness (Answer on a scale of 1 to 5, where 1 means total disagreement, and 5 means total agreement.)

- I like to take a chance.
- I like to try new and different things.
- When it comes to taking chances, I would rather be safe than sorry.
- I like to wait until something has been proven before I try it.
- If people would quit wasting their time experimenting, we would get more accomplished.
- When I see a new brand on the shelf, I usually pass right by.
- In general, I am the first (last) in my circle of friends to buy a new ____ when it appears.
- I like to buy new ____ before others do.

SOURCES: Items compiled from Goldsmith and Hofacker, 1991; Reynolds and Darden, 1971; and Goldsmith, Ronald E., and Charles F. Hofacker. "Measuring Consumer Innovativeness." *Journal of the Academy of Marketing Science* 19 (1991): 209–221; Reynolds, Fred D., and William R. Darden. "Mutually Adaptive Effects of Interpersonal Communication." *Journal of Marketing Research* 8 (November 1971): 449–454. See also Flynn, Leisa Reinecke,, Ronald E. Goldsmith, and Jacqueline K. Eastman. "Opinion Leaders and Opinion Seekers: Two New Measurement Scales." *Journal of the Academy of Marketing Science* 24 (Spring 1996): 137–47.

Innovation orientation differs not only among consumers but also among countries. In a cross-cultural study undertaken in 11 European Union countries, Steenkamp, Hofstede, and Wedel show that consumers in countries that are high on individualism and masculinity and low on uncertainty avoidance tend to be more innovative than countries that are collectivist, feminine, or high on uncertainty avoidance. You might recall that these are three of the five dimensions of cross-cultural values that we discussed in Chapter 2. Consumer innovativeness was also affected by the importance that the consumer attached to the value domain of conservation (security, conformity, and tradition) as compared to the domain of openness to change. Further, innovation also decreased with higher ethnocentrism (beliefs held by consumers about the appropriateness or morality of purchasing foreign-made products),[38] a more favourable attitude towards the past, and age. These differences across countries gives marketers a better idea of the kind of countries that they need to target when introducing an innovation, and also how to design strategies such as sampling, liberal return policies, or advertising so as to overcome these obstacles to innovation adoption.[39]

Innovators among Business Customers

Lead users
Innovative users of a product who use it in ways that suggest how the product should be modified for better utility.

Innovators and opinion leaders are just as important among business customers. Eric von Hippel calls them "lead users." **Lead users** use the products of today in ways that predict how those products should be modified to meet the needs of tomorrow. Thus, lead users use existing products to their maximum capacity with some unmet needs. Marketers can study these users and their needs and implement innovations in those products. Von Hippel cites the example of university students as the lead users of personal computers. The students had access to time-sharing terminals linked to mainframe computers at the university; these terminals were functional equivalents of what would be later known as personal computers. By studying their usage, marketers could have predicted the future popularity of desktop-based computer games among university students.

Adoption Process

Adoption (of an innovation)
Customer acceptance of an innovation for continued use.

The **adoption** of an innovation refers to customer acceptance of an innovation for continued use. Two principal factors that distinguish innovations from current products and cause people to be cautious are: (1) as new product categories, innovations lack evaluation criteria, so customers don't know how to appraise them; and (2) their benefits and negative outcomes are unknown or unestablished by experience. Therefore, customers engage in a long deliberative process before adopting the innovation. This adoption process has been characterized by the acronym, AIDA, which signifies a sequence of four stages, or four mental states, an adopter goes through: *awareness, interest, desire,* and *action*. Thus, customers first become aware of the innovation, then they become interested in it and feel a desire for it, and finally they take the necessary action to acquire it.

A related depiction of this process, emphasizing the customer's active mental process, has five steps: *exposure, information gathering, evaluation, trial adoption*, and *acceptance or rejection*. When the customer is exposed to an innovation, he or she gathers information, evaluates the innovation, decides to try it, and then finally accepts or rejects it. Contrary to the popular view, rejection does not make a person non-innovative. A true nonadopter is one who, following exposure, resists further evaluative processing of the innovation.

As one might expect, the incidence of early adopters in the general population declines as people get older, yet an Ipsos Reid survey found that in 2003, 48 percent of the 55-plus group had Internet access, but that number leapt to 60 percent in 2004. While the over-55s still lagged behind those aged 18 to 54 (at 83 percent in 2003 and 86 percent in 2004), the gap had certainly narrowed. Sixty-four percent of those 55 and older were also using high-speed Internet access to go online, compared to 50 percent in 2003. Seniors are using the Web to keep in touch with family and friends. Many in the older age group are also going online for information on health, travel, finances, retirement living, and even dating.[40] As computers become more user-friendly and seniors get more comfortable using the Web, their adoption rates will increase further.

Desirable Characteristics of Innovations

LO 5

Innovations vary along certain characteristics that render them easy or difficult for customers to adopt. The characteristics that consumers desire in innovations are as follows:

- *Relative advantage*—The **relative advantage** refers to how much better the innovation is compared to the current product that it will replace. For example, customers would adopt high-definition television sets only if they perceive them to satisfy the value they seek better than the conventional sets do.

Relative advantage The superiority of an innovation compared to the current product it will replace.

WINDOW ON **PRACTICE**

Characteristics of Early Adopters of the Internet Technology for Online Shopping

Data from a GVU survey was analyzed with reference to the adoption of online shopping as an innovation on the Internet. Respondents were classified as buyers/innovators based on the number of different product categories in which they had made online purchases within the previous six months. Of the 17 product categories, skeptics had not bought in any categories, triers had bought in fewer than three categories, and buyers/innovators had bought in three or more categories.

Three factors underlie people's perception of online vendors versus off-line vendors:

1. *Post-purchase expectations*—The post-purchase expectations dominate people's perceptions of online shopping in terms of the timely receipt of goods, billing, etc., and this concern is similar across buyers, triers, and skeptics.
2. *Benefits of purchasing online*—Buyers and triers tend to feel that there are greater benefits to buying online compared to the skeptics.
3. *Transaction costs*—Once again, buyers and triers have a more favourable perception of online transaction costs.

The distinguishing characteristic among the innovators (buyers), triers, and skeptics in adoption of online shopping was their primary reason for using the Web. Forty-six percent of innovators considered online shopping as their primary reason for using the Web, compared to 21 percent for triers and 8 percent for skeptics. Buyers represented 48 percent of those who spent 20 or more hours per week on the Internet, compared to 30 percent and 22 percent for triers and skeptics. Thirty-eight percent of buyers had more than 100 bookmarks on their browser, compared to 21 percent and 15 percent for triers and skeptics respectively. They found that in terms of demographic characteristics, buyers were more likely to be male,

(continued)

married, have higher incomes, and work in computer-related jobs. In a survey of online users, Ernst and Young also profiled the online shopper to be the male head of the household (49 percent), 40 years of age or older, have an annual income of over $50,000, and be better educated than the average householder.

In another survey posted on TechWeb, Yahoo!, Hermes, and 50 other sites, the authors explored the risk perceptions of users about the online medium and its impact on their intention to shop and provide vendors with personal information online. They collected data from users on the financial risks, privacy risks, and overall risks of shopping online. Data was also collected on the users' attitudes toward Web vendors, their willingness to buy from those vendors, and their willingness to provide information to the vendors. The authors found that perceived financial risk was a major determinant of perceived overall risks online. These risk perceptions influenced users' attitudes toward online vendors. When users had a negative attitude toward an online vendor, it affected their willingness to purchase from the vendor and their willingness to provide information to the vendor.

SOURCES: Adapted from Rangaswamy, Arvind, and Sunil Gupta. "Innovation Adoption and Diffusion in the Digital Environment: Some Research Opportunities." *eBRC Working Paper*, February 1999, http://www.ebrc.psu.edu/pubs.html; The Second Annual Ernst & Young Internet Shopping Study, 1999.

Perceived risk of an innovation
The uncertainty that the innovation might cause an unanticipated harm.

Complexity
The amount of effort required to comprehend and manage the product during its acquisition.

Communicability
The extent to which an innovation is socially visible, or the ease of communicating information about it in social groups.

Behavioural compatibility
The degree to which an innovation requires no change in existing behaviour.

Value compatibility
The degree to which an innovation is free from contradicting a person's deeply held values.

Trialability
The extent to which it is possible to try out an innovation on a small scale.

- *Perceived risk*—**Perceived risk of innovations** refers to the uncertainty about whether their relative advantage will accrue to the customer, and whether unanticipated harm will occur. Customers are less likely to adopt innovations with high perceived risk, such as laser surgery or the irradiation of food.
- *Complexity*—Customers prefer an innovation that is easy to comprehend. The easier it is to comprehend, the less **complexity** it has. For example, some customers may find the Internet too complex to understand, so they may decide not to adopt it.
- *Communicability*—**Communicability** refers to the extent to which an innovation is socially visible, or the ease of communicating information about it in social groups. The greater the ease with which customers can communicate information about an innovation, the more rapidly they are likely to adopt it. For example, taboo topics such as personal-hygiene products have low communicability, while hairstyles are more visible and, therefore, naturally more communicable.
- *Compatibility*—Customers want products that are compatible with their behaviour and values. **Behavioural compatibility** consists of qualities that do not require customers to alter their behavioural routine. **Value compatibility** is consistency with customers' deeply held values. Examples of behavioral incompatibility are vans that do not fit in the garage and electric cars that may require frequent battery charging. An example of value incompatibility is contraceptives for customers whose religion may prohibit contraception.
- *Trialability*—**Trialability** refers to the extent to which it is possible to try out an innovation on a small scale. For example, among birth-control methods, oral pills have trialability, whereas a vasectomy does not. Therefore, customers are likely to adopt vasectomy less rapidly.

Innovation Resistance

The terms that describe the diffusion of innovation have a pro-innovation bias.[41] Somehow it is assumed that adopting the innovation is good, while resisting it is bad. But as Edward Rogers has pointed out, regarding some innovations, "Many individuals, for their own good, should not adopt them."[42] In fact, people who desire not to change may be more rational than those who seek change for its own sake. The research evidence suggests that true innovators are more likely to be social deviants, abnormal in their drive to explore new things forever, always seeking change, and adopting innovations indiscriminately without any rational choice calculus. Therefore, marketers should understand the psychology of resistance for those individuals who resist change and focus on offering innovations that offer true value to customers, presented in a manner that responds to the customers' motivations for resistance.

Two factors account for resistance to innovation: habit and perceived risk. **Habit** is a learned sequence of responses to a previously encountered stimulus. Habits are efficient means of task execution since, by repetition, the skill has been perfected. The second factor, **perceived risk**, was defined before as the uncertainty about whether there would be any advantage and whether some unanticipated negative outcome might occur. These risks may take the form of **performance risk** (the probability that the product may not perform as expected or desired, or that there may be physical side effects or unwanted consequences) or **social risk** (the probability that the customer's significant others may not approve of the innovation adoption).

Habit
A learned sequence of responses to a previously encountered stimulus.

Perceived risk
The degree of potential loss (i.e., amount at stake) in the event that a wrong choice is made.

Based on these two factors, four types of innovation resistance can be found, as depicted in Figure 4.4.

When risk is low and habits are weak, there is likely to be virtually no resistance. Examples of these "no-resistance innovations" are soft soap or soap gel instead of the soap bar, better shaped razors and toothbrushes, change in the package design for sending overnight mail to business customers, etc. Some of these "no-resistance innovations" may be fads, so there might be little or no resistance to them, but there would also be no reason for rational consumers to adopt them.

Performance risk
The probability that the product may not perform as expected or desired, or that there may be physical side effects or unwanted consequences.

Social risk
The probability that a customer's significant others may not approve of the innovation adoption.

FIGURE 4.4 A Typology of Innovation Resistance

HABIT \ RISK	Low	High
Weak	1. NO RESISTANCE INNOVATIONS (New and improved versions of established products; fads and fashions)	3. RISK RESISTANCE INNOVATIONS (Discontinuous and replacement innovations)
Strong	2. HABIT RESISTANCE INNOVATIONS (Continuous and replacement innovations)	4. DUAL RESISTANCE INNOVATIONS (Social programs)

SOURCE: Sheth, Jagdish N. "Psychology of Innovation Resistance: The Less Developed Concept," *Research in Marketing* 4 (1981): 273–282.

Even when risk is low, habit for the old product may be well entrenched, and a new habit may be required for the new product. This category, called the "habit resistance innovations," includes many continuous innovations: for example, cars that work on electric power rather than gas and would therefore require consumers to recharge their batteries regularly. For consumers to learn this new habit, they would need substantial incentive, such as the prospect of significant savings in energy costs.

When habit for the existing alternative is weak (or the new alternative requires no habit), the risk may be high. An example of such "risk-resistance innovations" would be solar-energy home-heating systems. Once installed, using one or the other system entails no physical action, so habit is not a factor. But, there is risk that the solar system may not work. Documentation of the risk-free performance of new technology is required before rational consumers can be expected to adopt these innovations.

Finally, there are innovations that entail overcoming old habits as well as high risks. These "dual-resistance innovations" are the hardest for consumers to accept. Examples include social programs in developing countries, such as contraceptive practices. Consumers in these societies perceive health risks in the use of contraceptives, and using them requires learning new routines. Marketers should reengineer these innovations to minimize both the learning of new habits and the perceived risk.

For instance, research by the National Consumer Council in the U.K. shows that Internet security concerns are an important reason for consumers' slow adoption of e-commerce. Consumers are skeptical about providing their credit card and personal details to suppliers who might turn out to be fraudulent. Also, the inability to touch and feel products before purchase is a serious concern. These fears can be addressed by marketers and credit card companies by providing information about consumer liabilities in case of online fraud and legal recourse available to consumers in these cases.

The research showed that consumers try to minimize the risks of online shopping by relying on the trusted nature of brand names and well-known retailers. Twenty-eight percent of consumers surveyed stated that they would look for a well-known brand name when shopping online.[43]

LO 6 THE PERCEPTUAL AND LEARNING PROCESS AND THE THREE CUSTOMER ROLES

The perceptual and learning processes described in this chapter are experienced and exhibited by the customer in all three of his or her roles. Table 4.2 illustrates major areas where they apply.

Influence of Perception Processes

The general perceptual process depends on stimulus characteristics, the context, and the perceiver characteristics of prior knowledge and expectations. User evaluations of product-usage experience are perceptions inevitably biased by their knowledge of the brand name, the price, or the consumption situation. Many consumers swear how much they love their favourite brand and how they could never enjoy another brand, yet in blind tests they can't tell which brand is their favourite brand.

TABLE 4.2 The Perceptual and Learning Processes among the Customer Roles

Process	User	Payer	Buyer
PERCEPTION PROCESS			
General process	• Usage experience biased by prior expectations based on brand name, price, or consumption situation	• The price-value perception depends on brand-name and store contexts	• Perceptions of alternative brands biased by price, brand name, store, etc. Store distance perceptions are often biased
Just noticeable difference (j.n.d.)	• "New and improved" products must cross the j.n.d. barrier	• Price variations below j.n.d. are not noticed	• Package size reductions below j.n.d. are not noticed
Assimilation and contrast	• Distance to destinations, wait in service settings, etc., are assimilated or contrasted	• Price discrepancies from expected levels may be assimilated (acceptable) or contrasted (not acceptable).	• Store distances and customer service variations may be assimilated or contrasted
LEARNING PROCESS			
Cognitive learning	• User learns about the use of products by reading about them	• Payer learns about used-car prices from the NADA used-car price book	• Buyers learn about new stores by word of mouth and about brand ratings from *Consumer Reports*.
Classical conditioning	• Food preferences are acquired in early childhood	• Perceived fairness of price levels is classically conditioned	• Buyers are conditioned through continued patronage of the same vendors
Instrumental conditioning	• Users adopt new products if they find them beneficial	• Payers "buy cheap" at first, then experience shoddy performance and learn to "invest" more	• Buyers learn they can get better terms by changing vendors
Modelling	• Users model their clothing and car choices after people they admire	• Budgeting decisions mirror those of admired companies. Payers learn norms for tipping by observing others	• Buyers may switch preferences to stores and vendors that are trendy
Adoption of innovation	• Users adopt product and service feature innovations	• Payers adopt financing innovations (e.g., leasing, debit cards).	• Buyers adopt purchase procedure innovations (e.g., buying through the Internet)

Similarly, payers are intimately influenced in their perception of the price value by the context and their expectations. A price of $250 for a suit in a very upscale store such as Holt Renfrew would appear a bargain while the same price for the same suit in a discount store like Zellers or Wal-Mart would look unattractive. The psychophysics of price perceptions, discussed at length in this chapter, exemplifies the relevance of perceptual processes to the payer role.

Finally, the buyer role is also subject to the perceptual processes. The buyer's judgment of product quality from brand name, price, or store name is an indicator of the perceptual biases at work. Similarly, buyers perceive certain store locations to be too far compared to others despite equal distance and/or travel time. For example, in a city, stores accessible by an interstate highway or expressway are perceived by some to be farther away than those reachable by city roads, even though it might take longer to drive to those stores reachable by city roads.

The specific concepts we discussed in the perceptual process are also applicable to all three roles. For example, consider the concept of just noticable difference (j.n.d.). Users will not notice subtle differences (those that fall below the j.n.d. levels) between brands from the same vendor. The new and improved products should be improved beyond the j.n.d. levels rather than merely objectively. Similarly, buyers will not notice reductions in product size or quantity (a strategy marketers sometimes use instead of changing the price) as long as they are within the j.n.d. range. Finally, payers will not notice price variations across brands or for the same brand across purchase occasions if these variations are maintained within the j.n.d. levels. Similarly, the concepts of assimilation and contrast apply to all three roles. Will a patient expecting to wait at the doctor's office for about 15 minutes assimilate or contrast a 21-minute wait? Will a customer in the payer role, when confronted with a new product at a higher price, assimilate that price into his or her zone of acceptance, or, instead, contrast and reject it? These are the questions marketers need to consider when designing product and price changes and destination locations.

Influence of Learning Processes

The four models of learning are also general in nature, applicable to all three customer roles. However, the type of things the three roles need to learn differs. Users learn about the meaning of product attributes and the personal utility of products by reading information about them. Buyers learn about new stores and new vendors by word-of-mouth information, and about brand ratings from *Consumer Reports*, for example. And payers learn what is a good price value also by reading the price information. For example, suppose you wanted to buy a used car; you would learn the appropriate price by looking up a used-car price guidebook, such as the Canadian Red Book Vehicle Valuation Guide (http://canadianredbook.com).

Next, consider the other three models of learning: classical conditioning, instrumental conditioning, and modelling. As users, the examples of these learning modes abound, and were cited earlier in the chapter. We all acquire our preferences in foods, for example, by classical conditioning in early childhood. We adopt new products and use them repeatedly because of the rewards we obtain from them (instrumental conditioning), and we model our choice of clothing, houses, and cars after certain referents we admire.

As buyers, we continue to buy from the same vendors (classical conditioning) or decide to change vendors to obtain better terms (instrumental conditioning), or we mold our vendor choices following the trend leaders (modelling). The popularity of particular coffee houses, restaurants, and nightclubs soars and wanes, for example, based on which celebrities are or are not patronizing them. Business companies tout the identity of their illustrious customers, hoping to attract new customers for whom the current customers might serve as models.

Finally, as payers, we learn to view certain price levels as customary and fair (classical conditioning). For example, paying $2 for a cup of coffee in a gourmet coffee shop would not make us raise our eyebrows, but at a vending machine it would, even when labelled "gourmet coffee." Poor experiences teach us to spend more for better quality and consider the higher amount an investment (instrumental conditioning). Also, in many cases, how much the "admired others" pay becomes our own guideline through the process of modelling. For example, how much the business firm we admire spends on advertising might guide our own budgeting decisions, or our notions of how much to tip in a restaurant might have been molded by friends we consider to be socially savvy (or by those whose frugality we admire).

Customer Roles in Innovation Adoption

The last topic we discussed was the adoption of innovations. The applicability of the concepts within this topic to all three roles is rather obvious and straightforward. Innovations occur in relation to product features (for the user), in financing arrangements such as leasing and debit cards (for the payer), and in new modes of buying such as through the Internet (for the buyer). Innovators would adopt these because of the desirable characteristics we discussed earlier (e.g., relative advantage, trialability, etc.). Contrarily, users, payers, and buyers would resist their adoption if the innovation does not overcome the barriers of habit and perceived risk. For example, in regard to buying through the Internet, habit will not be a resistance factor for those who are already using the Internet for other purposes.

SUMMARY

In this chapter, we have described three processes of customer behaviour: perception, **LO 1, 2**
learning, and innovation adoption. In the perceptual process, we identified the influence of the characteristics of the stimulus, the context, and customers themselves. Next, we described three biases in the perception process: selective exposure, selective attention, and selective interpretation. We also illustrated these biases for marketing stimuli, such as perception of price and its biased association with quality.

In discussing the customer as a learner, we described four models of learning: cognitive **LO 3**
learning, classical conditioning, instrumental conditioning, and modelling. Classical conditioning occurs when a preexisting customer response to a stimulus (product or person) is transferred to another object or product the stimulus is constantly paired with. Instrumental conditioning occurs when customers learn to engage in a behaviour repeatedly because the behaviour is rewarding. Cognitive learning occurs when customers obtain new information. Modelling occurs by observing other customers whose behaviour we find worth imitating. Marketers take advantage of these learning models by structuring their market offerings and communications about them in a fashion conducive to most customer learning of desired responses.

Next, we discussed the customer as a responder to change. The market offers customers **LO 4, 5**
change in the form of new products, and the process of responding to the change is discussed in the context of diffusion of innovations. Customers desire certain characteristics in innovations: relative advantage, low perceived risk, low complexity, easy communicability, behavioural and value compatibility, and trialability. Customers adopt innovations easily when they conform to these characteristics. However, there are customers who resist innovation adoption, and two factors underlying this psychology of resistance are habit and perceived risk. Such resistance is overcome by redesigning the innovations to minimize both the learning of new habits and the perceived inherent risks.

Finally, we also discussed the roles and distinct qualities of innovators and opinion **LO 6**
leaders, suggesting ways to measure who is or is not an innovator or an opinion leader. Opinion leaders play a significant role in promoting innovations. The customer perspective—

how customers perceive, learn, accept or reject change, and make marketplace decisions—is detailed in this chapter. As marketers and students of customer behaviour, we will serve our purposes well by understanding this customer perspective and by using it as the basis of our response to customers.

KEY TERMS

Adoption 146
Assimilation and Contrast 133
Behavioural Compatibility 148
Classical Conditioning 138
Cognitive Learning 137
Communicability 148
Complexity 148
Conditioned Stimulus (CS) 137
Corporate Image 135
Country-of-Origin Effects 134
Diffusion Process 144
Expectations 130
Expertise 144
Forced Irrelevance 142
Habit 149
Habitual Purchasing 141
Imitation/Imitative Behaviour 140
Imitators 144
Information Content 129
Innovation 143
Innovators 144
Instrumental Conditioning 139
Interpretation 128
Just Noticeable Difference (j.n.d.) 132
Lead Users 146
Learning 130
Life-Status Change 142
Maturation 142
Modelling 140
Odd Pricing 133
Opinion Leadership 144
Organization 128
Perceived Risk 149
Perceived Risk of an Innovation 148
Perception 127
Perceptual Distortion 132
Perceptual Threshold 132
Performance Risk 149
Problem Routinization 141
Problem Solving 137
Psychology of Complication 141
Quality Cue 133
Reference Price 133
Relative Advantage 147
Rote Memorization 137
Sensation 128
Sensory 129
Social Risk 149
Stimulus 128
Trialability 148
Trustworthiness 144
Unconditioned Stimulus (UCS) 137
Value Compatibility 148
Weber's Law 133

DISCUSSION QUESTIONS AND EXERCISES

1. Why does classical conditioning work better for unknown brands than for known brands? What characteristics would you use to select a celebrity to pair with your brand? Or to be a spokesperson for your company?
2. What are the psychology of simplification and the psychology of complication? Think about your own life as a customer and identify two examples of each. Again, considering your marketplace behaviour, do you find yourself engaging more frequently in the psychology of simplification or in the psychology of complication? How? Why?
3. Evaluate the following products in terms of the characteristics of innovation that facilitate their adoption:
   a. Caller ID (identification) service on your phone

b. A shopping service where an employee from the firm will go to the supermarket with your phone order, buy your groceries, and deliver them to your home
c. A new clothing fashion of your choice
d. The business practice of just-in-time inventory management
e. The ISO-9000 standard of quality (assume it is not mandatory)

4. You are the marketing director of a local museum. You recall the concepts of instrumental conditioning, psychology of simplification and complication, boredom, maturation, etc., and wonder if any of these can help you develop ideas for getting your local museumgoers and the general population to visit the museum more often, and buy more items from the museum shop. List some ideas with their concepts.
5. Assume a clothing company in Russia has appointed you as a national marketing manager for introducing the designer clothing in your own country, Canada. The clothing line has sold well among Russian consumers, especially young adults, who view it as their own national alternative to a Western brand like Tommy Hilfiger or Calvin Klein. You also recall the concepts of innovators and opinion leaders, and want to use these to define your target markets. As you ponder the differences between consumers in the two countries, you also recall reading about "global youth," the idea that youth everywhere are becoming quite alike in their tastes as consumers. Prepare a marketing memorandum for the host country's top management, outlining your initial thoughts on these issues.

NOTES

1 http://www.dairyinfo.gc.ca/pdf_files/prof_milk_e.pdf.

2 http://arlafoods.com, news release 10/24/2003.

3 "Top 10 Beauty Sites," *emarketer 2000*, http://www.emarketer.com/elist/t10beauty/t10beaut_1.html.

4 Joel B. Cohen and Kunal Basu, "Alternative Models of Categorization: Toward a Contingent Processing Framework," *Journal of Consumer Research* 13 (March 1987): 455–72.

5 Quoted in Banwari Mittal, "Public Assessment of TV Advertising: Faint Praise and Harsh Criticism," *Journal of Advertising Research* 34, no.1 (January–February 1994): 35–53.

6 Lauer, David A., *Design Basics*. (New York: Holt, Rinehart & Winston, 1979).

7 L. W. Barsalou, "Ideals, Central Tendency, and Frequency of Instantiation as Determinants of Graded Structure," *Journal of Experimental Psychology: Learning, Memory and Cognition* 11 (October 1985): 629–54.

8 Maria Kalamas, Mark Cleveland, Michel Laroche, and Robert Laufer, "The Critical Role of Congruency in Prototypical Brand Extensions," *Journal of Strategic Marketing* 14 (September 2006): 193-209.

9 Valarie A. Zeithaml, A. Parasuraman, and Leonard L. Berry, "Problems and Strategies in Services Marketing," *Journal of Marketing* 49 (Spring 1985): 33–46.

10 "Internet Changing Financial Service Brand Perceptions," http://cyberatlas.internet.com/markets/finance/article/0,,5961_287291,00.html (accessed January 18, 2000).

11 "Building the B2B Foundation: Positioning Net Market Makers for Success," A. T. Kearney Report 2000, http://www.atkearney.com/main.taf?site=1&a=5&b=3&c=1&d=4.

12 Abhijit Biswas and Edward A. Blair, "Contextual Effects of Reference Prices in Retail Advertising," *Journal of Marketing* 55 (July 1991): 1–12.

13 William Boulding, Richard Staelin, Ajay Kalra, and Valarie Zeithaml, "A Dynamic Process Model of Service Quality: From Expectations to Behavioural Intentions," *Journal of Marketing Research*

30 (February 1993): 7–27; Michel, Laroche, Maria Kalamas, Soumaya Cheikhrouhou, and Adelaïde Cézard, "An Assessment of the Dimensionality of Should and Will Service Expectations," *Canadian Journal of Administrative Sciences* 21, no. 4 (December 2004): 361–375.

14 Eloise Coupey and Erin Sandgathe, "Rethinking Research on Communications Media: Information Modality and Message Structuring," *Advances in Consumer Research* 27 (2000): 224–29; Marie-Odile Richard, "Modeling the Impact of Internet Atmospherics on Surfer Behavior," *Journal of Business Research* 58, no. 12 (December 2005): 1632–1642.

15 Jean-Marc Léger and Dave Scholz, "Canadians Tuning Out on Ads," *Marketing*, Vol. 107, No 6, February 11, 2002.

16 Source: Internet Advertising Bureau of Canada, Newsletter, September 7, 2005. http://www.iabcanada.com.

17 eAdvertising Report, June 2000. http://www.emarketer.com; DoubleClick: Robin Greenspan, "Q1 2004 Ads Richer, Engaging," http://www.clickz.com (accessed May 11, 2004).

18 "Internet Advertisers Target Women," http://cyberatlas.internet.com/markets/advertising/article/0,,5941_288371,00.html (accessed January 19, 2000).

19 Stuart Henderson Britt, "How Weber's Law Can Be Applied to Marketing," *Business Horizons*, February 1975, 21–29.

20 Robert Jacobson and Carl Obermiller, "The Formation of Reference Price," *Advances in Consumer Research* 16 (1989): 234–40; Joel E. Urbany, William O. Bearden, and Dan C. Weilbaker, "The Effects of Plausible and Exaggerated Reference Prices on Consumer Perceptions and Price Search," *Journal of Consumer Research* 15 (June 1988): 95–110.

21 Valarie A. Zeithaml, "Consumer Perceptions of Price, Quality, and Value: A Means-End Model and Synthesis of Evidence," *Journal of Marketing* 52 (July 1988): 2–22; Carl Obermiller and John J. Wheatley, "Price Effects on Choice and Perceptions under Varying Conditions of Experience, Information, and Beliefs in Quality Differences," in *Advances in Consumer Research* 11, ed. Thomas C. Kinnear, 453–58 (Association for Consumer Research 1983).

22 Kent B. Monroe and R. Krishnan, "A Procedure for Integrating Outcomes across Studies," in *Advances in Consumer Research* 10, eds. Richard P. Bagozzi and Alice M. Tybout, 503–8 (Ann Arbor, MI: Association for Consumer Research, 1983).

23 For further reading on country-of-origin effects, see D. Tse and G. J. Gorn, "An Experiment on the Salience of Country-of-Origin in the Era of Global Brands," *International Marketing Review* 9 (1992): 57–76; W. K. Li, K. B. Monroe, and D. Chan, "The Effects of Country of Origin, Brand, and Price Information: A Cognitive-Affective Model of Buying Intentions," *Advances in Consumer Research* 21 (1994): 449–57; Sevgin A. Eroglu and Karen A. Machleit, "Effects of Individual and Product-Specific Variables on Utilizing Country-of-Origin as a Product Quality Cue," *International Marketing Review*, 6 (November 1998): 27–41; Michel Laroche, Nicolas Papadopoulos, Louise A. Heslop, and Mehdi Mourali, "The Influence of Country Image Structure on Consumer Evaluations of Foreign Products," *International Marketing Review*, 22, no. 1 (2005): 96-115; Michel Laroche, Nicolas Papadopoulos, Louise A. Heslop, and Jasmin Bergeron, "Effects of Subcultural Differences on Country and Product Evaluations," *Journal of Consumer Behaviour* 2, no. 3 (March 2003): 232–247.

24 Jay S. Niefeld, "Corporate Advertising," *Industrial Marketing* (July 1980), 64–74; "Two Different Animals: Brand Awareness and Corporate Image," *Forbes* 6, March 1989, 20.

25 Donna L. Hoffman and Thomas P. Novak, "Marketing in Hypermedia Computer-Mediated Environments: Conceptual Foundations," *Journal of Marketing* 60 (July 1996): 50–68; Marie-Odile Richard and Ramdas Chandra, "A Model of Consumer Web Navigational Behavior: Conceptual Development and Application," *Journal of Business Research* 58, no. 8 (August 2005): 1019–1029.

26 Leland C. Swenson, *Theories of Learning: Traditional Perspectives/Contemporary Developments* (Belmont, CA: Wadsworth Publishing Company, 1980), 13–30.

27 Gerald J. Gorn, "The Effects of Music in Advertising on Choice Behaviour: A Classical Conditioning Approach," *Journal of Marketing* (Winter 1982): 94–101.

28 Ronald E. Milliman, "Using Background Music to Affect Behaviour of Supermarket Shoppers," *Journal of Marketing* (Summer 1982): 86–91.

29 Neal E. Miller and John Dollard, *Social Learning and Imitation* (New Haven, CT: Yale University Press, 1941).

30 John A. Howard and Jagdish N. Sheth, *The Theory of Buyer Behavior*, (New York: John Wiley and Sons, 1961).

31 Jagdish N. Sheth and Atul Parvatiyar, "Relationship Marketing in Consumer Markets: Antecedents & Consequences," *Journal of the Academy of Marketing Science* 23, no. 4 (Fall 1995): 255–71.

32 P. S. Raju, "Optimum Stimulation Level: Its Relationship to Personality, Demographics, and Exploratory Behaviour," *Journal of Consumer Research* 7 (December 1980): 272–82; Richard and Chandra, *op.cit.*

33 Arvind Rangaswamy and Sunil Gupta, "Innovation Adoption and Diffusion in the Digital Environment: Some Research Opportunities," E-business Research Center Working Paper, http://www.ebrc.psu.edu/pubs.html (February 1999).

34 W. D. Hoyer and N. M. Ridgway, "Variety Seeking as an Explanation for Exploratory Purchase Behaviour: A Theoretical Model," *Advances in Consumer Research* 11 (1984): 114–99; L. McAlister and E. A. Pessemier, "Variety-Seeking Behaviour: An Interdisciplinary Review," *Journal of Consumer Research* 9 (December 1982): 311–22.

35 Arvind Rangaswamy and Sunil Gupta, *ibid.*

36 Alreck Pamala L. and Robert B. Settle, "The Importance of Word-of-Mouth Communications to Service Buyers," in *1995 AMA Winter Educators' Proceedings,* eds. David W. Stewart and Naufel J. Vilcassim, 188–93 (Chicago: American Marketing Association, 1995); Pamela Kiecker and Cathy L. Hartman, "Predicting Buyers' Selection of Interpersonal Sources: The Role of Strong Ties and Weak Ties," in *Advances in Consumer Research* 21, eds. Chris T. Allen and Deborah Roedder John (Provo, UT: Association for Consumer Research, 1994): 464–69.

37 Frank M. Bass, "A New Product Growth Model for Consumer Durables," *Management Science* 15 (January 1969): 215–27.

38 Terence A. Shimp and Subhash Sharma, "Consumer Ethnocentrism: Construction and Validation of the CETSCALE," *Journal of Marketing Research* 24 (August 1987): 280–89.

39 Jan-Benedict SteenKamp, E. M., Frenkel ter Hofstede, and Michel Wedel, "A Cross-National Investigation into the Individual and National Cultural Antecedents of Consumer Innovativeness," *Journal of Marketing* 63 (April 1999): 55–69.

40 Sarah Dobson, "The Oldster Boom," *Marketing*, Oct. 4–11, 2004, 4.

41 Adapted from Jagdish N. Sheth, "Psychology of Innovation Resistance: The Less Developed Concept (LDC) in Diffusion Research," *Research in Marketing* 4 (Greenwich, Conn.: Jai Press Inc., 1981): 273–82.

42 Everett M. Rogers, *Diffusion of Innovations*, 3rd ed. (New York: Free Press, 1983), 281–84.

43 "U.K. Consumers Wary of Online Security," http://cyberatlas.internet.com/big_picture/geographics/article/0,,5911_429671,00.html (accessed August 3, 2000).

CHAPTER 

Customer Motivation: Needs, Emotions, and Psychographics

LEARNING OBJECTIVES

After reading this chapter you should be able to:

LO 1 Understand the concept and process of customer motivation.

LO 2 Define customer needs, the three main hierarchies of needs (Maslow, Murray, Dichter), and the needs identified in marketing.

LO 3 Define the needs for arousal, cognition, and attribution.

LO 4 Define emotions, the eight types of emotions, moods, and deep involvement.

LO 5 Define psychographics and the VALS profile.

LO 6 Describe the motivational process and the three customer roles.

Reacting to the Germ Scare

In one of its routine consumer surveys a few years ago, Colgate-Palmolive discovered something unexpected: an unusually high level of consumer concern over germs and bacteria. Recent events had fueled the consumer paranoia about germs.

First, in the United States, there was the sudden death of moviemaker and Muppets creator Jim Henson from a bacteria-related illness. Then there were outbreaks of E. coli (a type of bacteria) from undercooked hamburgers, and even outbreaks of tuberculosis and cholera were reported. To top it off, in 1995, Hollywood released a movie called *Outbreak*, the story of a diseased monkey roaming the streets of New York City. And a made-for-TV movie called *Virus* aired on all major networks in North America. In late 1994, then-Quebec Premier Lucien Bouchard's bout with necrotizing myositis (commonly known as the "flesh-eating disease") cost him his left leg—and almost cost him his life. More recently, in 2003, Toronto was struck with a SARS (severe acute respiratory syndrome) crisis when several people got infected. There have been major concerns during the last few years about outbreaks of the West Nile virus and the avian flu, both causing some deaths or concern in Canada. With recurrent outbreaks of salmonella, E. coli bacteria, and the West Nile virus in the population, and the threat of a pandemic from the avian flu, people have been increasingly concerned about levels of cleanliness.

In response to this trend, Colgate and a host of other companies raced to the market with a bevy of antibacterial products. Playskool Frog Waterpal is a children's bath friend on the outside, but from the inside, it releases a powerful chemical defence that destroys the cell walls of bacteria, leaving them crippled and unable to multiply. Other antigerm weapons include Palmolive Ultra dish soap with "antibacterial" splashed across the label, Dial Corp.'s Brillo cleaning pads with patented microbe shield, Bristol-Myers Squibb Co.'s Keri antibacterial hand lotion, and Playskool's bacteria-fighting version of Soft Bear. Newer products continue to be introduced in the market, such as Clorox and Lysol antibacterial wipes. In 2004, Kimberly-Clark Corp. unveiled its Kleenex Brand Anti-Viral Tissue, less than a year after sales of sterile masks soared in the wake of a panic over SARS. And even a Web-based company, Go-Kit.com, has jumped on the bandwagon, selling the Go-Kit, a handy package for the bacteria-paranoid that fits into a purse or briefcase and claims to offer portable protection against SARS, avian flu, and the common cold.

Consumer phobia runs so high that one consumer in the Bristol-Myers study for the lotion is reported to have asked, "If I rub it on my nose, will it stop me from getting a cold?" This is just as Abraham Maslow proposed: physiological safety is one of human beings' most basic motivations.[1] The above-mentioned companies have developed products to meet this consumer motivation for physiological safety. In fact, newer products are introduced regularly to meet this need, with Clorox and Lysol antibacterial wipes being recent additions.

Marketers ask a number of questions in an attempt to understand why people behave the way they do: Why, in their roles of user, payer, and buyer, do customers use, pay for, and purchase what they do? What goals are they trying to achieve? What needs are they trying to satisfy? What feelings and emotions are they experiencing? How do these needs and emotions shape their lifestyles? How do their lifestyles relate to and explain their behaviour as customers?

This chapter addresses the ways in which marketers have attempted to answer such questions (see Figure 5.1). It begins by defining motivation and identifying three facets of customer motivation: needs, emotions, and psychographics. We then explore each facet. First, we summarize several models that categorize customer needs. Next, we define emotions and discuss their role in influencing customer behaviour. Finally, we define psychographics and introduce the major methods for classifying customers according to their values and lifestyles.

FIGURE 5.1 Conceptual Framework

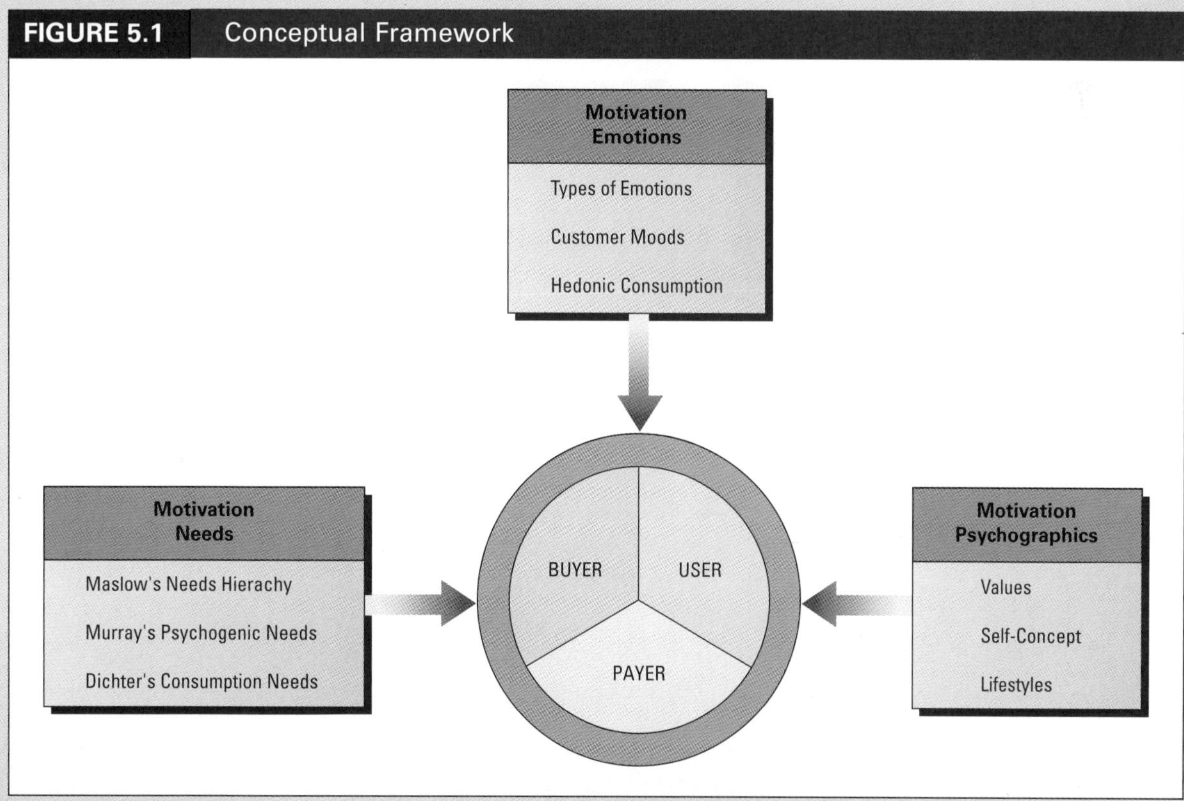

LO 1 MOTIVATION

Motivation
The state of drive or arousal that impels behaviour toward a goal-object.

Drive
An internal state of tension that produces actions purported to reduce that tension.

Goal-object
Something in the external world whose acquisition will reduce the tension experienced by an organism.

Purposive behaviour
The expending of energy to attain some goal-object.

Dr. Richard, why are you still prescribing *Zovirax* rather than *Valtrex*, the leading brand from our company? Ms. Nobel, why did you change the specs on this purchase order? Mr. Miodek, the CFO (chief financial officer), wants to know why you are recommending this vendor over the lowest-price bidder for the computer network installation contract.

What do these questions have in common? They all are looking for the underlying motivations for behaviours. The Window on Research explores the motivations for Web usage by customers.

Motivation is what moves people, the driving force for all human behaviour. More formally, it is defined as the state of drive or arousal that impels behaviour toward a goal-object. Thus, motivation has two components: (1) drive or arousal and (2) goal-object. A **drive** is an internal state of tension that produces actions purported to reduce that tension. A **goal-object** is something in the external world whose acquisition will reduce the tension. Arousal or drive provides the energy to act; goal-object provides the direction for one to channel that energy. A person with goal-objects but without the drive is just a daydreamer; one with energy but no goal-object is akin to a hyperactive child. When energy is expended to attain some goal-object, we call that use of energy **purposive behaviour**.[2]

Consumption without direction, such as alcoholism and unrestrained materialism, are non-purposive in nature.

WINDOW ON **RESEARCH**

Motivations for Web Usage

Korgaonkar and Wolin explore the motivations and concerns of Web users in three usage contexts: a) number of hours spent per day on the Web; b) percentage of that time spent for business versus personal purposes; and c) purchases made on the Web, specifically, the number of purchases made in the past year. The study lists the following reasons as motivations for Web usage, and these motivations correlate positively and significantly with the number of hours of Web usage and whether purchases are made on the Web:

1. *Social Escapism motivation*—Escape from reality; diversion and aesthetic enjoyment; relief from day-to-day boredom, stress, and loneliness.
2. *Information motivation*—Use of the Web for information and self-education needs.
3. *Interactive Control motivation*—Use of the interactive nature of the Web to control, customize, and personalize their experience on the medium.
4. *Socialization motivation*—Facilitate interpersonal communication and activities through e-mail, chat rooms, and virtual communities.
5. *Economic motivation*—Shopping and buying motivations: price savings, freebies.

The Social Escapism, Interactive Control, and Economic motivation factors correlate positively with the actual number of purchases made in the past year. The Interactive Control motivation correlates with the percentage of time spent on the Web for personal purposes. The respondents also voiced transaction-based security and privacy concerns (fear of providing credit-card information on the Web for purchase of products, and concerns about privacy of personal information) and nontransactional privacy concerns (overall concerns about privacy in terms of hackers and unsolicited e-mail).

SOURCE: Adapted from Korgaonkar, Pradeep K., and Lori D. Wolin. "A Multivariate Analysis of Web Usage." *Journal of Advertising Research* (March–April 1999):53–68.

THE PROCESS OF MOTIVATION

The motivational process, shown in Figure 5.2, begins when a stimulus engenders arousal or drive. The arousal can be *autonomic* (felt physiologically), such as when you suddenly feel hungry. It can be *emotive*: for example, when you are feeling lonely. Or it can be *cognitive*, such as when you are struggling to find a way out of a deal that you no longer find attractive.

FIGURE 5.2 A Model of the Motivation Process

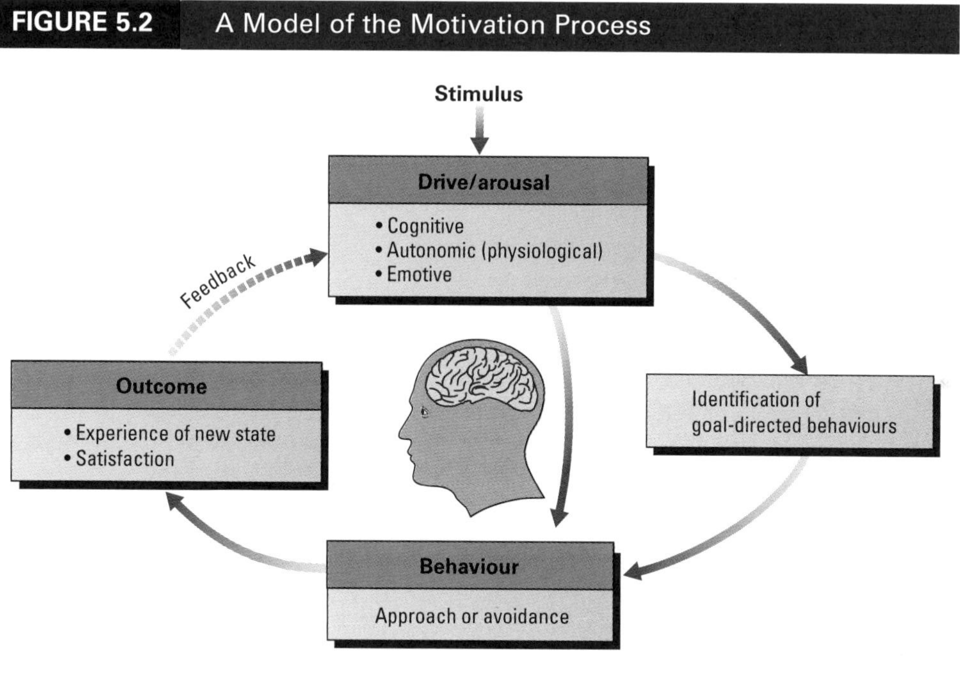

The arousal leads a person to act (i.e., to behave). Autonomic (physiological) or emotive arousal can elicit the relevant behaviour directly. For example, hunger pains will autonomically (i.e., automatically) make you search for food, and seeing something funny may make you immediately smile or laugh. Similarly, in a business context, when an executive sees an express mail envelope in the mail, his or her automatic response is to open that envelope first. Emotive feelings are aroused when we buy products that are made in our home country versus foreign countries. These feelings are magnified when there are tensions between the home country and a foreign country. For example, in 2003, France's refusal to participate with the United States in the Iraq war aroused strong negative feelings toward French products (mostly wines and other French luxury products) in the United States. Cognitive arousal would also elicit behaviour, but generally only after further cognitive activity to figure out possible goal-directed behaviours; for example, a person seeking a way out of a commitment will identify and deliberate about available options. Or a person with a broken-down car will deliberate about alternative ways of getting to the destination. In business, the onset of a new project causes cognitive arousal, and there is a request for proposals that are scanned and deliberated upon.

Following the automatic or selected behaviour, the final outcome will be the experience of a new state and a possible sense of satisfaction. This outcome, if positive, feeds back to calm the drive. If the new state is not satisfactory, the feedback recycles the process.

Approach/Avoidance Motives

Approach/avoidance motivation
The human desire to attain a goal-object and to avoid an object of negative outcomes.

Depending on whether the identified goal is something to embrace or avoid, the person will use either an approach or an avoidance behaviour. **Approach motivation** is the desire to attain a goal-object. Approach goal-objects (i.e., objects that attract us) are sought or even longed for. For example, most people seek vacations and good food. Their deprivation creates unhappiness. **Avoidance motivation** is the desire to protect oneself from an object. Avoidance goal-objects might include traffic tickets and the measles. E-tailing tries to cash in on the avoidance motivation of the buyer by building on his or her desire to avoid travelling long distances to purchase a product, paying high prices for a product, or conducting time-consuming comparison searches.

Marketers want to make their products approach objects. "No money down" purchase of products and pre-approved credit cards are examples of marketer approach features, and the high interest rates charged on these purchases and cards are the avoidance motives. Often, a tradeoff is involved—the product contains some approach and some avoidance outcomes. For example, the taste and sensory pleasure in candies elicit approach, but their fat and calorie content evoke an avoidance motive. Part of the consumer conflict is between immediate approach outcomes and distant, long-term negative side effects; for example, between the thrill of driving a car and its relatively low safety, or between an appliance that is low in initial purchase price but high in its cost of maintenance, or vice versa. The marketer's challenge is to minimize avoidance features while maximizing approach features, such as offering reduced-fat or reduced-calorie snacks without sacrificing the taste, or improving product quality without letting the costs rise.

In the business context, Application Service Providers (ASPs) provide services that make objects approachable for small- and medium-sized businesses. They provide the company with access to every required software application, from the simplest e-mail program to a sophisticated customized database that could, for example, track daily change in a company's sales figures by store or postal code and deliver it to wireless laptops anywhere in the country, all for a monthly fee. For the payer, it eliminates the cost of purchasing software and its upgrades. For the user, there is no headache of customizing, maintaining, integrating, and supporting software, yet there is access to all the software needed and the upgrades for it. Finally, for the buyer, it eliminates the hassle of evaluating suppliers and reduces risk.

FACETS OF MOTIVATION: NEEDS, EMOTIONS, AND PSYCHOGRAPHICS

Whatever the direction of motivation, it manifests in three facets: needs, emotions, and psychographics. Needs are gaps between the desired and the current state, and they lend themselves more readily to cognitive consciousness and appraisal. Emotions are more autonomic and engender more personal experience. Psychographics combine behaviours driven by both needs and emotions.

CUSTOMER NEEDS

LO 2

The concept of needs and wants is closely aligned to the concept of motivation. In Chapter 1, we defined *need* as the felt deprivation of a desired state. The desired state provides the goal-object, and its deprivation provides the drive. Researchers have suggested various *categories* of needs. Among the most relevant to marketers are Maslow's need hierarchy, Murray's psychogenic needs, Dichter's consumption needs, and various marketing scholars' lists of customer needs.

MASLOW'S HIERARCHY OF NEEDS

According to Maslow, human needs and wants are arranged in a hierarchy. Higher-level needs are dormant until lower-level needs are satisfied.

Maslow's hierarchy of needs consists of (from lowest to highest):

1. Physiological needs (hunger, thirst)
2. Safety and security needs (security, protection)
3. Belongingness and love needs (social needs)
4. Esteem and ego needs (self-esteem, recognition, status)
5. Need for self-actualization (self-development, realization)[3]

Maslow's hierarchy of needs
Psychologist Abraham Maslow's theory that human needs and wants exist in a hierarchy so that higher-level needs are dormant until lower-level needs are satisfied.

A person progresses to higher-level needs if lower-level needs are satisfied; he or she regresses to lower-level needs, should these needs become unsatisfied again. Maslow does not distinguish between needs and wants, but most contemporary psychology books do. According to this distinction, only the first two needs in Maslow's hierarchy would be needs, while the last three are wants.

Maslow's Needs for Household Customers

Physiological needs lead customers to strive for, purchase, and use food, clothing, and shelter. For many, such as those below the poverty line, these needs remain perpetually less than adequately met, so that they never become higher-level needs. Furthermore, many of the differences in what customers use and buy are due to physiological differences, as seen in Chapter 2 (i.e., genetics, race, gender, and age).

At the next level, safety and security needs are responsible for many people's fear of flying, for example, and for buying insurance against various uncertainties of life. Personal safety is a motive as old as survival itself, and in modern times, the use of home security systems is on the rise. Likewise, other safety concerns relate to automobile safety (e.g., side-impact curtains, a type of airbag, are becoming more common in new cars) and health-related safety, as consumers develop germ phobias.

Social motives of belongingness and love are evident when customers want to buy products that are well regarded by others, so that the use of those products brings the customers' peer approval, affection, and a sense of belonging. The kind of neighborhood you choose to live in, the kind of car you choose to drive, the designer logos on the clothes you wear, what school you send your youngster to, and the places you vacation are at least in part determined by how your peers and significant others will look upon these choices. Many products, such as greeting cards, flowers, and other kinds of gifts, are bought to promote relationships between individuals.

Next, we all work hard to gain success in our individual sphere of activity and to acquire the qualities others consider desirable and virtuous so that we may win our own and others' esteem. We also buy products we deem fitting of our esteem. Beyond impressing others, for example, we drive a car that, in our judgment, reflects who we are; we visit stores where we are treated with respect; and we even buy and give gifts to ourselves because we feel we deserve them.

Finally, once these physiological, social, and esteem needs are satisfied, people begin to explore and extend the bounds of their potential—that is, seek self-actualization. This self-actualization motive is what is behind a person engaging, for example, in self-improvement activities, such as taking an adult-education course or tenaciously pursuing a skill toward perfection, such as in competitive sports. This could also mean doing meditation to, according to Eastern philosophy, meet one's creator, to become what one was supposed to be, in a cosmic sense.

Maslow's Needs for Business Customers

Like household markets, customers in the business markets experience Maslow's hierarchy of needs. This can be seen at two levels: business customer as an enterprise and business customer as individuals working in firms. First consider business as an enterprise. As an enterprise, business firms need, for their physical survival, at least three resources: money, employees, and raw materials and equipment. Banks and venture capitalists who supply cash, recruitment agencies who supply employees, and suppliers of raw materials and equipment are catering to the survival needs of the business enterprise, akin to physiological needs of the individual.

Security needs for business firms translate into insurance against loss of property and assets and against liabilities that may arise in various business transactions. Indeed, safety and security are key concerns in government and business buying; for example, the safety features are of paramount importance when city governments procure vehicles for their police forces. In office buildings, elevators need to be inspected and maintained for safe operations.

Belongingness for business enterprises refers to recognition by peer organizations and being admitted to formal or informal membership groups of other similar organizations. Thus, to belong to *Fortune 500*, to be listed on the stock exchange, to belong to the Better Business Bureau, to be recognized as a leading contender in the field, or to be certified and recertified by formal certification agencies are examples of an enterprise's sense of belonging.

Esteem comes partly from being recognized by various bodies, but also partly from one's own sense of accomplishment, such as winning a Canada Award for Excellence or obtaining the AACSB (Association to Advance Collegiate Schools of Business) accreditation by a business school. Qualifying to belong to a group of enterprises or to attain certain status and awards, businesses need to buy, use, and pay for a range of products—for example, tightly controlled quality in raw materials, training for its employees, or reengineering services.

Finally, self-actualization is seen in business firms striving to become what they want to be, such as 3M as the innovative company, Ben & Jerry's as the environmental company, Levi Strauss as the diversity company, and Benetton as the social consciousness company. Firms that have these and other similar business firms as their customers must themselves reflect these values and deal in ways that further or help the customer companies to actualize their selves.

Now consider business customers as individuals working in organizations. Whatever they want to buy, they want to feel secure that it is a wise decision and be assured that the product will perform well and to the specifications. Whoever is making the purchase decision for the organization is held accountable for it, and often he or she is at risk of being perceived as being incompetent should an unwise purchase decision be made. Thus, business customers are likely to buy from someone they feel secure in dealing with. Next, many products are bought simply to satisfy a person's belongingness and esteem needs; for example, corporate membership in country clubs, corporate jets, the kind of hotel one chooses on business travel, and even the location and address of business premises. Finally, self-actualization reflects a person's personal value system and affects what s/he buys and whom s/he buys from—for example, buying from local suppliers.

MURRAY'S LIST OF PSYCHOGENIC NEEDS

Henry Murray proposed a list of 12 primary (or viscerogenic) and 28 secondary (or psychogenic) human needs. An illustrative sample of those psychogenic needs is shown in Table 5.1, along with an example of each. As can be seen from the list, Murray looks at human needs more microscopically so that each need is more focused, narrow, and specific compared with Maslow's needs, which are more broadly defined and, therefore, have fewer categories. Murray's list can be very useful in identifying more precisely the motivation underlying customers' specific marketplace behaviours, such as compulsive consumption (discussed later in this chapter).

TABLE 5.1 Murray's List of Needs: Examples of Psychogenic Needs

Need	Definition	Examples
Autonomy	To be independent and free to act according to impulse; to be unattached, irresponsible; to defy convention	Impulse buying, wearing unconventional clothing
Dominance	To direct the behaviour of others	Aggressively demanding attention in service establishments
Nurturance	To give sympathy and to feed, help, and protect the needy	Giving to humanitarian causes
Exhibition	To make an impression; to excite, amaze, fascinate, entertain, shock, intrigue, amuse, or entice others	Wearing high-fashion clothing
Cognizance	To explore, to ask questions, to seek knowledge	Visiting museums, learning about new technology and products
Exposition	To give information and explain, interpret, and lecture	Playing opinion leaders

SOURCE: Murray, Henry A. *Explorations in Personality* copyright 1938, renewed 1966 by Henry A. Murray. Reprinted by permission of Oxford University Press, Inc.

ERNEST DICHTER'S CONSUMPTION MOTIVES

Ernest Dichter, a strong believer in Freud's theory of personality, believed that unconscious motives play a significant role in people's consumption decisions. Based on in-depth interviews with consumers for more than 200 products, he identified a set of motives/needs that underlie an individual's consumption of diverse products (see Table 5.2). Since many of these motives are thought to influence consumption decisions unconsciously, the list is most useful for incorporating symbolism in product advertising.

TABLE 5.2 Dichter's List of Consumption Motives

Motive	Examples of Consumption Decisions
Mastery over environment	Kitchen appliances, power tools
Status	Scotch, owning a car in a third-world economy
Rewards	Candies, gifts to oneself
Individuality	Gourmet foods, foreign cars, tattoos
Social acceptance	Companionship: sharing tea drinking
Love and affection	Giving children toys
Security	Full drawer of neatly ironed shirts
Masculinity	Toy guns, heavy shoes
Femininity	Decorating (products with a heavy tactile component)
Eroticism	Sweets (to lick), gloves (to be removed by women as a form of undressing)
Disalienation	Listening to and calling in to talk shows (a desire to feel connected)
Moral purity/cleanliness	White bread, bathing, cotton fabrics
Magic, mystery	Belief in UFOs or the healing power of crystals, religious rituals, visiting the Elvis Presley museum, Graceland, and buying related products

SOURCE: Dichter, Ernest. *Handbook of Consumer Motivations.* New York: McGraw, 1964; Durgee, Jeffrey F. "Interpreting Dichter's Interpretations: An Analysis of Consumption Symbolism in the Handbook of Consumer Motivations." In *Marketing and Semiotics: Selected Papers from the Copenhagen Symposium,* edited by Hanne Hartvig-Larsen, David Glen Mick, and Christian Alstead, Copenhagen, 1991.

NEEDS IDENTIFIED BY MARKETING SCHOLARS

Working more directly on marketing problems and reflecting specifically on an individual's behaviour in the marketplace, several marketing scholars have identified and proposed their own classifications of needs. Geraldine Fennel identified consumer motives for product use based on use-situation—for example, aversive (to avert an adverse situation) or positive (to gain a reward) product-use situation. Morris Holbrook has discussed the hedonic (i.e., pleasure seeking) consumption motive, distinguishing it from the more utilitarian consumption. Similarly, Olli T. Ahtola has described utilitarian and hedonic consumer attitudes toward products. (Hedonic motive is discussed later in this chapter.)

Sheth, Newman, and Gross proposed that individual-choice behaviour stems from five needs:[4]

1. *Functional*—A product satisfies its physical or functional purpose (for example, soaps for cleansing and medicines for alleviating physical ailments).
2. *Social*—A product satisfies the social need through its association with selected demographic, socioeconomic, or cultural-ethnic segments of society (for example, wearing a Polo brand of shirt to identify with upper-income, successful people). Online communities like ivillage.com are attempting to fulfil social needs and, thereby, create strong emotional associations with the brand.
3. *Emotional*—The product satisfies this need by creating the appropriate feelings or emotions that a person experiences upon receiving a gift, such as joy, love, or respect.

4. *Epistemic*—The product satisfies the human need to know or learn something new (for example, buying and reading a newspaper, watching a TV news program, or purchasing an encyclopedia or books on history, science, or commerce). On the Internet, websites such as **http://AskMe.com** and **http://ExpertCentral.com** satisfy this need by inviting Web surfers to ask questions on any subject and having them answered by experts.
5. *Situational*—Certain products satisfy needs that are situational or contingent upon the time and place (for example, an emergency car repair on an out-of-town trip).

These classifications are valuable to study because they have been used in a number of consumer studies; for example, Sheth and his colleagues have applied the classification to consumers' transportation choices, to people's voting behaviour, and to an individual's smoking behaviour.

Finally, Janice Hanna has proposed a list of seven consumer needs:[5]

1. *Physical safety*—The need to consume products so as to avoid harm or danger in their use, and to preserve clean air and water in the environment.
2. *Material security*—The need to consume an adequate supply of material possessions.
3. *Material comfort*—The need to consume a large and/or luxurious supply of material possessions.
4. *Acceptance by others*—The need to consume products in order to be associated with a significant other or a special reference group.
5. *Recognition from others*—The need to consume products in order to be acknowledged by others as having gained a high status in his or her community.
6. *Influence over others*—The need to feel one's impact on others' consumption decisions.
7. *Personal growth*—The need to consume products in order to be or become one's own unique self.

NEED FOR AROUSAL, COGNITION, AND ATTRIBUTION

LO 3

Marketing scholars also have identified some specific needs that are especially influential in marketing. Three of these are the *need for arousal, need for cognition*, and *need for attribution*.

Arousal Seeking

One of the human needs that underlies a number of marketplace transactions is the need for arousal. The motive underlying hedonic consumption is the need to seek arousal. Humans have an innate need for stimulation. James Olds and Peter Milner demonstrated that when subjects were deprived of all sensory experiences, they could not survive in this environment for long; some of them reported hallucinations after enduring the environment for a few hours.[6]

There is an **optimal level of stimulation,** or a level at which a person feels neither bored nor overwhelmed. The process works like this: When we encounter a new stimulus, it interests us and holds our attention. However, as we continue to be exposed to it, we become used to it, or adapt to it; this condition is called the **level of adaptation** for any stimulus, the level of stimulation perceived as normal or average. Once the adaptation level is reached, there is no longer interest in the stimulus object. If new stimuli are all within the adaptation level, they arouse no interest, and the individual is starved of stimulation. If, on the other hand, he or she encounters too many new stimuli, the individual becomes overwhelmed and stressed, and

Optimal level of stimulation
The level at which balance is reached so that the person is neither bored nor overwhelmed by new experience.

Level of adaptation
The level at which a person develops adequate familiarity with a stimulus so that the stimulation is perceived as normal or average.

spontaneously acts to shut off additional sensory input (e.g., we close our eyes when watching a scary movie). Conversely, when the stimulation level falls below the optimum level, we feel bored and seek stimulating experiences.[7]

Arousal-seeking motive
The drive to maintain the organism's stimulation at an optimal level.

The **arousal-seeking motive** is the drive to maintain a person's stimulation at an optimal level. Some people characteristically seek more arousal than others. Raju, Steenkamp, and Baumgartner studied this motivation in consumers. They found that arousal-seeking consumers took more risks in life activities in general (e.g., gambling) as well as in their buying behaviour. They tended to adopt new products and switch brands just to try out a different brand. They also looked for more information about products and got bored when exposed to repetitive advertisements. Arousal seekers were also users of a greater assortment of options within the same product category, such as fast food.[8] Although no research has especially established this, we would expect arousal seekers to use more diverse products: perfumes and colognes, restaurants, clothing, vacation spots; likewise, among business customers, arousal seekers are likely to be open to alternative suppliers' pitches, be predisposed to attend trade shows and professional conferences, and actively search for better products.[9]

Curiosity: Need for Cognition

All humans are equipped with means for gathering and processing information for purposes of survival. The need for information, for understanding the world around us, and for knowledge are all derivative needs, i.e., needs in the service of the basic need for survival and safety.[10] This need for knowing is called **need for cognition.**

Need for cognition
The human need for information and for understanding the world around us.

Tolerance for ambiguity
The degree to which a person remains free from anxiety in the face of uncertainty and lack of complete information.

A related concept is **tolerance for ambiguity.** This trait refers to the degree to which lack of information or uncertainty makes a person anxious. Consumers intolerant of ambiguity are less likely to adopt new products than those with a high degree of this trait. Business executives and business customers low in this trait are likely to feel threatened when meeting other business associates and salespersons without a specific agenda and predeliberated items of information to be exchanged. The Internet has begun to play a crucial role in satisfying the need to obtain information and avoid ambiguity. The consumer is now able to very easily conduct comparison shopping across various purchase options, and there are also a number of general and specialized websites that make it simple for the consumer to obtain information about any topic. Retail banking and brokerage customers consider the Web a top media source for financial information and use it on a regular basis, according to a study by Cybertrends.

Need for cognition is real, and it has a vivid presence in the marketplace. The volume of news stories in the papers, on TV and radio, and the very survival of 24-hour Cable News Network (CNN) and C-Span assumes a high need for cognition. So do more than a thousand nonfiction magazines, both the ones in which the content is general news, and those with editorial material on special topics (e.g., *Popular Mechanics*, *Wired*, *Chemical Engineering*). We refer here not just to the need for knowing in order to make purchase decisions, such as the features of two vendor offerings or the timetable for the train between Geneva and Milan; rather, we refer also to the need to know for its own sake, like the game statistics for all the past games, the new developments in computer technology, or a visit to the National Archives. All the various magazines with news and gossip about celebrities (e.g., *People*, *Entertainment Weekly*, *National Enquirer*) also satisfy the need for cognition—knowing for its own sake.

Market mavens
Individuals who possess information about markets and disseminate it to other customers.

One specific significance of this phenomenon in marketing is the role of people who have been called *market mavens.* **Market mavens** have been defined as individuals who have information about many kinds of products, places to shop, and other facets of markets, initiate discussions with consumers, and respond to requests from consumers for market information.[11] Market mavens differ from opinion leaders (discussed in Chapter 4) in that opinion leaders' expertise and influence is limited to a specific product category or a group of related products (e.g., electronics), or a set of related topics. In comparison, market mavens are knowledgeable about the marketplace in general: what new products are available, what price deals are being offered, where you can find specific products or deals, and so on. To fulfill this self-assumed role, market mavens attend to diverse sources of marketplace information, do more window shopping, enjoy shopping, use coupons more, and frequently engage in market-related conversations with others.

Need for Attribution

Human beings are scientists. They want to know why something happened, the cause for someone's particular behaviour, or, for that matter, for their own behaviour. The process of assigning causes is called making attributions. **Attributions** are inferences that people draw about the causes of events, the behaviour of others, and their own behaviour.[12]

The motivation to assign causes is called **attribution motivation**. This motivation has implications for marketing. For example, when an appliance salesperson recommends a particular model, we, in our buyer roles, wonder why he or she is recommending it. We may attribute the cause to the salesperson's personal interest (e.g., a bigger commission), or to his or her genuine desire to serve our interests in order to build a long-term business relationship with us. This attribution will influence whether we patronize or shun the salesperson. We assign the cause of a person's behaviour either to the person himself or herself (internal) or to the situation (external). **Internal attributions** ascribe the cause of someone's behaviour to personal dispositions, traits, abilities, or motivations and feelings; **external attributions** assign the cause to situational demands or environmental constraints that were beyond the control of the individual.

Harold H. Kelley proposed a theory to explain when internal versus external attributions are made. He identified three conditions:

1. *Consistency*—If a person does something only once rather than consistently, we would be disinclined to attribute the cause to the person.
2. *Consensus*—If this person is the only one who does something (low consensus), then we will assign it to him or her.
3. *Distinctiveness*—If this person singles out this particular setting to behave this way, then we would not blame the person.

To summarize, in conditions of low consensus, high consistency, and low distinctiveness, we will tend to attribute the cause to the person (i.e., an internal attribution). In conditions of low consistency, or in conditions of high consistency accompanied by high consensus and high distinctiveness, the situation is likely to be blamed (i.e., an external attribution).[13]

Attributions
Inferences that people draw about the causes of events and behaviours.

Attribution motivation
The innate human need to assign causes to events and behaviours.

Internal attributions
Ascribing the cause of someone's behaviour to personal dispositions, traits, abilities, or motivations and feelings.

External attributions
Assigning the cause of someone's behaviour to situational demands or environmental constraints that were beyond the control of the individual.

EVALUATION OF NEED CATEGORIES

In the classical literature on human needs, many more perspectives and classification schemes are presented, applying perspectives ranging from economics and organizational behaviour to social psychology and cultural anthropology.[14] We have barely presented a few of these. A few points will help marketers evaluate the various models. First, different classification schemes are simply different ways of dividing the same pie. Second, the models differ in the level of detail. Finally, it is possible to cross-classify these need categories and, thus, relate one to the other. Maslow's need hierarchy is perhaps the best known as well as the most universal and general, but other schemes (e.g., Murray's list, Dichter's list) provide a more detailed and richer view of the tapestry of the complex web of human needs. We offer them here to enrich reader perspectives and to encourage a deeper reflection of your own needs and motivation as a customer.

LO 4 CUSTOMER EMOTIONS

Needs and emotions are closely related. Similar to needs, emotions are also capable of energizing the person toward relevant goal-objects. Felt deprivations of desired goal-objects (which engender the drive) are experienced in consciousness as negative emotions, and their attainment (which satisfies the drive) is experienced in consciousness as positive emotion. We all seek positive emotional experiences and avoid negative emotional experiences. Thus, positive emotions serve as approach motivations and negative emotions as avoidance motivations. Among several metaphors used to describe how consumers consume, the *Consuming as Experience* metaphor examines consumers' subjective emotional reactions to common objects. Therefore, it will be useful to gain some basic understanding of what emotions are and how they explain customer behaviour.

WHAT IS EMOTION?

As humans, we are creatures of emotion. Emotions lace our lives and guide everyday actions. Emotion is a complex set of processes, occurring concurrently in multiple systems of humans (i.e., both in the mind and in the body). **Emotions** are the consciousness of the occurrence of some physiological arousal, followed by a behavioral response along with the appraised meaning of both. This definition implies that emotions have three components: physiological, behavioral, and cognitive.[15]

Emotions
The consciousness of the occurrence of some physiological arousal, followed by a behavioural response along with the appraised meaning of both.

Let's say you are going about your day. Suddenly a stimulus appears before you (e.g., the shadow of some intruder in the dark, or your lottery number on the TV screen). Instantly and automatically, your nervous system is aroused: you feel a tremor in the visceral system, or butterflies in your stomach; you perspire; or you experience a sudden burst of energy. This is the physiological component, and because it occurs by reflex, almost automatically, it is called autonomic arousal. Then follows cognitive interpretation or meaning analysis—what does the stimulus mean? For example, is the intruder a friend or a foe? Is the winning lottery number real? Is it really the number on your ticket? This is the cognitive component.

Depending on your cognitive appraisal and the meaning you make of the initial stimulus, there can be further autonomic arousal (or reduced arousal, when the nervous system is calming down). If the intruder is a friend, your arousal calms down; if a foe, you experience more arousal. Next, but almost instantly, you act out a physiological response (or a behaviour). Thus, you flee if the intruder is a foe and approach if he or she is a friend. This is the behavioral component.

While all this autonomic and physiological arousal and response is going on, you also experience a consciousness of these changes in your body. You also perceive your response and interpret its efficacy and meaning, including the perception that a response is unavailable (i.e., you can do nothing about it). This consciousness, these perceptions of arousal and response, are accompanied by, and further produce feelings of, pleasure or pain. These feelings are called emotions.[16] For example, when a consumer faces a dissatisfying marketplace experience, the cognitive appraisal process starts first with the consumer's assessment of the significance of the dissatisfaction for his or her own well-being (whether the dissatisfying experience is relevant to deeply held goals, whether it inhibits goals, or whether it hurts his or her ego/self-esteem). If the experience is dissatisfying within these parameters, it causes stress. This cognitive appraisal of stress may lead directly to coping actions intended to manage the dissatisfying market experience, or to emotions that then lead to coping actions. Negative emotions arise due to the stress involved, and, depending on to whom the entire experience is attributed, the emotions are different. Emotions such as anger, disgust, or contempt arise when the dissatisfying experience is attributed to external factors and when they lead to problem-focused coping strategies, wherein people complain about the experience. Believing that the event could not have been helped leads to situational attribution and emotions of sadness and fear, while blaming oneself for the situation (internal attribution) leads to emotions of shame and guilt. The consumer does not complain when using an emotional coping strategy (a self-deception tactic such as denial of the problem, self-blame, or self-control in not complaining) or an avoidance coping strategy (such as quitting the situation).[17]

A MODEL OF EMOTION

Although a number of psychologists have tried to explain emotions, the prominent contemporary theory is **Schachter's two-factor theory**.[18] According to Stanley Schachter, the experience of emotion depends on two factors: autonomic arousal and its cognitive interpretation, or meaning analysis. In this model, we recognize that the initial stimulus can come from the external environment as well as from the inside of the organism, such as hunger pangs or a headache.

Schachter's two-factor theory
Psychologist Stanley Schachter's theory that the experience of emotion depends on two factors: autonomic arousal and its cognitive interpretation.

Marketers can adapt or respond to customer emotions by (1) designing the stimulus and (2) aiding the meaning appraisal. The first intervention takes the form of making product designs to fit appropriate consumption emotions. The second takes the form of communication, such as by attaching symbolism to products in advertising, or explaining certain aspects of the market offering or certain deviations from the expected marketplace events or outcomes. For example, positive attempts to help a customer's meaning appraisal process might include a physician explaining treatment procedures to a patient, or a server explaining why there is a delay in serving food at a restaurant.

TYPES OF EMOTIONS

Robert Plutchik has proposed eight primary emotions (see Figure 5.3), each of which can vary in intensity:

1. *Fear*—Ranging from timidity to terror. An individual customer might experience this if, when driving on the expressway, he or she discovers the car's brakes are not working. A business customer might experience fear upon learning that top management is looking into the problems experienced with the lower-cost computer network he or she was responsible for buying.

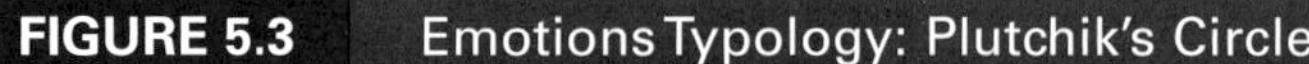
FIGURE 5.3 Emotions Typology: Plutchik's Circle

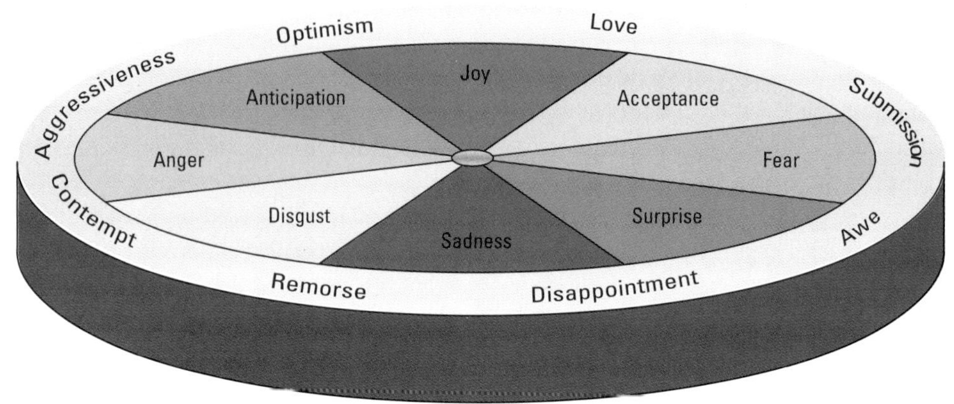

SOURCE: Adapted From: Weiten Wayne. *Psychology: Themes and Variations*, 4th ed. Pacific Grove, CA: Brooks/Cole, 1998, p. 413.

2. *Anger*—Ranging from annoyance to rage. For a household customer at the desk of a car rental agency, anger might result when the agency employee explains that the car the customer reserved is not available. A business customer might become angry upon realizing that his or her company's insurance agent sold the company a policy for more coverage than necessary.
3. *Joy*—Ranging from serenity to ecstasy. A household customer might experience joy in an auto dealership when spotting a rare model he or she has been looking for. A business customer might experience joy when his or her company's advertising agency delivers an "awesome" TV commercial.
4. *Sadness*—Ranging from pensiveness to grief. For a household customer, sadness might result from calling the airline for a last-minute reservation, only to be informed that the last seat was just sold. For a business customer, a cause of sadness might be the news that a favourite supplier has gone out of business.
5. *Acceptance*—Ranging from tolerance to adoration. For a household customer, acceptance might involve feelings about a favourite restaurant. For a business customer, the feeling might be preference for working with a particular salesperson.
6. *Disgust*—Ranging from boredom to loathing. A household customer might feel disgust at finding an insect in his or her cola. A business customer might be disgusted to learn that no insurance firm covers the risk of loss due to an act of war.
7. *Anticipation*—Ranging from mindfulness to vigilance. For a household customer, anticipation might include the wait for the announcement of the winning lottery number. For a business customer, it might include waiting for the results of a market research effort.
8. *Surprise*—Ranging from uncertainty to amazement. A household customer might feel surprise when his or her waiter announces that dessert will be on the house. For a business customer, surprise might be the response to a call from the company's media-buying agency, saying that a long-sought television spot on the final championship game has become available.

Primary emotions Basic human emotions that humans have acquired based on the evolutionary process.

These eight human reactions derive from the evolutionary process and define, according to Plutchik, basic human emotions. Hence, they are called **primary emotions.** Other emotions we experience are combinations of these; for example, joy and acceptance combine to produce the emotion of love; disgust and sadness combine as remorse. Table 5.3 shows a way to measure these emotions. The Window on Research discusses the Consumption Emotions Set associated with consumption of products.

TABLE 5.3 Scales to Measure Plutchik's Eight Emotions

Plutchik's emotions can be measured by rating the following triads of adjectives, each rated on a five-point scale, ranging from "not at all" to "very strongly." How do you feel at the moment?

Fear: threatened, frightened, intimidated

Anger: hostile, annoyed, irritated

Joy: happy, cheerful, delighted

Sadness: gloomy, sad, depressed

Acceptance: helped, accepted, trusting

Disgust: disgusted, offended, unpleased

Anticipation: alert, attentive, curious

Surprise: puzzled, confused, startled

Source: Havlena, William J., and Morris Holbrook. "The Varieties of Consumption Experience: Comparing Two Typologies of Emotion in Consumer Behaviour." *Journal of Consumer Research* 13, no. 3 (1986): 394–404. Reprinted with permission of the University of Chicago Press.

WINDOW ON **RESEARCH**

The Consumption Emotions Set

In a series of six studies, Marsha L. Richins developed a Consumption Emotions Set (CES). It reflects directly experienced emotions that result from the consumption of products, and excludes vicarious (aesthetic) emotions that are associated with artistic works like books, plays, and movies, or that may be induced by advertising. Consumers were asked to generate emotions that they experienced during six different types of consumption situations: use of a favourite possession; a recent important purchase; recent purchase of a clothing item, a food item, a durable good, or a service. The CES comprises a list of 16 emotions: *anger, discontent, worry, sadness, fear, shame, envy, loneliness, romantic love, love, peacefulness, contentment, optimism, joy, excitement,* and *surprise.*

SOURCE: Adapted from Richins, Marsha L. "Measuring Emotions in the Consumption Experience." *Journal of Consumer Research*, 24 (September 1997): 127–146.

CUSTOMER MOODS

Moods are simply emotions felt less intensely; they are also short-lived. They are easy to induce, and they appear and disappear frequently and readily. They are pervasive in that we are always in some kind of mood—we are always happy, sad, pensive, careless, irritated pleased, amused, bored, or one of many other moods. Moods affect our behaviour of the moment in general, as well as our response to the marketing activities to which we might be exposed at the time. For this reason, it is important for marketers to understand moods.

Moods
Short-lived and less intensely felt emotions.

Moods are induced by external stimuli as well as, internally, by autistic thinking; that is, recalling some past incident or fantasizing about some event. Among the marketing stimuli that can induce positive or negative moods are:

- the ambiance of the store or service delivery facility
- the demeanor of the salesperson
- the sensory features of the product
- the tone and manner of advertising
- the content of the salesperson's pitch itself or of the advertisement; whether it frustrates or fulfills one's goals in paying attention to that message (e.g., if the salesperson is not knowledgeable or if the advertisement is vain, the customer may feel frustration at having wasted time)

Mood states have consequences in terms of favourable or unfavourable customer response to marketer efforts. In research studies, customers have also been found to linger longer in positive mood environments, recall those advertisements more that had created positive moods, and feel more positive toward brands based on advertising that created feelings of warmth.[19]

Mood affects the strategies that consumers use to process information. However, one stream of research states that positive mood reduces the processing of stimulus information, while another states that positive mood enhances the learning of brand names better in comparison to a neutral mood. Brand-name recall is a prerequisite for the choice of the brand, and recall depends on the process by which the brand was first encoded into memory. Lee and Sternthal state that two factors important in the encoding process are *brand rehearsal*—"how frequently and recently the brand has been exposed in the memory as a member of a particular category"—and *relational elaboration*—"the process by which consumers link the brands to the specific categories they belong to." In a brand-learning task, they found that being in a positive mood helps consumers to cluster the brands that they are exposed to, by the categories they belong to. When the respondents are asked to recall as many brands as possible after this exposure, a positive mood helps them recall more categories and more brands as members of these categories, thus increasing the number of brands recalled compared to when they are in a neutral mood.[20] This finding is corroborated by the study by Barone, Miniard, and Romeo on the effect of positive mood on brand extension evaluations. They show that a positive mood influences the perceptions of similarity between the brand extension and the core brand (particularly for extensions that are moderately similar to the core brand) and the perceived competency of the manufacturer in producing the extension. Both of these factors are important determinants of extension evaluations, and positive mood enhances evaluation of brand extensions by influencing these determinants. Thus, marketers could use advertising, point-of-sale material, celebrity endorsements, free gifts, and several other strategies to induce positive moods in consumers to enable a more positive evaluation of a brand extension, thereby influencing choice.[21]

Marketers on the Internet attempt to overcome their inability to actually bring the customer into the store by creating the mood or ambience within the website. This might include the incorporation of store colours and background music aimed at entertaining the Web surfer and creating a favourable mood.[21a]

HEDONIC CONSUMPTION: SEEKING EMOTIONAL VALUE

Emotions and moods drive a host of consumption behaviours. While detergents, lawn mowers, microwave ovens, chain saws, insurance policies, investment portfolios, and computers are purchased and used for some utilitarian/functional end-states, products such as perfumes and colognes, diamonds, and bubble baths, and activities such as sports, theatre, movies, music concerts, and amusement parks are used or engaged in purely for the emotional or hedonic values they provide. In Chapter 1, we introduced the concept of emotional value as a discretionary value.

Hedonic consumption refers to the use of products for the sake of intrinsic enjoyment rather than to solve some problem in the physical environment. More specifically, hedonism refers to sensory pleasure. Thus, hedonic consumption is the use of products that give pleasure through the senses, that help create fantasies, and that give emotional arousal.[22] Here are some examples:

Hedonic consumption
The use of products for the sake of intrinsic enjoyment rather than to solve some problem in the physical environment.

- *Sensory pleasure*—taking a bubble bath; relaxing in a jacuzzi or sauna; using perfume and colognes; wearing exciting colors in clothing; enjoying strobe lights in a discotheque; choosing office decor; landscaping the corporate office building
- *Aesthetic pleasure*—reading poetry; visiting an art gallery; taking a course in Greek history; having original works of art in the corporate offices
- *Emotional experience*—watching movies or TV soap operas; taking a roller coaster ride; sending gifts; receiving gifts; visiting relatives; making or receiving long-distance social calls; dating; attending a class reunion; celebrating a silver wedding anniversary; celebrating the winning of a major business contract from a highly coveted client
- *Fun and enjoyment*—video game arcade; playing sports; dancing; vacationing; attending a business convention; entertaining a business customer in a game of golf; attending office Christmas parties

While North American teenagers are enamored by the newness and hedonic value of technological gadgets, European teenagers are concerned with their functional utility. They look at technology as a means to an end. The "end" they are interested in is social connectivity. They want to keep in touch with friends and develop relationships with peers, and they consider devices such as computers and cell phones to be a means to achieving this end.[23]

Deep Involvement

One special case of hedonic consumption is deep involvement in a product or activity. This describes customers' relationships with a select few products that are consumed with interest: the customer pauses to savour their taste, smell their aroma, feel their texture, or hear their sound. We like them; we enjoy them; we love them.

Everyone has a favourite activity, a favourite product, and a favourite brand. Some of us are fashion experts; others, car buffs; still others, computer jocks. We are eager to get to know these products (e.g., fashions, cars, and computers) and find out everything there is to know; we get excited whenever the topic comes up, and, of course, we want to use them whenever possible. This relationship we develop as users with selected products is called **deep involvement.** It can be defined as a customer's extreme and ongoing interest in a product.

Deep involvement
A customer's extreme and ongoing interest in a product.

Involvement
The degree of personal relevance of an object or product to a customer.

Enduring involvement
The degree of interest a customer feels in a product on an ongoing basis.

Situational involvement
The degree of a person's interest in a specific situation or on a specific occasion.

Involvement is a general term that can be defined as the degree of personal relevance of a product to a customer. Furthermore, involvement is a matter of degree—how relevant or how central a product is to a customer's life. Involvement, defined as the degree of interest, can be viewed as having two forms: enduring involvement and situational involvement. **Enduring involvement** is the degree of interest a customer feels in a product on an ongoing basis. In contrast, **situational involvement** is the degree of interest in a specific situation or on a specific occasion, such as when buying a product, or when consuming something in the presence of an important client or friend. Thus, Mary Chan was not much interested in dishwashers; she took the one in her kitchen for granted. But when she needed to buy a new one, she became extremely interested (i.e., involved) in dishwashers, attempting to learn about them, deliberating over various options, and weighing them vis-à-vis her own needs. In contrast, she is enduringly involved in gardening and in garden-related products, taking considerable interest in them and enjoying them. In a business context, a major infrastructure project in a company is an object of high situational involvement, and maximizing the lifetime value of its customers would be a matter of enduring involvement. (The general roles that enduring and situational involvement play in customer attitudes and decision making will be discussed in later chapters.)

The extreme form of enduring involvement is deep involvement. Deep involvement affects customer behaviour in a number of ways. First, deeply involved consumers are knowledgeable about the product and, thus, can act as opinion leaders. Second, they consume a greater quantity of the product and also buy related products. Third, they are less price-sensitive for that product and are willing to spend well. Fourth, they seek constant information about products. Fifth, they want to spend more time in related activities. It is easier to build more extended relationships with these customers. Consider, for example, Harley-Davidson motorcycle owners; there is a Harley Owners Group (HOG), and members participate in a wide range of activities, including charity work. The fanatic loyalty that favored IBM at one time, but now favours the Apple Mac, shows the deep involvement that these users have for the product. Finally, deeply involved customers can act as lead users for new products; they try products in innovative ways and, thus, are sources of new-product ideas.[24]

LO 5 PSYCHOGRAPHICS

Psychographics
Characteristics of individuals that describe them in terms of their psychological and behavioural makeup.

Along with needs and emotions, the third facet of motivation is psychographics. **Psychographics** are characteristics of individuals that describe them in terms of their psychological and behavioral makeup—how people occupy themselves (behaviour) and what psychological factors underlie that activity pattern. They are a manifestation of an individual's underlying motivations, and they, in turn, define them. For example, a person's need to seek affiliation or peer approval makes him or her engage, say, in going to the theatre or playing golf. Theatre going or playing golf, thus, becomes part of his or her psychographics. This psychographic, in turn, drives customer behaviour toward buying golf equipment or doing whatever is needed to implement that particular psychographic; it becomes motivational.

Psychographics have three components: **values, self-concept,** and **lifestyles**.

VALUES

When you think about what is important to you in life, you are thinking about your values. **Values** are end-states of life, the goals one lives for. In psychology, Milton Rokeach has identified two groups of these: terminal and instrumental. Terminal values are the goals we seek in life (e.g., peace and happiness) whereas instrumental values are the means or behavioural standards by which we pursue these goals (e.g., honesty).[25]

Values
The end-states of life; the goals one lives for.

Consumer researchers felt a need for values more directly relevant to everyday consumer behaviour. For this purpose, Lynn Kahle and his associates developed a List of Values (LOV) consisting of nine terminal values:

1. Self-respect
2. Self-fulfillment
3. Security
4. Sense of belonging
5. Excitement
6. Sense of accomplishment
7. Fun and enjoyment
8. Being well respected
9. Warm relationships with others[26]

This list of values corresponds well to the needs in Maslow's hierarchy, except that Maslow includes physiological needs, and LOV adds fun and excitement as values. Kahle argues that the nine values in LOV relate more closely to the values of life's major roles, such as marriage, parenting, work, leisure, and daily consumption, than do the values in Rokeach Value Survey.

In a number of studies, LOV has been found to be closely related to consumer activities. For example, Sharon Beatty and her associates found that people who value a sense of belonging especially like group activities. Those who value fun and enjoyment especially like skiing, dancing, backpacking, hiking, and camping, and they consume more alcohol than others. People who value a warm relationship with others tend to give gifts to others for no reason at all.[27]

Linking Product Attributes to Customer Values

One of the basic tenets of marketing has been that customers don't buy products; rather, they buy benefits. Thus, when consumers buy an automobile, they are not buying simply 2,500 kilograms of sheet metal. Rather they are buying transportation. They want a car with ergonomic seats because they want their body to feel comfortable, or they want a car with acceleration from 0 to 100 km per hour in 7 seconds versus 10 seconds, to experience the driving thrill. If we go one step further, transportation, comfort, and the driving thrill are important to consumers so that they can overcome the physical distance barrier, or escape to a more desirable place, or master the machine. Ultimately, then, the product features make sense only because they serve some more fundamental needs (such as the needs in Maslow's hierarchy) or values (as in the List of Values). Identifying the connections between product features on the one hand and customers' fundamental needs and values on the other is important if marketers are to design features that would offer value to customers.

Means-end chains Linkages between the product's physical features and customers' fundamental needs and values.

Laddering A research technique to identify means-end linkages.

This linking is accomplished by drawing means-end chains. **Means-end chains** are simply linkages between the product's physical features and customers' fundamental needs and values. They are identified by a research technique called **laddering**, in which potential customers are asked repeatedly in iterative sequence, "Why is that feature important to you?" For example, "Why is quick acceleration important to you?" If the answer is, "to maneuver out of traffic situations," we next ask, "and why is that important?" and so on.[28] Figure 5.4 shows an example of a means-end chain for a hypothetical customer.

SELF-CONCEPT

Self-concept A person's image of oneself—who he or she is

Actual self A person's self-image of who he or she is.

Ideal self A person's self-image of who he or she would like to be.

Everyone has a self-image of who he or she is. This is called **self-concept**. Furthermore, the self-concept includes an idea of what the person currently is and what he or she would like to become; these two concepts are respectively called **actual self** and **ideal self**. For some, the self-concept pertains to their intellectual and/or career accomplishments; for example, one wants to be a successful writer or an engineer or a financial executive on Bay Street.[29] For many, the self-concept pertains to the kind of material life they want to live.

These self-concepts influence a person's consumption deeply, for people live their self-concepts in large measure by what they consume. The *Consuming as Integration* metaphor describes how consumers are able to integrate their self-concepts and objects through a variety of consumption, self-extension, and personalizing rituals. For example, business students who are about to enter the corporate world start dressing more seriously in their senior year, or employees who are promoted to executive cadre change their wardrobe to include suits. Marketers can apply the principle of self-concept by obtaining a self-concept profile of customers in terms of selected personality traits, then obtaining the consumer's perceptions of a brand on the same traits, as shown in Table 5.4. From these two profiles, it is possible to identify the match or gaps between consumers' self-concept and their perceptions of the personality of the brand.[30] If the gaps are significant, the marketer may want to make changes to the product or to marketing communications about the product.

Businesses, too, have a self-concept. Some think of themselves as a company at the forefront of technology; others view their essence to be in communications wherever and in whatever form it may exist; still others define their essence as innovation. For example, Benetton's self-concept can be described as a clothing company for the young that promotes social issues. Basically, corporate self-concepts are expressed in mission statements.

Self-Concept as Users, Payers, and Buyers

Individuals have their self-concepts as individuals in general, but they also have a self-concept of themselves in their specific roles of user, payer, and buyer. Illustratively, a user could have the self-concept of a very discerning connoisseur user or a very involved (or alternatively, very detached) user. The payer could have the self-concept of being thrifty or financially prudent, or of having the attitude of "money is no object to me." Finally, the buyer could have the self-concept of being a convenience seeker or of being very time conscious.

FIGURE 5.4 A Means-End Chain for a Hypothetical Customer

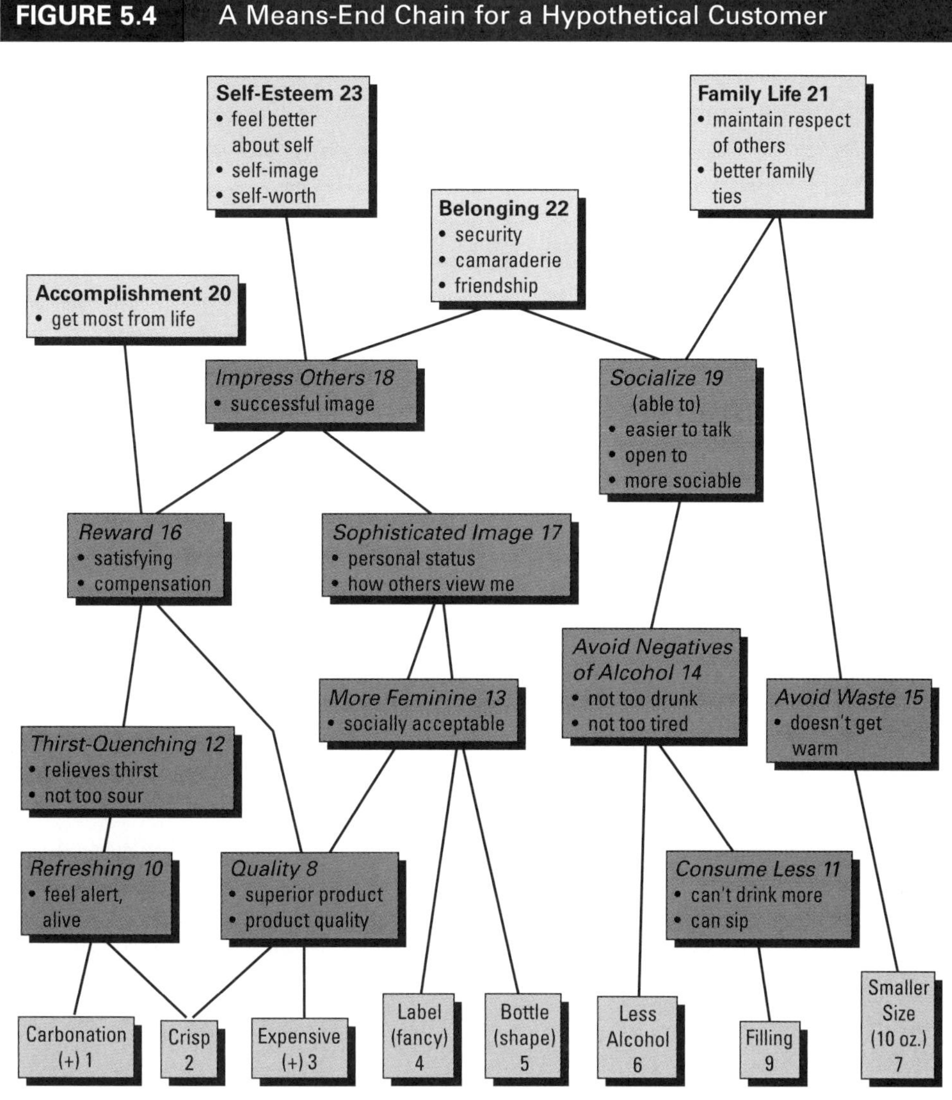

SOURCE: Thomas J. Reynolds and Jonathan Gardner, "Laddering Theory, Method, Analysis, and Interpretation." Reprinted from the Journal of Advertising Research 28 (February/March 1988), p.19. © 1988 Advertising Research Foundation.

TABLE 5.4 A Scale to Measure Self-Image and Product Image

Instruction: Rate yourself, as you see yourself, on the following descriptive word pairs, by circling a number in each row closer to the word that describes you.

1.	Rugged	1	2	3	4	5	6	7	Delicate
2.	Exciting	1	2	3	4	5	6	7	Calm
3.	Uncomfortable	1	2	3	4	5	6	7	Comfortable

(continued)

4.	Dominating	1	2	3	4	5	6	7	Submissive
5.	Thrifty	1	2	3	4	5	6	7	Indulgent
6.	Pleasant	1	2	3	4	5	6	7	Unpleasant
7.	Contemporary	1	2	3	4	5	6	7	Uncontemporary
8.	Organized	1	2	3	4	5	6	7	Unorganized
9.	Rational	1	2	3	4	5	6	7	Emotional
10.	Youthful	1	2	3	4	5	6	7	Mature
11.	Formal	1	2	3	4	5	6	7	Informal
12.	Orthodox	1	2	3	4	5	6	7	Liberal
13.	Complex	1	2	3	4	5	6	7	Simple
14.	Colourless	1	2	3	4	5	6	7	Colourful
15.	Modest	1	2	3	4	5	6	7	Vain

Note: To measure product or brand image, the entire scale is repeated with instructions to rate the specified product or brand.

SOURCE: Adapted from Malhotra, Naresh K. "A Scale to Measure Self-Concepts, Person Concepts, and Product Concepts." *Journal of Marketing Research* 18 (November 1981): 456–464.

LIFESTYLE

Lifestyles The way a person lives.

Along with what we think of ourselves and what we value, psychographics describes us in terms of **lifestyles**, or the way we live. Consider two consumers with different lifestyles. Thelma is a home- and family-oriented, traditional, educated, politically active, nonworking mother of two; she likes to cook, spends most of her time at home, and entertains relatives and friends over the weekend. Claire is a very outgoing, career-oriented, fashion-oriented, single mother of a 5-year-old; she likes to go out rather than stay at home, and dislikes household chores. Given different lifestyles, these customers have very different customer behaviours as well.

Lifestyles are determined by (a) a customer's personal characteristics (seen in Chapter 2), i.e., genetics, race, gender, age, and personality; (b) his or her personal context, i.e., culture, institutions and reference groups, and personal worth; and (c) needs and emotions. These three sets of factors together influence the pattern of our activities—how we spend time and money.

How do consumers live their lifestyles? How else but by doing activities that inevitably entail marketplace exchange and choices. Thelma obviously eats out less but buys more food items from the market than does Claire. Claire uses babysitting services more than does Thelma. Claire also uses drycleaning services more often, while Thelma buys laundry detergents more often. Claire is a frequent visitor to the fashion boutiques, while Thelma buys all of her own and her family's clothing at a department store. Because commercial products play a major role in customers' enactment of their lifestyles, lifestyles can significantly explain customer behaviour.

For instance, some consumers are extremely frugal in their consumption of goods and services. "Frugality is a unidimensional consumer lifestyle trait characterized by the degree to which consumers are both restrained in acquiring and resourcefully using economic goods and services to achieve long-term goals." Empirical research shows that the frugal are less susceptible to interpersonal influence, less materialistic, less compulsive in buying, and more price and value conscious. The frugal are not found to use coupons more often than regular customers; frugality affects customer decisions about "whether to buy" and "what to buy." Beyond buying, it also affects customers as users, since the frugal are more resourceful in using products (e.g., timing showers, packing a lunch for work).[31]

Catering to different consumer lifestyles are **lifestyle retail brands** like Gap, Benetton, and Laura Ashley. Their retail proposition is augmented with a set of added values that have symbolic meaning for the lifestyles of a specific group. In shopping at these stores, the consumer is projecting these lifestyles on his or her purchases, and with each different store the expectation is different, including store atmospherics. Laura Ashley represents "genteel English country lifestyle," while the Gap represents a "classic American, casual lifestyle" and the Polo/Ralph Lauren experience is the realm of "an exclusive gentleman's club and the country house."[32]

Lifestyle retail brands
Brands sold in retail stores that are sought by customers principally for symbolic value and meaning for their lifestyles.

Even in business, clothing can signify lifestyles. A professor might wear a tweed jacket on the university campus while an investment banker is likely to wear suits, and software professionals are likely to be dressed in business casuals. Some companies like IBM and Andersen Consulting ask their employees and consultants to dress conservatively, in dark suits and white shirts, which makes them look older than their real age and, thereby, adds credence when they meet with top executives of their client organizations.

Psychographics as Attitudes, Interests, and Opinions (AIO) Profiles

The appeal of psychographics in marketing from the outset has been its quantifiability: like demographics, psychographics were derived from quantitative measures. To measure psychographics (i.e., values, self-concepts, and lifestyles), researchers present a series of statements about possible activities, interests, and opinions (AOI). Respondents indicate their agreement or disagreement with these statements (see Chapter 7 for examples).

To analyze and interpret data from measures based on AIO statements, researchers group together people with similar responses. These groups, considered to have relatively similar lifestyles, values, and self-concepts, can then be described using certain AIO profiles, called psychographic profiles. These profiles are excellent indicators of how people are thinking and where they are going with their lives.

In an attempt to profile online shoppers, Ernst & Young charted their psychographic profile. They found that leisure time activities of the study's online buyers were not much different from the average household. Some differences were visible in movie attendance (37 percent of online shoppers go to movies frequently or regularly, compared to 26 percent of the average household), recreational travel (42 percent versus 32 percent), performing arts attendance (25 percent versus 17 percent), and family-time pursuits (57 percent versus 50 percent). A smaller percentage of online shoppers watch television (61 percent) compared to 65 percent of average households. Online shoppers are, however, similar to all households in volunteer activities, gardening, gourmet cooking, photography, and attending sporting events.[33]

Environics: Canadians' Social Values

Michael Adams, president of Environics Research Group and author of *Better Happy than Rich: Canadians, Money and the Meaning of Life,* uses polling methods to measure Canadians' social values, including attitudes about money. The survey asks respondents questions about their views of the world, their personal goals, wishes, hopes, dreams, and expectations. Adams says Canadian society is no longer homogeneous, but can be divided into 12 "tribes." Table 5.5 gives a profile of these "tribes." You can try the survey yourself on the Internet to see in which "tribe" you belong at **http://3sc.environics.net/surveys/3sc/main/3sc.asp**.

TABLE 5.5 Social Values of Canadians as per the Environics Research Group Clusters

Tribe	Fundamental Motivation	Key Values	Interesting Links for Tribe
Rational Traditionalists (54% of pre-boomers)	Financial independence, security, and stability	• Religiosity • Primacy of reason • Respect for historical tradition • Respect for authority • Duty • Guilt • Deferred gratification	Anglicans On-Line http://www.anglican.org/online Military History http://peacekeeper.kosone.com/milhist.hml Scientific American http://www.sciam.com
Extroverted Traditionalists (26% of pre-boomers)	Traditional communities, institutions, and social status	• Religiosity • Family • Respect for historical tradition • Respect for institutions • Duty • Fear • Deferred gratification	Info Seniors http://www.infoseniors.com Catholic Information Centre http://www.catholic.net Canadian Almanac http://www.canadainfo.com/history.html
Cosmopolitan Modernists (20% of pre-boomers)	Traditional institutions and experience seeking	• Global world-view • Respect for education • Desire for innovation	Golfmark http://www.golfmark.com Canada WealthNet http://www.nucleus.com/wealthnet The Globe and Mail's National Issues Forum http://forum.theglobeandmail.com/forum/nif
Autonomous Rebels (25% of boomers)	Personal autonomy and self-fulfilment	• Strong belief in human rights • Scepticism toward traditional institutions • Suspicion of authority • Freedom • Individuality • Respect for education	Electronic Frontier Canada http://insight.mcmaster.ca/org/efc/efc.html Adbusters http://www.adbusters.org/ New York Times http://www.nytimes.com/ Canadian Civil Liberties Association http://www.ccla.org/
Anxious Communitarians (20% of boomers)	Traditional communities, institutions, and social status	• Family • Community • Fear • Duty • Need for respect	Conversation Canada http://www.conversation.gc.ca/ Canadian Parents Online http://http://www.canadianparents.com/ United Way of Canada http://www.uwc-cc.ca/
Connected Enthusiasts (14% of boomers)	Traditional and new communities, and experience seeking	• Family • Community • Hedonism • Immediate gratification	Culture Net http://www.culturenet.ucalgary.ca/ E! Online http://www.eonline.com/ Epicurious http://epicurious.com/
Disengaged Darwinists (41% of boomers)	Financial independence, security, and stability	• Fear • Nostalgia for the past	Alberta Report http://albertareport.com

			The Fraser Institute http://www.fraserinstitute.ca/ Financial Post http://www.canoe.ca/FP
Aimless Dependents (27% of post-boomers)	Financial independence, security, and stability	• Fear • Desire for independence	Youth Resource Network of Canada http://www.youth.gc.ca/ Douglas Coupland Official Home Page http://www.coupland.com National Hockey League Home Page http://www.nhl.com/
Thrill-Seeking Materialists (25% of post-boomers)	Traditional communities, social status, and experience seeking	• Desire for money and material possessions • Desire for recognition, respect, and admiration	Pamela Anderson Lee http://la.yahoo.com/external/webceleb/anderson/ Fashion Television http://citytv.com/citytv/fashiontv/index.html ESPN SportsZone: NBA Information http://espnet.sportszone.com/nba
New Aquarians (13% of post-boomers)	Experience-seeking and new communities	• Egalitarianism • Ecologism • Hedonism	Greenpeace Canada http://www.greenpeacecanada.org Electronic Frontier Foundation: Cyberpunks http://www.eff.org/pub/Crypto/Security Hacking_cracking_phreaking/Net_culture_and_hacking/Cyberpunk/ Pagan Federation http://www.paganfed.demon.co.uk
Autonomous Post-materialists (20% of post-boomers)	Personal autonomy and self-fulfilment	• Freedom • Respect for human rights	South Park www.comcentral.com/southpark Zine Reviews www.interlog.com/~halpen/alphabet.html Friedrich Nietzsche Society www.swan.ac.uk/german/fns/fnslink.htm Amnesty International www.amnesty.ca/
Social Hedonists (15% of post-boomers)	Experience-seeking and new communities	• Aesthetics • Hedonism • Sexual permissiveness • Immediate gratification	Tribe Magazine http://www.tribe.ca The official Jacques Villeneuve website http://www.jacques.villeneuve.com/ Snowboarding http://pb.yahoo.com/recreation/sports/snowboarding

SOURCE: Connect to your tribe. http://www.erg.environics.net/tribe.

Four of the "tribes" define the boomer generation; the first is called *Autonomous Rebels.* Well educated and with higher-than-average incomes, the Rebels are skeptical of authority and motivated by self-fulfillment and personal autonomy. In their drive for fulfillment, they are cramming their jobs, families, parents, and leisure activities into hectic lives. They refuse to trade off living for today to save for tomorrow. They take several vacations a year; they buy season tickets to team sports or the theatre; they are always willing to spend for their home or their children. They are comfortable with the changes that have occurred during their lives: the sexual revolution, women's liberation, multiculturalism, gay liberation, and the technological revolution. They have two incomes, thus lots of money, but they are time-crunched as they try to do everything. Adams describes a second boomer tribe, the *Connected Enthusiasts*, as equally likely to look for instant gratification, but even more driven to experience seeking and self-exploration.

Not all boomers share in the affluence or the level of comfort with change of the *Autonomous Rebels.* Two other tribes, the *Anxious Communitarians* and *Disengaged Darwinists*, feel that Canada is moving away from traditional values. The *Darwinists* seek financial independence, security, and stability. They feel threatened by high crime rates and uncomfortable with a high-technology society, and they believe that only the fittest will survive. Adams names self-interest as their main motivation. They have a rational, cautious approach to money; they are careful savers, although they may not earn as much as the *Autonomous Rebels*. The *Darwinists* often marry *Anxious Communitarians*, who tend to be heavy spenders.[34]

VALS™

One of the most used psychographic profiling schemes is called VALS™. Developed by SRI International, Inc., its first version groups the entire population into nine groups, based on the identities they seek and implement via marketplace behaviours. According to SRI, people pursue and acquire products and experiences that provide satisfaction and give shape, substance, and character to their identities.[35] Even though this scheme has been replaced by a new VALS system with an eight-segment classification, it is important to understand the original scheme, which was introduced in 1978. That scheme used two dimensions for its conceptual foundation:

- Maslow's hierarchy—the theory that people rise from physiological, to safety, to social belonging, to self-esteem, to self-actualization needs.
- Riesman's Social Character Theory—a person is either inner-directed or outer-directed, deriving one's code of conduct respectively from oneself or from others. Inner-directed persons are more independent minded, whereas outer-directed persons are concerned with others' opinion of them (see Figure 5.5).

FIGURE 5.5 VALS 1: Nine Lifestyle Segments

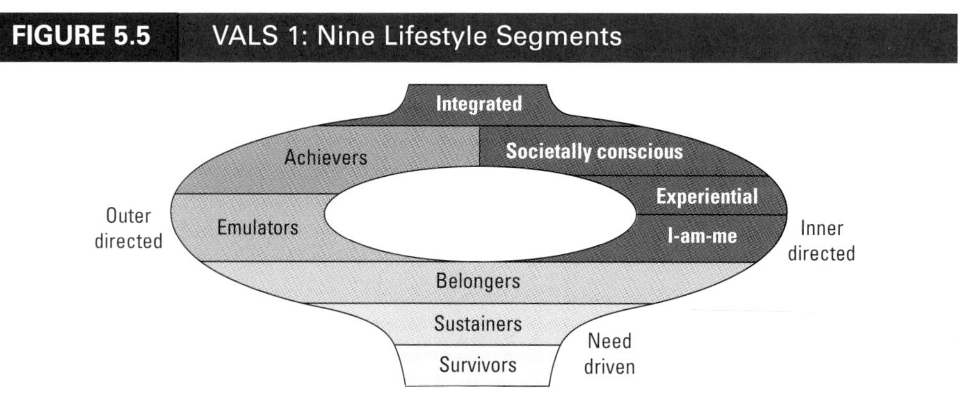

SOURCE: Wells, William, John Burnett, and Sandra Moriarty. *Advertising: Principles & Practice*, 191. Upper Saddle River, NJ. Reprinted by permission of Pearson Education, Inc.

At the bottom of the VALS hierarchy are *Survivors* and *Sustainers*, who are, respectively, the elderly poor and unemployed youth. *Belongers* is the next group, the largest of the nine groups and comprising middle-aged, middle-class, outer-directed individuals. Two other outer-directed groups are the *Emulators* and the *Achievers*. Achievers are affluent, successful professionals and businesspeople. In contrast, Emulators don't have as much money or success, but they try to emulate the lifestyles of Achievers. On the other side are three inner-directed segments, *I-am-me's*, *Experientials*, and *Societally Conscious*. I-am-me's are teenagers whose principal motto is rebellion against the established ways. Experientials are big on experiencing all the sensory and recreational experiences life has to offer—mountaineering, skiing, sports, travel, bungee-jumping, and so on. The Societally Conscious are concerned about and work for larger, societal issues, such as the environment, world peace, and racial harmony. Finally, the group at the top is the Integrateds, a small group that has gained material well-being and success in the material world and is, at the same time, working for larger issues or in jobs that give some intrinsic meaning to life rather than merely fame and wealth.

Today's VALS™

The current version of VALS groups U.S. customers into eight groups (see Figure 5.6). This grouping is based on two dimensions: self-orientation and resources.

FIGURE 5.6 Eight Lifestyles: VALS 2

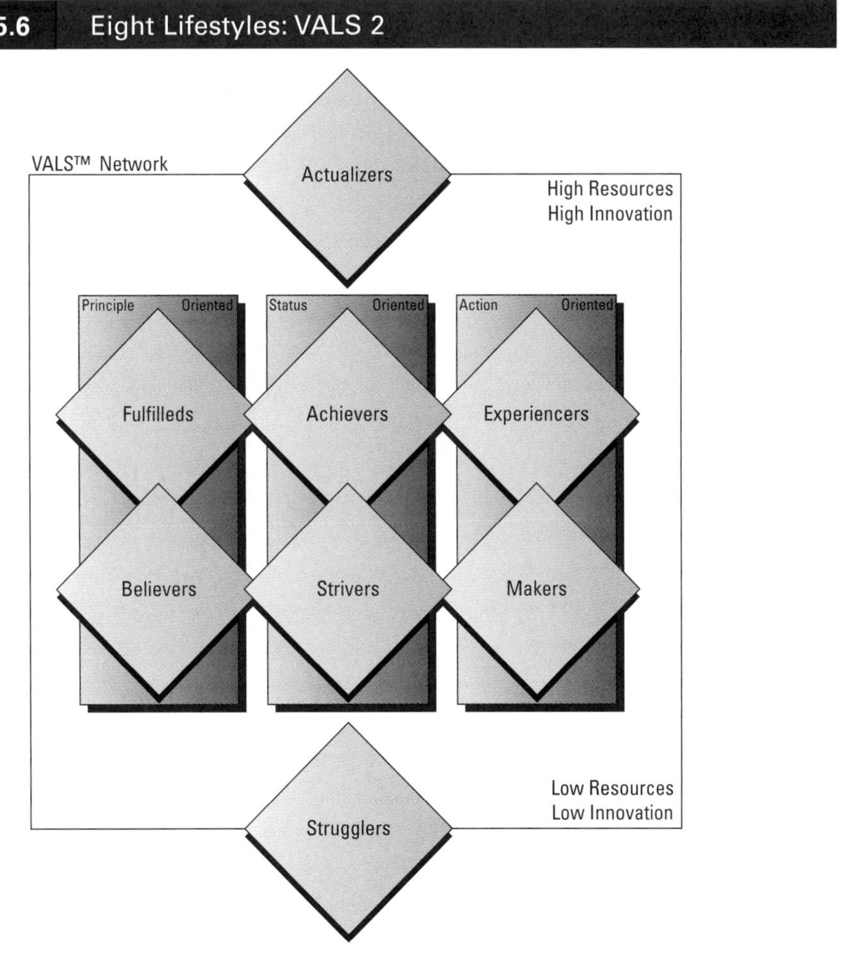

SOURCE: VALS framework. Principle, status, and action are the three dimensions of self-orientation proposed by SRI. Copyright 2001 by SRI Consulting Business Intelligence. Used with permission. All rights reserved.

Self-Orientation. According to SRI, people are motivated by one of three powerful self-orientations: principle, status, and action. Principle-oriented consumers are guided in their choices by abstract, idealized criteria, rather than by feelings, events, or desire for approval and the good opinion of others. Status-oriented consumers look for products that demonstrate the consumers' success to their peers. Action-oriented consumers are guided by a desire for social or physical activity, variety, and risk taking.

Resources. Resources refer to the full range of psychological, physical, demographic, and material means and capacities people have to draw upon. It encompasses education, income, self-confidence, health, and energy level. It is a continuum from minimal to abundant. Resources generally increase from adolescence through middle age but decrease with extreme age, depression, financial reversal (e.g., layoff), and physical or psychological impairment.

The Eight VALS™ Groups. Using the self-orientation and resources dimensions, VALS defines eight segments of adult consumers who have different attitudes and exhibit distinctive behaviour and decision-making patterns. These segments are Actualizers, Fulfilleds, Achievers, Experiencers, Believers, Strivers, Makers, and Strugglers. (Table 5.5 presents a list of questions that can be used to classify consumers into these VALS groups. You can try the survey yourself on the Internet at **http://www.sric-bi.com/vals/presurvey.shtml.**)

Actualizers are successful, sophisticated, active, take-charge people with high self-esteem and abundant resources. They are leaders in business and government and are interested in growth, innovation, and change. They seek to develop, explore, and express themselves in a variety of ways, sometimes guided by principle and sometimes by a desire to have an effect or to make a change. Image is important to them, not as evidence of status or power but as an expression of their taste, independence, and character. They possess a wide range of interests, are concerned with social issues, and show a cultivated taste for the finer things in life.

TABLE 5.5 Questionnaire to Assess VALS Type

Reply to the following statements with one of the four given caregories.

	Mostly Disagree	Somewhat Disagree	Somewhat Agree	Mostly Agree
1. I am often interested in theories.	___	___	___	___
2. I like outrageous people and things.	___	___	___	___
3. I like a lot of variety in my life.	___	___	___	___
4. I love to make things I can use every day.	___	___	___	___
5. I follow the latest trends and fashions.	___	___	___	___
6. Just as the Bible says, the world was literally created in six days.	___	___	___	___
7. I like being in charge of a group.	___	___	___	___
8. I like to learn about art, culture, and history.	___	___	___	___
9. I often crave excitement.	___	___	___	___
10. I am really interested in only a few things.	___	___	___	___

11. I would rather make something than buy it. ____ ____ ____ ____
12. I dress more fashionably than most people. ____ ____ ____ ____
13. The federal government should encourage prayer in public schools. ____ ____ ____ ____
14. I have more ability than most people. ____ ____ ____ ____
15. I consider myself an intellectual. ____ ____ ____ ____
16. I must admit that I like to show off. ____ ____ ____ ____
17. I like trying new things. ____ ____ ____ ____
18. I am very interested in how mechanical things, such as engines, work. ____ ____ ____ ____
19. I like to dress in the latest fashions. ____ ____ ____ ____
20. There is too much sex on television today. ____ ____ ____ ____
21. I like to lead others. ____ ____ ____ ____
22. I would like to spend a year or more in a foreign country. ____ ____ ____ ____
23. I like a lot of excitement in my life. ____ ____ ____ ____
24. I must admit that my interests are somewhat narrow and limited. ____ ____ ____ ____
25. I like making things of wood, metal, or other such material. ____ ____ ____ ____
26. I want to be considered fashionable. ____ ____ ____ ____
27. A woman's life is fulfilled only if she can provide a happy home for her family. ____ ____ ____ ____
28. I like the challenge of doing something I have never done before. ____ ____ ____ ____
29. I like to learn about things even if they may never be of any use to me. ____ ____ ____ ____
30. I like to make things with my hands. ____ ____ ____ ____
31. I am always looking for a thrill. ____ ____ ____ ____
32. I like doing things that are new and different. ____ ____ ____ ____
33. I like to look through hardware or automotive stores. ____ ____ ____ ____
34. I would like to understand more about how the universe works. ____ ____ ____ ____
35. I like my life to be pretty much the same from week to week. ____ ____ ____ ____

SOURCE: http://www.sric-bi.com/vals/presurvey.shtml. Used with permission of SRI Consulting Business Intelligence.

Fulfilleds are mature, satisfied, comfortable, reflective people who value order, knowledge, and responsibility. Most are well educated and in (or recently retired from) professional occupations. Content with their career, families, and station in life, their leisure activities tend to centre around the home. Fulfilleds have a moderate respect for the status quo institutions, but they are open to new ideas and social change. They tend to base their decisions on firmly held principles and, consequently, appear calm and self-assured. Fulfilleds are conservative, practical consumers, and the universal values for purchased goods or services of performance, service, and price are more important than personal values (e.g., social and emotional values).

Achievers are successful career and work-oriented people who like to feel in control of their lives. They value predictability and stability over risk. They are deeply committed to work and family. Work provides them with a sense of duty, material rewards, and prestige. Their social lives are structured around family, church, and career. Achievers live conventional lives, are politically conservative, and respect authority and the status quo. Image is important to them; they favor established, prestige products that demonstrate success to their peers.

Experiencers are young, vital, enthusiastic, impulsive, and rebellious. They seek variety and excitement, savoring the new, the offbeat, and the risky. Still in the process of formulating life values and patterns of behaviour, they quickly become enthusiastic about new possibilities but are equally quick to cool. At this stage in their lives, they are politically uncommitted, uninformed, and highly ambivalent about what they believe. Their energy finds an outlet in exercise, sports, outdoor recreation, and social activities. Experiencers are avid consumers and spend much of their income on clothing, fast food, music, movies, and video.

Believers are conservative, conventional people with commitment to family, church, community, and the nation. Living by a moral code is very important to them. As consumers, Believers are conservative and predictable, and favour American products and established brands. Their income, education, and energy are modest but sufficient to meet their needs.

Strivers seek motivation, self-definition, and approval from the world around them. They are striving to find a secure place in life. Unsure of themselves and low on economic, social, and psychological resources, Strivers are concerned about the opinions and approval of others. Money defines success for Strivers, who don't have enough of it and often feel that life has given them a raw deal. Strivers are impulsive and easily bored. Many seek to be stylish. They emulate those who own more impressive possessions, but what they wish to obtain is often beyond their reach.

Makers are practical people who have constructive skills and value self-sufficiency. They live within a traditional context of family, practical work, and physical recreation, and have little interest in what lies outside that context. Makers experience the world by working on it—building a house, raising children, fixing a car, or canning vegetables—and have enough skill, income, and energy to carry out their projects successfully. Makers are politically conservative, suspicious of new ideas, respectful of government authority and organized labour, but resentful of government intrusion on individual rights. They are unimpressed by material possessions other than those with a practical or functional purpose (such as tools, utility vehicles, and fishing equipment).

Strugglers tend to be chronically poor, ill-educated, low skilled, elderly, and concerned about their health. Preoccupied with the urgent needs of the present, they do not show a strong self-orientation. Their chief concerns are for security and safety: they are cautious consumers. They represent a very modest market for most products but they are loyal to favourite brands.

Applications of VALS™

Although SRI Consulting Business Intelligence (SRIC-BI), the company that currently runs VALS, has identified product consumption differences among the segments in each of the two VALS systems, the best use of VALS is in targeting marketing communications. Advertisers can use VALS to depict particular lifestyles the brand is attempting to target. SRIC-BI is also researching the generalizability of VALS to other cultures. One such application is for consumers in Japan (see the Window on Research).

WINDOW ON RESEARCH

The Japan VALS: A Portrait of Japan in Change

Japan VALS is the same scheme of grouping customers according to a psychographic profile, developed by SRI International specifically for understanding Japanese consumers. Japan VALS divides society into segments based on two key consumer attributes: life orientation and attitudes to social change. Life orientation is simply what interests or animates a person the most: life goals, occupational duties, or recreational interests. Japan VALS identifies four primary life orientations: *Traditional Ways, Occupations, Innovation,* and *Self-Expression.* Each orientation provides a life theme around which activities, interests, and personal goals are woven.

Cross-cutting the variety of life orientations, changing attitudes stratify society into distinct layers, like overturned bowls nested one inside another. The change-leading segments are found in the outermost layers of society, while the change-resisting segments are located at the centre. Change diffuses from one layer to the next, primarily along the channels created around different life orientations. The resulting classification identifies six groups of Japanese consumers:

- *Integrators* (4 percent of the population)—Highest on the Japan VALS measure of Innovation, these consumers are active, inquisitive, trend-leading, informed, and affluent. They travel frequently and consume a wide range of media print and broadcast, niche and foreign.
- *Self-Innovators and Self-Adapters* (7 percent and 11 percent of the population)—These consumers score high on self-expression, desire personal experience, seek excitement and daring ideas, are fashionable, and engage in social activities.
- *Ryoshiki Innovators and Ryoshiki Adapters* (6 percent and 10 percent of the population)—These groups score highest on occupations; education, career achievement, and professional knowledge are their personal focus, but home, family, and social status are their guiding concerns.
- *Tradition Innovators and Tradition Adapters* (6 percent and 10 percent of the population)—These consumers score highest on the measure of traditional ways and adhere to traditional religions and customs, prefer long-familiar home furnishings and dress, and hold conservative social opinions.
- *High Pragmatics and Low Pragmatics* (14 percent and 17 percent of the population)—These groups do not score high on any life-orientation dimension. They are not very active and not well informed, have few interests, and seem flexible or even uncommitted in their lifestyle choices.
- *Sustainers* (15 percent of the population)—These consumers score lowest on the innovation and self-expression dimensions. Lacking money, youth, and advanced education, these consumers dislike innovation and are typically oriented to sustaining the past.

SOURCE: Copyright 1996, SRI Consulting Business Intelligence. All rights reserved. Additional information available at http://www.sric-bi.com.

Likewise, to understand European customers as a unit, in the wake of unification, the advertising agency Backer Spielvogel Bates Worldwide runs a Global Scan, a program of surveys of consumers in 17 countries. It has identified five global psychographic types: *Strivers, Achievers, Pressureds, Adapters,* and *Traditionals.* It measures 250 attitudes (130 specific to one country, and 120 cross-culturally pertinent). Meanwhile, the advertising agency DMB&B did a 15-country survey and found four European groups: *Successful Idealists, Affluent Materialists, Comfortable Belongers,* and *Disaffected Survivors.*[36] The Window on Research presents an attempt at identifying lifestyle clusters in the Asian region. Thus, marketers are using VALS-based classifications and other psychographic measures to understand the customer worldwide.

WINDOW ON RESEARCH

Lifestyle Clusters in Asian Countries

Jiuan, Jung, Wirtz, and Keng review lifestyle research conducted in Japan, Malaysia, Singapore, Taiwan, and Thailand to develop Asian styles that could mirror the Eurostyles common to 15 European countries.

In Japan, the Dentsu Consumer Value Survey presented four lifestyle clusters: *Achievers, Intelligent, Group Merit,* and *Membership Dependent.* The clusters were derived from Japanese consumers' attitudes toward changes and norms in life. Some other clusters such as the *New Teenager*, the *New Singles*, the *New Jitsunen* (those in their 50s and 60s), and the *New Rich* represent the changing lifestyle in Japan.

In Malaysia, the Survey Research Group (SRG) identified seven clusters: *Yesterday People, Village Trendsetters, Chameleon, Loners, the New Breed, Yuppies,* and *Sleepwalkers.*

Seven clusters were identified in Singapore, but they are different from the seven clusters in Malaysia: *Aspirer, Pragmatist, Entrepreneur, Independent, New Age Family Oriented, Traditional Family Oriented,* and *Materialist.*

In Taiwan, the eight clusters defined by SRG are: *The Traditional Homebodies, The Confident Traditionalists, The Family-Centered Fatalists, The Lethargic, The Middle-Class Hopefuls, The Discontented Moderns, The Rebellious Young,* and *The Young Strivers.*

Finally, in Thailand, nine distinct segments were derived: *Today's Women, The Comfortable Middle Class, We Got The Blues, Mainstream Belongers, Young Achievers, Young At Heart, Trying To Make It, The Left Outs,* and *Almost.*

These clusters actually describe market segments, and the vast differences in the labels of such clusters across various countries shows that there are enormous differences in attitudes, traits, and values between these market segments. At the same time, descriptive characteristics of the clusters will also help to link these different countries together with respect to some attitudes, values, and traits. Yet, it is important for Western marketers in these countries to be cognizant of the many differences between such countries as they market products to their customers.

SOURCES: Wirtz, Jochen. "Special Session Summary: Lifestyle Research, Macro Trends and Consumer Behaviour in Asia." In *Asia Pacific Advances in Consumer Research* 3, edited by K. Hung and K. Monroe, 1–3. Duluth, MN: Association for Consumer Research, 1998; Jung, Kwon, Jochen Wirtz, Ah Keng Kau, and Soo Jiuan Tan. "The Seven Faces of Singaporeans: A Typology of Consumers Based on a Large-Scale Lifestyle Study." *Asia Pacific Journal of Management*, 16, no. 2 (1999): 229–248. Reprinted with permission from the author.

COMPULSIVE BUYING AND CONSUMING

The psychographic profile of some customers includes behaviour we call compulsive buying and consuming. These two categories of behaviour are distinct but related.

Compulsive Buying

Compulsive buying
A chronic tendency to purchase products far in excess of one's needs and resources.

We all know people who are compulsive buyers, always shopping, always buying things they may never use, or things they already have more of than they can use, and buying it even if they can barely afford it or even when they are short on money. Thus, we define **compulsive buying** as a chronic tendency to purchase products far in excess of both a person's needs and resources.

Benign compulsive buyers buy things whenever they are on sale, accumulating them for future use, but they are deliberative as to the value of the purchase, buying it only if the item represents a good bargain or a rare find; the compulsiveness resides in constantly looking for opportunistic merchandise. The less benign consumer buys without evaluation of future need and without regard for available means. Such people often accumulate huge debt and a large stock of unused products. For them, the act of buying becomes a thrill in itself.

It is this negative behaviour that detracts from individual welfare and, thus, deserves study. Researchers have defined this negative compulsive behaviour as chronic, repetitive purchasing that becomes a primary response to negative events or feelings.[37] (To try a measurement scale for compulsive buying, see the Window on Research on page 192.)

Compulsive buyers have been found to differ from other customers in a number of respects. Compared with others, compulsive buyers have lower self-esteem, are more depressed, show a greater tendency to fantasize, experience greater emotional lift at the time of purchase, experience remorse in the post-purchase phase, and accumulate a much higher debt. Moreover, research has found that compulsive buying is motivated less by a desire to possess things and more as a means of maintaining self-esteem.[38]

Compulsive Consumption

Beyond purchasing, some consumers are compulsive users of products. Whereas compulsive buying occurs for a broad range of products, compulsive consumption is limited to one or two related product categories (e.g., compulsive eating, drinking, or gambling). **Compulsive consumption** can be defined as an uncontrolled and obsessive frequent consumption of a product and in excessive amounts, likely to ultimately cause harm to the consumer or others. Here is how one consumer described her compulsive consumption behaviour:

Compulsive consumption
An uncontrolled and obsessive consumption of a product likely to ultimately cause harm to the consumer or others.

> When I was using drugs, they were the focal point of my whole life. They were all I thought about. Every two hours I would think, How can I do my drugs? . . . They were what I allocated my time to first, my money to first.[39]

In the consumer research literature, three characteristics of compulsive consumption have been reported. Compulsive consumers experience a drive or urge to engage in a behaviour, deny harmful consequences, and face repeated failure in attempts to control that behaviour.[40] A number of behaviours are examples of compulsive consumption: alcoholism, eating disorders, compulsive gambling, compulsive exercising, and compulsive sexuality.[41]

MATERIALISM

Do you want to own a lot of things, indulge in luxuries, live a very rich and comfortable life, and have lots of money, and do you consider your possessions an important aspect of your self-identify? If so, then you are what researchers call materialistic. The *Oxford English Dictionary* defines materialism as a devotion to material needs and desires, to the neglect of spiritual matters; a way of life, opinion, or tendency based entirely upon material interests. Russ Belk defines **materialism** as the importance a consumer attaches to material possessions.[42]

Materialism
The importance a consumer attaches to material possessions.

WINDOW ON RESEARCH

Are You a Compulsive Buyer?

Ronald J. Faber and Thomas C. O'Guinn have developed the following measurement scale to score customers on compulsive buying. If you want to score yourself, answer the questions, and then apply the formula given at the bottom of the table.

1. Please indicate how much you agree or disagree with each of the statements below. Place an X on the line that best indicates how you feel about each statement.

	Strongly Agree (1)	Somewhat Agree (2)	Neither Agree nor Disagree (3)	Somewhat Disagree (4)	Strongly Disagree (5)
a. If I have any money left at the end of the pay period, I just have to spend it.	___	___	___	___	___

2. Please indicate how often you have done each of the following things by placing an X on the appropriate line.

	Very Often (1)	Often (2)	Sometimes (3)	Rarely (4)	Never (5)
a. Felt others would be horrified if they knew of my spending habits.	___	___	___	___	___
b. Bought things even though I couldn't afford them.	___	___	___	___	___
c. Wrote a check when I knew I didn't have enough money in the bank to cover it.	___	___	___	___	___
d. Bought myself something in order to make myself feel better.	___	___	___	___	___
e. Felt anxious or nervous on days I didn't go shopping.	___	___	___	___	___
f. Made only the minimum payments on my credit cards.	___	___	___	___	___

To score yourself, enter your responses into the scoring equation and calculate the total:

Scoring equation = –9.69 + (*Q*1a × 0.33) + (*Q*2a × 0.34) + (*Q*2b × 0.50) + (*Q*2c × 0.47) + (*Q*2d × 0.33) + (*Q*2e × 0.38) + (*Q*2f × 0.31).

If your final score is less than or equal to 21.34, you are classified as a compulsive buyer. If you score this low, you may want to reflect on your motivations and resolve to identify strategies to overcome this psychographic aspect of your personality.

SOURCE: Adapted from Faber, Ronald J., and Thomas C. O'Guinn. "A Clinical Screener for Compulsive Buying." *Journal of Consumer Research* 19 (December 1992): 459–69. http://www.sltrib.com/98/feb/020298/utah_lif/20581.asp. Reprinted with permission of the authors.

Marsha L. Richins and Scott Dawson studied this consumer psychographic. Based on a review of the literature, they identified three dimensions of materialism as follows:

1. *Acquisition centrality*—The tendency to place material possessions and their acquisitions at the centre of one's life.
2. *Acquisition as the pursuit of happiness*—All consumers pursue happiness. However, some pursue it through other things, such as personal accomplishment; in contrast, materialists pursue happiness through the acquisition of possessions.
3. *Possession-defined success*—The tendency to judge one's own and others' success by material possessions.

Based on extensive research, Richins and Dawson designed a scale to measure these three dimensions of materialism (see Table 5.6).

TABLE 5.6 A Scale to Measure Materialism

Success Subscale

I admire people who own expensive homes, cars, and clothes.

Some of the most important achievements in life include acquiring material possessions.

I don't place much emphasis on the number of material objects that people own as a sign of success.

The things I own say a lot about how well I'm doing in life.

I like to own things that impress people.

I don't pay much attention to the material objects other people own.

Centrality Subscale

I usually buy only the things I need.

I try to keep my life simple as far as possessions are concerned.

The things I own aren't all that important to me.

I enjoy spending money on things that aren't practical.

Buying things gives me a lot of pleasure.

I like a lot of luxury in my life.

I put less emphasis on material things than most people do.

Happiness Subscale

I have all the things I really need to enjoy life.

My life would be better if I owned certain things I don't have.

I wouldn't be any happier if I owned nicer things.

I'd be happier if I could afford to buy more things.

It sometimes bothers me quite a bit that I can't afford to buy all the things I'd like.

SOURCE: Richins, Marsha L., and Scott Dawson. "A Consumer Values Orientation and Its Measurement: Scale Development and Validation." *Journal of Consumer Research*, 19, no. 3 (December 1992): 303–17. Reprinted with permission of the University of Chicago Press.

They also suggested characteristics of materialistic persons. First, materialists value acquisition of possessions more than they value other life goals and more than relationships with others. Second, materialistic people are self-centred and less likely to be sharing and giving. Furthermore, materialists lead a life of material complexity: reliance on technology,

Voluntary simplicity
A tendency to simplify life and adopt economic behaviours of low consumption and ecological responsibility.

positive attitude toward growth, and a lack of concern for nature. **Voluntary simplicity**, a tendency to simplify life and to adopt economic behaviours of low consumption and ecological responsibility, will be contrary to the spirit of materialism. Materialists tend to be less satisfied with life than others, for the lust for goods is insatiable; it always leaves materialists wanting more.

Using their scale of materialism, Richins and Dawson divided consumers into high and low materialists. They had these respondents choose and rank-order the four most important values out of a standard list of nine, and also indicate how much they would be willing to spend on categories such as buying things, giving to nonprofit organizations, and so forth. As expected, materialists tended to value financial security much more than non–materialists, and to place less value on warm relationships with others and a sense of accomplishment. Materialists were also likely to spend more on buying things than non-materialists but less on giving to charity and lending friends money.[43]

We have already referred to two metaphors related to consumption when we looked at the topics of emotions and self-concept; namely, *consuming as experience* and *consuming as integration*. Douglas B. Holt develops a typology of consumption practices with two other metaphors—namely, *consuming as classification* and *consuming as play*—and then conceptualizes materialism as a consumption style. When consumers use meanings associated with a consumption object (classifying through objects), or their interactions with the consumption object (classifying through actions) as means to classify themselves against relevant others, the *consuming as classification* metaphor is in use. With reference to spectators of a baseball game as consumers who are consuming the experience of the baseball game, classifying through objects would imply the use of souvenirs, photos, and insignia clothing to classify spectators into groups; classifying through actions would imply participating in conventions, predicting, mentoring, and expressing tastes with fellow spectators. *Consuming as play* involves using consumption objects to interact with fellow consumers. Spectators at a baseball game would commune as they shared mutually felt experiences with one another, and would socialize as they made use of experiential practices to entertain each other.

The author has conceptualized materialism as a "consumption style that emphasizes integrating practices over experiential practices (since integrating links possessions to the individual) and classifying through objects rather than classifying through actions (because objects are perceived as value laden) and de-emphasizes playing practices (because playing focuses on people rather than objects)." Thus, materialism is a distinctive consumption style in which "the focus is on consumption objects rather than experiences or other people."[44]

LO 6 THE MOTIVATIONAL PROCESSES AND THE THREE CUSTOMER ROLES

Needs, emotions, and psychographics are general characteristics of customers, applicable to all three roles (see Table 5.7). Consider needs first. For users, needs drive product usage. For example, locks and alarm systems are used for security needs, and flowers are sent as gifts for emotional value. Many of these same needs also motivate customers as payers. Payers often feel anxious about being cheated (which relate both to one's security and esteem needs). Donors often donate to worthy causes for self-esteem. Payers for gifts seek to satisfy social needs as well as gaining esteem; for example, the price of the gift might be viewed as reflecting on the value or worth of the gift giver. Donors to charity organizations satisfy their need for belonging, and feel self-actualized as the cause of charity is furthered. Finally, as buyers, customers are concerned with their personal safety in shopping areas, which is why buyers shun high-crime areas. Also, many buyers seek social interaction with salespersons or service-provider employees. They expect to be respected by salespersons and seek to maintain or bolster their self-esteem by interacting with polite and courteous service employees. For business customers in their buying roles, patronizing socially responsible vendors satisfies their self-actualizing needs.

TABLE 5.7 The Motivational Processes and the Three Customer Roles

	User	Payer	Buyer
Needs	• One or more needs constitute the primary purpose of product usage	• Fear of being ripped off (security, esteem) • Donors to worthy causes (esteem) • Payers for gifts (esteem, social needs)	• Personal safety in shopping areas • Seek social interaction with salespersons and service providers • Need to protect and look to enhancing self-esteem in marketplace experiences
Emotions	• Emotional value from products	• Emergency expenses and involuntary expenses cause negative emotions • Debt causes grief to many payers • Spending on self and for loved ones causes positive emotions	• Shopping activity is sometimes enjoyable, and, at other times, boring • Finding a deal gives a thrill
Psychographics	• Users seek and use many products to live their lifestyles, to fit in with their psychographics	• Being a spendthrift or a big spender, being a credit card user, accumulating debt or being eager to stay debt-free are psychographics	• Comparison shopper, shop-'til-you-drop shopper, and late-night shopper types

Emotions also surround and suffuse all three roles. Illustratively, talking to a parent or a close friend long-distance on the phone is joyful; attending a church mass is spiritually uplifting; wearing a diamond necklace for the first time is ecstatic; flying in an airplane is, for some, fearful. For a business traveller, flying first class or using a corporate jet is an emotional experience. As payers, customers experience negative emotions when faced with some emergency expenses (e.g., a sudden breakdown of the car's transmission) or involuntary spending (e.g., a heavy fine for speeding or a steep increase in tuition fee). Likewise, mounting debt causes grief to many payers. On the flip side, positive and pleasant emotions are experienced by payers for spending money on self and on loved ones. Finally, in their buyer roles, customers sometimes enjoy shopping while at other times they find it boring. Many encounters with sales employees are emotionally rewarding. And, buyers get a thrill in finding a deal.

Psychographics, the third facet of customer motivations, applies to all three customer roles as well. Customers use many products to put together a lifestyle, to weave a psychographic profile, so to speak. Many product categories (e.g., mountain bikes, golf equipment, nature trips, tattoo parlors) are targeted to users with specific lifestyles, and many brands in mature product categories are differentiated by the lifestyles and psychographics of their purported users (e.g., Tilley Endurables for upscale, adventurous travellers and Armani for upscale celebrities). For the payer, relevant elements of psychographics are individual traits such as being a spendthrift or a big spender, being or not being a credit-card user, accumulating a debt or being eager to stay debt-free. Finally, for the buyer, traits such as being a comparison shopper or an impulse buyer or being a compulsive shopper (i.e., shop 'til you drop), late-night shopper, and so on, are aspects of the buyer's psychographics. Buyers in business markets might have the self-concept of being very successful negotiators. Similarly, the shopper classification mentioned in Chapter 1 (i.e., personal shopper, convenience shopper) are also elements of psychographics for buyers.

Summary

LO 1, 2, 3 This chapter dealt with customer motivations—why customers buy, pay for, and use specific products. We organized this topic into three sections, one each on needs, emotions, and psychographics. Needs are felt deprivations of desired states. We discussed some of the prominent classifications of needs by scholars. Maslow's hierarchy of needs classification is perhaps the most well known of these, but we also outlined Murray's social needs system and Dichter's list of subconscious needs (or motives). Finally, we discussed some needs classifications adapted by marketing scholars such as Sheth and Holbrook, with a synthesis by Hanna.

LO 4 Human emotions also play a significant role in motivating human behaviour. We explained Plutchik's emotional classification system and discussed the concept of hedonic consumption and the related phenomenon of product-use involvement. Hedonic consumption offers customers intense emotional satisfaction and makes them highly involved in product use. This involvement turns into enthusiasm and accounts for heightened participation by customers in marketplace activities related to those products (e.g., Harley Owners Group).

LO 5, 6 Psychographics, the third facet of customer motivation, describes customers' profile of needs, emotions, and resulting behaviours, and as such explains much of customer behaviour. Psychographics includes self-concept, personal values (what aspects of life are important to us), and lifestyles (how we spend time and money, and what activities we participate in). We discussed ways of measuring lifestyles or ways of graphing the psychological makeup of the customer (hence, the name psychographics). Finally, we discussed one particular classification of lifestyles (called the VALS system) for both North America and Japan. In conclusion, we reviewed all the concepts covered in the chapter and illustrated their applicability to each of the three roles of the customer.

KEY TERMS

Actual Self 178
Approach Motivation 162
Arousal-Seeking Motive 168
Attribution Motivation 169
Attributions 169
Avoidance Motivation 162
Compulsive Buying 190
Compulsive Consumption 191
Deep Involvement 175
Drive 160
Emotions 170
Enduring Involvement 176
External Attributions 169
Goal-Object 160
Hedonic Consumption 175
Ideal Self 178
Internal Attributions 169
Involvement 176
Laddering 178
Level of Adaptation 167
Lifestyle Retail Brands 181
Lifestyles 180
Market Mavens 168
Maslow's Hierarchy of Needs 163

Materialism 191
Means-End Chains 178
Moods 173
Motivation 160
Need for Cognition 168
Optimal Level of Stimulation 167
Primary Emotions 172
Psychographics 176
Purposive Behaviour 160
Schachter's Two-Factory Theory 171
Self-Concept 178
Situational Involvement 176
Tolerance for Ambiguity 168
Values 177
Voluntary Simplicity 194

DISCUSSION QUESTIONS AND EXERCISES

1. Compare and contrast terminal and instrumental values. Give five examples of each of these two types of consumer values, and, for each one, provide an example of a company that stresses the achievement of that value in its advertising messages.
2. What is attribution theory? Why is it so important to consumer researchers? How would you use this theory if you were a marketing manager for:
   a. A weight-reduction exercise and diet plan
   b. A car dealership's car service division
3. Do you anticipate any major changes in your lifestyle five years from now? If so, what are these likely to be, and in which VALS 2 segment are you likely to belong five years from now? Explain your response.
4. Construct a hypothetical means-end chain model for the purchase of an engagement ring. How might a jeweller use this approach to develop a promotional strategy?
5. Assume that you are the director of marketing for a major credit-card company. You are interested in sending more targeted promotions to your customers and have been able to analyze your best customers in more depth. On the surface, it appears that a comparison of customer groups reveals a number of similarities in terms of several demographic variables, such as age, gender, and income (e.g., a 40-year-old male plumber and a 40-year-old male lawyer, each making $80,000 per year). However, upon more careful analysis, you find that their spending patterns and choice of goods and services vary greatly. Upon consulting your consumer research staff, you realize that this is due to psychographical differences. What might some of these differences be for the lawyer and the plumber segments, and why is understanding these differences important for you?

NOTES

1 Tara Parker-Pope, "Fear of Disease Has Consumers Resorting to Germ Warfare," *The Wall Street Journal*, February 7, 1997, A1, A4.

2 John W. Atkinson, *An Introduction to Motivation* (New York: D. Van Nostrand Company, 1964); Edward J. Murray, *Motivation and Emotion* (Englewood Cliffs, NJ: Prentice Hall, 1964).

3 Abraham H. Maslow, "A Theory of Human Motivation," *Psychological Review* 50 (July 1943): 370–96; Abraham H. Maslow, *Motivation and Personality* (New York: Harper & Row, 1970).

4 Jagdish N. Sheth, Bruce I. Newman, and Barbara L. Gross, *Consumption Values and Market Choices: Theory and Application* (Cincinnati: South-Western Publishing Co., 1991), 16–79.

5 Janice Hanna, "A Typology of Consumer Needs," *Research in Marketing* 3, ed. Jagdish N. Sheth, (Greenwich, Conn.: JAI Press, 1980), 83–104.

6 James Olds and Peter M. Milner, "Positive Reinforcement Produced by Electric Stimulation of Septal Area and Other Regions of Rat Brains," *Journal of Comparative and Physiological Psychology* 47 (1954): 419–27.

7 Lyle E. Bourne and Bruce R. Ekstrand, *Psychology: Its Principles and Meanings* (New York, NY: Holt, Rinehart, and Winston, 1979), 255–57.

8 P. S. Raju, "Optimum Stimulation Level: Its Relationship to Personality, Demographics, and Exploratory Behaviour," *Journal of Consumer Research* 7 (December 1980): 272–82; Jan-Benedict, E. M. Steenkamp, and Hans Baumgartner, "The Role of Optimum Stimulation Level in Exploratory Consumer Behaviour," *Journal of Consumer Research* 19 (December 1992): 434–48.

9 Maslow, *Ibid.* Meera P. Venkatraman and Deborah J. MacInnis, "The Epistemic and Sensory Exploratory Behaviours of Hedonic and Cognitive Consumers," *Advances in Consumer Research* 12, eds. Elizabeth C. Hirschman and Morris B. Holbrook, 102–7 (Provo, Utah: Association for Consumer Research 1985).

10 Maslow, *Ibid.*

11 Lawrence F. Feick and Linda L. Price, "The Market Maven: A Diffuser of Marketplace Information," *Journal of Marketing* 51, no. 1 (January 1987): 83 97.

12 Wayne Weiten, *Psychology: Themes and Variations* (Belmont, Calif.: Wadsworth, 1989), 596.

13 Harold H. Kelley, "Attribution Theory in Social Psychology," *Nebraska Symposium on Motivation* 15 (1967): 191–241; Harold H. Kelley, "The Process of Causal Attribution," *American Psychologist* 28 (1973): 107–28.

14 Janice Hanna, *Ibid.*

15 P. T. Young, *Motivation and Emotion* (New York: John Wiley and Sons, 1961); Edward J. Murray, *Motivation and Emotion* (Englewood Cliffs, NJ: Prentice Hall, 1964).

16 George Mandler, *Mind and Body* (New York: Norton, 1984); Carroll E. Izard, *Human Emotions* (New York: Platinum, 1977).

17 Nancy Stephens and Kevin P. Gwinner, "Why Don't Some People Complain? A Cognitive-Emotive Process Model of Consumer Complaint Behaviour," *Journal of the Academy of Marketing Science* 26, no. 3 (1998): 172–89.

18 Wayne Weiten, *Psychology: Themes and Variations* (Belmont, Calif.: Wadsworth, 1989), 374–77.

19 Rajeev Batra and Douglas M. Stayman, "The Role of Mood in Advertising Effectiveness," *Journal of Consumer Research* 17, no. 2 (September 1990): 203–14.

20 Angela Y. Lee and Brian Sternthal, "The Effects of Positive Mood on Memory," *Journal of Consumer Research* 26 (September 1999): 115–12.

21 Michael J. Barone, Paul W. Miniard, and Jean B. Romeo, "The Influence of Positive Mood on Brand Extension Evaluations," *Journal of Consumer Research* 26 (March 2000): 386–400.

21a Marie-Odile Richard, "Modeling The Impact of Internet Atmospherics on Surfer Behavior," *Journal of Business Research 58*, no. 12 (December 2005): 1632-42.

22 Morris Holbrook and Elizabeth Hirschman, "The Experiential Aspects of Consumption: Consumer Fantasies, Feelings, and Fun," *Journal of Consumer Research* 9 (September 1982): 132–40; Elizabeth Hirschman and Morris Holbrook, "Hedonic Consumption: Emerging Concepts, Methods, and Propositions," *Journal of Marketing* 46 (Summer 1982): 92–101.

23 Becky Ebenkamp, "The Ugly American URL? (European Teens Not Interested in Generic Web-Marketing)," *Brandweek* 41, no. 36 (September 18, 2000).

24 John H. Antil, "Conceptualization and Operationalization of Involvement," in *Advances in Consumer Research* 11, ed. T. C. Kinear, 203–9 (Provo, Utah: Association for Consumer Research 1984).

25 Milton Rokeach, *The Nature of Human Values* (New York: Free Press, 1973); David E. Vinson, Jerome E. Scott, and Lawrence Lamont, "The Role of Personal Values in Marketing and Consumer Behaviour," *Journal of Marketing* 41 (April 1977): 44–50.

26 Lynn R. Kahle, Sharon E. Beatty, and Pamela Homer, "Alternative Measurement Approaches to Consumer Values: The List of Values (LOV) and Values and Life Style (VALS)," *Journal of Consumer Research* 13 (December 1986): 405–09; Sharon Beatty, Lynn R. Kahle, Pamela Homer,

and Shekhar Misra, "Alternative Measurement Approaches to Consumer Values: The List of Values and the Rokeach Value Survey," *Psychology & Marketing* 2 (Fall 1985): 181–200.

27 *Ibid.*

28 Thomas J. Reynolds and Jonathan Gutman, "Laddering Theory, Method, Analysis, and Interpretation," *Journal of Advertising Research* 28 (January–February 1988): 11–31.

29 Robert A. Snyder and Ronald R. Williams, "Self-Theory: An Integrative Theory of Work Motivation," *Journal of Occupational Psychology* 55 (1982): 257–67.

30 M. Joseph Sirgy, "Self-Concept in Consumer Behaviour: A Critical Review," *Journal of Consumer Research* (December 1982): 287–300; M. Joseph Sirgy, "Using Self-Congruity and Ideal Congruity to Predict Purchase Motivation," *Journal of Business Research* 13 (June 1985): 195–206.

31 John Lastovicka, Lance A. Bettencourt, Renee Shaw Hughner, and Ronald J. Kuntze, "The Lifestyle of Tight and Frugal: Theory and Measurement," *Journal of Consumer Research* 26 (June 1999): 85–98.

32 Deborah Helman and Leslie De Chernatony, "Exploring the Development of Lifestyle Retail Brands," *The Service Industries Journal* 19 (April 1999): 49–68.

33 The Second Annual Ernst & Young Internet Shopping Study, 1999, 9.

34 http://erg.environics.net/news/default.asp?aID=489.

35 VALS description on the Internet, at http://www.sric-bi.com.

36 Rebecca Piirto, "Global Psychographics," *American Demographics* 12, no. 12 (December 1990): 8.

37 Thomas C. O'Guinn and Ronald J. Faber, "Compulsive Buying: A Phenomenological Exploration," *Journal of Consumer Research* 16 (September 1989): 147–57.

38 *Ibid.*

39 Elizabeth C. Hirschman, "The Consciousness of Addiction: Toward a General Theory of Compulsive Consumption," *Journal of Consumer Research* 19 (September 1992): 155–79.

40 Faber and O'Guinn; also Dennis W. Rook, "The Buying Impulse," *Journal of Consumer Research* (September, 14, 1987): 189–99.

41 Hirschman, *Ibid.*

42 Russell W. Belk, "Materialism: Trait Aspects of Living in the Material World," *Journal of Consumer Research* 12 (December 1985): 265–80.

43 Marsha L. Richins and Scott Dawson, "A Consumer Values Orientation and Its Measurement: Scale Development and Validation," *Journal of Consumer Research* 19, no. 3 (December 1992): 385.

44 Douglas B. Holt, "How Consumers Consume: A Typology of Consumption Practices," *Journal of Consumer Research* 22 (June 1995): 1–16.

CHAPTER 

Customer Attitudes: Cognitive and Affective

LEARNING OBJECTIVES

After reading this chapter you should be able to:

LO 1 Define attitudes and describe their characteristics.

LO 2 Describe the three-component model of attitudes.

LO 3 Explain attitude molding and the three routes (cognitive, affective, conative).

LO 4 Describe the different psychological processes underlying attitude change.

LO 5 Describe the Rosenberg and Fishbein models of attitudes.

LO 6 Explain the functional theory of attitudes.

Managing Attitudes

As with any e-transformation, technology is not the only stumbling block; user attitudes create significant problems as well. Air Canada faced a challenge in getting computer novices to accept e-learning. "What's a mouse?" was a question that arose more than once. In Montreal, Air Canada held open houses, serving coffee and doughnuts in the same area where the computers were set up so that users could become more comfortable with the technology. The younger employees who frequently accessed the Net at home and were more comfortable with computers helped their older colleagues through this technology-adoption process.

Bell Canada Enterprises (BCE), an employer of more than 65,000 people across Canada, faced major training challenges when it shifted its e-learning training from 20 percent to 80 percent online in 2001. BCE had to determine how to dramatically reduce training costs while providing a sufficient amount of training to achieve productivity gains. Shifting training to online delivery was a way of achieving this goal. BCE then launched its "Click & Learn" program. Courses were offered at no charge to employees and with very low charge-back rates to the various departments in which they worked. Besides being supported by executive sponsorships, BCE's "Click & Learn" program was also heavily marketed and branded in-house to encourage adoption within the company.[1]

These examples show how managing user attitudes is extremely important for the success of technology in business. Likewise, managing customer attitudes is important in every sphere of business. When the sweatshop crusade began against several retailers like Nordstrom, Gap, Wal-Mart, and The Bay, these organizations had to take concrete steps so that they could make customer attitudes toward their products favourable again.

Marketers are interested in knowing customer attitudes about their products and other elements of the marketing mix, since such knowledge helps predict customer behaviour. This chapter introduces the current state of marketing knowledge about attitudes. (See Figure 6.1 for our framework.) First, we define and discuss attitude as a global concept. Next, we present a three-component view of attitude and discuss three hierarchies in which the three components are organized. Following this, we discuss various strategies for influencing customer attitudes, using current knowledge of how the three components are interrelated. This is followed by an explanation of the underlying psychological processes and the various theories that capture these processes. Next, we discuss a class of models (called multiattribute models) that account for how customers might combine several beliefs about something into a global attitude. In one of these models, we also discuss how global attitude combines with social pressures to produce customer action. Next, we discuss the functional theory of attitude. Knowing what functions an attitude serves will help us understand the deeper motivation for customer attitudes. Finally, we discuss a special application of attitudes to marketing; namely, how to use knowledge of customer attitudes in order to plan and promote social change. In the concluding section, we outline the relevance of various topics covered in this chapter to each of the three customer roles.

FIGURE 6.1 Conceptual Framework

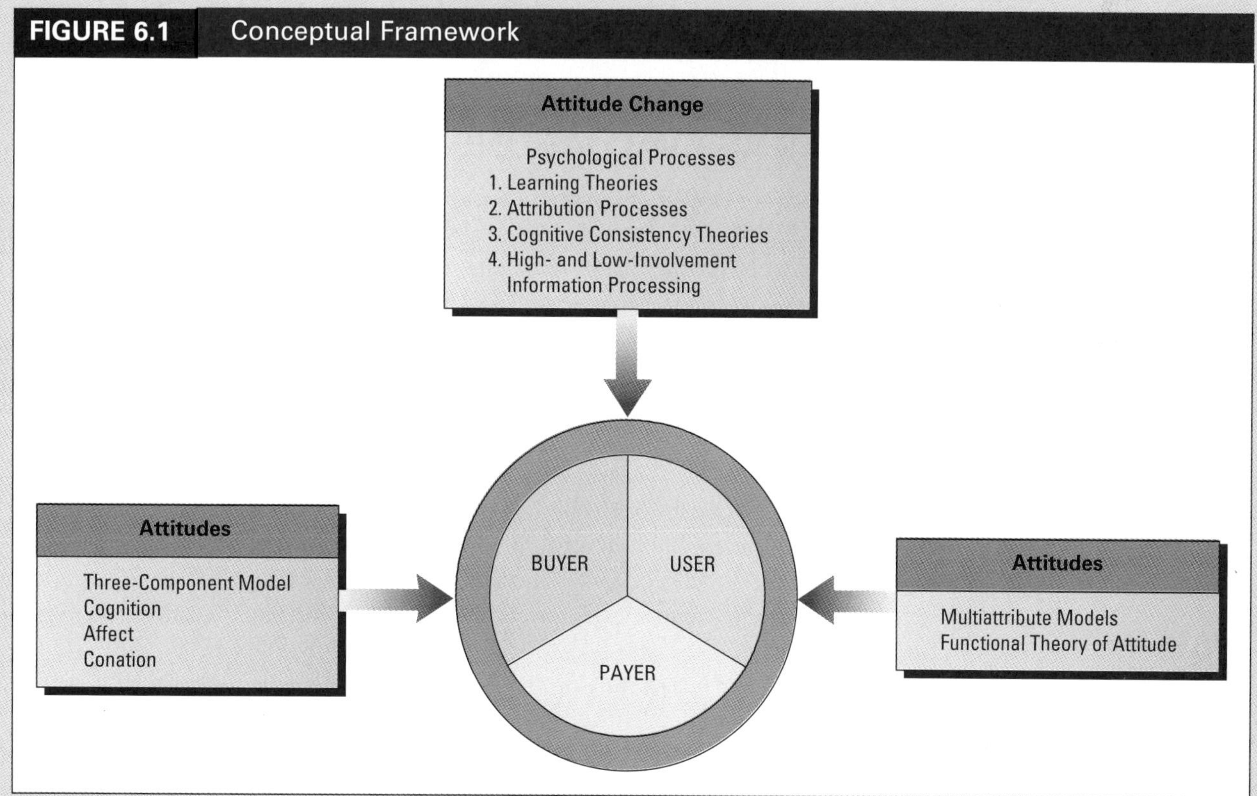

LO 1 ATTITUDE: DEFINITION AND CHARACTERISTICS

Attitude
A learned predisposition to respond to an object or class of objects in a consistently favourable or unfavourable way.

To fully understand the significance of attitudes, let us first review a classic definition of attitudes, offered by Gordon Allport: "**Attitudes** are learned predispositions to respond to an object or class of objects in a consistently favourable or unfavourable way."[2]

This definition has several implications:

- Attitudes are learned. That is, they get formed on the basis of some experience with or information about the object.
- Attitudes are predispositions. As such, they reside in the mind.
- Attitudes cause consistent response. They precede and produce behaviour.

Therefore, attitudes can be used to predict behaviour. For example, if you show a favourable attitude toward a new product concept, then marketers predict that when the new product is made available, you are likely to buy it.

Alternatively, behaviour can be used to infer the underlying attitudes. For example, if you buy a ticket for a fine-arts show, marketers infer that you have a favourable attitude toward the fine arts; a fundraising letter is then sent to you in the hope that your attitude (inferred to be favourable) toward the fine arts implies support for the arts category in general. Thus, your purchase of the ticket has been used to infer your underlying attitudes toward the arts in general.

ATTITUDES AS EVALUATIONS

Attitudes, then, are our evaluations of objects, people, places, brands, products, organizations, etc. People evaluate these in terms of their goodness, likability, or desirability. As such, it is easy to measure attitudes by getting customers to rate statements such as the following:

Please check how you feel about Olestra, [a fat substitute used by Procter & Gamble as a cooking medium for snack products]:

I dislike Olestra very much. ☐ ☐ ☐ ☐ ☐ I like Olestra very much.

Toward Olestra, I feel unfavourably. ☐ ☐ ☐ ☐ ☐ Toward Olestra, I feel favourably.

My opinion about Olestra is:

Negative ☐ ☐ ☐ ☐ ☐ Positive

Attitudes are held by customers both in household and business markets. In household markets, many customers hold an attitude toward salespersons in general (for example, "Salespeople are basically all hucksters"), and a business customer might hold an unfavourable attitude toward offshore companies or toward vendors as a group (e.g., "Vendors are, in general, opportunistic").

With e-commerce burgeoning on the Web, the customer's attitude toward a website is an important consideration. Attitude toward a site is "the Web surfer's predisposition to respond favourably or unfavourably to Web content in natural exposure situations." Chen and Wells developed a six-item scale to measure consumers' attitudes toward a particular site (Table 6.1). They also determined the factors leading to a favourable attitude toward the site, and found that Entertainment (fun, exciting, cool, imaginative, entertaining, flashy), Informativeness (informative, intelligent, knowledgeable, resourceful, useful, helpful) and Organization (not messy, not cumbersome, not confusing, not irritating) are most important.[3]

TABLE 6.1 Measures for Attitude Towards the Website

After you have visited a given website, the following statements measure your general favourability toward the website you just visited. Circle the number that best indicates your level of agreement or disagreement with each statement.

	Definitely disagree			Definitely agree	
The website makes it easy for me to build a relationship with this company.	1	2	3	4	5
I would like to visit this website again in the future.	1	2	3	4	5
I am satisfied with the service provided by this website.	1	2	3	4	5
I feel comfortable in surfing this website.	1	2	3	4	5
I feel surfing this website is a good way for me to spend my time.	1	2	3	4	5
	One of the worst			One of the best	
Compared with other websites, I would rate this one as	1	2	3	4	5

SOURCE: Chen, Qimei, and William D. Wells. "Attitude towards the Site." *Journal of Advertising Research* (September–October 1999): 27–38.

In Britain, the independent home and garden products chain Robert Dyas is defining new ways of using its floor space to augment the customer's Internet experience. It has created a showroom in the dead space of the store's basement, where customers can experience the products. Customers then take the specifications home to check if the product will fit in the space for which it is intended. If they are satisfied, they can purchase the product from the store's website and the product is delivered to their home in 24 hours. Thus, the store has taken the risk out of the Internet purchase and, at the same time, provided the customer with the convenience of electronic shopping. The physical environment also helps create brand presence. This is, therefore, an example of using the physical and virtual environment to create a favourable attitude about the brand in the mind of the customer.

Another example of managing different customer attitudes towards a brand can be seen at John Lewis department stores, also in the U.K. Adjacent to the women's dressing rooms, a "boyfriend area" has been introduced, where partners can sit down and listen to CDs, read newspapers, and have coffee. Thus, the store is not only making sure that the actual customer has a fantastic retail experience, but is also ensuring that the person accompanying the customer also feels good about the shopping experience, thus creating positive attitudes for the brand for both parties.[4]

THREE-COMPONENT MODEL OF ATTITUDE

LO 2

The previous view of attitude as an overall evaluation of objects treats attitude as a single dimensional global concept. This view informs us how a person feels in overall terms about an object, but not why he or she feels that way or what underlies that specific attitude. Psychologists have identified three underlying dimensions to global attitude: *cognition, affect,*

Beliefs
Expectations that connect an object to an attribute or quality.

Brand belief
A thought about a specific property or quality associated with a brand.

and *conation* or, respectively, knowledge, feeling, and action. That is, when we hold an attitude about an object, typically it is based on some knowledge and beliefs about the object. We feel some positive or negative emotion toward it, and we want to act in a certain way toward it—either embracing it or spurning it, for example.

Cognitions or thoughts about brands or objects are also called beliefs. More specifically, **beliefs** are expectations as to what something is or is not, or what something will or will not do. Statements of belief connect an object (person, brand, store) to an attribute or benefit. Accordingly, a **brand belief** is a thought about a specific property or quality of the brand. Customers' beliefs about purchasing foreign and domestic products are captured in a construct called ethnocentrism. The Window on Research elaborates on the characteristics of ethnocentrics and draws pointers to help marketers tackle these attitudes.

WINDOW ON **RESEARCH**

Ethnocentrism

Shimp and Sharma use the ethnocentrism construct to represent the beliefs held by Americans about the appropriateness, or morality, of purchasing foreign-made products. Ethnocentric consumers believe that purchasing foreign-made goods hurts the domestic economy through loss of jobs, and, hence, it is unpatriotic to purchase foreign-made goods. They developed an instrument called the CETSCALE that measures consumers' ethnocentric tendencies toward purchasing foreign-made versus American-made products. They found that consumer ethnocentrics had significantly lower educational achievements, incomes, and social-class attainments compared to nonethnocentrics.

Netemeyer, Durvasula, and Lichtenstein measured ethnocentric tendencies using the CETSCALE with samples from the United States, France, Japan, and Germany. They found that the attitude toward home country had a significant effect on consumer ethnocentrism. People with strong positive attitudes toward their home country were likely to display more ethnocentric tendencies than others. After the fall of communism in Russia, Netemeyer, Andrews, and Durvasula conducted studies across sample regions in the U.S. and Russia. Russian consumers were found to be less ethnocentric than U.S. consumers. They were more positive about foreign-made products, and also more accepting of them than U.S. consumers. Another study of Polish customers after the removal of trade barriers in Central Europe shows that patriotism as a dimension of ethnocentrism is related to preference for Polish products. However, social status as a dimension of conspicuous consumption is related to a preference for Western products.

How is knowledge of "ethnocentrism" useful for multinational firms? It follows from this discussion that if consumers in a country are highly ethnocentric, the firm should focus on product and brand attributes, and not on the product's country of origin. Multinationals can also apply the ethnocentrism scale within a country to determine which regions are more ethnocentric and tailor marketing strategies accordingly.

SOURCES: Adapted from Shimp T. A., and S. Sharma. "Consumer Ethnocentrism: Construction and Validation of the CETSCALE." *Journal of Marketing Research* 24 (August 1987): 280–289; Netemeyer, R. G., S. Durvasula, and D. R. Lichtenstein. "A Cross-National Assessment of the Reliability and Validity of the CETSCALE." *Journal of Marketing Research* 28 (August 1991): 320–327; Durvasula, S., J. C. Andrews, and R. G. Netemeyer. "A Cross-Cultural Comparison of Ethnocentrism in the United States and Russia." *Journal of International Consumer Marketing*, 9, no. 4 (1997): 73–93; Marcoux, J. S., P. Filiatrault, and E. Cheron. "The Attitudes Underlying Preferences of Young Urban Educated Polish Consumers Towards Products Made in Western Countries." *Journal of International Consumer Marketing* 9, no. 4 (1997): 5–29.

There are three types of beliefs: *descriptive, evaluative,* and *normative.* **Descriptive beliefs** connect an object or person to a quality or outcome; for example, "This computer has a large memory," or "This airline is often late." **Evaluative beliefs** connect an object to personal likes or dislikes, preferences, and perceptions. Some statements expressing evaluative beliefs are: "This computer is very user-friendly" or "The service at this store is outrageous." **Normative beliefs** invoke moral and ethical judgments in relation to someone's acts, as in the following examples: "Cigarette companies should not advertise in a way that would appeal to youth," or "It is unfair for businesses to take advantage of innocent customers."

Affect is the feelings a person has toward an object, or the emotions that object evokes in the person. Finally, **conation** is the action a person wants to take toward the object.

Table 6.2 presents examples of each attitude component for attitudes about two services. Researchers can measure attitudes by asking respondents to rate how well each statement describes them or their beliefs.

Descriptive beliefs An association in a customer's mind that links an object or person to a quality or outcome.

Evaluative beliefs An association in a customer's mind that links an object to personal likes or dislikes, preferences, and perceptions.

Normative beliefs Beliefs that invoke moral and ethical judgments in relation to someone's acts.

Affect The feelings a person has toward an object, or the emotions that object evokes in the person.

Hierarchies in Attitude

If attitudes have three components, we need to know how, if at all, they are related. Do you think first and then act, or do you act first and think afterward? Marketers have addressed such questions by looking for an attitude hierarchy. **Attitude hierarchy** refers to the sequence in which the three components occur.

TABLE 6.2 Illustrative Measures of the Three-Component Model of Attitude

	Attitude Object	
Attitude Component	**DHL, for Shipping a Business's Small Packages**	**Shopping for Airline Tickets on the Internet**
Cognitions or Beliefs	• DHL's service is very reliable • DHL is more economical than other package-carrier services • DHL is able to customize its service to my shipping needs	• For my airline tickets, shopping on the Internet is very convenient • You can find the cheapest fares by shopping on the Internet • Internet-based travel agents do not offer you a comprehensive set of airline and flight options
Affect or Feelings	• When I ship by DHL, I feel secure • I am very happy to be using DHL for my shipping needs • I don't care if DHL goes out of business	• Shopping on the Internet is: (please circle as many as apply) Totally cool Confusing Boring A pain in the neck Enjoyable Terrible
Conations or Actions	• I use DHL for my shipping more than I use other carriers • I often recommend DHL to other business associates • I am looking for alternative carriers.	• I have used the Internet for my travel airline tickets recently • I often search the Internet for planning my travel itinerary

Conation
The action a person wants to take toward an object.

Attitude hierarchy
The sequence in which the three components of attitude (cognition, affect, and conation) occur.

Learning hierarchy
A sequence of attitude components wherein a person thinks first, feels next, and acts last.

Learning Hierarchy

The most commonly discussed hierarchy is the learning hierarchy. In the **learning hierarchy,** cognitions come first, affect next, and action last. (See Figure 6.2.) That is, you think first, feel next, and act last. The learning hierarchy assumes that brand beliefs underlie our feelings toward the brand. Brand beliefs lead to brand feelings, which then cause brand purchase and use (or avoidance).

Consider an example. Let us say that you need to decide where to go for spring break: Palm Beach, Florida; Quebec City; Cancun, Mexico; or Whistler, B.C. Suppose you were to first collect information, such as how far these places are in terms of the travel time, the cost of travel, hotel room cost, and the kinds of activities offered by each site. Then you make a judgment based on such information about the destination that will be good for you, whether you like Quebec City better or Whistler, whether the idea of going to Palm Beach excites you, or whether it is Cancun that you really feel the urge to visit. Based on these feelings, you then choose one of these four destinations. You are using the learning hierarchy, also known as the rational hierarchy. In business, you may attend a trade show and collect brochures from different vendors for some products that you intend to purchase. You could evaluate each of these vendors on several parameters and then make a rational decision as to whom you should award your contract. This is the learning hierarchy.

Emotional Hierarchy

Emotional hierarchy
A sequence of attitude components in which a person first feels an emotion toward an object, then acts on it, and then becomes knowledgeable about it.

However, if you said, "The last time I decided my spring break plans . . . well, what happened was that we were a bunch of friends watching this show on cable TV, called MTV Spring Break; it was basically a live scene from Palm Beach, where lots and lots of college students were having one big party on the beach. And we said, 'That's it. That's where we're going'"—if you said that, you were engaged in the **emotional hierarchy.**

This description of your attitude feelings, action, and thoughts toward Palm Beach illustrates a different process, the **emotional hierarchy** of attitude. Here you feel first, then act, and think last. Based on your emotions—attraction or repulsion by certain brands or persons or things—you avoid them, or you embrace, buy, and use them. Finally, through experience, you learn more about them. Thus, in this hierarchy, affect comes first, conation next, and cognition last. (See Figure 6.3.)

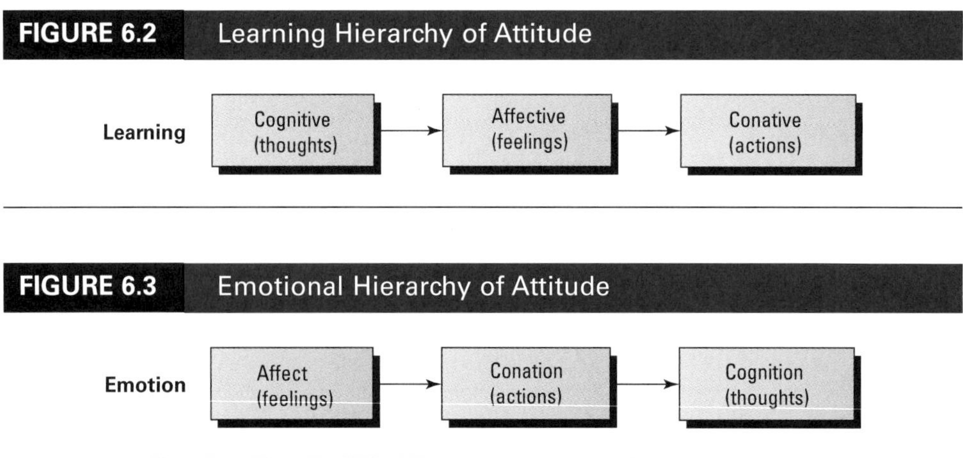

These hierarchies happen just as much for business customers. The same scenarios may be observed, for example, when a business manager chooses a site for the next national sales meeting. The manager may follow the rational route, choosing the site primarily on cost considerations, for example. Alternatively, he or she may follow an emotional route, choosing the site primarily based on the allure of the place.

Low-Involvement Hierarchy

The learning and emotional hierarchies are *high-involvement hierarchies* because the attitude object generates high involvement. As we defined *involvement* in Chapter 5, it can be viewed as the degree of importance of an object to you, the stakes you have in the object, or how much owning the object matters to you. The spring-break site or an international trip is a high-involvement object for you, and, hence, you want to have the attitude that you can feel committed, whether you reached this attitude state via the rational or the emotional hierarchy.

In contrast is the *low-involvement* mode where not much is at stake, and it would not matter much if your attitude happened to be wrong. **Low-involvement attitude hierarchy** refers to the sequence in which the three attitude components occur in a person's acquisition of attitude toward objects that are of low prominence or importance in his or her life. This model has the sequence of conation, affect, cognition, as shown in Figure 6.4.

Low-involvement attitude hierarchy A sequence of attitude components in a person's acquisition of attitude toward objects that are of low prominence or importance.

Suppose that you are in the neighbourhood bakery and you notice a new kind of bread; it has multigrains and some seeds in it, and its appearance is inviting. The bread is new, so you don't have an attitude toward it. Now, do you have to know a whole lot about it or really feel attracted to it before you buy it? Not likely. Thus, neither the rational nor the emotional hierarchy is likely to apply. Instead, what you are likely to do is just put it in your shopping basket, bring it home, take the first bite, and say that it is good and that you like it. Then you pause to feel what kind of grains it has and what flavour it has, and then maybe you even read the ingredients label and the nutrition information. Thus, in this case of a low-involvement product, action comes first (buying and using the bread), feelings next (the bread is good), and cognitions or thoughts last (noticing the ingredients). A similar example is the case of some demonstration software that you might receive in the mail. Action comes first since you use it first. Depending on whether it is of use to you, you feel good or bad about it, and then you check for various features included in the software, thus forming cognitions about the product.

Two clarifications are in order. One, involvement is not a property of the product; rather, it is the importance of it to a customer. Thus, the same product could be low-involving for some and high-involving for others. In our example, bread could indeed be a high-involvement product for some consumers. These consumers will then first read the label and try to learn as much as possible about the bread. Based on this information, they will like it or not like it, and then, based on this feeling, they will choose to buy it or not. That, of course, is the high-involvement attitude acquisition process described earlier.

FIGURE 6.4 Low-Involvement Hierarchy of Attitude

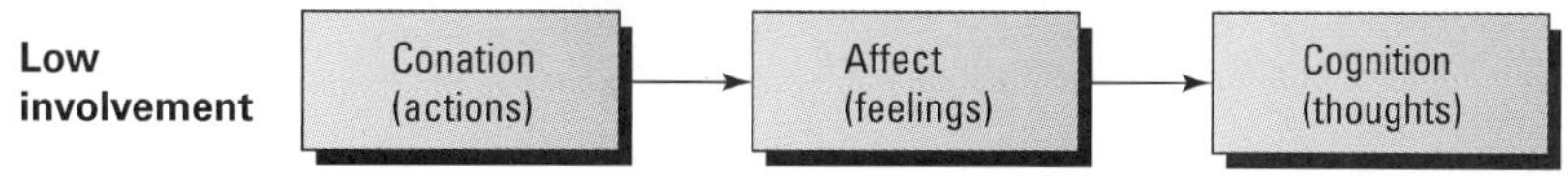

Low involvement: Conation (actions) → Affect (feelings) → Cognition (thoughts)

The second clarification is that involvement is not dichotomous (a strict choice between very high and very low). Rather, it is a matter of degree. The low-involvement hierarchy occurs at the very low-involvement end when something is utterly of no consequence to the consumer. In the middle range, the high-involvement hierarchies occur, but with less intensity of processing. The emotional hierarchy still begins with affect, but at the middle range, it is likely to begin with a mood rather than a deep emotion. And the rational hierarchy is still relevant, except that instead of the extensive cognitions of the high-involvement condition, fewer cognitions will drive the affect. (See Figure 6.5.) This is why relatively lower-involvement products are advertised by citing only one or two features.

Consistency Among the Three Components

Although the three components develop in terms of hierarchies, they imply one another. A person tries to make the three components consistent and to maintain consistency among them. Certain cognitions inevitably give rise to certain affect tendencies and then certain action tendencies, and vice versa.

Attitude valence
The favourableness and unfavourableness of attitudes, i.e., of thoughts, feelings, and actions about an object.

The consistency can be related to two factors: valence and intensity. **Attitude valence** refers to favourable and unfavourable thoughts, feelings, and actions. Thus, favourable cognitions will be associated with positive affect, and unfavourable cognitions with negative affect, regardless of the sequence in which they might have arisen initially. Likewise, favourable action tendencies will be associated with positive affect and positive cognitions. If one of them needs to be modified, then the other components will need to be modified as well. For example, suppose that you have recently tried a new kind of multigrain bread, and after several uses, you don't like its taste anymore; then you will have to modify some cognitions (e.g., the grains don't really taste as good as they first did) and conation, too (e.g., I won't buy it in the future).

FIGURE 6.5 Degrees of Involvement and Types of Attitude Hierarchy

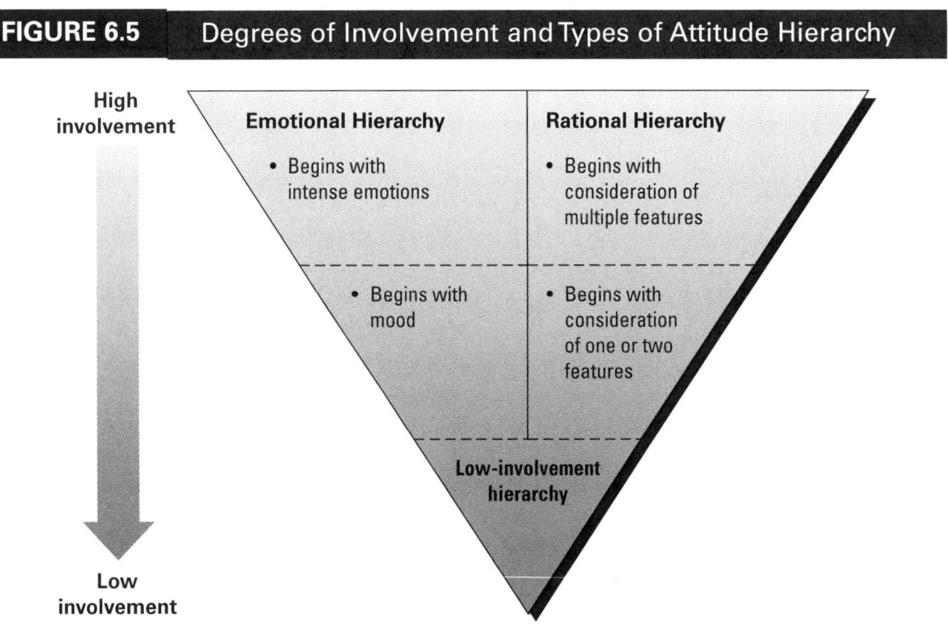

The second dimension on which the three components have to be consistent is intensity: the *strength* with which they occur. Some beliefs are strong; others are weak. Likewise, some feelings are deep; others are mild. Finally, there is strong action commitment toward some things and "take it or leave it" stance toward others. **Attitude strength** refers to the degree of commitment one feels toward a cognition or feeling or action. Just as with valence, so too with strength: the three components have to be balanced. Strong beliefs produce strong feelings and very committed action tendencies, and vice versa.

Attitude strength
The degree of commitment one feels toward a cognition, feeling, or action.

Since these three components must be mutually consistent, regardless of their initial sequence or hierarchy, they continue to mold one another. Accordingly, it is informative to depict them as mutually interdependent and mutually influential. Thus, in contrast to the previous hierarchy models, Figure 6.6 shows the arrows going in both directions among all three of the components.

MOLDING CUSTOMER ATTITUDES

LO 3

The two dimensions of consistency—valence and intensity—have implications for how marketers may help mold customer attitudes. Since the three components—cognition, affect and conation—are mutually consistent, it is possible to mold an attitude (all three components) by first molding or changing any component. By **attitude molding,** we mean both helping to form an attitude where none existed before and changing a preexisting attitude. Accordingly, there are three avenues of attitude molding: (1) via cognitive change, (2) via affective change, and (3) via behavioural change.

Attitude molding
Forming a new attitude or changing a preexisting attitude.

COGNITIVE ROUTE TO ATTITUDE MOLDING

To follow the cognitive route, the marketer provides an association about the product (e.g., Brand A has property X); if the consumer accepts that association, then a brand belief is formed. Brand belief is a unit of thought that associates a brand with a property: for example, that the Head and Shoulders brand of shampoo is really effective in eliminating dandruff, or that the Makino brand of hydraulic controls is very reliable. When a brand belief is formed, the cognitive component of attitude is formed. This component then produces compatible affective and conative components. The same process works in altering a cognition if the customer already had one; that is, if you give the customer new facts on something, he or she would likely change his or her old beliefs. Suppose you thought that a potato is fattening and has no good qualities. Now, suppose we were to tell you that it is fattening only when fried (as in potato chips or french

FIGURE 6.6 Three Attitude Components in Mutual Interdependence

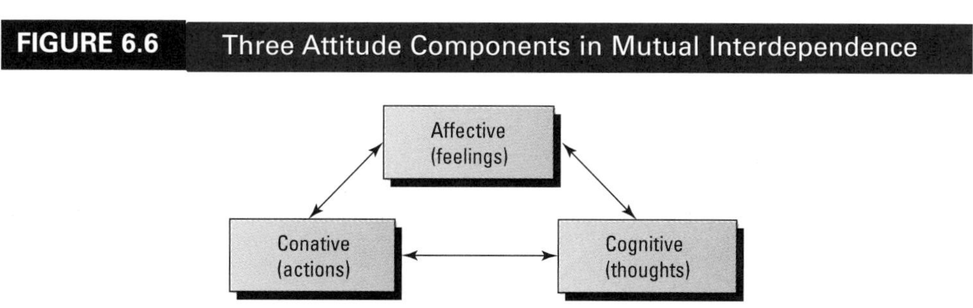

fries) and not by itself and that, further, it has much-needed carbohydrates. This is likely to change your prior beliefs about potatoes (cognitive attitude change). As commerce grows on the Internet, a similar change in beliefs about security and privacy issues on the Internet is occurring among Internet users. They were initially wary of providing credit card and personal information to vendors on the Web. But with marketers providing information on secure encryption methods for transmitting credit card information and also posting statements protecting privacy of personal information, customer beliefs on these issues are undergoing change.

AFFECTIVE ROUTE TO ATTITUDE MOLDING

The marketer may also mold attitudes by attempting to create an emotional connection with the consumer in the context of the product being promoted. (See the Window on Research box for an example of how antismoking ads shape adolescents' long-term attitudes toward smoking.) Domestic marketers of both household and industrial products could appeal to a sense of patriotism. Products such as soft drinks, colognes, and food are often presented with upbeat, mood-inducing music. Some car models appeal to the customer's sense of exploration and fun, as in the Saab campaign entitled "Find your own road." For business customers, IBM had long played upon what came to be known as the FUD factor—fear, uncertainty, and doubt—to promote its computers as the safest bet.

Just as affect is generated by any of the above methods that result in evaluation of an alternative, research shows affect is generated by engaging in the processing activity involved in the evaluation—termed as **process-induced affect.** As cognitive effort involved in the processing of an alternative increases, negative process-induced affect is generated. Hence, between equivalent alternatives, consumers tend to choose the alternative whose evaluation takes less effort. This effect is intensified under time pressure and, hence, has implications for the ways in which marketers should present information to consumers for evaluation in a time-constrained world.[5]

Process-induced affect
Affect (i.e., feelings) that is generated when a customer processes information about a product.

WINDOW ON **RESEARCH**

What Makes Kids Think Smokers Are Cool?

Is it possible to change customers' attitudes toward something—a product or category of persons—by giving them information on the undesirable aspects of it? Is it possible, for example, to modify adolescents' attitudes toward smoking and smokers by exposing them to antismoking messages in advertising? This question was researched in a pair of studies by Cornelia Pechman and S. Ratneshwar.

In Study 1, they showed seventh-graders either antismoking ads, cigarette ads, or ads not related to smoking. Each seventh-grader saw only one type of advertisement, and research participants were randomly assigned to see one of these ads. The ads were embedded in a mock-up of a magazine, and the research was presented as an evaluation of the magazine. After rating the magazines, respondents participated in a second study. A computer presented information about an unnamed person, Student A, who was described to all the respondents as having three habits: watches TV, rides a bike, and goes to the mall. The interesting twist on this research design was that half of the seventh-graders in each of the three groups from Study 1 were told of only these three habits, while the other half were additionally informed that Student A was a smoker. All the participants were told certain traits of Student A; the traits were a mix of positive and negative traits, and every seventh-grader was told the same traits.

Did the viewing of the antismoking ads in Study 1 affect participants' perceptions of Student A when Student A was described as a smoker versus a nonsmoker? Pechman and Ratneshwar measured this by asking participants to rate Student A on such characteristics as *smart, intelligent, healthy, grown-up, mature, good-looking, attractive, exciting, adventuresome, popular, has friends,* and *cool.* They were also asked whether they (the seventh graders) might personally like the target. The results? The seventh-graders who had seen the antismoking ads rated Student A much lower when Student A was described as a smoker than when he or she was described as a nonsmoker. This deterioration in the rating of Student A was much greater among the participants who had seen the antismoking ads than among those who had seen either the pro-smoking ads or the smoking-unrelated ads.

Each student saw only one type of ad, and was asked to rate only one instance of Student A. Thus, each student was totally unaware of the experimental manipulation (in that Student A was being presented in two different ways). The students were also unaware that the two studies were related (they were conducted by different research staff). Rather than seek reactions to the ads or to the idea of smoking, researchers measured consumer reactions to a person who happened to be a smoker or a nonsmoker. This clever research procedure went to the heart of the issue in antismoking advertising: Can antismoking advertising shape adolescents' long-term attitude toward smoking so that they don't view smoking in attractive terms as the cigarette advertising purports to show? The answer, based on this research, is a reassuring yes.

SOURCE: Adapted from Pechman, Cornelia, and S. Ratneshwar. "The Effects of Anti-smoking and Cigarette Advertising on Young Adolescents' Perceptions of Peers Who Smoke." *Journal of Consumer Research* 23 (December 1994): 236-251. Additional information available at http://www.tobaccofreekids.org.

CONATIVE ROUTE TO ATTITUDE MOLDING

Finally, in this third approach, behaviour is influenced directly, for example, by free product sampling, or by giving incentives such as rebates, coupons, and discounted prices. Once the behaviour is influenced (e.g., the consumer buys a brand because he or she has coupons for it), the cognitions and feelings will fall into place. Part of the appeal of this approach is that it can be easier to induce someone to try a sample (or mandate that they do something) than to convince them to think or feel in a new way. "Just try it," marketers urge, confident that the experience will win the customer over. Risk-free trials are becoming more common in business markets. Marketers urge customers to try a product completely free for 30 days and if dissatisfied, the customer can return it, no questions asked. Netscape used this strategy to corner the browser market. Methods of influencing the customer's behaviour directly are incentives, structuring the physical environment, business procedures, government mandates, and information structuring.

Incentives

As already mentioned, special price promotions, coupons, rebates, etc., are a frequently used means of inducing the desired behaviour. Three types of behavioural change due to incentives can be distinguished:

1. In low-involvement choices, as for many supermarket items, where the customer has no brand preference and hasn't thought much, he or she buys the brand on sale.

2. If a product is not necessarily low in involvement, but two or more brands are comparable and the customer is equally likely to buy either of them, the price incentive would channel the behaviour of many. For example, some people buy either Coca-Cola or Pepsi, depending on which brand is on sale during a particular week. This strategy may be even more common in business markets as companies switch between carriers such as FedEx and UPS, depending on the deals available.
3. If the attitude is already favourable but not yet strong enough to impel action, the financial incentive gives that extra push; it tilts the customer preference toward the brand with the incentive. Cash rebates on cars are an example. A consumer doesn't buy just any car because of a rebate, but rather, only the car he or she was already considering buying.

Structuring the Physical Environment

The physical facility surrounding the customer may be designed to induce behaviour directly, either as an impulse purchase or as subconscious behaviour.[6] Examples of the former are the display of candies, magazines, or novelties in the checkout lines in the supermarket. An example of a physical environment designed to induce subconscious behaviours would be an inviting store design, with pleasing colours, spacious aisles, and subtle lighting conditions.

In an experiment by Ronald E. Milliman, a supermarket played fast-paced music on certain days and slow-paced music on other days.[7] The days of fast and slow music were rotated so that each type of music was played on each of the weekdays; for example, on Wednesday of one week fast music was played, and on Wednesday of the following week slow music was played, and the same with other weekdays or weekend days). What happened to customer behaviour? Compared to fast-paced music days, on slow-paced music days, customers moved with a slower pace, spent more time in the store, and had a larger average bill! All of this occurred without customers' being aware that all this was happening. This strategy of molding behaviour is called **ecological design.**

Ecological design A strategy of influencing behaviour by the design elements of the physical facility surrounding the customer.

On the Internet, the physical environment is created by the text, graphics, colours, and layout of the website. An attempt is often made to recreate the company's store-feel on the website by use of relevant colours, symbols, and layout. Companies such as Dell.com, a pure online company, compensate for the assistance provided by a store assistant by prominently displaying a toll-free number on every page of their website.

Government Mandates

An important means of eliciting some desired behaviours is *government mandates.*[8] Making consumption or non-consumption mandatory might be the only means available when (1) consumers lack the knowledge or competence to judge their own interests (e.g., automobile insurance policies and seatbelts are examples of mandated consumption, and a smoking ban is an example of mandated non-consumption) and (2) individual benefits are remote and are outweighed by collective public benefits, such as with recycling, observing speed limits, and using unleaded gasoline.[9] Among business customers, many workplace environmental and hiring practices are followed because of the presence of possible legal penalties.

Business Procedures

Customer behaviour can also be modified by business procedures.[10] Marketers mold customer behaviour by instituting business procedures that prescribe certain behaviours and bring them to customers' attention. These behavioural prescriptions include store hours of operation, which force customers to shop during certain hours; "take a number" queue-management procedures; visibility of in-store surveillance devices; and dress requirements for participating as customers (e.g., shoes and shirts are required to enter a store).

Information Structuring

Finally, information can be structured in such a way as to channel the customer behaviour toward the desired target. Some salesmen or retailers adopt the practice of selectively presenting information, such as declaring the item as being the last one in stock, or displaying the store brand in conjunction only with those brands that would make the store brand seem a better choice. In the business context, information can be structured in presentations to prospective clients.

Foot-in-the-Door versus Door-in-the-Face

An interesting variant of this information-structuring method is what is called the twin procedures of foot-in-the-door and door-in-the-face. In the **foot-in-the-door strategy,** the customer is first asked for a small favour. Since the favour is small, the customer typically complies, even if unenthusiastically. Later, he or she is asked for a bigger favour. Research has found that when a favour is presented after a small request, the bigger request is generally granted more often (or by more customers) than if the bigger request had been made at the outset. An example of this is charity organizations' seeking help from volunteers and donors. Typically, they begin by asking for a small amount of help, too small to be refused, and then follow it up by a subsequent appeal for larger assistance.

Foot-in-the-door strategy
A strategy of eliciting a behaviour by first asking for a small favour, whose acceptance is followed by a larger request.

The opposite to the foot-in-the-door strategy is the **door-in-the-face strategy.** Here the first request is large, almost certain to be refused (hence called "door-in-the-face"). This is followed by a much smaller request. The assumption is that the customer would have denied the smaller request, except that she or he feels bad, maybe even a little guilty, about the first refusal. That feeling increases the chance of the second request being granted. Not much research has been done to identify the conditions under which one approach would be better than the other.

Door-in-the-face strategy
A strategy of eliciting a behaviour by first making a large request whose refusal is followed by a small request.

THE PSYCHOLOGICAL PROCESSES UNDERLYING ATTITUDE CHANGE

LO 4

The approaches to attitude molding or change are descriptions of what an external agent (such as the marketer) does to elicit the desired attitude changes. For example, the marketer provides information, presents emotion-arousing stimuli, structures the environment, imposes procedures or government mandates, and manages information. In response to such actions, certain internal (i.e., psychological) processes occur to produce these attitude changes. The effort to explain these processes has generated four major groups of theories:

1. Learning theories
2. Attribution theory

3. Cognitive-consistency theories
4. High- and low-involvement information processing modes

LEARNING THEORIES

The four learning theories described in Chapter 4 explain how attitudes are *formed*. In addition, learning is a pathway to attitude *change*. Those four learning theories were *classical conditioning, instrumental conditioning, modelling,* and *cognitive learning*.

Classical conditioning methods can be used to reposition a brand by associating it with new celebrities and situations. Thus, milk was repositioned from an image of being a children's drink to being an adult drink by advertising that paired it with adult celebrities. This learning method is the explanation for (a) creating new associations (i.e., beliefs) by presenting the brand in constant conjunction with well-liked celebrities, situations, or user groups; (b) influencing the affective component directly by presenting emotional stimuli, such as the Saab campaign mentioned earlier; and, (c) using the environmental structuring method, which was described earlier. IBM has successfully repositioned itself from being a "hardware provider" to a supplier of e-business solutions through an e-business ad campaign. It spent millions of dollars on the campaign and targeted businesspeople, IT decision makers, and their related influencers such as business partners and software developers. The campaign has helped establish IBM as the company that can help businesses move to the next generation of e-business with the help of its specialists in the areas of strategy, digital branding and marketing, interactive design, Web application development, knowledge management, and system integration.[11]

Instrumental conditioning can also be used to change attitudes. For example, the marketer might offer frequent-use rewards on a previously unpopular product. Also, giving a free sample induces initial behaviour; the outcome of this behaviour, if positive, is then instrumental in sustaining that behaviour. If a computer manufacturer were to sell computers with a free one-year maintenance contract thrown in, this company would be more favourably viewed compared to competitors vying for the same business.

Similarly, modelling can change attitudes. For example, fashions come and go, and then they reappear. Their fast diffusion upon reappearance is a prime example of attitude change by modelling. This method creates desired association (e.g., clothing with the grunge look is cool), and/or emotional arousal, such as the urge to wear clothes like those worn by rap musicians whose song lyrics feature themes of rebellion. In businesses, the lead customer of an organization usually prompts attitude change in other customers through a process of modelling. For example, once a new software has been adopted by a well-respected organization, other companies follow suit.

Finally, the cognitive-learning method is a very potent method for altering attitudes because of its capacity to engage the attitude holder in a conscious reexamination of beliefs underlying his or her old attitude. Information from external sources and from one's own experience acts to change beliefs.

Inference making Reaching a judgment about an object based on incomplete information.

Information is also generated by a process of reasoning. This is called **inference making.** For example, a consumer may reason: "This pair of shoes is twice as expensive, so it must be more durable." Offshore software is usually subject to such inference-making as well: "Since it is offshore software, it must be cheap." In this manner, based on some initial information and some logical expectations, the person generates further information internally in order to fill in missing information. Thus, whether from an external source or internally generated, new information influences our attitude.

ATTRIBUTION PROCESSES

In Chapter 5, we described the attribution motivation as motivation to assign causes and to explain things. In the context of attitude molding, attribution processes are set in motion when the customer first engages in some behaviour that is incongruent with his or her initial attitude. The customer then resolves the inconsistency between what his or her supposed initial attitude and the attitude-incongruent behaviour. This forces the consumer to reread and reinterpret his or her attitude, bringing it more in line with the behaviour.

A marketer can get the customer to engage in an attitude-incongruent behaviour if the latter's prior attitude is not overly negative, or is only mildly unfavourable and the incentive given to engage in the behaviour is not large. Under these circumstances, the inferred post-behaviour attitude is likely to swing in the positive direction. This process is explained by Daryl J. Bem's **self-perception theory,** which proposes that sometimes people do not know or are unsure of what their own attitudes really are. When queried about their attitudes, they reflect on their behaviour and infer what their attitude must be. For their behaviour, they could assign the causality to an external agent or to themselves—that they did it on their own volition. When they assign it to themselves, they consequently infer that their attitude must have been positive, even at the outset.

Self-perception theory
The idea that people often infer their attitude by observing their own behaviour—thus making attitude an inference from behaviour rather than a cause of it.

A marketing implication of this is that when consumers buy a less-preferred brand because they have a coupon for it, their attitude toward the purchased brand will become more positive only if the coupon was for a small amount. If the coupon has a large face value, people tend to make the external attribution that they bought the item because of the coupon. If the coupon has a small face value, however, they tend to see the small savings as insufficient cause for purchase, and therefore they assign the cause to their feelings about the product itself, rereading their attitude as being more positive than it might otherwise have been.

Attribution theory explains the foot-in-the-door strategy and the door-in-the-face strategy to attitude change. In the foot-in-the-door strategy, the consumer complies with a small request first, even if somewhat unenthusiastically. Later, she or he attributes (i.e., credits) this accommodation to her or his own volition and, hence, to her or his own favourable attitude. Subsequently, when she or he is asked for a bigger favour, the re-interpreted positive attitude impels further accommodation. This accommodation, in turn, readjusts the attitude further.

In the door-in-the-face strategy, cognitive processes are set in motion following a behavioural act of the customer shutting the door in the marketer's face. Specifically, two theories can be advanced, both based on cognitive processes: One theory, advanced by John C. Bowen and Robert Cialdini, is called norm of reciprocity.[12] **Norm of reciprocity** refers to an expectation that an act of favour or concession toward someone must be returned by a comparable act of favour. In effect, the customer says, "If you are willing to give up something, then I will give up something." Thus, when the marketer makes a large request and then follows it up by a smaller request, she or he creates the impression that what was really needed was the large request; however, the marketer is making a big sacrifice in now making a substantially reduced request. The customer feels obligated, in turn, to make some concession and accede to that second request. Another example is a restaurant sending a gift certificate to a customer for her or his birthday.

Norm of reciprocity
An expectation that an act of favour or concession toward someone must be returned by a comparable act of favour.

The other cognitive theory that can account for this phenomenon is attribution theory. At the initial refusal of the large request, the customer embarks on self-scrutiny of his or her refusal behaviour and surmises two possible reasons for refusal: that she or he is too selfish, mean, or unhelpful, or that the request was too unreasonable. The customer is not willing to consider that she or he is mean, etc., and, hence, reasons that she or he would have acceded to the request if it had been reasonable. In the wake of this self-serving attribution, one's helpfulness is reaffirmed in one's consciousness. A smaller request then challenges the person to prove that helpfulness, thus making it likely that the smaller request will be granted.

COGNITIVE CONSISTENCY THEORIES

The general concept of cognitive consistency is that various cognitions people hold have to be consistent with one another. Inconsistency among ideas causes tension or drive, which people are moved to reduce by bringing the inconsistent cognitions into consistency. People accomplish this by changing one of the cognitions in order to make it consistent with another. Two specific theories based on the cognitive-consistency principle are Festinger's dissonance theory and Heider's balance theory.

Festinger's Dissonance Theory

Buyer's remorse
The regret a customer feels after buying a product because he or she is unsure if buying it was wise.

Cognitive dissonance
A tension between two opposite thoughts, typically manifested after a customer has bought something but is uncertain whether a correct choice was made.

Festinger's dissonance theory
The theory that two cognitions are in dissonance (i.e., in conflict): the cognition that the decision has been made, and the cognition that the decision may not have been the best choice.

When you buy something, do you sometimes feel some uncertainty as to whether you made the right choice? If you do, this is quite normal; most customers experience it. In popular language, it is called **buyer's remorse.** In psychology, it is called **cognitive dissonance.** Leon A. Festinger observed that the customer first makes a decision based on a certain evaluation of the object; next, post-decision doubt arises. Finally, the customer resolves that doubt by upgrading the evaluation in the positive direction. This happens, according to **Festinger's dissonance theory,** because two cognitions are in dissonance: the cognition that the decision *has been* made (i.e., that the brand has been bought) and the cognition that the decision may not have been the best (i.e., that brand may not be the best choice). Assuming that the behaviour cannot be undone (the purchased brand cannot be returned, or there is no certainty that another brand would be better), the only way to achieve consistency is to think that the decision is actually much better than previously realized (e.g., that the brand is actually a very good choice). That is why the post-decision evaluation becomes more favourable.[13]

One frequently observed customer behaviour is that customers become more attentive to product or brand information after they have already bought the product. This is explained by the dissonance theory. Customers are looking for positive information to resolve their dissonance.

Rationalization used to overcome dissonance is common in business, too. There is statistical evidence that 80 percent of acquisitions are deemed failures.[14] Yet, there are few companies that admit to an acquisition being a failure. They generally try to rationalize the decision with arguments and figures, and to make it appear as if the acquisition was one of the wisest decisions ever taken. A similar case is that of the multimillion-dollar Enterprise Resource Planning (ERP) systems adopted by companies. Sometimes, the systems do not provide the company with the benefits expected, but companies rationalize their decision by stating that they must have the systems to be competitive in the twenty-first century.

Heider's Balance Theory

According to **Heider's balance theory,** based on the principle of cognitive consistency, when a respected opinion leader endorses an attitude not initially favoured by a person, either that person's opinion of the opinion leader is lowered, or his or her opinion of the endorsed attitude becomes more favourable. If the issues are value-laden and/or the initial opinions are deeply negative, the endorser must be held in strong esteem to overcome the negative opinion.

Heider's balance theory The principle that a person will modify some of his beliefs to make them balanced or congruent with the rest of his or her beliefs.

For example, in business markets, consider a small company that buys machine tools from a Japanese supplier, believing that domestic machines are of poor quality. One day it learns that the industry leader whom it respects actually patronizes a domestic supplier. As a result, it stops respecting the industry leader, at least as far as the latter's opinion about the quality of the domestic supplier goes. Alternatively, of course, the firm could modify its opinion in favour of the domestic supplier.

HIGH- AND LOW-INVOLVEMENT INFORMATION-PROCESSING MODES

Within the cognitive explanation of attitude formation and change, the second mode is the information-processing mode. When customers are exposed to an ad or other marketing communications, they process the information via either of two routes: central or peripheral. This has been termed the *Elaboration Likelihood Model* (ELM). In the **central processing route,** the customer attends to and scrutinizes message *content* actively and thoughtfully. The consumer elaborates upon the message to examine and interpret it. Therefore, the quality of evidence presented to support the product claims plays a key role. In contrast, in the **peripheral processing route**, the consumer attends to the message only cursorily, and tends to make quick inferences by simply looking at the elements in the ad (such as the quality of the music, the setting, or the spokesperson). The *form* of the message determines consumer attitude more than does the message's substance. The central route is followed in a high-involvement mode, and the peripheral route in a low-involvement mode. See the Window on Research box on central and peripheral routes to attitude formation.

Central processing route Message content is attended to and scrutinized actively and thoughtfully.

Peripheral processing route A message is interpreted cursorily by attending to its form rather than its content.

WINDOW ON RESEARCH

Central and Peripheral Routes to Attitude Formation

To test the occurrence of central and peripheral routes to attitude formation, Richard E. Petty, John T. Cacioppo, and David Schumann performed an experiment. They prepared an ad booklet containing 10 ads—some familiar, others new. The sixth ad, for a fictitious brand (Edge) of razor, was different in two versions of the booklet: In one booklet, the ad featured a famous endorser (e.g., "Professional athletes agree . . .") and five strong and product-relevant message arguments: a new, advanced honing method creates unsurpassed blade sharpness; a special, chemically formulated coating eliminates nicks and cuts; the handle is tapered to prevent slipping; in tests, the Edge gave twice as many close shaves; and the unique angle placement of the blade provides a smoother shave. The other version featured ordinary citizens and weak message arguments: the razor floats in water without rusting; comes in various colours, sizes, and shapes; is designed with the bathroom in mind; in direct-comparison tests, Edge gave no more of a close shave than the competition; and can only be used once, but will be memorable. Half the respondents were given one version and the other half were given the second version.

Subjects were placed in either the high-involvement or low-involvement mindset by telling them a cover story. Half were told that the product would be available in their part of the country soon, while the other half were informed of the opposite. Furthermore, the first group was offered a free gift of a disposable razor while the other group was offered a free gift of an unrelated product. The first group was called a high-involvement group, and the second was a low-involvement group.

After they had looked through the booklet, respondents answered a questionnaire pertaining to their evaluation of the advertised brands. Logically, the strong-arguments ad produced a more favourable brand attitude, but the absolute power of the argument's strength and quality was not under research here. What was of interest was how the low- and high-involvement groups differed in their attitude. The findings here were most fascinating: Strong arguments produced a positive attitude both among the low- and high-involvement groups; however, the weak arguments produced a more favourable attitude among the low-involvement group compared to the high-involvement group! The reason, argue Petty and Cacioppo, is that the weakness of the weak arguments was transparent only to high-involvement respondents, since only they processed the ad via the central route.

SOURCE: Adapted from Petty, Richard E., John T. Cacioppo, and David Schumann. "Central and Peripheral Routes to Advertising Effectiveness: The Moderating Role of Involvement." *Journal of Consumer Research* 10 (September 1993): 135–146.

J. L. Aaker and D. Maheswaran assessed the cross-cultural generalizability of the persuasion effects predicted by the above dual-process models. They conducted a comparative study using data sets from Hong Kong (a collectivist culture) and the U.S. (an individualistic culture), and found that the central and peripheral processing models are effective in predicting persuasion effects across cultures.

Attitudinal and behavioural differences across cultures are explained by the differences in the perceived importance of heuristic cues across cultures. In collectivist cultures, opinions of others, or group norms (consensus-related heuristic cues), are emphasized more, and, hence, play a larger role in persuasion (compared to attribute-related information used in individualistic cultures). Therefore, even under high-motivation conditions, when faced with incongruent information from consensus and attribute-related cues, members of the collectivist culture tend to use consensus-related information to form attitudes because they perceive these cues to be more important than the individual attribute-related information. However, when the attribute and consensus cues are congruent, the attribute-related information is used to form attitudes just as is expected in individualistic cultures.[15]

Attitude persistence The extent to which initial attitudes, formed through exposure to ads, persist over time until the actual purchase decision is made.

After initial attitudes are formed through exposure to ads, it is imperative that these attitudes persist over time until the purchase decision is made. This is attitude persistence. **Attitude persistence** is more closely associated with high-involvement than low-involvement processing because the customer goes through a more thorough interpretation of the message in the high-involvement condition. However, since most advertising is processed in the low-involvement condition, it is important for marketers to find out the conditions under which attitude persistence occurs, even under conditions of low involvement. Research shows that peripherally processed cues, like brand names and celebrity endorsers, can lead to attitude persistence when they are related to the product category advertised.[16]

MULTIATTRIBUTE MODELS OF ATTITUDE

LO 5

In the cognitive route to attitude change, how do various cognitions or beliefs about a product or brand combine to produce a global attitude? This question is answered by multiattribute models. The **multiattribute models of attitude** suggest that overall attitude is based on the component beliefs about the object, weighted by the evaluation of those beliefs. There are three such models: the Rosenberg model, the Fishbein model, and the extended Fishbein model.

Multiattribute models of attitude
A rule that suggests that overall attitude is formed on the basis of component beliefs about the object, weighted by the evaluation of those beliefs.

THE ROSENBERG MODEL

Milton Rosenberg developed a model based on cognitive consistency theory. According to the **Rosenberg model,** an object may be instrumental in helping us achieve certain values. Our attitude toward that object is a function of the extent to which the object is instrumental in obtaining various values, weighted by the relative importance to us of those values:

$$A_o = \sum_{j=1}^{n} I_j \times V_j$$

where A_o is the overall attitude toward the object, I_j is the importance of value j, V_j is the instrumentality of the object in obtaining value j, and n is the number of values.

Consider a business customer's attitude toward buying from a minority or domestic supplier. To find the customer's attitude, add together each of the values this behaviour might satisfy (e.g., patriotism, encouraging the disadvantaged, rewarding the spirit of enterprise, nurturance, etc.), weighted by the importance of the value to him or her.

Rosenberg model
Psychologist Milton Rosenberg's formulation that attitude toward an object is a function of the extent to which the object is instrumental in obtaining various values, weighted by the relative importance of those values.

THE FISHBEIN MODEL

Martin Fishbein tried to explain the formation of overall attitude by seeing the object as having a set of consequences, which could be desirable or undesirable. In the **Fishbein model,** attitude is the sum of these weighted consequences, where each consequence is weighted by the evaluation of that consequence (i.e., how good or bad that consequence is):

$$A_o = \sum_{i=1}^{n} B_i \times E_i$$

where A_o is the overall attitude toward the object, B_i is the belief that object i has a certain consequence, E_i is the evaluation of that consequence, and n is the number of consequences.

As an example, assume a customer rates two Internet service providers, Bell Canada and America Online (AOL), as shown in Table 6.3. Using the data from the table, we can compute the customer's attitude toward each service provider by using Fishbein's formula:

$$A_{AOL} = 3(3) + 2(4) + -3(3) + -1(2) = 6$$

$$A_{Bell} = 3(5) + 2(3) + -3(3) + -1(5) = 7$$

In this example, the customer's attitude toward both services is positive, but it is more positive toward Bell Canada. Other customers would have different perceptions about the four attributes, as well as different values for the attributes, so that they would have different attitudes.

Fishbein model
Psychologist Martin Fishbein's formulation that attitude toward an object is the sum of the consequences of that object, weighted by the evaluation of those consequences.

TABLE 6.3 Example of Customer Attitudes: Two Internet Service Providers

ATTRIBUTE	Evaluation of Attribute (Unlikely 1 2 3 4 5 Likely) AMERICA ONLINE	BELL CANADA	EVALUATION OF CONSEQUENCES
1. Connection will be established successfully every time.	3	5	+3
2. The connection will be established speedily.	4	3	+2
3. The connection will be dropped in the middle of the session.	3	3	−3
4. The price (monthly fee) will be high.	2	5	−1
(Very bad -3 -2 -1 0 +1 +2 +3 Very good)			

FISHBEIN'S EXTENDED MODEL OF BEHAVIOURAL INTENTION

Fishbein's extended model of behavioural intention Psychologist Martin Fishbein's formulation that a person's intent to engage in a behaviour is the weighted sum of his or her own attitude toward that behaviour, and others' expectations about his or her performing that behaviour.

Martin Fishbein has also proposed an augmented model of attitude, which emphasizes behaviour. **Fishbein's extended model** measures attitudes toward behaviours and defines the role of these attitudes in determining behaviours. Figure 6.7 is a schematic of this model. In general, a person's attitudes and subjective norms about a behaviour lead to a behavioral intention, and that behavioral intention is the impetus for a behaviour.

To examine this model in more detail, begin at the upper left quadrant of Figure 6.7. A person's beliefs about the consequences of a behaviour, multiplied by his or her evaluation of the consequences, generate an attitude. This is similar to the previous multiattribute model, except that the model is not concerned with attitude toward the object per se, but with attitude toward a specific *behaviour*. This distinction is important in Fishbein's view because we may hold multiple attitudes toward different behaviours for the *same* object. For example, suppose a city wants to build a new stadium for its football team and holds a referendum on it. A person (1) may dislike the idea of a stadium, (2) may approve of the stadium but does not like the idea of campaigning for it, (3) may not like to contribute to it, or (4) may not mind contributing but does not want a mandatory tax levy. Thus, rather than measuring customer attitude toward the stadium (or the idea of having it in the city), Fishbein's model measures attitude separately toward each of these behaviours in relation to the stadium.

Subjective norms A person's perception about what others expect from him or her.

Along with attitude, a person's behaviour depends on social norms, called **subjective norms**, or others' desires or expectations from us. Thus, someone may *personally* have an unfavourable attitude toward donating to an abortion clinic, but may end up doing so because of the expectations of his or her co-workers or neighbours. Subjective norms are the product of beliefs about others' norms or expectations, multiplied by one's motivation to comply with these norms (see the bottom left quadrant of Figure 6.7). In a business context, a purchasing agent might disregard the plant engineer's wishes concerning the choice of vendor because there may be no motivation to comply with the plant engineer's wish.

FIGURE 6.7 Schematic of Fishbein's Extended Model

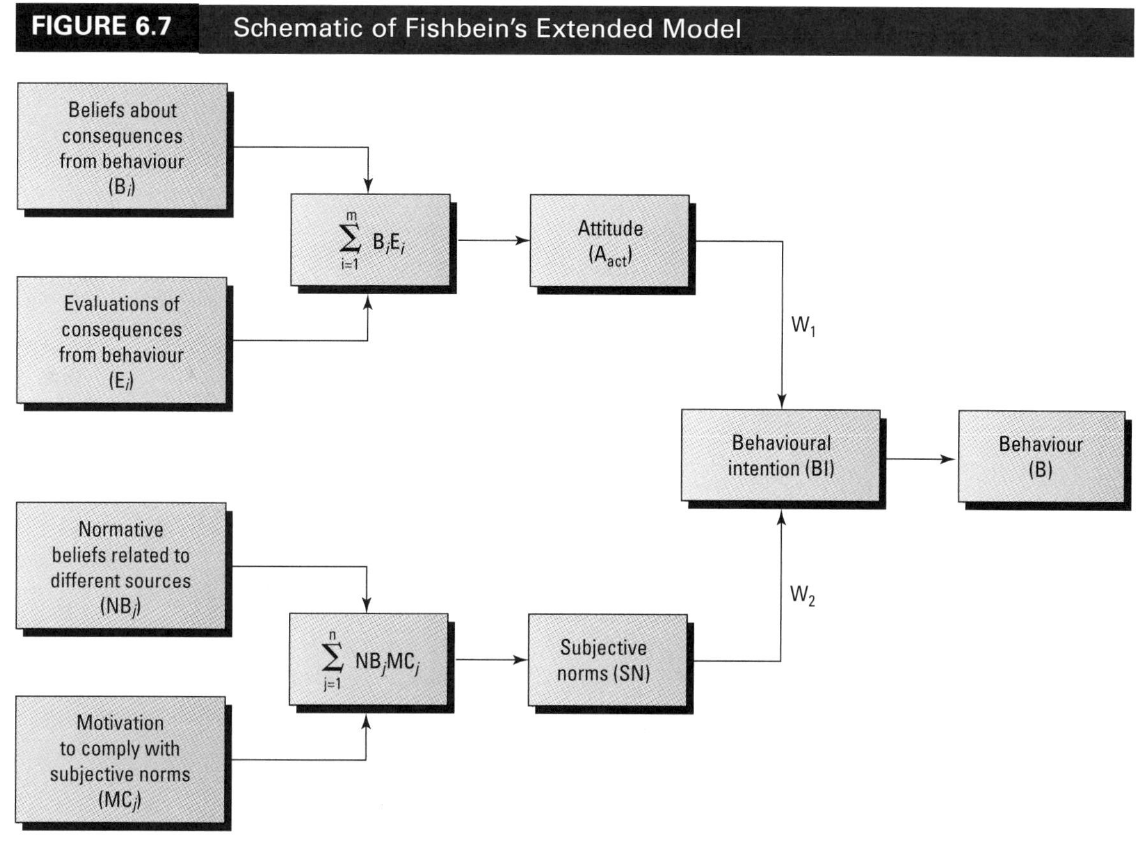

To find the person's behavioural intention, the person's attitude and subjective norms are each weighted; then the two are added together. (For a particular situation, the weight would be obtained through empirical research.) Finally, the model uses behavioral intention as an approximation of behaviour since attitude and subjective norms can only predict an intention; actual behaviour also depends on the specifics of the situation. Table 6.4 summarizes the equations used in this model.

The distinctive advantage of Fishbein's extended model is that it accounts for social normative pressures as well as one's own internal beliefs about the consequences of the behaviour. Explain to a teenager all you want about how utterly injurious to health smoking is, yet if the teenager's peers consider smoking cool, your fact-laden pleadings are probably going to fall on deaf ears.

Social norms influence business behaviour as well. A firm buying legal and auditing services, for example, may be expected to sign a contract with the most prestigious firms in town, even if, on objective performance, other firms are comparable or better. Thus, normative expectations mold, in important ways, customers' own internal desires for specific products. It is important for marketers, therefore, to understand social sanctions and rewards surrounding their products.

TABLE 6.4 Fishbein's Extended Model of Behaviour

B	=	$f[(BI) = (A_{act})w_1 + (SN)w_2]$
where		
B	=	overt behaviour (i.e., brand purchase)
BI	=	behavioral intention or purchase intention
A_{act}	=	attitude toward purchase of brand
SN	=	subjective norm
w_1 and w_2	=	empirically determined evaluation weights
A_{act}	=	$\sum_{i=1}^{m} B_i E_i$
where		
B_i	=	belief that performance of a certain behaviour brand purchase will lead to an anticipated outcome
E_i	=	evaluation of an anticipated outcome, either a positive benefit or the avoidance of a negative consequence
i	=	anticipated outcome 1, 2, ... m
SN	=	$\sum_{j=1}^{n} NB_j MC_j$
where		
SN	=	subjective norm—the motivation toward an act as determined by the influence of significant others
NB_j	=	normative beliefs—belief that significant others (j) expect the consumer to engage in an action
MC_j	=	motivation to comply—the extent to which the consumer is motivated to realize the expectations of significant others (j)
j	=	significant other 1, 2, ... n

In a qualitative study of prostitute patronage in Thailand and the resulting problem of AIDS in that country, Belk, Ostergaard, and Groves challenge the underlying assumptions of Fishbein's beliefs-based extended model of behavioural intention. The study shows that although a high level of knowledge about HIV risks leads to a change in beliefs, it still does not affect actual condom use among tourists and students in Thailand. This inconsistency between beliefs and behaviour can be attributed to cultural values (pertaining to fidelity or romance), rituals (consumption of alcohol before visiting a brothel, or unprotected sex), sex roles (culturally stronger for men than for women), and emotions in the Thai context.[17]

USE OF MULTIATTRIBUTE MODELS

Whether or not they are extended to include social norms, the multiattribute models of attitude have advantages over the models of global attitude, which could have been measured by a couple of simple scales such as dislike/like, favourable/unfavourable, and so forth. In the global attitude measure, we know only that the customer attitude is favourable or unfavourable, but we do not know why. In the multiattribute models, we know what beliefs underlie customer attitudes and how those beliefs are weighted to yield overall attitudes. Thus, multiattribute models explain attitudes, rather than simply index them. They add **diagnosticity**—the ability to diagnose why certain attitudes are the way they are.

Diagnosticity
The ability to diagnose why certain attitudes are the way they are.

Since the multiattribute models specify what underlies attitudes, they offer a handle on how, in the cognitive mode, we can change or influence customer attitudes. According to the multiattribute model, we can change customer attitudes in three ways:

1. By changing a specific component belief, which can be done by changing the perception of the corresponding attribute level or associated consequence.
2. By changing the importance customers assign to an attribute or the evaluation of that consequence.
3. By introducing a new attribute (i.e., evaluation criterion) into customers' evaluation process.

These three strategies can be applied to the preceding example of America Online (AOL). Suppose AOL wants to influence a particular customer's attitude toward itself relative to Bell Canada. It can improve its connection success rate and communicate this improvement to the customer. (If its connection success rate is already comparable to that of Bell Canada, then it can communicate this to correct the current misperception.) Since, in the example, AOL has a superior rating on speed, it can try to emphasize the desirability of high speed, thus raising the speed's evaluation from the current rating of +2 to, say, +3. Finally, if AOL offers very good customer support, it could communicate that customer support should be an important consideration in choosing an Internet service provider. In the face of a competitive bid for business, an account executive from an advertising agency would use these three strategies to convince the customer that his or her agency is a better choice compared to the competition.

THE FUNCTIONAL THEORY OF ATTITUDE

LO 6

The process of forming attitudes does not fully explain differences in attitudes and in people's willingness to change them. Some of this variation is related to the reasons behind people's attitudes. Daniel Katz called this perspective the functional theory of attitude. According to Katz's theory, people hold certain attitudes (or come to acquire those attitudes) because the attitudes serve certain functions. Katz proposed four such functions: **utilitarian, ego defense, value expressive,** and **knowledge.** Table 6.5 provides definitions and examples for each of the four functions.

Utilitarian function
An object's degree of usefulness.

Ego-defense function
An attitude that is held to protect a person's ego.

Value-expressive function
The degree to which an object helps express a customers' personal values and tastes.

Knowledge function
The degree to which an object adds to a person's knowledge.

APPLICATIONS OF THE FUNCTIONAL THEORY

An understanding of these functions of attitudes helps explain why certain attitudes are resistant to change, as well as why attitudes about the same object, person, or brand vary from one customer to another. Someone may have a prejudice about immigrants, for example, thinking that immigrants take jobs away from native-born people (utilitarian function). Someone else may hold a favourable attitude toward immigrants because they provide a cheap source of labour, particularly for menial household chores, such as babysitting or cooking and cleaning (again, a utilitarian function). Yet another person may hold a favourable attitude toward immigrants because they offer a window on another culture (knowledge function). Similarly, offshore software made in Singapore or India might be preferred by businesses since it is relatively cheaper than American- or Canadian-made software (utilitarian function).

TABLE 6.5 Functions of Attitudes

Function	Definition	Example
Utilitarian	Related to whether the object is useful	I prefer no-crease jeans because they are easy to care for
Ego-defensive	Held to protect a person's ego	My income may not be high, but I can buy this luxury car
Knowledge	Related to whether the object adds to a person's knowledge	I like to work with this salesperson because he spends a lot of time learning my needs and explaining how his company's products will help our company
Value-expressive	Manifesting one's existing values	Every year I donate to the art institute and a local dance theatre because the arts are a vital part of this community

Stereotypes themselves are attitudes toward a *category* of objects or persons. We hold them toward a category of people (e.g., Asian-Canadians) and toward a group of products, such as those made in Korea or China. Customers use stereotypes to efficiently order the world around them—to give some structure to the world, to understand it in terms of what is what.

Stereotypes serve the knowledge function of attitudes. For example, depending on your vantage point, you might hold the stereotype that immigrants from Russia are hard to understand, unsophisticated, and spendthrift people, or that they are hard-working, intelligent, and successful career professionals. Traditionally, customers and marketers alike have stereotypes. For example, there used to be a broad stereotype of Internet users as "computer geeks." Early business websites were designed with these so-called "geeks" in mind. But as Internet demographics change and the Internet user resembles the common North American more and more, it is necessary for Web content to cater to the regular customer and the new adopter of the Internet. The regular customer has concerns about the security of credit card information, privacy of personal data, shipping costs, and disclosure of return policies, and websites need to provide this information upfront. If businesses on the Web do not move away from their stereotype of the Internet user, they will lose business.[18]

Stereotypes are even more prevalent in business. American car makers once believed that the Japanese could not make good quality cars, and they lost the market. India is in the same situation today with respect to the software business. It was considered to be an avenue for the basic coding of U.S. and Canadian software, but now companies in India are competing against the U.S. and Canadian software companies with their own software solutions. Once formed, stereotypes help you deal with newer instances. In other words, stereotypes as attitudes help you deal with the world efficiently (but not always accurately).

Even in modern societies, there are plenty of people who are unfamiliar with, or do not accept, explanations provided by modern science, and who look to scriptures or mythology for answers. To these people, Greek mythology or the Hindu scriptures are valuable sources of knowledge about the workings of the universe. This knowledge function of the scriptures accounts for a very favourable attitude these people hold toward the scriptures and toward the myths. Thus, it is difficult to alter people's attitudes because they are often rooted in some critical function they serve for the individual. Only by understanding such functions can we hope to mold that attitude in the desired direction.

Applying the Theory of Attitudes: Planned Social Change

In every society, some individual behaviours are not in the long-term interests of the society as a whole. Examples include individuals not practicing contraception in high-population countries, producing excessive garbage, littering, driving beyond the local speed limits, and polluting the environment. Sometimes individual behaviours are not even in the long-term interest of the individuals themselves, even though these individuals may enjoy them at the moment. Examples include unhealthy eating, smoking, drinking and driving, and not taking preventive health measures, such as vaccinations or breast examinations for cancer.

Governments and other agencies that want to protect the societal and individual interests engage in programs designed to alter these individual behaviours. These programs are called planned social change programs. **Planned social change** refers to active intervention by some agency with a conscious policy objective to change some social or consumption behaviour among the members of a population. The agency implementing such programs is called a **change agent,** and people whose behaviour a change agent attempts to alter are called **change targets.** Gerald Zaltman and Philip Kotler have argued that some principles and tools of marketing can be applied to planned social change. This application is termed **social marketing.** Social Marketing is even more important in the current era. The Internet could promote unwanted customer behaviour by allowing the free trade of goods that may be subject to social controls in the off-line world. For instance, selling cigarettes over the Internet allows minors to purchase them freely while simultaneously allowing purchasers to avoid the high taxes that the government has been employing as a tool to discourage smoking.[19]

Planned social change
Active intervention by an agency with a conscious policy objective to bring about a change in some social or consumption behaviour among the members of a population.

Change agent
A person or organization that brings about a planned social change.

Change targets
People whose behaviour change agents attempt to alter.

Social marketing
The application of the principles and tools of marketing for planned social change.

Planned social change programs use a number of strategies, and we review them here to understand how they relate to the attitude change models we have discussed in the preceding section. The social marketing literature has identified eight strategies of planned social change:

1. *Informing and educating*—This strategy consists of dissemination of objective information without drawing conclusions. Examples would be information about daily nutrition requirements, or how to perform a breast self-examination. To promote energy conservation, utility companies offer to audit a business customer's production and office faculty, and recommend steps to conserve energy.
2. *Persuasion and propaganda*—This entails a dramatic, and sometimes biased, presentation of information while stressing the recommended behaviour. Government, especially in nondemocratic societies, has often used this strategy to get the cooperation of its people in nation building.
3. *Social controls*—This entails using group and peer pressure to adopt the group's values, norms, and behaviours. Examples include a blood drive by a work group in which co-workers would communicate their expectation of each co-worker, or a neighbourhood

campaign for fundraising or recycling, and so forth. With regard to the Internet, Canada favours self-regulation and is pressing the Advertising Standard Council to develop a set of codes for advertising and marketing on the Internet. This is akin to using social controls to make users conform to a specified set of behaviours.

4. *Delivery systems*—This entails making it easy for individuals to engage in prosocial behaviour. Examples include convenient placement of trash cans to prevent littering, mobile blood collection or vaccination units, and more flexible public health-clinic hours.
5. *Economic incentives*—This entails giving monetary incentives for prosocial behaviour, such as giving tax credit for home insulation or use of a solar heating system, or even offering a cash incentive for undergoing a surgical procedure for birth control.
6. *Economic disincentives*—This strategy entails adding to the financial costs of continuing with undesirable behaviour. Examples include increased taxes on cigarettes and liquor and increased fines for speeding and littering.
7. *Clinical counselling and behaviour modification*—This entails one-on-one psychiatric and psychoanalytic programs for individuals, or programs of small-group therapy that bring about the unlearning of socially undesirable behaviours, or the learning of socially desirable behaviours. Examples include quit-smoking clinics and Alcoholics Anonymous, a group in which persons with severe drinking habits discuss their problems and seek social support in their effort to overcome their addiction.
8. *Mandatory rules and regulations*—The government may enact laws to restrict the undesirable behaviour, specifying punitive measures for noncompliance. Examples include mandatory reproduction restriction, smoking prohibition in public buildings, and fire safety codes in building construction.[20]

CHOICE OF STRATEGY

How does a manager know which strategy is appropriate for a specific social change program in a specific population? This question is answered by considering a person's attitudes about the change program. Basically, a person's attitude may be positive or negative; for each case, moreover, the person may or may not be engaged in the desired behaviour. Using these attitude and behaviour statuses, customers can be classified into four groups, as shown in Table 6.6. A different strategy is appropriate for each of these groups.

TABLE 6.6 A Typology of Strategy Mix for Planned Social Change

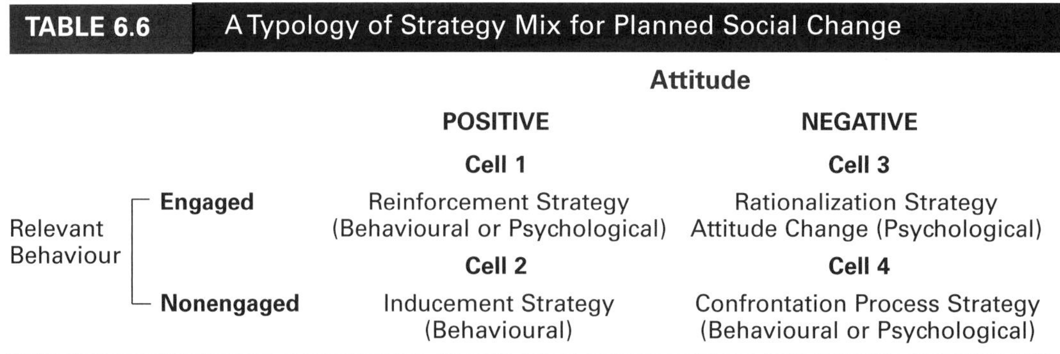

		Attitude	
		POSITIVE	**NEGATIVE**
Relevant Behaviour	**Engaged**	**Cell 1** Reinforcement Strategy (Behavioural or Psychological)	**Cell 3** Rationalization Strategy Attitude Change (Psychological)
	Nonengaged	**Cell 2** Inducement Strategy (Behavioural)	**Cell 4** Confrontation Process Strategy (Behavioural or Psychological)

SOURCE: Sheth, Jagdish N., and Gary L. Frazier. "A Model of Strategy Mix for Planned Social Change." *Journal of Marketing* 46, no. 1 (Winter 1982): 15–26.

When attitude is positive and behaviour is present (Cell 1), what is needed is a reinforcement strategy, a strategy that will reward the person for his or her behaviour and encourage him or her to maintain the positive attitude. The reinforcement may be either behavioural (e.g., economic incentives for participation in the prosocial program) or psychological (e.g., praise).

If attitude is positive but behaviour is absent (Cell 2), then an inducement strategy is needed. Basically, the behaviour needs to be facilitated (since the attitude is already positive). Therefore, the social-change programs should try to remove whatever is holding back the behaviour, such as some organizational, socioeconomic, time, or place constraints. Delivery systems become important, making it convenient for the customer to engage in the prosocial behaviour.

When attitude is negative and yet the person is engaging in the desired behaviour (Cell 3), a rationalization strategy is called for. This situation may occur due to lack of choice (e.g., wearing a helmet while riding a motorcycle because that is the law) or due to a temporary situation (e.g., carpooling due to a temporary shortage of fuel). Social change agents need to aid and stimulate the rationalization of the behaviour; that is, the person tries to justify the behaviour as desirable rather than merely necessary under the circumstances.

Finally, Cell 4 shows the situation where attitude is negative and the behaviour is absent. Here, a confrontation process strategy is needed. Two types of confrontations are behavioural and psychological. In the behavioral confrontation, the change agency uses its power to block the current behaviour, thus leaving the desired behaviour as the only viable option. In the psychological confrontation, the change agency directly attacks the person's existing attitudes toward the desired behaviour. Although the ultimate goal is to move change targets from Cell 4 to Cell 1, this may be too radical to attempt in one step. If so, the change targets may be moved first to Cell 2 or Cell 3 and then, in the next phase, to Cell 1.

The general lesson of this discussion is that it is important to understand the attitudes underlying a particular behaviour, and also to recognize the nature of the attitude-behaviour gap. Depending on the direction of any discrepancy, the task may be to mold the attitude first or the behaviour first. In either case, certain strategies may be more appropriate than others.

Customer Attitudes and the Three Customer Roles

The concepts of attitudes discussed in this chapter apply to all three customer roles. Customers hold attitudes relevant to each of their roles (see Table 6.7). As users, for example, we like certain products (e.g., vegetables if we are health-conscious, and power tools if we are do-it-yourselfers) and dislike others (e.g., cigarettes if we are nonsmokers). As payers, we have attitudes toward credit: some of us like it while others don't like it. Finally, as buyers, we like certain stores, vendors, and purchase methods while we dislike others.

In each of these instances, our attitudes exist in their three components. As users, our attitudes comprise beliefs we hold about products (e.g., "Toyota cars are reliable," or "Sun Microsystems has versatile connectivity"), determine our feelings toward them (e.g., "I love my Toyota," or "I like doing business with Sun Microsystems"), and manifest corresponding approach or avoidance behaviour (e.g., "I will always buy a Toyota," or "My current preferred network service provider is Sun Microsystems"). Then, as payers, we have beliefs about specific credit cards, have favourable predispositions toward them, and we use certain cards and reject others. Finally, as buyers, we have beliefs about certain vendors, like some and dislike others, and patronize those we like and avoid those we dislike. For example, some of us may like to shop at warehouse club stores, believing that they offer good selection and price, while others among us may avoid them because of the belief that they offer a low level of service. Fishbein's extended model points to the role of subjective norms—the expectations of significant others—and these norms also influence each of the three roles. As users, we are concerned about whether significant others will like what we use. We buy the cars our neighbors will not frown upon, wear clothing our friends and co-workers will admire, eat our vegetables to appease our parents, and (as business customers) fly economy class to comply with the company's new cost-saving measures. As payers, our debt behaviour is shaped by parents' expectations during our teenage years, when we first acquire our own credit cards. Furthermore, we are expected to spend money within a normative range for specific products; for example, our spouse would expect us not to be spendthrift, and gift recipients would expect us to spend at least a certain amount on the gift. Finally, subjective norms also influence our choice of vendors as well as our shopping strategy. For example, we shop at some of the same stores as our friends and people of our social class. We don't shop around too much if we have a friend along. And government-funded projects specify a list of approved vendors.

Involvement, an attitudinal state of the customer, is also manifested in all three roles. As users, we are highly involved in some products, exhibiting fanatic consumption of these, such as an art collection. As payers, we differ in our concern with what happens to the money we give. Some parents, for example, might give their children an allowance and not worry about how they spend it, while other parents may want to keep a close eye on how that money is being spent. As donors to charity organizations, we might be uninterested in the exact uses of that money, or we might want to be on the board of directors so that we may influence the distribution of funds. Finally, as buyers, we might shop disinterestedly, or we might enjoy shopping or take a keen interest in making the most judicious purchase. As business customers, we might routinely reorder from the existing vendor, or we might diligently search for new vendors.

TABLE 6.7 Attitudes and the Three Customer Roles

	User	Payer	Buyer
Customer attitudes	• Users like products they use, and dislike products they avoid.	• Payers have attitude toward credit.	• Buyers like some vendors more than others.
Three-component-model	• Users hold beliefs about products, have feelings toward them, and manifest approach or avoidance behaviour.	• Payers have beliefs, feelings, and behaviours toward specific credit cards and other forms of payment methods.	• Buyers have beliefs about the attributes of vendors, like or dislike them, and patronize or ignore them accordingly.
Fishbein's extended model	• Subjective norms dictate customer use or nonuse of many products.	• Subjective norms influence a person's debt behaviour and also spending norms for specific purchases. Tipping behaviour.	• Subjective norms influence one's choice of vendors. Government has list of approved vendors.
High- and low-involvement	• Users are very involved with some products, exhibiting fanatic consumption.	• Payers differ in their concern about what happens to the money they pay.	• Some buyers are highly involved, and others are not.

These examples cover only the main concepts of attitude. Other concepts discussed in this chapter—the multicomponent model, attribution processes, cognitive dissonance and consistency, and the functional theory of attitude—also are relevant to the three roles. For example, as a payer, we might like and use a particular credit card simply because that card has offered us a higher credit limit, even though we would never even come close to exhausting the much lower limit of a competing card; we may do so because it serves our ego-defense function. Or we might prefer a credit card because of its higher prestige (value-expressive function). We leave it to you to reflect on and tease out the relevance of these and other attitude concepts to the three customer roles.

SUMMARY

This chapter dealt with the concept of attitude and how it applies to customer behaviour. **LO 1 2 3** Attitudes were described as customers' likes and dislikes toward various products and their predispositions to respond to them (approach or avoidance). These attitudes have three components—cognition (thoughts), affect (feelings), and conation (actions). Customers acquire these three components in a specific sequence, and three such sequences were identified: rational, emotional, and low-involvement. Because the three components usually exist in harmony (i.e., consistency), changing any one of them would usually drive a change in others.

Accordingly, we have identified three routes to attitude change: the cognitive, affective, and **LO 3** conative routes. In the conative route, behaviour is shaped or encouraged by such means as incentives, information structuring, and regulation. Corresponding thoughts and feelings then follow, to become consistent with the shaped behaviour.

Various psychological processes underlie attitude change. First, attitudes are changed when we **LO 4** learn something; accordingly, all four methods of learning (classical conditioning, instrumental conditioning, modelling, and cognitive learning) also become methods of attitude change. Attitudes change because humans have an innate need for attribution of causes (i.e., to understand causality) and seek cognitive consistency (e.g., Heider's balance theory, Festinger's dissonance theory). Furthermore, low- and high-involvement learning processes lead to attitude change in very different manners.

Multiattribute models of attitudes seek to capture the arithmetic of how object beliefs (i.e., **LO 5** cognitions) combine to form an overall attitude or evaluation of the object. Two major models have been developed by Rosenberg and Fishbein. Fishbein's model also has an extended form, which adds a normative component to the basic model's cognitive component. Together, these predict a customer's behavioural intention.

Next, we discussed a functional theory of attitude. Advanced by Daniel Katz, this theory **LO 6** expounds on the motivational reasons why customers hold an attitude at all. They hold it, according to Katz, because these attitudes serve one or more of the four functions: utilitarian, value-expressive, ego-defense, and knowledge. Applications of these functions for customer behaviour were discussed.

These attitude concepts have been applied to the task of planned social change. Concerned with changing people's behaviours so that the acquired behaviours are in the interests of the customers themselves or society at large, planned social change can use diverse strategies of social marketing. The appropriateness of these strategies depends on the nature of attitude-behaviour gaps.

In the last section, we highlighted the applicability of various attitude concepts covered in the chapter to each of the three customer roles and the market values they seek.

KEY TERMS

Affect 205
Attitude Hierarchy 206
Attitude Molding 209
Attitude Persistence 218
Attitude Strength 209
Attitude Valence 208
Attitudes 202
Beliefs 204
Brand Belief 204
Buyers' Remorse 216
Central Processing Route 217
Change Agent 225
Change Targets 225
Cognitive dissonance 216
Conation 206
Descriptive Beliefs 205
Diagnosticity 223
Door-in-the-Face Strategy 213
Ecological Design 212
Ego-Defense Function 223
Emotional Hierarchy 206
Evaluative Beliefs 205
Festinger's Dissonance Theory 216
Fishbein Model 219
Fishbein's Extended Model 220
Foot-in-the-Door Strategy 213
Heider's Balance Theory 217
Inference Making 214
Knowledge Function 223
Learning Hierarchy 206
Low-Involvement Attitude Hierarchy 207
Multiattribute Models of Attitude 219
Norm of Reciprocity 215
Normative Beliefs 205
Peripheral Processing Route 217
Planned Social Change 225
Process-Induced Affect 210
Rosenberg Model 219
Self-Perception Theory 215
Social Marketing 225
Subjective Norms 220
Utilitarian Function 223
Value-Expressive Function 223

DISCUSSION QUESTIONS AND EXERCISES

1. What are consumer attitudes? What are the two primary uses of the concept of consumer attitudes in marketing? How can marketers use an understanding of customer attitudes to better satisfy customer needs? Since attitudes are learned predispositions to respond (i.e., engage or not engage in a specific behaviour), why don't marketers and market researchers simply measure purchase response (i.e., behaviour) and forget about attitudes?
2. How does the central mode of attitude processing differ from the peripheral mode? What differences in attitude might accrue as a result of processing in one way or the other? Provide one example of central processing being stressed by a company in its communications, and another example of a company where peripheral processing is stressed. Under what conditions should a marketer select one route versus another in attempting to change consumer attitudes?
3. Put the three-component model of attitude to work by providing three measurement statements for each component of the model for the following three objects: (a) Nike running shoes, (b) surfing the World Wide Web, and (c) McDonald's fast-food restaurants.

4. Describe an attitude you recently developed toward a product in terms of classical conditioning, instrumental conditioning, modelling, and cognitive learning theory. Give one example of your acquiring an attitude in each of these four learning modes.
5. Assume the role of strategic marketing manager for a new line of South Korean automobiles. You are very familiar with the problems that your predecessors, such as Hyundai and Kia, have had in creating a high-quality automobile image among North American customers. In South Asia and Europe, your new line has tested very well, and you are confident that your cars will succeed in Canada, given that you can properly shape attitudes toward Korean auto imports. Given your knowledge about the attitudes of Canadian consumers toward their cars, which of the three alternative routes to attitude molding will you take in your promotional campaign? Why have you chosen this route? Briefly describe the types of attitudes you hope to invoke in your target customers.
6. Despite the raging war against the tobacco industry and the generally negative sentiments toward cigarette smokers, nearly 20 percent of Canadians continue to smoke. Based on the model of planned social change presented in this chapter, evaluate various strategies and identify the ones you would recommend for an antismoking marketing program of action.

NOTES

1 http://www.thomson.com/learning/learning_trends.jsp.

2 Gordon W. Allport, "Attitudes," in *A Handbook of Social Psychology,* ed.C.A. Murchinson, 798–844 (Worcester, MA: Clark University Press, 1935).

3 Qimei Chen and William D. Wells, "Attitude Towards the Site," *Journal of Advertising Research* (September–October 1999): 27–38; Marie-Odile Richard, "Modeling The Impact of Internet Atmospherics On Surfer Behavior," *Journal of Business Research* 58, no. 12 (December 2005): 1632–42.

4 Neil Whitehead, "Terms of Engagement," *Brand Strategy,* 09/01/2000.

5 Ellen C. Garbarino and Julie A. Edell, "Cognitive Effort, Affect, and Choice," *Journal of Consumer Research* 24 (September 1997): 147–58.

6 Philip Kotler, "Atmospherics as a Marketing Tool," *Journal of Retailing* 49 (Winter 1973–74): 48–64; Robert Donovan and John Rossiter, "Store Atmosphere: An Environmental Psychology Approach," *Journal of Retailing* 58 (Spring 1982): 34–57.

7 Ronald E. Milliman, "Using Background Music to Affect the Behaviour of Supermarket Shoppers," *Journal of Marketing* 46 (Summer 1982): 86–91; Ronald E. Milliman "The Influence of Background Music on the Behaviour of Restaurant Patrons," *Journal of Consumer Research* 13 (September 1986): 286–89; James J. Kellaris and Robert J. Kent, "The Influence of Music on Consumers' Temporal Perceptions: Does Time Fly When You Are Having Fun?," *Journal of Consumer Psychology* 1, no. 4 (1992): 365–76.

8 Jagdish N. Sheth and Banwari Mittal, "A Framework for Managing Customer Expectations," *Journal of Market-Focused Management* 2 (1996): 137–58.

9 Robert E. Krapfel, "Marketing by Mandate," *Journal of Marketing* 46 (Summer 1982): 79–85; Jagdish N. Sheth, *Winning Back Your Market: The Inside Stories of the Companies that Did It* (New York: John Wiley, 1985), 59–72.

10 Jagdish N. Sheth and Banwari Mittal, "A Framework for Managing Customer Expectations," *Journal of Market-Focused Management* 2 (1996): 137–58.

11 Sam Albert, "A New, Nimbler IBM?," *Midrange Systems;* Spring House; September 4, 2000, 46.

12 John C. Mowen and Robert Cialdini, "On Implementing the Door-in-the-Face Compliance Strategy in a Marketing Context," *Journal of Marketing Research* 17 (May 1980): 253–58.

13 Leon A. Festinger, *A Theory of Cognitive Dissonance* (Evanston, IL: Row, Peterson, 1957).

14 Charles A. O'Reilly III and Jeffrey Pfeffer, *Hidden Value: How Great Companies Achieve Extraordinary Results With Ordinary People* (Harvard Business School Press, 2000).

15 Jennifer L. Aaker and Durairaj Maheswaran, "The Effect of Cultural Orientation on Persuasion," *Journal of Consumer Research* 24 (December 1997): 315–28.

16 Jaideep Sengupta, Ronald C. Goodstein, and David. S. Boninger, "All Cues Are Not Created Equal: Obtaining Attitude Persistence Under Low Involvement Conditions," *Journal of Consumer Research* 23 (March 1997) 351–61.

17 Russell W. Belk, Per Ostergaard, and Ronald Groves, "Sexual Consumption in the Time of AIDS: A Study of Prostitute Patronage in Thailand," *Journal of Public Policy and Marketing* 17, no. 2 (Fall 1998):197–214.

18 Kevin Featherly, "E-Demographics Survey Reveals Continental Shifts," September 20, 2000, http://www.emarketer.com.

19 http://www.emarketer.com.

20 Jagdish N. Sheth and Gary L. Frazier, "A Model of Strategy Mix for Planned Social Change," *Journal of Marketing* 46, no. 1 (Winter 1982): 15–26.

CHAPTER 

Researching Customer Behaviour

LEARNING OBJECTIVES

After reading this chapter you should be able to:

LO 1 Explain the qualitative research methods (focus groups, in-depth interviews, customer visits, motivation research).

LO 2 Describe interpretive research.

LO 3 Explain the quantitative research methods (surveys, experiments, simulation), and their main applications.

LO 4 Explain the information-processing research methods (information boards, mechanical).

LO 5 Describe the various databases used in secondary research.

LO 6 Describe virtual-reality research methods.

LO 7 Explain the relationships between research methods and the three customer roles.

How Research Helped Intrawest Identify and Reach Their Savvy Passionate Experts

With premier resorts ranging from towering mountains to championship golf courses and pristine beaches, and with over 8 million skier visits on 10 mountains, thousands of golfers on 36 championship golf courses, and thousands more visiting lakeside and ocean beaches, Intrawest is a leader in the leisure industry. These resorts pose a major challenge to Intrawest's marketing and research teams as they try to capture the opinions and demographic information of their visitors. Knowing their demographics and receiving customer feedback help them improve their facilities, accommodate customer requests, and put on events that people are interested in attending. A positive resort experience is essential to bringing people back and ensuring that they recommend the resort to their friends and family. "The idea is the more that we know what you like, the more we hope to be able to position relevant offers to you," says Linda Denis, vice-president, customer relationship marketing.

After studying its ski and snowboarding resort customers, Intrawest identified six segments based on needs, attitudes, and behaviour. It found that "valuable detached experts"—regular skiers, possibly people who own a home at an Intrawest property—make up 14 percent of customers; they respond best to clear and direct communications with value positioning. "Mixed personality skiers"—also known as mass customers—make up 24 percent of customers; they want to avoid crowds and long lineups and they tend to ski at only one resort. "Family value vacationers"—who make up 17 percent of customers—comparison shop, look for bargains, and respond to images of social experiences and offers of ski, spa, and restaurant packages. "Family value renters" (16 percent) are less-confident novice skiers who want simple lodgings, lessons, and rental packages, and reassurance in their communications. The biggest group, "occasional tentative renters," at 19 percent, tend to take day trips and focus on lessons and rentals. Lapsed "savvy passionate experts" make up only 9 percent of customers, but are big spenders who ski at any time of the year or in any conditions, and are willing to trade up to season passes, heli-skiing, or advanced lessons.

In February 2004, Intrawest underwent a direct mail test aimed at 50 percent of "savvy passionate experts," using "steep and deep" imagery and copy that read "awesome terrain and four high alpine bowls open for business." The results were a 78 percent increase in purchase rate and an 81 percent jump in revenue. "We found an incredible lift over the generic messages that were going out into the marketplace," says Jane Osier, executive director, market development for Intrawest. "Yet if you put that 'savvy passionate' message out to the generic marketplace it probably would not have worked."[1]

In a competitive environment, with mounting pressures on firms to do more with less, the firms that will survive will be those, like Intrawest, that research and understand their customers well, the values customers are seeking, and how they judge and find those values in the marketplace. Thus, researching customer behaviour is critical for marketing success. (See Figure 7.1 for the conceptual framework.)

FIGURE 7.1 Conceptual Framework

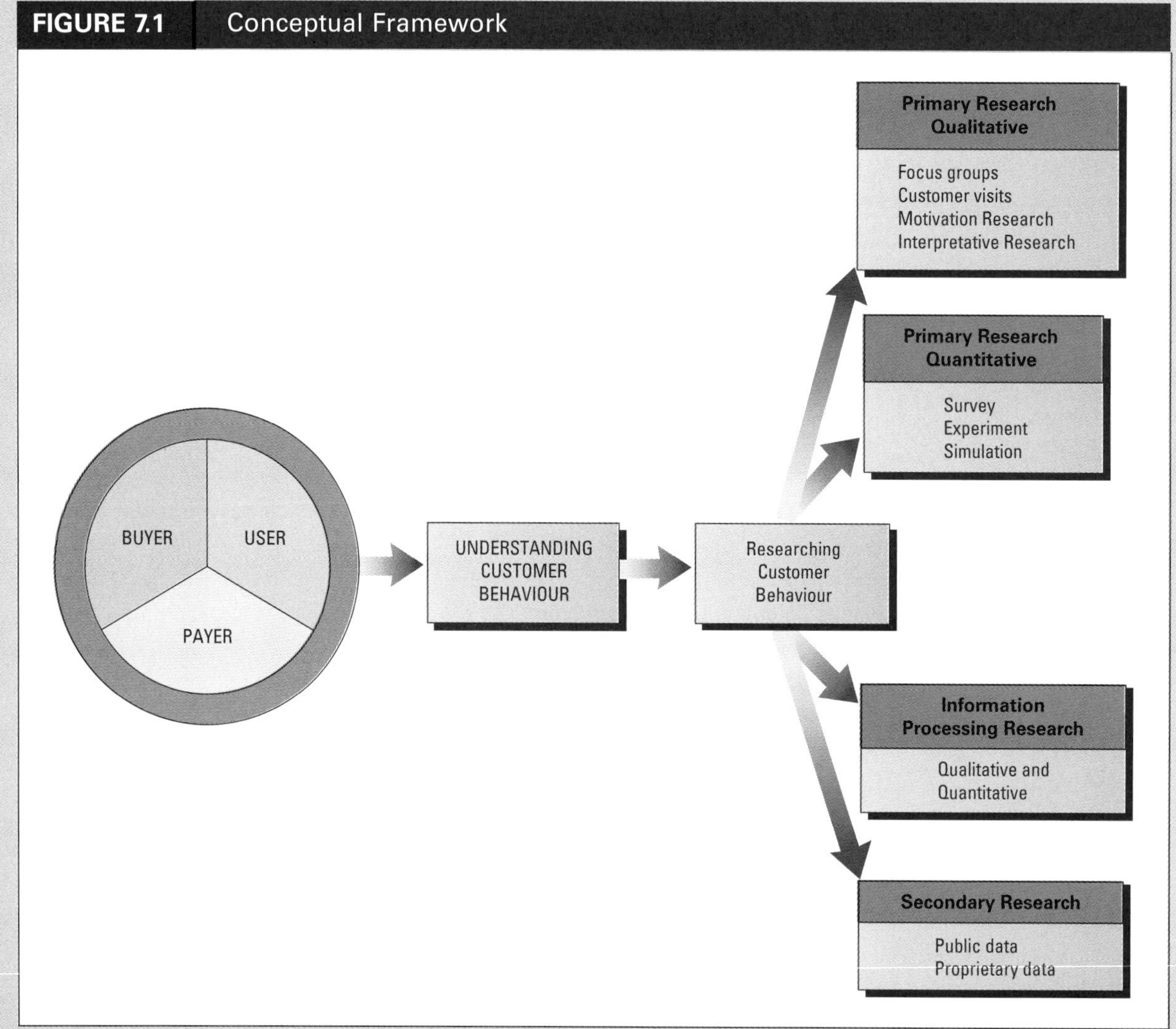

This chapter introduces the means by which marketers conduct research to understand customer behaviour. It begins by describing the many methods available for conducting the two broad categories of research:

- *Qualitative*—measuring in terms of general descriptions and categories.
- *Quantitative*—measuring in terms of numbers.

We also describe research methods for investigating the ways people process information and techniques for simulating customer behaviour. The chapter then covers secondary research, which uses existing data, such as that available in a library or database. We explore some recent innovations in market research, specifically applications of virtual reality and the collection of data on the Internet. The Internet is being used by marketing researchers because of its increased accessibility (depending on the target segment) via e-mail, speed of communication, and convenience. With the growth in the number of Net users, an estimated 30 to 40 percent of marketers are expected to use online primary research by 2007 and online methods are projected to generate 50 percent of revenue for market research firms.[2] Finally, we consider the ways in which customer behaviour research can shed light on the three customer roles.

QUALITATIVE RESEARCH

LO 1

In using **qualitative research,** the researcher does not ask the respondent to limit his or her answers to preassigned response categories. The answers are verbal rather than numerical, and the respondent is requested to state the answer in her or his own words. As a student, when you answer a true/false or multiple-choice question, you are providing a quantitative answer. But when you answer an essay question, you are providing a qualitative answer. In fact, the researcher or marketer may not even know what the possible answers might be; and, indeed, that is why the researcher chooses a qualitative research approach. This approach allows researchers to discover customers' consumption values, motives, attitudes, opinions, perceptions, preferences, experiences, actions, and future intentions.

Qualitative research
A method of gathering data wherein the respondent answers questions in his or her own words rather than being limited to preassigned response categories.

Several specific methods or techniques are available for implementing qualitative research. These include focus groups, customer visits, motivation research, and interpretative research.

FOCUS GROUPS

With **focus groups,** a small group of customers is assembled in a room, and a moderator steers the group discussion around certain questions of interest to the marketer. The group members can range in number from 6 to 15, and are generally chosen by **convenience sampling** (a method in which respondents are recruited based on simple availability) but are prescreened to represent the target market. The moderator is a trained market research professional, and she or he generally uses a discussion guideline (a list of issues to probe). A good moderator endeavours to avoid biasing the opinions expressed by the group members. He or she also tries to ensure that no one member of the group dominates the discussion, that all group members get a chance to have their say, and that the discussion stays focused on the topic at hand. The discussion room is generally specially equipped with a one-way mirror on one of its walls. Behind the mirror, client companies' executives can sit and watch the group session. Also, the focus group is generally audio- and/or video-recorded for later review and analysis of data. Focus groups are often used both in business and household markets, to understand customers' views about the topic at hand.

Focus groups
A research method wherein a small group of customers participate in a group discussion, steered by a moderator, on specified issues.

Convenience sampling
A method wherein a group of customers are recruited based simply on availability.

Since focus groups are not a random sample of the target population, the findings of focus group research cannot be extrapolated to the entire target population. Rather, focus groups offer a window into the customer's mind, bringing to the surface things the marketer may not have known about the customer and her or his view of the product. What the marketer discovers through focus groups (and other qualitative research methods), she or he can then use to design specific questions for a subsequent large-scale quantitative research study. Thus, the principal utility of focus group research is to explore the customer behaviour about which marketers didn't know much to begin with. In this role, focus groups have several applications:

- Generating ideas for product improvements or new products. A discussion of the problems customers currently face in using the product, or of how the product can be made more convenient to use, can suggest new directions for product research and development (R&D). Some customers use the product innovatively; conversations with these customers about their use of the product can also suggest new product uses.
- Understanding customer perceptions of competing brands. A firm can display its own brand (keeping the sponsor's identity unrevealed) and competing brands, and engage the customer group in comparing these.
- Testing new concepts. New product concepts, packaging prototypes, new distribution channels, new brand names, and, certainly, advertising photo boards or finished commercials can all be presented to focus-group members for their feedback.

"Imagine a focus-group discussion without the participants really present in the same room. This is focus group *online.*" The Internet facilitates a virtual meeting of discussion groups in Internet "chat rooms" in real time through services like AOL, EarthLink, and MSN. Depending on the topic of the discussion, participants are recruited from different usegroups or from specific websites. The moderator and participants log in at a prespecified time, and the focus group is conducted as it would be in a regular research setting—the only difference being that the participants are in their own homes or workplaces—continents apart from each other.

The advantages of online focus groups compared to their conventional counterpart are time savings, cost savings, and the ability to bring together customers or users from around the world. The focus group can also be made extremely interactive by presenting new product concepts or advertisements using realistic computer graphics as opposed to a paper-and-pencil concept description. (This feature of computer graphics can be used in face-to-face discussion groups as well.) Disadvantages of online focus groups include lack of a face-to-face interpersonal dynamic, which could sometimes lead to nonresponse. There is also a greater reliance on verbalizable responses, and hence, it is difficult for marketers to get a feel for the emotional responses generated by the product concept or advertisement.[3]

Online focus groups constitute an interesting use of information technology. However, as is true with any new application of a technology, customer researchers should be aware of some still-unanswered questions about this method. Is an online focus-group moderator able to establish rapport with and communicate trust to the discussion group members? In comparison to face-to-face focus groups, do online respondents assume that they are being exposed to a large number of online users, or do they assume anonymity because no one can identify them? Finally, does such anonymity bring forth more candid or less candid responses? As experience with the method grows, these questions will be answered.

In-Depth Personal Interviews

In-depth personal interviews are one-to-one interviews of a respondent with a trained interviewer. There are at least three types of situations when focus groups are neither appropriate nor feasible:

- The research deals with a population at risk. For example, children are often distracted in a focus group environment, and require individualized attention.
- The research deals with a very specific topic to be discussed, and if it is a very sensitive topic (e.g., sexual issues, hygiene or health problems), it may be too embarassing to be discussed in a group.
- The research deals with a difficult population. For example, it is almost impossible to recruit executives or other professionals for focus group discussions because of their time commitment.

CUSTOMER VISITS

Any activity that entails visiting a customer, observing him or her, and discussing his or her experience with the product is a kind of **customer visit.** However, we describe the customer visit in terms of the specific program of research that was designed, implemented, refined, and documented by Edward F. McQuarrie.[4]

Customer visits
A research program wherein a marketing firm's managers visit customer firms to interview buyers as well as users of their product and to observe their product in use.

A typical program involves visiting a dozen or so customer firms to hold interviews with customers and observe each customer's experience with the supplier's product. The visits are made by cross-functional research teams comprising people from the design, production, logistics, and marketing departments. (Thus, the research task is not delegated to the market research department.) The visits are closely planned, with a thoughtful selection of the team members, the sample of customer firms, and the personnel to interview. Specific objectives for the visit are developed and communicated to the customer firms ahead of time. The purpose of the visit is solely to learn about the customer's experience with the product and requirements, not to sell anything.

During the visit, the vendor research team holds interviews with design engineers, production engineers, shop floor supervisors, assembly workers, craftspeople, and others who handle the vendor's product, as well as with purchasing managers and those who participate in the selection of suppliers. These interviews are loosely structured dialogues. However, the team uses a discussion guide that identifies areas of questioning. In addition, the vendor research team takes plant tours in order to observe firsthand the vendor's product in use.

Advantages of Customer Visits

The program offers several advantages. First, it affords a good opportunity to understand customer requirements. Face-to-face interaction between the customer's and vendor's engineers helps to develop the specs jointly so that the product may better fit the overall customer requirements and may be easier for the vendor to produce.

A second advantage of a face-to-face visit is that it enables the technical staff of the vendor firm to understand and respond to the customers' thought-world. Typically, vendors and customers live in different thought-worlds, even if their technical specialty is the same. A face-to-face visit helps to align the thought-world of a design-and-production engineer (revolving around bits, bytes, and baud rates in a computer-manufacturing company) to that of a customer engineer who is more end-use or task oriented, and whose thought-world, therefore, is made up of, for example, the speed of data processing or the format of the printed report.

Furthermore, a customer visit will help the technical personnel become more market/customer oriented by having them understand customers' needs as well as their psychology firsthand, rather than learning about them indirectly from reading a report done by the marketing department or an outside research firm. Here is what an R&D manager had to say about the benefits of customer visits:

> There is a lot I get out of visiting customers. I get unfiltered information. In addition, I have a different set of eyes; I can hear things that are different from what my marketing and sales counterparts hear. The customer is the one who has the information I need to design products.[5]

Certain things can be learned not by interviews, but only by observing the product as it is handled or used at the customer firm, and only through an observation done by a person directly involved with the design and/or production of a particular aspect of the product. In fact, such potential learning opportunities may be missed not only by a marketing research specialist but also by the user-customer him- or herself. For example, only a logistics and packaging person from the vendor firm may, while observing how the firm's product is being unloaded and handled by the customer, identify a better way of packaging and/or shipping the product. That is why a program of customer visits includes a plant tour by a cross-functional team from the supplier organization.

Obviously, the utility of a program of customer visits varies from industry to industry, and from one business firm to another. But one of the factors that will determine its usefulness is the skill with which these visits are planned and the investment the supplier makes in establishing mutual *trust* with the customer personnel before and during customer visits.

Applications of Customer Visits

This type of research program is primarily suited to business-to-business marketers (as opposed to households), and it is especially beneficial to the producers and vendors of high-tech or otherwise complex products (such as computers, communication networks, defense equipment, aircrafts, health insurance, and delivery systems). Currently, it is practiced by such firms as Hewlett Packard, IBM, Sun Microsystems, and CIGNA Insurance.[6]

It should be noted that customer visits are *discovery* research. They are not needed where customer requirements are quite simple, stable, and well-met by current offerings (i.e., where there is not much to be discovered). And, it is not suitable for *confirmatory* research, where the objective may be to test the acceptability and profitability of, say, a new product concept.

MOTIVATION RESEARCH

Motivation research (MR)
A research method directed at discovering the conscious or subconscious reasons that motivate a person's behaviour.

Motivation research (MR) is directed at discovering the reasons, or motives, for a person's behaviour. In customer behaviour, motivation research is conducted to find out the conscious or subconscious reasons why people do or do not buy a particular product or brand, patronize or avoid a store, and accept or reject a marketing communication. Since most motivation research entails the use of the techniques of clinical psychology, some researchers reserve the term MR only for these techniques. However, MR is defined by the research purpose (namely, to discover customers' reasons for particular marketplace responses), not by the research technique. Accordingly, as shown in Table 7.1, a variety of techniques are useful for MR.

TABLE 7.1 Techniques for Motivation Research

STRUCTURED?		DISGUISED? Yes	DISGUISED? No
	Yes	Disguised Structured Techniques	Nondisguised Structured Techniques
	No	Disguised Nonstructured Techniques	Nondisguised Nonstructured Techniques

Nondisguised-Structured Techniques

The research design may make the research purpose obvious and may seek responses along prespecified response categories. Such designs are called **nondisguised-structured techniques.** To infer someone's reasons for a particular marketplace behaviour, customer researchers often ask for opinions or attitudes on pertinent topics. For example, to understand customers' preferences among various car makes, especially between domestic and foreign makes, the researcher can simply ask questions concerning people's beliefs about buying Canadian, by asking for a rating of such statements as: "Canadian goods are of equal or better quality than foreign-made goods", "Buying foreign automobiles is bad for the Canadian labour force", etc. The answer categories are prestructured, such as agree/disagree or true/false. Thus, neither is the purpose of the study disguised, nor is anyone looking for unexpected reasons or explanations of behaviour. Rather, we simply want to know the proportion of customers to whom a particular (preknown) reason or motive applies. Political polls and referendums are other common examples of this technique.

Nondisguised-structured technique
A technique that makes the research purpose obvious and seeks responses along prespecified response categories.

Nondisguised-Nonstructured Techniques

With other techniques, called **nondisguised-nonstructured techniques,** the purpose of the study is not disguised, and the customer response categories are not predetermined. The questioning is open-ended and broad, encouraging the respondent to supply whatever answer he or she thinks fit. This set of methods is known as unstructured interviews, qualitative interviews, nondirective interviews, etc. The researcher simply names a broad topic and encourages the respondent to talk about whatever she or he knows, thinks, and feels about the topic. For example, customers may be asked to talk about cars to learn about how individual customers relate to automobiles and what place automobiles occupy in their lives.

Nondisguised-nonstructured technique
A technique in which the purpose of the study is not disguised; however, the customer response categories are not predetermined.

Disguised-Structured Techniques

In **disguised-structured techniques,** the real intent of the question is disguised, but the response categories are provided. The question is one whose answer is not supposed to be known to the respondent, who is therefore supposed to guess the answer. It is in the guessed

Disguised-structured technique
A questionnaire design wherein the real intent of the question is disguised, but the response categories are provided.

answer that the respondent unknowingly reveals her or his own biases toward the marketer's product or brand. For example, a researcher might ask, "Of the following, who is most likely to own a motorcycle: (a) a professor, (b) a student, (c) an actor, or (d) a mechanic?" The respondent's answer will reveal the image he or she holds of a motorcycle owner. The Window on Research describes a classic study that illustrates this method well.

WINDOW ON **RESEARCH**

Why Housewives Didn't Buy Instant Coffee: The Mason Haire Classic Study

When the Nescafé brand of instant coffee was first introduced in the 1940s, customer response was less than enthusiastic. When asked in a conventional questionnaire whether they (the customers) liked instant coffee, and if not, why not, a typical response was that they did not like its taste. This answer would seem an obvious and logical answer, so it was unclear whether it represented a true answer, or whether it was simply a sensible-sounding answer respondents thought appropriate to justify their rejection of the brand. To find out more about customers' real motives behind the rejection of the brand, the firm sought the help of Mason Haire.

Haire prepared two shopping lists that were identical, except that one had Nescafé Instant Coffee written on it and the other had Maxwell House Coffee (drip ground). The researchers showed one list to a random sample of customers and showed the other list to another, matching sample. Each group was unaware of the existence of the other list. The respondents were asked to guess the type of person whose shopping list it was, and to describe the personality of that person.

The responses were verbal and elaborate. Here are some of the responses about the woman who bought Maxwell House coffee:

> "I'd say she was a practical, frugal woman. She must like to cook and bake.... She is probably quite set in her ways....[The purchase of Del Monte canned peaches indicates that] she may be anxious to please either herself or members of her family with a treat. She is probably a thrifty, sensible housewife."

Statements describing the woman who bought Nescafé instant coffee included these conclusions:

> "This woman appears to be either single or living alone. I would guess that she had an office job.... She seems to be lazy because of her purchases of canned peaches and instant coffee. I think the woman is the type who never thinks far ahead.... The girl may be an office girl who is just living from one day to the next in a sort of haphazard sort of life."

Note that the inclusion of instant coffee on the list influenced the inferences drawn from other items (e.g., canned peaches) as well. Thus, many of the attributions made to the shoppers with the list were not even acknowledged as coming from the inclusion of instant coffee. In this way, the disguised-structured techniques help bring to the surface stereotypes that would otherwise not be acknowledged in a straightforward questionnaire. Haire coded the results of these interviews to indicate whether responses were made by women who had instant coffee in their own homes. The following table summarizes Haire's findings:

The woman who buys Nescafé is seen as:	**By women who HAD instant coffee in the house**	**By women who did NOT have instant coffee in the house**
Economical	70%	28%
Can't cook or does not like to	16%	55%
Lazy	19%	39%
Good housewife	29%	0%
Poor housewife (doesn't care about family)	16%	39%

Jagdish N. Sheth replicated the study in the late 1960s and found the same negative perceptions about the instant coffee user:

	Description of women who would shop with	
	Instant coffee list	Regular coffee list
Lazy	12.3%	3.8%
Poor planner	15.4%	11.4%
Good planner	1.6%	6.1%
Good wife	4.8%	11.4%
Doesn't like to cook	12.3%	2.3%
Busy	28.7%	9.2%

Note that while the negative perceptions persisted (e.g., poor planner, not a good wife, etc.), the gap in the perceptions of the two groups had narrowed. Moreover, respondents tended to excuse the instant-coffee user as being busy and uninterested in cooking.

SOURCE: Adapted from Haire, Mason. "Projective Techniques in Marketing Research." *Journal of Marketing* (April 1950): 649–56.

Disguised-Nonstructured Techniques

In the set of techniques called **disguised-nonstructured techniques,** the research purpose is not apparent to the customer, nor are the response categories prestructured. The general characteristic of these techniques is that the respondent is given a fairly vague stimulus, and is then asked to interpret that stimulus. Since the stimulus is vague, interpreting it requires that the research subject project himself or herself into the stimulus situation. These techniques are, therefore, called projective techniques. From this self-projection, the researcher is able to infer a customer's motives for a particular marketplace behaviour. This set of techniques is especially helpful in uncovering motives that respondents would not knowingly and voluntarily reveal. The specific techniques are word association, sentence completion, and story completion.

Disguised-nonstructured technique
A questionnaire design wherein the research purpose is not apparent to the customer, nor are the response categories provided.

Word Association. In the **word association technique,** the researcher either reads or flashes a set of words before the customer, who is instructed to respond with whatever word comes to mind. For example, the expression "instant coffee" might bring out such associations as *tasteless, ordinary,* or *cheap,* revealing the reason this group of customers may not buy instant coffee; another group of respondents might respond with such words as *convenient, quick,* and *invigorating,* revealing why this group of customers includes heavy users of instant coffee.

Word association
A research technique wherein the respondent is asked to state what associations are invoked by the presentation of each word in a set.

Sentence Completion. The **sentence completion techniques** are similar to word association. Here, though, the customer is presented with an incomplete sentence and is asked to fill in the blank. For example, an incomplete sentence like, "I drink instant coffee only when I am ... " might elicit such responses as *in a hurry* or *in the office;* or alternatively, such responses as *entertaining at home* or *relaxing.* These two sets of responses will reveal two different sets of motives for consuming instant coffee, and vastly divergent perceptions about it.

Sentence completion techniques
Research techniques wherein the customer is presented with an incomplete sentence and asked to fill in the blank.

Thematic apperception test (TAT)
A series of ambiguous pictures shown to respondents who are then asked to describe the story of which the picture is a part.

Story Completion. The most common form of story completion is the **thematic apperception test (TAT),** which consists of a series of ambiguous pictures shown to the customer. The customer is then asked to describe the story of which the picture is a part. To continue with the coffee example, a customer might be shown someone preparing a cup of instant coffee and asked to describe the story surrounding this situation. Someone might say, "The customer shown in the picture is an office secretary preparing coffee for a high-level executive meeting;" or the customer's story might instead be that the person in the picture is a bored housewife, getting ready to watch daytime TV. These two stories illustrate two very different sets of perceptions, attitudes, and motives for or against the consumption of instant coffee. A related use of this technique in marketing would be to show a customer or a group of them in a product-buying or usage situation apparently looking at some product information, or talking about the product. The researcher then asks respondents to fill in the thoughts of people shown in the picture.

Zaltman metaphor elicitation technique (ZMET)
Consumer researcher Gerald Zaltman's patented research technique to help respondents identify and report the rich imagery they hold as a result of their experience in the consumption of a product.

Hybrid Techniques. Customer researchers often experiment with hybrid techniques that are in part disguised and nondisguised, and likewise in part structured and nonstructured. Thus, the respondent is told the topic of research, e.g., dieting (nondisguised), but not what specific dieting behaviours or product-use issues are being investigated (disguised); the respondent is guided to some extent, such as, "Think about the people you know who diet and those who don't" (structured), but is still asked a very broad question to elicit the most individualistic responses possible, for example, "How would you describe the dieters as a group?" (nonstructured). One innovation in such hybrid techniques is what is called the ZMET method. The **Zaltman metaphor elicitation technique (ZMET)** is a method of guiding customer respondents to collect and build pictorial images (i.e., metaphors) that capture their thoughts about a product or about shopping, etc. The respondents are subsequently questioned by structured techniques such as laddering, a method of asking a series of questions to elicit causal linkages for a specific response: for example, Why did you want that?; why is that important to you?; and what do you gain by getting this thing that you said is important to you?[7] See the Window on Research entitled "Seeing the Voice of the Customer: The Zaltman Metaphor Technique."[8]

WINDOW ON **RESEARCH**

Seeing the Voice of the Customer: The Zaltman Metaphor Elicitation Technique

Let us say that you are a customer, and you have agreed to participate in our research project. We make an appointment for you to visit us at our research site 7 to 10 days from now. In the interim, we ask you to collect a minimum of 12 images representing your thoughts and feelings about the research topic. The topic can be what you think of a particular brand or company, what your experience is when you use a product or brand, how you feel about a new product concept, etc. However, you are to avoid pictures that directly show the product under discussion.

Armed with these images, you come on the appointed day and time. What follows is a two-hour one-on-one interview. During this interview, you will begin by describing each image, telling a story of how each image or picture relates to the topic, any particular image you may have had in mind but were unable to locate, any image that is *not* representative of the topic, and what in each image is most representative of the topic.

The next step uses a technique called Kelly repertory grid. In this technique, you will be asked to select three images at random, and then identify how any two are similar and yet different from the third.

Suppose you said that the two pictures are similar in showing trust. A technique called laddering is then used to identify the causes of trust. In laddering, you will be asked what leads to trust, then what leads to whatever leads to trust, etc.

In the next step, you will be asked to create a mind's-eye video incorporating some of the more important ideas you have expressed so far. In the final step, you will be asked to create a collage summarizing all your thoughts and feelings. This collage is created by digital-imaging techniques, with the help of a computer technician. As input for this step, all your images will have been scanned into the computer, and the technician will help you manipulate these digital images until a composite collage is obtained that captures all your feelings and thoughts on the topic. This concludes your participation in the research.

Sound like fun? It is. Nearly 2,000 diverse customers have gone through this process. This interesting research method, pioneered by Gerald Zaltman and Robin Higie Coulter, is called the Zaltman Metaphor Elicitation Technique (ZMET). A metaphor is something that stands for something else. Zaltman believes that metaphors are not only ways of hiding or expressing thoughts, but they also actively create and shape them. Among the other beliefs at the foundation of this method are: most social communication is nonverbal; thoughts occur as images; and metaphors can capture these images better than the verbal responses most often sought in customer research. Thus, the patented ZMET method is inherently better for capturing the rich imagery customers hold and experience in the consumption of a product.

The final research report is equally unusual. The entire data is stored on a digital disk, with commentaries and interpretations by researchers that can be accessed interactively by managers. Additional information is located at http://www.hbs.edu/mml/zmet.html.

SOURCE: Adapted from Zaltman Gerald. "Metaphorically Speaking." *Marketing Research* 8, no. 2 (Summer 1996): 13–20.

An example of a hybrid technique in Web-based data collection is presented by Englis and Solomon. Most of the data collection on the Web tends to be verbal in nature; however, this technique called "Life/Style Online" is visual in nature and suitable for a variety of customer research applications. "Life/Style Online" was initially developed to explore how fashion trends take root and diffuse among young female customers. Another important objective was to understand the linkages between the customers' fashion choices and their other lifestyle choices.

In this technique, the respondent is aware of the project objective, but the Web-based data-collection process allows each respondent to express her unique tastes and preferences through a choice of several visual images of products. The respondent first selects an "ideal" person image and then navigates through the rooms of that person's house, making product selections for every room of the house, associated with different social scenarios. For example, if the respondent's task were to help the "ideal" person prepare for a dinner party for business associates, the respondent would go to the closet and select an outfit, shoes, and other items. Then she would move to the living room and select furnishings, music, artwork, etc. Finally, the respondent would move to the dining room to select table settings, entrées, beverages, and so on. Once the respondent completes this process, she is asked to complete a questionnaire that probes her perceptions of the social category the "ideal person" belongs to, and her perceptions of the assortments and their constituent elements. This technique is extremely useful for marketers because it allows aggregation of responses from a large number of respondents. This gives the marketer a feel for how a particular concept is perceived by a reasonably large number of respondents in that particular target segment. New product development, packaging design, advertising testing, store layout, and brand equity studies can also be conducted using this methodology.[9] What results from such hybrid methods is a research insight into customers' mindset, comprising both verbal and nonverbal, well-formed and conscious as well as unconscious or vague and undefined ideas, motivations, perceptions, attitudes, and preferences.

LO 2 INTERPRETATIVE RESEARCH

Interpretative research
A method of research in which a researcher observes a group of consumers in their natural setting, and interprets their behaviour based on an extensive understanding of the social and cultural characteristics of that setting.

With **interpretative research,** another qualitative method, a researcher observes a customer or a group of customers in their natural setting, and interprets that behaviour based on an extensive understanding of the social and cultural characteristics of that setting. The researcher spends extensive time understanding the culture and becomes a participant observer of the scene. These types of studies are also called *ethnographic* studies. The term *ethnographic* means taking the cultural perspective of the population being studied. Thus, the behaviour of specific customers is interpreted from the vantage point of the customers themselves. The question the researcher asks is: What meaning does a particular customer behaviour have for the customer himself or herself? How does it make sense within the context of the culture that the customer group shares?[10]

Interpretative research is an example of what has been termed *post-modern research.* The focus of post-modern research is on understanding the meaning of a product or consumption experience in a customer's life. The purpose here is not limited to the buying decision, but rather it covers the customer's lifestyle, his or her well-being, satisfaction, and the role that material objects and worldly activities play in her or his life.[11]

The Consumer Behaviour Odyssey

Consumer behaviour odyssey
A qualitative research project undertaken in the late 1980s in the United States that involved personal visits by an interdisciplinary team of academic consumer researchers to a variety of consumer sites.

An eminent example of this kind of research is what has come to be known as the Odyssey project. The **Consumer Behaviour Odyssey** was a qualitative research project involving personal visits by an interdisciplinary team of academic customer researchers to a variety of customer sites. The project was undertaken in the summer of 1986 by a group of leading consumer researchers (trained in such disciplines as sociology, psychology, anthropology, consumer behaviour, and market research) who traveled in a recreational vehicle (RV) from coast-to-coast on a journey of discovery, so to speak. The data collection methods consisted of taped interviews, still photos, on-site recording of diaries, and day-end writing of reflections in personal journals. Researchers visited department stores and garage sales, county fairs and tourist resorts, opera performances and rock concerts, and picnics and weddings (i.e., virtually any consumption site that came their way). The objective was to observe in a *non*intrusive way the acquisition, consumption, and disposition of products wherever these occurred.[12] Two examples of the kind of customer knowledge that projects of this nature can yield are the swap meet and the techno-consumers.

The Psychology of Buyers and Sellers at a Swap Meet

Why do consumers frequent flea markets and garage sales? Who sells at the swap markets, and why? And, beyond the commercial exchange of pre-owned and used goods, are there other cultural and community rituals transpiring here that draw participants like a magnet to these events? These questions warrant a qualitative discovery study, and the Odyssey researchers did just that. Three Odyssey researchers spent a weekend at a swap meet at Red Mesa and reported the following findings and observations:

- The swap meet is a forum for the exchange of goods, services, and ideas. In addition to being a site of lateral recycling (i.e., where the product passes on from one consumer to another), retailing, and wholesaling, it is for many sellers a temporary residential area with a feeling of community. And for buyers, it is a festival or a fair.

- Both buyers and sellers feel a special kind of freedom. They enjoy being free from the confining sites of indoor retail stores, from having to pay income tax, and from the formal rules of behaviour in regular malls or shopping plazas. Although the swap administration imposes rules (e.g., no pets allowed, or limitations on the number of lights used), there is deliberate pleasure taken in selectively breaking and flouting rules. The exercise of a strong sense of individual freedom was evidenced, for example, in vendors wearing sidearms or knives to defend themselves and their merchandise.
- The roles of buyers and sellers interchange. Many vendors themselves become buyers of others' merchandise. Some products are produced on the spot (e.g., the imprinting of logos on T-shirts). Both buyers and sellers enjoy people-watching.
- For many sellers, selling personal possessions amounts to transforming what was once a sacred object (one's prized possession, beyond commercial valuation) into a profane good. While the need to dispossess the object may be strong, there exists a strong desire to resist undervaluing it by selling it at a throwaway price. A low price seems to be interpreted as a detraction from one's personal self, whose part the merchandise once formed. This is in sharp contrast to the absence of any such feeling for those merchants who are selling items not personally pre-owned.

Cultural Objects

Based on three years of observations of visitors to the Vancouver Museum of Anthropology (MOA), Robert Kelley found an interesting pattern: Almost one-third of the visitors to the museum who come on a tour bus and pay the admission fee to the museum never visit the exhibits gallery. Instead, they directly go to the museum shop, buy something representative of the museum, and go back to the bus and wait there. Most of them were foreign visitors on their first visit to the museum and came with recommendations from friends to visit the museum. The researcher identified these as **techno-consumers.** Techno-consumers are those who derive consumption satisfaction merely from having been to a high-culture place. In contrast, trads (short for traditionals) are educated in high-culture exhibits, have a taste for high culture, spend time visiting the exhibit galleries, and derive their satisfaction merely from being there.[13]

Techno-consumers consumers who derive consumption satisfaction merely from having been to a high-culture place.

Advantages and Disadvantages of Interpretative Research

The advantages of interpretative research are manifold. First, the researcher is able to encounter customers and consumption activities in their natural settings, thus eliminating the artificialness of surveys, focus-group rooms, or laboratory settings. Further, one observes a customer for one hour or one day or one week as necessary, rather than for a few minutes. The researcher observes firsthand the customer activity, rather than asking respondents about it. Even when the respondent is interviewed, the researcher's own observations supplement the respondent's answers. Besides, the questioning is much more open-ended and qualitative rather than close-ended and quantified. Because of the extended mutual exposure between the researcher and the customer, a greater trust is built, which then leads to customer answers being more sincere. Finally, the customer activity being analyzed and questioned is much more immediate and physically present. For example, a researcher who observes certain possessions in a customer's house can actually point to them rather than ask the question in the abstract.

This method also has some shortcomings. It requires highly skilled and well-trained researchers who are less preoccupied with recording but more directed to constantly interpreting what they are observing. It is very time-consuming and expensive. In addition, the interpretation of data is subjective, despite following certain analytic procedures. Finally, the methods are good at generating hypotheses, but not at confirming hypotheses or suggesting generalizable principles.

LO 3 QUANTITATIVE RESEARCH METHODS

Quantitative research
A research method wherein a person's answers are obtained on a numerical scale.

In **quantitative research,** the consumer's answers are given on a numerical scale, such as a scale of 0 to 10. The comparability of numerically scaled answers allows us to research a large number of customers and then pool their answers to come up with an overall measure of whatever aspect of consumer behaviour we are researching.

Quantitative research can use either of two broad methods: survey and experiment.

SURVEY

In the survey method, respondents are simply asked to respond to a questionnaire. The researcher reads (on the phone or in face-to-face settings) a series of predetermined questions, one at a time, and records the consumer's answers. Alternatively, in a self-administered questionnaire (sent by mail or given in person), respondents write in the answer themselves.

Basically, the method is useful to elicit customers' beliefs, opinions, attitudes, and perceptions. One limitation of this method is that respondents tend to give the answers they consider safe to give. Thus, information they consider personal will not be given. Also, respondents do not like to appear ignorant and will, therefore, make up an answer even if they have never before thought about the topic. When the topic might be one in which consumer motivations might be hidden or where consumers may hesitate to candidly share their opinion, qualitative disguised techniques discussed before are more appropriate.

Verbatim
The recording of respondent answers exactly in their own words.

Surveys typically use prespecified numerical scales for answer categories, so we discuss this method as a quantitative technique. However, surveys can be used just as well for eliciting respondent answers **verbatim** (i.e., in their own words). In many cases, questionnaires contain a few questions that seek open-ended verbatim responses, even though the majority of the questions seek numerical responses.

The basic form of online surveys over the Internet involves sending personalized e-mails to potential respondents with a questionnaire, or posting a set of questions on a website, to which a customer can respond. Today there are several websites, such as Inetsurvey.com and zoomerang.com, which offer researchers the hassle-free option of conducting online surveys. For a fee, these sites will provide several options for the different kind of questions that you want to use on the survey—including Likert scales and questions for preferential mapping or cluster analysis. They will host the survey at their website and also help in the analysis of the responses. Once the questionnaire is ready, the researcher contacts the respondents through e-mails which contain a link to the survey. The respondent clicks on the link and is directed to the survey. All responses are collected in a database that has been designed for the particular questionnaire, and the data is collected for analysis.[14]

Firms that have conducted both online and traditional surveys find that the cost per respondent of online research is lower than offline research since production and mailing/interviewing costs are reduced, and lower respondent incentives are needed. Online research is faster, since responses to surveys can come almost instantaneously, or, at least, less than 24 hours after the survey has been posted. Online surveys also tend to have less "yea saying," and the responses are more frank, resulting in lower purchase intent, satisfaction scores, higher price sensitivity, and more "don't know" responses.

The Internet does allow the marketer to get responses from a more geographically dispersed sample, but a major disadvantage of online surveys is that online samples may not be representative of the target population. There is no master list of Internet users and, as mentioned in Chapter 2, Internet users tend to be more educated and from higher-income households. However, with higher levels of PC penetration and the increasing diversity of users online (with respect to the different demographic parameters), this problem should be reduced. Marketers are trying to overcome this problem by choosing samples from large representative Internet user panels maintained by research agencies like NFO Interactive, NPD, Greenfield Online, and Cyber Dialogue. Other research firms are developing techniques that allow them to adjust results from online surveys for differences between the online sample and the actual target population. Prequalifying respondents through e-mail solicitation, putting links to surveys at popular Internet portals, and offering incentives to participation are some other methods used to get representative online samples. Online surveys are, without a doubt, best for all research related to the Internet, such as the effectiveness of Web advertising, evaluation of a website, etc.[15]

There are some ethical concerns that surround online survey research. As Fred Bove of Socratic Technologies puts it: "Spam is starting to do the same thing to e-mail surveys that telemarketing did to phone surveys in the 1980s." As marketers gather e-mail addresses from newsgroups and purchase data from websites, sometimes without permission of the customers, privacy has become an extremely important issue. With more and more websites asking for personal information for customization of offerings of customers, websites that are able to balance information gathering and personalization, along with privacy concerns of users, stand a much better chance of success in the online marketplace.[16]

EXPERIMENT

One limitation of survey methods is that questionnaires are limited to assessing consumer opinions and thoughts. In respect to *behaviour*, survey questionnaires can only measure what respondents say they will do, not what they will actually do. For that purpose, experimental methods are employed. An **experiment** is a method in which the researcher places respondents in a situation that does not normally occur, and then observes or records their response.

Experiment
A research method in which respondents are placed in a controlled situation, and then their response is observed or recorded.

A prime example of experimental research in marketing is test marketing. **Test marketing** is a method of testing a marketing mix on a limited market as a precursor to deciding whether to implement that mix in the entire market. Suppose, for example, that you wanted to launch a new product. Rather than launch it in the whole of Canada (and incur huge losses in case the product does not sell), you could launch it in two cities and observe customer response. Or let us say that you simply wanted to test the relative appeal of two types of packages, or two different price levels, or two different advertisements, or any combination of these. You could select two matching cities (i.e., cities similar in their demographic profiles) and place one package, price, or advertisement (called a stimulus) in one city and the second stimulus in the second city, and observe which elicits a more favourable customer response. While a fuller discussion of these methods is beyond the

Test marketing
A research method of testing a marketing mix on a limited market as a precursor to deciding whether to implement that mix in the entire market.

scope of this book, we may note that experiments such as these can be performed also in laboratory settings. Representative customers are invited to come to a research site where they are exposed to alternative stimuli, and their reactions—verbal as well as behavioural—are recorded.[17] We discuss virtual test marketing in the final section on virtual-reality techniques in this chapter. In the online world, experiments are possible at very low cost and with instant feedback. For example, an e-tailer could vary the prices of products based on the day of the week, the time of day, or the profile of the buyer, and could "test" various products, promotions, and prices in real time. The Window on Practice presents the case of Amazon.com.

Simulation

Simulation
A research method wherein real-world conditions are created in a laboratory to study the behaviour of customers.

Simulation is a quantitative, experimental method, in which researchers create real-world conditions in a laboratory to study the behaviour of consumers. By observing their behaviour in this laboratory setting, marketers are able to forecast how the consumers would behave in the real marketplace. Just as astronauts use a flight simulator to train for the real flight, so, too, marketers simulate the marketing mix (i.e., create the market mix on a smaller scale in the laboratory) before investing money in the full-fledged marketing program.

Pretest market lab simulation is a specific procedure for testing new-product concepts and prototypes. In a typical procedure, consumers who are representative of the target market are recruited by mall intercepts and invited to view a TV program and look at some product samples. They are also shown a 15-minute program segment, a pretaped TV program with one change: one of the commercials has been substituted by the test commercial. After viewing the program, the consumers are surveyed on their perceptions of the commercial and how persuasive they find it. Next, they are given some shopping money and are requested to examine the mock-up store display that contains the new test brand as well as other brands. Customer purchases are recorded, and later consumers are called to obtain their reactions to the test product. The data can then be analyzed by statistical models to predict the performance of the new product in the real world. For details about an actual simulation model, see the Window on Practice.

Advanced computer technology (including graphic ability) is now available to simulate the entire procedure on the computer; that is, computers are used not only for running the data through statistical models, but also for information display and data collection. To do this, the real-world store environment is mimicked on the computer. For example, the computer can show store shelves with the test brand and other brands displayed exactly as they would be in the real store. The advertisements, end-of-aisle displays, shelf tags, store specials, point-of-purchase advertisements, manufacturers' coupons, and store coupons are all displayed and made available on the computer. The respondent sits at a computer terminal and goes on a weekly shopping trip. His or her purchases are automatically recorded by the computer.

WINDOW ON **PRACTICE**

Assessor: A Simulation Model

A simulation model called ASSESSOR was designed by Glen L. Urban and Alvin J. Silk. The ASSESSOR research process consists of the following steps.

1. Respondents are screened and recruited.
2. Respondents' existing attitudes and perceptions about the product category are measured by a self-administered survey questionnaire. This includes finding out what brands respondents consider relevant to their need (i.e., what is their consideration set), what attributes and criteria they use to evaluate various brands in the product category, the relative weight they place on these criteria, and their current brand preferences.
3. Customers are exposed to advertising for existing brands and the new brand, usually in a studio.
4. Customers' reactions to the advertising material are measured by a questionnaire. Questions asked include whether they liked the advertised brand or not, and why. This allows the researcher to know not only the effectiveness of the advertisement but also diagnostic information as to which aspects of the advertised brand or of the advertisement itself were viewed favourably or unfavourably.
5. Customers are given shopping money and exposed to a simulated store display of the new brand and its competitors.
6. An observer records the brands the consumer purchased, or the fact that no purchase was made.
7. Respondents not buying the test brand are given a sample of the brand for use at home.
8. Respondents are called back after a few days to survey their experience with the product. At this stage, satisfaction or dissatisfaction with the new brand is measured. Also, customer perceptions of various attributes of the new brand are obtained. Finally, new preference ratings for the new brand and other established brands are assessed.
9. Data is analyzed via computers, using statistical models to forecast repeat buying rates and market share.

SOURCE: Silk, Alvin J., and Glen L. Urban. "Pre-Test Market Evaluation of New Packaged Goods: A Model and Measurement Methodology." *Journal of Marketing Research* 15 (May 1978): 171–191. Reprinted with permission of American Marketing Association. See http://www.mit.edu.

In an interesting experiment, some researchers simulated the exact store conditions that had existed in specific stores in a neighbourhood over the previous seven months. The purpose of the experiment was to investigate the degree to which such simulations correctly predicted the real-world behaviour. During the six months preceding the experiment, all shopping receipts were collected from customers. The computer simulated week-by-week store merchandising programs of the previous six months; that is, in the same sitting, consumers went through about 25 weekly shopping trips. The results suggested that in the simulation, consumers tended to buy more of the products featured that week than they actually did in the real world under similar circumstances. They also tended to buy store brands to a lesser extent (perhaps due to having no real money constraints), and tended to switch brands less often. More important, however, the lab results performed very well in predicting market share. This study, therefore, attested to the utility of simulation tests.[18] Virtual reality simulations are addressed at the end of the chapter in a separate section.

APPLICATIONS OF QUANTITATIVE RESEARCH

Quantitative research on consumer behaviour uses a variety of concepts and numerical scales. As shown in Figure 7.2, typical ones include attitude research, image and self-concept measurement, multiattribute attitude models, and perceptual and preference mapping.

Attitude Research

As described in Chapter 6, attitudes are evaluations of an object, such as a brand or person. It is easy to measure attitudes by various scales. For example, the *semantic differential* scale asks respondents to rate the object in terms of pairs of traits:

FIGURE 7.2 Selected Applications of Quantitative Research

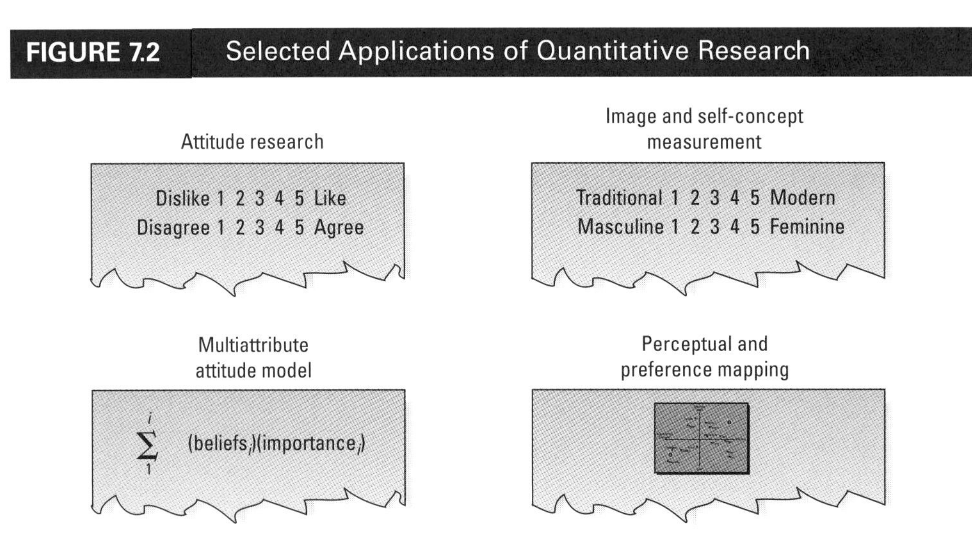

Brand A office equipment is:

Poor	1	2	3	4	5	Excellent
Ineffective	1	2	3	4	5	Effective
Uneconomical	1	2	3	4	5	Economical
Bad	1	2	3	4	5	Good
Low quality	1	2	3	4	5	High quality

My opinion of this brand of office equipment is:

Unfavourable	1	2	3	4	5	Favourable
Negative	1	2	3	4	5	Positive
I dislike	1	2	3	4	5	Like this brand very much

Similarly, *Likert scales* request a numerical rating, but they ask respondents the degree to which they agree or disagree with statements:

Please express your opinion on the following questions about seatbelts, by circling an appropriate number.

1. Strongly Disagree
2. Disagree
3. Feel Neutral
4. Agree
5. Strongly Agree

■ Seatbelts prevent injuries.	1	2	3	4	5
■ Seatbelts are inconvenient.	1	2	3	4	5
■ Seatbelts can trap you in case of an accident.	1	2	3	4	5

The attitude scales can also be pictorial, rather than numerical. Such a scale is particularly useful for less literate respondents, for children respondents, or those who speak a different language. When the research purpose is to measure the emotions the respondent experiences, pictures of various facial expressions can be used.[19] (See Figure 7.3.)

Pictorial scales are especially useful for researching children as customers. One particular variety of pictorial scale was developed recently by Yvonne Cariveau Karsten and Deborah Roedder John. This type of scale is called a **behaviourally anchored scale** because these scales are anchored in specific behaviours that children are likely to relate to. The consideration behind

Behaviourally anchored scales Measurement scales that use descriptions of specific behaviours, to which the respondents express their reactions.

FIGURE 7.3 Pictorial Scales to Measure Customer Attitudes

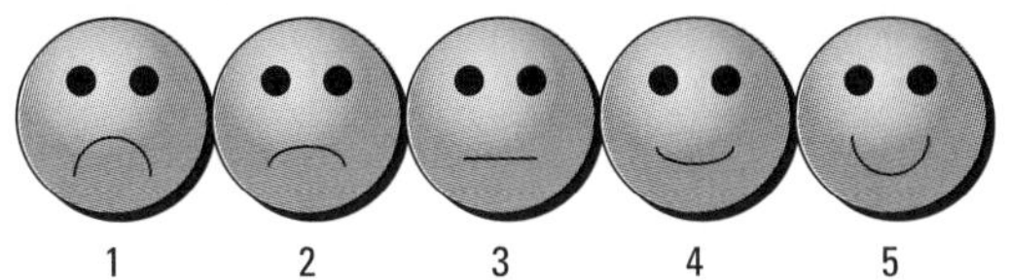

these scales is that children will be able to report their attitudes more accurately if they are presented with representations of situations depicting the kind of behaviours they will engage in when they experience those attitudes. Two scales meant to elicit children's attitudes toward cereals are shown in Figures 7.3 and 7.4, along with their verbal interpretations in Table 7.2.

FIGURE 7.4 Behaviourally Anchored Rating Scales

A. "Shopping" Scale (BARS1)

B. "Sharing" Scale (BARS2)

SOURCE: Karsten, Yvonne Cariveau, and Deborah Roedder John. "Measuring Young Children's Preferences: The Use of Behaviourally Anchored Rating Scales." Marketing Science Institute. *Report Number 94-122.*: November 1994. Cambridge, MA.

Image/Self-Concept Measurement

Consumers' own self-image, as well as their image of specific products and brands, can be measured by using a semantic differential scale, such as the following:

Modern	___	___	___	Traditional
Economic	___	___	___	Uneconomic
Pleasant	___	___	___	Unpleasant
Feminine	___	___	___	Masculine

TABLE 7.2 Description of Behavioural Incidents in Figure 7.4

		PREFERENCE
Setting	**Level**	**Description**
Shopping	Like a lot	Child asking Mom for cereal
		Jumping up and down
	Like	Child putting cereal box into cart
	Neutral	Child looking at cereal box
	Dislike	Child looking at cereal, gesturing dislike
	Dislike a lot	Child throwing cereal box on floor

Sharing	Like a lot	Child hugging cereal box, with a full bowl of cereal in front of him or her; other child has empty bowl
	Like	Child hugging cereal box, with a moderately full bowl of cereal in front of him or her; other child has a small amount of cereal in bowl
	Neutral	Both children have bowls with equal amounts of cereal in them
	Dislike	Child pushing cereal box and bowl away; other child has a full bowl of cereal
	Dislike a lot	Child pushing cereal box and bowl to the floor; other child has full bowl of cereal

SOURCE: Karsten, Yvonne Cariveau, and Deborah Roedder John. "Measuring Young Children's Preferences: The Use of Behaviourally Anchored Rating Scales." Marketing Science Institute. *Report Number 94-122.*: November 1994. Cambridge, MA.

As seen in Chapter 5, psychographics describes us in terms of lifestyles, or the way we live. To measure psychographics (i.e., values, self-concepts, and lifestyles), researchers present a series of statements about possible activities, interests, and opinions (AOI). Respondents indicate their agreement or disagreement with these statements. Some sample activities, interests, and opinions defining a few lifestyle categories are presented below.[20]

Child-Oriented

When my children are ill in bed, I drop almost everything else in order to see to their comfort.

My children are the most important things in my life.

I try to arrange my home for my children's convenience.

I take a lot of time and effort to teach my children good habits.

Financial Optimist

I will probably have more money to spend next year than I have now.

Five years from now the family income will probably be a lot higher than it is now.

Price Conscious

I shop a lot for specials.

I find myself checking the prices in the grocery store, even for small items.

I usually watch the advertisements for announcements of sales.

A person can save a lot of money by shopping around for bargains.

Fashion Conscious

I usually have one or more outfits that are of the very latest style.

When I must choose between the two, I usually dress for fashion, not for comfort.

An important part of my life and activities is dressing smartly.

I often try the latest hairstyles when they change.

Multiattribute Attitude Model

According to the multiattribute attitude model, a consumer's attitude toward a product is the weighted sum of her or his beliefs about the extent to which the product possesses a set of attributes or characteristics. Each belief is weighted to measure the importance of the attribute to the person. Thus, one first needs to measure consumers' perceptions or beliefs about the attributes of the product, and then measure the importance consumers assign to these attributes. The following scale is designed to measure perceptions of attributes:

Please rate Brand A long-distance phone company on the following characteristics, using a number from 1 to 5, where 1 means "very poor," and 5 means "excellent."

Sound quality	1	2	3	4	5
Speed of connection	1	2	3	4	5
Operator assistance	1	2	3	4	5
Payment plan	1	2	3	4	5

The following question then measures the importance of each attribute:

And how *important* are these attributes to you? Please circle a number from 1 to 5, where 1 means "not important" and 5 means "very important."

Sound quality	1	2	3	4	5
Speed of connection	1	2	3	4	5
Operator assistance	1	2	3	4	5
Payment plan	1	2	3	4	5

Perceptual and Preference Mapping

Perceptual and preference mapping
An analytical technique for obtaining a visual map in a multi-dimensional space that shows consumer perceptions of similarity among and preference for various product alternatives.

To understand what attributes and criteria consumers use to judge and evaluate alternative brands, products, retailers, or vendors, researchers can use **perceptual** and **preference mapping.** These analytical techniques provide a visual map in a multidimensional space that shows how similar or different various brands are considered to be by the consumer. The miracle of these analytical methods (collectively called multidimensional scaling) is that they enable a researcher to plot the alternative brands in a perceptual space without knowing beforehand what the dimensions of this space are; that is, without knowing what dimensions consumers base their judgments on.

Suppose you were to ask consumers how similar or different a number of beverages are, e.g., on such attributes as sweetness, carbonation, pungency, viscosity, and colour. How do we know that consumers use these attributes in beverage evaluation; for example, does viscosity matter to them? And are these the only attributes they use? Could not aroma be one of the attributes, or aftertaste? Finally, are we sure they can judge magnitude differences on individual attributes; for example, is Beverage A sweeter than Beverage B? Multidimensional scaling avoids this problem by requiring consumers to tell the researcher only which of the two brands are more similar than some other pair, without probing the basis of judging such similarity. Alternatively, instead of similarity, we can ask consumers to indicate which of a pair of brands they prefer. Table 7.3 shows the format in which these data may be collected.

A computer program then performs the mapping technique. It locates the alternative brands in a space so that the distances between the brand locations represent brand differences. That is, more similar brands are plotted close to each other. The computer has to determine how many dimensions this space will have. To do this, it attempts to place the brands in one-dimensional space, then in two-dimensional space, three-, and so on. Each time, it indicates the stress each solution represents. To understand this, consider that if three chairs were lying at the same distance from one another, it would be difficult to locate these along a single line; however, it would be easy to plot them perfectly in two dimensions as points of an equilateral triangle. Likewise, four objects that are equidistant would require a three-dimensional space. Thus, when a number of brands have been rated as pairs, their relative similarity or dissimilarity creates constraints that make the solution fit better in a space of a particular dimensionality.

TABLE 7.3 Methods of Measuring Customer Perceptions and Preferences

Perception Measurement 1

Brand A of soda is more similar to: ___ Brand B or ___ Brand C

Brand A of soda is more similar to: ___ Brand C or ___ Brand D

Brand B of soda is more similar to: ___ Brand C or ___ Brand D

Brand B of soda is more similar to: ___ Brand A or ___ Brand D

Perception Measurement 2

In the following matrix, place 1 in the cell for the pair of brands most similar, 2 for the next most similar, and so on.

A B C D E . . .

A

B

C

D

E

Preference Measurement 1

Which brand do you prefer more in each pair (circle one brand in each pair)?

A or B

B or C

A or C

A or D

B or D

C or D

Preference Measurement 2

Please rank the following brands from the most preferred (1) to the least preferred (5).

Brand A ___

Brand B ___

Brand C ___

Brand D ___

Brand E ___

After determining the number of dimensions, the computer plots the resulting maps two dimensions at a time. These maps allow us to visually see how a specific brand compares to the others. See Figure 7.5 for a perceptual map (which is based on similarity-perception judgments). Although it is not necessary to know the dimensions of the perceptual space to draw these maps, the researcher does want to know what these dimensions possibly represent. There are two ways of making this inference. First, by looking at the brands clustering together, a marketing manager might be able to infer the identity of the underlying dimensions. For example, if all the soda drinks that were at the high end of an axis were cola drinks, one could label that axis to be "cola-ness."

Alternatively, a marketer could also ask the respondents to rate all the drinks on a set of attributes and then superimpose a plot of these attributes on the perceptual map obtained earlier. Figure 7.6 provides an example; the attributes are shown as vectors (arrows indicating magnitude). The attributes are plotted such that the vertical projections of the brands on these attribute vectors represent the relative magnitudes of brand ratings on these attributes. By inspecting which attribute vectors cluster around the axes of the space, the researcher can interpret and identify the perceptual maps' dimensions.

In the preference map, it is possible to locate the ideal point of individual consumers. An ideal point is a brand alternative that, if available, would meet the consumer's requirement perfectly. This is done by locating a point such that, for each pair of brands, the brand more preferred is always closer to this ideal point than is the other brand in the pair. When all the respondents are plotted in this manner (i.e., one ideal point for each consumer), it is then possible to identify segments of consumers with differing preferences (see Figure 7.7 on page 258).

FIGURE 7.5 A Perceptual Map

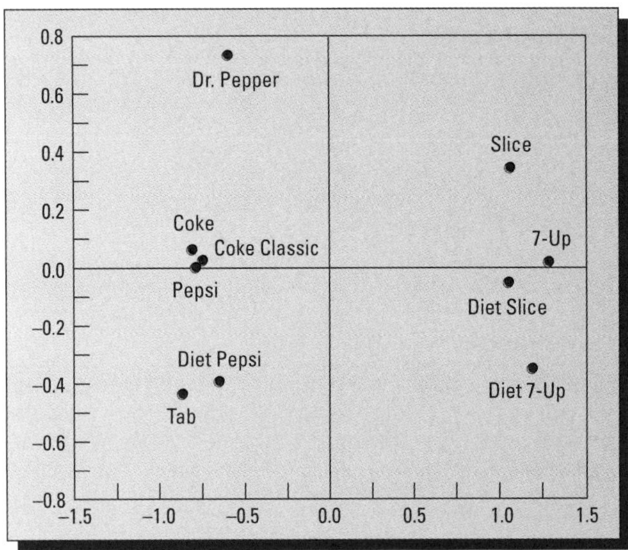

SOURCE: Malhotra, Naresh K. *Marketing Research: An Applied Orientation*, 695. © Reprinted by permission of Pearson Education, Inc., Upper Saddle River, NJ.

Perceptual and preference maps are very useful in identifying new-product concepts, in perceptually repositioning a brand, and in identifying the market segments best suited to one's own brand.

INFORMATION PROCESSING RESEARCH

LO 4

Information processing research A class of research whose focus is on studying the information customers process for reaching a decision.

Rather than asking direct questions about decisions consumers make, **information processing research** studies what information consumers are looking for, looking at, paying attention to, considering, and using to make decisions. Ultimately, they hope to discover what information led consumers to choose certain brands or products. The advantage of this method is that the researcher comes closer to understanding what goes on inside the mind of the consumer. It tells the researcher what effect certain information has on the final decision. It offers guidance on how to present product information to consumers. This method can offer valuable insight on consumer decisions. The disadvantage is that it is very time-consuming.

A number of methods are available for conducting such research. We can quietly observe consumers, keeping an eye on the information they are acquiring and evaluating; or we could ask them to share with us their information acquisition and processing behaviour. The techniques that have been developed for studying consumers' information-processing activity include information boards; measures of eye movement, galvanic skin response, and brain activity; visual image profiles; and protocols. These methods can be quantitative or qualitative.

FIGURE 7.6 A Perceptual Map with Product Attributes

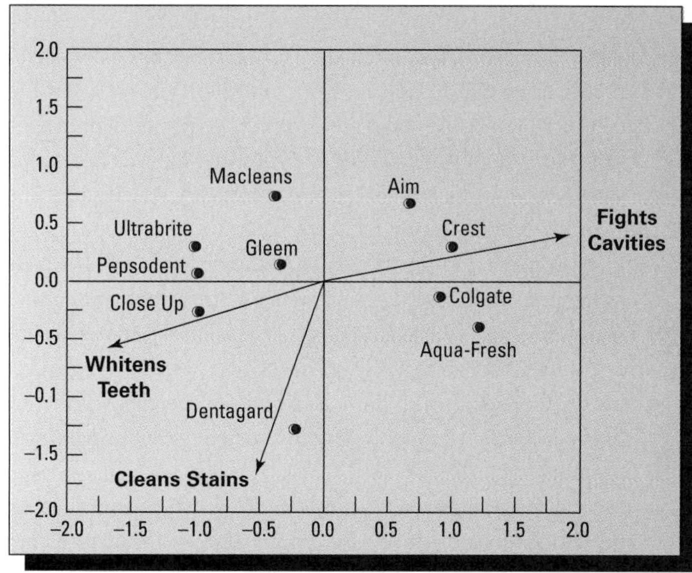

SOURCE: Malhotra, Naresh K. *Marketing Research: An Applied Orientation,* 695. © Reprinted by permission of Pearson Education, Inc., Upper Saddle River, NJ.

FIGURE 7.7 A Perceptual Map with Ideal Points (I_1 & I_2) Shown

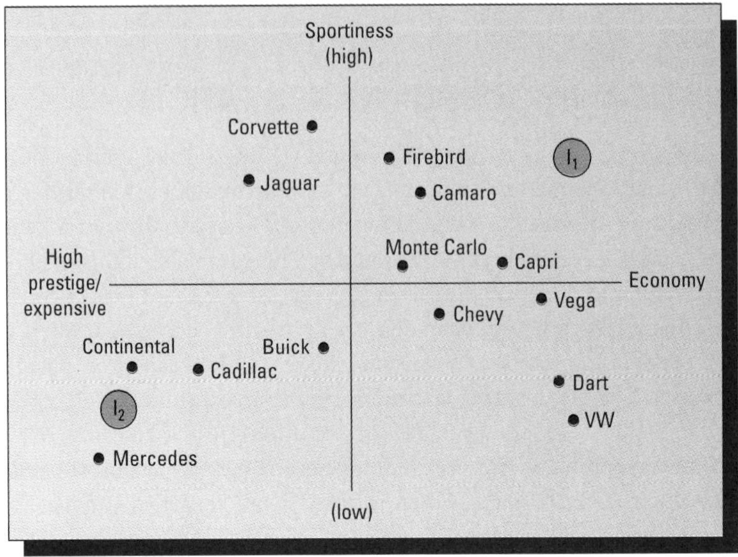

SOURCE: Malhotra, Naresh K. *Marketing Research: An Applied Orientation*, 695. © Reprinted by permission of Pearson Education, Inc., Upper Saddle River, NJ.

INFORMATION BOARDS

Information board
A table of information in which the cells contain the information about the extent to which the brand specified in the corresponding row contains the attribute specified in the corresponding column.

An **information board** is a table of information with brand names in the rows and attribute names in the columns (see Figure 7.8). Cells contain the information about the extent to which the brand specified in the corresponding row contains the attribute specified in the corresponding column. The attribute information could be in the natural units of the attribute (e.g., miles per gallon for car fuel efficiency, or 200 calories for a food item) or on a common rating scale (e.g., poor to excellent). Initially, all cell entries are covered; the respondent in the research study is asked to make a brand decision by uncovering the cells in whatever order she or he desires, and as many or as few cells as he or she feels necessary to come to a decision. Some brand names may be hypothetical (often designated by letters, e.g., Brand K), or one brand may be the sponsor's brand. As the customer uncovers the cells, the sequence of this uncovering is recorded.

Later, the researcher analyzes consumers' sequence of information acquisition. Based on the sequence, the researcher draws inferences about the evaluative criteria consumers use in appraising alternative brands, the comparison process they employ in making their choice (e.g., do they compare two brands on the same attribute, or weigh two or more features for the same brand?), and the judgment model (compensatory or noncompensatory) they utilize to form their final judgment.

This kind of research helps a marketer understand which product features are important to consumers and which features should be emphasized in marketing communications. It is possible, for example, that the very last attribute uncovered on the information board was the one on which the marketer's brand was edged out by a competitor's brand, even though the former was superior on all the preceding attributes. The marketer now has the choice of either improving this last-considered feature in his or her brand or educating the consumer about her or his brand's considerable superiority on all the features taken as a group.

FIGURE 7.8 Information Board

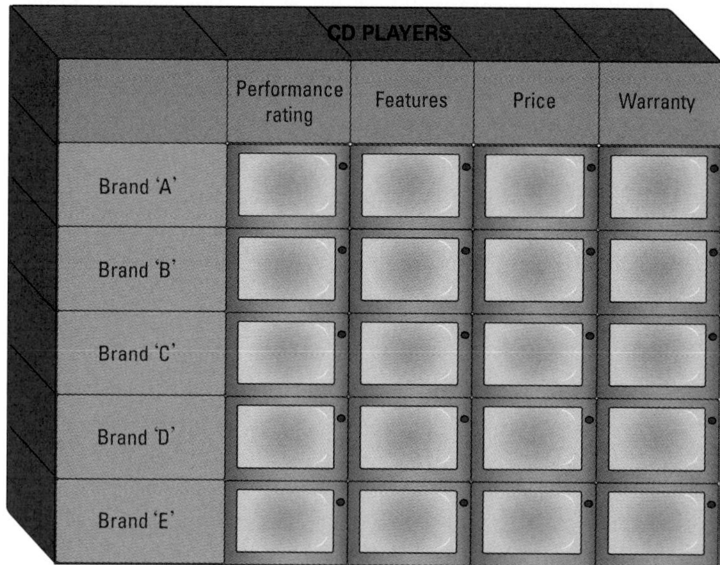

An information board *can* be a simple card or wooden board with pegs on the cells for hanging information cards. More often, it is an electronic information board created and displayed on a computer. The research participant simply clicks on the desired cell to reveal the information. The computer automatically records the sequence of uncovering the information cells.

A variation on this is a menu-driven microcomputer-based program for information search experiments, such as the program called Search Monitor. Search Monitor enables the consumer to obtain information on various alternatives by offering a battery of such questions as:

Q. What type of ________ does brand ________ have?

Q. What price is brand ________ in store ________?

Q. Does brand ________ have a ________?

The customer chooses a question from the list and fills in the blanks with the desired brand, store, and feature name. Then the answer appears on the screen. In some applications, the researcher can build in delays in response times in order to make the respondent realize that information search will consume time just as it does in the real world. The program permits the researcher to design the question menu, key in the answers according to the product and brands being studied, and vary the waiting times before the answer will appear on the screen.[21]

EYE MOVEMENT

Another device to capture customers' information processing is an eye camera. The camera records the pupil movement as the customer looks through a piece of information. This method can be used to study customer's information acquisition while reading or viewing an advertisement, looking at aisle displays, and examining package information on products in a supermarket, or participating in an experiment such as an information board. The researcher uses data gathered by the eye camera to identify the information at which the customer gazed longest. Such data helps the researcher pinpoint the selective appeal and use of information by the customer.

GALVANIC SKIN RESPONSE

Galvanic skin response (GSR) measures the amount of skin resistance to electric current between two electrodes. When a customer reacts to any stimuli, his or her sweat glands are activated; this, in turn, reduces the skin resistance. Thus, GSR activity indicates customer response to a stimulus, such as an item of information (e.g., price) or an emotional story line in an advertisement.

BRAIN ACTIVITY

When customers process any information or react to any marketing stimulus, electric impulses are generated in the brain. These impulses can be measured by sensors attached to the skull, which generate electroencephalographic (EEG) measures, or by using brain-imaging techniques. One of the brain activities measured in this way is called alpha activity. Alpha activity inversely measures the degree of the brain's attentiveness. When we are sleeping, resting, or otherwise inactive, the alpha activity is high; when we are paying attention to a commercial, the alpha activity is low. During the viewing of different ads, viewers' alpha activity levels will vary, and, accordingly, they will serve as indicators of the ad's ability to attract and hold viewer attention.

The two main brain imaging methods are computed tomography (CT scan) and magnetic resonance imaging (MRI). In CT scans, the participant is exposed to a source of X-rays and a series of detectors measure tissue density. Patterns of brain activity, for example, while the participant is watching a TV program, are seen as hues of grey (e.g., grey matter is light grey, white matter is medium grey, and cerebral-spinal fluid is medium grey to black). In MRI, radio waves sent in short burst into the magnet where the participant is placed create different reactions from the protons contained in body tissues. The MRI machine then creates still images of the brain at different intervals. By studying these images, areas that are activated by viewing an ad, for example, can be mapped.[21a]

VISUAL IMAGE PROFILE

Measurement of CT, MRI, alpha activity, GSR, and eye movement get at the physical responses to stimuli, and questionnaires asking consumers to describe their reactions address their conscious, cognitive responses. However, much communication is nonverbal, and much of its content is emotional. Respondents may have difficulty describing their visual (nonverbal) and emotional responses to stimuli.

Visual image profile
A research technique to elicit the nonverbal response of customers by presenting them with visual images of human emotions to identify their own emotional experiences.

To elicit nonverbal responses, therefore, some firms are using nonverbal methods such as the **visual image profile.** The Foote, Cone, & Belding and BBDO ad agencies use a set of pictures illustrating facial expressions that represent a wide range of human emotions. They ask customers to identify which pictures best reflect how they themselves felt when they were watching the commercial. The cards selected by the customer can be counted and scored to reflect a customer's reaction to the ad.

PROTOCOL

Information boards indicate to the researcher only what information the customer acquired, not what information was processed, much less *how* it was processed. For example, after uncovering a cell in the information board study, the consumer may simply decide to discard that information from further consideration, but the researcher has no way of knowing this.

The protocol method, in contrast, allows a peep into the consumer's mental processes. In the **protocol** method, the consumer is asked to speak her or his thoughts out loud. For example, a customer making a selection in a supermarket aisle would be asked to say what information she or he is looking at, thinking of, or deciding about. The researcher accompanying the respondent and recording his or her spoken thoughts would periodically prompt the respondent with questions like "Now what are you thinking?" "Why did you just look at that?" "Why did you put that brand down?" or "Why did you finally select that?" These consumer thoughts, spoken aloud and recorded, are called protocols. The protocols are later analyzed to gain insight into consumers' decision-making processes.

Protocols
Customers' verbatim responses to certain information-processing tasks, often elicited by asking the respondent to speak her or his task-related thoughts aloud.

There are two types of protocols: concurrent and retrospective. **Concurrent protocols** are the consumer thoughts recorded at the time of decision making, such as in the supermarket aisle when the customer is actually making a brand selection. Concurrent protocols can also be combined with data from information boards so that we gain information on both consumers' information *acquisition* and *processing*. **Retrospective protocols** are consumers' reports on the decision *process* for a decision they made in the recent past. For example, a researcher might contact recent car buyers and ask them to describe the process of information search and alternative evaluation they went through in making their car purchase. The researcher would begin by asking such questions as "When did you begin thinking of buying a car?" "What cars did you consider in the very beginning?" and "Then what did you consider about these cars, and how did you narrow down the field?" In effect, the consumer is remembering and reconstructing the decision process. Obviously, the less time elapsed since the decision was made, and/or the more significant the decision, the more accurate the protocols would be.

Concurrent protocols
A record of respondent thoughts at the time of decision making.

Retrospective protocols
Respondents' reports of their thought processes about a decision made in the past.

An obvious criticism of concurrent protocols is that they might interfere with the actual information processing; that is, if the customer didn't have to verbalize his or her thoughts, her or his information processing may have been different. Researchers have found, however, that after a few initial minutes of performing the required speak-out task, respondents return to their normal way of making shopping decisions.

SECONDARY RESEARCH

LO 5

So far, we have been describing forms of primary research—research to gather data that does not already exist. When the marketer is considering the launch of a new product, for example, the marketer would not know how consumers will react to the particular product without conducting primary research. However, many questions can be answered more efficiently with **secondary research**—an examination of data that already exist (that is, secondary data).[22] A researcher's first attempt should always be to study secondary data, since they already exist and can save the expense of collecting primary data. However, often the secondary data is outdated, or information relevant to research issues at hand may simply not exist. In such cases, managers have to resort to primary data.

Secondary research
An examination of secondary data to answer the questions that are of interest to the marketer.

There are two types of secondary data: *public* and *proprietary.* These types refer to the source of the data.

PUBLIC DATA

Secondary data in the public domain is that collected mostly by the government and other domestic, foreign, and international public organizations. These reports are available in most public libraries or are obtainable for free or at nominal cost from the various organizations that collect them. Statistics Canada is the primary statistical agency of Canada, publishing statistical information relating to the commercial, industrial, financial, social, economic, and general activities and conditions of the people of Canada. Statistics Canada's website offers more than 530 Internet titles, available in html and pdf formats, of which more than 330 are accessible free of charge. Its website provides links to government departments and agencies. Table 7.4 outlines some selected Canadian government publications.

TABLE 7.4 Selected Canadian Government Publications

1. The *Census of Canada*, conducted every five years, provides the population and dwelling counts not only for Canada but also for each province and territory, and for smaller geographic units such as cities or districts within cities. The census also provides information about Canada's demographic, social, and economic characteristics.
2. The *Marketing Research Handbook* provides current statistics on the changing demographics, standards of living, and economic characteristics of Canadian society. The handbook helps businesses locate target markets, track their market share, and assess their competitive position. It provides basic socio-economic data, retail trade, employment/earnings, per capita expenditure by household, construction, and more.
3. Statistics Canada's *Survey of Household Spending* and the *Family Food Expenditure in Canada* report are good sources of statistics on goods and services spending.
4. The *Annual Demographic Statistics* publication provides the most recent population estimates by age group and sex, as well as data on births, deaths, and migrations. It groups the information by province and territory, census metropolitan area, census division, and economic region. It also provides estimates of population by marital status and for census families for the provinces and territories.
5. The CANSIM data base contains literally millions of time series of Canadian data compiled by Statistics Canada. Series cover a broad array of economic, demographic, and social statistics data. Time coverage varies, but series may cover decades.
6. *Canadian Social Trends* is a series of articles on demographic trends, including the latest statistical indicators.
7. The *Daily* is Statistics Canada's official release bulletin. The *Daily* issues news releases on current social and economic conditions and announces new products. It provides a comprehensive one-stop overview of new information available from Statistics Canada.
8. *Canadian Economic Observer. Statistical Summary* covers National Accounts, Labour Markets, Prices, International Trade, Goods-Producing Industries, Services, Financial Markets, and Provincial data.
9. Industry Canada's Strategis (http://www.strategis.gc.ca), Canada's business and consumer information site, provides access to company directories, trade and investment information, consumer information, regulatory information, economic analysis, business support, and financial and consumer information.
10. The *Canadian Consumer Handbook* (Strategis) offers information and advice about consumers' rights, and is intended to help them make informed decisions and protect themselves against unscrupulous merchants. The handbook includes corporate, consumer, and government and non-government contacts.
11. The *Annual Survey of Manufacturers* classifies each commodity that is produced by an establishment and provides summaries of principal statistics for commodities.

Other sources of secondary data include public reports by other governmental agencies and not-for-profit agencies, such as the Conference Board of Canada, which publishes and disseminates research on economic and social issues. Other not-for-profit organizations providing research to marketers are the Interactive Advertising Bureau of Canada (IABcanada.com) which produces semi-annual surveys to measure the size of the Internet advertising industry, and Media Awareness Network (Mnet) which provides an extensive database about the role of the Internet in the lives of young Canadians. International agencies are also a source of public data. If a pharmaceutical company wants, for example, information on the incidence of various diseases in a foreign country, it can find that information in World Health Survey, published by the World Health Organization, an agency of the United Nations. The Organization for Economic Cooperation and Development (http://www.oecd.org) and the Eurostat website (http://www.europa.eu.int/comm/eurostat) offer comprehensive European statistics as well.

The Internet is a rich source of information for researchers, with a variety of websites that offer information on trends in technological, political, competitive, and economic contexts. Secondary research is relatively easier on the Internet since the data is indexed and searchable using a variety of general and specialized search engines (Yahoo.ca, Google.ca). Sites like http://www.gdsourcing.ca provide links to a comprehensive list of websites that provide Canadian Internet data. Several websites, such as emarketer.com, cyberatlas.com, and digitrends.net, provide access to general statistics relating to Internet usage and commerce on the Internet; and market research companies such as the Gartner Group, Media Metrix, and Forrester Research also offer research reports that may be purchased at their respective websites. Archives of news groups are another source of online information for marketers. There are, however, limitations to conducting secondary research on the Internet. Web coverage for specific issues may not be extensive with general-purpose search engines, and there is no guarantee of "freshness of links." Secondary research on the Internet also means that the researcher will need to sift through a large amount of information that has no bearing on the actual objective of the research. Finally, the researcher must be careful to verify the quality of this information before it is used.[23]

PROPRIETARY DATA

Marketers may also use **proprietary data,** or data collected by private business firms for their own use or by firms that are in the business of collecting and marketing information of interest to a class of clients. A brief description of some important secondary databases is provided in Table 7.5. There are a host of website companies conducting marketing research such as, for example, http://www.surveysite.com. There are two kinds of proprietary data: *syndicated* and *customized.*

Proprietary data
Data collected by private business firms that are in the business of collecting and marketing information of interest to a class of clients.

Syndicated Data

Syndicated data is data of interest to a potentially large number of users, collected by standardized procedures at regular periods. The type of information collected remains the same for successive surveys. The compiled reports are then sold to whoever may want to buy them without any exclusive right to use the data.

An example of a syndicated report is the BBM TV ratings report. The BBM Bureau of Measurement monitors people's TV-watching behaviour via placing a portable people meter (PPM) in the homes of a sample of Canadian TV households. PPMs are pager-size devices

Syndicated data
Data that is of interest to a potentially large number of users, regularly collected by standardized procedures and made commercially available to all interested marketers.

TABLE 7.5 Selected Sources of Commercial Data

1. Print Measurement Bureau: Canadian magazine readership, consumer patterns and media habits.
2. Financial Post Canadian Markets. Toronto: Financial Post Corporation Services. Contains forecasts for consumer spending as well as economic and demographic information.
3. Ipsos Reid Group Inc.: Syndicated studies, polls, and research.
4. Market Facts: Produces the Household Flow of Funds report.
5. Bureau of Broadcast Measurement (BBM) (http://www.bbm.ca): Radio and TV audience reports.
6. Newspaper Audience Data Bank (NADbank): Newspaper readership.
7. ACNielsen Canada (http://www.acnielsen.ca): Provides data on products and brands sold through retail outlets (e.g., MarketTrack, Fresh Track, Toy Track, Homescan) and data on television audiences (Media Research Services).
8. Other commercial research houses selling data to subscribers include: Starch, CARD, Equifax.

that detect inaudible codes imbedded in television programs. At the end of the day, participants place their PPM into base stations for recharging and sending the data to BBM for tabulation. This tabulation (along with data collected via diaries that the households fill in) are then compiled and published as BBM TV ratings reports. These reports enable advertisers to select programs and media vehicles that would best reach their target audience.

Other examples of syndicated data are the PRIZM scheme by the Claritas Co., which consists of 40 demographic and lifestyle clusters in Canada, and the PSYTE Canada Advantage cluster of MapInfo, which categorizes every Canadian neighbourhood into 60 clusters (see the Window on Research). These databases enable marketers to target specific postal codes and also to decide which media to use to research the selected postal codes.

WINDOW ON RESEARCH

PSYTE Canada Advantage

Most marketers are familiar with the geo-demographic neighbourhood classification system, i.e., people with similar cultural backgrounds, means, and perspectives form relatively homogeneous communities. Its basic premise is the maxim "birds of a feather flock together." Once settled in, people naturally emulate their neighbours, adopt similar social values, tastes and expectations and, most important of all, share similar patterns of consumer behaviour toward products, media, and promotions. This behaviour is the basis for the development of classification systems such as LIFESTYLES, PRIZM, CLUSTER PLUS, and MapInfo's PSYTE, all of which classify neighbourhoods and their households into clusters or groups of neighbourhoods, based on their underlying socio-economic and demographic composition. PSYTE Canada Advantage is MapInfo's new geo-demographic market segmentation system that classifies Canadian postal codes and Dissemination Areas into lifestyle groups and mutually exclusive neighbourhood types. PSYTE Canada Advantage is built on a 2001 Canadian Census base in addition to various other third-party data inputs. The resultant clusters represent snapshots of Canadian neighbourhoods. The PSYTE Canada database has 60 clusters that are organized into 15 major groups. Each cluster is associated with one of four settlement types: Urban, with 23 clusters; Suburban, with 17 clusters; Towns, with 8 clusters; and Rural, with 12 clusters. The 60 PSYTE groups are listed in the table on the next page, ranked by relative affluence.

Additional information is provided for each cluster. For example, *Cluster 04, Urban Gentry* are affluent and well-educated, and tend to be mature singles, couples, or small families. The Saab 900 is their favoured car; they drink scotch and sparkling water. Big on culture, *Urban Gentries* can be found living in million-dollar houses squeezed onto small lots near downtown cores where art galleries, theatres, and fine restaurants await their patronage. On the other hand, for the *Cluster 34, Pick-Ups and Dirt Bikes,* the preferred dwelling is a farm with dogs, some all-terrain vehicles, and a satellite dish. They spend their disposable income, which is less than the national average, on hunting, snowmobiling, and vacationing in an RV. They like to fix their own car, which is likely to be a pick-up.

PSYTE CANADA CLUSTER DEMOGRAPHICS

Group	Cluster	Name	% of Can.HH	Income Level	Age Group	HH Type	Education	Occupation	Housing Type	Housing Tenure	Dominant Language	Projected 5 Year Growth
U1	1	Canadian Establishment	0.17	Elite	45+	Families	University	Executive	Single Detached	Own	English	Low
	2	The Affluentials	0.65	Elite	35-64	Families	University	Executive	Single Detached	Own	English	Medium
	4	Urban Gentry	1.80	Upscale	45+	Mixed	University	Executive	Single Detached/Other	Own	English	Low
S1	3	Suburban Executives	1.67	Upscale	35-54	Large Families	University	Executive	Single Detached	Own	English	High
	6	Mortgaged in Suburbia	1.54	Upscale	25-44	Large Families	University/College	Executive	Single Detached	Own	English	High
	7	Technocrats & Bureaucrats	3.22	Upscale	25-54	Large Families	University	Executive/White Collar	Single Detached	Own	English	High
	9	Asian Heights	0.76	Upscale	35-54	Large Families	University/College	Management	Single Detached/Other	Own	English/Other	High
S2	5	Boomers & Teens	1.85	Upscale	35-54	Large Families	University/College	White Collar/Management	Single Detached	Own	English	High
	8	Stable Suburban Families	1.39	Upscale	45-64	Families	University/College	Management	Single Detached	Own	English	Low
	15	Small City Elite	1.81	Upper Middle	35-54	Families	University/College	White Collar/Management	Single Detached	Own	English	High
	16	Old Bungalow Burbs	1.70	Upper Middle	45-64	Families	College/University	Grey/White Collar	Single Detached	Own	English	Low
S3	10	Suburban Nesters	1.63	Upper Middle	50+	Families	University/College	Management/White Collar	Single Detached	Mixed	English	Low
	12	Brie & Chablis	1.11	Upper Middle	Mixed	Singles & Couples	University	Executive	Condominium/Apartment	Mixed	English	High
	17	Aging Erudites	1.51	Upper Middle	50+	Singles & Couples	University	White Collar/Management	Single Detached/Other	Mixed	English	Medium
S4	14	Satellite Suburbs	3.31	Upper Middle	25-54	Large Families	College	Grey Collar/Management	Single Detached/Other	Own	English	High
	23	Kindergarten Boom	2.85	Middle	<45	Large Families	College/High School	Grey/White Collar	Other/Single Detached	Mixed	English	High
T1	13	Blue Collar Winners	2.68	Upper Middle	35-60	Families	High School/College	Blue Collar/Management/Farm	Single Detached	Own	English	High
	19	Town Boomers	1.06	Upper Middle	30-54	Families	College/High School	Mixed	Single Detached	Own	English	Medium
	27	Old Towns' New Fringe	4.03	Middle	25-44	Families	College/High School	Grey/White Collar	Single Detached	Own	English	High
S5	18	Participaction Quebec	3.30	Upper Middle	25-54	Large Families	College/University	Mixed	Single Detached	Own	French	High
	24	New Quebec Rows	1.17	Middle	<45	Mixed	College	Grey/White Collar	Other	Mixed	French	High
	30	Quebec Melange	2.64	Middle	45-64	Mixed	College/High School	Grey/White Collar	Other/Single Detached	Mixed	French	Medium
	32	Traditional French Can. Families	2.72	Middle	25-54	Families	High School/College	Blue Collar	Single Detached	Own	French	High
R1	11	Northern Lights	0.49	Upper Middle	<40	Families	College/High School	Natural Resource/ Blue/White Collar	Single Detached/Other	Mixed	English	Medium
	22	The New Frontier	1.54	Middle	<45	Mixed	College/High School	Blue Collar/Natural Resource	Single Detached	Mixed	English	Low
	26	Rustic Prosperity	1.91	Middle	45-64	Large Families	High School/College	Blue Collar/Farm	Single Detached	Own	English	Low
	34	Pick-ups & Dirt Bikes	1.87	Middle	35-64	Families	High School	Blue Collar/Natural Resource/Farm	Single Detached	Own	English	Decline
	37	Quebec's Heartland	1.03	Lower Middle	35+	Families	High School/<Grade 9	Blue Collar/Farm	Single Detached	Own	French	Low
	38	The Grain Belt	0.68	Lower Middle	45+	Large Families	High School	Farm	Single Detached	Own	English	Decline
U2	21	Europa	1.30	Middle	45-64	Large Families	<Grade 9	Blue/Grey Collar	Other/Single Detached	Mixed	English/Other	Medium
	25	Asian Mosaic	1.41	Middle	Mixed	Families	Mixed	Grey Collar	Other/Single Detached	Mixed	English/Other	Medium
	41	High Rise Melting Pot	1.39	Lower Middle	<40	Mixed	Mixed	Mixed	Apartment	Rent	English/Other	Low
U3	28	Conservative Homebodies	3.45	Middle	50+	Singles & Couples	College/High School	Mixed	Single Detached/Other	Own	English	Low
	33	High Rise Sunsets	1.27	Middle	60+	Singles & Couples	Mixed	Retired/Management	Apartment	Rent	English	High
U4	20	Young Urban Professionals	1.72	Upper Middle	<35	Singles	University	Management/White Collar	Other/Apartment	Mixed	English	Medium
	29	Young Urban Mix	1.98	Middle	<35	Mixed	College/University	White/Grey Collar	Other/Apartment	Rent	English	Medium
	36	Young Urban Intelligentsia	1.60	Lower Middle	<35	Singles	University	White Collar/Executive	Apartment/Other	Rent	English	High
	40	University Enclaves	1.81	Lower Middle	<35	Singles	University	White/Grey Collar	Other/Apartment	Rent	English	Medium
	51	Young City Singles	1.89	Low	<35	Singles	College/University	Grey Collar	Apartment/Other	Rent	English	High
	56	Urban Bohemia	1.07	Low	Mixed	Singles	University	Grey/White Collar	Other/Apartment	Rent	French/ English/Other	Medium
T2	31	Old Leafy Towns	2.61	Middle	50+	Singles & Couples	College/High School	Mixed Single	Detached	Own	English	High
	35	Town Renters	0.81	Lower Middle	<40	Families	High School/College	Grey Collar	Other	Rent	English	Medium
	39	Nesters & Young Homesteaders	2.16	Lower Middle	<25 & 65+	Singles & Couples	College/High School	Grey Collar	Other/Single Detached	Mixed	English	Medium
	44	Young Grey Collar	0.79	Lower Middle	<30 & 65+	Mixed	High School/College	Grey Collar	Other/Single Detached	Mixed	English	Low
	46	Quiet Towns	2.03	Lower Middle	<25 & 65+	Singles & Couples	High School	Grey Collar	Single Detached/Other	Mixed	English	Medium
R2	43	Agrarian Blues	0.22	Lower Middle	50+ Large	Families	<Grade 9	Farm/Blue Collar	Single Detached	Own	English/French	Decline
	47	Rod & Rifle	2.36	Lower Middle	55+	Families	High School/<Grade 9	Blue Collar/Natural Resource/Farm	Single Detached	Own	English	Low
	49	Down, Down East	0.74	Lower Middle	Mixed	Large Families	High School/<Grade 9	Blue Collar/Unemployed/ Natural Resource	Single Detached	Own	English	Decline
	50	Big Country Families	1.49	Lower Middle	45+	Large Families	High School/<Grade 9	Blue Collar/Farm/White Collar	Single Detached/Band	Own	English	Low
	52	Quebec Rural Blues	2.52	Low	50+	Families	<Grade 9	Blue Collar/Natural Resource	Single Detached	Own	French	Low
	55	Old Canadian Rustics	0.96	Low	65+	Singles & Couples	High School/<Grade 9	Blue/Grey Collar/Farm	Single Detached	Own	English	Decline
U5	42	Euro Quebec	0.94	Lower Middle	Mixed	Mixed	<Grade 9/High School	Blue/Grey Collar	Other	Rent	French/Other	Low
	45	Old Quebec Walkups	1.74	Lower Middle	<30 & 55+	Mixed	<Grade 9/High School	White/Grey Collar	Other	Rent	French	Low
	53	Quebec Town Elders	2.66	Low	<30 & 55+	Mixed	<Grade 9/High School	Grey Collar	Other/Single Detached	Mixed	French	Medium
	54	Aging Quebec Urbanites	0.27	Low	<30 & 60+	Singles	<Grade 9/High School	Grey/White Collar	Other/Apartment	Rent	French	Medium
	57	Quebec's New Urban Mosaic	2.15	Low	<35 & 60+	Mixed	<Grade 9/High School	Grey Collar	Other	Rent	French	Low
U6	48	Struggling Downtowns	2.90	Lower Middle	<35 & 65+	Mixed	High School	Grey/Blue Collar	Single Detached/Other	Mixed	English	Low
	58	Aged Pensioners	1.11	Low	<30 & 60+	Singles	<Grade 9/High School	Grey Collar	Apartment/Other	Rent	English	Medium
	59	Big City Stress	1.06	Low	<35	Mixed	High School/<Grade 9	Grey Collar/Unemployed/ Blue Collar	Other/Apartment	Rent	English/Other	Decline
	60	Old Grey Towers	0.48	Low	65+	Singles	<Grade 9	Retired	Apartment	Rent	English	High

SOURCE: ©2001 MapInfo Corporation (http://www.mapinfo.com), PSYTE Brochure, Canada.

Customized Data

Customized data Data that is collected at the behest of a small group of pre-identified customers, and made available only to sponsoring companies.

The other category of proprietary data is **customized data.** This type of data is collected at the behest of a small group of pre-identified consumers, and their use is generally restricted to the sponsoring companies. Research companies collect customized data to answer specific research questions. Therefore, the collection is done on a project-by-project basis, with both the survey questions and the research method identified individually for each study.

Some of the more prominent suppliers of customized information are research companies with a customer panel. For example, a market research firm like Ipsos Reid (Canada's Access Panel: http://www.ipsos.ca) has consumer panels of over 50,000 household—more than 130,000 individuals. The data from these consumer panels is compiled to make reports that are used by companies. Internet portals like Yahoo.ca have developed consumer panels to understand how people use the World Wide Web. This information helps Yahoo! design new content and products to meet customer's needs.

Tracking Services

Some secondary research supplier firms provide tracking services. They survey customers to track their opinions and attitudes on a longitudinal basis. For example, Ipsos Reid has been tracking the book publishing industry (Ipsos Book Trends).

Figure 7.9 shows an example of clustering of Toronto households using the PSYTE Advantage Neighbourhood Segmentation System for the imported beer market. Any cluster that indexes above 100 is considered to have a high propensity to use a particular product, whereas an index less than 100 means the cluster has a below-average propensity to use the product compared to the benchmark. From this clustering one can identify two distinct target groups: one, older and more affluent, and the other, younger and well educated.

Single-Source Data

A common problem marketers face is having to combine sources for different pieces of the information puzzle. For example, the MRCA household panel report gives the marketer information about what households with different demographic profiles are buying, but not on what media they are viewing or reading. On the other hand, BBM TV reports provide data on the audience profile of particular TV programs, but not on their buying preferences. This necessitates that marketers match aggregate information from two diverse sources. To overcome this problem, some research suppliers now offer what are known as **single-source data.** This data directly links consumers' exposure to advertising with their purchase response at the individual consumer level.

Single-source data The organization of both purchase incidence and consumer characteristics data in a single integrated record.

One company that offers this service is Information Resources Inc., with its behaviour-scan system, in which matched samples of population in the sampled geographic markets are recruited as panel members. The members are given ID cards for shopping at the area's supermarkets. The two samples are fed, via their home cable TVs, TV programs that are identical except for one of the commercials, which is different between the two samples. Since the panel members use their shopping ID at the supermarket where they shop, their purchases can be tied to the viewing of the commercial. The marketer can find out which commercial was more effective. Furthermore, since an individual panel household's demographic profile is prerecorded in the database, the purchase response data can be analyzed by demographics. That is, the marketer knows not only which commercial was more effective but also whether it was more effective for some demographic groups than others. A brief outline of behaviour-scan and other single-source systems is presented in Figure 7.10 on page 268.

FIGURE 7.9 Example of Clustering Using the PSYTE System

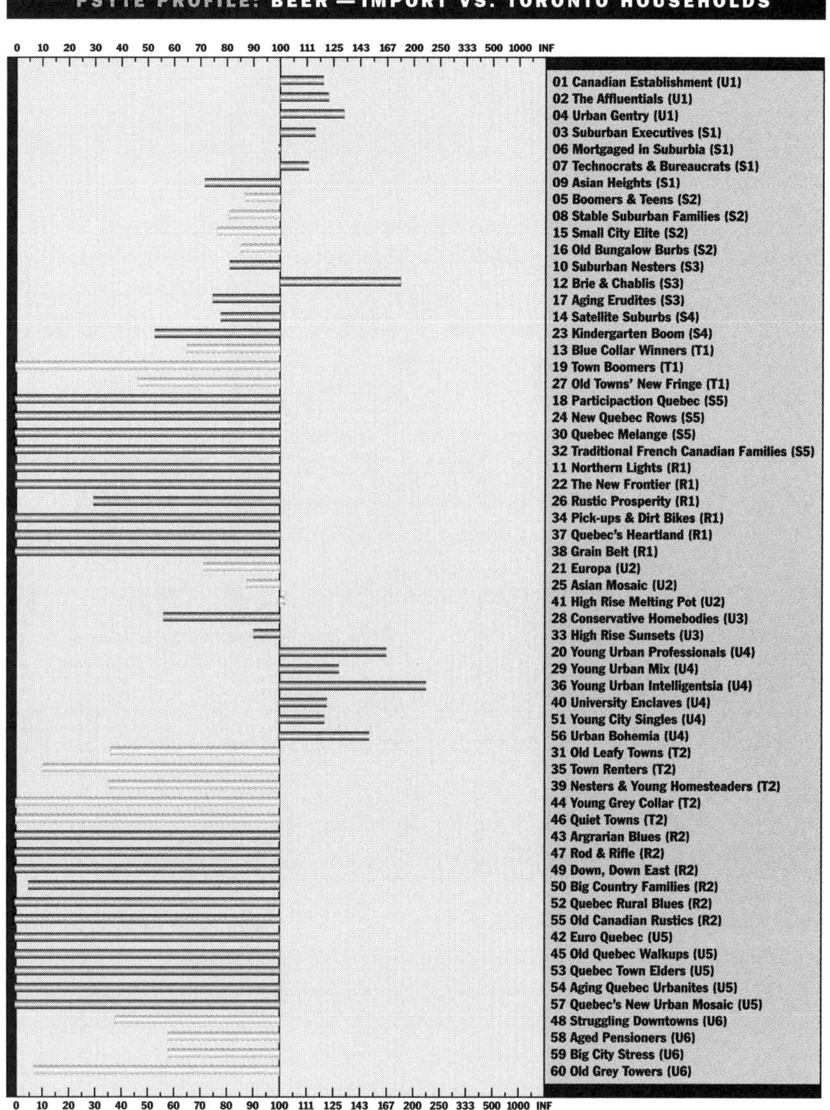

SOURCE: Thompson, Paul. "Leveraging the Target Market Cycle to Grow and Strengthen your Business." *MapInfo Magazine,* 2004, 8, no. 1 (http://www.mapinfo.com/magazine).

Another type of single-source data is the scanner data that links consumer identity with products bought. When you go to a supermarket, the cashier scans the universal price code (UPC) on the package, and the computer automatically identifies the product and supplies the price information. The store can collect this scanner data and use it to track product sales. Some retailers link this scanner data to household data for its shoppers. To do this, they issue the shopping households a membership card, which would be scanned every time the household made the purchase.

FIGURE 7.10 The Process of Single-Source Data Collection

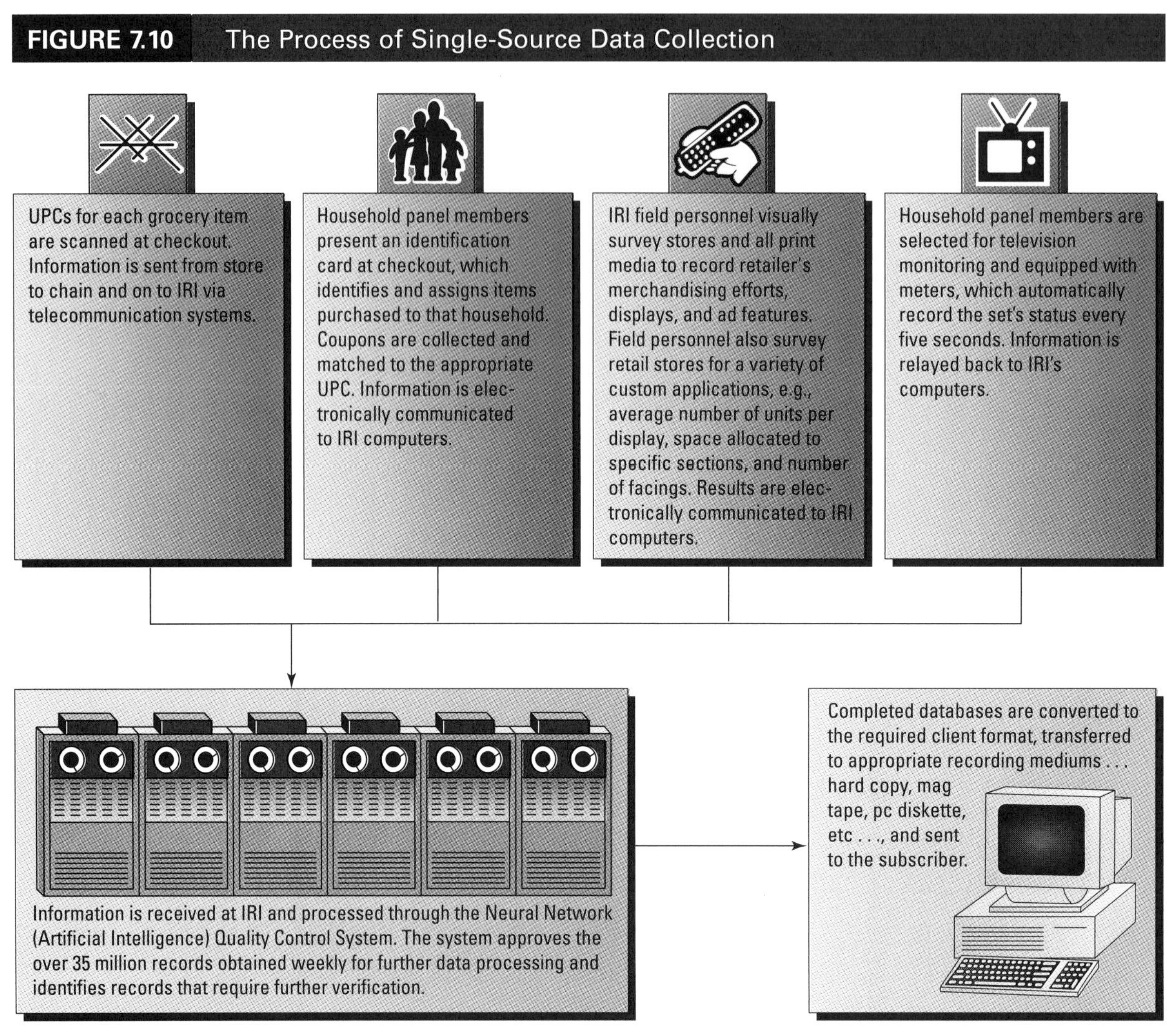

UPCs for each grocery item are scanned at checkout. Information is sent from store to chain and on to IRI via telecommunication systems.
Household panel members present an identification card at checkout, which identifies and assigns items purchased to that household. Coupons are collected and matched to the appropriate UPC. Information is electronically communicated to IRI computers.
IRI field personnel visually survey stores and all print media to record retailer's merchandising efforts, displays, and ad features. Field personnel also survey retail stores for a variety of custom applications, e.g., average number of units per display, space allocated to specific sections, and number of facings. Results are electronically communicated to IRI computers.
Household panel members are selected for television monitoring and equipped with meters, which automatically record the set's status every five seconds. Information is relayed back to IRI's computers.
Information is received at IRI and processed through the Neural Network (Artificial Intelligence) Quality Control System. The system approves the over 35 million records obtained weekly for further data processing and identifies records that require further verification.
Completed databases are converted to the required client format, transferred to appropriate recording mediums . . . hard copy, mag tape, pc diskette, etc . . ., and sent to the subscriber.

SOURCE: Aaker, David A.,, V. Kumar, and George S. Day, *Marketing Research.* Toronto: John Wiley & Sons, Inc., 1995): 152. Reprinted by permission of John Wiley & Sons, Inc.

DATABASE RESEARCH

Addressability
A feature of a database wherein each customer's address is known in order to enable a marketer to address marketing communications individually, on a one-on-one basis.

Marketers may also build their own database containing the names of and relevant information about their current or prospective customers. This information is obtained by a number of means, such as warranty cards, sweepstake entries, rebate forms, special surveys, asking customers to return for free products, and premiums. The most significant feature of such a database is consumer **addressability.** That is, each customer's address is known. This feature enables a marketer to address marketing communications individually, on a one-on-one basis.

Equally important is the potential of this database for customer research. Analysis can reveal customer purchase patterns by customer groups, by geography, by demographics, by seasonality, by product clusters, and so forth. For example, a credit card company can identify heavy travellers or heavy users of fine dining; it can analyze the data for whether those who patronize fine dining restaurants are also heavy users of theatre performances, beauty parlors, or educational seminars, for example. This type of analysis of customer profiles and clustering of products bought by individuals can be very useful to marketers in planning and directing their communications and product offerings to customers.

VIRTUAL REALITY: A NEW TOOL OF CUSTOMER RESEARCH

LO 6

Virtual reality refers to interactive, immersive, computer-generated 3D visual and sound display. The virtual reality equipment consists of a stereoscopic head-mounted display, body suit, and glove to provide tactile and sensory input. With virtual reality, test environments can be simulated to be indistinguishable from their real (physical) versions.

Virtual reality
An interactive, immersive, computer-generated 3D visual and sound display of stimuli and situations representative of their real (physical) versions.

VIRTUAL REALITY TECHNIQUES IN CONSUMER RESEARCH

Let us describe two typical applications of virtual reality: *virtual shopping* and *virtual test marketing.*

Virtual Shopping

Using computer technology, a store aisle can be simulated on the computer. Sitting in front of a video-game type of screen, customers can walk through the aisle, look at a shelf display, examine a product, read the label, request additional information, learn if a coupon is available, put the item back on the shelf, or place it in a cart (depicted by a visual icon), all with the click of a mouse. The computer displays whatever information the customer wants and, in turn, keeps a record of customer activity. Thus, it is a useful tool for studying customers' information-seeking behaviour as well as customer responses to alternative shelf displays. A version of this system, called Visionary Shopper, is currently being tested in the United Kingdom. It will cost a fifth of the conventional simulated test-marketing approaches.

An example of the use of the "Visionary Shopper" to examine a key category management topic, namely, shelf layout, is a study conducted in the frozen-foods section of a store to show how a simple rearrangement of shelf layouts could be beneficial for customers, manufacturers, and retailers. At the time of the study, it was common practice to stock frozen-food shelf sections by segments—single-serve entrées, family-style entrées, kids's entrées, pot pies, etc. The manufacturer felt that stocking by brand instead of segment would increase the time that consumers spent at the shelf and make shopping easier for them as well. As a part of the experiment, two layouts were created for the shelf, in addition to the existing layout. In the first layout, brands were blocked together, and then segments within the brand were blocked. In the second layout, brands were blocked, and key competitive items between the manufacturer and their main competitors were stocked together on the shelf in a "competitive" set. The results of the experiment were extremely positive. The manufacturer's brand dollar sales increased by 16 percent in the "competitive set" layout over the "only brand-blocking" layout. (The manufacturer had a price and size advantage over the competitor). Brand blocking also increased retailer's dollar sales by 18 percent and the competitive layout increased sales by 16 percent.[24]

Virtual Test Marketing

In an actual virtual-reality test marketing project, the goal was to evaluate demand for electric cars. Respondents were placed in front of a multimedia display. The screen flashed newspaper stories from an imagined future time. This was done to move respondents *forward in time.* Respondents then interacted with the program and its laser disc full of an array of verbal, pictorial, text, and video material. Respondents could look at the car display, walk around it, talk to salesmen, read press reports, and talk to other customers. After this simulation, they were asked to drive a conventional car, but with the engine replaced by an electric engine. Following the real-world test drive, they returned to their computers to answer questions on their attitudes and preferences. The proprietary name of this technique is the Information Acceleration, designed by Glen Urban and his colleagues, who also operate a Marketing Simulation Lab that is equipped to create virtual shopping environments. The technique has been adapted to test new services (as opposed to goods). Called SERVASSOR, the technique employs simulation of a service on the computer such as telebanking.[25]

ADVANTAGES OF VIRTUAL REALITY TECHNIQUES

Virtual-shopping research has several advantages over other methods. Compared to focus-group and concept-test research, the virtual-shopping method is able to simulate the real-world shopping environment much more realistically. In the virtual-shopping experiment, the customer is exposed to very realistic shelf displays, complete with the clutter of competing brands; even the hustle-bustle and the sight and sound of other shoppers can be simulated. Another advantage is that the computer is able to record much more detailed data about shopper behaviour. This data includes the amount of time the shopper took to examine the product and make a decision, the content of information he or she sought and considered, the sequence in which the information was examined, and the sequence in which brands were examined and products chosen.

The method also has advantages over the conventional store-simulation methods. In the conventional method, a small-scale physical model store (or store shelf) is created, without the benefit of electronic display and manipulation of information. The virtual-shopping research tool presents the store information not only more realistically but also more economically. It costs much less to program and create virtual images and also to record customer processing data. Moreover, the computer records the data unobtrusively (i.e., without the consumer being conscious of being observed).[26] The Window on Research illustrates these advantages.

DATA TRAIL FROM SHOPPING ON THE INTERNET

Shopping on the Internet is a use of technology that is widening its appeal. Customers can access product information on websites or home pages created by business firms. With electronic commerce (or e-commerce), consumers can use the Internet to pay with their credit cards, and companies can get bank authorization for credit payments. Among the firms that are trying out this capability is Uncover, Inc., a database company that offers table-of-contents information for thousands of journals. The company has experimented with offering the information on the Internet to preapproved customer accounts. E-commerce leaves a rich data trail. Since the information about every transaction is tracked by cookies (unique identifiers), it will be possible to analyze this data for customer profiles and patterns of purchasing,

WINDOW ON RESEARCH

A Virtual-Reality Consumer Research Project

A snack manufacturer wanted to find out if its line of snacks included items that consumers perceived as close substitutes. If two or more items were perceived as substitutes, then the firm could trim the line without reducing sales (but reducing the costs). On the flip side, the firm wanted to know what snack products of the competition were perceived to be substitutes of the firm's own products. If there was a competitor's snack product against which the firm's product was briefly compared but then rejected as not being a good substitute, this would suggest a gap in the firm's own product line. The firm could fill this hole by bringing out a new product.

To answer these questions, the firm employed a virtual-shopping experiment. Four hundred consumers were recruited from six shopping malls. They were invited to the local simulation lab repeatedly to buy snack products from a virtual vending machine. Since they were invited for several shopping trips, it was possible to first study their preferences and then custom-design the vending machine inventory to force a reconsideration of their choices. For example, in a subsequent shopping trip, the vending machine display was manipulated to show the item of a particular customer's preference as being out of stock. The customer was, thus, forced to consider substitutes (although she or he was free to buy or not buy a substitute). This enabled the researcher to study customer perceptions of what was a close substitute for their favourite brand versus what was not.

This method had three advantages: First, it was much less costly to set up vending machine displays on the computer screens than would have been the case with physically real displays. Second, the out-of-stock manipulation could be custom designed for each consumer based on the knowledge of what his or her current preference was. Finally, the consumer perception and preference data could be collected *unobtrusively*.

SOURCE: Adapted from Burke, Raymond R. "Virtual Shopping." *ORMS Today 22,* no. 4 (August 1995): 28–34. http://www.vendline.com.

including the cluster of products different individuals buy. This enables sites to customize data for the customer when he or she visits the site again, and also to send the customer information relating to her or his interests. Thus, Internet-based commerce will make available one more tool of research for insight into customer behaviour.

CUSTOMER BEHAVIOUR RESEARCH AND THE THREE CUSTOMER ROLES

LO 7

Adopting a customer orientation implies that marketers assess the needs and wants of customers in each of their three roles (see Table 7.6). Thus, research concerning customer behaviour should cover not only the user role but also the payer and buyer roles. Much of the research in the past has focused on users, such as the research to identify potential needs and wants that new products might satisfy. For payers, research is needed to understand the price sensitivity of various customer segments, or their reference prices (i.e., the price they expect to pay and the price they consider fair). Research is also needed to understand customer preferences for alternative financing options (e.g., leasing). Finally, research is needed on the attitudes of buyers toward shopping, alternative vendors, and alternative means of making marketplace transactions (e.g., home-shopping networks, banking on the ATMs, and Internet shopping). For business customers, we need to research their attitudes toward and experience with electronic data interchange (EDI) systems used in purchasing.

The different research techniques discussed in this chapter are also applicable to the three roles, although some are more suited to one particular role than others. Qualitative research methods of focus groups and customer visits are useful primarily for user roles to identify unfulfilled needs and wants. But topics explored during focus groups and customer visits can include payer concerns (e.g., perceived value, reference prices, and affordability) and buyer concerns (e.g., perceptions of alternative vendors). Motivation research is likely to be useful primarily for users, to identify their subconscious motives.

The quantitative research technique of survey research has the widest applicability across three roles. The content of the survey can pertain to users (to elicit users' beliefs, attitudes, and behaviours), to payers (questioning them about their desired price in order to determine target pricing), and to buyers (to assess their attitudes about vendors). The experimental method is often used and is very useful for users. Blind taste tests are designed to elicit customer preferences for new products per se, and then again for new products under specific brand names. On the other hand, test markets (a form of experimental research) are designed primarily to test buyer response to new products and the related marketing mix.

TABLE 7.6 Researching Customer Behaviour and the Three Customer Roles

	User	Payer	Buyer
Need to Research Customer Behaviour	• Researching user needs and wants for new product designs.	• Researching price-sensitivity of customers. • Researching customer preferences toward leasing. • Researching customers' reference prices.	• Researching customer attitudes toward alternative vendors (e.g., home-shopping network) • Researching buyer use of an experience with EDI systems
Specific Research Methods			
Focus groups Customer visits	• To explore user views and to identify alternative unfulfilled needs and wants.	• Perceived value and reference price as discussion topics in focus group and customer visits.	• Perceptions of vendors can be explored
Motivation research	• To identify subconscious motives of users		
Survey research	• To elicit users' beliefs, attitudes, behaviours, etc.	• Survey of customers for target pricing, price awareness, and so on	• Survey of buyers to assess vendor attitudes
Experimental research	• Blind taste tests. • Product use tests		• Test markets
Information processing research	• Research on how viewers process advertising messages.		• Primarily applicable to study the information processing by buyers

So far, information-processing research has been used primarily for buyers. For example, it has sought to answer such questions as: Do shoppers pay attention to nutrition information? Do they compare brands by attributes or by overall brand ratings? How many stores and brands do they examine? Recently, advertising research has adopted this method. Typically, customers are shown advertisements and asked what they remember of the message and what impressions they form. This is researching the user, since the advertising message has to appeal to the user who has to accept the advertised product as meeting his or her needs.

SUMMARY

The various methods of researching customer behaviour are either qualitative or quantitative. Qualitative methods include focus groups, customer visits, motivation research, and interpretative research. Quantitative methods entail surveys or experiments. Surveys find out what customers think, know, or feel already. Experiments, in contrast, present some stimuli and seek customer reactions to these stimuli. Some major topics researched by quantitative methods are customer attitudes, image or self-concept measurement, multi-attribute models, and perceptual and preference maps. **LO 1, 2, 3**

Along with these specific quantitative and qualitative methods, there are several special streams of research in the customer behaviour field: information-processing research, simulation, secondary research, and research using virtual reality and the Internet. These methods range from qualitative (verbal, unordered responses) to quantitative (numerically scalable responses), exploratory (discovering hitherto unknown response possibilities) to directed (finding out the incidence of previously known responses), secondary (using published data) to primary (collecting new data), low-tech (e.g., face-to-face interview) to high-tech (e.g., using virtual reality), and from objective (e.g., measuring eye movement) to subjective (e.g., interpretative research, such as Consumer Behaviour Odyssey). **LO 4, 5, 6**

Although these methods differ in their techniques as well as their goals, they have a common purpose: to help marketers understand the customer, get inside her or his mind, know what concerns him or her, what market values she or he seeks, what he or she likes and dislikes, how she or he perceives various marketing stimuli, how he or she responds to them, and why she or he responds that way. In other words, marketers want to know why customers manifest the particular marketplace behaviours that they do. Such an understanding of customers and of the market values they seek is a prerequisite to designing a good marketing program.

KEY TERMS

Addressability 268
Behaviourally Anchored Scales 251
Concurrent Protocols 261
Consumer Behaviour Odyssey 244
Convenience Sampling 235
CT Scan 260
Customer Visit 237
Customized Data 266
Disguised-Nonstructured Techniques 241
Disguised-Structured Techniques 239
Experiment 247
Focus Groups 235
Information Board 258
Information Processing Research 257
Interpretative Research 244
Motivation Research (MR) 238
MRI 260

Nondisguised-Nonstructured Techniques 239
Nondisguised-Structured Techniques 239
Perceptual and Preference Mapping 254
Proprietary Data 263
Protocols 261
Qualitative Research 246
Quantitative Research 235
Retrospective Protocols 261
Secondary Research 261
Simulation 248
Single-Source Data 266
Syndicated Data 263
Techno-consumers 245
Test Marketing 247
Thematic Apperception Test (TAT) 242
Verbatim 246
Virtual Reality 269
Visual Image Profile 260
Word Association 241
Zaltman Metaphor Elicitation Technique (ZMET) 242

DISCUSSION QUESTIONS AND EXERCISES

1. Recently, companies have been disappointed by the results of traditional quantitative market research data. Many companies, such as Honda, Mattel, Sony, and Yamaha, have adopted "live learning labs," where they can mingle with, talk to, and directly observe consumers using their products, and can learn firsthand about these users' likes and dislikes. This approach is called interpretative research. Discuss the advantages and disadvantages of this method of customer inquiry.
2. Assume you are a product manager in charge of launching a new chain of pizza outlets. One of the needs that customers have identified in the past is the desire to "make their own" pizzas in the restaurant when they come in to eat. To gain deeper insight into this customer need, you decide to conduct some customer research. Develop a list of research questions you would want to have answered, and outline appropriate research methods.
3. Recently, companies have been creating huge customer databases to better understand their customers, to analyze patterns of customer purchases, and to enable marketers to better target their one-on-one communications. What databases are you a part of? How did the company get its information about you? What kinds of communications have you been receiving from it? Have these communications been effective at getting you to buy the company's products?
4. Interview ten consumers, and for each, create a perceptual map for the following products, using two different dimensions to distinguish at least six brands for each product: (a) breakfast foods, (b) pizza, and (c) alcoholic beverages. How do these maps help the marketers of these products?.
5. What type of research—qualitative or quantitative—is most appropriate for the following situations and why? What type of sample should be used? What method would you use to contact respondents? Explain each of your answers.
   a. Unilever wants to determine whether a new brand of fabric softener will be accepted by consumers.
   b. Calvin Klein wants to find out what new fashion designs will be most appealing to university students.
   c. Imperial Tobacco wants to gain some insight into the attitudes toward smoking among teenagers and young adults.
6. Using the Internet, access the website of Statistics Canada: http://www.statcan.ca. Document the kind of information that is available from this resource.

NOTES

1 Eve Lazarus, "Intrawest Digs Deep," *Marketing,* 109, no. 19 (May 31, 2004): 4. http://www.Intrawest.com.

2 Dana James, "The Future of Online Research," *Marketing News* (January 3, 2000): 1–11, Quoted by Judy Strauss, Raymond Frost in *E-Marketing,* Upper Saddle River, NJ: Prentice Hall, 2000.

3 Margaret R. Roller, "Virtual Research Exists, But How Real Is It?," *Marketing New* (January 15, 1996): 13.

4 Edward F. McQuarrie, *Customer Visits: Building a Better Market Focus* (Newbury Park, CA: Sage, 1993).

5 Gary McWilliams, "A Notebook That Puts Users Ahead of Gimmicks," *Business Week* (September 27, 1993) 92.

6 Johnny K. Johansson and Ikujiro Nonaka, "Market Research the Japanese Way," *Harvard Business Review,* May/June 1987, 16–19.

7 Thomas J. Reynolds and Jonathan Gutman, "Laddering Theory, Method, Analysis, and Interpretation," *Journal of Advertising Research* 28, No. 1 (February/March 1988): 11–31.

8 Gerald Zaltman and Robin Higie Coulter, "Seeing the Voice of the Customer: Metaphor-Based Advertising Research," *Journal of Advertising Research,* July/August 1995, 35–49.

9 Basil G. Englis and Michael R. Solomon, "Life/Style Online: A Web-Based Methodology for Visually-Oriented Consumer Research," *Journal of Interactive Marketing* 14, no. 11 (Winter 2000): 2–14.

10 Bobby J. Calder and Alice M. Tybout, "Interpretive Qualitative, and Traditional Scientific Empirical Consumer Behaviour Research," in *Interpretive Consumer Research,* ed. Elizabeth C. Hirschman, 199–208 (Provo, UT: Association for Consumer Research, 1989).

11 Elizabeth C. Hirschman and Morris B. Holbrook, *Postmodern Consumer Research: The Study of Consumption as Text* (Newbury Park, CA: Sage, 1992).

12 Russell W. Belk, John F. Sherry, and Melanie Wallendorf, "A Naturalistic Inquiry into Buyer and Seller Behaviour at a Swap Meet," *Journal of Consumer Research,* March 1988, 14: 449–70.

13 Robert F. Kelley, "Culture as Commodity: The Marketing of Cultural Objects and Cultural Experiences," *Advances in Consumer Research* 14, eds. Paul Anderson and Melanie Wallendorf, 347–51 (Provo, UT: Association for Consumer Research).

14 Judy Strauss and Raymond Frost, *E-Marketing* (Upper Saddle River, NJ: Prentice Hall 2000).

15 Raymond R. Burke, Arvind Rangaswamy, and Sunil Gupta, "Rethinking Marketing Research in the Digital World," eBRC Research Center Working Paper, January 1999, http://www.ebrc.psu.edu/publications/researchpapers.html.

16 Maryann Jones Thompson "When Market Research Turns into Marketing," *The Industry Standard,* August 23, 1999, 68–70.

17 Naresh K. Malhotra, *Marketing Research: An Applied Orientation* (Upper Saddle River, NJ: Prentice Hall, 1996); David Aaker, V. Kumar, and George S. Day, *Marketing Research* (New York: John Wiley & Sons, 1995).

18 Raymond Burke, Barbara E. Kahn, Leonard M. Lodish, and Bari A. Harlam, "Comparing Dynamic Consumer Decision Processes and Real and Computer-Simulated Environments," Report Number 91-116, June (Cambridge, MA: Marketing Science Institute, 1991).

19 Gilbert A. Churchill, *Marketing Research: Methodological Foundations,* 6th ed. (Fort Worth, TX: Dryden, 1994).

20 Adapted from William D. Wells and Douglas J. Tigert, "Activities, Interests, and Opinions," *Journal of Advertising Research* 11 (August 1971): 35. Reprinted from the *Journal of Advertising Research* © 1971, by the Advertising Research Foundation.

21 Merrie Brucks, "Search Monitor: An Approach for Computer-Controlled Experiments Involving Consumer Information Search," *Journal of Consumer Research* 15 (June 1988): 117–21.

21a Carolyn Yoon, Angela H. Gutchess, Fred Feinberg, and Thad A. Polk, "A Functional Magnetic Resonance Imaging Study of Neural Dissociations between Brand and Person Judgements," *Journal of Consumer Research* 33 (June 2006): 31–40.

22 David W. Stewart and Michael A. Kamins, *Secondary Research: Information Sources and Methods* (Newbury Park, CA: Sage, 1993).

23 Raymond R. Burke, Arvind Rangaswamy, and Sunil Gupta, "Rethinking Marketing Research in the Digital World," eBRC Research Center Working Paper, January 1999, http://www.ebrc.psu.edu/publications/researchpapers.html.

24 Stephen P. Needel, "Understanding Consumer Response to Category Management Through Virtual Reality," *Journal of Advertising Research* 38 no.4 (July/August 1998): 61–67.

25 Leslie de Chernatony and Philip J. Rosenberger III, "Virtual Reality Techniques in NPD Research," *Journal of the Market Research Society* 37, no. 4 1995: 345-54.

26 Raymond R. Burke, "Virtual Shopping," *ORMS Today* 22, no.4 (August 1995): 28–34.

PART 3 Customer Decisions and Relationships

CHAPTER 8

Individual Customer Decision Making

LEARNING OBJECTIVES

After reading this chapter you should be able to:

LO 1 Understand the individual decision maker.

LO 2 Describe the five-step consumer decision process.

LO 3 Identify the sources of decision information, and explain search strategies and the determinants of the amount of search.

LO 4 Describe the four non-compensatory models, and explain how and when each one is used.

LO 5 Relate consumer decision making to the three consumer roles.

Cultural Differences in the Buying Process

In a study of Chinese customers in Montreal, interviews were conducted with recent buyers of electronic equipment (e.g., audio systems, VCRs, and televisions). The study found that the most notable cultural characteristic of this group of customers was the high value they placed on thrift and the habit of saving. Buying by debt financing was generally disapproved of, and, consequently, the impulse purchase of an expensive item was rare among the Chinese. Credit cards were used for convenience, not for credit; most Chinese customers paid off their entire balances monthly. This is in sharp contrast to North American customers, who usually finance their major purchases by credit. This norm of not buying on credit makes every major purchase a three-stage process for Chinese customers: (1) budgeting for the purchase, (2) accumulating the savings, and (3) implementing the purchase. Information search takes on a different character during these stages. In the budgeting and saving stage, the search is lengthy, broad in scope, and leisurely. The customer is broadly scanning the environment rather than focusing on a specific aspect. The purpose of this search is to become familiar with the product category and various brands available in the market in order to learn price points, to seek others' general impressions about various brands and features, and to decide on the amount they would like to spend. In the second stage, the search virtually stops, and the customer focuses on saving the amount needed. Finally, in the third, post-saving stage, which begins after the needed budgeted amount has been saved, the search is short, intense, and directed at specific information about specific brands and models.

The study also observed some differences in the information sources used by Chinese customers. They distinguished between factual and evaluative information.

FIGURE 8.1 Conceptual Framework

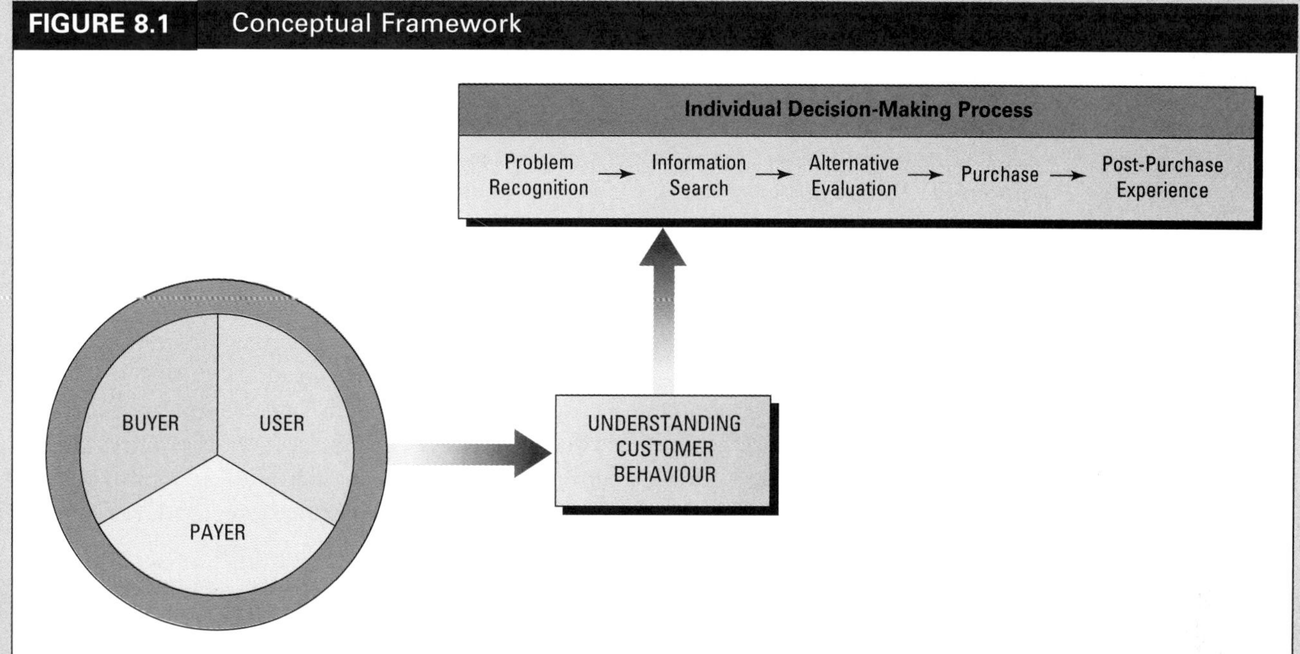

They relied on salespersons for the former but not for the latter. Thus, they could ask the salesperson about product features and other objective features, but for judgments about overall product quality, they sought independent sources like *Consumer Reports* and personal sources like friends and relatives. This general distrust of salespersons also required them to rely much more on their own product inspection, even for objective features. Thus, Chinese customers tended to search for product information in stores where they could browse without being approached by salespersons.

Because the implementation of the decision process is influenced by cultural background, it is important that marketers study the decision-making process for customers in different countries, and for customers of different cultural backgrounds within the same country.[1]

As a customer, understanding your own decision processes might improve your future decisions (see Figure 8.1 for the conceptual framework). As a marketer, understanding the process helps organize marketing efforts in a fashion that is responsive to the customer's decision-making imperatives.

To lay the foundation for such an understanding, this chapter begins by describing the role of the individual decision maker. It identifies the steps in the decision process, including the types of decisions relevant to customer behaviour and the ways in which customers gather information. We present several models for the process of evaluating alternatives, and we identify conditions under which a customer is likely to use each model. Finally, the chapter analyzes purchase and post-purchase behaviour as part of the decision process.

THE INDIVIDUAL DECISION MAKER

LO 1

Purchase decisions are sometimes made by individuals in households; at other times, they are made by groups of people, such as spouses, or by committees in business organizations. The next chapter deals with group decisions; this chapter focuses on *individual* decision makers. This focus includes situations when the individual decision maker is making a decision about any product in any context, as long as she or he is making the decision about a product for his or her own use. Thus, it includes purchase decisions customers make not only in their personal capacity but also in their capacity as an employee in a firm. For example, employment-related travel purchases, when made by individual employees (rather than by a corporate travel officer), are considered individual purchase decisions even though they occur in an organizational context, and even though someone else pays for them. Of course, individual decisions are made using somewhat different criteria when someone else is the payer (as in business travel) compared to when the decision maker himself or herself is the payer. In the former case, the decision maker may be less concerned with the economic and financing values compared with the other values. But the decision process remains the same.

ROLES OF THE DECISION MAKER

In individual decision making (as opposed to organizational decisions), the three customer roles (payer, user, and buyer) could all be played by a single individual, or each could be played by a different individual. Often, at least two of the roles of a customer—those of buyer and user—come together within a single person. In these cases, the individual decision maker must be concerned with at least four of the six market values of our framework (i.e., the market values relevant to the user and the buyer roles). In addition, the payer role is often played by the same individual so that all six market values—performance, social/psychological, convenience, service, economic, and financing—come into play in individual decision making. The individual may also be the buyer and payer but not the user in some situations. But even when the same individual plays all three roles, the concerns may differ for each role, creating internal role conflict. This chapter covers the decision processes of all individual customers, whether they are playing one, two, or all three roles.

When we think of an individual making a choice, we tend to limit our attention to the benefits of a product (i.e., values it will satisfy), whether these be performance-related or social/emotional outcomes. This is a limited view, confining the decision maker to the user role. In reality, to the individual decision maker, the buyer and payer roles are also pertinent, so that the service, convenience, economic, and financing values (i.e., market values relevant to the buyer and payer roles) become equally important. In some situations, some of these values might determine the choice.

LOCATION AND COST OF AN INDIVIDUAL'S DECISION

Individual consumption can occur in three places: (1) at home, (2) in business organizations (e.g., at work or at school), and (3) in public places (e.g., a restaurant, an airplane, on the road, or in a park). For products consumed at home, purchase decisions tend to be made in advance, substantially ahead of time. Consumption in organizational settings and in public places is much less separated in time from the purchase decisions. When purchase decisions are made close to the time of consumption (or for immediate consumption), convenience value acquires much more importance for the person in the buyer role. That is why individual customers readily buy a can of soda from a vending machine for one dollar when they are on the road; the same customers might choose their supermarket based on a 20-cent deal on a case of Coke or Pepsi for consumption at home.

Likewise, consumption in public places tends to bring into prominence the social values of the user relative to the values of the payer. Price sensitivity is lessened in favour of how good the product will look in public. Purchase of items like a Rolex watch or a Jaguar car reflect these social values. However, the price value for the payer gains prominence while shopping on the Internet since the convenience value for the buyer is taken care of. People are more willing to spend time comparing prices across retailers from the comfort of their home than actually visiting multiple physical locations. The online competition for a consumer's money is just a click away instead of miles away.

When products are given away free, whether by government or by organizations, the decision criteria change. Free public roads become quickly congested, whereas toll roads encourage car pooling. At one extreme, customers will willingly accept any type of freebies, such as a free coffee mug, disregarding its low quality; while at the other extreme, if they are not the payers (for example, when employees are buying something for self-use), they would want the best quality, making user values most salient.

The more you combine the user, the payer, and the buyer roles, the more conflicting the decision process becomes. It is in individual buying decisions, then, that the values of the three roles interplay, and tradeoffs become integral to the decision process, making it an intriguing process to study.

CUSTOMER DECISION PROCESS

LO 2

Customer decisions are decisions customers make in the marketplace as buyers, payers, and users. Typically, these decisions include *whether* to purchase, *what* to purchase, *when* to purchase, from *whom* to purchase, and *how* to pay for it. *Whether* to purchase something is the first level of decision that entails weighing alternative uses of money and time resources. Customers have finite amounts of money and time, and they must allocate them judiciously. Alternative demands on time, such as work deadlines, may constrain a customer to postpone or dismiss a purchase altogether, such as a vacation plan. Allocating *money* resources entails weighing alternative needs at the level of the product category. For example, a family may have to choose between taking a cruise and investing in remodelling the house. This product-level choice involves deciding both *whether* to purchase and *what* to purchase.

Customer decisions Decisions customers make in the marketplace as buyers, payers, and users.

An important customer behaviour at this category-level of decision is **mental budgeting**—how the budget that customers set for a product category guides their subsequent behaviour as a customer. This concept of mental budgeting is explained in the Window on Research box. The concept of mental budgeting highlights the importance of the payer role. The payer role (regardless of whether it is the customer or someone else in the payer role) imposes relatively inflexible budget limits, and in this way, imposes some self-discipline on the user, whose needs and wants can sometimes be infinitely expandable. Unfortunately, research on mental budgeting is limited, and it is based solely on Western consumers. It is entirely possible that consumers in other cultures, and/or consumers who live from hand to mouth, might not practice the concept of mental budgeting, or might implement it in a flexible way, adjusting the budget at the time of the purchase. This is an issue that needs cross-cultural research.

Mental budgeting The idea that customers mentally set aside budgets for product categories.

Nevertheless, the concept of mental budgeting can guide marketers' positioning efforts; a product may be positioned in one category rather than the other to take advantage of the budget earmarked for each category. For example, a frozen dinner of lobster may be viewed by the customer as an expensive food item; the marketer might, in contrast, present it as a relatively economical entertainment (compared to going out to eat at a restaurant).

Following the choice at the product level, the customer makes another "what to purchase" decision: a choice among brands. That is, if a product category-level decision is made—namely, "take the cruise"—the next decision is which brand to purchase (e.g., which travel destination to select and which cruise line to purchase tickets on).

These decisions at various levels of hierarchy can all be framed in a general way: these are all *alternatives,* and the customer task is to decide among alternatives. Thus, this section uses the term *alternatives* generically to refer to product categories, brands, stores, suppliers, and so on, and deals with customer choice decisions among alternatives.

The process of customer decision making consists of the steps shown in Figure 8.1.

STEP 1: PROBLEM RECOGNITION

The decision process begins with a customer recognizing a problem to be solved or a need to be satisfied. The customer notices, for example, that she or he is hungry and needs to get some food, that the light bulb has blown out and needs to be replaced, that the roof has begun to leak and needs to be repaired, or that the office copier has run out of paper and needs to be refilled.

WINDOW ON RESEARCH

Mental Budgeting and Customer Behaviour

Do people set a budget for different categories of consumption, such as entertainment, clothing, food, and investment? And what happens if the money budgeted turns out to be too much or too little? Do these budgets become limiting? Do they result in under-consumption of one product category and over-consumption of another? Interestingly, the answer to all these questions is yes.

Consider two consumers, A and B. Consumer A has put aside some money for clothing to purchase a pair of slacks. After finding no acceptable slacks, he can easily put that money into another product category; instead, he just goes ahead and purchases a sweater that he had no prior intention of buying. Consumer B has allocated some money for entertainment. She receives an invitation to join a dinner group but discovers that the money she has allocated to the entertainment category is not adequate to cover the cost of dinner with the group. So she declines, even though she could have easily moved some money from another consumption category. For Consumer A to buy a sweater just to use the budget for clothing is an example of over-consumption. For Consumer B to decline the dinner invitation even though she knew she would have enjoyed the event is an example of under-consumption.

Chip Heath and Jack B. Soll asked a group of consumers a set of questions about how much they had set aside to spend and how much they would spend if certain hypothetical incidents had occurred. Their questions and respondents' answers are best illustrated by this example. Suppose a respondent said at the outset that she had set aside $100 for entertainment this week. Now suppose she had already spent $30 on a dinner: how much did she expect to spend on entertainment for the rest of the week? The answer, as expected, was about $70. Now, what if the dinner was paid for by a friend; the respondent still wanted to spend about $100 rather than about $70. What if the respondent had to unexpectedly buy someone a $30 birthday gift? She still expected to spend $100 for entertainment. This pattern of response demonstrates the mental budgeting effects. Heath and Soll obtained this pattern of responses from a majority of their research respondents.

SOURCE: Adapted from Heath, Chip, and Jack B. Soll. "Mental Budgeting and Consumer Decisions." *Journal of Consumer Research* 23, no. 1 (June 1996): 40–52. Reprinted with permission of the University of Chicago Press. http://www.journals.uchicago.edu/JCR.

As these examples illustrate, a customer problem is not necessarily a physical problem, such as a hungry stomach or dirty laundry. Rather, a **customer problem** is any state of deprivation, discomfort, or wanting (whether physical or psychological) felt by a person. **Problem recognition** is a realization by the customer that he or she needs to buy something to get back to a normal state of physical or psychological comfort.

Customer problem Any state of deprivation or discomfort or wanting (whether physical or psychological) felt by a person.

Problem recognition A realization by the customer that he or she needs to purchase something to get back to the normal state of comfort—physically and psychologically.

Stimuli for Problem Recognition

Problem recognition has two types of source: an internal stimulus or an external stimulus. **Internal stimuli** are perceived states of discomfort, and can be physical or psychological (e.g., hunger or boredom, respectively). **External stimuli** are marketplace information items that lead the customer to realize the problem. Thus, an advertisement about multivitamins or the sight of a Pizza Hut can serve as external stimuli to arouse the recognition of a need. The Window on Practice box provides examples of how banks have attempted to use such stimuli.

Internal stimuli Perceived states of physical or psychological discomfort that cause problem recognition.

External stimuli Marketplace information that causes problem recognition.

The terms *external* and *internal stimuli* are commonly used in psychology; however, more apt terms would be problem stimuli and solution stimuli. A problem stimulus is one in which the problem itself is the source of information. This source could lie *within* the customer (as in hunger pangs) or *outside* the customer (as in dirty laundry). The solution stimulus is the information emanating from a solution itself; exposure to a potential solution arouses the recognition of the need or the problem. For example, the smell of fresh-baked cinnamon rolls from a bakery might arouse your desire for cinnamon rolls. Marketing communications, product samples, window shopping, etc. have their utility precisely because they serve as problem-recognition stimuli. On the Internet, broadband providers (cable and DSL) use banner advertising with messages like "You are wasting your time" and "Your Internet connection is too slow" to try to make people aware of faster alternatives to their current ISP.

As customers, you can expect to encounter solution-stimuli in three states of mind:

1. When you have already recognized the problem and are looking for a solution; for example, suppose you have dandruff and are looking for a more effective shampoo than the one you are using currently; or you find your current food service contractor for the company cafeteria unsatisfactory and are planning to find a new contractor.
2. When the problem had been recognized in the past, but it was just not salient (i.e., not at a top-of-the-mind awareness level) at the moment of the exposure to the solution. For example, you might be thinking of buying some exercise equipment, but you have not pursued the thought actively; an infomercial or product display or the fact that a friend bought exercise equipment rekindles the need you had previously recognized.
3. When you never recognized the need in the past, but exposure to the solution-product makes you realize that the product would solve a condition now perceived as a problem. Thus, a display of a caller-ID device in a store and the salesperson's explanation of its use might make you realize that not knowing who is calling has always been a frustrating experience, even though until now you never viewed it as a problem. For a health-conscious customer, information on dietary requirements obtained during exploratory browsing of the Internet could act as problem-recognition stimuli. The consumer might now perceive a problem in his or her eating habits and change them accordingly.

Life situations that cause inconvenience but have no solutions are generally not viewed as problems; they are simply viewed as life conditions, taken for granted. Only when a solution appears on the horizon does the life condition become a problem. For example, before the invention of the microwave ovens, the slow process of conventional ovens was not perceived as a problem. Or before the home delivery of pizza, going to the pizzeria was not perceived as a problem. Before e-mail and fax, the effort, cost, and delay in getting messages from one person to another was not perceived as a problem.

Primary demand Demand for the product category itself.

This distinction is important for two reasons. First, it underscores the role of what is known as educational or pioneering marketing. Pioneering marketing and communications promote a new product by educating the customer about what the product will do and how it can solve a hitherto unsolved or unrecognized problem. Some of these marketing efforts are intended to create primary demand rather than secondary demand. **Primary demand** is

WINDOW ON **PRACTICE**

Problem Recognition: A Key to Selling Bank Loans

Often the trickiest part of generating a demand for a product is helping customers make the connection between that product and their needs. This connection is not always obvious to the customer, and marketers sometimes miss this opportunity. Take, for example, bank loans. Most banks market them predominantly by advertising the interest rate and other terms of financing. That works if consumers are already looking for a loan. But looking for a loan and needing a loan are not the same thing. Customers may want to do things for which they need money, but if the customer does not see those things as legitimate reasons to obtain a bank loan, then the idea of getting a bank loan for that purpose may not occur to them. So there may be a customer need (i.e., a problem), and there may be a solution available. But the customer problem and the marketplace solution remain unconnected in the customer's mind. To establish that connection is to facilitate problem recognition. And some banks have done just that.

One category of bank loans is the home equity loan—money that banks lend using the borrower's house as the collateral. It is a desirable type of loan for the bank because the collateral makes the loan less risky. And it appeals to the customer because the rate is generally lower than other types of loans. Yet most customers think that a home equity loan is for financing the purchase of a home, or at most, for financing a home improvement project, and for no other purpose. That is, home equity loans are perceived the same as mortgage loans.

A number of major banks realized this quirk in customer assumptions only recently. They realized why rate advertising was not creating new demand for loans. People's Heritage Bank of Portland, Maine is a case in point. The bank ran an advertising campaign that educated the customer about the various uses for which a home equity loan could be obtained. The bank developed three advertisements that featured people who achieved their dreams with the help of a home equity loan. In one advertisement, a veterinarian opened her practice with the home equity loan. In another advertisement, a customer bought the guitar he had always wanted. In a third advertisement, a teenager and her dad were featured with the computer they bought with the home equity loan so they could explore Europe on the Internet. By the end of the advertising campaign, which involved print and radio as well as more targeted direct mail, the bank had tripled the average number of home equity loan sales each month.

Reflecting on the situation, a senior product manager commented: "There was a lot of rate advertising in the market when we introduced this product. We were offering a good competitive rate, yet we wanted to offer customers something more. We wanted to show them that our product had value." In other words, the bank needed to make a connection between the things customers valued and the product the firm offered.

SOURCE: Adapted from Morrall, Katherine. "Marketing Loans that Make Consumers' Dreams Come True." *Bank Marketing*, April 1996, 19–24.

demand for the product category itself, seeking to convert non-buyers of the product category into buyers. **Secondary demand** (also known as **selective demand**), in contrast, is simply to deflect demand from one brand to the other.

Secondary demand Demand for a specific brand of product.

There is a noteworthy controversy on this issue in cigarette advertising. The government and anti-tobacco groups claim that cigarette advertising is targeted at young people, promoting the primary demand for smoking among new customers. If this is true, then cigarette advertising is a solution stimulus arousing a problem recognition among youth by presenting the product as a solution to their enduring need to be seen as cool by their peers. The tobacco industry, on the other hand, argues that it is merely creating secondary demand for specific brands, rather than enticing and recruiting new smokers. Advertising on comparison sites like MySimon.com, Dealtime.com, and Bizrate.com are attempts by advertisers to switch demand from another brand to theirs (secondary demand). To reduce the risk involved in shopping from "unknown" vendors, MySimon, Dealtime, and Bizrate rate the sellers to give buyers a degree of confidence. The distinction between primary and secondary demand for products is visible in emerging versus mature markets as well. Several products like automobiles, cellphones, and video cameras already have a secondary demand in the mature Western markets, while marketers are still trying to create primary demand for these products in the emerging markets in Asia.

The second implication of solution versus problem stimulus goes to the heart of a basic controversy in marketing. An often-asked question is, "Does marketing create a need or merely satisfy one?" In arguing that it indeed *creates* needs, critics note that no one needed a VCR, a video camera, a cellular phone, a $150 pair of Nike shoes, or an overnight document delivery service until advertising came along, parading these products in an enticing way.

Our view is that a need ought to be defined in terms of the function the product serves, rather than in terms of the product itself (as in "no one needed a VCR"). When needs are properly defined in terms of the function, it is easy to see that the only products that would be successful in the marketplace are those that serve some function. Thus, a VCR serves the function of enabling time-shifted viewing, and the need to be able to watch a program at the viewer's convenience was always a need, albeit unrecognized as a problem and, as such, relegated from consciousness simply as a life condition. The invention of the VCR, like all other inventions, helped bring that latent need to the surface. Likewise, in the world of business, there is a product to which every executive and every staff member is addicted—Post-it® notes. Yet before their invention, no one even sensed the problem now addressed by this innovative product.

Problem Recognition by Each Customer Role

Problem recognition can occur for each customer role and for each of the six values customers seek. The VCR and Post-it® examples illustrate the latent needs of the user role. For business consumers, 3M has a Post-it® easel pad which can be stuck on the wall like a white board, used, and peeled off without any paint peeling off the walls. This is clearly fulfilling a latent need of the business customer. For the buyer role, the example of problem recognition is the home delivery of pizza, which offers convenience value. Similarly, online shopping offers the convenience of searching for information and completing the purchase from the confines of one's home. For the payer, the availability of leasing automobiles to individual customers or for a corporate fleet has improved affordability. Also, availability of credit makes many customers realize the need to buy a *new* car or furniture.

A Typology of Problems

To see the variety of problems customers recognize, we can classify them along two dimensions: familiar versus novel and vivid versus latent (see Table 8.1). Familiar problems are generally caused by what is commonly called stock depletion; for example, a hungry stomach or a worn-out tire. Novel problems arise generally with life events that mark passage from one stage to another, as discussed in Chapter 4. Examples include a new job, a marriage, or international relocation; or, for business customers, the life-stage changes occur when firms go public, change ownership, or form alliances.

Vivid problem situations are immediately obvious and recognized, as in a just-emptied cereal box, the arrival of the back-to-school month, power outages, or network traffic on Web pages causing the server to shut down. A latent problem is not immediately obvious and needs shaping, either by self-reflection or, more likely, by an external agent such as a salesperson. Examples of a latent problem are regular car tune-ups, preventive maintenance and scheduled repairs and replacements for machines, or the ability to know who is calling you on the phone. Availability of the caller ID service from the local phone company makes the latent need salient (i.e., recognized). Thus, recognition of novel-latent problems is stimulated by solution stimuli, generally in the form of new technologies and new products. In addition, the recognition of latent problems (whether familiar or novel) generally requires educational marketing efforts (e.g., counselling by a salesperson about the need for a life-insurance policy).

STEP 2: INFORMATION SEARCH

Once the need has been recognized, customers search for information about various alternative ways of solving the problem. That search rarely includes every brand in existence. Rather, as shown in Figure 8.2, customers consider only a select subset of brands/suppliers that are available in a market, organized as follows:

Awareness set
Brands that a customer is aware of.

Evoked set
Brands in a product category that the customer remembers at the time of decision making.

Consideration set
All the brands in a product category that a customer will consider assessing for purchase.

- The **awareness set** consists of the brands/suppliers a customer is aware of, i.e., the brand name is known by the customer.
- An **evoked set** consists of the brands/suppliers in a product category that the customer remembers at the time of decision making.
- The **consideration set** consists of the brands/suppliers from the evoked set that a customer will consider buying after the brands/suppliers that are considered unfit have been eliminated. The brands that are not considered would fall into three categories: (1) the customer knows the brand/supplier, but does not have any information about it (*foggy set*); (2) the brand is rejected because it is is deemed unsatisfactory to the customer needs (*reject set*); (3) the brand is set aside because the customer has incomplete information or the price/quality relationship is unsatisfactory (*hold set*).[2]

TABLE 8.1 Four Situations for Problem Recognition

	Vivid	Latent
Familiar	Stock depletion	Educational marketing
Novel	Life-stage change	New product technology

Initially, customers seek information about the consideration set of brands, which is a subset of the evoked set. New information can bring additional brands/suppliers into the awareness, evoked, and consideration sets. It should be the minimum objective of all marketing communications to place the brand in the consideration set (rather than merely in the awareness or evoked set) of its target customers. Consideration sets will include alternatives from different categories when the consumer experiences goal conflict (a single category cannot deliver on all salient and conflicting goals) or goal ambiguity (a lack of salient goals). For example, when the salient goals for a car are maximum fuel efficiency and the capability of driving off-road, the consumer may find that one category does not satisfy all salient goals. Subcompacts may offer fuel efficiency but not off-road driving, and four-wheel-drive trucks would do the opposite. Similarly there is goal ambiguity when the consumer has a fuzzy goal like appeasing hunger or a need for personal transportation. Products from several categories could be used to form a consideration set to satisfy these goals.[3]

One of the most significant outcomes of the Internet revolution is the "democratization of information" across the vast customer population. Information search is one of the first uses of the Internet. A vast number of alternatives are available to the customer, and it is common to find most consumer decisions being researched on the Internet before the products are bought offline or online. Thus, the fundamental benefit of "Interactive Home Shopping" (IHS—shopping from home via the Internet) is the low cost of information search. Yet Alba et al. state that the growth of IHS is dependent on several other factors:

1. *Selection:* Customers should be able to access a large set of items fairly quickly.
2. *Screening:* Consumers should be able to screen the available options effectively. If they are not able to do this, then the benefits of a vast selection will be offset by the high cost of the search.
3. *Reliability:* The customer should be able to easily understand the benefits of the products in the IHS shopping format. If experiential information available from stores is better than the information from IHS, and the consumer is not satisfied with the information available through IHS to make a purchase decision, the IHS format will lose the customer to the store.
4. *Product comparison:* The IHS format should provide the consumer with superior methods for comparing alternatives in order to make the purchase decision.[4]

FIGURE 8.2 Awareness, Evoked, and Consideration Sets

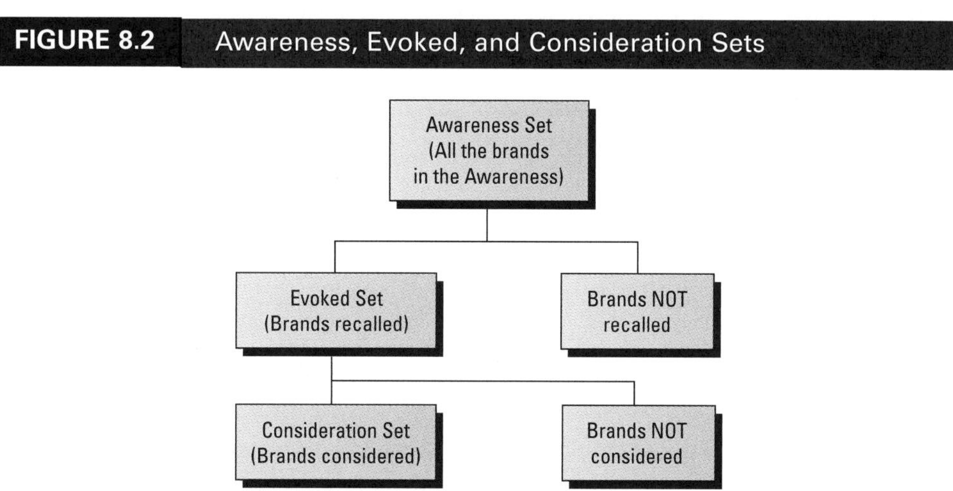

Three elements characterize the information-search phase of the decision process: (1) *sources of information,* (2) *search strategies,* and (3) *amount of search.*

LO 3

SOURCES OF INFORMATION

Marketer sources Communication sources that act on behalf of the marketer of the product itself.

Advocate sources Communication sources that have a vested point of view to advocate or promote.

Non-marketer sources Communication sources that are independent of marketer influence.

Sources of information may be categorized as *marketer* or *non-marketer.* (See Table 8.2.) **Marketer sources** are those that come from the marketer of the product itself. These consist of advertising, salespersons, product literature and brochures, and in-store displays. One of the latest marketer sources is the Internet. More and more companies have opened a home page on the Internet, a site customers can visit at their convenience. Since these sources have a vested interest in providing favorable information, these are also referred to as **advocate sources** (i.e., sources that have a vested point-of-view to advocate or promote). As such, these sources have lower credibility compared with non-marketer sources.

Non-marketer sources

Non-marketer sources are those that are independent of the marketer's control. They include personal sources and independent sources. Since these have no vested interest in biasing the information, they are viewed as non-advocate sources and are deemed more credible. Friends and other acquaintances with past experience and the customers' own past experience with the product are credible sources of information. Independent sources are usually publications and organizations with relevant expertise. For example, *Consumer Reports* provides performance data based on product trials by independent judges and systematically collected reports of other past users' experiences. Online sites like **http://www.epinions.com** attempt to recreate the informal social information-gathering experience by using their Web of Trust. Online sites are willing to pay independent rating sites like Bizrate (**http://www.bizrate.com**) and Gomez (**http://www.gomez.com**) to get reviewed. Professional appraisers/advisors are sometimes used for very large purchases. Thus, home appraisers are used by home buyers, and car mechanics are used to appraise used cars. In business-to-business buying, such as for plant and equipment, engineering consultants are utilized as sources of information.

TABLE 8.2 Sources of Information for Customers

Marketer Sources	Non-Marketer Sources
Advertising	**PERSONAL**
Salespersons	Friends and other acquaintances
Product brochures	Past experience
Store displays	
Company websites	
	INDEPENDENT SOURCES
	Public information (e.g., *Consumer Reports*, Better Business Bureau, news reports in media, government publications such as *The Census of Canada*)
	Product experts (e.g., auto critic, home appraiser, pharmacist), Internet (bulletin boards)

There are marketer and non-marketer sources for every conceivable product on the Internet, from businesses to alternative medicine. For example, for prospective car buyers, there are hundreds of sites, sponsored by auto manufacturers, dealerships, government agencies, insurance industry groups, consumer and car-buff magazines, newspapers, and financial institutions, as well as an assortment of new and used-car price information services. Two of these, **http://www.edmunds.com** and **canadianredbook.com,** offer vehicle valuations guides; Autobytel.ca (**http://www.autobytel.ca**) is an Internet-based, purchasing program for new and pre-owned vehicles in Canada, featuring general information and links to finance and insurance vendors; **http://www.canadiandriver.com** is an online automotive magazine offering general automotive information and a guide to Canadian automobile resources online; **http://www.autonet.ca** is a portal offering automotive information, dealer directories, and financing and insurance tools.

Search Strategies

The choice of information sources depends partly on the customer's search strategy. A **search strategy** is the pattern of information acquisition customers use to solve their decision problems. Since information acquisition has costs in terms of time, and physical and mental effort, customers weigh the costs against the likely gains from information acquisition. That comparison helps them decide how much information they will acquire and from what sources.

Search strategy
The pattern of information acquisition by customers to solve their decision problems.

Routine, Extended, and Limited Problem Solving

Based on the amount of search deemed necessary, customer decision strategies may be routine, limited, or extended problem-solving strategies. **Routine problem solving** is a strategy in which no new information is considered. This strategy is used for purchase problems that have occurred and have been solved previously. Consequently, when these problems recur, they are solved simply by repeating a past choice, as in purchasing the brand bought in the past. Information search is minimal. This is common in business because search costs are enormous. Sometimes, non-strategic supplies are outsourced. **Extended problem solving** occurs when the search is extensive and deliberation prolonged. This strategy becomes necessary for purchases never made before or made long ago, or where risks of wrong choice are high. Examples are the purchase of a new home or, in a business context, a building for a new factory. Finally, **limited problem solving** is a strategy wherein the customer invests a limited amount of time and energy in searching and evaluating alternative solutions. Customers adopt this strategy when purchases are nontrivial, the risk is limited, and the product is not complex or technical in terms of its features. There is some familiarity with the product class, but a desire for variety (e.g., buying a new dress) or the unavailability of previous solutions (e.g., stock-out of your usual brand) necessitates some amount of search. In the business context, users might request a change in the products offered in the vending machine placed in the office cafeteria. The company would have to undertake limited problem solving to look for vendors who can accomodate the choices requested. Textbook adoption by professors in a business school would also involve limited problem solving.

Routine problem solving (RPS)
A product selection strategy wherein the customer considers no new information, and instead simply repeats previously made choices.

Extended problem solving (EPS)
A product selection strategy wherein the customer engages in an extensive information search and prolonged deliberation in order to minimize the risk of a wrong choice.

Limited problem solving (LPS)
A product selection strategy wherein the customer invests a limited amount of time and energy in searching and evaluating alternative solutions.

These three strategies are related to the problem typology discussed earlier. Generally, familiar-vivid problems are likely to be solved with routine problem solving. Novel-latent problems would tend to be solved with extended problem solving. Familiar-latent problems (e.g., starting to get your car regularly tuned) may entail routine (go to your regular mechanic) or limited problem solving (comparison shopping with coupons). Finally, novel-vivid problems may entail limited or extended problem solving, depending on the risk involved and/or prior familiarity. Note that the familiar-novel/vivid-latent typology has to do with the genesis of problem *recognition,* whereas the routine/extended/limited continuum has to do with search efforts.

Systematic versus Heuristic Search

Systematic search
A comprehensive search and evaluation of alternatives.

Heuristics
Quick rules of thumb and shortcuts used to make decisions.

So far, the description of search strategies may seem to suggest that customers prefer systematic strategies. **Systematic search** consists of a comprehensive search and evaluation of alternatives. Systematic searchers have been found to search information extensively, consult with a variety of sources, shop with others, take a long time, and deliberate a lot, and they are especially price-comparison shoppers. However, customers also use a contrasting search strategy, termed heuristics. **Heuristics** are quick rules of thumb and shortcuts used to make decisions.[5]

Heuristics can be implemented in a variety of ways:

- Broad inferences are quickly drawn from partial information (e.g., price may be used to judge quality). Technical-sounding terms may be used to infer overall brand superiority (e.g., many customers may not know what Dolby sound in stereos or even pH-balanced in shampoos means, but they would conveniently infer that these imply advanced products). Another trademark that is used to infer quality of products is "UL Listed," (Underwriters Laboratories, a well-known testing firm) and the phrase "Intel Inside" for computers instills confidence in the purchase.
- Past experiences are considered adequate.
- Others' judgments are sought and summarily adopted as final choice. In business, companies benchmark against competitors or seek consultants to give them advice.
- Brand names/suppliers are heavily relied on, and further attribute information is not sought.

Interattribute inference
A process wherein the customer infers the value of one attribute based on another attribute.

Evaluative consistency
A process wherein the missing attribute is assumed in order to conform to the overall evaluation of the brand.

Other-brand averaging
A process wherein the missing attribute value is assumed to be an average of its values across all other brands.

Negative cue
An inference-making strategy wherein the customer simply treats the missing information as a negative cue, which then affects the overall judgment negatively.

Although these strategies are not systematic, they are also not irrational. They are rational to their users in terms of their perceived cost-versus-benefit tradeoffs.

Consider inferences, for example. Customers often have to make their decisions on partial information about various product alternatives. In these situations, customers make product assessments by supplying the missing information in the form of inferences. Various strategies customers use for handling missing information are:

- **Interattribute inference**—The value of one attribute is inferred based on another attribute. For example, thickness of the fabric in an item of clothing might be used to infer crease resistance. Refinement of chemicals may imply purity.
- **Evaluative consistency**—The missing attribute is assumed to conform to the overall evaluation of the brand/supplier. Thus, if a brand is positively evaluated in overall terms, the brand is assumed to be good on the missing attribute as well.
- **Other-brand averaging**—The missing attribute value may be assumed to be an average of its values across all other brands. This is likely to occur, however, only if the variance in the values of this attribute for other brands is low.
- **Negative Cue**—The customer may simply treat the missing information as a negative cue and then use one of two sub-strategies: avoid the option with the missing information

altogether, or assume a low or poor value for this attribute. A customer may look for the ISO 9000 certification in a supplier and consider the absence of the certification as a negative cue.

The Window on Research box discusses the application of intuitive theories to these strategies.

The extent and type of inference made will depend on several factors. One is the need for inference; that is, how critical is the attribute considered for product assessment? Another factor is customer involvement in the purchase; that is, how critical is it to make the right choice? Finally, the use of inferences will depend on the customer's product category knowledge. More knowledgeable customers are more likely to infer the missing information.

Determinants of the Amount of Search

Imagine that you are in the market for an HD (high-definition) television set, or a pair of shoes, or a greeting card, or a catering service for an office party, or business consulting services or training. How much information will you seek? How much effort will you put into processing this information? Actually, this depends on several factors. These factors include perceived risk, involvement, familiarity, expertise, time pressure, the functional versus expressive nature of the product, information overload, and relative brand uncertainty.

Perceived Risk

The **perceived risk** is the degree of loss (i.e., amount at stake) in the event that a wrong choice is made. There are five types of risks:

Perceived risk
The degree of loss (i.e., amount at stake) in the event that a wrong choice is made.

1. *Performance risk*—The product may not perform well or not as well as some other alternatives. Examples are plastic surgery undertaken to improve one's looks or software bought for a specific purpose.
2. *Social risk*—Reference group members and significant others may not like it. Clothing and country club memberships may be subject to social risk.
3. *Psychological risk*—The product may not reflect oneself. A foreign product purchase may not reflect you as well as Canadian-made products.
4. *Financial risk*—The alternative may be overpriced; there may exist a better choice from the cost perspective. There may be some alternative that you did not consider from competitors that you are not aware of, which may be cheaper than what you purchased.
5. *Obsolescence risk*—The alternative may be replaced by newer substitutes. Fashion and software are subject to obsolescence risk.

The financial risk is of most concern to the payer, whereas other risks are of concern to the user. The greater the perceived risk, the more extensive the search and deliberation. Marketers, therefore, attempt to overcome these risks by various strategies: performance warranties to overcome performance risks, price guarantees (matching a competitor's price or refunding the difference) to overcome price risks, and product upgrades and trade-in of old models to overcome obsolescence risk. Social and psychological risks are addressed by liberal return, exchange, or refund policies. Consumers contemplating buying products through the Internet face the added risk of not seeing and touching a physical product before making their purchase. This presents a bigger challenge for marketers on the Internet compared to the "brick and mortar" ones.

Similarly, for business customers, marketers attempt to free customers from various perceived risks by assuming the risks themselves. For office machines, for example, performance risk is minimized by offering a lifetime repair maintenance contract. Financial and obsolescence risks are minimized by offering the product on lease. Many consulting firms and advertising agencies guarantee certain results for the client, and some even make their fees contingent on the degree to which intended results are achieved.

Involvement

Purchase-decision involvement
The degree of concern and caring that customers feel in a purchase decision.

On the positive side of the equation, involvement is defined as the perceived importance of the product. There are some products that we just purchase routinely, while others, which we consider important, we purchase with great care. In business, there are strategic and non-strategic decisions.

Consumer researchers have distinguished between two general types of involvement: purchase decision involvement and enduring involvement. **Purchase-decision (or situational)**

WINDOW ON RESEARCH

Intuitive Theories in Customer Inference Making

An important research issue concerning inferences is the extent to which customers' intuitive theories play a role in inference making. For example, people generally expect the length of a warranty to be positively related to a product's reliability (i.e., the longer and better the warranty, the more reliable the product is likely to be). But what if we did not find this to be true in a specific case? For example, suppose you were shopping for a camera and you found that across different brands of cameras there was no correspondence between reliability and warranty. Brands that had poor warranties had just as good or poor a reliability record as brands with exceptional warranties. However, another attribute, say shutter speed, was perfectly correlated with reliability record; that is, the model that had a high shutter speed also had more reliability. Note that there is no logical connection between shutter speed and reliability. It just so happens that for all the models you examined, the reliability record happens to be correlated not to warranties but to shutter speed. Now, suppose you encounter another brand and find reliability information missing. How are you going to infer its value? Is your inference going to be based more on data (i.e., in the models examined, reliability related with shutter speed was a mere coincidence) or is it going to be based more on your general intuitive theory, which tells you that, logically, reliability should be related to warranty?

This important question was examined by Susan M. Broniarczyk and Joseph W. Alba, who presented customers with information about alternative brands of cameras to choose from. After they made the choice, customers were presented with information about a new set of brands, except that the information on their reliability record was missing. In choosing from these new, incompletely described brands, customers could make inferences about the missing attribute either from their knowledge of the value of the missing attribute in an otherwise identical brand in the previous set (which would be in conflict with intuitive theory), or they could base such an inference on intuitive theory. The experimental subjects' choices revealed that in inferring the missing information, customers drew on their intuitive theory, even when the previously exposed data was in conflict with the logical theory.

Of course, further research is needed; but this important finding implies that marketers should understand their customers' intuitive theories about the relationships among diverse brand attributes in particular, and about various marketplace phenomena in general.

SOURCE: Adapted from Broniarczyk, Susan M., and Joseph W. Alba. "The Role of Consumers' Intuitions in Inference Making." *Journal of Consumer Research* 21 (December 1994): 393–407 (http://www.ConsumerReports.org). Reprinted with permission of the University of Chicago Press.

involvement is the degree of concern and caring that customers bring to bear on the purchase decision or situation. Purchase decision involvement is high for most of the high-ticket items, but price and involvement do not have one-to-one correspondence. What brings in purchase involvement is the degree of risk, whether performance, financial, or social. For most products, customers' involvement ends when the purchase is made. After buying an appliance, for example, most customers just use it without deliberation. For some products, however, the involvement continues well beyond the purchase, into the product use. This is termed **enduring involvement,** or ongoing interest in the product. Researchers refer to this state of enduring involvement as deep involvement. In the business context, service contracts and single sourcing are examples of enduring involvement with suppliers. Consider this quote from Morris Holbrook, where he speaks as a consumer himself, specifically as a fanatic consumer of jazz music:

Enduring involvement
The degree of interest a customer feels in a product on an ongoing basis.

> I just want to hear the music. What I do need is music in every location where I might spend any appreciable amount of time (say five minutes). This includes the living room, my study, Christopher's room, Sally's office, Sally's desk, the Oldsmobile, and [my other] house in Pennsylvania. For other locations and for traveling, I also keep a backup collection of portable radios and tape players.[6]

Table 8.3 illustrates measures of these two forms of involvement.

The relationship between purchase involvement and enduring product involvement is that enduring product involvement will create high purchase involvement, but high purchase involvement does not necessarily involve enduring product involvement. For example,

TABLE 8.3 Illustrative Measures of Consumer Involvement

Product Involvement or Importance:

This product is

Unimportant	________	Important
Means nothing to me	________	Means a lot to me
Unappealing	________	Appealing
Worthless	________	Valuable
Unexciting	________	Exciting

Enduring Product Involvement (Example: consumer involvement with cars):

- Cars offer me relaxation and fun when life's pressures build up.
- I prefer to drive a car with a strong personality.
- To me, a car is much more than an appliance.
- I enjoy conversations about cars.

Purchase Involvement:

- In choosing this product, I would not care at all/would care a lot about which brand, make, or model I buy.
- How important would it be for you to make a right choice of this product? Not at all/Extremely important
- It is not/it is a big deal if I make a mistake in choosing (the product name).

SOURCES: Compiled from Bloch, Peter H. "An Exploration into the Scaling of Consumers' Involvement in Product Class." In *Advances in Consumer Research*, Vol. 8, edited by K. Monroe, (Provo, UT: Association for Consumer Research) 61–65, 1981; Zaichkowsky, Judith Lynne. "Measuring the Involvement Construct." *Journal of Consumer Research* 12 (December 1985): 341–352; Mittal, Banwari. "Measuring Purchase Decision Involvement." *Psychology and Marketing* 6 (1988): 147–62.

purchases like a washer-dryer could be highly involving without the product itself eliciting any enduring, long-term involvement. In contrast, if a music lover wants to buy a stereo sound system, his or her enduring interest in music raises his or her purchase involvement, and his or her involvement in the product continues beyond the purchase occasion.

Purchase decision involvement directly affects the extent of information search and processing. Enduring product involvement, on the other hand, leads customers to develop expertise on the product category, to search information on an ongoing basis, to take interest in product care, and to augment and upgrade it. Marketers expect these people to become opinion leaders and advocates for the brand, to purchase add-on options, to build a bonding relationship with the company, and to participate in new-product idea generation. Nintendo and KOOL-AID® coordinate membership clubs to channel product fans' enthusiasm.

Familiarity and Expertise

Customers have familiarity and expertise as a result of prior information acquisition and prior personal experience. The relationship between prior experience and external information search is generally inverse; with increasing prior experience, less external search occurs. Prior experience also implies that the purchase problem is solved in the routine problem-solving mode, as happens with most of the day-to-day purchases of staple items. However, even with high prior experience, routine problem solving may not be considered a desirable strategy under these conditions:

- If the experience with the prior purchase was not positive (e.g., last year's lawn maintenance service was unsatisfactory or the past training or consulting was not up to the mark).
- If the technology has changed substantially since the last purchase, thus rendering prior experience obsolete (e.g., a newer generation of computers and servers).
- If the goal is to build an assortment rather than replace the older or prior purchase (e.g., the purchase of clothes or a music CD collection).
- If the purchase is infrequent and long after the last purchase so that there is a natural desire to explore what is new (e.g., an automobile, factory equipment, business consultants).
- If the product is a high-risk purchase so that there is a need to optimize the purchase anew; the optimal choice at the time of the last purchase may not be the optimal choice now (e.g., investment portfolios, new generation equipment).
- If the product is one of high-interest/high-enduring involvement, so it is inherently enjoyable to search information about the alternatives in the product class (e.g., antiques). In these instances, information search is likely to occur despite prior experience.

It is useful to distinguish between prior experience and expertise. Prior experience refers simply to the history of purchase and consumption, and to information obtained with respect to that product. In contrast, expertise refers to the *understanding* of the attributes in a product class and knowledge about how various alternatives stack up regarding these attributes. Once a customer judges prior experience to be inadequate for the impending purchase and decides that a new information search is needed, expertise comes into play in determining how much search will be undertaken.

Interestingly, the role of prior expertise is counter-intuitive. At first, marketers thought customers with low prior expertise would seek more information to overcome their knowledge deficit (the deficit hypothesis). However, it turns out that customers with prior expertise seek even more information about the impending purchase than do those less knowledgeable.[7] For example, in a study of 1,400 car buyers, it was found that the amount of prior experience was negatively correlated with the amount of search effort customers undertook prior to making their choice. However, customers' general interest in cars was positively correlated with their product knowledge (i.e., expertise), and both interest and expertise were *positively* correlated with the amount of search effort.[8] This tendency of less knowledgeable customers to seek less information rather than more is the **ignorance paradox.** The ignorance paradox occurs in that those who do not know also do not know that they do not know.

Ignorance paradox The tendency of less knowledgeable customers to seek less information rather than more.

A survey of 3,000 online shoppers by ebates.com/Harris Interactive shows that buying behaviour on the Internet reflects this trend. Table 8.4 presents a classification of shoppers on the Internet based on their shopping behaviour. The Newbies are the smallest group online, and are most apprehensive about shopping on the Internet due to lack of familiarity and prior experience. However, as consumers gather experience, they gravitate toward different modes of shopping on the Internet—the Time-sensitive Materialists look for fast checkouts and one-stop shopping, while the Brand Loyalists visit the site of their choice, and the Hunter-Gatherers undertake comparison shopping for the best deals for a family.[9]

Time Pressure

One of the most conspicuous characteristics of the customer is time pressure. Time has become and is becoming more and more scarce, due to (a) both spouses working, (b) many customers being employed in more than one job, (c) many customers re-enrolling in school to acquire new skills necessary for a more complex employment market, and (d) new leisure activities enabled by technology. Some have called the always-on-the-go customer the harassed decision maker. Time pressure is making customers look for more convenient shopping outlets (e.g., home-shopping networks, catalogue shopping, and the Internet). In addition, time-pressed customers are likely to cut short their information search, comparison shopping, and decision-making time.[10] Some grocery stores offer online purchase of groceries

TABLE 8.4 A Classification of Shopping Types on the Internet by Harris Interactive

Shopping Type	Description	Percentage of Total Online Shoppers
eBivalent Newbies	Newest to the Internet; do not spend a lot online and like online shopping the least	5%
Hooked, Online and Single	Likely to be young males; have been online the longest; bank, invest, and shop online the most often	16%
Time-Sensitive Materialists	Most interested in convenience and saving time; want fast check-out and one-stop shopping	17%
Brand Loyalists	Go directly to the site of the merchant they know; spend the most online	19%
Hunter-Gatherers	Ages 30–49 with two children; use sites that compare and provide analysis	20%
Clicks-and-Mortar Group	Shop online but prefer to buy offline; concerned with online privacy and security; visit shopping malls the most	23%

SOURCE: http://www.emarketer.com/estats/dailyestats/b2c/20001101_shoptypes.html.

such as some IGA supermarkets in Quebec (**http://magasin.iga.net/index_en.html**) and **onlinegrocer.ca** in Ottawa, with an aim to creating more free time for busy individuals and families by striking at one of the important home tasks, i.e., grocery shopping. By setting up regular shopping lists that users can update on a weekly/regular basis through the Web, grocers can make it easier to shop, saving time and effort in the process.

Relative Brand Uncertainty

Moorthy, Ratchford, and Talukdar propose that relative brand uncertainty is also an important factor determining the amount of search undertaken by a customer. They state that "Relative brand uncertainty is the uncertainty about which brand is best among a set of brands, while individual brand uncertainty is the uncertainty about what each brand offers." Consumers feel the need to search for information only when they experience relative brand uncertainty. A consumer has a utility distribution for every brand. When the consumer perceives the brands in his consideration set to be completely differentiated, she or he can clearly identify the best brand, implying that the consumer does not experience any relative brand uncertainty. Hence, there is no search. Similarly, when the top two brands in the consideration set are perceived to be identical, the consumer has to search for information on only one brand. This search gives information about all other brands, since the brands are homogeneous. Thus, there is no relative brand uncertainty, and hence, no search. The authors show that relative brand uncertainty is nonzero only when the consumers perceive brands to be partially differentiated, or when the top two brands are perceived to have homogeneous utilities, but are not considered identical. In both these cases, the consumer has to search between brands to select—the best brand among the set.[11]

Functional versus Expressive Nature of Products

In Chapter 1, we distinguished between performance value and social and psychological value. This distinction highlights the fact that people buy some products primarily for their physical performance, whereas others are bought primarily or significantly for their social image or for their hedonic (sensory enjoyment) utilities. These two end goals in product purchases have implications for evaluation criteria.

Information processing mode (IPM)
A decision mode wherein the customer acquires, evaluates, and integrates information about brand attributes to arrive at an overall brand evaluation.

Affective choice mode (ACM)
A decision mode wherein affect or liking for the brand results in a choice based not on attribute information, but on holistic judgments.

Specifically, only performance value products (detergents, appliances, and financial investments, for example) lend themselves to choice by information processing. In the **information processing mode (IPM),** the customer is thought to acquire information about brand/supplier attributes, form evaluative criteria, judge the levels of these attributes in various brands/suppliers, and combine these attribute levels for overall brand/supplier evaluation.[12] Sites like **http://www.cellmania.com** help users navigate through the many choices of cell phones and plans by asking ten simple questions about intended use. Based on the user responses, it returns a list of plans that meets the user's requirements. Users can then compare and contrast these plans and features side by side to make an informed decision.

Products sought for social and psychological values (for example, perfumes, clothing, jewellery, country clubs, and trade shows) are chosen in contrast by an affective choice mode. In the **affective choice mode (ACM),** affect or liking for the brand results in a choice based not on attribute information, but on judgments that are holistic, self-implicative, and difficult to articulate. That is, the overall style and appearance matters (holistic); the product is judged in relation to oneself, as in "How will I look in this dress?" (self-implicative); and the decision cannot be verbalized since it is the nonverbal cues and emotional experience (vicarious at the time of choosing) that lead to choice. For business customers, the purchase of raw materials, components, and equipment uses IPM, while the purchase of a corporate jet, office furniture, and even an office location, say with a prestigious street address, are driven to a large extent by ACM. It will be interesting to see whether sites like **http://www.bluenile.ca** (which sells diamonds and fine jewellery) will be able to persuade people to part with significant amounts of money (usually more than $1,000) for a decision that often follows ACM.

There are two implications of this distinction. First, for social/psychological value-fulfilling products, customers would not seek much feature information, though the deliberation time may still be just as much as in the IPM strategy. Second, marketers should not burden the customer with a lot of attribute information. Instead, they should focus on showing the product in its entirety (i.e., holistically), stressing supplier reputation, which is holistic in nature, and creating social/psychological symbolism via nonverbal communication and via association with positive role models.

Information Overload

Information overload is the condition of being exposed to too much information—so much so that you are unable to process it to make a decision. To illustrate this phenomenon, let us review how researchers study it. Typically, some customers are asked to participate in a research study. They are provided information about a number of attributes of various brands/suppliers and are asked to make a brand/supplier selection. Some customers are provided more information; others not as much. Researchers then analyze these customer decisions in terms of their accuracy. Although the results of various studies are not conclusive, the findings tend to show that as the number of attributes or alternatives were increased, customers experienced information overload and made sub-optimal decisions.

Information overload
Customers are exposed to so much information that they are unable to process it to make a decision.

A general principle of the customer information search is that customers are *selective* in their acquisition of information, and because of this selectivity, they may not always make the best decisions. There is an important lesson here for marketers: they should carefully consider what information they should provide. Marketers should not overload the customer with information, should organize the information so that it is easy to process, and should ensure that the subset of information presented is still adequate for the customer to make an informed choice.[13] Advertising, catalogues, and in-store displays aid exploratory visual information search. Here, attention for the focal object is a function of the competition for attention created by the non-focal information. Hence, in a catalogue, for instance, marketers can draw attention to focal items by not just increasing the size of the focal object or removing other items from the page, but by rearranging items on the page in such a way that the entire display is not visually competitive.[14]

A study shows that factual information about products has more impact on choices made online than in traditional supermarkets. Brand names are found to be important in online decision making when information on other attributes is not available.[15] As consumers face an information overload on the Web, the type of information provided for decision making will decide whether the customer will buy from a website or leave the site. In fact, a specialized discipline called "Human Computer Interaction" has come into place, and university courses are offered on the subject so that Web developers and companies interface better with the customer.

STEP 3: ALTERNATIVE EVALUATION

Now that the customer has all the information, how does she or he use it to make a choice? In this section, we discuss the specific manner in which customers select one of several alternatives (e.g., brands or suppliers) available to them. These specific processes and steps are referred to as choice *models.* There are two broad categories of choice models: *compensatory* and *non-compensatory.*[16] Consumers also use affect to evaluate a target object by asking themselves: "How do I feel about it?" This mode of evaluation is particularly used by consumers for consumption behaviours that are "intrinsically rewarding" compared to behaviours that are undertaken to achieve goals (reading a book for pleasure versus reading a book to pass an exam). When consumers are faced with non-comparable alternatives, and when they believe that their feelings are representative of the target object, and not attributable to any external reasons such as the background music in the store or a pleasant salesperson or store atmosphere, positive feelings toward the target object lead to a favorable evaluation of the object.[17]

The Compensatory Model

Compensatory model
A decision rule and process wherein a customer makes a choice by considering all of the attributes and benefits of a product and mentally trading off the alternative's perceived weakness on one or more attributes for its perceived strength on other attributes.

In the **compensatory model,** the customer arrives at a choice by considering *all* of the attributes and benefits of a product and mentally trading off the alternative's perceived weakness on one or more attributes for its perceived strength on other attributes. A customer may go about making this calculation in two ways. One method of arriving at a choice is simply to add the number of positive attributes and subtract the number of negative attributes each alternative has, and then choose the one that has the most positive and fewest negative attributes. However, often, the individual does not consider each plus or a minus equally significant. Some considerations are clearly more important than others, and every minus may or may not cancel a plus on some other feature. A second and more systematic approach is to weigh every attribute for each alternative in terms of its relative importance. To implement this approach, the decision maker also estimates the degree to which the alternative possesses each positive or negative attribute. This can be done either on a numerical scale of, say, 0 to 10 where 10

TABLE 8.5 Use of the Compensatory Choice Model by a Business Customer

		SUPPLIER RATINGS		
Attribute	**Weight**	**Supplier 1**	**Supplier 2**	**Supplier 3**
Quality	4	Average (2)	Excellent (4)	Poor (1)
Fit with desired performance standards	3	Good (3)	Poor (1)	Good (3)
Customer support	1	Poor(1)	Good (3)	Excellent (4)
Price	2	Good (3)	Average (2)	Poor (1)
Total		4(2) + 3(3) + 1(1) + 2(3) = 24	4(4) + 3(1) + 1(3) + 2(2) = 26	4(1) + 3(3) + 1(4) + 2(1) = 19

means a perfect performance on that attribute, or in verbal rating categories such as poor, average, excellent, etc. The latter ratings are then multiplied by the relative weight of the attribute. The sum of these products for each alternative provides a total score for that alternative. The alternative with the highest score is then chosen. Table 8.5 provides an example of how business customers could use the compensatory model for vendor selection (use of a vendor score card). In this example, Vendor 2 has the greatest total score, so the business customer would choose Vendor 2.

This model is called compensatory because a shortfall on one attribute may be compensated by a good rating on another attribute. For example, a vacation spot that has less learning opportunity but more activities for fun for the whole family might receive the same overall rating as another destination with few family fun activities but more learning opportunities.

Non-compensatory Models

LO 4

While there are several non-compensatory models identified in the literature, four are the most common and useful. These are called *conjunctive, disjunctive, lexicographic,* and *elimination by aspects.*[18]

The Conjunctive Model

In the **conjunctive model,** the customer begins by *setting the minimum cutoffs for all salient attributes.* For each attribute, every alternative is then examined, and any alternative that meets the minimum cutoffs for all attributes can potentially be chosen. If an alternative fails the cutoff, even for one attribute, it is dropped from further consideration. If all alternatives fail to meet the cutoff levels, then the customer may revise his or her minimum cutoff levels or use another decision model. On the other hand, if more than one alternative meets all the minimum cutoff levels, the customer might resort to another decision model to further eliminate alternatives until only one survives the process.

Conjunctive model A decision-making procedure wherein the customer examines all the alternatives in a set of attributes or evaluative criteria in order to identify an alternative that would meet minimum cutoff levels for each attribute.

Consider a customer buying a car. She or he might want a car that is priced below $20,000, gets at least 45 miles per gallon, has at least an average reliability and repair record, and has at least a good safety rating. (These latter two ratings can be read from *Consumer Reports,* for example.) The customer eliminates cars that fall below these cutoff levels. If more than one car satisfies all these cutoffs, the customer may next decide on the basis of style, or may simply raise the desired cutoffs on one or more attributes. Online resources like MSN's Carpoint (**http://www.carpoint.ca**) and Autotrader (**http://www.autotrader.ca**) allow consumers to specify the minimum features/criteria that they want in an automobile and then provides a list of products that meet these criteria, thus helping the customer with his or her conjunctive model in decision making.

The conjunctive model can be used by both household and business customers. Since businesses often buy components and raw materials that have to fit into finished products and production processes, meeting the minimum specifications becomes a necessity. For example, in the chemical industry, required chemicals have to meet certain minimums on such attributes as purity, side-effects, and disposability. Business-to-Business exchanges like ChemConnect (**http://www.chemconnect.com**) allow businesses to specify their minimum criteria and generate efficiencies and cost savings through the Internet. Such indispensable minimums serve as cutoffs in the conjunctive model. The conjunctive model is, therefore, especially important in business-to-business markets.

The Disjunctive Model

Disjunctive model A decision-making procedure that entails tradeoffs between aspects of choice alternatives.

The **disjunctive model** entails *tradeoffs between aspects of choice alternatives.* Sometimes the customer is willing to trade off one feature for another. For example, a home buyer might say that the house she or he would consider buying should have either five bedrooms or, if it has only four bedrooms, it should have a finished basement. A business customer buying a copy machine might be willing to trade off copying speed if the machine has dual-side copying capability because, in a sense, automatic dual copying saves time and inconvenience. Although these tradeoffs are made also in the compensatory model, there are important differences. First, the disjunctive model considers the sheer presence or absence of attributes, rather than the degree or amount in which these attributes are present. Thus, the attributes tend to be those that do not vary on a graduated scale. For example, gas mileage rating tends to be used in a compensatory fashion, whereas the presence or absence of a finished basement tends to be traded off in a disjunctive model. This categorical (Is it present or not?) rather than graduated (How much of it is there?) appraisal of an attribute makes the disjunctive model simpler to execute than the other models. Customers could use attributes such as country of origin as a required attribute and drop all alternatives that are foreign made. Similarly, when customers came to know that Nike shoes were manufactured by underpaid and underage workers, the presence of this information was enough to drop these products from their choice set.

Second, in the compensatory model, the attributes traded off need not serve the same purpose while in the disjunctive model they tend to. Thus, in the compensatory model, lower gas mileage of a car can be compensated by superior rating on a totally unrelated attribute, such as safety. In the disjunctive model, on the other hand, gas mileage could be traded off only with other cost-saving features, such as low-maintenance costs. Or for copiers, the high speed and the dual-copying capability address the same time and convenience utility.

The Lexicographic Model

Lexicographic model A decision model wherein the available alternatives are compared in sequence by the rank-ordered attributes.

Another model customers use to make a choice is termed the **lexicographic model.** In this model, *attributes of alternatives are rank-ordered in terms of importance.* Customers examine all alternatives for the most important criterion and identify the one with the highest level for that criterion. If more than one alternative remains in the choice set, then they consider the second most important criterion and examine the remaining alternatives with respect to that criterion. The process continues until only one alternative remains.

For an example of business-to-business service, consider a business traveller (a salesperson, say) deciding on a hotel for an out-of-town trip. The most important criterion might be location within the downtown business district (rather than in the outlying areas of the city); therefore, he or she does not even bother looking at the listings of the outlying area hotels. (In the CAA guide books, hotels are listed in separate sections for downtown and outlying areas.) If there are several hotels in the business district listing, he or she next considers the second most important criterion: availability of office and business services (fax, copying, a DVD-equipped TV monitor in the room, high-speed Internet connection, etc.). Suppose only four hotels in the CAA listing meet this criterion. He or she next considers the third most important criterion, say price. The business traveller then chooses the one with the lowest price, and the decision is made. But if two (or more) hotels had the same low price, the customer would have to go through the next round of processing the alternatives for the criterion next in importance, such as the availability of a health spa on the hotel property. The process stops when one alternative is identified.

Elimination by Aspects

The **elimination by aspects (EBA)** model, first proposed by Amos Tversky, is similar to the lexicographic model but with one important difference. The customer rates the attributes in the order of importance and, in addition, defines cutoff values. She or he then examines all alternatives first for the most important attribute, admitting for further consideration only those that satisfy the minimum cutoff level for this most important attribute. If more than one alternative meets this requirement, then the customer goes to the next step, appraising the remaining alternatives on the second attribute, delineating those that meet the minimum cutoff level on this attribute, and so on.[19]

Elimination by aspects (EBA)
A decision-making procedure wherein the customer examines all alternatives, one attribute at a time, in the ranked-order sequence with minimum cutoff attribute values.

How and When the Models Are Used

Several concepts shed light on how and when various choice models are used. These are *processing by brand/supplier or by attribute, comparative features of various choice models, the two-stage choice process, rapid heuristics,* and *satisficing.*

Processing by Brand or by Attribute

Customers making choice decisions employ various models according to the choice situation facing them. An important characteristic of these models is the manner in which the evaluation proceeds: one brand/supplier at a time, or one attribute at a time (e.g., in Table 8.5, by rows or by columns). Conjunctive models entail considering one brand at a time with respect to all the attributes. The process of assessing one brand/supplier entirely before moving on to the second brand is called **processing by brands.** Note that the term *brand* is being used here to connote any alternative from which the choice must be made. Thus, the model is applicable to supplier choice as well as to choice of products.

Processing by brands (PBB)
The process of assessing one brand entirely before moving on to the second brand.

In contrast to conjunctive models, the lexicographic and EBA processes entail **processing by attributes** (i.e., processing all the brands simultaneously on one attribute at a time). This is simpler to execute than processing by brands. However, processing by brands allows a more thorough evaluation of brands than does processing by attributes. Furthermore, the lexicographic model is simpler to execute than the EBA, but the lexicographic loses the opportunity to purchase a brand that may be superior on the next set of attributes.

Processing by attributes (PBA)
The process of assessing brands wherein all the available brands are compared simultaneously for one attribute at a time.

In processing by attributes, brands are also subject to a "direction-of-comparison effect." When two brands are compared, one brand becomes the focal object of comparison, while the other brand is the referent of comparison. This process of comparison naturally elicits more thoughts about the focal brand compared to the referent brand. As a result of this process, the unique attributes of the focal brand gain prominence in the comparison, and if these attributes are positive, they gain more weight in the evaluation of the two brands. The attributes of the referent brand are compared against these attributes of the focal brand, and given that the referent brand does not have the unique attributes of the focal brand, it is more likely that the focal brand will be preferred over the referent brand. In the same way, when the unique attributes of the focal brand are negative, they work against the focal brand's favour, and the referent brand is preferred. The direction-of-comparison effect is stronger in judgments made by people who have a high need for cognition because they are more likely to use an attribute-based processing strategy. This effect occurs the least when consumers use an attitude-based processing strategy that involves the use of general attitudes, summary impressions, intuitions, or heuristics to make judgments.[20]

Comparative Features of Various Choice Models

The conjunctive, disjunctive, lexicographic, and EBA models are all *non*-compensatory models, since the deficiency for one attribute is not allowed to be made up for by excess for another. An alternative may be eliminated in the first step for being only marginally inferior to an otherwise substantially better alternative for the second most important attribute; it doesn't matter that the eliminated alternative is much superior for all other attributes. The compensatory model eliminates the possibility of making such suboptimal choices. The compensatory model is more burdensome to execute, however, because the customer has to consider several dimensions or attributes at the same time, and somehow weigh them in his or her mind. Typically, therefore, the compensatory model is used sparingly and only for important decisions.[21] Most low-ticket items are likely to be chosen with the help of non-compensatory models. Thus, a customer may buy table salt based simply on a single criterion, such as familiarity with the brand or whether it is iodized, or perhaps on price alone. Another customer buying an entrée might use fat content as the important criterion and then either choose the one with the lowest fat content (thus employing a lexicographic model) or consider all entrées with fat content not exceeding 15 percent of total calories (thus employing EBA). Calories per serving might then be used as the second criterion, and, if need be, price as the third.

In terms of the three routine/limited/extended problem-solving strategies, the compensatory model is likely to be used generally for extended problem solving. Non-compensatory models are likely used for limited and routine problem-solving situations. Furthermore, non-compensatory models may also be used in the initial stage of an extended problem-solving decision situation, as explained next.

Two-Stage Choice Process

Phased decision strategy
A two-stage decision procedure wherein the alternatives are first eliminated, and then the remaining alternatives are compared for a final choice.

For the more important decisions, a customer might first use a non-compensatory model and then, to further identify the choice, a compensatory model. Bettman and Park have described the customer decision process as a two-stage process, termed **phased decision strategy.**[22] In the first stage, termed the *alternative-elimination stage,* customers narrow the set of alternatives for closer comparisons. In the second stage, termed the *alternative-selection stage,* the smaller set of alternatives is further examined. The objective of the first stage is to identify the *acceptable* alternatives, whereas the second stage is meant to identify the *best.*

Since non-compensatory models are easier to execute, a large number of alternatives can be examined relatively quickly, particularly if processing is done by attributes rather than by brands. In the second stage, when only three or four alternatives remain, customers can more efficiently employ the compensatory model. Even here, if one or more attributes are matching across the alternatives, one simply ignores this attribute and applies the compensatory model on the smaller set of attributes. In this way customers can take advantage of the compensatory model to make an optimal decision without incurring the information-overload cost that would have accrued if all of the initially available large number of alternatives were to be processed by the compensatory model throughout.

Rapid Heuristics

For a common, repeat purchase of low-risk, low-ticket items such as shampoo, snacks, cereals, or office supplies in the business context, customers are unlikely to spend much time or effort. These purchases are perceived to be low-risk, low-involvement decisions. As such, hardly any information is examined, and brand choice is made by using a heuristic (simple rule of thumb). Examples of heuristics used for such repeat purchase items are: "Purchase the known brand only;" "Purchase whichever brand is on sale;" and "I saw my friend using this brand, so I too will purchase this one."

Wayne D. Hoyer (U.S. customers) and Siew Meng Leong (Chinese customers) observed customers in a supermarket selecting a couple of common, repeat purchase items (namely, detergent and shampoo) and later approached and asked them what was the basis of their decision.[23] In a subsequent experimental study, customers were given a product that could be examined by taste (namely, peanut butter in one study and cheese in another). Of the three brands presented to research customers, one was a well-known brand. The researchers found that customers in the supermarket study spent very little time (less than 15 seconds) to complete their in-store decision, examined a small number of packages (about 1.5 on an average), made few brand comparisons, and looked at only a few shelf tags. When asked why they chose the brand they did, an overwhelming majority (approximately 95 percent) mentioned a single reason. This single reason, for the largest majority, was: "It worked better." When customers were making a new choice (since none of their usual brands were in the choice set), and one of the three brands was known but the other two were not, customers overwhelmingly (97 percent) chose the known brand. Thus, "purchase the known brand" is a choice heuristic customers use most often, especially in a new choice task of a low-ticket, common, repeat-purchase item. Not in vain, then, do advertisers spend considerable amounts of money keeping their brands in the top-of-the-mind awareness of their target customers.

Satisficing

No matter what decision model they use, customers as decision makers can never consider and appraise all of the alternatives exhaustively. Indeed, customers *do not* typically make the most optimal choice. As already pointed out, the use of lexicographic, EBA, or other non-compensatory model might eliminate a brand from further consideration based on the first attribute even though the brand's other features could have made the brand more attractive overall. Yet customers are perfectly happy making a choice by non-compensatory models. This is a concept that Herbert Simon calls satisficing.[24] **Satisficing** refers to the customer's (or decision maker's) acceptance of an alternative that she or he finds satisfying, rather than pursuing the arduous search for the most optimal alternative. Thus, even the ardent comparison shoppers finally give up and buy the product they find most acceptable from among those they have considered so far, even though they recognize that there might well be a slightly or even substantially better product or deal at the next store. In the business context, the cost of searching for information for a myriad of alternatives and then evaluating them can be enormous. Hence, satisficing is common even in the business context.

Satisficing
The customer's (or decision maker's) acceptance of an alternative that he or she finds satisfying, rather than an arduous search for the most optimal alternative.

STEP 4: PURCHASE

Once the customer has evaluated the alternatives, she or he makes the purchase. This at first appears a straightforward step, but even here customer behaviour at times becomes intriguing. In fact, this behaviour can be broken down into three substeps. The first occurs when the customer identifies the most preferred alternative, based on the alternative evaluation process just described. The next substep is to form a purchase intent—a determination to buy that product. The final substep is implementing the purchase. This entails arranging the terms of the transaction, seeking and obtaining the transfer of the title or ownership from the seller, paying for the product, and receiving possession of the good or the service commitment from the seller.

The first substep (choice identification) is the conclusion of a process wherein the customer's user role and his or her needs and wants as user become most salient. Although the payer's concern (e.g., whether it is affordable) and buyer's concern (e.g., where to obtain it). may also be taken into account, the emphasis is likely to have remained on the fit between the product and the performance, and whatever social/psychological values the customer seeks in the user role.

In the second substep (purchase intent), the payer's concerns become most salient. If the payer is different from the user, a formal budget approval may be needed. The payer may have to assess whether the product is overpriced, whether the required cash or credit is available at this time, whether it sits well with established guidelines for allocating the budget over different categories of products or whether it offers equity to other users (e.g., other members of the household or other employees in the organization) who may have claims on the budget pool.

Finally, the purchase implementation substep activates the buyer role and is influenced most by the concerns of the buyer. The buyer's market values (convenience and service values) become the determining forces. This may influence the store or supplier from whom the preferred item is bought, the day and time it is bought, how soon or late it is bought, and whether it is bought at all. For example, a 13-year-old boy wants to attend a space camp run by NASA. He calls the camp organizers, gets the brochures, identifies the specific program he wants to attend, and gets his parents to agree to pay for the trip. The final task of filling out and sending the application is left to the older brother, who procrastinates until the deadline has expired. Even when the same person plays the payer, user, and buyer roles, the buyer role may hinder the implementation of the choice identified and approved by the other two roles. Thus, as the above example shows, the customer journey from choice identification to purchase implementation does not always proceed in predictable ways. Sometimes, the purchase intention may not be implemented, as, for example, when a customer almost decides to join a particular weight-reduction program but somehow never gets around to actually doing it. But even if the purchase implementation eventually occurs, the customer journey may take a different route. Two factors can potentially derail the journey: postponement or delay in implementation, and deviation from the identified choice. The business procurement process is discussed in detail in Chapter 9.

Delay in Implementation

Delays in implementation occur at various stages of the customer decision process, from problem recognition through alternative evaluation to purchase. We discuss those that occur at the purchase step here for convenience, and because it is the purchase step that is ultimately delayed. A study by Eric A. Greenleaf and Donald R. Lehmann identified the reasons consumers give for delay in their purchase decisions. They interviewed recent buyers of such products as home appliances, electronics, personal computers, clothing, furniture, sports equipment, and automobiles. The consumers were asked to describe why they delayed the decision to buy these products, and also how they subsequently closed the decision. These factors, along with their importance ratings in this study, are described in Table 8.6. The top three reasons for delay in buying the products were time pressure, need for more information, and inability to afford the product at the time. Top reasons for closure were deciding on another alternative and finding the time to make the decision.

TABLE 8.6 Reasons for Delay and Decision Closure

Reason	Mean Importance	Customer Role
REASONS FOR DELAY		
Time pressure; too busy to devote the time	3.91	User, payer, buyer
Needed more information	3.43	User
Couldn't afford at the time	3.19	Payer
Not sure if needed the item	2.75	User
Social and psychological risk if a wrong choice is made	2.70	User
Felt another product at home would do	2.70	User
Performance and financial risk if a wrong choice is made	2.65	User, payer
Expected price reduction or product modification in the near future	2.52	User, payer
Needed others' consent	2.41	User, payer
Find shopping unpleasant	2.34	Buyer
REASONS FOR DECISION CLOSURE		
Decided on another alternative	3.84	User
Found the time	3.62	User, buyer
Need had become passing	3.51	User
Lower price became available	3.10	Payer
Tired of shopping further	2.70	Buyer
Found a good store	2.41	Buyer
Was able to justify the expense	2.32	Payer
Obtained the advice and consent I needed	2.14	User, payer
Due to good word of mouth	2.01	User

SOURCE: Adapted from Greenleaf, Eric A., and Donald R. Lehmann. "Reasons for Substantial Delay in Consumer Decision Making." *Journal of Consumer Research* 22, no.2 (1996): 186–199.

Delays in purchase implementations occur among business customers as well. One reason for such delay is a change in management: the new management may want to review all capital equipment procurement plans and/or redesign the procurement policies. Another possible reason is declining financial performance; if sales and profits fall below projected levels, then some capital equipment purchase plans may be put on hold. Decisions may be delayed because of fourth-quarter syndrome: businesses typically postpone making major purchases until the last quarter of the accounting year; thus, purchase decision making may be delayed until the fourth quarter, either to avoid committing money early in the year, or because time pressure did not permit decision making earlier. Interest rates and the economic situation—domestic or global—may also cause delays in purchase implementations.

An ATKearney report states that four out of five shoppers abandon their shopping carts on the Internet. Customers stated that the top reason for not completing the purchase was that the site required too much personal information before making the purchase. This shows that customers are not very comfortable sharing a large amount of personal information on their first visit to a site. They are willing to part with more information only when they trust the retailer and believe that providing more information will lead to increased benefits. Reluctance to give credit card details, website malfunction, and an inability to find the desired products are other reasons stated by customers for incompletion of a purchase.[25]

Understanding these reasons is important for marketers because it helps them facilitate the customer journey from problem recognition to purchase. By identifying the particular reason and the step where it has a delaying effect, marketers can work to overcome that barrier. Furthermore, marketers can implement separate actions directed individually toward the three roles of the user, payer, and buyer.

Deviation From the Identified Choice

The second factor that may derail the customer purchase implementation is deviation from the identified choice. Several conditions may account for this. First, the preferred brand may be out of stock, thus forcing the customer to buy a brand different from the one identified, especially if one needs the product immediately. Second, new in-store information may reopen the evaluation process. Third, financing terms may render a purchase infeasible, forcing the customer either to abandon the purchase altogether or to choose a lower-level model or another brand available on preferred terms. In the business context, stock-outs at the regular supplier may force a switch to another supplier. Financing of the project, say from the World Bank or Export Development Canada, may change the options considered. These conditions may also shift the relative impact of the customer roles. While the values of the user are most influential in the alternative evaluation phase, the values of the buyer (e.g., convenience of buying) or of the payer (e.g., the financing available) become influential at the purchase stage.

STEP 5: POST-PURCHASE EXPERIENCE

The customer's decision process does not end with the purchase. Rather, the experience of buying and using the product provides information that the customer will use in future decision making. In some cases, the customer will be pleased with the experience and will buy the same product from the same supplier again. In other cases, the customer will be disappointed and may even return or exchange the product. The consumer may also experience *regret* as a result of comparing one's outcome with a better outcome that would have occurred had a different alternative been selected. Regret has a negative influence on satisfaction with the chosen alternative and on repurchase intentions for the chosen alternative.[26] In general, the post-purchase process includes four steps: *decision confirmation, experience evaluation, satisfaction or dissatisfaction,* and *future response* (exit, voice, or loyalty), in that order.

Decision Confirmation

After a customer makes an important choice decision, she or he experiences an intense need to confirm the wisdom of that decision. The flip side is that she or he wants to avoid the lack of confirmation. One of the processes that occurs at this stage is *cognitive dissonance,* discussed in Chapter 6, which is a post-purchase doubt the buyer experiences about the wisdom of the choice.

Two methods of reducing dissonance and confirming the soundness of one's decision are: seeking further positive information about the chosen alternative, and avoiding negative information about the chosen alternative. Thus, customers reread product literature reviewing the brand's positive features, and avoid competitors' advertisements or negative information from others. They ask their friends about the purchase, hoping that their friends will validate their decision by praising the selected brand. Marketers can put this principle to use: After the purchase (say, during product delivery), salespeople can review with customers all the features of the product, and this review during the post-purchase phase is likely to bring to customer attention a few positive features previously ignored, thus improving the perceived attractiveness of the product. In the business context, the company could arrange for a formal celebration with customers or could provide customer testimonials in its advertisements to reassure prospective customers.

Experience Evaluation

Following purchase, the product is actually consumed. Marketers need to know whether customers consume it routinely or while consciously evaluating it. This depends on the level of enduring involvement in the product and the finality of the preference that caused this purchase.

Earlier in this chapter, enduring involvement was defined as the interest customers take in the consumption of the product on an *ongoing basis.* We use most products routinely and notice them only if something does not work as expected. On the other hand, we are very enthusiastic about some products. In consuming these, we are conscious of the consumption experience, appraising and relishing it continually (e.g., wine drinking by connoisseurs). These, then, are the products that undergo conscious evaluation during use. In the business context, companies would be enduringly involved in a service contract or a single-source supplier, but the appraisal and evaluation would be more formal than in the case of an individual customer's evaluation of a product in which he is enduringly involved.

Secondly, customers buy some products on a trial basis, without making their preference final yet. These products, even if not of enduring involvement, are the ones that the customer is likely to use with an eye to appraisal. Free samples received are usually used routinely, without conscious appraisal of the performance of the product. Sampling is productive when the product's superiority is substantial and would be conspicuous in consumption, and when the samples are targeted at customers who are not satisfied with the current solutions. Because of their dissatisfaction, they would actively appraise the sampled product. Airbus, the European consortium producing passenger airplanes, is using this strategy and offering its products to several U.S. airlines on a trial basis to break into the market.

Satisfaction/Dissatisfaction

Whether or not they actively evaluate a product during use or consumption, users do experience the usage outcome. This outcome is characterized as satisfaction or dissatisfaction. Measuring overall satisfaction/dissatisfaction is easy. Customer researchers can simply ask, "How satisfied or dissatisfied are you with___(the product name)?" What is more challenging is to understand *why* customers feel the way they do. There are two approaches to this challenge. One is to get the customer to rate a product on its various attributes, such as, for a car, handling, gas mileage, acceleration, and braking. Satisfaction or dissatisfaction with these product attributes can then be used to explain the customer's *overall* satisfaction or dissatisfaction with the product.

But this approach raises another question: What causes satisfaction or dissatisfaction with individual attributes? This question is successfully addressed by a theoretical approach to understanding satisfaction. Scholars have proposed that satisfaction depends not on the absolute levels of performance on various attributes but rather on how the actual performance compares with the *expected* performance. Thus, if the product experience fulfills prepurchase expectations, then satisfaction results, and if doesn't, dissatisfaction results. Therefore, satisfaction or dissatisfaction stems respectively from the confirmation of our expectations, or the lack thereof. The theory makes intuitive sense in our everyday experience. For example, we may find a particular level of cleanliness unsatisfactory in a Four Seasons hotel but quite satisfactory in, say, a Motel 6. This is because our expectations about the Four Seasons are quite high compared to those we hold for Motel 6.

A new type of market-based performance measure for firms, industries, economic sectors, and national economies, named the American Customer Satisfaction Index (ACSI), was first introduced in the fall of 1994, with information on 40 industries and seven major sectors of the U.S. economy. The index is produced through a partnership of the University of Michigan Business School, the American Society for Quality, and the CFI Group. It is a national economic indicator of customer satisfaction with the quality of goods and services available to household consumers in the United States. "An individual firm's ACSI represents its customers' overall evaluation of total purchase and consumption experience, both actual and anticipated." An industry ACSI represents an industry's customers' overall evaluation of its market offering; a sector ACSI is an overall evaluation of that sector, and the national ACSI gauges the nation's total consumption experience. Hence, ACSI represents "a cumulative evaluation of a firm's market offering, rather than a person's evaluation of a specific transaction." The American Customer Satisfaction Index uses a 100-point scale and presently measures satisfaction with 164 companies and 30 government agencies. The score fell from the baseline level of 74.2 in 1994 to an all time low below 71.0 in Q1 1997. Since then the value of the index increased until the first quarter of 2004 but it dropped dramatically in the fourth quarter of 2004 after a two-year period of steady improvement. After Q1 2005, the index increased dramatically to 74.1 for Q1 2006 thanks to significant increases in consumer spending.[27]

In the online context, a study of "e-satisfaction"—customers' satisfaction with e-retailing—by Szymanski and Hise shows that shopping convenience (total shopping time, convenience, ease of browsing), site design (uncluttered screens, easy search paths, and fast presentations) and financial security of online transactions are the three most important drivers of e-satisfaction. Surprisingly, product information (quantity and quality of information) had a very small impact on e-satisfaction, and product offerings (number and variety of offerings) had no impact at all.[28] The cost and effort of voicing dissatisfaction online with products is also rapidly declining for customers. With services like PlanetFeedback (**http://www.planetfeedback.com**) and the Better Business Bureau (**http://www.bbbonline.org**), it is much easier for customers to voice their grievances. This puts added pressure on marketers since the impact of dissatisfied customers is also magnified through the medium of the Internet (higher reach).

The theory of satisfaction has important implications for shaping expectations.[29] If marketing communications and other elements of the marketing mix (e.g., advertising, salespersons, price, appearance of the store) promise too much, they may create expectations that the product would almost surely fail to fulfill, thus risking customer dissatisfaction. Of course, if the expectations are too low, the sale may not result. The right strategy, therefore, ought to be to create realistic expectations, implying a performance level that the target market finds attractive enough to select the brand. To assess whether they are on target, marketers may use a measure of satisfaction such as the one illustrated in Table 8.7.

TABLE 8.7 Measuring Satisfaction in Terms of Expectations

A hotel might ask: How did we do? How was our:

	Fell Below Expectations	Met Expectations	Exceeded Expectations
Room appearance	O	O	O
Room cleanliness	O	O	O
Registration speed	O	O	O
Friendliness of staff	O	O	O
Room service promptness	O	O	O

Future Response: Exit, Voice, or Loyalty

Following the experience of satisfaction or dissatisfaction, customers have three possible responses: *exit, voice,* or *loyalty.*

Exit

If customers are dissatisfied with their experience with a brand, they may decide never again to buy the brand. This places them back at the start of the decision process the next time the problem recognition arises. They have to go through the arduous process of information search, alternative evaluation, and so on, all over again. This "churn" in customers is very common in credit-card services, and long-distance carriers as customers tend to switch from suppliers when they are dissatisfied.

Voice

Dissatisfied customers may complain and then decide either to give the brand or marketer another chance or simply to exit.

What accounts for customers' tendency to complain or not complain? The likelihood that a customer will complain depends on three factors: dissatisfaction salience, attributions to the marketer, and customers' personality traits (see Figure 8.3).

- *Dissatisfaction salience*—Not all dissatisfaction is salient (i.e., bothersome to customers). Generally, small gaps between performance and expectations are ignored; moreover, even substantial gaps are not likely to be noticed if the product is trivial. Thus, the importance of the product and the width of the performance-expectations gap determine dissatisfaction salience, which, in turn, determines the likelihood of customer complaints. Malfunction of the vending machine at a supermarket or the non-availability of the desired product in the vending machine is a matter that causes dissatisfaction, but not enough for it to be salient.
- *Attributions to the marketer*—Customers make attributions about who is to blame for poor product performance. For example, in the case of airlines, delays are more often than not attributed to the marketer, even though the actual delay may have been caused by weather problems. If customers blame themselves or circumstances, then they will not complain; on the other hand, if they attribute failure to the marketer, then they are likely to complain. Furthermore, if customers thought that the failure was not likely to

FIGURE 8.3 Determinants of Complaining

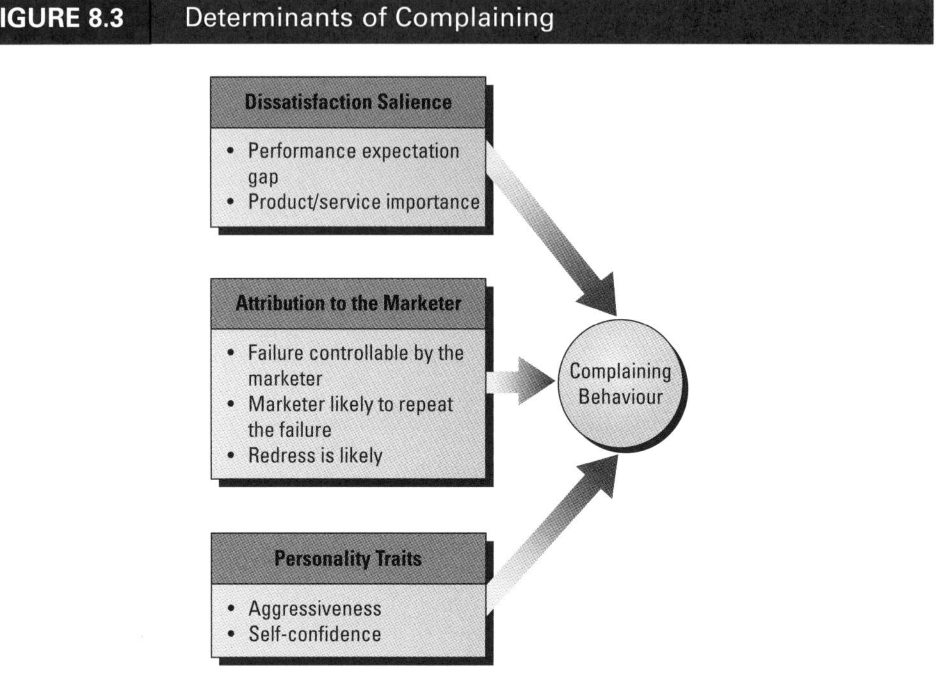

be repeated, they would be less motivated to complain. Finally, customers must also believe that the marketer is likely to take the corrective action; if they think that redress from the marketer is unlikely, they may consider complaining a waste of effort.

- *Customers' personality traits*—Customers' personality traits play an important role in complaining. Customers differ in self-confidence and in their degree of aggressiveness or submissiveness. Complaining requires self-confidence, and aggressiveness drives customers to assert themselves. These traits, therefore, lead customers to complain rather than meekly accept poor marketer performance.

Following the complaint, negative word-of-mouth is less likely and repatronage more likely if the complaint is successfully redressed. An important concept here is perceived justice. **Perceived justice** is a customer's perception that he or she was treated with respect during the conflict resolution process, the policy and procedures followed were fair, and the decision itself was fair.[30] When perceived justice seems not to have occurred, then hostility increases.

Perceived justice Customers' perception that they were treated fairly during the conflict resolution process, and that the outcome itself was fair.

Research has found that customer complaint is actually good for the marketer. According to one study, about 19 percent of dissatisfied customers complain; of the complaining customers, a significant majority continue to buy the product, compared to those who are dissatisfied but do not bother to complain. Thus, complainers care enough to complain. Non-complainers simply walk out, taking their patronage to a competitor.

Loyalty

The third response is, of course, loyalty. Customer loyalty means the customer buys the same brand repeatedly. The concept of loyalty has been debated in the literature in various definitions of *brand loyalty.* First, brand loyalty can be defined simply as the consistent repurchase of the same brand. This definition has two problems. First, in many product categories, customers buy an assortment of brands to satisfy their need for variety in the consumption experience. For example, eating the same cereal every day or eating lunch every day in the office cafeteria may not be satisfying. This problem of variety can be handled by asking customers if the focal brand is consistently at least a part of the assortment the customer buys, if not an exclusive purchase. In the business context, companies are loyal to multiple vendors.

The second problem with defining and measuring brand loyalty as a consistent repurchase is that one does not know if the consistent repurchase is merely due to convenience, is a routinization of the purchase decision, or reflects genuine preference for the brand. To overcome this uncertainty, some researchers have defined brand loyalty in attitudinal terms: the brand attitude underlying the re-purchase. Only if a favourable brand attitude underlies re-purchase is brand loyalty thought to exist. This topic is discussed more fully in Chapter 11.

At first thought, one would think that if customers are satisfied, they will not switch brands. Thus, a satisfaction rating may be deemed to ensure loyalty. Research has shown, however, that while customers are less likely to switch when they are satisfied than when they are not, being satisfied does not guarantee loyalty. One study showed that despite satisfaction, as many as 30 percent of customers were likely to switch suppliers.[31]

There are several reasons why satisfied customers may still switch. First, customers report being satisfied with a brand, but they may also be satisfied with some other brands. The implication of this is that one should measure customer satisfaction with a brand *relative* to competitors' brands. The second reason is that the marginal utility of a repeated use may decline simply due to familiarity, and need for variety can drive brand switching. Research shows that increasing the variety in the context—that is, providing variety in a different product category that is purchased simultaneously with the focal category—may reduce variety seeking in the focal category. This happens because consumers try to achieve an optimal level of stimulation by balancing the stimulation that comes from variety seeking and the stimulation available from the context.[32] Finally, customers may switch brands because they expect to receive even greater value or satisfaction from some other brand.

INDIVIDUAL CUSTOMER DECISION MAKING AND THE THREE CUSTOMER ROLES

LO 5

In this section, we pull together various concepts covered in the chapter and illustrate their relevance to the three customer roles (see Table 8.8). First, we talked about the setting of individual decision making. By definition, the user and buyer roles, and often the payer role as well, are played by the same individual. Since buyer and user roles are combined in the same individual, the user has more control over what to buy, and where to buy it. At the same time, the convergence of the buyer and user roles may also cause some sacrifice in weak user values. For example, if the individual feels too lazy to go out (a buyer role) to eat (a user role), she or he has to make do with a home-delivered pizza that may not be as good in quality or taste. Sometimes the payer role is separated, as in the consumption of free public services; with someone else as payer (government or employers), the users tend to consume more as well as evaluate the product less stringently.

The three roles also come into play in the stages of the decision-making process: problem recognition, information search, alternative evaluation, choice or purchase, and post-choice experience. Although most products are bought in response to the problem recognition by the user role, the other two roles can also be the source of problem recognition. When the buyer values are violated (for example, lack of pre-purchase assistance or rude store employees) or

TABLE 8.8 Individual Customer Decision Making and the Three Customer Roles

Concepts	User	Payer	Buyer
Individual Decision Maker	• User in control of buying role as well; strong user values rule over payer/ buyer values	• With someone else as payer, users tend to consume more; also, user evaluation is less stringent	• Role convergence sometimes causes sacrifice in weak user values
Decision Process			
Problem recognition	• Users are the most frequent problem recognizers	• Buyer dissatisfaction with service, convenience, and personalization values can cause problem recognition • New delivery channels serve as solution stimuli to cause problem recognition by buyers	• Awareness of better price value from competitors causes payer role problem recognition
Information search	• Information pertaining to user values is sought	• Payer role seeks information about competitors' prices	• Inadequate buyer motivation to expend search efforts constrains user's and payer's desire for more information
Search determinants:			
Perceived risk	• User-felt risk causes more information search	• Payers willing to pay more to avoid user risks	• Buyers lean on trustworthy sources
Involvement	• User involvement may demand sacrifice in buyer/payer values		• Involved buyers do extensive information search
Familiarity	• User familiarity enables greater use of available information		• Familiarity lulls buyers into less search effort
Time pressure	• Users seek time-saving features in products		• Time pressure most affects buyers who seek efficient exchanges
Alternative evaluation	• Users' values are most important evaluation criteria	• For parity products (i.e., with user indifference), payers seek to maximize price value	• For parity products, buyer values become important criteria
Decision mode is:			
Compensatory	• Users participate actively		
Non-compensatory	• One or the other role may be most important	• Payer value may be exercised through use of some non-compensatory model	• To minimize cognitive effort, buyers like to use non-compensatory model
Functional/expressive Product	• For expressive products, users must participate in evaluation		

Purchase		• Lack of agreement on financing may hinder purchase	• This stage is most relevant to the buyer role
Post-choice processes: Buyer's remorse/ decision confirmation			• Buyer role subject to remorse; seeks more favourable information before decision confirmation
Experience evaluation	• Product use experienced by the user role		
Satisfaction	• Determined largely by satisfaction of user values		
Exit, voice, loyalty	• User satisfaction leads to loyalty • Users spread word-of-mouth		• Loyalty simplifies buyer's task
Complaint	• User dissatisfaction motivates complaints		• Buyer aggressiveness determines if complaint will be made

if a new means of obtaining the product becomes available (such as home delivery of groceries), the buyer's problem recognition is triggered. Payers recognize the problem when a competitor brings home the point that they are paying too much for their current product.

In the information-search stage, information is sought that is relevant to user and payer values. While some information is received without the buyer's effort (e.g., information from advertisements), the information that requires visits to the store or going to the library, etc., depends on the buyer motivation to make the effort. The buyer's values (i.e., his or her desire to limit the search effort) then constrain users' and payers' desire to maximize its values. Buyers who enjoy browsing help the user identify new solutions. Buyers who are comparison shoppers help the payer find the best price value. Various determinants of search (namely, perceived risk, involvement, familiarity, and time pressure) also implicate the three roles differently.

Perceived risk generally necessitates a search regarding brand features, the concern of the user. To ensure risk-free product for the user, payers may be willing to sacrifice on payer value. Buyers may want to limit consideration to suppliers they have dealt with, and whom they trust. Involvement with the product again emphasizes the user, whose concern with getting the best product (in the case of high involvement) demands sacrifice in payer and buyer values, if necessary. High involvement, again, leads to extensive search.

Buyers' roles can also vary in involvement. Some customers simply dislike shopping while others enjoy it, reading product labels in the store and comparing products on features. Involved shoppers, thus, end up doing extensive information search. Uninvolved shoppers (i.e., buyers) would lead users to make do with less information. Familiarity with the product enables the user to more easily absorb the current information that the user comes across, such as in advertising, but the buyer may feel less need to make the effort to search for new information. Time pressure is most relevant to the buyer role in the information-search stage, and also in the purchase stage, as the buyer would seek time-saving means of acquiring the product. Time pressure on users is also a factor, and it will affect the performance criteria inasmuch as the users will seek time-saving features in products, such as ready-to-eat meals or faster cycle machines.

In the alternative evaluation stage, since the buyer is the same as the user, the market values the user seeks become the overriding criteria. Only in the case of parity products do the buyer's market values (e.g., convenience) become determinant so that, in this example, the buyer buys whatever is most conveniently purchased. Furthermore, given user indifference to alternatives (which happens with parity products), the payer's concern with obtaining the best price value also becomes a prominent decision criterion.

Decision models also implicate the roles differently. Compensatory models require simultaneous consideration of various criteria, mostly comprising user values; therefore, users participate actively in the decision. Non-compensatory models generally emphasize one or the other of the three roles; for example, in seeking the lowest price as the sole factor (lexicographic model), the payer role is being given prominence. Buying whatever is available (another lexicographic rule) makes the buyer role the determinant.

Functional versus expressive products also influence the interplay of the three roles. Expressive products can be evaluated only by the user, much more than is the case for functional products. For functional products, the user can specify the performance criteria, and then let the buyer match the product against those criteria; in contrast, for expressive products, product evaluation against the desired social/emotional values can be done only by the user, not the buyer. Of course, users can subsequently routinize their choice by brand name for functional and expressive products alike and let the buyer simply execute it.

In the next stage, purchase, the values of the buyer and the payer become most important. Sometimes when the decision is made outside the store, or if the purchase cannot be executed as soon as the user decision is made, the buyer may delay buying the product or may fail to implement the decision, sometimes foregoing the purchase altogether. The payer value of best price and good financing or credit may sometimes hinder the purchase of the user's choice; for example, when price negotiations fail. The purchase may be blocked by the buyer's skill at negotiating price, payment, and delivery terms, or the payer's ability to receive credit or meet the payment terms.

In the post-purchase stage, dissonance (or buyer's remorse) and the consequent decision confirmation are processes experienced by the buyer. Experience evaluation is done by the user. Buyer and payer values received in the transaction are soon forgotten, but the user values persist. Satisfaction is largely determined by the extent to which the user gets the expected value during the product's use. Satisfactory user experience simplifies the buyer's task for the future; she or he can now simply execute the future purchases in the routine problem-solving mode. Favourable or unfavourable word of mouth ensues from satisfied or dissatisfied customers in the user role. Satisfied users display loyalty behaviour; dissatisfied users seek exit from their current supplier and trigger the buyer role of finding a new source. If dissatisfied, the user can feel enough anger to motivate a complaint, but the aggressiveness of the buyer will determine whether or not the complaint is actually made.

The Elimination by Aspects (EBA) model is most sensitive to the user, payer, and buyer roles. Whichever role has the opportunity to influence the decision uses EBA to emphasize its own value. If the customer is most concerned with user values, then the user's market values become the first EBA criterion. On the other hand, if the customer's constraints as a payer or the buyer are insurmountable, then those roles' market values become the first EBA criterion. Thus, if the user value is most important, then the customer gets to buy his or her favourite brand, say of clothing or computers. Thus, a popular or reputed brand name becomes the first

EBA criterion. On the other hand, if the payer constraints are strong, then budget constraints or economic value (good value for the money) become the first EBA criterion. Finally, if the buyer role's constraint become the key decision influencer, then convenience or service values become the first EBA criterion.

SUMMARY

In this chapter, we studied customer decision making as a five-step process: problem recognition, information search, alternative evaluation, choice, and post-choice. The customer decision problem begins with problem recognition. The problem recognition occurs when the customer receives internal cues from unfulfilled motives or from the external stimuli of these motives. A typology of problems was suggested—namely, familiar-latent, familiar-vivid, novel-latent, and novel-vivid—and its marketing implications were discussed. Once problem recognition occurs, the customer (a) either relies on prior knowledge and previously learned solutions or (b) searches for new solutions through the acquisition of new information and the evaluation and integration of that new information. In the information-search stage, there are several determinants of information search, such as perceived risk, involvement, familiarity and expertise, and the functional versus expressive nature of products. **LO 1, 2**

Evaluation of alternatives entails use of compensatory and non-compensatory decision models. The latter include conjunctive, disjunctive, lexicographic, and elimination-by-aspects models. The outcome of these evaluation processes is the identification of a preferred brand and the formation of a purchase intent. Such purchase intent is then implemented by the actual purchase act, but it was suggested that the purchase act does not always occur as planned. Sometimes, substantial delays occur in purchase implementation, and at other times, the brand actually bought is different from the one planned because of stock-outs or new information at the time of purchase. In the post-choice phase, the processes of decision confirmation, satisfaction/dissatisfaction, exit, voice (complaining), and loyalty responses were discussed. **LO 3, 4**

The individual purchasing behaviour is determined by a person's individual characteristics, such as demographics, personality, and motives (see previous chapters). This chapter focused on the process itself—how the individual buying behaviour unfolds. Understanding this process should help you be aware of your own marketplace behaviour in the future. And understanding the individual buying behaviour is helpful to marketing managers, as reflected in the many applications and implications we outlined throughout the chapter. Ultimately, it behooves marketers to structure their offerings and their communications in a fashion that responds to and resonates with customers' decision-making processes. **LO 5**

KEY TERMS

Advocate Sources 288
Affective Choice Mode (ACM) 296
Awareness Set 286
Compensatory Model 298
Conjunctive Model 299
Consideration Set 286
Customer Decisions 281
Customer Problem 283
Disjunctive Model 300
Elimination by Aspects (EBA) 301

Enduring Involvement 293
Evaluative Consistency 290
Evoked Set 286
Extended Problem Solving 289
External Stimuli 283
Heuristics 290
Ignorance Paradox 295
Information Overload 297
Information Processing Mode (IPM) 296
Interattribute Inference 290
Internal Stimuli 283
Lexicographic Model 300
Limited Problem Solving 289
Marketer Sources 288
Mental Budgeting 281
Negative Cue 290
Non-Marketer Sources 288
Other-Brand Averaging 290
Perceived Justice 310
Perceived Risk 291
Phased Decision Strategy 302
Primary Demand 284
Problem Recognition 283
Processing by Attributes 301
Processing by Brands 301
Purchase-Decision Involvement 292
Routine Problem Solving 289
Satisficing 303
Search Strategy 289
Secondary (Selective) Demand 285
Systematic Search 290

DISCUSSION QUESTIONS AND EXERCISES

1. Reflect on your customer behaviour, drawing on examples from each consumption location where individual decision making can occur—at home, at work, and in public places. Discuss which of the three customer roles and six customer values become more influential in different situations.
2. Reflect on how you might choose each of the following products:
   a. An MBA degree
   b. A restaurant for an anniversary dinner with your spouse, or with your boyfriend or girlfriend on his or her birthday
   c. A hotel for a business trip to France
   d. A toothpaste during a business trip to an Asian country where none of your usual brands are available
   e. A photocopier/scanner/fax machine for your home office.

   For each, please indicate whether you will use:

   i) a two-phase or a single-phase decision strategy
   ii) a compensatory or a non-compensatory model, or both
   iii) a heuristic; identify the heuristic you have in mind.
3. Assume that you recently made these three customer decisions: (1) after evaluating three lawn-maintenance service companies, you just gave the contract to one of them; (2) you wanted to watch a movie on your hotel room TV and rented one from the choice of two; and (3) at the restaurant, you debated briefly between iced tea and Coca-Cola and ordered iced tea. For which of these decisions are you likely to have experienced cognitive dissonance? Why or why not? What actions are you likely to have taken to reduce that dissonance? What can a marketer do, in each case, to help you overcome that dissonance?
4. You are intrigued by the concept of mental budgeting that you read about in this chapter. One issue that is nagging you is that the concept has been studied only in a Western country. You wonder if customers in other cultures set mental budgets and whether their

mental budgets are as inflexible as those reported here. To find out, you want to interview five customers from a different country (say China) living in Canada; for example, foreign students or employees. Prepare a discussion guideline for such interviews. Pay special attention to what happens for those instances of mental budgeting where the payer is a different member of the household than the user and/or buyer. Are mental budgets in such instances more or less flexible? Then, conduct the interviews and write your report, summarizing your findings. If you do not have access to foreign customers, then interview any five customers to find out to what extent they engage in mental budgeting.

5. Interview two customers on each of the following: (a) a recent major appliance purchase and (b) a recent supermarket product that was purchased for the first time. Query them on how they went about making their brand selection. Then identify for each the decision model they used, contrasting the two customers as well as contrasting the two types of purchases for each customer.
6. Interview five customers about their most recent complaint. (Every consumer has complained at one time or another.) Identify what led them to complain in terms of the model of complaining presented in the chapter. Then try to assess how they felt after the complaint and whether it depended on how the complaint was resolved.

NOTES

1 Adapted from Kathleen Brewer Doran, "Exploring Cultural Differences in Consumer Decision Making: Chinese Consumers in Montreal," in *Advances in Consumer Research,* vol. 21, eds. Chris Allen and D. John, (Provo, UT: Association for Consumer Research, 1994): 318–22.

2 Michel Laroche, Maria Kalamas, and Qinchao Huang, "Effects of Coupons on Brand Categorization and Choice of Fast Foods in China," *Journal of Business Research* 58, no. 5 (May 2005): 674-686; Michel Laroche, Ikuo Takahashi, Lefa Teng, and Maria Kalamas, "Modeling the Selection of Fast-Food Franchises Among Japanese Consumers," *Journal of Business Research* 58, no. 8 (August 2005): 1121-1131.

3 S. Ratneshwar, Cornelia Pechmann, and Allan D. Shocker, "Goal-Derived Categories and the Antecedents of Across-Category Consideration," *Journal of Consumer Research* 23 (December 1996): 240–50.

4 Joseph Alba, John Lynch, Barton Weitz, Chris Janiszewski, Richard Lutz, Alan Sawyer, and Stacy Wood, "Interactive Home Shopping: Consumer, Retailer and Manufacturer Incentives to Participate in Electronic Marketplaces," *Journal of Marketing* 6 (July 1997): 38–53.

5 Shelly Chaiken, "Heuristic Versus Systematic Information Processing and the Use of Source Versus Message Cues in Persuasion," *Journal of Personality and Social Psychology* 39 (November 1980): 752–66; David H. Furse, Girish N. Punj, and David W. Stewart, "A Typology of Individual Search Strategies among Purchasers of New Automobiles," *Journal of Consumer Research* 10, no. 4 (March 1984): 417–31.

6 Morris D. Holbrook, "An Audiovisual Inventory of Some Fanatic Consumer Behavior: The 25-Cents Tour of a Jazz Collector's Home," in *Advances in Consumer Research* 14 (Provo, UT: Association for Consumer Research, 1987), eds. M. R. Wallendorf and P.F. Anderson, 144–49.

7 C. Whan Park and V. Parker Lessig, "Familiarity and Its Impact on Consumer Decision Biases and Heuristics," *Journal of Consumer Research* 8 (September 1981): 223–30; James R. Bettman and C. W. Park, "Effects of Prior Knowledge and Experience and Phase of Choice Process on Consumer Decision Processes: A Protocol Analysis," *Journal of Consumer Research* 7 (December 1980): 234–48.

8 Narasimhan Srinivasan and Brian T. Ratchford, "An Empirical Test of a Model of External Search for Automobiles," *Journal of Consumer Research* 18 (September 1991): 233–42; Rajan Sambandam and Kenneth R. Lord, "Switching Behaviour in Automobile Markets: A Consideration-Sets Model," *Journal of the Academy of Marketing Science* 23, no. 1 (1995): 57–65.

9 http://www.emarketer.com/estats/dailyestats/b2c/20001101_shoptypes.html.

10 Peter L. Wright, "The Harassed Decision Maker: Time Pressure, Distractions, and the Use of Evidence," *Journal of Applied Psychology* 59 (October): 555–61; C. Whan Park, Easwar Iyer, and Daniel C. Smith, "The Effects of Situational Factors on In-Store Grocery Shopping Behaviour: The Role of Store Environment and Time Available for Shopping," *Journal of Consumer Research* 15 (March 1989): 422–33.

11 Sridhar Moorthy, Brian T. Ratchford, and Debabrata Talukdar, "Consumer Information Search Revisited: Theory and Empirical Analysis," *Journal of Consumer Research* 23 (March 1997): 263–78.

12 Banwari Mittal, "The Role of Affective Choice Mode in the Consumer Purchase of Expressive Products," *Journal of Economic Psychology* 9 (1988): 499–524.

13 Jacob Jacoby (1984), "Perspectives on Information Overload," *Journal of Consumer Research* 4 (March 1982): 432–35; Naresh K. Malhotra, "Reflections on the Information Overload Paradigm in Consumer Decision Making," *Journal of Consumer Research* 10, no. 4 (March 1984): 436–40.

14 Chris Janiszewski, "The Influence of Display Characteristics on Visual Exploratory Search Behaviour," *Journal of Consumer Research* 25 (December 1998): 290–301.

15 Alexandru M. Degeratu, Arvind Rangaswamy, and Jianan Wu, "Consumer Choice Behaviour in Online and Traditional Supermarkets: The Effects of Brand Name, Price, and Other Search Attributes," *International Journal of Research in Marketing* 17 (March 2000): 55–78.

16 James R. Bettman, *An Information Processing Theory of Consumer Choice* (Reading, Mass.: Addison-Wesley, 1979), 173–228.

17 Michael Tuan Pham, "Representativeness, Relevance and the Use of Feelings in Decision Making," *Journal of Consumer Research* 25 (September 1998): 144–59.

18 Hillel J. Einhorn "Use of Nonlinear, Noncompensatory Models in Decision Making," *Psychological Bulletin* 73 (1970): 221–30; Michel Laroche, Chankon Kim and Takayoshi Matsui, "Which Decision Heuristics are Used in Consideration Set Formation?" *Journal of Consumer Marketing* 20, no. 3 (2003): 192-209.

19 Amos Tversky, "Elimination by Aspects: A Theory of Choice," *Psychological Review* 79 (July 1972): 281–99.

20 Susan Powell Mantel and Frank R. Kardes, "The Role of Direction of Comparison, Attribute-based Processing and Attitude-based Processing in Consumer Preference," *Journal of Consumer Research* 25 (March 1999): 335–52.

21 Peter L. Wright, "Consumer Judgment Strategies: Beyond the Compensatory Assumption," in *Proceedings of the Third Annual Conference,* ed. M. Venkatesan (Chicago: Association for Consumer Research, 1972): 316–24.

22 James R. Bettman and Michel A. Zins, "Constructive Processes in Consumer Choice," *Journal of Consumer Research* 4 (September 1977): 75–85; James R. Bettman and C. Whan Park, "Effects of Prior Knowledge and Experience and Phase of Choice Process on Consumer Decision Processes: A Protocol Analysis," *Journal of Consumer Research* 7 (December 1980): 234–48.

23 Wayne D. Hoyer and Siew Meng Leong, "Consumer Decision Making for Common, Repeat-Purchase Products: A Dual Replication," *Journal of Consumer Psychology* 2, no. 2 (1995): 193–208.

24 Herbert A. Simon, *Models of Man* (New York: John Wiley & Sons, 1957); also see Peter L. Wright, "Consumer Choice Strategies: Simplifying Versus Optimizing," *Journal of Marketing Research* 11 (1975): 60–67.

25 Blake Rohrbacher, "Top Reasons for Abandoned Online Purchases," 01/17/2001, http://www.clickz.com/article/cz.3178.html.

26 Michael Tsiros and Vikas Mittal, "Regret: A Model of its Antecedents and Consequences in Consumer Decision Making," *Journal of Consumer Research* 26 (March 2000): 401–17.

27 Claes Fornell, Michael D. Johnson, Eugene W. Anderson, Jaesung Cha, and Barbara Everitt Bryant, "The American Customer Satisfaction Index: Nature, Purpose and Findings," *Journal of Marketing* 60 (October 1996): 7–18, http://www.bus.umich.edu/research/nqrc/acsi.html; http://www.theacsi.org/scores_commentaries/commentaries/Q1_06_comm.htm.

28 David M. Symanski and Richard T. Hise, "e-Satisfaction: An Initial Examination," *Journal of Retailing* 76, no. 3 (2000): 309–22.

29 Jagdish N. Sheth and Banwari Mittal, "A Framework for Managing Customer Expectations," *Journal of Market-Focused Management* 1 (1996): 137–58.

30 C. Goodwin and I. Ross, "Salient Dimensions of Perceived Fairness in Resolution of Service Complaints," *Journal of Satisfaction, Dissatisfaction, and Complaining Behaviour* 2 (1989): 87–92.

31 Bradley T. Gale, *Managing Customer Value* (New York: The Free Press, 1994).

32 Satya Menon and Barbara E. Kahn, "The Impact of Context on Variety Seeking in Product Choices," *Journal of Consumer Research* 22 (December 1995): 285–95.

CHAPTER 

Institutional Customer Decision Making: Household, Business, and Government

LEARNING OBJECTIVES

After reading this chapter you should be able to:

LO 1 Describe the steps in the family buying process.

LO 2 Explain how husband-wife decision roles are determined and how conflicts are resolved.

LO 3 Explain children's influence in family decision making.

LO 4 Explain consumer socialization and intergenerational influence.

LO 5 Explain the components of the business buying process.

LO 6 Explain the government buying process.

Pester Power

Today's kids have more autonomy and decision-making power within the family than in previous generations, so it follows that kids are vocal about what they want their parents to buy. "Pester power," or "the nag factor," refers to children's ability to nag their parents into purchasing items they may not otherwise buy. But while children's scope of influence has traditionally been limited to youth-friendly items such as breakfast cereals, snack foods, and running shoes, today's youngsters are both informed and outspoken enough to provide opinions on everything from family vacations and financial services to automobiles and cell phones.

Research by Corus Entertainment indicated that kids influence about $20 billion in household spending in Canada each year and have memorized between 300 and 400 brand names by age 10. It also showed that time-pressed and guilt-ridden parents respond favourably to 75 percent of kids' requests.[1] The study also found that 91 percent of tweens (kids aged 9–14) said they had asked their parents to purchase snack food in the past six months, while 90 percent had asked to go to a specific fast-food restaurant and 89 percent had asked for clothing. Those are all decisions upon which kids have traditionally exerted considerable influence, but the report also indicated that a high number of kids had also made requests for items more often purchased by adults. These included household groceries (79 percent), family trips (64 percent), home entertainment/electronics equipment (56 percent), batteries (53 percent), cameras and film (36 percent), and even the family car (17 percent).

One adult-oriented marketer that has already dabbled in advertising on youth channels is RadioShack. While the bulk of the electronics retailer's TV advertising is typically aimed at the male 25-to-54 demographic (computer and wireless phones account for the bulk of its sales, with toy sales accounting for about 5 percent), in early 2003 the company adopted a strategy to target children with its Christmas advertising. RadioShack ran two 30-second ads on the youth channels YTV and Teletoon. One spot promoting its line of ZipZaps micro remote-control cars, and the other one, its larger scale remote-control toys, ran for three weeks before migrating to other youth-friendly channels and then conventional TV. RadioShack wanted to get to the influencers. Children are a big influence on where to shop and what items are going to be the hot items. By getting out into the market and getting visibility early, RadioShack could start to encourage that "nag factor" early. The results were overwhelming, as RadioShack had the best sell-through of toys in its history, including a 100 percent sell-through of the ZipZap cars.[2]

The family decision-making process is different from the individual decision-making process that was studied in Chapter 8 in that the buying decision is shared, with members influencing that decision at various stages of the decision process. Our focus in this chapter is on group customer decision making in households, in business, and in the government. (See Figure 9.1 for our conceptual framework.) The chapter first explains the roles husbands and wives, mothers and daughters, fathers and sons, and boyfriends and girlfriends play in influencing each other's marketplace choices. It discusses the various methods people use to resolve their differences over what to buy and explains how families and households buy.

We then examine the decision-making processes of business and government customers. The challenge of marketing to organizational customers is to understand their decision-making process as end users, payers, and buyers. These customers include business and government customers, as well as institutions (both private and public) such as universities, hospitals, religious groups, and charitable organizations, which purchase products for use by their employees, members, or clients. The chapter discusses the components of the business buying process, including the steps in, influences on, and participants in the process, and their conflict resolution techniques.

The next part of the chapter covers the buying behaviour of government. It explores ways in which business buying behaviour and government buying behaviour differ from and resemble one another. It describes procedures and regulations that characterize government buying, as well as the challenges and rewards of doing business with the government. Finally, we explore developments in government buying.

FIGURE 9.1 Conceptual Framework

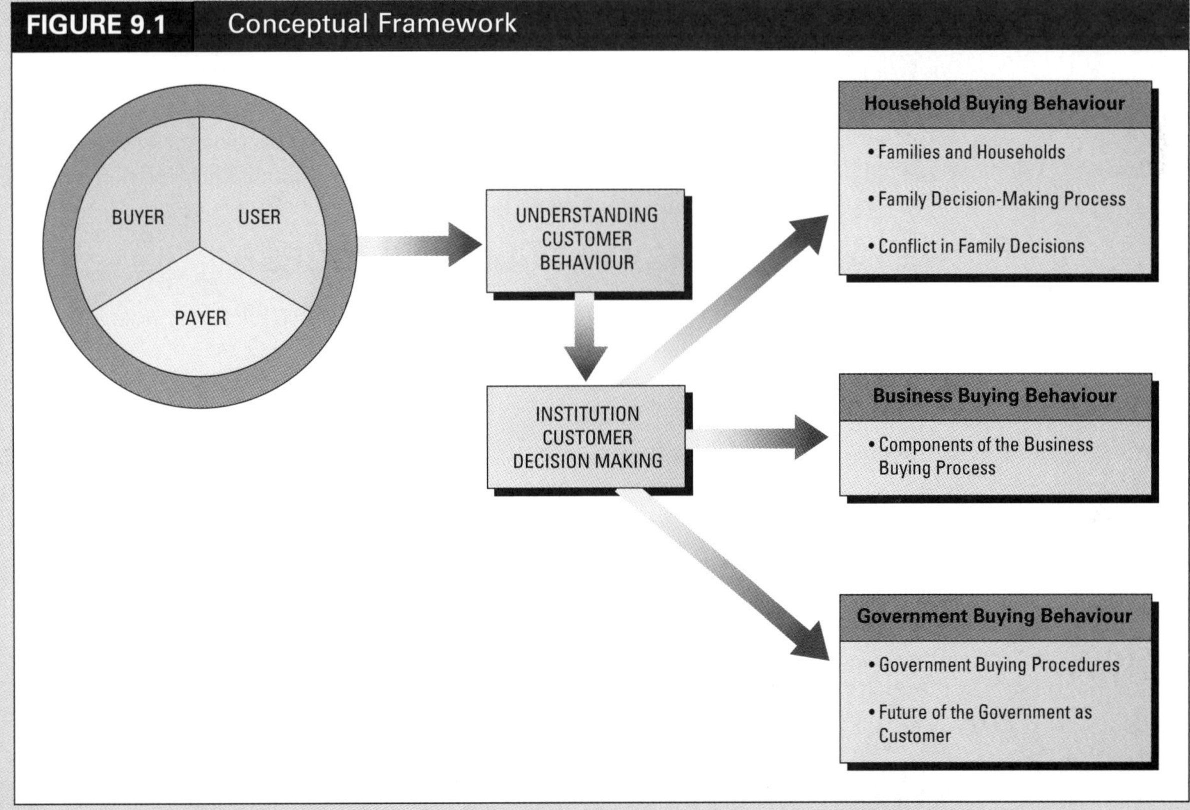

LO 1 HOUSEHOLD BUYING BEHAVIOUR

Household
A consumption unit of one or more persons, identified by a common location with an address.

Households are the basic unit of buying and consumption in a society. A **household** is a consumption unit of one or more persons identified by a common location with an address, such as the McGoldrick residence. While a number of customer decisions are, no doubt, made by individuals for their personal consumption, their decisions as members of a household are more complex, since these decisions must accommodate the diverse needs and wants of various household members. Household decisions are also important to study because it is possible to separate the three customer roles: the user, the payer, and the buyer. In the individual buying decisions, all three roles often merge in one person. When these roles separate, as they generally do in household buying behaviour, the marketer has to appeal separately to different members of the households, differentiating the selling appeal according to the role the family member plays. These role allocations are dynamic, varying from time to time, from one product to another, and from one family type to another. That is why it is important for a marketer to understand how an individual family changes over its lifetime, how households are changing in the aggregate, and how different members of these changing households make purchase decisions.

FAMILIES AND HOUSEHOLDS

Family
A group of persons related by blood and/or marriage.

Non-family household
A household that does not contain a family.

We will discuss two types of households: *family* and *non-family.* A **family** is a group of persons related by blood and/or marriage. Among family households, four types are most common: (1) married or common-law couples alone, (2) married or common-law couples with children, (3) a single parent with children, and (4) extended family, which may include parents, children's spouses, and/or grandchildren, and occasionally cousins. A **non-family household** is a household that contains people who are not at all related. Examples of non-family households are (1) a single person living alone in a dwelling unit, (2) roommates, two persons living in the same dwelling unit, including persons of the opposite sex sharing living quarters, and (3) boarding houses (three or more unrelated persons living in the same dwelling unit). We focus on decision making in family-type households since decision making in a family household is influenced by several members and it is different from individual decision making.

THE FAMILY DECISION-MAKING PROCESS

Family decisions differ from individual decisions in two ways. First, the payer, buyer, and user roles are distributed across family members (the same family member may not have all three roles). In addition, these roles are shared by various family members (a single role may be jointly held by more than one individual). Given the distribution and sharing of the three roles among family members, how is the purchase decision process implemented? Specifically, who decides what to buy, when to buy, which brand to buy, and so on?

STEPS IN FAMILY BUYING DECISIONS

Think back to a recent marketplace decision made in your household. You might recall that various members undertook various activities en route to the final decision. Several scholars have identified and described the family buying process as consisting of the following steps:[3]

1. Initiation of the purchase decision
2. Gathering and sharing of information

3. Evaluating and deciding
4. Shopping and buying
5. Conflict management

The first four steps are self-explanatory and similar in interpretation to those described in the previous chapter. Therefore, these will be discussed here only briefly. The fifth step is particularly salient in all group decision making (and the family is a group). Therefore, that step will be discussed in detail in a later section.

Regarding the first four steps, although their basic operation is similar to that in individual decision making, the actual dynamics are more involved. Different members of the family play different roles in the decision process. Thus, one member might initiate the purchase decision by making a product request; another might collect information, and a third might evaluate and decide. Yet another member might make the actual product purchase. Finally, someone might take the responsibility of resolving any differences of preference and conflicts that may arise. One solution to avoiding conflict is to find a product brand that satisfies every family member's unique preferences. Throughout this process, different family members may influence the decision to varying degrees. Of particular interest is the influence of spouses and children.[4]

HUSBAND-WIFE DECISION ROLES

LO 2

With regard to the roles of husband and wife, five patterns of relative influence are possible: (1) autonomous decision by the husband, (2) husband-dominated decision, (3) syncratic decisions (equal role for both), (4) wife-dominated decision, and (5) autonomous decision by the wife. **Autonomous decisions** are decisions made independently by the decision maker. **Syncratic decisions** are decisions in which the husband and the wife play equal roles in making the decision.

Autonomous decisions
Decisions that are made independently by the decision maker.

Syncratic decisions
Decisions in which each family member plays an equal role.

In a study of 200 households for the purchase of three products (washing machine, carpeting, and television), the wife's influence was stronger for washing machines and carpeting, while the husband's was greater for televisions. But even for TVs, husbands claimed more influence compared to wives, who reported more *joint* decision making. For each product, however, more families use joint decision making than autonomic decisions. The relative influence shifts during the decision stages. Generally, one spouse initiates the purchase consideration, but the process becomes more joint as the decision moves to advanced stages, such as information gathering. Although the study is old, it provides a point of comparison. Has the pattern of relative influence between the spouses changed since then? In what manner?

Joint Decision Process

Joint decisions are those in which more than one decision participant made the decision. When couples report they made joint decisions for a specific purchase, it is not easy to visualize exactly how each member participated in the joint decision. In fact, C. W. Park has termed joint decisions as a muddling-through process. His study of home buying revealed very interesting patterns of interpersonal dynamics among the spouses. Park studied the decision-making process for 45 couples soon after they had bought a home.[5] Among his findings:

Joint decisions
Decisions wherein more than one decision maker participates.

- The similarity between the decision plans of the spouses is relatively low.
- When spouses agree on features that the product must have, this agreement on must-have features leads them to perceive that their decision plans are similar (even when they

disagree on other optional features). Contrarily, when spouses disagree on must-have features, they perceive conflict.

- Individual spouses are more satisfied with some features of the product purchased than with others, and the features with which the spouses are satisfied differ between the spouses. Each spouse feels greater satisfaction with the feature whose inclusion was influenced more by that spouse.
- Spouses agree more with each other on salient objective dimensions (e.g., number of bedrooms, presence of a swimming pool) than on subjective dimensions (e.g., interior design, amount of insulation).
- Spouses grant each other role specialization with respect to the feature about which they are expert or should have a say. A husband might be viewed by both spouses as an expert on insulation, but the wife might be considered to be the expert on interior design. (Or vice versa, of course.) On these role-specialized features, spouses acknowledge the partner's relative influence. On other features, each believes she or he influenced the decision more than the other partner did.

To understand a couple's joint decision process, Park constructed a decision plan net as shown in Figure 9.2. A decision plan net is a tree diagram of the criteria that the decision maker will use and the sequence and manner in which she or he will use them.

Factors Influencing Interspousal Influence

Several factors affect the pattern of decision sharing between spouses. Factors that have been identified include gender-role orientation, the wife's employment status, family life cycle stages, time pressure, the importance of the purchase, and the socioeconomic development of the population.

Gender-Role Orientation

Gender-role orientation
The degree to which specific behaviours and norms are linked to a person's gender rather than being shared across genders.

Gender roles among spouses can be placed on a continuum of traditional to modern. The degree to which specific behaviours and norms are linked to a person's gender, rather than being shared across genders, is called **gender-role orientation.** The traditional view is one of sharply dichotomous roles for the husband and wife, while the modern view is one of more sharing of responsibilities between the two sexes.[6] In Canada, there is a trend toward merging of buyer, payer, and user role in the same person, and sharing of a single role (e.g., payer) by both spouses. Even in traditional households, Asian or Middle Eastern, purchase decisions are domain-specific: cooking-related materials are the domain of women though perhaps bought from the market by men.

Wife's Employment Status

The wife's employment status significantly influences gender-role orientation. In families where a wife is employed outside of the home, there is greater acceptance of her role in important family decisions. She makes autonomous decisions, and she is consulted on others because she contributes to family finances and because she is knowledgeable from her exposure to the world outside.

FIGURE 9.2 Decision Plan Nets for a Husband and Wife

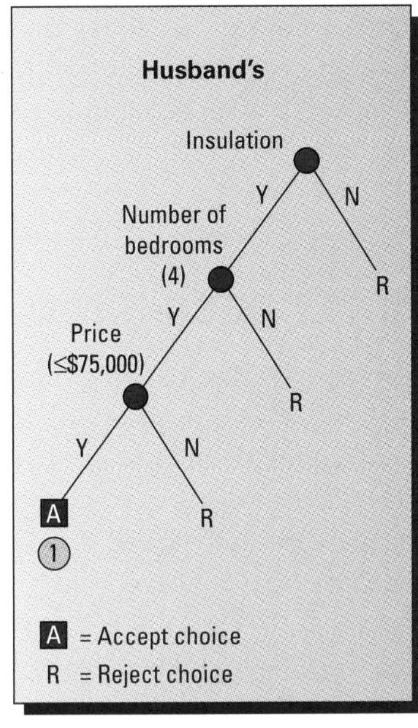

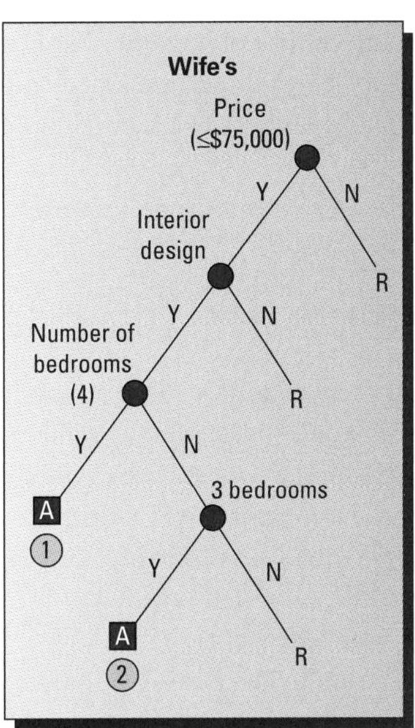

SOURCE: Park, C. Whan. "Joint Decisions in Home Purchasing: A Muddling-Through Process." *Journal of Consumer Research*, 9 (September 1982): 151–162. Reprinted with permission of the University of Chicago Press.

Stage in Family Life Cycle

Family life cycle, i.e., the stages a family goes through life, has also been found to influence decision making in families. Recently married couples tend to make more joint decisions; as the marriage ages, the chores become allocated along with the purchases that accompany those chores (e.g., grocery supplies for cooking, car wax for car washing) and get to be decided autonomously. However, the age of the marriage is not likely to affect decision making for important purchases.

Time Pressure

Families with high time pressure tend to rely less on joint decision making since autonomous decision processes are generally perceived to be more time-efficient. However, such decisions may sacrifice effectiveness; the decision may not be optimal.

Importance of Purchase

Purchase importance refers to how important the family perceives the product to be. The importance of the purchase may stem from the financial outlay or from the centrality of the product to the life of the individual who chooses it. The more important the purchase, the more the decision making is going to be a joint one because it involves using common family resources, and it is a decision that family members may have to live with for a long time.

Socioeconomic Development of the Population

Gender roles and role specializations vary from one culture and country to another. Specifically, the culture of a country is related to the stage of socioeconomic development of the population. Thus, underdeveloped countries have more traditional gender roles than do more developed countries. With development and the resulting modernization, urbanization, and concomitant increasing employment of women outside of the home, women's influence on marketplace decision making increases.

LO 3 CHILDREN'S INFLUENCE IN FAMILY DECISION MAKING

Children as family members constitute an important target market for marketers of all household products. Collectively, the 2.5 million tweens (9–14 years old) spend $1.9 billion a year of "their own" money, but they also influence about $20 billion of household expenditures. Their influence impacts everything from small-ticket purchases such as snack foods to major buys like cars.[7] Children's influence increases with age. One study found that 21 percent of mothers of 5-to-7-year-olds yielded to their children's requests, while 57 percent of mothers of 11-to-12-year-olds yielded to children's requests.[8]

Children influence household buying in three ways. First, children express individualistic preferences for products paid for and bought by parents (e.g., small children demanding particular toys or cereals). Second, children in their teen years begin to have their own money and become their own payers and buyers of items of self-use. Third, children influence their parents' choice of products that are meant for shared consumption (e.g., family vacation or home entertainment system) or even products used by a parent, by exerting expertise influence (e.g., clothes, perfumes). The Window on Research describes findings of a study on children's influence.

Social-oriented families
Families that are more concerned with maintaining discipline among children than promoting independent thinking.

Concept-oriented families
Families that are concerned with the growth of independent thinking and individuality in children.

Authoritarian families
Families where parents exercise strict authority over children; children learn to obey their elders in all matters.

According to Mnet's 2001 survey *Young Canadians in a Wired World* among 5,272 students grade 4 to 11, only 15 percent of Canadian teens had made online purchases. As mentioned in Chapter 2, lack of credit cards is restricting online purchasing by kids and teenagers, but some of the "teen com" sites allow teens to earn points that can be redeemed as discounts, while others provide alternatives to credit cards for Web purchases by teens, usually by allowing their parents to create debit accounts. But nowadays, more and more teens are obtaining credit; for example, Visa and American Express launched credit cards for kids aged 12 to 18 in 2000.[9]

George P. Moschis studied the role that children play in family decision making. One of his insights is that children's influence in the family decisions depends on whether the family has a social or concept orientation. **Social-oriented families** are the ones more concerned with maintaining discipline among their children, whereas **concept-oriented families** are those that are concerned with the growth of independent thinking and individuality in their children. Children from families with social orientation are less likely to make independent decisions and less likely to be involved in family decisions. Those with concept orientation are likely to have greater product knowledge, have a higher regard for their parents' opinion, and a preference for objective sources of information such as *Consumer Reports.*[10]

Another way of classifying families is by how authority is exercised in the family. On this basis, families worldwide can be classified into four types:[11]

1. **Authoritarian families**—The head of the household (mother in matriarchal societies and father in patriarchal societies) exercises strict authority over children, and children

always obey their elders. Although a culture of obedience to elders is considered to be a virtue, especially in Asian cultures, it does curb individuality among children and, consequently, their influence on family buying decisions.

WINDOW ON RESEARCH

Children's Influence on Family Decisions

Ellen Foxman, Patria Tanshuhaj, and Karin Ekstrom studied the role of adolescent children in family purchase decisions and found the following:

- Adolescents had more influence on products for their own use.
- The greater the teenager's financial resources, the greater the influence she or he exercised.
- The greater the perceived knowledge, the greater the perceived influence.
- The greater the importance to the teenager of the product category, the greater the teenager's influence.
- Teenager's influence was greater in dual-income families.
- Teenagers exercised more influence at the initiation stage than at the search and decision stages.
- Mothers attributed less influence to their children than did children themselves. This discrepancy was less between mothers and their daughters than between mothers and their sons.

In an extension of this research, Sharon E. Beatty and Salil Talpade analyzed purchases of durables (TV, stereo, phone, and furniture) made for family use versus those of items primarily for use by the teenager. Some of their findings were as follows:

- The financial resources of teenagers influenced only those durable purchases that were for the teenager's own use (as opposed to family use) and only in the purchase initiation stage, not in the search and decision stages.
- Children's product knowledge was influential only in the initiation of purchase consideration and only for products intended for teenager use. For family purchases, teenager influence was significantly enhanced with product knowledge but only in the search and decision stages and only for stereos (not for the other products investigated).
- Importance of purchase to teenagers affected their influence for both for-family and for-teenager purchases, and in the initiation, search, and decision stages.
- When teenagers were the major users of for-family durables, they exercised more influence (than if they were not going to be the major user) in the initiation, search, and decision stages.
- Children had greater influence in dual-income families than in single-income families; however, this influence was significant only for purchases made for shared family consumption. For purchases for their own use, children had influence alike in both single- and dual-income families.

SOURCE: Adapted from Foxman, Ellen R., Patriya S. Tanshuhaj, and Karin M. Ekstrom. "Family Members' Perceptions of Adolescents' Influence in Family Decision Making." *Journal of Consumer Research* 15 (March 1989): 482–91; Foxman, Ellen R., Patriya S. Tansuhaj, and Karin M. Ekstrom. "Adolescents' Influence in Family Purchase Decisions: A Socialization Perspective." *Journal of Business Research* 18 (March 1989): 159–72; Belch, George E., M. A. Belch, and G. Ceresino. "Parental and Teenage Child Influences in Family Decision Making." *Journal of Business Research* 13 (1985): 163–76. (see http://www.aafcs.org)

TABLE 9.1 Children's Role by Family Type

	CHILDREN'S ROLE			
	For Own-Use Products		For Family-Use Products	
FAMILY TYPE	DIRECT CONTROL	SHARED INFLUENCE	DIRECT CONTROL	SHARED INFLUENCE
Authoritarian	Low	Low	Low	Low
Neglectful	High	High	Low	Low
Democratic	Moderate	Moderate	Moderate	Moderate
Permissive	High	Moderate	Moderate	Moderate

Neglectful families Families having parents who remain distant from their children and neglect them.

Democratic families Families where every family member has an equal voice and self-expression, autonomy, and mature behaviour are encouraged among the children.

Permissive families Families wherein children are given relative independence in conducting their own affairs, especially in their adolescent years.

2. **Neglectful families**—The parents are distant from their children; they neglect their children because they place more priority on their own individual affairs. Single-parent families risk this behaviour most, some due to time pressure, and others due to the undisciplined lifestyle of the single parent. Of course, not all single parents neglect their children. Children exercise no influence on their parents' purchases in such families and are able to exercise relative autonomy for their purchases, if they have the resources.
3. **Democratic families**—Every member is given an equal voice. Most family matters are discussed among the family members, especially those who would be most affected by the decisions. The final decision could be a joint one, or it could be exercised by the family head(s). Self-expression, autonomy, and mature behaviour are encouraged among the children. Children share influence with other members in democratic families.
4. **Permissive families**—Children are given relative independence in conducting their own affairs, especially in their adolescent years. Unlike parents in the neglectful families, however, permissive parents closely watch children's interests and exercise of freedom.

The relative prevalence of these types differs across different countries, and their proportions would change in the same country over time. Also, families could have partial tendencies of more than one type. Depending on whether the product is for the children's own use or for shared use in the family, the degree of influence children will have in each of the four types of families is shown in Table 9.1. Marketers can use this classification as a tool to understand family decision making in different countries. However, the classification has been studied in relation to family buying decisions only in one study, limited to preschoolers in one city.[12] The foregoing relationships between the four family types and children's relative influence are our intuitive judgments.

LO 4 LEARNING THE CUSTOMER ROLES

Families, especially parents and respected elders, are the first source of information about how to carry out the three customer roles. Even as we become adults, we often seek the influence of family members with greater experience or expertise. Primary modes of learning customer roles are, therefore, *consumer socialization* and *intergenerational influence.*

CONSUMER SOCIALIZATION

How do children learn to become consumers? How do they become socialized to engage in marketplace exchanges? And they do become socialized to an amazing degree. One study found that children 7 to 12 years old possessed strong brand preferences. And children who cannot yet read have been found to be able to recognize brand symbols, such as McDonald's golden arches, the Joe Camel cartoon character from Camel cigarette ads, and Tony the Tiger, mascot for Kellogg's Frosted Flakes.[13]

Consumer socialization refers to the acquisition of the knowledge, preferences, and skills to function in the marketplace.[14] That is, consumer socialization occurs when one or more of the following are learned or acquired by children:

Consumer socialization The acquisition of the knowledge, preferences, and skills to function in the marketplace.

- preferences among alternative brands and products;
- knowledge about product features and the functioning of the marketplace;
- skills in making smart decisions, such as making price and product comparisons, discounting advertising and salespersons' claims, and evaluating tradeoffs across options (including the option to buy or not to buy).

Deborah Roedder John suggests that "consumer socialization can be viewed as a developmental process that proceeds through a series of stages as children mature into adult consumers." She identifies three stages of consumer socialization: perceptual, analytic and reflective.

In the *perceptual stage* (age 3–7 years), children tend to emphasize perceptual thought over abstract or symbolic thought. Their consumer knowledge is characterized by perceptual features and distinctions, usually based on a single dimension or attribute. They can recognize brands and retail stores in the market, but do not have any in-depth understanding about them. In terms of influence strategies and decision making, children are able to look at things only from their own perspective. They may be aware that others do not share the same perspective, but they are not able to incorporate their views into their decision-making process.

In the *analytical stage* (age 7–11 years), children are able to approach situations in a more detailed and analytical manner. An increase in information-processing abilities and better understanding of the marketplace in terms of product categories, prices, advertising, and brands mark this stage. Children are now able to use more than one dimension or attribute in their evaluations, and their decision-making approach is more adaptive and flexible as they weave perspectives of family and friends into the process.

In the *reflective stage* (age 11–16 years), children focus on understanding the social meanings that exemplify the marketplace. Their information-processing and social skills are well developed, and they have a clear understanding of brands, prices, advertising, and promotions. There is complete awareness of other people's perspectives, and consumer decisions are made adaptively, depending on the situation and the task at hand. Their influence strategies are also strategic, based on what they think will be best received by the person being influenced.[15]

Thus, we can conclude that two types of factors play a role in consumer socialization of children: *cognitive* and *environmental.* Cognitive factors are age-related mental abilities. Cognitive development proceeds with age, and so does children's consumer socialization. Environmental factors are socialization agents (sources of information and influence): mass media, peers, and family. Family has been the strongest influence on children's socialization in general, not just on their socialization as consumers.[16] As the child becomes older, peer influence and media influence grows, and the influence of family likely declines. The weakening of family influence with advancing years is less prevalent in Asian and traditional countries than in the more industrialized Western countries. Research by YTV as shown in Figure 9.3 shows that over 80 percent of Canadian teens learn of "cool" new products and brand names on TV, with TV commercials the most commonly mentioned source of product information.[17] The Window on Research reflects on the consumer socialization of children in China.

FIGURE 9.3 How Teens Learn about Cool New Products and Brand Names

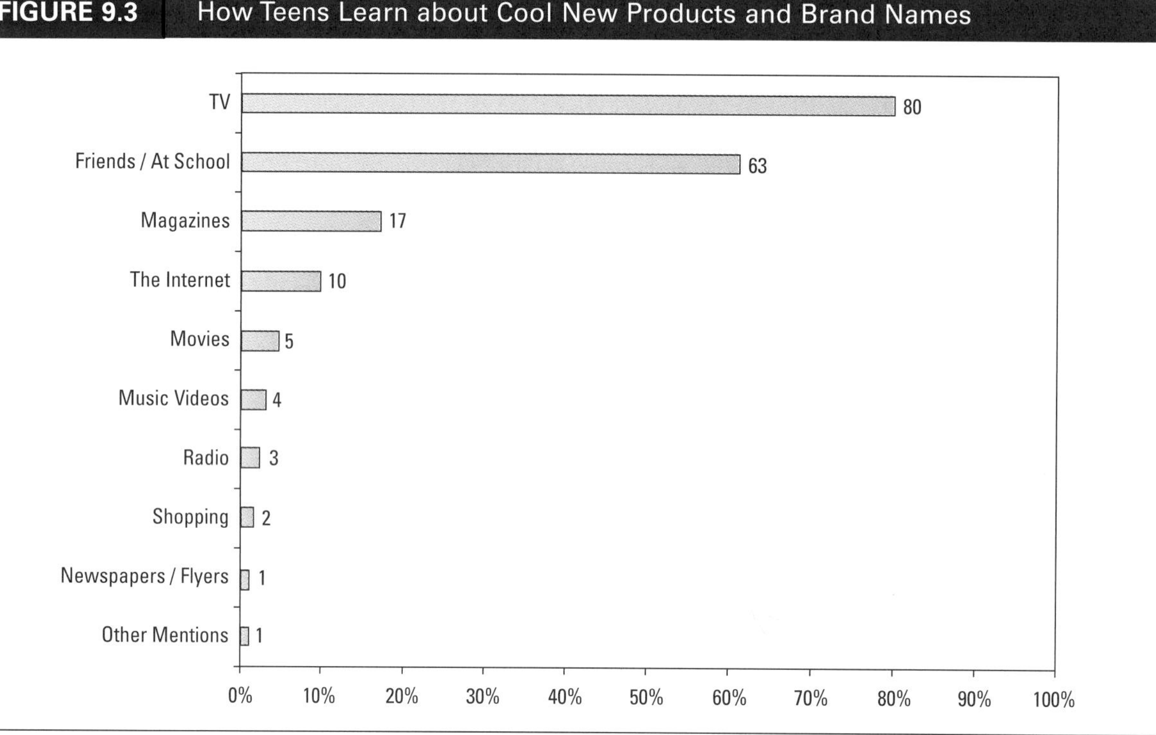

SOURCE: YTV Tween Report 2002: Special; Kidfluence Edition

Learning Mechanisms

The socialization of children by parents occurs basically through the learning mechanisms described in Chapter 4: instrumental conditioning, modelling, and cognitive learning. These three mechanisms correspond to the three bases of reference-group influence (a topic covered in Chapter 2): *utilitarian, value-expressive,* and *informational,* respectively.

Instrumental conditioning refers to learning to do those things that are rewarded. Children learn those behaviours and the underlying values that bring rewards from their parents. The second mechanism is modelling. Here children look up to their parents as role models and try to internalize and adopt their values, roles, and attitudes. The cognitive mechanism of learning toward socialization can occur at two levels: low involvement and high involvement. In the low-involvement mode, there could be undeliberated adoption of product choices because of familiarity or because these products were used by one's parents. At the high-involvement level, socialization influence can result from communication and education by parents about various brands or buying strategies. Learning from the media can occur through cognitive (communication and education) and/or modelling (identification with models) processes. Learning from peers occurs predominantly via modelling, but occasionally it can be through cognitive means (information) or through instrumental conditioning (reward of approval).

WINDOW ON RESEARCH

Socialization of Chinese Children as Consumers

China adopted the one-child policy in 1979. As only children, Chinese children exert great influence on the spending of their families and spend a considerable amount of their own money in the marketplace. It has been found that Chinese children's overall index of influence on family spending of 25 items is around 68 percent. Socialization of children as consumers involves gaining an understanding of the marketplace, one aspect of which is knowledge of sources of information about products. James McNeal and Mindy Ji conducted a study of 460 children between the ages of 8 and 13 years in the Beijing area to understand Chinese children's use of new product information sources and their perceptions of the relative importance of each information source. The children were provided with a list of products and asked where they learned about each product. Children were also asked to rank their most important sources of information from a predefined list of sources, and data on their media use was collected from the parents.

Children identified television to be the most important source of information about products. Parents and stores were also identified as information sources, but they were not relied upon as much as television. It is believed that "the family in the Chinese culture would be the most instrumental in introducing children to products new to them due to the fact that in China the family is the basic social unit." But this finding shows that television, though a relatively new medium, is powerful in its influence in China. (See the box on Symbolic Consumption of Products: Television in China in Chapter 1.) Penetration of television sets is very high in China, and children spent 17.2 hours each week watching television, compared to 2.7 hours reading newspapers, 2.6 hours reading magazines, and 6.3 hours listening to the radio. With its potent combination of entertainment and information value, or what has been termed "infotainment," the television is the most valued source of new product information for children in China. The researchers state that two models of communication exist in Chinese families: "media to children and children to parents," and "media to parents and parents to children."

Marketers need to set aside their stereotypes and focus on the new influences on the emerging consumer generation in China. These influences are more commercial than interpersonal and they are affecting consumer socialization.

SOURCE: Adapted from McNeal, James U., and Mindy F. Ji. "Chinese Children as Consumers: An Analysis of Their New Product Information Sources." *Journal of Consumer Marketing* 16, no. 4 (1999). http://www.emerald-library.com.

An example of learning from the media through a cognitive process occurred in the fall of 2002, when Canada Investment & Savings, purveyor of Canada Savings Bonds, wanted to teach young Canadians the important rules of saving money. That meant letting them know that by saving money they can reach both their long-term and short-term goals, and that saving money can both be cool and have a payoff at the end. To teach something as dry as saving money, YTV and CI&S ran an unconventional online approach to kids and tweens. At **ytv.com** there was a CI&S mini-site, Buck Save-A-lot's interactive trip to Toonieville. It featured multiple-choice questions and outcomes (answering correctly taught users the three rules of saving money); a savings calculator showing the power of compound interest; and on-line entry for "The Great Canadians Save" contest.[18]

Socialization Outcomes

Whether the socialization agents are the family, peers, or the media, there are several possible outcomes. First, children can adopt products and brands simply by noticing them being used in the house or seeing them in advertisements, and can firm up preferences based on satisfactory use experience. Children can learn about desirable product features, alternative products, brands, stores, and other options, and can make this information a part of their stock of marketplace knowledge. Finally, children can learn the knowledge and skills to make smart choices. They can learn to clip coupons, comparison shop, and select items from mail catalogues.

INTERGENERATIONAL INFLUENCE

Intergenerational influence (IGI) Influence of family members and the transmission of values, attitudes, and behaviours from one generation to another.

The **intergenerational influence (IGI)** of family members refers to the transmission of values, attitudes, and behaviours from one generation to another.[19] Numerous studies have shown that transfer of market values in terms of product preferences occurs for many products, including banks, auto insurance, grooming products, and supermarket items.[20] (See the Window on Research.) IGI can take place in two directions: forward (from parents to children) and reverse (from children to parents). Forward IGI occurs both when the child is young and lives with the parents, and during the adult years, when the parents and grown children live in separate households. Typically, researchers have studied forward IGI during early childhood (that is, during consumer socialization). In contrast, forward and reverse IGI during the adult years of sons and daughters has not been studied much.

Reverse Influence

The *reverse influence* begins to occur as children grow up and are exposed to new knowledge and new role models. Consequently, they begin to depend less on their parents as role models or for guidance, and begin to carve out their individual identities.

This influence can occur for two reasons. First, the offspring begin to influence their parents' preferences and marketplace choices because on certain products children acquire greater knowledge and expertise than their parents, which their parents acknowledge. The second mechanism of children-to-parent influence occurs due to what can be called democratic justice. **Democratic justice** refers to a family norm in which each family member is given a voice in family decisions. Thus, in the purchase of common assets (e.g., car, furniture), and for products consumed exclusively by children, many families may consider it legitimate to give youngsters a voice and, thus, to allow them to influence parents' preferences.

Democratic justice A family norm in which each family member is given a voice in family decisions.

However, democratic justice as a mechanism of children-to-parent influence can cause tensions in a family when the offsprings' preferences become incongruent with their parents' values. For example, when offspring want to get a punk-style haircut or turn a room into a discotheque, or when the children's preferences make excessive demands on parents' resources, parents' sense of propriety is likely violated, and conflict results. Both these sources of conflict are mediated, of course, by who controls the resources. If offspring depend entirely on parents for financial support, then the rejection of the former's preferences is more likely. On the other hand, if they contribute to the family's financial resources, or at least earn part of their living, then parents are likely to allow more leeway. But the value incongruence does not disappear with resource sharing.

WINDOW ON RESEARCH

Research Findings on Intergenerational Influence

Bank preference. A study found that 93 percent of college freshmen patronize the same bank as their parents do.

Financial planning. The extent to which families pre-plan their financial goals and then act to fulfill those goals was found to be consistent over three generations studied.

Auto insurance. In one study, 40 percent of married couples had purchased automobile insurance from the same company as the husband's parents. In another, 32 percent of adult men dealt with the same auto insurance agency as did their fathers. This influence decreased with the age of adult children: 62 percent among men in their 20s, and 19 percent among men 50 years of age or older.

Grocery items. In a study of 49 female college students and their mothers, brand preferences between mothers and their grown daughters were found to be more similar for grocery items with high brand-name visibility (e.g., toothpaste, facial tissues, pain reliever, and peanut butter) than for products with low brand-name visibility (spaghetti sauce, canned vegetables, coffee, and frozen juices). For high-visibility brands, 49 percent of mothers and daughters agreed on their brand preference, compared to only 31 percent agreement for low-visibility brands. There was also similarity on such choice rules (i.e., the rules of thumb consumers employ to make their buying more efficient) as buying items on sale, brand loyalty, relying on others for advice or information, and pre-purchase planning. Moreover, mothers' and daughters' marketplace beliefs were similar, such as the beliefs that there is a positive price-quality relationship, marketer-given information is useful, advertising has positive value, and private brands and sale merchandise are good value.

SOURCES: Adapted from Moore-Shay, Elizabeth S., and R. J. Lutz. "Intergenerational Influences in the Formation of Consumer Attitudes and Beliefs about the Marketplace: Mothers and Daughters." *Advances in Consumer Research*, vol. 15, M. Houston, ed., (Provo, UT: Association for Consumer Research, 1988), pp. 461–67; Fry, J., D. C. Shaw, C. H. von Lanzenauer, and C. R. Dipchard, "Customer Loyalty to Banks: A Longitudinal Study." *Journal of Business* 46: 517–25; Woodson, L. G., T. L. Childers, and P. R. Winn. "Intergenerational Influences in the Purchase of Auto Insurance." in *Marketing Looking Outward: Business Proceedings*, edited by W. Locander, 43–49. Chicago: American Marketing Association, 1976. See http://www.usadata.com.

Family Characteristics That Influence IGI

Forward and reverse IGI are both influenced by family relationship and relative expertise across generations. **Family relationship** refers to the degree of mutual respect and trust between parents and their adult offspring, and the harmony of relations and communication among them, in all areas of life (not just about products and shopping activities). *Relative expertise* is the acknowledgment by the children that parents possess expertise about a product (or, for reverse IGI, that parents acknowledge their offsprings to be experts).

Family relationship
The degree of mutual respect and trust between parents and adult offspring, and the harmony of their relations and communication.

Based on these two characteristics, four IGI states can occur (see Table 9.2).[21] When perceived expertise is high but the family relationship is negative, there will be disaffected IGI. This means the person acknowledges the soundness of the expert advice in principle, but does not act upon the advice because he or she psychologically rejects the adviser. When perceived expertise is high and the family relationship is positive, there will be high IGI. Children and their parents will seek out and act on one another's advice. In contrast, when perceived expertise is low and family relationship negative, there will be no IGI. Finally, when perceived expertise is low and family relationship is positive, there will be discounted IGI, meaning the person receives the advice politely but discounts it as not being credible.

TABLE 9.2 Intergenerational Influences (IGI)

		FAMILY RELATIONSHIP	
		Negative	**Positive**
Perceived Expertise	**High**	Disaffected IGI	High IGI
	Low	No IGI	Discounted IGI

IGI across Households

A special case of IGI occurs when children have formed their own households separate from the parents. This can be termed *IGI across households.*[22] IGI occurs across households mainly because of *expertise.* If grown offspring still consider their parents experts on the purchase of a specific product (e.g., a house, life insurance, stocks, or traditional rituals), they will turn to them for advice, despite household separation. Conversely, on matters where adult offspring are perceived to possess expertise (e.g., computers, CD players, or even cars), parents will seek their advice. Another reason for IGI across households is *lifestyle similarity* between the generations. For example, a mother returning to the workforce might appreciate her successful daughter's insights on what chic people wear to work. Yet another factor, *resource control,* refers to who finances the expense for the purchase under control. When parents finance the purchase, they will exercise IGI. On the other hand, if retired parents depend on their grown children, then reverse IGI occurs.

These three factors correspond closely with the three types of reference group influences we studied in Chapter 2: informational, identificational, and normative or instrumental. Informational influence occurs when the influencing agent provides useful information that guides, facilitates, or alters the choices the influence recipient makes. Identificational influence occurs when the influenced person identifies with the influencer, viewing the latter as a role model and emulating his or her behaviour. Finally, instrumental influence occurs due to the ability of influence agents to reward or punish the influence target. This also includes what has been called normative influence: the expectations of significant others. As mentioned earlier, for any of these influences to operate, there must also be a positive family relationship. It is a necessary condition, and the others are sufficient conditions.

Conflict in Family Decisions

Family decision making may give rise to conflict, whether the customer roles are distributed among family members or shared by family members. Conflict among *distributed roles* arises when the user, payer, and buyer roles are played by different family members, and alternatives (such as brands/suppliers) do not satisfy the goals (market values) of each.

Conflict due to *shared roles* arises when a single role is shared by multiple family members and their goals (market values) diverge. For example, when both husband and wife play the payer role as they draw on common family funds, they may experience conflict on how much can be spent on home refurnishing.

TABLE 9.3 Types of Conflict

		GOALS/VALUES	
		Convergent	**Divergent**
Perceptions/ Evaluations	**Divergent**	Solution conflict (family vacation)	Compounded Complex, important purchases (home buying)
	Convergent	No conflict (daily consumption items)	Goal conflict (what to buy) (product-level conflict)

TYPES OF CONFLICT

When the family decision process entails joint decision making, conflict is inevitable if family members disagree on either goals (market values) or perceptions (evaluation of alternatives). The nature of the conflict will differ according to whether there is disagreement in one or both of these areas (see Table 9.3). When goals are in agreement but alternative evaluations differ, solution conflict crops up. When both goals and perceptions diverge, conflict is *compounded.* This would happen in buying a condominium when spouses may desire different goals (e.g., the husband may want a city view, and the wife may prefer a view of the lake) and also perceive two condominiums differently on a common goal (e.g., they may differ on which of the two condominiums they examined is more aesthetic).[23] When both values and evaluations converge across family members, conflict does not appear; choice of many daily consumption items exemplify this setting. When goals diverge but perceptions of solutions are in agreement, goal conflict is created. This occurs when the husband may want a stylish, youthful car but the wife wants a large, safe car.

CONFLICT RESOLUTION

Four strategies of conflict resolution have been suggested by scholars: problem solving, persuasion, bargaining, and politicking (see Table 9.4). Problem solving entails members trying to gather more information or to add new alternatives. When motives/goals are congruent and only perceptions differ, obtaining and sharing information (i.e., problem solving) often suffices to resolve conflicts. Persuasion requires educating about the goal hierarchy; the wife might argue that a safe, large car is in the best interest of the whole family since the car is needed to transport children. Bargaining entails trading favours (husband gets to buy a house

TABLE 9.4 Conflict Resolution Techniques

		GOALS/VALUES	
		Convergent	**Divergent**
Evaluations	**Divergent**	Problem solving	Politicking Bargaining
	Convergent	No conflict	Persuasion

with a den and the finished basement, provided the car he buys is one of his wife's preference). When goals and evaluations are so divergent that even bargaining is infeasible, politicking is resorted to. Here, members form coalitions and subgroups within the family and, by so doing, simply impose their will on the minority coalition.[24] Marketers can help household members resolve a conflict by aiding the problem-solving mode; they can provide additional information about alternatives, especially in interpersonal selling situations.[25] Research has focused on the interpersonal dynamics of how household members such as spouses influence each other in joint decisions. (See the Window on Research.)

WINDOW ON RESEARCH

How Spouses Influence Each Other's Decisions

In one study of married spouses' influence strategies, Margaret C. Nelson identified the following repertoire of influence strategies spouses used.

1. Punishments, threats, authority, and negative emotions
   - Refuses to do chores
   - Threatens punishment
   - Becomes angry
   - Questions spouse's right to disagree
2. Positive emotion and subtle manipulation
   - Puts the spouse in a receptive mood
   - Appeals to spouse's love and affection
   - Promises to do something nice in return
   - Acknowledges that it would be a favour
3. Withdrawal and egocentrism
   - Denies affection, acts cold
   - Clams up
   - Looks hurt, sulks
4. Persuasion and reason
   - Uses logic
   - Persists in arguing and requesting compliance
5. Miscellaneous others
   - Simply gives in
   - Argues that she or he knows more
   - Compromises; meets in the middle
   - Pleads or begs
   - Comes up with a new solution acceptable to both

SOURCE: Adapted from Margaret C. Nelson. "The Resolution of Conflict in Joint Purchase Decisions by Husbands and Wives: A Review and Empirical Test." In *Advances in Consumer Research*, vol. 15, edited by Michael J Houston, Provo, UT: Association for Consumer Research (1988): 436–41. http://acr.webpage.com.

A GENERAL FRAMEWORK FOR UNDERSTANDING FAMILY BUYING DECISIONS

It is useful to bring together the major topics covered in this chapter in an organizing framework. Figure 9.4 presents such a framework. Since we have already discussed most of the variables contained in this figure, we describe the model only briefly here.

DECISION PROCESS

The linchpin of the model is the decision process, which can be either autonomous (i.e., decision made by a single family member), or joint decision making. It is the joint decision making that distinguishes household buying from individual buying. The decision is joint if family members exercise any degree of influence during any of the stages of the decision process. These decision-process stages (not shown in Figure 9.4) are initiation, information gathering, evaluation and decision, shopping and buying, and conflict resolution. Conflict

FIGURE 9.4 A Framework for Understanding Family Buying Decisions

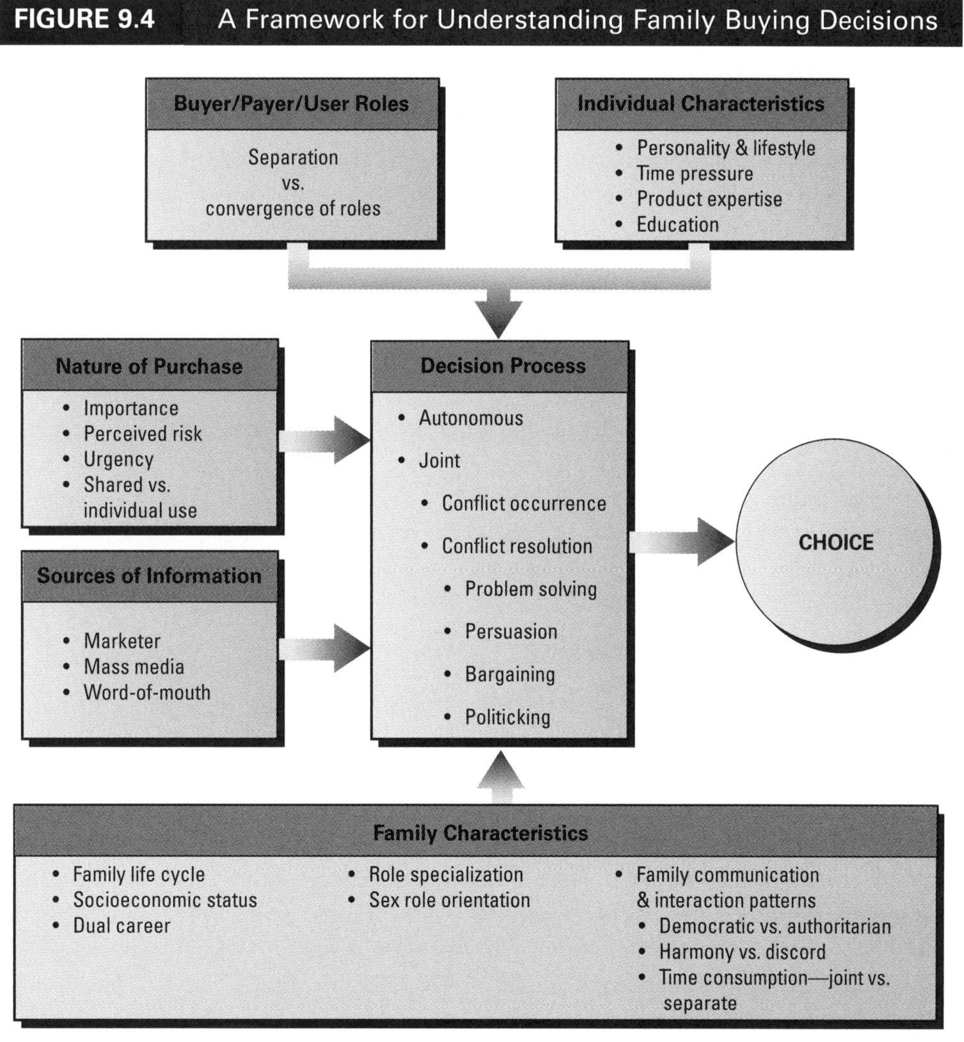

occurrence is a significant component of the decision process. The conflict may arise either because the family members do not agree on purchase goals and criteria or because they disagree on their perceptions as to which alternatives would best meet these goals and criteria. Its resolution would typically follow one of the four strategies discussed earlier: problem solving, persuasion, bargaining, or politicking.

INFLUENCES ON THE DECISION PROCESS

The extent to which a decision process will be autonomous rather than joint, or vice versa, will depend on the nature of the purchase, separation of the buyer, payer, and user roles, individual member characteristics, and family characteristics. And, of course, sources of information will influence the decision process. Different members may be exposed differently to different sources of information, and their individual perspectives and perceptual distortions make the decision process less or more involving and conflicting.

Nature of the Purchase

Consider the Nature of the Purchase

If the purchase is important and if there is high perceived risk associated with the purchase, then the decision will more likely be a joint decision. If the product is required urgently, then the time-consuming process of joint decision will be avoided in favor of autonomous decisions. Finally, if the product to be bought is for shared consumption among the family members, then the process is likely to be a joint one.

Separation of the Three Roles

The extent to which the three customer roles are separated in a household will influence the customer decision. In some households, one spouse assumes all three roles, while in others the spouses divide the role responsibility or jointly share each role. Likewise, the influence of children varies from household to household. Where the three roles do not converge in the same person, or where household members do not delegate their roles to others, joint rather than autonomous decisions are more likely, and, consequently, conflicts too are more likely.

Individual Characteristics

Among the individual characteristics, the first factor is whether any given individual in the family carries all three role responsibilities: buyer, payer, and user. If these roles converge in the same individual, then the decision making is likely to be autonomous. The more these roles are distributed across the family members, the more the decision process is likely to be a joint one.

Other characteristics of the individual are personality and lifestyle, time pressure, product expertise, and education. These influence both the extent of joint decision making and the way in which the conflicts are resolved. Time pressure on one or more members will lead to less joint decision making. If individual members have a lifestyle and personality that is individualistic rather than sharing and inclusive (i.e., a "me" rather than "us" personality), then autonomous decisions are more likely. Of course, product expertise of individuals will bring them more into family decisions. Finally, education will influence the interaction and the conflict management. Spouses and parents with more education will likely keep the conflicts manageable and solve them via rational arguments and persuasion, rather than by politicking.

Family Characteristics

One set of family characteristics that would affect the decision process includes family life cycle (FLC), socioeconomic status, and dual versus single career. Consider FLC: Newly marrieds have generally been found to use the joint process to a much greater extent than couples with aging marriages. Adolescent children begin to make more autonomous decisions for products for which they are the primary users. Socioeconomic status (SES) influences the extent of joint process and also how the conflicts may be resolved. Although conclusive research evidence on this has not appeared, for products meant exclusively for an individual member's use, the decision is more likely to be an autonomous one for both upper-class and lower-class (compared to the middle-class) households—the upper class because they can afford it, and the lower-class because funds are controlled by the head of the household.

A second set of family characteristics is the gender-role orientations and role specialization. In families where gender roles are traditionally oriented, many more decisions will be made autonomously. Also, with role specialization, purchases will tend to be assigned for autonomous decisions by those perceived to possess the most specialized knowledge of the topic. A related variable is dual versus single career in the family. In dual-career families, gender-role orientation is less likely to be traditional, making the decision process a joint one between spouses.

The last set of family characteristics includes the communication and interaction patterns. Does the head of the household govern and manage the family in an authoritarian or democratic way? The decisions would be more joint in the latter than in the former type of household. Also, are day-to-day communications among the family members marked with harmony or discord? That would affect whether influence attempts by one member will be accepted by other members, as stated in discussing intergenerational influence (IGI). Conflict resolution would be closely influenced by democratic versus authoritarian management style and harmony versus discord in everyday communications within the family. Finally, the more family members share time and lifestyle, the more they are likely to engage in a joint decision process.

It should be remembered that our description of the family's customer behaviour is founded on research in North America. Students of customer behaviour need to deliberate over how the concepts described in this chapter would be adapted for families in other nations and in other cultures.[26]

BUSINESS BUYING BEHAVIOUR

A **business** is a licensed entity engaged in the activity of making, buying, or selling products for profit or nonprofit objectives. This definition considers any organization that makes and sells something to be a business. As customers, businesses buy products (raw materials, components, supplies, support services, and machinery) to provide value for their customers, end users, resellers, value-added resellers, employees, or owners (i.e., the key stakeholders).

Business
A licensed entity engaged in the business of making, buying or selling products for profit or nonprofit objectives.

Business buying typically differs from household buying in several key ways: greater role specialization, more formalization of the buying process, more formal accountability for decisions, greater internal capabilities, and more complex requirements (see Table 9.5).

TABLE 9.5 Comparison of Household and Business Buying

Characteristic	Household Buying	Business Buying
Specialization of customer roles	Combined or slightly specialized	Moderately to very specialized
Formalization of the buying process	Informal	Slightly formal (small businesses) to formal (large businesses)
Accountability for decisions	Usually not formally measured	Strict measures
Internal capabilities	Weak	Weak (small businesses) to very strong (large businesses)
Complexity of requirements	Little complexity	Operational and strategic complexity

SPECIALIZATION OF CUSTOMER ROLES

As we explained in Chapter 8, individual buying requires that the three customer roles—payer, buyer, and user—be combined in a single individual, whereas in household buying decisions, these roles may be held by a single person or distributed among various group members. Such role specialization is even more marked in business buying. An exception to this pattern is a one-person entrepreneur, who makes decisions equivalent to individual decision making.

FORMALIZATION OF THE BUYING PROCESS

Business buying is formalized with respect to policy, procedures, and paperwork. Generally, businesses have written policies and rules to guide the solicitation of price quotes, preferential treatment to a certain class of vendors (e.g., minority businesses), and the way the decisions are to be made in the buying firm. This degree of formalization is rare in family buying behaviour.[27] The degree of formalization may vary from business to business—slightly formal in small businesses to very formal in regulated industries and in the government. Large businesses tend to be somewhere in the middle.

ACCOUNTABILITY FOR DECISIONS

Unlike household buying, business buying holds accountable those who are in charge of paying and buying. This results in more formal evaluation of and feedback on these purchase decisions. This greater accountability in business arises because ownership is divorced from management, and buying is divorced from usage. Therefore, business buying encourages formal supplier ratings and scorecards, as well as constant feedback and communication to its suppliers.

INTERNAL CAPABILITIES

More often than households, business customers are capable of producing certain items in-house rather than buying them from others. This capability requires business customers to analyze the economics of the make-versus-buy options.

COMPLEXITY OF REQUIREMENTS

The buying behaviour of business customers is complex both in its operation and its strategy. Operationally, complexity results from the number of employees participating in the buying process, from the need to adhere to government rules and regulations, and because decisions involve multiple authority and expertise levels. Additionally, procurement is often a strategic function since it is the single largest cost centre to a business organization. It is also strategic because it is responsible for buying both capital goods and materials, so the risks associated with failure are enormous.

COMPONENTS OF THE BUSINESS BUYING PROCESS

With purchasing being such a significant and complex function, all but the smallest organizations have formal systems for carrying it out. These systems, called procurement systems, have several components—nature of the purchase, organizational characteristics, buying centre, rules and procedures, and a decision process. These components also exist in small businesses, but tend to be simpler and less rigidly defined. By determining the way the components fit together in a particular business, marketers can describe the business's customer behaviour.

NATURE OF THE PURCHASE

The way an organization makes a purchase decision depends to a large degree on the nature of the purchase. This nature is defined by the **buyclass** (type of purchase need); the significance of the decision in terms of perceived risk, importance, and product complexity; and the time pressure faced by the decision makers.

Buyclass
Type of purchase need, rated in terms of its newness to the business.

Buyclass

For an individual, purchase needs may require routine problem solving, limited problem solving, or extended problem solving. Similarly, businesses have three types of procurement needs, or buyclasses: straight re-buy, modified re-buy, and new task.

A **straight re-buy** is a need that has been processed and fulfilled before. It is for an item that is needed repeatedly and has been bought before. Examples include shop supplies (e.g., lubricants), worker uniforms, and office stationery. If the outcomes of prior purchase have been satisfactory, the business simply places the order with one of the past suppliers because the gains in savings from a new search of suppliers is unlikely to outweigh the costs of the effort. Thus, businesses often negotiate an annual purchasing agreement for these items with automatic reordering.

Straight re-buy
A product that has been purchased before, and needs to be re-purchased without any modifications.

Some tremendous efficiencies can be realized by automating straight re-buys. Most companies use the airline websites for direct corporate travel bookings. Firms such as Wal-Mart and Procter & Gamble collaborate so that inventory can be restocked as it falls below predetermined levels. In order to maintain a reliable connection to its thousands of suppliers, Wal-Mart transformed Retail Link, its traditional dial-in supplier network, into an Internet application. Wal-Mart's suppliers now have quick and easy access to inventory systems, resulting in faster replenishment, a product mix attuned to customer needs, and lower inventory costs. The network also helps keep prices low and maintains inventory on the shelves. Ingram Micro, a wholesale provider of technology products and supply chain services, has also set up an online procurement platform called Rosetta to make the procurement process faster and more streamlined, and to lower transaction costs. Similarly, specialized business-to-business exchanges such as **Foodservice.com** and **Restaurantpro.com** for the restaurant industry aim to do the same thing.

Modified re-buy
A purchase item that is similar to the previously purchased item, but entails some changes either in design/performance specifications or in the supply environment.

A **modified re-buy** represents a need that is similar in broad nature to the previously fulfilled needs, but it entails some changes either in design/performance specifications or in the supply environment. For example, the firm wants to buy more desktop computers; although the firm has bought these before, it wants to reexamine the latest technology available, or the firm wants to evaluate a new supplier of higher reputation who has entered the market. Made-to-order online purchases allow the business customer with this ability to execute modified re-buys without expending a lot of time and effort. For example, with more and more companies offering online ordering for off-the-shelf products, customers can register with several suppliers and be provided with a password-protected page at these supplier's sites where they can create purchase orders and buy products. The product images and technical specifications are given on the website, and it becomes a matter of sifting through the required set of products at different sites to change from one supplier to another in a modified re-buy.

New task
A purchase item new to the buying organization.

New task purchases pertain to those needs that are new to the organization. This item has not been purchased before, and, indeed, there has never been a need for it. Now, therefore, there is considerable uncertainty about the design/performance requirements, which are still being assessed. Also, suppliers may not already be on the company list, and, at any rate, new suppliers may need to be added and all suppliers may have to be appraised anew. Deciding on new technology for a process or a new design would be an example of a new task purchase.

The concept of buyclass is important because the purchase process is different across the three buyclasses (see Table 9.6). On a continuum of straight re-buy to modified re-buy to new task, the more the purchase is of the new-task type, the more the buying group:

- perceives the need for information;
- is large;
- is deliberative and patient;
- is concerned with finding a good solution;
- underplays low price and assured supply as evaluation criteria;

TABLE 9.6 Buying Behaviour Associated with Buyclasses

Buyclass	Description of Need	Buying Centre Size	Information Search
Straight re-buy	Item is frequently needed and has been satisfactorily bought before	Very small; ordering may even be automated	Brief or nonexistent; new suppliers rarely considered; technical expertise rarely sought
Modified re-buy	Need is broadly similar to one that has been fulfilled before but requires some change in specifications or the supply environment	Moderate	Some information is gathered; new suppliers may be considered; technical experts may have input into decision
New task	Need is completely new to the organization	Large	Extensive; new suppliers, often considered experts, usually have major input into decision

- will consider new suppliers;
- will value the influence of technical persons, relative to the influence of buying agents.[28]

Perceived Risk, Importance, and Complexity

Each type of purchase involves a different level of perceived risk, importance, and complexity for the decision maker.

Perceived risk refers to the expected probability that the purchase may not produce a satisfactory outcome. It is a product of two factors: (1) the degree of uncertainty that a choice may be wrong, and (2) the amount at stake should a wrong choice occur. Uncertainty stems from the absence of prior design/performance specifications and from lack of experience with potential suppliers. Thus, new tasks have the most uncertainty, and straight re-buys have the least. Amount at stake is the financial loss or performance loss from a sub-optimal choice. Financial loss depends on the purchase price in absolute terms (the more expensive the purchase, the greater the financial loss) as well as from a less advantageous price (the supplier chosen may not be the best-priced supplier). Performance loss comes from the product not performing to standards, which may, in fact, cause systemwide damage (e.g., a chemical ingredient of lesser purity than required might damage the processing equipment).

Perceived risk
The degree of loss (i.e., amount at stake) in the event that a wrong choice is made.

The **importance of purchase** is a combination of the amount at stake and the extent to which the product plays a strategic role in the organization. The higher the amount at stake, and the more strategic the product's role, the more important the purchase. Thus, a large fleet of transportation vehicles might cost more than a communication network; yet the latter might be viewed as a more important purchase due to its strategic role in equipping the customer firm for the information age.

Importance of purchase
How important a purchase is in the customer's life.

Complexity refers to the extent of the effort required to comprehend and manage the product during its acquisition. Complexity has two dimensions: (1) the number of performance dimensions and (2) the technical and specialist knowledge required to understand those dimensions. Thus, a single-dimensional product such as a chemical is simpler than a multidimensional item such as a personal computer (even though the risk might be greater with the purchase of a chemical than with that of a computer). Office furniture is less technical than surgical sutures. The latter require more specialist knowledge to understand the design/performance characteristics and the supplier information.

Complexity
The extent of the effort required to comprehend and manage the product during its acquisition.

As the foregoing examples suggest, importance, complexity, and perceived risk are often but not always, related. Together, these influence how extensive and involved the purchase decision process will be. (See the Window on Research.)

Time Pressure

Customers behave differently when they are under time pressure. Time pressure refers simply to how urgently the item is needed. When the item is needed urgently, the purchase decision will tend to short-circuit the usual process, make the process less deliberative, and give more direct role to the user/requisitioner.

ORGANIZATIONAL CHARACTERISTICS

Four organizational characteristics of the customer firm affect buying behaviour: (1) size, (2) structure, (3) purchase resources, and (4) purchase orientation.

Size

The size of the business determines not only the customer's potential dollar volume, but also the sophistication of its buying process. Small business organizations behave more like a family in their buying behaviour; entrepreneurial firms usually consist of a one-person purchasing group and, thus, resemble an individual buying decision. Large organizations, in contrast, have larger buying groups and more formalized procedures.

Structure

Structure refers to the number of departmental units, geographical locations over which the units are spread out, and its degree of centralization. The more departments a business has, the larger the buying group is likely to be, and the more prolonged the buying process is likely to be. Multi-location buying firms create more complexity for the seller than single-locale firms. For example, a firm selling construction equipment may have to visit the administrative headquarters of a construction firm as well as its construction site managers.

Purchase Resources

Purchase resources refer to the availability of professional buyers and the extent to which the purchase office is staffed with the required type and number of experts as well as equipment (e.g., computerized supplier information system). Generally, large and professionally managed (as opposed to owner-managed) firms would have better-resourced purchasing departments leading to well-evaluated decisions and formal and rigorous vendor evaluation.

WINDOW ON **RESEARCH**

What Perceived Risk Does to Business Buying Behaviour

Researchers have extensively studied the impact of perceived risk on buying behaviour. Their findings support the view that when business customers perceive high risk, they adjust their buying behaviour to protect themselves and their organizations.

For example, with higher perceived risk, the buying group (centre) becomes more complex. That is, more people are involved in the purchase decision throughout the purchase process, and they are drawn from a greater variety of departmental and/or organizational interests. Additionally, buying-centre participants will generally be of higher organizational status and authority; if not, the buying centre will not have the authority to make the final purchase decision. Instead, its function will be (1) to gather and evaluate relevant information and (2) to make recommendations to upper-level management.

Participants in a high-risk purchase decision process are more educated and experienced in their area of expertise. Also, since the purchase decision is important, participants are motivated to expend greater effort and deliberate more carefully throughout the purchase process.

High-risk decisions favour sellers who offer proven products and solutions. Product quality and post-sale service will be of the utmost importance. Price will be considered only after product criteria have been fully met. If (after careful scrutiny) two or more sellers appear equally capable of satisfying purchase requirements, price will play a dominant role in the purchase decision.

(continued)

Information search is active, and a wide variety of information sources are used to guide and support the purchase decision. Buying-centre participants may rely more heavily on impersonal, commercial information sources (e.g., trade publications, sales literature) during the earlier stages of the decision process. As the procurement decision progresses, personal, non-commercial information sources (e.g., consultants, other organizations that have already made similar purchases) may become more important.

Within the buying firm, conflict between buying-centre participants increases. One reason is that more departments (through their representatives) are involved in the purchase decision. Also, since the purchase outcome is important, buying-centre participants will be reluctant to make concessions without some form of reciprocal reward. Therefore, buying-centre participants will most likely use a bargaining negotiation strategy.

Role stress among decision makers also increases. One cause is the size and complexity of the buying centre, resulting in greater conflict among participants with differing perspectives and motivations. Also, in a highly visible (important) purchase where the outcome is uncertain, the chances of making a wrong decision and the associated consequences of a wrong decision intensify participant stress.

SOURCE: Adapted from Johnston, Wesley J., and Jeffrey E. Lewin. "Organizational Buying Behaviour: Toward an Integrative Framework." *Journal of Business Research* 35 (January 1996): 1–15. http://www.elsevier.com/wps/find/journal_browse.cws_home.

Purchase Orientation

The organization's purchase orientation refers to its purchasing philosophy along a continuum. This continuum begins with viewing purchasing simply as an administrative function that finds the most economical sources of materials needed when they are needed, and at its end, views purchasing as a strategic, managerial function whose goal is to add value to the organization's offerings. As a strategic function, purchasing is engaged in several key activities:

- Scrutinizing make-versus-buy decisions. It questions the very need to buy something, or even whether it may not be better to buy the whole thing, rather than buying an intermediate product and then converting it into a final marketable product.
- Continually finding better products, materials, and technology.
- Developing long-term sources of supply and building relationships with the suppliers.

THE BUYING CENTRE

In all but the smallest organizations, purchase decisions are handled by a formal or informal **buying centre**—a multi-function, multi-level internal organization that is responsible for the centralized purchasing function. The buying centre represents a subset of *roles* within the organization, which participate in the buying process. Several roles have been identified:

Buying centre All the members of a customer firm who play some role in the purchase decision.

- *User*—This is the user department that would use the product to be purchased by an organization.
- *Buyer*—The buyer, alternatively called purchasing manager or purchasing executive, has the formal authority to execute the purchase contract and place a purchase order.
- *Analyzer*—One who performs a technical analysis of suppliers by using tools such as cost analysis and value analysis.

- *Influencer*—By their expert advice, these role holders influence the evaluative criteria and supplier ratings and/or the final decision itself. Typically, they are design engineers and external consultants.
- *Gatekeepers*—They regulate the flow of information from suppliers to the other members of the buying centre. They permit or deny salespersons access to design and user departments or to other executives. Sometimes, the legal department in an organization is a gatekeeper.
- *Decider*—The deciders make the final decision. This role may be played by a formal buying committee, or by the CEO, CFO, or purchasing executive alone. Sometimes, the user and engineering departments short list and rank the suppliers, and then a high-level executive who may or may not be a member of any buying committee makes the final decision.

The buying centre roles (e.g., user, influencer) are roles, not titles, and not necessarily single persons; also, an individual may play multiple roles, such as influencer and gatekeeper. Although various executives may play a crucial role in the buying decision, personnel from three departments are typically involved more extensively: purchasing, manufacturing, and quality control. The buying centre is a concept and should not be confused with buying committees, which many organizations have. Where buying committees exist, persons other than those on the formal committee may influence the decision and are, therefore, deemed to be a part of the buying centre concept. Where buying committees do not exist, buying centres still exist as virtual groups.

Firms that decide to target large companies as customers have to deploy more resources to go through the decision process. This process is typically longer, but it results in larger dollar value sales. For example, ICG Commerce, an e-procurement company that targets Global 1000 companies, would have longer sales cycles than companies that target small and medium companies.

RULES AND PROCEDURES

Businesses generally set up elaborate policies (e.g., favouring a minority supplier), rules (e.g., purchase needs must be consolidated for the entire organization), and procedures (e.g., a minimum number of bids required). The degree of formalization and decision freedom varies from buyer to buyer. If the buying firm is less obligated to adhere to prescribed rules and procedures, a marketer has more freedom to innovate and add value to offerings and educate the buyer about them.

DECISION PROCESS

Like individual and household buying decisions, organizational buying decisions entail a multistage process. Business buying decisions comprise the following stages:

- *Need assessment*—Deciding the technical and performance specifications for the needed item.
- *Development of choice criteria*—Identifying supplier selection criteria.
- *Request for proposals (RFPs)*—Calling for proposals by publishing requests for quotes (RFQs) and inviting suppliers to submit bids. Additional suppliers are actively solicited if adequate suppliers are not already on the list. For suppliers who submit proposals,

information is collected about their capabilities and past performance. This information comes from suppliers themselves and, more important, from other independent sources such as consultants, trade associations, word-of-mouth, and formal rating reports from independent sources. E-procurement service providers like ICG Commerce offer eRFPs and eRFQs. Such firms also allow forward and reverse auctions. These allow qualified bidders to compete on price in an anonymous online auction. These services drastically reduce the time for the process as well as the prices the company can get from suppliers.

- *Supplier evaluation*—Rank-ordering vendors. Some negotiations may occur toward reconciling differences both on technical matters and on price variations among various bidders or suppliers.
- *Supplier selection*—Awarding the contract or placing an order.
- *Fulfillment and monitoring*—Monitoring for smooth fulfillment in a timely fashion and to the satisfaction of the buyers and users.

These steps are similar to individual decision making except that there is a lot more formal analysis as well as use of more structured procedures. (See the Window on Research.)

WINDOW ON RESEARCH

How Businesses Award Long-Term Contracts for Repeat-Purchase Items

To study the process of selecting a vendor for long-term contracts, Niren Vyas and Arch Woodside interviewed managers in six buying firms. Among the 18 products included in the study were corrugated boxes, metal bars, rubber gaskets, fuel oil, and electric cables—a sample of all three buyclasses. Based on their findings, they described the vendor selection decision as comprising five steps:

1. *Identifying the suppliers*—For straight re-buy and modified re-buy items, the buyer firm already had a list of potential suppliers. For new task items, potential suppliers were identified from prior experience, advice from design engineers, and trade journals.
2. *Qualifying the suppliers*—Buyers assessed suppliers on factors such as capacity, location, manufacturing facility, and financial resources judged from brochures, information from salespeople, and plant visits. To qualify suppliers, buyers applied conjunctive decision rules (a list of required minimums). Some buyers had a policy of including minority suppliers in the list even if this necessitated relaxing some criteria.
3. *Inviting bids*—The buyers issued RFQs (requests for quotations), which detail the design specifications and product performance criteria. The specifications are generated by design and production engineers, based on their technical need and their knowledge of what is available. Buyers preferred to have at least three bidders. If the list of qualified suppliers was long, the conjunctive decision rule was made more demanding (i.e., the required minimums were raised). If this step left more than three bidders, buyers tried to eliminate other suppliers with a lexicographic rule (i.e., eliminate the supplier with the least-attractive value on the most desirable criteria).
4. *Bid evaluation*—Bids were evaluated on both technical and commercial criteria. Commercial evaluation, done by the purchasing department, entailed checking items such as payment terms, price escalation, labour-contract expiration dates, and shipping terms. Technical evaluation was done by

(continued)

user departments and design engineers, generally without the price information, so that the technical evaluation was unbiased. A chief goal was to determine the amount of price premium to allow the consideration of suppliers for superior quality and service. None of the firms used a formal evaluation system, so the price premium decision was simply an intuitive judgment by the buying centre.

5. *Bid selection*—If only one bid was received, buyers started immediate negotiations with the bidder on price and delivery schedule. With multiple bids, the first decision was whether to patronize more than one supplier. Buyers often preferred the bargaining advantage of two (or more) suppliers. Factors that affected the final selection were successful experience with a bidder, supplier reputation, and location of the service organization. These factors were weighed against the quoted price in a compensatory decision rule (i.e., the lack of one factor is compensated by superiority on others). The lowest bidder was often selected, but bidders with as much as a 6-percent price premium over the lowest bidder were sometimes awarded the contract. When multiple suppliers were selected, the current supplier was given more than 50 percent of the annual order.

SOURCE: Adapted from Vyas, Niren, and Arch G. Woodside. "An Inductive Model of Industrial Supplier Choice Process." *Journal of Marketing* 48 (Winter 1984): 30–45. http://www.marketingjournals.org/jm/.

Various roles in the buying centre participate more in some stages than others (see Table 9.7). Generally, users exercise more influence at the need assessment and choice criteria stages; buyers shoulder the major responsibility at the RFP, supplier search, and fulfillment stages; analyzers help most at the supplier evaluation stage; influencers, at the supplier evaluation and selection stages; and decision makers, at the vender selection stages. Gatekeepers, of course, would be active throughout, depending on the inflow of information, influence, and salesperson communications, all vying for the decision makers' attention. However, the exact pattern of influence each member exercises at each decision stage varies from case to case.

It is the task of a business-to-business salesperson and marketer to identify and map this pattern for each business client individually. According to a survey, engineering and technical staff participate more during the need identification and specification generation stages, whereas purchasing agents/managers participate more in the later stages of identifying the sources of supply and evaluating and choosing them.[29]

TABLE 9.7 Varying Influence of Buying Centre Roles

	BUYING CENTRE ROLES					
	User	**Buyer**	**Decider**	**Analyzer**	**Influencer**	**Gatekeeper**
Need assessment	XX		X		X	
Vendor search		XX	XX		XX	XX
Choice criteria	X	X		X	XX	
RFP		XX				
Supplier evaluation				XX	XX	
Selection	X	X	XX	X	X	XX
Fulfillment/monitoring	XX	XX				

X = Some Influence; XX = Strong Influence.

Procurement Costs

In business buying, when decision makers weigh costs, they consider the total costs of a purchase. These costs include acquisition costs, possession costs, and usage costs. The elements in these three component costs are listed in Table 9.8.

As a business-to-business supplier, a firm should understand and know these costs for a specific customer, then design market offerings in a way that reduces the customer's total costs, rather than just the selling price.

Psychology of Decision Makers

The decision-making process is primarily driven by two psychological processes occurring in the decision makers: (1) their expectations and (2) their perceptual distortions.

Expectations

One factor that sets organizational decision making apart from individual and household decision making is that each member of the buying centre tend to have his or her own set of different expectations. These expectations are influenced by background and by the level of satisfaction or dissatisfaction with past purchases.[30]

The background that shapes expectations comprises educational and work experiences. Persons with different technical backgrounds emphasize different decision criteria (e.g., engineers focus on technical factors, and buyers focus on price factors). Expectations also are created by role orientations; for example, expectations of a proactive buying agent would differ vastly from that of an agent playing a reactive role. The second source of individual expectations, namely satisfaction with prior buying experiences with suppliers, focuses on the price and quality of previously purchased products.

Perceptual Distortions

Business customers, like individual consumers, encode incoming information selectively (attending to some and ignoring other information) and in a biased manner. This tendency is called *selective perceptual distortion.* Expectations play a major role in selective perceptions.

TABLE 9.8 Components of a Business Customer's Total Costs

Acquisition Costs	Possession Costs	Usage Costs
Price	Interest cost	Field defects
Paperwork cost	Storage cost	Training cost
Shopping time	Quality control	User labour cost
Expediting cost	Taxes and insurance	Product longevity
Cost of mistakes in order	Shrinkage and obsolescence	Replacement costs
Pre-purchase product evaluation costs	General internal handling costs	Disposal costs

SOURCE: Cespedes, Frank V. "Industrial Marketing: Managing New Requirements." *Sloan Management Review* (Spring 1994) by permission of the publisher.

Thus, some buying centre members might expect that only engineers are able to understand product specifications; they might then discount as unreliable any information that salespeople provide, assuming they do not have an engineering background.

Conflict and Its Resolution

When expectations of members in the buying centre differ, conflicts arise. These may concern either the relative weight of the evaluative criteria or the rating of different suppliers on these criteria. When conflicts arise, they may be resolved in the four ways introduced in the section on household decision making: problem solving, persuasion, bargaining, and politicking.[31]

Problem solving
A rational approach to conflict resolution wherein participants search for more information and deliberate on the new information.

Persuasion
A rational method of conflict resolution wherein some members persuade others by demonstrating how the other person's position will lead to a sub-optimal outcome.

Bargaining
A method of conflict resolution, based on distributive justice for all, wherein the dissenting members negotiate a give and take.

Politicking
A conflict resolution method wherein members form partisan coalitions and then "manage" the decision with behind-the-scenes manoeuvering.

Problem solving is a rational approach to conflict resolution. It entails a search for more information, further deliberation on the new information, and possibly consideration of new suppliers. If the conflict is due to disagreements on what is to be expected from the suppliers and their products, then the conflict will likely be resolved in the problem-solving manner.

Persuasion, also a rational method of conflict resolution, is used when there is a disagreement on specific criteria for supplier evaluation (but overall agreement on what is to be expected of them). In this method, additional information is not gathered, but further deliberation among parties continues, and may even proceed to the inclusion of an outside party to resolve the conflict.

When the difference between the buying parties centres on basic goals and objectives, the conflict resolution method shifts from a rational orientation to **bargaining,** which hinges on distributive justice for all. This method is quite common in the case of a new task purchase. Resolution begins by a recognition and acceptance of differences in goals of dissenting members who negotiate for give and take.

In **politicking,** resolution comes through back-stabbing techniques and centres on the use of an efficient, nonrational approach to dealing with conflicts. Members form partisan coalitions and then manage the decision with behind-the-scenes manoeuvring. The organization suffers when this method is used, as decisions are either delayed or resolved in a manner not consistent with the overall goals and objectives of the organization.

A COMPREHENSIVE MODEL OF ORGANIZATIONAL CUSTOMER BEHAVIOUR

To bring together the individual components of the business procurement system, we can diagram a comprehensive model of organizational buyer behaviour, such as the one in Figure 9.5.

As Figure 9.5 shows, the nature of purchase and organizational characteristics (including rules and procedures) influences the structure of the buying centre, such as whether a formal buying centre exists, how many members it has, who its members are, and what its charge may be. The buying centre is constituted within the framework of buying policies, rules, and procedures (which are determined by the organizational characteristics), and the buying centre, in turn, influences these by interpreting, implementing, and/or deviating from them. The decision process is influenced by the buying centre as well as by the policies, rules, and procedures. Sources of information form an input at the supplier search stage of the decision process. This input is routed, of course, via the gatekeeper, and is filtered through the perceptual-distortion processes of the buying-centre members. Conflicts may occur at the supplier evaluation and selection stage, and if they do, they are resolved by one of the four methods described earlier.

FIGURE 9.5 A Comprehensive Model of Organizational Customer Behaviour

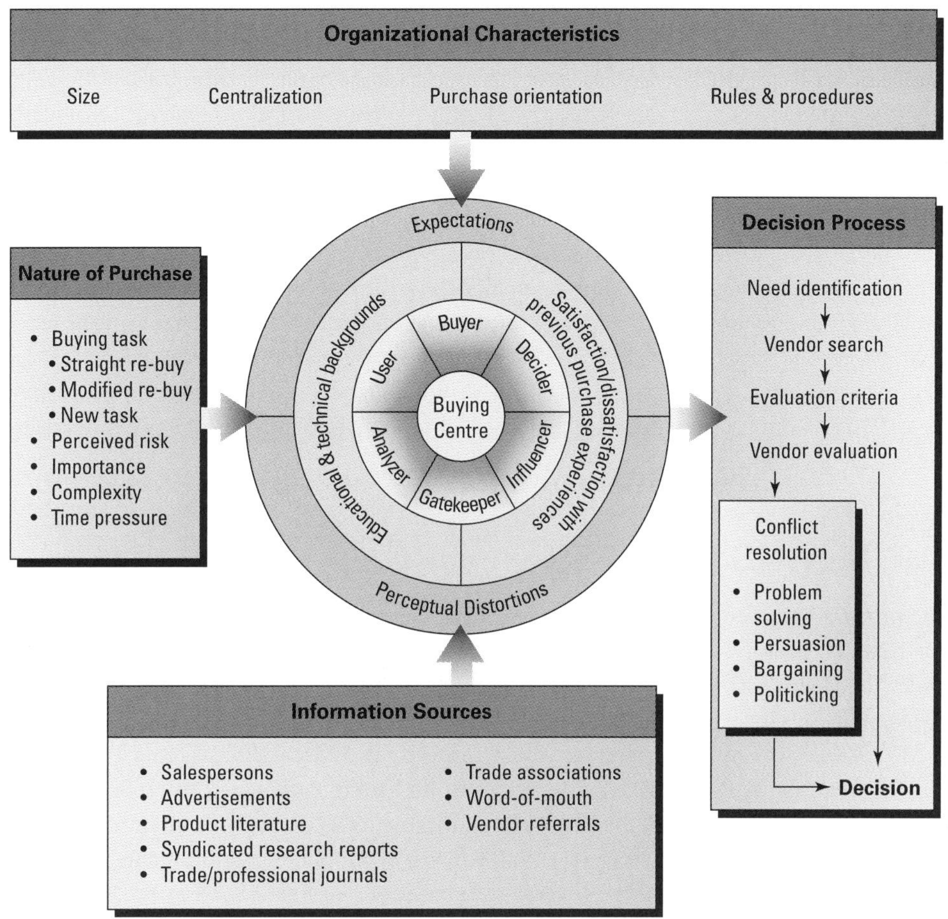

One factor not shown in the figure is the macro-environment. It consists of the economic, political, legal, cultural, technological, and marketplace environments (i.e., suppliers and competitors). These envelop the entire buying system. For example, legal restrictions might exist against seeking foreign sources of supply. Economic uncertainty might engender a shortage or surplus of certain products. Technology that suppliers use to offer product information (e.g., the Internet) or that buyers require (e.g., electronic ordering) might render some suppliers and buyers unsuitable for each other. And certain suppliers or supplier cultures (especially involving cross-national dealings) might mandate certain styles of negotiations (e.g., misrepresenting information) unacceptable. Thus, the entire procurement system is facilitated and constrained within the framework of the macroenvironment surrounding it.

GOVERNMENT BUYING BEHAVIOUR

LO 6

Governments are legal entities empowered to organize and govern people, processes (e.g., free trade), and infrastructures (e.g., highways) by the resources and compliance mechanisms they possess as monarchs, dictators, elected presidents, prime ministers, or

Government
Legal entities empowered to organize and govern a city, state, or nation.

governors, the military, and the civil service, along with the many democratically elected or administratively appointed bodies (e.g., parliament, congress, assembly, or the city council).

In every country, the government buys many products; sometimes it is likely to be the single biggest buyer. It buys heavy equipment, appliances, jets, road vehicles, ships, telecommunication equipment, food grain, prepared food, clothes and uniforms, scientific equipment, maintenance parts, supplies, paper, furniture, transportation, and communication services, to name a few. It buys at every level: national, provincial, and municipal. The Government of Canada buys approximately $14 billion worth of goods and services every year from thousands of suppliers. There are over 85 departments, agencies, Crown corporations, and Special Operating Agencies (SOAs). Public Works and Government Services Canada (PWGSC) is the government's largest purchasing organization, averaging 60,000 contracts totalling $10 billion annually. While PWGSC buys goods for most departments of the federal government, the departments buy most services themselves. A sizeable part of service contracting is directly done by the end users: SOAs, individual departments, and Crown corporations. PWGSC only contracts for a portion of all services bought from the private sector by the federal government.

THE BUYING PROCESS

The procurement and contracting policies of the Government of Canada are established by the Treasury Board. Government contracting must comply with Canada's trade obligations under the North American Free Trade Agreement (NAFTA), the World Trade Organization Agreement on Government Procurement (WTO-AGP), and the Agreement on Internal Trade (AIT). Government contracts must respect the Federal Contractors Program for Employment Equity (FCP). Federal departments do a lot of their own contracting for goods up to $5,000 and for most of their services requirements. Federal government departments and agencies have a number of ways to find sources of supply for requirements they handle directly. They can:

- access the SRI (Supplier Registration Information) service. The SRI service is a directory of vendors who want to do business with the federal government;
- refer to publications such as telephone books and trade directories;
- access their own source lists of companies;
- publicly advertise their requirements in MERX™ (**http://www.merx.com**), the Internet-based electronic bulletin board that provides information on bid opportunities for several governments across Canada and distributes bid documents to interested vendors;
- use SELECT (for architectural and engineering consulting services, services related to real property and construction services only). SELECT is a computerized system that contains a list of pre-qualified real property firms identified by their expertise and the services they provide.

For the most part, federal government buyers use MERX™ for higher dollar value requirements and purchases that are subject to a trade agreement. For low-dollar value purchases they use telephone and trade directories as well as databases developed by their departments.

Individual departments may buy directly from suppliers through their procurement or acquisition division for services contracts. They may contract up to $400,000 competitively or up to $100,000 without competition. They may also buy competitively, up to $2 million when they advertise their requirements through MERX™. Under the federal government's trade agreement obligations, departments must publicly advertise opportunities subject to these agreements. Some may advertise other services requirements as well. Crown corporations contract for services on their own and have more flexible procedures than line departments. PWGSC has the highest approval limit for services with up to $20 million competitively, and $3 million without competition.

GOVERNMENT BUYING PROCEDURES

Governments follow well-specified and rule-driven buying procedures. Most governments insist that agreements with suppliers be drafted using their standard terms. In the case of Canada's federal government, the Standard Acquisition Clauses and Conditions (SACC) manual is the source of most contract language. Other governments often include "pro forma" agreements in their procurement documents. As an example, we briefly describe the procurement process of PWGSC. Additional information can be obtained from the Business Access Canada website (http://contractscanada.gc.ca/en/how-e.htm).

PWGSC Buying Process

PWGSC, the government's principal purchasing arm, uses a step-by-step process to buy products. These steps include checkpoints for clearance at various levels of authority, depending on the value of the contract. What follows is an overview of how the process works. The *Supply Manual* (http://www.pwgsc.gc.ca/acquisitions/text/sm/toc-e.html) describes in detail the supply activities of PWGSC and contains relevant laws, regulations, and government and departmental policies.

The process starts when an organization in a department or agency requires goods or services and issues a requisition for the purchase of such products. Subject to the value of the requisition, the department may have the delegated authority to make the purchase itself; if not, the requisition will be sent to PWGSC for action.

PWGSC advertises most opportunities worth $25,000 or more on MERX™, the electronic tendering service. Increasingly, however, opportunities valued at less than $25,000 are also advertised on MERX™. PWGSC also advertises on MERX™ most architectural and engineering consulting services worth $84,000 or more, services related to real property worth $84,000 or more, and construction opportunities valued at $100,000 or more. For some requirements valued at less than $25,000, and for certain contracts that require pre-qualified bidders, source lists of known suppliers may be used.

Requirement for architectural and engineering consulting services, and services related to real property valued at less than $84,000, as well as construction requirements valued at less than $100,000 are handled through the computer-assisted selection and contract award system SELECT. When any of these services are required, SELECT matches the specifics of the requirement with firms that have the required expertise and are within a prescribed geographic range. Depending on the requirement, either one firm may be given the opportunity to accept or decline the work, or multiple firms may be given the opportunity to compete for the contract.

The Bidding Process

Depending on the dollar value and the particular requirements of the proposed contract, the procurement officer and the client (e.g., government agency) may choose one of the following bid solicitation methods outlined below. When bid solicitations are national in scope or originate from an office that is obliged to serve the public in both official languages pursuant to the Act and Regulations, all documents must be provided in both official languages. Most procurement of goods and services is to be carried out using the general conditions and supplemental general conditions found in the *SACC* manual. The conditions to be used depend on the nature of the procurement.

Telephone buy (T-buy)

PWGSC uses these for small competitive purchases valued at under $25,000 when it gets a requisition for something that can be easily identified over the phone and must be delivered quickly. The PWGSC officer phones at least three companies who give their bids over the phone. The one that offers the lowest price and fulfills all of the terms of the requirement wins the contract.

Request for Quotation (RFQ)

PWGSC normally sends out RFQs when a requisition is received for goods and services valued at less than $25,000. The bid documents are kept simple so that the contract can be awarded quickly. Quotations are not technically offers to supply. To form a contract, there must be an offer and formal acceptance of the offer.

Invitation to Tender (ITT)

PWGSC sends out ITTs to bidders when the opportunity is worth $25,000 or more and has fairly straightforward requirements, such as a request for off-the-shelf goods and many construction requirements. The lowest-priced responsive bid (the lowest bid that complies with all the mandatory requirements specified in the ITT document) will be awarded the contract.

Request for Proposal (RFP)

A RFP, while generally used for requirements of $25,000 or more, is often employed for purchases where the selection of a supplier cannot be made solely on the basis of the lowest price. A RFP is used to procure the most cost-effective solution based on evaluation criteria identified in the RFP in these circumstances: (1) when only one source is being solicited; (2) when it expects to have to negotiate with one or more bidders about certain aspects of the requirement; or (3) when the requirement is not clear-cut and suppliers are then invited to propose a solution to a problem, requirement, or objective, and contractor selection is based on the effectiveness of the proposed solution rather than on price alone. Proposals are evaluated in accordance with specific criteria set out in the RFP. A RFP is likely to be issued when the product is new or complex, and/or when it entails large sums of money.

Request for Standing Offer (RFSO)

This bid method is very different from the others. When PWGSC sets up a standing offer with a supplier, the latter is offering to provide a given product at a specified price during a certain time period. Standing offers are not contracts. If and when the government issues a call-up against the standing offer, then a contract takes place. They are usually employed when (1) the government repetitively orders the same products, and the actual demand is not known in advance; or (2) when a need is anticipated for a range of goods or services for a specific purpose, but the actual demand is not known yet, and delivery is to be made when a requirement arises. Standing offers are most suited to products that can be clearly defined, in order to allow suppliers to offer firm pricing.

Request for Supply Arrangement (RFSA)

A RFSA is a method of solicitation where clients, under the framework of the resulting arrangement, may solicit bids from a pool of pre-screened vendors. A supply arrangement is used when a commodity is procured on a regular basis and when clients can negotiate price reductions from the ceiling price quoted by the supplier.

Sole-Sourcing

Whenever possible, the government seeks to award contracts through competition. However, a contract may be awarded without competition subject to obligations under the trade agreements or Government Contracting Regulations (GCRs).

Bid Specifications

Each bid document is unique. It specifies all requirements for the job. All bid solicitations must specify the bid closing date, time, and location. It contains requirements that must be met; otherwise, the bid will be considered non-responsive. Bid documents specify the dates, times, and locations of the bidders' conferences, if any. Bidders' conferences are intended to ensure that bidders have a clear understanding of the technical, operational, and performance specifications, as well as the financial and contracting requirements. Standard clauses and conditions are used according to the *SACC* manual. For some contracts and standing offers, e.g., those requiring access to sensitive or classified material or information, or to government buildings, the buyer may require that the supplier be cleared or screened for security or reliability.

Bid Receipt

Bids are received in the designated bid receiving area identified in the bid solicitation. All bids submitted to PWGSC are rigorously controlled, date- and time-stamped, and released only to the official authorized to undertake the evaluations. Late bids are not accepted.

Bid Evaluation

The bids received are evaluated using criteria specified in the bid document. Mandatory requirements are evaluated objectively on a simple pass/fail basis. If a bidder does not meet the mandatory criteria, then the bid is not given further consideration. For RFPs, point-rated criteria are used to determine the relative technical merit of each proposal. PWGSC uses point-rated criteria to evaluate the "value added" factors, over and above those that meet the minimum requirements of the RFP. The maximum points that can be achieved for each criterion are identified in the RFP. Once the evaluation is complete, a bidder will be recommended for contract award.

Bid Award

As a rule, the bidder who fulfills all the terms and conditions of the requirement, and offers the best value or lowest price (or as stipulated in the bid documentation), is generally selected. If only one bidder is responsive, PWGSC may negotiate contract terms and prices with that individual or company. Before a contract is awarded, the expenditure has to be approved by the appropriate level of authority, usually within PWGSC. In the case of large and complex contracts, Treasury Board approval must be obtained. For all publicly advertised procurements, award notices are generated automatically and published on MERX™.

Contract

The contract document will depend on the type of bid requested and received. RFSOs and RFSAs are two types of non-binding agreements between the federal government and potential suppliers for the supply of specified goods or services. These agreements outline the terms and conditions that will apply to future requirements to be ordered on an "as-and-when-required" basis.

PROCUREMENT BY PROVINCIAL GOVERNMENTS

Provincial governments are, collectively, responsible for a huge procurement budget. Each province has its own guidelines for doing business. Many provinces make vendor information available on their Internet website. For example, Ontario's Ministry of Government Services's website (http://www.ppitpb.gov.on.ca) provides information on Ontario's procurement policies and procedures and samples of procurement documents such as Request for Proposal, Contracts, etc. It also provides a link to MERX™ (http://www.merx.com).

SIMILARITIES BETWEEN GOVERNMENT AND BUSINESS PROCUREMENT[32]

Government spending, especially at the federal level, involves large amounts of money, complex procedures, and red tape in even the smallest purchase. However, there are some parallels between business buying and government buying: in the matters of buyclass, buying steps, and procurement management goals.

In business buying, the purchase task was classified as straight re-buy, modified re-buy, and new task. In government, the buying tasks can be viewed as non-developmental, modified non-developmental, and developmental. These classifications are based on the level of analysis and the degree of buyer attention they require. Generally speaking, buying decisions for both business and government buyers involve either repetition of a previous purchase, some variation of a previous purchase, or a new purchase situation.

The steps in the buying process for business and government buying are similar except for some differences in nomenclature. Both processes begin with the definition of a need, and must make those needs known to interested suppliers and invite them to develop offers and bids. Next, a selection process takes place, with some kind of follow-up after the order is placed.

Both business and government buyers pursue the same objectives in managing their procurement responsibilities and in reaching their supplier decisions. Both exist to fulfill the material needs of their user departments, seek to develop competent and reliable sources, must procure at prices most advantageous to the buying organization, must minimize inventory costs, and must encourage competition for their business.

HOW GOVERNMENT CUSTOMERS DIFFER FROM BUSINESS CUSTOMERS

While there is similarity on the goals and the overall nature of the procurement task between the business and government sectors, there are also a number of differences. These differences arise mainly in how the tasks are *procedurally* implemented.

Size of the Average Purchase and Standardization

The size of the average purchase by the Canadian government is huge, even for simple supplies such as stationery. Because large quantities are needed at various locations by various agencies, centralized purchasing is used wherever possible. Governments issue standard specifications for a large number of commercial items, and there is stricter adherence to them in government than in the private sector. The size of business that the government can provide has brought the dot-coms to the C2G (consumer-to-government) business sector as well. The city of Vancouver (http://www.city.vancouver.bc.ca), for example, offers an array of services online, ranging from local government job listings to government auctions, and it facilitates online payment for city services, parking tickets, and property taxes.

Legal Restrictions and Compliance Reviews

Laws regulate government procurement procedures in areas such as competitive bidding, budgetary limitations, auditing of accounts, and the use of standard specifications. Along with the regulations come extensive compliance reviews. Any government procurement contract involves numerous specialists and inspectors who monitor and audit records as well as contractor operations. The audits are intended to uncover any irregularities the government procurement agency may have committed in the awarding of the contract, as well as any deviations in compliance by a supplier. The government even has the legal authority to regulate contractors' hiring practices and the manner in which they do business with their subcontractors. Such legal jurisdiction over contractor operations is unheard of and unthinkable in private-sector procurement.

Solicitation of Sellers

Government buyers are obligated to seek suppliers widely and extensively. The *Government Contracts Regulations* (GCR) require the competitive soliciting of bids before any contract is entered into. However, contracts may be entered into without soliciting under well-defined situations. All bidding purchasing are posted in MERX™. The Government of Canada is committed to allowing small and medium enterprises (SMEs) to compete for government business. The Office of Small and Medium Enterprises (OSME) supports SMEs by working to reduce barriers and by simplifying requirements for SMEs that want to do business with the Government of Canada. Although business buyers also engage in soliciting competitive bidders, nothing in the business sector is comparable to the active solicitation of potential suppliers in government procurement.

Open-Access Information

Unlike what occurs in the business sector, government purchases in Canada take place in a goldfish bowl. In fact, since 2004, in accordance with a new policy, PWGSCs must provide information on government contracts over $10,000 awarded during the previous three months.

Diffusion of Authority

There is much greater diffusion of authority in government than in most private-sector procurement. One reason is that government procurement uses input from multiple users and advisors. In addition, authority for sub-tasks is separated. If the purchase task is a modified non-developmental task, and certainly if it is a developmental task, the government seeks input and assistance from a number of expert groups: accountants, engineers, lawyers, and other high-level officials. In comparison, in the business setting, technical, engineering, and production staff who generate specifications often serve on the *buying centre* and actively participate in joint decision making, and the purchasing manager or the user department who may jointly make the supplier selection also authorizes payments. Thus, in the private sector, there is much less diffusion of authority, perhaps because there is less need for checks and balances.

Procedural Detail and Paperwork

Finally, there is the inevitable paperwork, substantially more voluminous in government than in business procurement. Government's invitation to tender forms can be voluminous. Then there is need for strict adherence and legendary red tape. The product specifications tend to be exhaustive. Detailed specifications give the government ample ground to reject suppliers found unqualified.

THE TRAVAILS AND REWARDS OF SELLING TO THE GOVERNMENT

When faced with all the rules, regulations, and mountains of paperwork required in government contract bidding, it is easy to be discouraged. However, many of the quirks and nuances in government procurement stem from the responsibilities and obligations of public policy and public expenditures. Public projects of the developmental-tasks type are still in the evolutionary phase of planning, and, thus, the process of need identification is prolonged. Public procurement is funded by taxpayers' money, and the government is obliged to spend it wisely. Most important, government is responsible for implementing its procurement function in a socially responsible way. Finally, the rules require detailed paperwork so that everything is in writing; this helps to protect the government as well as the bidder.

Although there is room for reform in government procurement, consider some of the unique benefits of doing business with government:

- *Stability*—The economy affects private businesses much more than government. Government buys in bad as well as good economic times. Thus, doing business with the government can give a contractor stability.

- *Security*—As a customer, government has the best credit in the world. Suppliers to a stable government, such as Canada, don't even have to ask for credit references. Sometimes the government will even pay part of the costs in advance as progressive payments.
- *Size*—Government buys a lot of things and buys them in large quantities. Hundreds of businesses, including some of the biggest, such as Bombardier and IBM, have benefited from government contracts.
- *Breakthrough R&D Work*—Some government contracts entail funding the development of new technology and new applications, which can later be used for wider commercial applications. For example, Teflon nonstick cooking surfaces and Tang instant breakfast drink were developed for the space program.
- *Challenge*—The government is a stickler for cost efficiency and performance specifications. Satisfying the government requires total quality management, mastery of details, an ability to plan long term, and the perseverance required to do the job (including the daunting paperwork) right. There can be no better training ground than this. If a business firm can successfully do business with the government, it can compete anywhere else.

FUTURE OF THE GOVERNMENT AS A CUSTOMER

Just as corporate Canada is going through changes in its purchasing function, so too government procurement is experiencing pressures to change. The resulting changes include downsizing and restructuring.

Downsizing and Restructuring the Government

As businesses have improved their efficiency through downsizing and restructuring, people are demanding that their governments do the same. As a payer, the government is becoming more cost conscious, and is more concerned about fraud, waste, and mismanagement. Downsizing is one of the most basic tactics used by government departments and agencies to scale down their budgets. One way governments are getting by on reduced funding is through combinations of privatization and outsourcing. Privatization involves converting government operations, such as telecommunications, railroads, airlines, television, and postal services, into private businesses. In Canada, privatization is extending to airports, highways, and healthcare. Outsourcing involves contracting with private business (with relevant expertise) for the handling of certain tasks. Governments have outsourced to the private sector functions such as building maintenance, computer maintenance, and information technology services. Public-private partnerships (PPPs) are becoming a common tool to bring together the strengths of both sectors. In addition to maximizing efficiencies and innovations of private enterprise, PPPs can provide much needed capital to finance government programs and projects. Examples of PPP projects are the Confederation Bridge, the Highway 407 Electronic Toll Route, the Moncton Water Treatment Plant, the commercialization of the St. Lawrence Seaway, Kelowna Skyreach Place, and the Bruce Nuclear Power Plant lease (see http://www.pppcouncil.ca).

HOUSEHOLD, BUSINESS, AND GOVERNMENT DECISION MAKING AND THE THREE CUSTOMER ROLES

Household Buying Behaviour

Nearly all of the concepts discussed in this chapter have relevance to the three customer roles. Some apply to all three roles; others acquire more or less salience depending on the role. These are outlined in Table 9.9.

TABLE 9.9 Household, Business, and Government Decision Making and the Three Customer Roles

Concepts	User	Payer	Buyer
		HOUSEHOLD CUSTOMERS DECISIONS: UNIQUE ASPECTS	
Family and non-family households	• In non-family households, user and payer roles reside more likely in the same individual • User values are normatively influenced by nonuser family members	• In families where user and payer roles often separate, users need to persuade payers	• In non-family households, members may alternate buyer role across situations, but users may not surrender their choice-decision responsibility
Family decisions	• Users initiate and gather information about desirable alternatives	• Payers approve or disapprove category purchase	• Buyers often influence brand choices
Children's influence	• Very young children as users depend on parents as payers and buyers • Adolescent children influence user decisions on products for common use	• Children on allowances look for price and value	• Teenagers assume purchase task, including brand decisions, for routine shopping and seek convenience value the most
Consumer socialization of children	• Observation of adults and mass media socialize children into becoming users	• Payer-role socialization is the hardest to achieve • Debt accumulation on credit cards is a major concern of parents	• Accompanying parents on shopping trips helps socialize children into buying roles
Intergenerational influence	• User values considerably influenced by and between the generations • Influence based on product expertise or taste	• Financial resources enable payers to influence user choices across generations	• Types of stores one shops at can be influenced by intergenerational influence
Conflict resolution	• User-user conflict on items for common use • Usually resolved by problem solving (e.g., finding an acceptable alternative)	• User-payer role separation is principal source of conflict, often resolved by bargaining	• Buyers imposing their own user values can cause conflict
		BUSINESS CUSTOMERS DECISIONS: UNIQUE ASPECTS	
Role specialization	• Users focus on performance value evaluation	• Payers focus on budget allocations	• Buyers, often separate from users and payers, specialize in buying task
Formalized process	• Users submit a formal requisition and technical specifications	• Payers use sound budgeting practices	• Buyers follow well-laid-out policies and processes
Accountability	• Users are accountable for correct specifications	• Payers are accountable for not overspending	• Buyers are accountable for professional buying
Internal capabilities	• User capabilities may lead to in-house production	• Strong financial position can gain favorable terms for suppliers	• Buyers with low skills may draw on external advice

Complexity	• Need identification may be an extended process		• Buyers may need to coordinate with multiple suppliers
Buyclass	• Users may automate the requisition for re-buys	• For new task buys, payers may have to juggle money	• Re-buys may be routinized and automated. New task buys would require professional talents of buyers
Buying centre	• Buying centre brings all roles together	• Payers often are the deciders in the buying centre	• Buyers bring vendors and users together
Decision process	• Users are most active at the specification and vendor screening stages	• Payers are most active at the decision stage	• Buyers are active throughout the decision process
Conflict resolution	• Three roles are often in conflict	• Payers are often overly concerned with cost minimization	
		GOVERNMENT CUSTOMERS DECISIONS: UNIQUE ASPECTS	
RFPs	• User specifications are extensive in RFPs		• Buyers act as gatekeepers
Bid evaluation	• Users conduct technical evaluation	• Payers engage in cost evaluation of the bid	• Buyers coordinate and intensely participate in price evaluation
Acquisition teams	• Users play important role on acquisition teams		• Buyers handle principal responsibility for acquisition
Acquisition reforms	• Greater authority to users for direct purchase	• With rising concern about waste, payers would have to do budget allocations more conscientiously	• Buyer's job is made more more efficient

Households are classified into *family* and *non-family* types. In non-family households, payer and user roles are more likely to reside within the same individual, while in family households earning members support non-earning members. The separation of user and payer roles often found in family households brings forth a need for users to persuade payers, and the marketer needs to appeal to them by offering good price and credit and financing values. Regarding the buyer role, in family households, there are joint buying trips or role specialization by product categories. In non-family households, in contrast, role specialization is less likely, and, instead, each member may take turns performing the buyer role.

In *family decision making,* different family members contribute to the decision differently, according to the role they shoulder, based on their skills and resources. Individuals playing the user roles generally initiate the purchase request or the need recognition, and also gather information about available alternatives. Payers approve or disapprove the very idea of buying a specific product category. Buyers influence brand choices. *Children* influence family purchases, not only for products for which they themselves are users but also for products meant for common use in the family. In contrast to the user values, the payer values are not much influenced by children except when children spend their own money. Finally, children definitely influence the buyer values as teenagers increasingly assume the payer role for family groceries, making brand decisions and seeking convenience value.

Socialization of children as consumers is easy and natural in respect to the user role; children learn both by observation of consumption by parents in the household and also from mass media and peers. It is the payer role that is hard to socialize the children into; this takes some judicious shaping (such as asking children to pay rent). Finally, buyer-role socialization also occurs relatively easily as children accompany parents on shopping trips.

With regard to *intergenerational influence,* parents influence grown sons' and daughters' user values (and vice versa) on products that they have expertise on. Furthermore, in their payer roles, members of one generation influence the choices of other generations, in either direction, by controlling financial resources. Finally, buyer roles are also influenced in terms of selection of outlets.

Conflicts among family members are common even where the same member discharges all three roles and when multiple family members share the user role for the same product. User-user conflicts are typically resolved by problem solving (e.g., by identifying alternatives that are acceptable to all members). Next, user-payer role separation is the principal source of conflict, wherein payers exercise their power by ruling whether or not a particular product category will be bought. This conflict is often resolved by bargaining. Finally, buyers are often in a position to control the brand choice since they are the ones who implement the acquisition transaction or their own user values, which can also cause conflict. Such conflicts are generally resolved by the use of logic and persuasive arguments.

Business Buying Behaviour

Role specialization is more pronounced for business customers than for household customers because business buying requires specialist knowledge to evaluate each of the six market values. Users focus on technical performance evaluations; payers focus on organization-wide budget allocations; and buyers specialize in buying tasks, especially finding and appraising alternative sources. To ensure that maximum user values are obtained at lowest total costs, organizations lay down a *formalized process* that each role holder has to follow. Users must obtain budget approval from payers and submit a formal requisition, payers must use sound budgeting practices, and buyers must ensure that vendor selection follows the stipulated process. Each role holder is *accountable* for his or her part in the job—users for ensuring correct specifications for maximum performance value, payers for not overspending, and buyers for making the procurement more efficient and effective. *Internal capabilities* are relevant for all three roles. Users may produce the item in-house, and payers with deep pockets can gain more favourable terms from suppliers. As to the buyer role, if the buyer is not adequately skilled, the procurement itself may be outsourced. *Complexity* makes both user and buyer tasks more demanding as ensuring the fit with the requirements becomes crucial. For complex purchases, buyers may need to coordinate with multiple suppliers for complementary portions of the job.

Buyclass affects all three roles. Users may automate the requisition process for straight re-buys, but for new tasks, they would need to generate product specifications, perhaps for the first time. For straight re-buy, the budget is easily approved or earmarked; but for new tasks, payers may have to juggle money, including raising new capital. For re-buys, buyers rely on current suppliers; for new tasks, buyers need to go through an extensive process of identifying and evaluating all qualified vendors, bringing professional buying skills and talents to bear on the process.

The *buying centre* is a concept unique to business buying, and it is founded on the idea that the three roles may be, as they often are, separated and allocated among different personnel. Payers (such as senior management) often play the decider role, while buyers bring vendors and users together for exploring the technical fit. In the *decision process,* users are most active at the need-specification and vendor-screening stages, payers at the decision stage, and buyers throughout for coordinating the entire process. *Conflicts* may arise among users, buyers, or payers, if each of these roles is itself shared among more than one individual. Conflicts may also arise among the three roles. For example, buyers may want to keep certain vendors out of the process, while users may insist on certain preferred vendors. Payers may be driven unduly by price considerations, constraining optimal choices for users.

Government Buying Behaviour

In government procurement, user specifications are extensive in seeking RFPs. Bid evaluation is handled in two independent parts: *technical evaluation* and *price evaluation.* Users play a dominant role in the former while costing experts in the buyer department handle the second part. Each is accountable for his or her part, and, thus, each task is handled more rigorously. The acquisition team itself comes from different departments and, thus, from all three roles. Acquisition reform in the Canadian government will simplify the buying process, raising the dollar threshold for adopting routinized buying procedure, and giving greater authority to user departments for direct purchase. This will simplify the buyer task and also give more flexibility to users who will need less lead time to order. As public concern with government waste rises, payers would have to become more cautious in ensuring judicious use of available budgets.

SUMMARY

We began this chapter with a discussion of the importance and challenge of studying household buying decisions. Principally, these decisions are complex because the user, payer, and buyer roles are shared among different household members. We then defined various types of family and non-family households.

LO 1, 2, 3

The family buying process was described as one in which different members of the family influence various stages of the decision process. Particularly, the relative influence of spouses in joint decision making was described as a muddling-through process. The exact influence of either spouse was determined by such factors as gender roles, wife's employment status, family life cycle, time pressure, importance of purchase, and the socioeconomic development of the relevant population. Children influence parental choices of products and receive influence from parents in their own marketplace preferences. The latter process is captured in the concept of consumer socialization of children.

LO 4

After childhood, the mutual influence of parents and children on each other continues into the children's adult years. This influence in either direction is termed intergenerational influence (IGI). IGI occurs because one generation (whether living in the same or a separate household) controls the household resources for another, has greater expertise than another, or offers a power of identification over the other. Since family buying decisions are shared decisions with different members vying for influence and control, inevitably conflicts occur. We discussed various types of conflicts among the user, payer, and buyer roles. We also discussed four strategies of resolving these conflicts: problem solving, bargaining, persuasion, and politicking.

We then described a general framework for understanding family buying decisions. It views the choice as an outcome of autonomous or joint decision process with or without a conflict occurrence, which is then resolved by one of the four strategies. The decision process is affected by family characteristics, individual characteristics of various family members, the nature of purchase, and sources of information used.

LO 5 In contrast to household buying, the customer behaviour of a business involves greater specialization of customer roles, a more formalized buying process, greater accountability for decisions, more sophisticated internal capabilities, and more complex requirements.

The business buying process has several components: the nature of the purchase, organizational characteristics, a buying centre, rules and procedures, and a decision process. The nature of the purchase is defined by the buyclass (straight re-buy, modified re-buy, or new task), perceived risk, importance, and product complexity, and the time pressure faced by the decision makers. A business customer spends the most time and effort investigating a new task purchase, and/or a purchase that involves relatively great perceived risk, importance, and complexity. In contrast, time pressure will shorten the decision process and increase the impact of the user's input.

Buying behaviour is also affected by four organizational characteristics of the customer: size, structure, purchase resources, and purchase orientation. Small organizations behave more like individuals or households, whereas large organizations use more formalized buying procedures. Structure refers to the number of departments in the organization, where they are located, and how centralized they are. Organizations with many departments in multiple locations engage in more complex buying behaviour. Purchase resources are the organization's professional buyers and ordering equipment. Purchase orientation is the organization's purchasing philosophy, ranging along a continuum from viewing purchasing as an administrative function to viewing it as a strategic function. A purchasing department with a strategic role is more active in the decision-making process.

The buying centre is a multi-function, multi-level internal organization responsible for the centralized purchasing function. Rather than a department or committee, it is a concept, defining the variety of roles involved in a purchase: user, buyer, analyzer, influencer, gatekeeper, and decider. Most businesses set up policies, rules, and procedures that limit the decision criteria and decision process.

Business buying decisions take place in several stages: need assessment, development of choice criteria, request for proposals (RFPs), supplier evaluation, supplier selection, and fulfillment and monitoring. These steps involve more formal analysis than in the typical household buying decision. Total procurement costs, rather than price alone, are an important factor in most business buying decisions. The decision process is primarily driven by buyers' expectations and perceptual distortions. Conflicts are resolved through some combination of problem solving, persuasion, bargaining, and politicking.

LO 6 Government is a major customer in every country. Governments are powerful customers because their orders are large and their power to make and enforce laws gives them substantial control over the buying process. In Canada, the federal government buys through a highly structured process. Marketers to the federal government must operate within the strict guidelines of these procedures. Provincial governments are also sizable customers. Each province has its own guidelines for marketers to learn and follow.

Government procurement and business procurement resemble each other in terms of buyclasses, buying steps, and procurement management goals. However, government buyclasses are called non-developmental, modified non-developmental, and developmental. Also, the government process may be more formal. In other ways, government procurement and business procurement differ. Government purchases tend to be larger and more standardized. They involve more legal restrictions and compliance reviews. Unlike businesses, governments must solicit suppliers widely. Government purchases also involve open access to information, greater diffusion of authority, and more paperwork. Nevertheless, selling to the government offers the advantages of stability, security, size, access to breakthrough R&D work, and a quality-inspiring challenge.

The government's role as customer is undergoing change. Governments are increasingly engaged in downsizing and restructuring, which may include privatization, outsourcing, and acquisition reform.

KEY TERMS

Authoritarian Families 326
Autonomous Decisions 323
Bargaining 350
Business 339
Buyclass 341
Buying Centre 345
Complexity 343
Concept-Oriented Families 326
Consumer Socialization 329
Democratic Families 328
Democratic Justice 332
Family 322
Family Relationship 333
Federal Contractors Program for Employment Equity (FCP) 352
Gender-Role Orientation 324
Government 352
Government Contract Regulations (GCR) 357
Household 322
Importance of Purchase 343
Intergenerational Influence (IGI) 332
Invitation to Tender (ITT) 354
Joint Decisions 232
Modified Re-Buy 342
Neglectful Families 328
New Task 342
Non-Family Household 322
Perceived Risk 343
Permissive Families 328
Persuasion 350
Politicking 350
Problem Solving 350
Public-Private Partnerships (PPPs) 359
Request for Proposal (RFP) 348
Request for Quotation (RFQ) 354
Request for Supply Arrangement (RFSA) 355
Request for Standing Offer (RFSO) 354
Social-Oriented Families 326
Standard Acquisition Clauses and Conditions (SACC) 353
Straight Re-Buy 341
Syncratic Decisions 323
Telephone buy (T-Buy) 354

DISCUSSION QUESTIONS AND EXERCISES

1. As demographic changes occur throughout the world, particularly as customer roles within the family change, marketers must keep abreast of these changes and alter their marketing strategies accordingly. Identify two or three changing customer roles within the family in your own country, and give an example of what marketers ought to do in response to these changes.
2. Conduct an informal interview with a few children between 13 and 17 years old. Ask them how they developed their preferences for their favorite brands of the following products:
    a. Breakfast cereal
    b. Sneakers
    c. Clothing
    d. Restaurants (fast food)

3. Examine ads from one of the following product-marketing companies: breakfast cereals, toys, personal care, home appliances, cooking products, athletic performance products (e.g., sporting goods), and clothing. Determine whether these companies use the concept of IGI, and describe how they do so. If they do not currently use IGI, make a case for whether they should begin to do so, and describe how.
4. When people emigrate to a new country, one of the first things they have to learn is how to go about acquiring the products they need in the unfamiliar, new marketplace. Find three families who have come to Canada from another country and one Canadian-born family. Ask them how they made their decisions about which products and brands to buy. Ask whether they were influenced by their parents' earlier education and socialization in terms of specific customer values. Finally, ask them whether they were influenced by any other agents (e.g., peers, the media) in their choice of certain types of products and specific brands. What differences exist across immigrant families from different countries? What differences exist between immigrant families and native-born families in terms of buying behaviours acquired from parents and from countries of past residence versus behaviours adopted anew in the new country?
5. Assume you are senior vice president of procurement for a large multinational consumer products company. In your attempt to influence others in senior management that your department managers should be given more authority and resources, you bring up the recent notions of "procurement as a core competency" and "global sourcing." What exactly do you discuss with your colleagues?
6. You have recently been hired by the Canadian government to be in charge of procurement for all Canadian embassies abroad. Although you have had enormous experience with procurement in general, your work experience has always been in the business sector, not the government sector. What are some of your concerns about the differences regarding the procurement task in these two contexts? What will you have to keep in mind in terms of the procedural implementation of the tasks in your new job?

NOTES

1 YTV's *Tween Report, Wave 8, 2002,* Special Kidfluence Edition.

2 Chris Powell, "Under the Influence," *Marketing,* February 16, 2004, 109, no. 6, 9.

3 Jagdish N. Sheth, "Models of Buyer Behaviour: Conceptual, Quantitative, and Empirical," in *A Theory of Family Buying Decisions,* 17–33 (New York: Harper & Row).

4 *Ibid.*; Harry L. Davis, "Decision Making Within the Household," *Journal of Consumer Research* 2 (March 1976): 241–60.

5 C. Whan Park, "Joint Decisions in Home Purchasing: A Muddling-Through Process," *Journal of Consumer Research* 9 (September 1982): 151–61.

6 Dennis L. Rosen and Donald H. Granbois, "Determinants of Role Structure in Family Financial Management," *Journal of Consumer Research* 10 (September 1983): 253–58; Charles Schaninger and Chris T. Allen, "Wife's Occupational Status as a Consumer Behaviour Construct," *Journal of Consumer Research* 8 (September 1981): 189–96; Mary Lou Roberts and Lawrence H. Wortzel, "Role Transferral in the Household: A Conceptual Model and Partial Test," *Advances in Consumer Research* 9 (Provo, UT: Association for Consumer Research, 1982): 261–66.

7 http://www.corusmedia.com/ytv/kidfluence/index.asp.

8 Pierre Filiatrault and J. R. Ritchie, "Joint Purchasing Decisions: A Comparison of Influence Structure in Family and Couple Decision Making," *Journal of Consumer Research* 7 (September 1980): 131–40.

9 "How Marketers Target Kids Online," http://www.media-awareness.ca.

10 George P. Moschis, "The Role of Family Communication in Consumer Socialization of Children and Adolescents," *Journal of Consumer Research* 11 (1985): 898–913; George P. Moschis and Gilbert A. Churchill, "Consumer Socialization: A Theoretical and Empirical Analysis," *Journal of Marketing Research* 15 (1978): 599–609; George P. Moschis, A. E. Prahasto, and L. G. Mitchell, "Family Communication Influences on the Development of Consumer Behaviour: Some Additional Findings," in *Advances in Consumer Research* 13, ed. R. J. Lutz, 365–69 (Provo, UT: Association for Consumer Research, 1986).

11 Adapted from Conway Lackman and John M. Lanasa, "Family Decision Making: An Overview and Assessment," *Psychology and Marketing* 12, no. 2 (March–April 1993): 81–93; Les Carlson and Sanford Grossbart, "Parental Style and Consumer Socialization of Children," *Journal of Consumer Research* 15, no. 1 (June 1988): 77–94.

12 Carlson and Grossbart.

13 Moschis and Moore (1982), Bahn (1986); James U. McNeal, "The Littlest Shoppers," *American Demographics* 14, no. 2 (February 1992): 48–53; P. M. Fischer; M. P. Schwartz; J. W. Richards Jr; A. O. Goldstein; T. H. Rojas, "Brand Logo Recognition by Children Aged 3 to 6 Years: Mickey Mouse and Old Joe the Camel," *JAMA* 266 (Dec 1991): 3145–3148.

14 Moschis and Churchill (1978), *Ibid.*

15 Deborah Roedder John, "Consumer Socialization of Children: A Retrospective Look at Twenty-five Years of Research," *Journal of Consumer Research* 26 (December 1999): 183–213.

16 Moschis and Moore; Scott Ward and Daniel Wackman, "Children's Purchase Influence Attempts and Parental Yielding," *Journal of Marketing Research* 9 (August 1972): 316–19; Jan Møller Jensen, "Children's Purchase Requests and Parental Responses: Results from an Exploratory Study in Denmark," in *European Advances in Consumer Behaviour* vol. 2, ed. Flemming Hansen, 61–68 (Provo, UT: Association for Consumer Research, 1995); Les Carlson and Sanford Grossbart, "Parental Style and Consumer Socialization of Children," *Journal of Consumer Research* 15 (1988): 77–94.

17 http://www.corusmedia.com/ytv/kidfluence/index.asp.

18 "Money in the bank for CSB," *Marketing,* Oct. 6–13, 2003, S7.

19 Reshma H. Shah, "Toward a Theory of Intergenerational Influence: A Framework for Assessing the Differential Impact of Varying Sources of Influence on the Preferences and Consumption Values of Adult Children," Unpublished working paper, University of Pittsburgh, 1992.

20 Ruby Roy Dholkia, "Intergenerational Differences in Consumer Behaviour: Some Evidence from a Developing Country," *Journal of Business Research* 12, no. 1 (1984): 19–34; Patricia Sorce, Philip R. Tyler, and Lynette Loomis, "Inter-generational Influence on Consumer Decision Making," *Advances in Consumer Research* 16 (Provo, UT: Association for Consumer Research, 1989): 271–75.

21 Shah (1992); D. Riesman and H. Roseborough, "Careers and Consumer Behaviour," in *Consumer Behaviour, Vol. 2: The Life Cycle and Consumer Behaviour,* ed. L. H. Clark (New York: New York University Press, 1995).

22 Adapted from Reshma H. Shah and Banwari Mittal, "The Role of Intergenerational Influence in Consumer Choice: Toward an Exploratory Theory," in *Advances in Consumer Research,* eds. Merrie Brucks and Debbie MacInnis, 55–60 (Provo, UT: Association for Consumer Research, 1997).

23 Kim P. Corfman and Donald R. Lehmann, "Models of Cooperative Group Decision-Making and Relative Influence: An Experimental Investigation of Family Purchase Decisions," *Journal of Consumer Research* 14 (June 1987): 1–13; Rosann L. Spiro, "Persuasion in Family Decision Making," *Journal of Consumer Research* 10 (March 1983): 393–402.

24 James G. March and Herbert A. Simon, *Organizations* (New York: Wiley, 1958).

25 Jagdish N. Sheth, "A Theory of Family Buying Decisions," in *Insights in Consumer and Market Research,* ed. Paul Pellemans, 32–48 (Namon University Press, 1971).

26 Michel Laroche, Zhiyong Yang, Chankon Kim and Marie-Odile Richard, "How Culture Matters in Children's Purchase Influence: A Multi-Level Investigation," *Journal of the Academy of Marketing Science* (2007, in press).

27 Philip Kotler, *Marketing Management: Analysis, Planning, Implementation, and Control* (Englewood Cliffs, NJ: Prentice-Hall, 1991), 247.

28 Based on research by Erin Anderson, Wujin Chu, and Barton Weitz, "Industrial Purchasing: An Empirical Exploration of the Buyclass Framework," *Journal of Marketing* 51 (July 1987): 71–86.

29 "Purchasing Pros Do Select Suppliers Really," *Purchasing,* April 3, 1997, 22.

30 Jagdish N. Sheth, "A Model of Industrial Buyer Behaviour," *Journal of Marketing* 37 (October 1973): 50–56.

31 Jagdish N. Sheth, "A Model of Industrial Buyer Behaviour," in *Marketing Theory: Classic and Contemporary Readings,* eds. Jagdish N. Sheth and Dennis E. P. Garrett, 539–50 (Cincinnati: South-Western Publishing Co., 1986).

32 Adapted from Jagdish N. Sheth, Robert F. Williams, and Richard M. Hill, "Government and Business Purchasing: How Similar Are They?," *Journal of Purchasing and Materials Management* (Winter 1983): 7–13.

CHAPTER 10

Relationship-Based Buying

LEARNING OBJECTIVES

After reading this chapter you should be able to:

LO 1 Explain the motivations for relationship-based buying.

LO 2 Explain the supplier-customer relationship and the outcome of relationship buying.

LO 3 Describe the IMP models.

LO 4 Explain the determinants of trust and commitment from business customers.

LO 5 Explain relationship-based buying with suppliers.

LO 6 Explain supplier-customer partnering.

LO 7 Relate customer relationship management and the three customer roles.

It's More than Just a "Sale"

The philosophy of sheet steel buying is changing at Ford Motor Co. The company is now focusing on building relationships with a small set of sheet steel suppliers worldwide who will be partners with Ford in initiatives such as continuous improvement programs and e-procurement. To this end, Ford is trying to improve internal organizational processes that help to identify world-class suppliers, order and distribute metal to fabrication sites, and streamline its supply chain. Ford has regional operations in North America, South America, Europe, and Asia—with different material procurements by region. Sheet steel is a key commodity, costing the company almost $3 billion annually, and accounting for 90 percent of the total steel buy at Ford.

Ford's Total Cost Management (TCM) Center already helps sheet steel suppliers adjust to the lean manufacturing systems at Ford, and the Supplier Technical Assistance (STA) personnel provide guidance on product quality issues. In addition to this, Ford buyers are also advising sheet steel suppliers on new levels of expected technical services, product transportation, delivery services, and inventory control.

Cost-cutting is the main goal at Ford, and suppliers who will work with Ford on cost-cutting measures through various initiatives will survive with Ford as partners. Hence, Ford sets quality and productivity targets for suppliers in negotiations to improve efficiency and reduce costs. Ford's online information portal—the Ford Supplier Network (FSN)—sends updates to suppliers on company efforts such as quality, cost avoidance, new-technology implementation, and supplier development. Suppliers can log into the portal using a pre-specified ID and password and access key, purchasing related data and information relevant to their business needs. The site also provides a link to Ford's Lean Resource Center, a comprehensive library and resource service for suppliers. In a few years, the Ford Supplier Network Online site is expected to have 100,000 to 200,000 supplier users from 1,100 production and 500 non-production supplier companies. The online Ford Supplier Network has also helped in developing a global virtual training institute for suppliers called the Ford Supplier Learning Institute (FSLI). Ford is now a part of the Covisint—the automotive industry's Internet based e-procurement marketplace and the FSN site has a hot link for suppliers to access Covisint. Ford has been working to link steel suppliers and buyers online even before it starts buying through Covisint. It is working with Newview, an online steel business-to-business exchange, to streamline its purchase of steel products, and Newview will oversee Ford's order fulfillment, claims, financial controls, and audit reporting across its manufacturing and assembly operations.

Bob Mateer, the global manager of raw materials purchasing for Ford, says "teaching, communicating, and sharing are fundamental principles of supplier relationships at Ford." And that fits with the company's online supplier's guide, which says "Collaboration, not confrontation; teamwork, not make-work; cooperation, not competition—those ideas characterize our guidelines for working with suppliers. Ford firmly believes that these principles form the foundation that will deliver dividends for our suppliers and us." (Tom Stundza, 2001)[1]

Seeking and winning long-term patronage—satisfying a customer rather than merely making a sale—is the objective of relationship marketing as in the Ford example above. In a way, this has always been the goal of marketing *per se*. Relationship marketing has rekindled an awareness of this basic purpose of marketing. Increasingly, marketers are pursuing relationship marketing practices. To do so, however, they must understand relationship marketing from the customers' point of view. That is, why would customers want to engage in relationship-based buying?

In this chapter we examine customers' relationship-based buying behaviour (see Figure 10.1 for our framework). We begin by outlining the value to businesses of relationship-based buying. Next, a model of customers' relationship-based buying behaviour is presented. We discuss certain special determinants of trust and commitment applicable specifically in business markets. We also discuss the practice of nurturing suppliers and the place of such nurturing in relationship buying.

FIGURE 10.1 Conceptual Framework

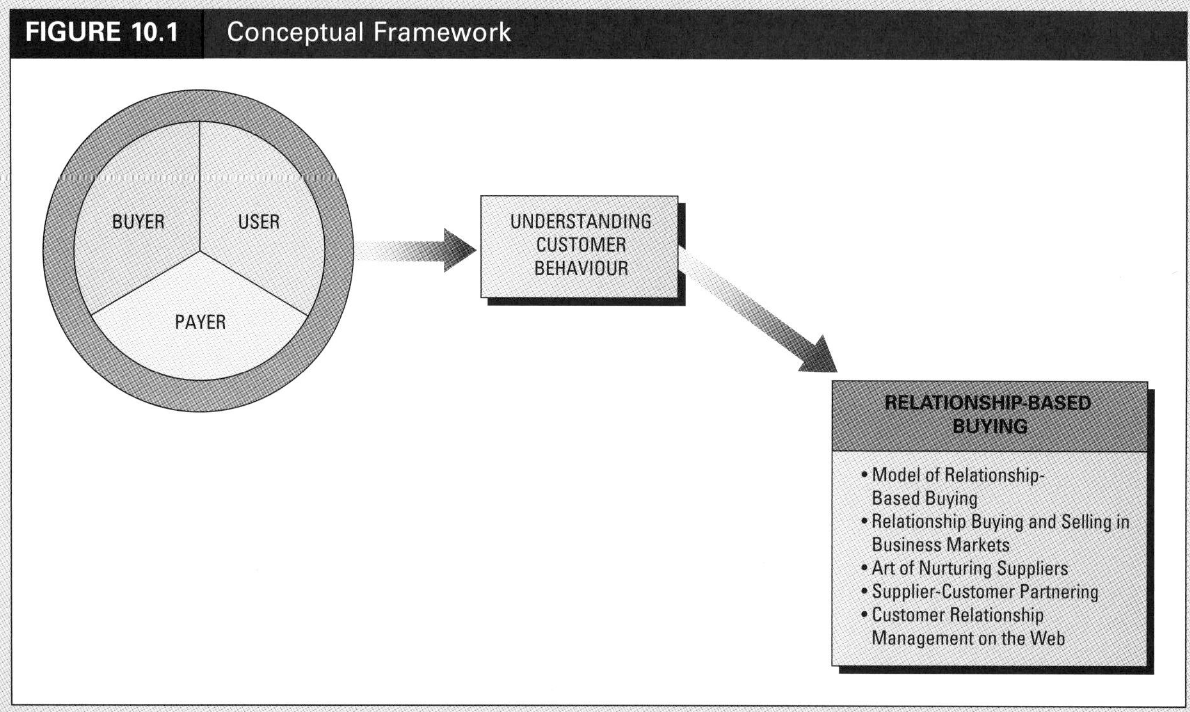

A MODEL OF RELATIONSHIP-BASED BUYING

LO 1

Relationship-based buying
The customer practice of limiting his or her choice to a single supplier.

Customers who engage in the practice of **relationship-based buying** limit their choice to a single supplier and depend on this supplier to handle their needs for a product. Why would customers limit choices and not take advantage of a competitive marketplace with multiple suppliers, attempting to gain the best product at the lowest price? The reason is that exercising choices can be wasteful—it costs time, money, and energy; and there is no guarantee that the alternative supplier is better than the old supplier. As a result, customers are powerfully motivated to voluntarily limit their choice of suppliers.

The model of relationship buying shown in Figure 10.2 summarizes these motivations and the resulting customer behaviour. The model has three sections: (1) antecedents, or the motivations that drive relationship-based buying; (2) the concept of relationships; and (3) the outcomes of the relationship. The two categories of antecedents (cost-benefit factors and sociocultural factors) influence people's decisions about whether to enter into a buying relationship. If such a relationship is characterized by mutual trust and commitment, and leads to positive outcomes, the customer may have such post-purchase attitudes and behaviours as increased buying, loyalty to the supplier, and even willingness to pay more for the supplier's offerings.

CUSTOMER MOTIVATIONS FOR RELATIONSHIP-BASED BUYING

The antecedents in the model are customer motivations for engaging in relationship-based buying. These motivations can be grouped into two broad categories: *cost-benefit factors* and *sociocultural factors*.

Cost-Benefit Factors

When customers make buying decisions, including whether to enter an ongoing relationship with a supplier, they weigh the potential costs and benefits. Jagdish N. Sheth and Atul Parvatiyar have proposed that many of these decisions are driven by the desire to reduce choices.

FIGURE 10.2 A Model of Relationship-Based Buying

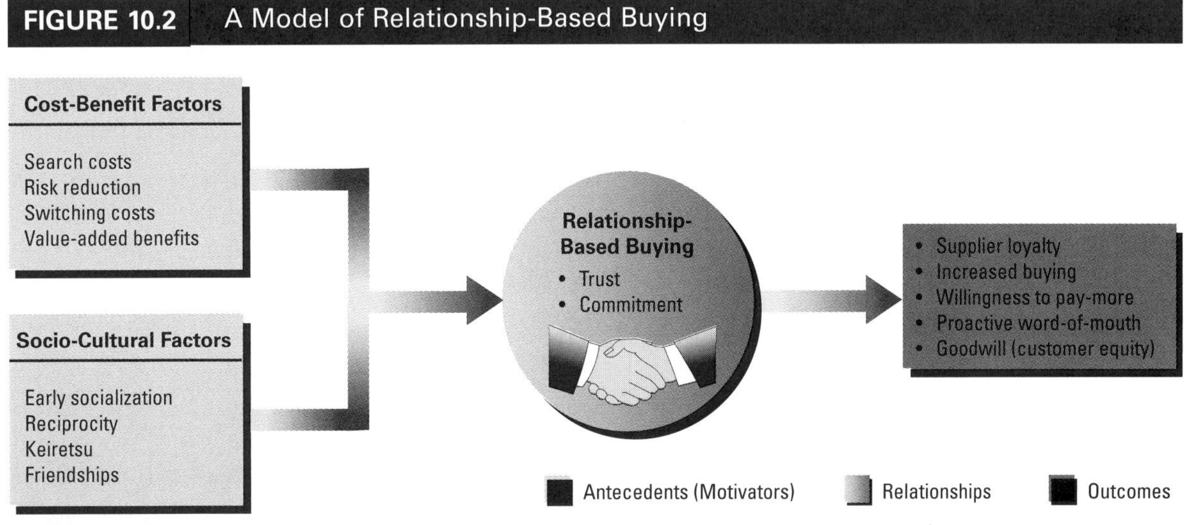

- Customers favour relationship buying when it saves time, effort, and inconvenience, and they avoid considering new choices if doing so will entail extensive search and information processing. Similarly, if a new supplier makes switching easy (as when a credit card company offers to transfer balances), consumers may consider making a change.
- Customers favour relationship buying if they expect positive reinforcement from it.
- Customers favour relationship buying if they perceive that it will help them avoid risk.
- Customers maintain buying relationships if a change involves costs, such as legal penalties or loss of peer-group approval.
- People tend to resist change because change involves effort. Consequently, they maintain buying relationships out of inertia.

In the model in Figure 10.2, the cost-benefit factors that drive decisions about relationship-based buying include the search costs, the perceived risk, the switching costs, and the value-added benefits of the relationship.[2]

Search Costs

The principal cost of breaking free from a relationship with a marketer is the cost of *finding* a new product or supplier. Purchasing is problem solving; customers buy a product to solve a problem. Initially, to find a solution, customers expend the necessary effort. Once they find an acceptable solution, they don't want to exert the effort anew to solve the same problem again and again. As discussed in Chapter 5, problem simplification by routinization of the problem-solving task is a basic consumer motive. Thus, once they identify a product that meets their needs, customers don't want to exert any unnecessary effort.

Perceived Risk

A basic factor in all decisions is the perceived risk, the possibility that the decision may not yield the expected outcomes or may result in negative consequences. Whenever a choice is to be made among alternatives, the magnitude of negative or sub-optimal outcomes and uncertainty as to its likelihood constitute risk. Among the various types of risks (discussed in Chapters 8 and 9), several are particularly relevant:

- *Performance risk*—The product may not do the job it is supposed to do.
- *Financial risk*—The chosen alternative may not be the best-priced alternative.
- *Social risk*—The firm's reputation may be at risk if it chooses a substandard supplier.

When a customer continues to do business with the same firm, these risks are minimized. But if a customer chooses to do business with new suppliers, then risks are likely. These perceived risks tend to motivate customers to stay with their current supplier.

Switching Costs

Switching costs
Costs a customer would have to incur if he or she switched suppliers.

Along with search costs for future suppliers, changing suppliers may generate **switching costs,** costs directly related to switching suppliers. For example, the purchase contract may stipulate termination penalties. In addition, the buyer may not have fully recovered its sunk costs, meaning some costs of writing off investments are not recovered yet. Partner-specific investments, discussed near the end of the chapter, constitute such costs. Finally, getting set up for the new supplier may generate new costs. For example, a change in supplier may entail some retooling of the production process, some retraining of workers, some new software to run the automatic reordering process, etc. Knowledge of these potential switching costs, therefore, serves as a second motivation for staying with the current supplier. Switching costs may be combined with perceived risk to shed light on patterns of relationship-based customer behaviours (see the matrix in Figure 10.3). In each quadrant, the customer purchasing strategies are different, so marketer strategies also ought to be different in order to retain the customer's repatronage.

When both switching costs and perceived risk are low, the customer prefers transactional exchange. As in the case of most supermarket items, switching to a different brand does not entail extensive information search, and the investment is low. The customer is mainly interested in lower prices, tends to engage in opportunistic buying, and has no stake in continued repatronage. Indeed, his or her preference may be for a *transactional exchange*. To increase the risk of switching, the marketer could offer some extra value (for example, better service), thus differentiating his or her offering from competitors. A supermarket could differentiate itself, for example, by offering delivery to a customer's car.

The combination of high risk and low switching costs exists in the purchase of, for example, a cruise tour. There is a high risk that the chosen cruise may be unsatisfactory, but switching to a new cruise company has no costs. Because the untried alternatives are deemed to be risky, the customer is motivated to maintain continued patronage; at the same time, however, she or he is open to switching (since there are no switching costs) if a reputable competitor offers substantial cost savings. Thus, the customer is in a *vulnerable relationship* with the current supplier. To increase loyalty, the marketer (current seller) should reinforce the product's proven quality and performance.

High switching costs plus no perceived risk combine in the case of airlines that offer frequent-flyer benefits. You can buy your travel on any airline (they are all about equal in safety and other features, so there is no risk); but you may not be able to cash in mileage awards unless you accumulate enough of them. In this case, the customer is constrained in the present relationship. Current sellers must ensure continued customer satisfaction. They may also strive to further deepen the customer's investments or stakes in the present relationship, for example, by increasing the rewards for continued patronage.

The strongest barriers to customers switching their patronage arise when switching costs and perceived risk are both high. Here the customer is in relational buying. Customers are so strongly motivated to maintain a relationship with their present supplier that they may wish to iron out problems rather than switch, unless the present suppliers ignore their satisfaction level and remain unresponsive to changing customer needs or to complaints about product failures. Marketer strategies should focus on continued quality maintenance and on a positive complaint-response system.

FIGURE 10.3 Combinations of Perceived Risk and Switching Costs

Switching Costs		Perceived Risk of Alternatives: Low	Perceived Risk of Alternatives: High
	High	Constrained in relationship	Relational buying
	Low	Transactional exchange	Vulnerable relationship

Value-Added Benefits

When you buy repeatedly from a supplier or marketer, you treat that supplier as a preferred supplier. In turn, to retain you as a customer, the supplier tends to treat you as a preferred customer. For example, many hotels and car rental agencies have instituted a frequent-guest program. When you become a member of these programs, the hotel or car rental agency is happy to upgrade you to a better room or a bigger car without any extra charge.

For business customers, firms differentiate themselves on the basis of added benefits, especially when the core product remains the same. For example, all suppliers may offer the same product at the same price; however, a firm may customize a financing plan for you, or it may customize the way it does business with you. These added benefits, obtainable from a firm only if there is assurance of repeat business, serve as a motivation for customers to engage in relationship-based buying.

Sociocultural Factors

As seen in previous chapters, buying decisions are not purely rational economic decisions based on objective data. For example, a person's culture, business, and personal relationships influence buying decisions. For example, in some cultures such as Latin America, Asia, and Eastern Europe, establishing a personal relationship is often a prelude and a prerequisite to doing business with anyone. (See the Window on Practice box about building relationships in Russia.) With regard to relationship-based buying, the sociocultural factors that influence the formation of a customer relationship include *socialization, reciprocity, networks*, and *friendships*.

Early Socialization

One reason why customers choose to engage in relationship-based buying is that they are socialized into it from the time they first begin to use that product. As individual customers, many of the choices we learn during childhood socialization (Chapter 9) result from behavioural patterns picked up from role models such as parents and other family members. Many of our choices of brands, products, and suppliers are based on our observations of our families.

As business customers, too, we learn our choices early from what the organization and other role models in it are using. As our supervisor grooms us in our job, we learn from him or her which document delivery service to use; which restaurants to use when entertaining a specific category of client; and which attorneys, auditors, and consultants to hire when we need their services. These role models implicitly validate the quality and risk-free character of these socialization-based choices. Hence, continuing with these choices appears to be a safe practice.

Reciprocity

Reciprocity
The customer practice of buying from a supplier because he or she (the supplier) in turn buys something else from the customer.

In some cases, a customer buys from a particular supplier because the supplier in turn buys something from the customer. This practice is called **reciprocity**—the basis of barter trade. Even today, a number of market exchanges occur on this basis. For example, employees patronize the company they work for; for example, General Electric (GE) employees tend to buy GE appliances. Among business-to-business customers, reciprocal buying is equally prevalent.

Networks

Networks are a group of firms that deal with each other on a preferential basis. The firms are linked into the network either by common ownership (such as Mitsubishi Industries) or by contractual arrangement. *Keiretsu* is a Japanese term for such networks, and this is a prevalent business practice in Japan. The firms in *keiretsu* enjoy a lifetime of relationships when there is a mutual understanding that each company will receive orders from the other for its lifetime. For example, in a study of suppliers of U.S. and Japanese automakers, Japanese suppliers reported that they had a 92 percent chance of re-winning the business when their car models changed; in contrast, U.S. automakers' suppliers believed that their chance of re-winning was only 69 percent. In this climate of close-knit supplier-customer networks, it is very difficult for outside suppliers to break in, as has been the experience of many North American and European companies trying to get a foothold in Japan.

Networks
A group of firms that deal with each other on a preferential basis.

Similar networks are being established in other business markets. The very idea of supplier partnership is one of building *keiretsu*-style arrangements. For example, in North America, the ChryslerDaimler Corporation now gives most of its suppliers business for the life of the car model. That way, instead of worrying about bidding and winning on the next year's business, suppliers can work toward cost reduction and can share in the resulting savings. This pattern of relationships and the benefits that accrue from it is another way in which customers are strongly motivated to engage in relationship-based buying.[3]

WINDOW ON **PRACTICE**

Getting to Know You: Building Relationships in Russia

H. Ned Seelye and Alan Seelye-James narrate this case story about the importance of relationships: In the aftermath of perestroika, a British engineering firm struck a deal with the Russians to support them in a plant start-up. To staff this project, the firm appointed two Britons, Diana and Horace, who would use interpreters. In the remaining slot of a site consulting engineer's position, Nigel Johnson was appointed. Johnson was a brilliant engineer, plus he spoke Russian fluently. His only drawback was that he was dark, short, and young. This conflicted with Russians' expectations that consultants are tall, light-skinned, and have grey hair and wrinkled faces, reflecting years of experience and wisdom. A middle-aged British colleague had warned him that there may be a problem.When Johnson arrived at the plant, he gathered plant managers and supervisors and spent the whole morning talking to them, not at all about engineering and the plant, but rather about himself and his family, asking his audience about their families and answering their questions about life in England and other matters, related to the business at hand or not. This perplexed Johnson's own supervisor, who admonished Johnson not to waste any more time in non-business talk. Johnson paid no heed and continued with the relaxed pace and informal conversations for the next few days. Then, Johnson was asked into a meeting with the Russian managers and supervisors, and his advice was sought on a particular problem. Although the plant director did not agree with all of his advice, the director let it be known that he was happy to have Johnson help them.

What to Johnson's supervisor was a waste of time was, in fact, time well invested in establishing relationships. In countries and cultures such as Russia, relationships are a prelude to doing any business at all. Business customers in such relationship-oriented cultures want to spend time with you in social and informal situations and assess your character in order to judge your trustworthiness. Without trustworthiness, they will do no business with you. In such customer cultures, a seller who gets right down to business would likely scare off more than a few customers.

SOURCE: Adapted from Seelye, H. Ned, and Alan Seelye-James. *Culture Clash: Managing in a Multicultural World.* Lincolnwood, IL: NTC Business Books, 1995. Reproduced with the permission of McGraw-Hill Education.

Buying Based on Friendship

Many purchases are made on the basis of friendship. Thus, if your neighbour or friend is an insurance agent, you are likely to buy your insurance from him or her. If your friend is an Avon salesperson, you are going to patronize her for all your cosmetics. Similarly, in business markets, many customers are obtained by referral from friends. Lunch meetings of professional associations are primarily intended to expand a person's network of prospective customers. In many cultures, business is done strictly on the basis of friendship.

Ingmar Bjorkman and Soren Kock have studied business buying practices in China. Much business buying, especially of large contracts with foreign firms, occurs within the friendship and social networks called *guanxi*. These differ from business networks in that the latter are concerned with relationships between organizations. *Guanxi*, the networks of individuals based on social exchange, are key to gaining access to both initial information about a prospective buyer's needs and also to subsequent decision-making units (DMUs) and their influencers. Buying decisions based on friendships and social networks are literal instances of relationship-based buying.[4] The Window on Research provides more information on *guanxi*.

WINDOW ON RESEARCH

Mapping Relationships: *Guanxi* in China

Guanxi defines the concept of "relationship" in China. It is defined as "pre-existing relationships of classmates, people from the same native-place, relatives, superior and subordinate in the same workplace, and so forth." It involves a hierarchically structured network of relationships embedded with mutual obligations through a self-conscious manipulation of "face, *renqing* (favour) and related symbols." The basis of *guanxi* is the concept of obligation. One is expected to oblige friends, relatives, and people from the same native-place, and failure to oblige brings shame on the person and his family. The concept of "face" is defined as "the process by which one gains and maintains status and moral reputation." If you do not fulfill your obligations, you "get dirt on your face," while if you meet your obligations, you "put gold on your face." The word "*renqing*" means "a resource allocated to another person as a gift" and also connotes a set of social norms to guide an individual to get along well with other people.

Business alliances in China are structured as *guanxi* networks. Organizations that are part of a *guanxi* network cooperate with each other on different areas, are very close to each other, and defend other members of the network. Marketers need to be cognizant of the fact that business alliances in China are driven by personal relationships. Research shows that *guanxi* can be represented as a set of four insider-outsider psychological processes, namely *testing, trial, teaming*, and *trust*.

In the testing quadrant, each party considers the other party an outsider, and tests the other party's intentions or reactions. In the trial quadrant, each party evaluates its position in terms of its dependence on the other party and the degree of trust in the other party, and bargains from this position of power. When a strong *guanxi* relationship exists between parties, these two initial quadrants are skipped, and parties directly work from the teaming quadrant and then move to the trust quadrant.

In dealing with Chinese business partners, time taken to build relationships will be directly proportional to the time taken to traverse through these quadrants. If you begin the relationship as an outsider, you will need to go through the four quadrants, but if you are considered an insider, it is relatively easier to build relationships.

The implementation and effectiveness of guanxi can also be explained through six dimensions involving a harmonious combination of "mind" and "heart" (the yin-yang harmony). Contact, conflict, and compromise are the three dimensions of the "mind" approach. Contact to build relationships requires time. Conflict is avoided via *renqing* (favour). Compromise is a mutual adaptive behaviour.

Centrality, convergence, and creativity are the three dimensions of the "heart" approach. Centrality in relationships makes Chinese treat foreigners as outsiders. Convergence of yin and yang thinking is necessary to understand Chinese business people. Creativity, in this sense, is knowing the best time to deal with aggressors in a relationship.

Guanxi is a manifestation of Chinese culture, traditions and social organization, and doing business in China requires an understanding of *guanxi*. It is evident that building relationships in China takes time, but the concept of *guanxi* ensures that they will be long-lasting.

SOURCE: Adapted from Wong, Y. H., and Jackie L. M. Tam. "Mapping Relationships in China: Guanxi Dynamic Approach." *Journal of Business and Industrial Marketing* 15, no. 1 (2000). http://www.emerald-library.com; Simmons, Lee C. "Is Relationship Marketing Culturally Bound: A Look at *Guanxi* in China." *Advances in Consumer Research* 23 (Provo, UT: Association for Consumer Research, 1996): 92–96. http://www.acrweb.org.

THE SUPPLIER-CUSTOMER RELATIONSHIP

LO 2

Trust and commitment are the twin legs of relationship-based buying. For a customer to be engaged in relationship-based buying at all, the customer has to trust the marketer and then make a commitment to the marketer.

Trust

The most essential ingredient in any relationship, whether a business or a social relationship, is trust. It is also a key arbitrator of commitment. If there is no trust, there will be no commitment.

TABLE 10.1 Trust and Commitment: Various Definitions

Trust

- We conceptualize trust as existing when one party has confidence in an exchange partner's reliability and integrity (Morgan and Hunt, 1994).
- Trust is defined as a willingness to rely on an exchange partner in whom one has confidence (Moorman, Deshpande, and Zaltman, 1993).
- [Trust is] a generalized expectancy held by an individual that the word of another can be relied on (Rotter, 1980).
- The firm's belief that another company will perform actions that will result in positive outcomes for the firm, and will not take unexpected actions that result in negative outcomes (Anderson and Narus, 1990).

Commitment

- The exchange partner's belief that an ongoing relationship with another is so important as to warrant making a maximum effort to maintain it. That is, the committed party believes that the relationship is worth working on to ensure that it endures indefinitely (Morgan and Hunt, 1994).
- An enduring desire to maintain a valued relationship (Moorman, Zaltman, and Deshpande, 1992).

SOURCES: Morgan, Robert M., and Shelby D. Hunt. "The Commitment-Trust Theory of Relationship Marketing." *Journal of Marketing* 58 (July 1994): 20–38; Moorman, Christine, Gerald Zaltman, and Rohit Deshpande. "Relationships Between Providers and Users of Market Research: The Dynamics of Trust Within and Between Organizations." *Journal of Marketing Research* 29 (August 1992): 314–38; Moorman, Christine, Rohit Deshpande, and Gerald Zaltman. "Factors Affecting Trust in Market Research Relationships." *Journal of Marketing* 57 (January 1993) 81–101; Anderson, James C., and James A. Narus. "A Model of Distributor Firm and Manufacturer Firm Working Partnership." *Journal of Marketing* 54 (Spring 1990): 42–58; Rotter, J. B., "Interpersonal Trust, Trustworthiness, and Gullibility." *American Psychologist* 35 (1980): 1–7.

Trust
A willingness to rely on the ability, integrity, and motivation of the other party to act in the best interests of the trusting party.

Marketing scholars have recognized trust to be so important a building block that they have attempted to define and describe it. (For various definitions, see Table 10.1). We extract and adapt from these a common-denominator definition: **Trust** is a willingness to rely on the ability, integrity, and motivation of the other party to act to serve one's needs and interests as agreed upon implicitly or explicitly. Several elements of this definition are noteworthy:

- The person with trust is willing to rely on and act upon the confidence that comes with trust.
- Trust concerns all three aspects of a partner's characteristics: ability, integrity, and motivation. Thus, you judge the partner to be competent to carry out his or her obligations and to serve you. Second, you judge the partner to have integrity; you can believe in the partner's word. Finally, you believe the partner has the motivation not to act against your interests; the partner appreciates the stakes involved in the relationship, and will behave rationally.
- The trusted person will look after both parties' needs and interests, not his or her needs and interests alone.
- The partner's behaviours will comply with mutual expectations, both explicit (as stipulated in a contract, for example) and implicit. That is, the partner's behaviours will go beyond the mere letter of the contract; she or he will also honor the spirit of the agreement.[5]

Commitment

Commitment
An enduring desire to continue a relationship, and to work to ensure its continuance.

Long-term customer relationships are also characterized by **commitment**, that is, *an enduring desire to continue the relationship, and to work to ensure its continuance.*[6] In household markets, for example, a customer who is committed to his or her long-distance phone service supplier would not switch suppliers just to gain a temporary price deal. In business markets, commitment is not merely the carrying out of certain contractual obligations (such as a reseller displaying the product according to the manufacturer's written requirements); rather, it requires making every effort to promote the partner's business. The commitment manifests in cooperative behaviours, but it goes beyond individual acts of cooperation. It refers to a mind-set of pledging to do nothing that would harm the relationship and doing everything needed to nurture it.

OUTCOMES OF RELATIONSHIP-BASED BUYING

As Figure 10.2 shows, the outcomes of successful relationship-based buying are supplier loyalty, increased buying, willingness to pay more, proactive word of mouth, and customer equity or goodwill. The most direct outcome of relationship-based buying is supplier loyalty: customers prefer this supplier and consistently buy from the same supplier.

Initially, customers may engage in relational buying with a particular supplier for a specific product; with the relationship well founded, however, customers may progress to buying more of the same product from the supplier, and then to buying other products from the supplier as well. Cross-selling is a practice wherein salespeople try to sell other lines of the company's products to the customers of a specific product. For example, an advertising agency that has been developing creative work for a business client may, after a few years, also solicit and obtain media buying work from the client. Moreover, preference for the relational supplier grows, so that customers begin to perceive substantial superiority in this supplier's offering. Eventually, many customers become willing to pay a premium price for the supplier's products.

Proactive word of mouth also increases. Word of mouth is an outcome when customers are satisfied. But, with relational buying, such positive word of mouth acquires a more proactive character because the positive supplier experience is repeated often in frequent re-purchase encounters. Finally, suppliers that keep a customer satisfied enough to receive his or her relational buying acquire **customer equity** or **goodwill**, customer support for the supplier's well-being. These are the positive outcomes that flow to the firm from relational buying by its customers.

Customer equity (goodwill) Customer support for a supplier's well-being.

RELATIONSHIP BUYING AND SELLING IN BUSINESS MARKETS

Business customers tend to place larger orders than individual consumers do. This makes customer relationships especially important in business markets. However, the historical model of purchasing by business organizations has been transaction-oriented, with each purchase being a disjointed transaction, without regard to those that preceded it or those that would follow it. Meanwhile, the goal of buyers has been to ensure that a source of supply will be available. Now this buying practice is changing in many forward-looking organizations toward relationship-based buying.

The model of buyer behaviour described in Chapter 9 focuses on a *discrete* purchase. That model helps us understand things like how buying centres choose suppliers, what information they process, and how their members interact and make joint decisions. Because that model focuses on the decision-making processes that lead up to a single purchase event, it needs to be supplemented by an understanding of the *long-term relationships* that develop between buyers and sellers. It is not unusual for a business buyer to purchase from the same supplier firm for 5 or 10 years. When this happens, a relationship develops. The dynamics of relationship building and maintenance brings into the picture certain other variables and factors that marketers need to understand.

PROCESS OF RELATIONSHIP BUYING: THE IMP MODEL

LO 3

A few years ago, a group of European researchers studied the buying process in business organizations. The group, called the Industrial Marketing and Purchasing (IMP) group, used case studies of business buying. On the basis of case studies of some 300 companies in five European countries, the IMP group established that *long-term* patronage is quite common in business buying. Organizational buying entails interactions at the individual, departmental, and company levels. They sought to study, therefore, a relational model of buying: a model that describes the processes or steps in the development of relationships in a series of interactions.[7]

Characteristics of Relational Buying

The IMP model has identified three key factors that characterize all relational buying by business customers:

Transaction-specific investments (TSIs) Any special equipment or technology or human resources that need to be dedicated to meeting the needs of a particular customer/supplier partner.

Power dependence The relative dependence of one party on the other because of the resources the other party possesses.

Asymmetrical power One party has more power over the other.

Role formalness The degree to which interactions between the supplier and customer are limited to the formal roles of the parties.

1. *Transaction-specific investments/adaptations*—Any special equipment, technology, or human resources that need to be obtained and dedicated or set aside only for meeting the needs of a particular customer/supplier partner. Similarly, adaptations mean any specific changes a firm needs to make to accommodate the other partner.
2. *Power dependence*—The relative dependence of one party on the other because of the resources the other party possesses. If the customer is going to finance the suppliers' production equipment or R&D work, for example, then the supplier develops a dependency relationship with the customer. On the other hand, if the supplier is going to provide training and technical assistance, then the supplier has the power, and the customer becomes dependent. Often the power between the two parties is balanced, in that each has a resource the other values. However, when one party depends more on the other than the converse (such as when there is a monopolistic supplier), the power dependence is *asymmetrical*.
3. *Role formalness*—The degree to which the interactions between the supplier and customer are close and personal or, instead, limited to the formal roles of the parties.

These three variables define the character of supplier-customer relationships. Thus, a relationship may be marked by few or extensive dedicated investments, symmetrical or asymmetrical power dependence, and close-personal or role-formal interactions.

Steps in Relationship Development

Based on the case studies of business buyers and sellers, the IMP group also identified the steps that companies go through in building a relationship. These comprise need complementarity, interactions/exchanges, outcomes, satisfaction, investment, and commitment.

1. *Needs Complementarity*—First, the parties mutually recognize that each depends on the other for resources it does not have.
2. *Interactions*—Repeated personal contacts or repeated interactions/exchanges serve to build and further the relationship.
3. *Outcomes and Satisfaction*—These interactions result in business and social outcomes. If these outcomes generate satisfaction, then the parties choose to make transaction-specific investments.
4. *Investments*—When dedicated to the other party, investments signify faith that the other party will reciprocate.
5. *Commitment*—With investments, especially when they are reciprocal, commitment to the other partner deepens, and, consequently, the relationship-buying process is perpetuated.

Among business firms, the relationship progresses from initial trial exchange to commitment. The buyer realizes that the vendor has the unique skills and capability to produce the product it needs, and the vendor realizes that the buyer assures a market for its special skills. With the trial purchase, both are satisfied. To produce the product in quantities required by the buyer, the seller would then need to invest in additional equipment; and the buyer would have to place an engineer at the seller's factory to assist in the setup of quality control processes. Each decides to invest, and with this dedicated investment, the commitment of each deepens the relationship.

REASONS FOR RELATIONSHIP DEVELOPMENT IN BUSINESS BUYING

In addition to the motivations for relationship-based buying described earlier, business customers may also have a few special reasons for relationship-based buying. First, businesses may need a long-term exchange contract to ensure long-term supply, and this implies relationship buying. This is helpful generally when the product is crucial to a customer's production processes or other operations, and an ongoing supply is critical.

Business customers also want to reduce the cost of buying transactions, particularly such activities as inventory monitoring and order placement, so they transfer this task to the seller organization. This requires the two parties to invest in automated ordering and order-fulfilling systems, and to link each others' computers and information systems. Assumption of such responsibility requires a long-term commitment to the relationship. Buyers and sellers may also have quality and cost goals that require collaboration. The buyers and suppliers can pursue these goals jointly much more effectively than each party acting alone. Such joint pursuit requires relationship buying.

A related factor is the need to form an alliance, or pool resources, to jointly develop the future product, in order to nurture the supplier. Sometimes, customers desire more than improved quality and cost reduction; they desire new-product development and innovation. Suppliers would be unwilling to invest in R&D work unless assured of a long-term buying commitment. (See the Window on Practice box for details on how the auto industry has been applying these principles.)

DETERMINANTS OF TRUST AND COMMITMENT FROM BUSINESS CUSTOMERS

LO 4

Some factors that cause and sustain relationship commitment and trust are specific to business markets. These factors, listed in the left column of Table 10.2, are switching costs, partner-specific investments, mutually shared goals, communication and product support, and avoidance of opportunistic behaviour. Of these, switching costs have already been discussed. The remaining factors are described below.[8]

TABLE 10.2 Determinants of Trust and Commitment in Business Relationships

Determinants for the Customer	Determinants for the Supplier
Switching costs	Supplier-specific investments
Partner-specific investments	Customer avoidance of opportunistic behaviour
Mutually shared goals	Single-source policy
Communication and product support	Data sharing and nurturance
Supplier avoidance of opportunistic behaviour	

WINDOW ON **PRACTICE**

Successful Relationship Buying at Toyota

In October 2000, *Fortune* published its annual rating of the most admired carmakers in the world. Toyota was ranked first in the list, which included 14 manufacturers such as Ford and General Motors. Much of Toyota's success in the U.S. and other world markets can be attributed directly to the synergistic performance of its policies in human resources management and supply-chain networks. Supply chain relationships among Asian manufacturers are based on a complex system of co-operation and equity interests. Some Asian manufacturers, such as Toyota, have been able to transcend western cultural and institutional barriers and superimpose Asian models of supply chain management and cooperation elsewhere. The company's sustained competitive advantage in the car industry in large measure is directly attributable to the precision with which Toyota has been able to schedule and coordinate the activities of its network of 300 components suppliers. Toyota has a world-class network of suppliers in both Japan and North America, and a highly efficient and effective just-in-time (JIT) inventory system that is heavily dependent upon the coordination of its supplier network. Toyota also nurtures its suppliers by providing in-depth support when they have severe problems and, if needed, Toyota technical personnel are sent to supplier plants to help them overcome serious issues.

SOURCE: Adapted from Reza Vaghefi, Louis Woods, and Michael N. DaPrile. "Creating Sustainable Competitive Advantage: The Toyota Philosophy and its Effects." *Financial Times*, FT.com, September 5, 2002.

Partner-Specific Investments

Partner-specific investments Investments that one party makes on processes dedicated to the other party.

The parties build and sustain relationships when they make **partner-specific investments**, that is, investments that one party makes in processes dedicated to the other party. Suppose that the use of a new material requires some investment in R&D and/or process equipment; that investment may be made by the supplier or jointly by the two partners. The developmental outcome will be useful only for the customer involved, thus making it a partner-specific investment. Even if the supplier alone shoulders the investment, this exhibits the supplier's commitment, which, in turn, will bring forth the customer's commitment. In many cases, the customer bears the capital costs in equipment dedicated to doing business with the particular supplier. For example, Wal-Mart installed computer systems networked to Procter & Gamble's order receiving and delivery system. These investments build customer trust in suppliers and their commitment to the relationship.

Mutual Goals

Mutual goals Those goals that require each exchange partner's cooperation and by whose achievement each partner profits.

Long-term relationships are also strengthened by **mutual goals**, or goals that require each exchange partner's cooperation and through whose achievement each partner profits. For example, if a supplier succeeds in developing a new material that would improve the customer's end-product, it may increase the customer's market share in the end-user market. If the customer's sales increase, the supplier's sales will increase in turn. This then is a mutual goal that will profit both the partners. Consequently, both the partners should be committed to working toward the accomplishment of that goal.

Communication and Product Support

If there is open communication, then the customer acquires more knowledge about the supplier activities and knows that the supplier is not secretive. In communicating openly, the supplier confides in the customer. The customer responds by extending the same confidence and trust. In the same vein, the more product support the supplier offers, the more the customer sees supplier behaviour that is helpful to the customer. This too strengthens the customer's trust.

Avoidance of Opportunistic Behaviour

To cultivate an ongoing relationship, the supplier must avoid engaging in opportunistic behaviour. Opportunistic behaviour concerns unilateral acts whereby the supplier profits from opportunities that may arise and that were not stipulated in the contract. Suppose, for example, in developing a particular new material for the customer (with customer-financed R&D work), the supplier's R&D personnel come across a spinoff byproduct that will be independently commercially profitable. If the supplier were to transfer some of the customer-financed R&D resources to getting this spinoff byproduct market-ready, and if the supplier were not to discuss this with the customer, this would constitute opportunistic behaviour. Trust and relationships require that the plans for profiting from opportunities be shared. Worse will be the case when one partner takes the opportunity to profit at another's cost (i.e., even when the act would harm the partner's interests).

DETERMINANTS OF SUPPLIER TRUST IN CUSTOMERS

Suppliers also need to trust their customers. If they believe that their customers have no commitment to them and that they (the customers) would themselves engage in opportunistic buying, then suppliers would not have any trust in customers. Consequently, suppliers will not be committed to the relationship. The factors for supplier trust in the customer are similar to the factors for customer trust in the supplier. Some of these factors are the same; others are somewhat different. These are listed in the right column of Table 10.2. Two of the factors have already been discussed; these are supplier-specific investments and nonopportunistic behaviour. The other two are single-source policies and data sharing and nurturance.

Perhaps the most important factor is *single-source policy*. If the customer is constantly looking for new suppliers, then the supplier would not trust the customer, especially if the supplier needs to make investments to offer better value to the customer. To engender supplier trust, the customer should seek to rationalize the procurement policies, realizing the benefits of dealing with fewer, rather than more, suppliers. Relying on a single supplier often necessitates mutual nurturance. Particularly if the customer is more resourceful than the supplier, the customer may have to provide developmental support to the supplier. Or, if no one can meet the customer's requirement at present, the customer may have to induce and assist a potential supplier to become one. This is an instance of "nurturing suppliers," discussed in the next section.

Along with providing general nurturance, customers need to share their internal data with suppliers in order for suppliers to make long-term plans. For example, customers need to involve suppliers in their own long-term plans so that suppliers can, in turn, adjust their own production capabilities to meet the future needs of customers. If customers are secretive about their long-term plans, then the suppliers would suspect that the customer is planning to switch suppliers or is developing other suppliers.

Thus, trust is a two-way street. Trust begets trust. In relationship buying, each party has to engage in trust-building behaviours, and each has to seek and motivate similar behaviours in the other. Each has to make investments specific to the other partner. The roles of mutual trust, investment, and interdependence have been highlighted in a number of studies, as the Window on Research box shows.

LO 5 RELATIONSHIP-BASED BUYING: THE ART OF NURTURING SUPPLIERS

The mutuality of goals and behaviours makes a long-term exchange relationship more bi-directional. Often the distinction between who is the buyer and who is the supplier is blurred. One party may have to market itself more than the other. Sometimes the marketer may be the customer, marketing itself to the supplier.

One of the key determinants of a firm's profitability is how well the firm is able to procure its inputs. In *Competitive Strategy*, Michael Porter has suggested that a firm's bargaining power with its suppliers is one of the four forces that determine the firm's profitability and performance. The other forces are threat of new entrants, rivalry among the existing firms, and threat of substitute products. Thus, organizations that can establish and maintain mutually cooperative relationships with suppliers are better positioned in a competitive marketplace.

To have good suppliers is to be blessed with good resources. A firm needs suppliers that can produce the product to the high-quality requirements that its own internal standards require. It needs suppliers that can constantly bring down costs, will continuously innovate, will grow as the customer firm's needs grow, and will be ready to change when the customer's needs change. For example, Dofasco, a supplier of steel to the automotive industry, launched in 1997 North America's "body-in-white" initiative. The stripped-down shell of a major automotive customer's best-selling vehicle was purchased for the purpose of showing the car manufacturer how new steel technology could reduce weight, cut costs, and strengthen overall design. This program resulted in improved strength, a 25 percent reduction in weight, and a three percent lower production cost. Dofasco's "body-in-white" program began a new trend that has since become an industry standard. When a high-caliber supplier does not exist, the customer firm must develop, maintain, and motivate suppliers, current or prospective, to set themselves up as long-term suppliers.

WINDOW ON **RESEARCH**

Nurturing a Buyer-Seller Relationship

Many scholars have studied the factors that help nurture relationships between buyers and sellers. A study conducted by Shankar Ganesan surveyed 124 retail buyers responsible for buying the merchandise for their stores, ranging from men's and women's clothing, to jewellery, silverware, and perfume. He also surveyed 52 vendors from whom the surveyed retail-store buyers bought the merchandise. The purpose was to verify whether certain factors hypothesized in the relationship-marketing literature were or were not helpful in the development of buyer-seller relationships. Of the 124 retailer buyers, 76 (61 percent) were asked to answer questions with respect to a vendor with whom they had a long-term relationship, and 48 (39 percent) with respect to vendors with whom they had a short-term relationship. All respondents were questioned on such factors as the buyer firm's trust in the vendor, its dependence on the vendor, its perception of the vendor's dependence on the retailer, transaction-specific investments (TSIs) by the retailer, perception of vendor TSIs, the reputation of the vendor, and satisfaction with the past outcomes.

The data showed that the retailer's long-term orientation in its dealings with the vendor were positively influenced by the vendor's credibility and trustworthiness, and by the extent to which the retailer was dependent on the vendor; however, if the vendor firm itself was perceived to be dependent on the retailer, then the retailer tended to adopt a short-term orientation. These factors were, in turn, affected by TSIs by both parties. Specifically, trustworthiness was positively influenced by the vendor's reputation and the TSIs made by the vendor. And, the retailer's dependence on the vendor was positively influenced both by the TSIs made by the retailer firm itself and by the vendor.

Many of these same results were mirrored in the data from vendors. For example, in order to adopt a long-term orientation in their dealings with the retailer firm, vendors needed to perceive the retailer to be trustworthy, and also perceive each party to be dependent on the other. Moreover, the retailer was seen to be dependent on the vendor if it (the vendor) had made some TSIs. Vendors were also likely to trust the retailers more if they (the retailers) made some TSIs. The TSIs by the retailer included investments in displays, salesperson training, and the time and effort in learning about the vendor's method of operation. Correspondingly, TSIs by the vendor included support to the retailer in display materials, in the training of salespeople, and in acquiring knowledge about the retailer's operations.

SOURCE: Adapted from Ganesan, Shankar. "Determinants of Long-Term Orientation in Buyer-Seller Relationships." *Journal of Marketing* 58, no. 2 1–19. http://www.marketingjournals.org/jm/.

NURTURING THE SUPPLIER

That is the challenge that McDonald's faced when it entered the Russian market in the late 1980s. McDonald's works on the principle of short supply meaning having everything to hand. In Russia, the fast-food giant had to contend with the then Soviet Union's erratic, centralized supply doctrine. Russia was often plagued by shortages and in some cases ingredients, such as iceberg lettuce, did not exist in the country. Faced with this challenge, McDonald's built the McComplex, in a joint venture with the Moscow city council. The company was the only party capable of providing the investment required to manage such a huge operation. (The complex cost US$45 million to build.) The 10,000 m^2 complex in a suburb of Moscow contained everything McDonald's would need to serve its then 20 stores. From a bakery line churning out the Big Mac buns, to a "liquid" line for making the special sauce. In other words, everything that was needed to keep up with demand for 40,000 meals a day under one roof with its highly prized consistency.

But as the company expanded (in 2005, McDonald's had 134 restaurants in 37 cities in Russia, with 500,000 customers a day), the McComplex had to evolve. So McDonald's made the strategic move of developing locally, finding local entrepreneurs, working with them to grow their business so that eventually they could move the supply core elements entirely over to them. In doing so, it cemented the McDonald's brand as innovative and supportive. Local suppliers' capacity has increased so much thanks to the golden arches that they now supply other brands, and even export to Europe—something that was unthinkable just 15 years ago. By investing in a strong local supply chain and teaching local producers, McDonald's has earned itself an almost unassailable position, with 80 percent of the Russian fast-food market.[9]

This art of nurturing suppliers is clearly needed when the existing suppliers cannot meet the required quality, quantity, price, service, and delivery objectives. Rather than select from the slate of existing suppliers, the purchaser task is then to *create* suppliers. Thus, this process is an aggressive and imaginative approach to achieving supply objectives. The purchaser takes the initiative in making the proposal. It is the purchaser's proposal (rather than the seller's) that becomes the agenda for discussion and negotiation.[10]

Creating new sources of supply and persuading current suppliers to build new capabilities to fulfill the customer's objectives is not limited to industrial suppliers. It is feasible for business services as well. For example, convention and meeting organizers do not have to accept standard hotel packages. Once they know what facilities and services will suit them best, they can look for suppliers willing to adapt their standard services to meet specific customers' needs.

Reasons for Nurturing Suppliers

Businesses engage in the process of nurturing suppliers for several reasons. These include the need to meet future needs, compliance with government policies, good citizenship, promoting environmental policies, ensuring quality, and cost reduction.

Meeting Future Needs

When the existing suppliers are unable to meet future needs, a firm may have to develop specific suppliers by helping them to acquire the capability. This is exactly what McDonald's did in the example above. Another situation occurs when a customer firm is planning an expansion of its operations and wants to assure an increased supply of raw materials and parts. If the current vendor needs to invest significantly to expand its own capacity, then the customer firm would engage in motivating, and, in fact, helping the vendor set up for the expanded capacity.

Government Policy Compliance

Federal and provincial governments may require the development and patronage of local or domestic suppliers. Yet these suppliers may not be good enough to meet a customer firm's needs and supplier criteria. The customer firm would then develop the capabilities of the local or domestic vendor firm.

Good Citizenship

Often, business firms want to do the right thing even without the government edict: they want to engage in socially responsible or helpful corporate behaviour and, thus, show good citizenship.

Promoting Environmental Policies

This reason is similar to the foregoing two reasons except that attention is now focused on the supplier firm's environmental record. The buyer firm must motivate and educate the potential supplier firms to adopt environmentally friendly policies as a condition of doing business. For example, Dofasco, which in 2005 was once again, for the sixth consecutive year, the only steel company in the world to be listed on the Dow Jones Sustainability World Index, promotes the procurement of products that have minimal adverse impact on the environment, and works with vendors to identify and implement improvements in their formulations.

Quality Assurance

For more than two decades now, business firms around the globe have been pursuing very high-quality standards in the products they produce. A critical requirement of quality output products is that the input materials and parts themselves be of high quality. While large manufacturing firms have the resources to upgrade their equipment and processes for high-quality output, often small vendors of input materials and parts do not have such resources. Therefore, the customer firm with greater resources and greater motivation to obtain the quality input materials undertakes to develop the quality capability in the supplier. This may entail supporting the supplier firm with financial resources, managerial skills, technical training, and development resources. The supplier firm needs to be persuaded (i.e., sold on the idea) to invest its own time and effort to meet the quality needs of the customer firm.

Cost Reduction

The final reason for nurturing suppliers is the pursuit of cost reductions. The buyer may analyze the supplier's production costs and identify ways the supplier can save enough on production costs that it can charge less yet maintain or improve its own profit margins. But for the supplier firm to engage in the activities necessary to reduce costs may require some persuasion. An example of a customer firm seeking cost containment via the art of nurturing suppliers is this statement by Texas Instruments:

> "We are a company in a highly competitive environment. For us to survive and prosper we need to be able to bring our long-term costs down significantly as fast as we can. To the best of our knowledge, in view of increasing volume and technological and other improvements, it should be possible for you to achieve the following targets for the next three years. Should you agree, we are counting on you to achieve these targets. We are willing to assist you in a variety of ways to make sure you will achieve this. However, if you do not believe you can meet our future objectives, there is no point in making a deal with us now, even though you may be fully competitive now."[11]

Advantages of Nurturing Suppliers

Since this process begins with the customer's rather than the supplier's proposal, the customer may seek whatever advantages are important to its strategy. Typically, companies nurture suppliers to obtain some combination of substantially improved quality, substantially improved performance, lower costs, better delivery schedule, and extended service support.

SUPPLIER-CUSTOMER PARTNERING

LO 6

Supplier-customer partnering
Establishing a partnership-like relationship with one's supplier or with one's customer.

Supplier-customer partnering is establishing a partnership-like relationship with one's supplier or with one's customer. The supplier and customer firm do not merge ownership. Rather, they come together and agree to collaborate so that each partner works to the advantage of the other (which, in turn, helps each partner itself). The principal focus of the process of nurturing suppliers was to motivate the supplier to do business with one's company, even when the supplier was not in that kind of business. In supplier-customer partnering, the focus is on redefining the way two parties deal with each other.

Models for Dealing with Suppliers

The traditional model of dealing with the suppliers is for the customer to focus on his or her own efficiency and cost minimization. In contrast, in supplier-partnership arrangements, the focus is on optimizing the efficiency of the entire value chain (i.e., the entire system, from the supplier to the end user). In the traditional arm's-length dealings model, the customer firm's focus is on minimizing the price it pays; in the partnering model, the emphasis is on reducing the total system cost and, at the same time, improving quality. In supplier partnering, there is a joint effort to define needs and solutions, and information about cost and about demand and capacity data is freely shared between the partners. In partnering, partners make customized investments in each other (what were earlier called transaction-specific investments), and contracts are more flexible, signifying that the parties trust each other and are willing to commit to working toward common goals.

Such supplier partnering had its beginning in the Japanese auto industry, whereas traditionally the North American auto industry has followed the model of arm's-length dealings with the suppliers, although this practice is now changing. Even though North American companies are now increasingly following the supplier-partnering model, for illustrative purposes, the traditional North American model of arm's-length dealings with suppliers and the Japanese model of supplier partnering are worth comparing. (This comparison is presented in Table 10.3.)

Whether or not the parties are already in business with each other, and whether or not they already have a long-term buying contract, the goal of supplier-customer partnering is to broaden the scope of interactions between the two firms at all levels and across all functions. In arm's-length transactional dealings, the supplier and customer firms' contact point is limited to two types of interaction: the supplier's sales staff interacts with the buyer's purchasing department, and the buying firm's users interact with the supplier's service personnel.

In the partnering model, the two organizations' interactions are broad-based, with each function dealing with its counterpart in the partnering firm. Buyers and the buying firm's engineers get involved in the design and development of the seller's product. Conversely, suppliers want to be in on the ground floor when an end product is being designed so that they may suggest changes that would help them produce the component part for the customer more economically. Other departments interface with their counterparts in the customer firm. Thus, engineering and production personnel interface with their counterparts to identify next-generation product and process improvements. Warehousing and materials management personnel deal with the manufacturing and shipping personnel to explore the most efficient logistics. Information-system designers work to interlock their firms' computer systems. Even credit and accounting managers team up with the accounting people from the customer's firm to identify methods of automating the invoice and payment system.[12]

TABLE 10.3 Vendor Relations in Japan and North America

Traditional North American Model	Japanese Partnering Model
Department or firm focus, optimize firm efficiency.	Business system focus (include supplier/customer economics), optimize value chain efficiency.
Emphasis on unit cost/price (minimum quality standards).	Emphasis on full value chain (systems) costs as well as on improving quality.
Manufacturer defines needs; specialization of activities; sequential planning.	Joint efforts to define needs and problem solve; highly integrated operations and planning.
Communication is sporadic, problem driven; little sharing of information or assistance.	Communication is frequent and planned; continuous sharing of information and assistance.
General investments; uniform approach.	Customized investments to meet unique customer or supplier needs (e.g., in information systems, people, manufacturing equipment).
Precise contracts that split economic benefits beforehand.	Flexible contracts that adjust to split economic gains fully as market conditions change.

SOURCE: Reprinted from Dyer, Jeffery H., and William G. Ouchi. "Japanese-Style Partnerhips: Giving Companies a Competitive Edge." *Sloan Management Review* (Fall 1993): 54. By permission of the publisher.

Either party can take the initiative. Either a customer may initiate and spearhead the drive to partner with the supplier, or a supplier may initiate the partnering effort. Illustratively, a customer might invite supplier engineers to be on its design team, or the supplier may seek such an invitation. Likewise, a customer may offer to collaborate on the supplier's product design, or the supplier may motivate the customer to contribute to the supplier firm's product design efforts.

Factors for the Growth of Supplier Partnering

Four factors would influence customers to seek supplier partnering:

1. *Competitive intensity*—Business in the established product categories becomes more competitive. Competitive intensity would increase due to market saturation, deregulation, privatization of more and more sectors of the economy, and globalization (firms selling and competing worldwide).
2. *Pressure on market prices*—As competitive intensity increases, businesses want to be able to compete on prices. They, therefore, want to reduce the total cost of inputs (i.e., raw materials, parts, components, and manufacturing supplies). Target costing (designing products and making them to meet certain cost goals or targets) would be on the rise, which would further put pressure on costs of inputs. To reduce purchasing costs,

centralized buying will be adopted increasingly. This will make buying more of a corporate and strategic function in the pursuit of cost-reduction goals.

3. *Concern with quality*—Competitive intensity will also necessitate that firms differentiate themselves on quality. To build quality in the finished products, firms would need an assurance of quality in the input materials and components. To enable consistently high quality, buyers would need to guide and assist suppliers on an ongoing basis.
4. *Enabling technology*—The foregoing three factors offer a reason for businesses to buy more efficiently and more effectively, and supplier partnering is an avenue for it. Yet supplier partnering would remain an elusive goal were it not for modern enabling technology. In particular, customers and suppliers can link computer networks and communications technology to their databases and processes.

Future business buying will be increasingly relational and based on a strategic plan for supplier development. The customer will have to motivate the supplier to do business in a way that produces greater value for both partners. In the future model of business buying, the customer seeks to link all of his or her firm's business processes to the supplier's identical business processes. In such relational and partnering exchanges, customers and suppliers collaborate to explore avenues of greater profitability for both.

LO 7 CUSTOMER RELATIONSHIP MANAGEMENT AND THE THREE CUSTOMER ROLES

In this section, we bring together various concepts of the chapter and relate them to the three customer roles. The illustrative relevance of selected concepts is shown in Table 10.4. Traditional marketplace transactions have considered the sale to be the endpoint of all marketing actions. The true contribution of relationship marketing is that it goes beyond the consummation of the sale per se. In so doing, it brings the user role again into focus following the sale. The goal of relationship marketing is to satisfy the user.

TABLE 10.4 Customer Relationship Management and the Three Customer Roles

Concepts	User	Payer	Buyer
General concept of relationship marketing	• Marketer refocuses on the user after the sale		
A model of relationship-based buying			
Motivations			
Search costs			• Search entails time and effort of the buyer role
Risk reduction	• Performance risk to user is reduced		
Switching costs	• Usage learning of product from new supplier	• Retooling costs	• Effort to learn to deal with the new supplier
Value-added benefits	• Add-on benefits for the user.	• Better financing plan may benefit the payer	
Early socialization	• User socialization		• Buyer socialization

Reciprocity		• Payment through reciprocal exchange assured	• Source availability assured
Networks	• Suppliers in network more trustworthy with product/ service quality	• Firms in network are accommodating in financial exigencies	• Easier to do business with
Friendships	• Friendly supplier assures quality product		• Friendly vendors give friendly service
Nurturing suppliers	• Better performance value	• Lower costs over the long run	
Supplier partnering	• Better performance value; data sharing; joint planning helpful to user	•Total cost reduction	• Buying function becomes more efficient

The central concept in the chapter is the model of relationship-based buying, which comprises customer motivations for and outcomes of relationship-based buying. Among the motivations are cost-benefit factors (search costs, risk reduction, switching costs, and value-added benefits) and sociocultural factors (early socialization, reciprocity, networks, and friendships). Search costs occur in terms of the time and effort of the buyer role. Risk reduction is a benefit to the user in that the current product from the current supplier, tried and tested, is devoid of uncertainty as to its performance. Switching costs can relate to each of the three roles. Penalties for breaking the contract, if any, and the costs of new investments, such as retooling to become compatible with the new supplier, are costs to the payer. Time and effort expended to learn to do business with the new supplier are costs to the buyer. Learning to use the new supplier's product is a cost to the user. Finally, value-added benefits offer an advantage generally to the user, but if these relate to, say, an improved financing plan or terms of payment, then the payer role is benefited as well.

Among the sociocultural factors, early socialization is the learned behaviour both of using a product and of buying from a particular source (i.e., it is a socialization of both the user and buyer roles). Reciprocity affects at least two of the three roles, the buyer and the payer. The buyer is assured of a source and its commitment since the latter (i.e., the supplier) depends on the buyer for receiving the product it (the supplier) in turn needs. The payer is certain to be able to pay since it has the resource the other party values, namely its own product. Networks affect all three roles. Buyers find it easy to do business with other firms in the network due to a history of interaction. Users gain by being assured of performance, and suppliers in the network are accountable to one another for delivering the quality product, and they command the social approval as a source. Payers are affected by getting an improved price value over time, by being assured of getting credit terms favourably altered in case of future financial exigencies, and by knowing that firms in the network will not abandon the customer in times of financial hardship. Finally, friendship helps all three roles in the same way as do networks. The user can trust the friend for product performance, the buyer gets friendly service, and the payer might get a better price and better credit terms.

The process of nurturing suppliers is driven by the buyer search for both user and payer values. We enumerated the benefits of this process as substantially improved quality, substantially improved performance, better delivery schedule, extended service support, and lower costs over the long run. Of these, the first four are benefits to the user role, and the fifth is a benefit to the payer role.

These same benefits occur from supplier partnering. Because suppliers are on board from the design stage, better performance value results from customized design of components and parts or service. Mutual data sharing improves joint production planning for the user role. The payer role benefits from the joint pursuit of long-term total-cost reduction goals. And since the users interface closely with suppliers on a continual basis, the buyer role becomes more efficient; ordering and delivery transactions can also become automated.

SUMMARY

LO 1 In this chapter, we have examined the customer's motivation to patronize the same marketer repeatedly, on an enduring basis. To view the consumer as someone always looking for a better deal, always open to competing suppliers' pitches and, always eager to do business with a new marketer makes the marketer resort to a wheeling-and-dealing strategy of marketing. This view is not entirely inaccurate (and for this reason, the marketer should always strive to offer better value to its current customers); however, it is only half of the story. There are powerful forces that make a customer want to patronize the same marketer repeatedly. It is possible and fruitful for marketers, therefore, to learn to keep customers returning for business again and again (i.e., to build long-term relationships with their customers).

LO 2 This requires understanding about what motivates customers to engage in relationship-based buying. We integrated these motivations in a model of relationship-based buying. In this model, two groups of factors constitute the motivations: (1) cost-benefit factors that comprise search costs, risk reduction, switching costs, and value-added benefits, and (2) sociocultural factors that comprise early socialization, reciprocity, networks, and friendships. These antecedent factors result in supplier-customer relationships that are characterized by commitment and trust. The outcome of these relationships is customer loyalty to the supplier, increased buying, willingness to pay more, favourable word of mouth, and customer equity or goodwill.

LO 3 Next we discussed relationship buying and selling in business markets. The process of relationship buying in business markets was captured by the Industrial Marketing and Purchasing (IMP) group (a group of European researchers). In the IMP model, three key factors are recognized: transaction-specific investments/adaptations made to meet the need of a specific customer; power dependence that reflects the dependence of one partner on the other; and role formalness that indicates how personal or impersonal the interactions between the partners are. Following this, we identified a set of reasons for relationship development in business buying. These reasons include business customers' need to ensure long-term supply, to reduce the cost of transactions, and to pursue quality and cost-reduction goals.

LO 4 Next, we described the determinants of trust and commitment, identified earlier as key elements of business relationships. Business customers trust their suppliers when suppliers make partner-specific investments, strive for mutual goals, offer open communications and product support, and avoid opportunistic behaviours. Conversely, suppliers also need to be able to trust their customers, and this trust depends on customers adopting a single-source policy and engaging in data sharing and nurturance.

We also discussed the process of developing and nurturing suppliers. This is needed when future needs would not be met by existing suppliers, when specific but unprepared suppliers need to be patronized, when certain environmental policies need to be promoted, when vendors need quality assurance support, or when a program of cost reduction is needed. **LO 5**

We elaborated on the topic of supplier-customer partnering—the establishment of partnership-like relations with one's customers or one's suppliers. Four sets of factors encourage business firms to engage in supplier partnering: competitive intensity, pressure on market prices, high concern with quality, and the availability of enabling technology. Reviewing the emerging trends, we suggested that future business buying will increasingly be relational and based on a strategic plan for supplier development. **LO 6, 7**

KEY TERMS

Asymmetrical 380
Commitment 378
Customer Equity or Goodwill 379
Mutual Goals 382
Networks 375
Partner-Specific Investments 382
Perceived Risk 372
Power Dependence 380
Reciprocity 374
Relationship-Based Buying 371
Role Formalness 380
Supplier-Customer Partnering 387
Switching Costs 372
Transaction-Specific Investments/Adaptations 380
Trust 378

DISCUSSION QUESTIONS AND EXERCISES

1. The chapter describes the perceived risk/switching costs model of relationship buying. Based on this model, identify for each of the following businesses what a company can do to encourage relationship-based buying by its current customers:
   - **a.** A credit card company
   - **b.** A long-distance phone company
   - **c.** A supermarket
   - **d.** A package-delivery company, such as FedEx for its business customers
   - **e.** A health insurance company dealing with employers as customers.
2. Trust and commitment are advanced as two essential ingredients in relationship-based buying. Write your boss a memo outlining all the actions your company can take to improve its trust and commitment scores with its major customers.
3. Think about your own experiences as a customer, or the experiences of your company as a customer. Think of five or six companies that you (or your company) do business with as a customer. What does the company do or not do to encourage or discourage you regarding relationship-based buying from it? Make a list, and compare it across the companies you have considered.
4. Contact the purchasing director of a company, and interview him or her to determine whether the firm engages in any one of the following: (a) supplier partnering, (b) supplier nurturing marketing or supplier development, or (c) long-term contract buying.

Query him or her about (1) the advantages and disadvantages of this manner of dealing with its suppliers, (2) how the firm goes about establishing this relationship, and (3) what each partner does to satisfy and maintain the commitment of the other.

5. A friend has just graduated from university in liberal arts; a company has offered him a job as an assistant to the director of purchasing. He is wondering how it relates to marketing, his main interest. Unlike him, you took a class in customer behaviour where the strategic role of procurement was emphasized and such developments as supplier partnering were discussed. Would you advise your friend whether or not the job he is offered is a marketing job? How would you explain to him the significance of his job to a career in marketing?

NOTES

1 Adapted from Tom Stundza, "Ford Shakes Up Its Steel Buy," *Purchasing*, March 8, 2001, 27–32.

2 Adapted from Jagdish N. Sheth and Atul Paravatiyar, "Relationship Marketing in Consumer Markets: Antecedents and Consequences," *Journal of the Academy of Marketing Science* 23, no. 4 (Fall 1995): 255–71.

3 James C. Anderson, Hakan Hakansson, and Lars Johanson, "Dyadic Business Relationships Within a Business Network Context," *Journal of Marketing* 58 (October 1994): 1–15.

4 Ingmar Bjorkman and Soren Kock, "Social Relationships and Business Networks: The Case of Western Companies in China," *International Business Review* 4, no. 4 (1995): 519–35.

5 Banwari Mittal, "Trust and Relationship Quality: A Conceptual Excursion," in *The Contemporary Knowledge of Relationship Marketing*, eds. Atul Parvatiyar and Jagdish N. Sheth, 230–40 (Atlanta, GA: Emory University, Center for Relationship Marketing, 1996); Jagdish N. Sheth and Banwari Mittal, "A Framework for Managing Customer Expectations," *Journal of Market-Focused Management* 1, no. 2 (1996): 137–58.

6 Wilson, 1995; Dwyer, Schurr, and Oh, 1987; Moorman, Zaltman, and Deshpande, 1992.

7 IMP Group, "An Interaction Approach," in *International Marketing and Purchasing of Industrial Goods*, ed. H. Hakansson (John Wiley & Sons, Chichester (U.K.), 1982).

8 Neeli Bendapudi and Leonard Berry, "Customers' Motivations for Relationships with Service Providers," *Journal of Retailing* 73, no. 1 (1997): 15–37.

9 Adapted from "Case Study: McDonald's Russia," *Brand Strategy*, November 2, 2005, 29.

10 *Ibid.*, 2; Alan J. Magrath and Kenneth G. Hardy, "Building Customer Partnering," *Business Horizons*, January February, 1994, 24 28.

11 *Ibid.*, 136–37.

12 Alan J. Magrath and Kenneth G. Hardy, "Building Customer Partnering," *Business Horizons* (January–February 1994): 24–28.

PART 4

Building Loyalty and Customer Value

CHAPTER 11

Customer Loyalty to Products, Brands, and Stores

LEARNING OBJECTIVES

After reading this chapter you should be able to:

LO 1 Understand the concept of brand loyalty, and how it is measured.

LO 2 Describe the contributors to brand loyalty.

LO 3 Describe the detractors from brand loyalty.

LO 4 Explain the concept of brand equity.

LO 5 Describe the model of store loyalty.

LO 6 Explain how store choice is made.

LO 7 Describe the concept of one-stop shopping.

Are You True to Your Brand?

What began as a doughnut shop in an Ontario steel town has grown into the nation's top food-service chain, with nearly 2,500 locations across the country and $2.9 billion in revenues. Celebrating its 40th anniversary in 2004, Tim Hortons, one of Canada's most iconic brands, has become "the people's restaurant," and is a part of everyday life for millions of consumers. Rob Wilson, a professor at Ryerson University, notes, "People don't go for coffee at Tim Hortons, they go for a Tim's." For the second year in a row, in the 2005 Survey of Canada's Best and Worst Managed Brands commissioned by *Canadian Business* magazine and *Marketing Daily*, Tim Hortons topped the list of Canada's best-managed brands, with 52 percent of respondents choosing the purveyor of coffee and doughnuts—up from 42 percent in 2004. Despite its American ownership (it was sold in 1995 to Wendy's International Inc.), the brand has become a large part of Canadian culture—at least in Ontario and the East, where most of its outlets are concentrated.[1]

As a $5 billion retail leader in automotive, sports and leisure, and home products, one of Canadian Tire's greatest assets is its brand. Canadian Tire is the country's most-shopped retailer: 90 percent of Canadians shop there, and 40 percent shop there weekly. Canadian Tire touches the lives of more than 3 million customers every week. The retail chain has a very loyal base, from young Canadians to retirees. Ninety-nine percent of Canadians recognize the Canadian Tire brand. In the 2005 Survey of Canada's Best and Worst Managed Brands, the brand stood tall among the top five most-recognized brands in the country. Canadian Tire "Money" is an integral part of its marketing mix, and it has one of the country's most successful and popular customer reward programs, with a 90 percent redemption and participation level.[2]

Savvy retailers, such as M&M Meat Shops, use loyalty cards to track customer purchases and offer instant discounts, making repeat visits likelier. Each Valentine's Day, M&M franchises have the option of delivering a bouquet of roses and a box of candy to their top customers, and every Christmas those customers also receive personally signed holiday cards. A majority of M&M customers use the loyalty card, making it one of the more useful loyalty programs from a customer intelligence standpoint.[3]

A study conducted by the International Mass Retail Association showed that consumers shopping for a power screwdriver were more concerned about the product having a national brand name than its price. Contractors and professional tradesmen have always been fiercely loyal to their power tool brands, and now the same kind of loyalty is being seen in the consumer market as well.[4]

Customer loyalty toward products is manifest in the loyalty that groups of customers are known to exhibit toward the diet-foods product category, the caffeine-free product category, or the organic-foods category. Businesses also show such exceptional product loyalty when it comes to computer systems, machinery (analog vs. digital), and software. Products such as Macintosh, Nintendo, BlackBerry, Nike, McCain, Tylenol, Lise Watier, Singapore Airlines, and Club Med, as well as retail stores such as Sears, The Bay, Roots, Jacob, Gap, and the Body Shop have loyal followings.

On the flip side of the coin, not all customers are loyal to any one product or store, nor is any one customer loyal to everything he or she buys and uses. Based on ACNielsen data collected from 14 product areas containing 80 categories in 38 markets worldwide, private label goods (which is an indicator of lack of loyalty to manufacturers' brands) comprised 17 percent of total value sales for the 12 months ending the first quarter of 2005, up from the 15 percent level of 2003. In terms of growth, private labels more than doubled the growth rate of manufacturer brands, 5 percent to 2 percent. In fact, in more than two-thirds of the markets studied, private label value sales grew faster than manufacturer brand counterparts. While private label still commands only 17 percent of the global marketplace, in some markets it is far higher. For example, in Switzerland, private label share of value sales was at its highest level of 45 percent, while in Canada it was 19 percent and in the Unted States 16 percent.[5]

Why such variation in customer loyalty? Why are customers loyal to some brands and stores and not to others? What can marketers do to win their customers' loyalty? These questions are the subject matter of this chapter. (See Figure 11.1 for the conceptual framework.)

FIGURE 11.1 Conceptual Framework

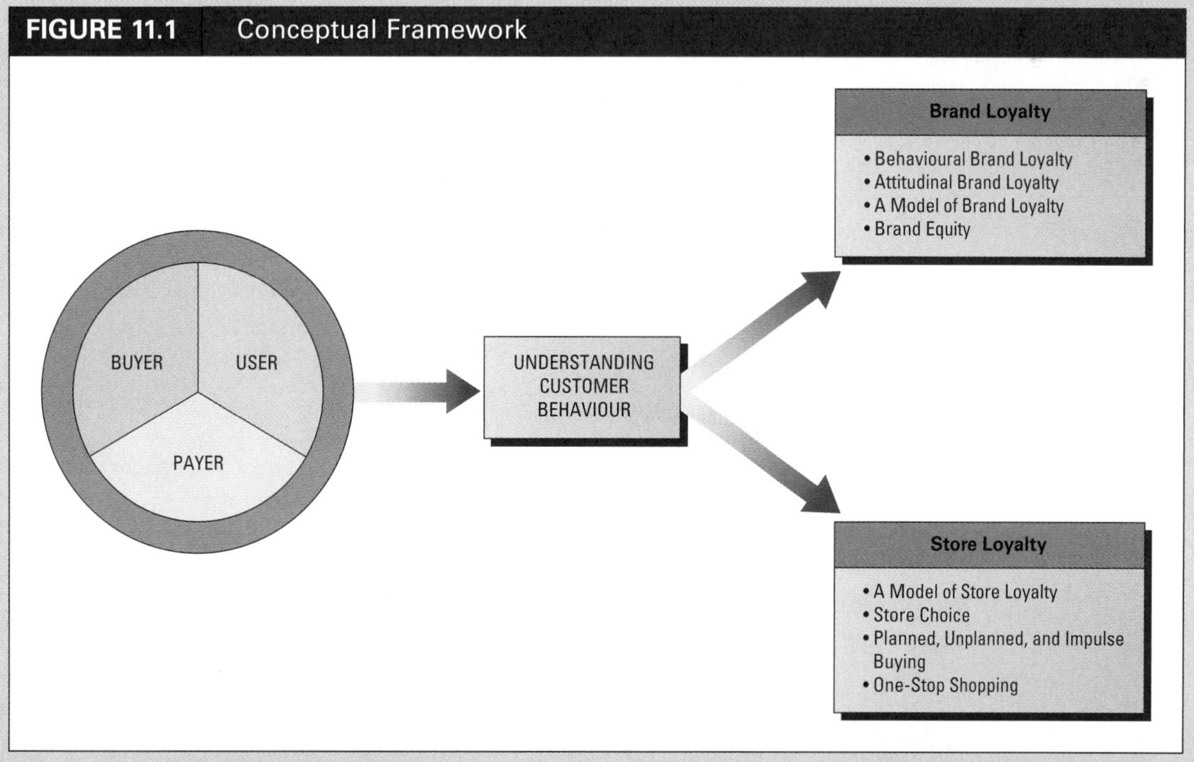

We begin by defining brand loyalty and describing ways to measure it. Next, we introduce a model of brand loyalty that brings together its diverse determinants. In business markets, the brand name is equivalent to the supplier, and supplier loyalty would involve considerations similar to brand loyalty in the consumer markets. We then describe the concept of brand equity and discuss its significance for marketers. Next, we present a model of customers' store loyalty, describing the underlying factors. We also consider customers' shopping behaviour in terms of the decision process for choosing which stores to shop at; diverse shopping motives; and a specific customer behaviour, namely one-stop shopping.

LO 1 DEFINITION AND MEASUREMENT OF BRAND LOYALTY

There are two ways to think of brand loyalty: brand loyalty as a behaviour, and as an attitude. That is, marketers define brand loyalty in terms of what brands people buy and how they feel about brands.

BEHAVIOURAL BRAND LOYALTY

In behavioural terms, brand loyalty is simply a customer's consistent re-purchase of a brand. Every time a customer re-purchases a product (shampoo, wine, jeans, frozen pizza, motor oil, automotive tools, computers, mail delivery service, plumbing service, or car insurance), if the customer buys the same brand of that product, we consider that customer a brand-loyal customer for that product category. This consistent re-purchase of this brand is called **behavioural brand loyalty.**

Behavioural brand loyalty
A customer's consistent re-purchase of a brand.

Completely consistent re-purchase of the same brand would show perfect behavioural brand loyalty, but in practice even brand-loyal customers may deviate from their regular brand by occasionally buying an alternative. To allow for imperfect consistency, marketers have measured behavioural brand loyalty in several ways: *proportion of purchase*, *sequence of purchase*, and *probability of purchase.*

Proportion of Purchase

Marketers sometimes measure loyalty as a percentage: the number of times the most frequently purchased brand is purchased divided by the total number of purchases. Thus, if the most frequently purchased brand is purchased 7 out of 10 times, then brand loyalty is 70 percent.

Sequence of Purchase

Another measure is based on the consistency with which the consumer switches between brands. Consider the following sequences between two brands, A and B: AAABAAABBB and ABABABABABA. Both are patterns of divided loyalty between the two brands, with 60 percent loyalty toward brand A; however, the first pattern shows more consistent sequence than the second pattern. Accordingly, the customer exhibiting the first pattern would be deemed to be more brand loyal than the customer exhibiting the second pattern.

Jacob Jacoby designed a more elaborate measure of loyalty using panel data, where he looked at both the sequence and frequency of purchases as a measure of loyalty. For example, Jacoby defined undivided loyalty as six consecutive purchases of the same brand. However, if the consumer made six purchases that switched back and forth between two brand names, then the consumer had divided loyalty. If the consumer made three purchases and switched to something else, the consumer had what Jacoby called unstable loyalty. He referred to any other pattern as non-loyalty.

Probability of Purchase

Marketers also may combine proportion and sequence measures to compute the probability of purchase based on the customer's long-term purchase history. First, the marketer computes a proportion of purchase for the long-term history. Then, at some point in time, the proportion is adjusted to reflect the most recent purchase. Every time the customer purchases a specific brand, the purchase increases the statistical probability that he or she will re-purchase that brand on the next occasion.

ATTITUDINAL BRAND LOYALTY

The problem with behavioural brand loyalty is that it simply shows that customers re-purchase the same brand, not whether they actually like the brand more than other brands. A customer could buy the same brand simply out of habit or convenience, without thinking much about it. This kind of loyalty cannot be stable; if a competing brand offers a price deal, the customer would readily buy the other brand. On the flip side, on a particular occasion, if we notice a customer buying a brand different from his or her regular brand, we would interpret it as a lack of brand loyalty. However, the customer may, in fact, have been forced to switch brands, for example, due to a stock-out of his or her regular brand.

For these reasons, marketing scholars have argued that in measuring brand loyalty, we should assess customers' attitude toward the brand. Only if the customer attitude for a brand is more favourable than for the competing brands should that customer be considered brand loyal to that brand. This way of looking at brand loyalty—that is, a greater liking for the brand—can be termed **attitudinal brand loyalty.** This can be measured by asking customers to rank various brands in terms of how much they like them, or which brand they prefer.

Attitudinal brand loyalty
A customer's consistent re-purchase of a brand due to his or her preference for it.

Brand Loyalty as Attitude-Based Behaviour

Soon, scholars who had earlier proposed behavioural measures of loyalty began to view loyalty jointly in behavioural and attitudinal terms. Jacoby himself proposed a new definition of brand loyalty: **Brand loyalty** is the biased (i.e., non-random) behavioural response (i.e., purchase), expressed over time by some decision-making unit, with respect to one or more alternative brands out of a set of such brands, and is a function of psychological (decision-making, evaluative) processes.[6] George S. Day defined brand loyalty as consisting of repeated purchases prompted by a strong internal disposition. The phrase *internal disposition* refers to a favourable attitude. Thus, true loyalty incorporates both a behaviour and an attitude.[7] Note that here we employ the term *attitude* to refer to the overall liking and predisposition rather than the three-component view discussed in Chapter 6.

Brand loyalty
A customer's commitment to buy and use a given brand repeatedly.

Based on this definition, some measures of brand loyalty are shown in Table 11.1. In that table, the first two statements capture attitudinal bias toward the brand, the next two statements reflect consistent behaviour, and the last statement taps commitment. Susan Fournier refers to a construct similar in spirit to brand loyalty—"*brand relationship quality*." It can be

TABLE 11.1 Illustrative Measures of Brand Loyalty

These statements may be rated on a five-point scale (where 1 means Strongly Disagree and 5 means Strongly Agree); a stronger agreement shows higher loyalty.

1. I like this brand very much.
2. In this product category, I have a favourite brand.
3. When buying (product) I always buy my favourite brand, no matter what.
4. In the past, almost all of my purchases of (product) have been this brand.
5. If my favourite brand of (product) is not available in the store, I would go to another store rather than buy a substitute brand.

defined as "relationship oriented view of customer-brand interactions which are positively held, voluntarily engaged, long-term, and affectively intense (in short, brand-loyal relations) in nature." Brand relationship quality has six facets:

1. *Love/Passion*—Strong affective ties with the brand.
2. *Self-Connection*—Degree to which the brand delivers on important identity concerns, tasks, or themes expressing a significant aspect of the self.
3. *Commitment*—High commitment in terms of an intention to behave in a manner supportive of the relationship longevity.
4. *Interdependence*—High degree of interdependence between brand and consumer, involving frequent brand interactions (using a brand many times in a day), increased scope and diversity of brand-related activities (e.g., purchasing extensions of the brand), and heightened intensity of individual interaction events (e.g., considering the use of the brand to be an occasion in itself).
5. *Intimacy*—Brand relationship memory of personal associations and experiences, and the intimacy that comes from these elaborate meanings.
6. *Brand Partner Quality*—Consumers' evaluation of the brand's performance in the partnership role.[8]

A MODEL OF BRAND LOYALTY

What makes a customer brand-loyal? Several factors induce brand loyalty; others work against it. The degree of brand loyalty is the net outcome of these positive and negative factors (see Figure 11.2).

LO 2 CONTRIBUTORS TO BRAND LOYALTY

As shown in Figure 11.2, several factors contribute to brand loyalty. The three major contributors are the perceived brand-performance fit, social and emotional identification with the brand, and habit combined with a long history of using the brand.

Thus, favourable brand attitude and brand loyalty result primarily from the satisfaction of user values, namely, (1) performance and (2) social and emotional identification. Some insights on customer satisfaction and loyalty to brands in several international markets are presented in the appendix.

FIGURE 11.2 A Model of Customers' Brand Loyalty

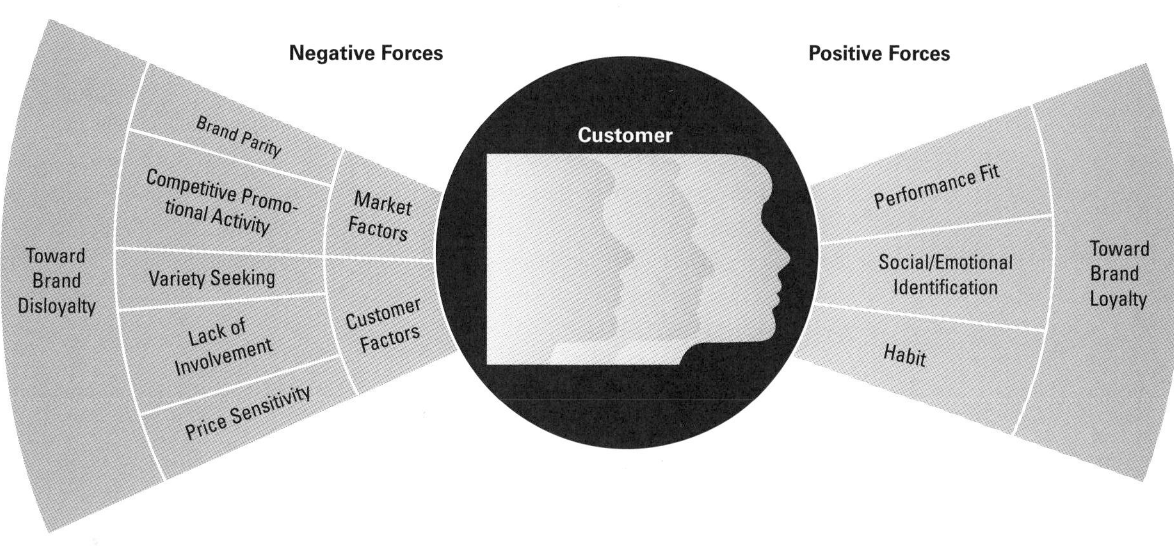

Perceived Brand-Performance Fit

Basically, customers like brands that meet their needs and wants well. If they have a positive usage experience, customers want to seek that reward again.

Brands differ not only in the quality of their performance (e.g., how well a shampoo cleans hair, or the reliability of a network communication system) but also on specific performance dimensions (e.g., shampoo that gives hair body versus one that eliminates dandruff, or a network's data capacity, transmission speed, and portability). Furthermore, customers have different needs for specific performance features (e.g., shampoo for oily, dry, thick, or thin hair; speed versus data volume in a network). Consequently, brand loyalty depends not merely on whether a brand does what it is intended to do, but also on the degree of fit between the customer's specific performance requirements and the brand's performance capability. Brands targeted at specific customer segments are likely to fit better than those mass-marketed to the public at large. That is why customer loyalty is generally higher in niche markets compared with mass markets.

Another measure of a brand's performance is its overall quality (e.g., workmanship, durability, reliability). Perceived brand quality is a very important factor in a person's preference for and loyal patronage of the brand. Motorola, Toyota, Xerox, and Fairmount Hotels are examples of brands well known for their quality. Once customers experience the quality of these brands, they become loyal users.

Social and Emotional Identification with the Brand

The second category of user values is social and emotional identification with the brand. Brands come to acquire certain social images through marketing communications and/or by real-world observations of who is buying which brands. Such associations are particularly inevitable and, indeed, quite strong for conspicuous products such as clothing, cars, office furniture, and places of leisure and recreation. Brands that reflect social self-concept—the kind of person you like to be seen as—win over the user-customer's loyalty.

Emotional identification with the brand is related to customers' self-concept. User-customers enjoy some brands so much that they begin to see those brands as part of themselves. They identify themselves with the brands. The classic case of "old" Coke's brief withdrawal from the marketplace resulted in a groundswell of public protest from the brand's loyal fans, who believed that the brand's absence had created a void in their personal lives! Brand communities on the Web also help foster social and emotional identification with the brand. For example, Molson (**http://www.molsoncanadian.ca**) allows individuals to become insiders and "go to the wall" where they can chat with other insiders, play hockey, or "get exposed" by submitting pictures or videos. By creating online communities relating to their brands, companies are forging stronger relationships with their customers.

Habit and History

Finally, brand loyalty arises from habit and a long history of brand usage. Customers acquire some of their preferences simply by repeated use. This can happen for three reasons. First, we become familiar with the brand, and we feel comfortable with it. As in the case of services, we like to stick to the same doctor, the same accounting firm, the same restaurant, and even the same hair salon.

We also develop a taste for a brand by conditioning. For example, initially we may not like Mexican or Japanese food, but after several tastings, we may learn not only to like it but, in fact, to crave it. Likewise, the same may occur for certain brands of wine, certain food items, certain perfumes and colognes, certain music styles, or even certain artists. This acquired taste is the reason why many brands try to catch user-customers young. If an individual uses a brand while growing up, he or she is likely to remain loyal to it lifelong, such as to Colgate toothpaste or Life cereal.

Finally, if customers saw a brand being used in their parental home as they were growing up, they are likely to view this history of use by parents as testimony to the brand's goodness. Intergenerational influence by family members, seen in Chapter 9, is an important determinant of acquired brand loyalty.

LO 3 DETRACTORS FROM LOYALTY: ATTRACTION OF ALTERNATIVES

While performance fit, social and emotional identification, and history of use engender and contribute to brand loyalty, another set of factors detracts from it. This group of factors is called **attraction of alternatives**—that is, how attractive a customer finds alternative brands to be. Attraction of alternatives depends on factors relating to the market environment, and others pertaining to the customer personally.

Attraction of alternatives How attractive a customer finds alternative brands to be.

Market Factors

The market influences attraction of alternatives through brand parity and competitive promotional activity. **Brand parity** refers to how similar and mutually substitutable the brands are. The more alike the brands in a product category are, the less motivation there is for a customer to stick with a particular brand. Of course, the parity matters, not in its absolute form, but rather as perceived by the customer, and customers may evaluate parity in terms of performance utility or their social and emotional identities. Credit cards are a good example of a product category with very similar and mutually substitutable brands.

Brand parity The concept of how similar and mutually substitutable the brands are.

Competitive promotional activity refers to the special price deals available on competing brands. These price deals provide the motivation to switch from a favourite brand to a featured

Competitive promotional activity Special price deals available on competing brands.

brand. Generally, this switching is limited to brands that the customer perceives to be comparable to his or her chosen brand. Of course, customer response to promotional activity depends on the customers' price sensitivity. Long-distance telephone services and beer are examples of categories that have constant promotional activity prompting customers to switch between brands.

Customer Factors

The second group of detractors is customer factors: variety seeking, product involvement, price sensitivity, multi-brand loyalty, withdrawal from the product category, and change in needs. As noted in Chapter 4, some customers like to seek variety in their experience because they are bored with the same product or life experience; they may not be dissatisfied with the first brand's performance itself, or other values. The more variety-seeking a customer is, the less brand-loyal he or she is likely to be.

Product involvement defines how central to a customer's life the customer considers a product to be. Many products, such as light bulbs, salt, sugar, and cotton swabs are considered trivial, while others such as clothing, hairstyles, cars, and movies are deemed to be central to our lives. For these products, the customer would like to obtain maximum value repeatedly, so he or she is likely to develop a favourite brand and, accordingly, show brand loyalty. For products of low importance and involvement, there is no reason to favour a brand, so brand loyalty will be low. Sharon Beatty and Lynn Kahle have shown that customer involvement in a product is a direct determinant of brand commitment (i.e., brand loyalty).[9]

Customers also differ in their price sensitivity. Some customers check the prices even on small items and notice even small price differences. A number of marketing studies have found consumers' price sensitivity to be negatively related to brand loyalty and positively related to coupon use.[10] Of course, not all consumers are equally price sensitive. Accordingly, they differ in their brand-loyalty behaviour and in their response to competitor's promotional activities. (For more on the link between price sensitivity and customer loyalty, see the Window on Practice.)

Finally, the customer may purchase more than one brand in the same category regularly and, thus, not be completely loyal to either. The customer may also withdraw from a category—stop smoking, for instance—and, thus, his or her loyalty to a brand of cigarettes may cease. Also, as the customer moves from one stage of the life cycle to another, his or her needs may change and loyalty to brands may also change.

WINDOW ON **PRACTICE**

Customer Segments by Loyalty

A. C. Nielsen Company did a study of British supermarket shoppers and, based on their attitude toward price and promotions, identified the following five groups of customers:

1. *Branded EDLP Seekers (19 percent)*—Strapped for cash due to restricted income, they shop around to get the best price on their favourite brands, generally seeking everyday low prices (EDLP) rather than promotions that require them to alter their buying patterns (e.g., bulk buying). Thus, they score low on store loyalty scales but high on brand loyalty.

(continued)

2. *Low-Price Fixture Ferrets (23 percent)*—These are young families whose financial resources are strained by their growing expenses (e.g., mortgage). Very budget-conscious, they use coupons and seek price deals (but dislike bulk buys). They respond well to store-loyalty schemes and are store-loyal, tend to switch brands, and spend a lot on store brands.
3. *Promotion Junkies (18 percent)*—These customers will do anything to get the lowest shopping bill. They switch back and forth between national and store brands, and have loyalty to neither stores nor brands. They experience a thrill in finding a bargain, and pride in telling others where the bargains are. Nielsen describes them as a peril to retailer and manufacturer alike, as there is no long-term gain from them.
4. *Stockpilers (21 percent)*—These shoppers are affluent and are unconcerned about the size of their bill. Their store selection is driven by location, product assortment, and product quality rather than by price or promotions. They tend not to switch brands due to promotions; however, they will take advantage of promotions on their favourite brands, happily buying in bulk to stockpile and save money. Nielsen describes them as a retailer's and manufacturer's Nirvana due to their loyalty to both brands and stores.
5. *Promotionally Oblivious (18 percent)*—This group is driven by habit, settled on brands and stores, and not interested in better deals. Promotions and special deals just pass them by, and while they might occasionally indulge in soft deals such as a free item or coupons, they dislike aggressive promotions and deals. They are not a source of growth for manufacturers or stores, but they are reliable and, as Nielsen puts it, the bedrock of their franchises.

SOURCE: Adapted from Rachel Miller. "Does Everyone Have a Price? Consumer Types and Their Attitudes to Promotion." *Marketing,* April 24, 1997, 30. http://www.sainsburys.co.uk, http://www.safeway.co.uk.

LO 4 BRAND EQUITY

A few years ago, when Marriott Hotels built a new chain of mid-priced inns, they tested two alternative names for the property: Fairfield Inn and Fairfield Inn by Marriott. Survey respondents who saw the property under the second name estimated a reasonable price that was 35 percent more than that estimated by the other group of respondents, who were shown the same property but under the first name. This power of the brand name is referred to as brand equity.

TWO VIEWS OF BRAND EQUITY

Brand equity can be considered from two points of view: investors' and customers'. David Aaker offers a definition that encompasses both points of view. According to Aaker, brand equity is a set of brand assets and liabilities linked to a brand, its name, or its symbol, that add to or subtract from the value provided by a product to a firm and/or to that firm's customers.[11] Let us look at the value to the firm (or its stockholder investors) and the value to its customers separately.

Brand valuation
The financial worth of a brand name.

From the investors' standpoint, brand equity is called **brand valuation,** and is measured as the financial worth of a brand name. If we take a new soft drink, for example, and attach the brand name Coca-Cola to it, then, over the new soft drink's lifetime, how much additional earnings will the brand name Coca-Cola generate over and above the earnings from the same soft drink if sold as a no-name brand? This is brand valuation. Indeed, according to a recent study, the Coca-Cola brand name was valued at $68 billion. In Canada, the most valued brand is the Royal Bank at $4.5 billion. Among the other top 10 brands are Loblaw ($3.3 billion), Bell ($3.1 billion), Canadian Imperial Bank of Commerce ($2.8 billion), Toronto-Dominion Bank ($2.8 billion), Bank of Nova Scotia ($2.2 billion), Bank of Montreal ($1.8 billion), Canadian Tire ($1.7 billion), Esso ($1.5 billion), and Telus ($1.4 billion).[12]

From customers' point of view, brand equity is the value of that brand to the customer compared to other brands. **Brand equity** may be defined as the enhancement in the perceived utility and desirability that a brand name confers on a product. It is the customer's perception of the superiority of a product carrying that brand name compared with other brands. Customer perceptions of a brand's superiority are based on the brand associations that the customer makes (for example, that Head & Shoulders shampoo is very effective in eliminating dandruff; that Xerox copiers work reliably; that Tommy Hilfiger clothing is for very contemporary, self-confident young adults; that Roots clothing represents the great Canadian outdoors and activity in a casual style; or that Mercedes is a subtle statement of success). These associations are at the heart of brand equity, and are the outcomes of a long history of brand communications and the image projected in these communications, as well as from personal use experience.[13]

Brand equity
The enhancement in the perceived utility and desirability that a brand name confers on a product.

Brand equity reflects the greater confidence that customers place in the brand than they do in the competing brands. This confidence then translates into customer preference for the brand, brand loyalty, and even a willingness to pay a premium price for the brand. For example, a study by McKinsey & Company and Intelliquest Inc. found that consumers tend to buy brands with low brand equity, like Packard Bell, only at a price discount compared to such brands as Compaq or IBM. The resulting market share and profit potential translate into financial gains, so much so that the holding company's net worth is raised.

BRAND EQUITY VERSUS BRAND LOYALTY

The concepts of brand equity and brand loyalty are related but also distinct. Brand loyalty is a consistent re-purchase of the brand accompanied by a favourable brand attitude. Brand equity itself does not include brand purchase, although customers who perceive a higher brand equity in a brand should obviously buy that brand. Rather, brand equity is a mental concept of a brand's superiority. Brand attitude, a component of brand loyalty, is also a mental concept, but because it is an attitude, by definition it is a general evaluation of the brand and predisposition to buy it. In comparison, brand equity is based more on specific brand associations and a consideration of the value those associations represent. Thus, the emphasis in studying brand equity is on the brand associations and value.

COMPONENTS OF BRAND EQUITY

What considerations underlie customer perceptions of brand equity? This question was answered in a study by Walfried Lassar, Banwari Mittal, and Arun Sharma.[14] They identified five dimensions of brand equity:

1. *Performance*—a customer's judgment about a brand's fault-free and long-lasting physical operation and flawlessness in the product's physical construction.
2. *Social image*—the consumer's perception of the esteem in which the consumer's social or reference groups hold the brand.

3. *Value*—the brand's perceived utility relative to its costs, based on a comparison of what is received with what is given up.
4. *Trustworthiness*—the trust the brand has won from the customer—trust that the brand will maintain its strengths, and will not compromise its quality or otherwise take advantage of its customers. An example of a trust-failure is the press story about Sears automotive shops doing unneeded repairs on cars; this story detracted from Sears's brand equity.
5. *Identification*—the degree to which customers identify themselves with the brand or feel some attachment to it. In effect, consumers would say that it is their brand; it is the kind of brand they would be happy to be associated with. Often, identification occurs because the brand is associated with things, persons, ideas, or symbols we find engaging. In particular, celebrities and role models are often used to develop identification.

In many cases, brand identification springs from the social policy the brand's makers promote (e.g., diversity in hiring, environmental friendliness). Benetton has long employed shocking images associated with various social issues (e.g., AIDS research, racial harmony); it hopes to generate bonds of identification among its core customers in whom such images strike an emotional chord. Identification suffers when the brand marketer adopts some policy that goes against the value system of its customers.[15]

Marketers can measure the components of brand equity by seeking customer ratings of brands on these aspects. Table 11.2 shows a sample measurement scale. Brand equity will be highest when the brand scores well on all five components. Managers can identify which components are weak and can work to improve those aspects of the brand. Thus, measurement of these components helps managers to map their own brands vis-à-vis competitors, then take action to improve the deficient component.[16]

TABLE 11.2 Illustrative Measures of Components of Brand Equity

State your opinion on the following statements by rating them 1 through 5, where 1 means strong disagreement and 5 means strong agreement:

Performance

P1 From this brand of television, I can expect superior performance.

P2 During use, this brand of television is highly unlikely to be defective.

P3 This brand of television is made so as to work trouble-free.

P4 This brand will work very well.

Social image

SI1 This brand of television fits my personality.

SI2 I would be proud to own a television of this brand.

SI3 This brand of television will be well regarded by my friends.

SI4 In its status and style, this brand matches my personality.

Value

V1 This brand is well priced.

V2 Considering what I would pay for this brand of television, I will get much more than my money's worth.

V3 I consider this brand of television to be a bargain because of the benefits I receive.

Trustworthiness

T1 I consider the company and people who stand behind these televisions to be very trustworthy.

T2 In regard to consumer interests, this company seems to be very caring.

T3 I believe that this company does not take advantage of consumers.

Attachment

A1 After watching this brand of television, I am very likely to grow fond of it.

A2 For this brand of television, I have positive personal feelings.

A3 With time, I will develop a warm feeling toward this brand of television.

SOURCE: Lassar, Walfried, Banwari Mittal, and Arun Sharma. "Measuring Customer-Based Brand Equity." *Journal of Consumer Marketing* 12, no. 4 (1995): 11–19.

CUSTOMER LOYALTY

The concept of loyalty that marketers have developed for brands applies equally well to stores, service suppliers, and other vendors. To refer to all these targets of loyalty, we can use the general term *customer loyalty*. Thus, **customer loyalty** is a customer's commitment to a brand, store, or supplier based on a strong favourable attitude and manifested in consistent re-patronage. The Window on Research presents some insights on customer loyalty online.

Customer loyalty
A customer's commitment to a brand, store, or supplier, based on a strong favourable attitude, and manifested in consistent re-patronage.

This definition of loyalty includes both behaviour and attitude. These two components define four possible situations, as shown in Figure 11.3. When both attitude and behaviour are weak, no loyalty exists. Weak attitude means the customer does not have any liking or preference for the brand. Weak behaviour means purchase of the brand is sporadic (i.e., the same brand is not purchased consistently). When both are strong (i.e., attitude is very favourable and the same brand is purchased consistently), strong loyalty exists. The remaining two cases are more interesting.

When behaviour is high but attitude is low, the customer has spurious loyalty—loyalty that is incidental and not well-founded. The customer buys the same brand again and again or shops at the same store regularly, but he or she feels no preferential attitude toward it. Thus, the brand or store is chosen because of convenience or mere inertia, since the customer perceives all brands to be more or less the same. In such a case, given more choice or a price deal on competitive brands, the consumer might switch. To move this customer into the loyalty quadrant, the marketer would have to strengthen the customer's perception of the brand's image.

Finally, in the quadrant with high attitude and low behaviour, the customer has latent loyalty. He or she likes the brand but has been unable to buy it; perhaps the price is too high or the customer lacks access to the brand or the store. Here, the marketer needs to tap into this hidden potential market by lowering whatever barriers prevent customers from buying this desired brand.

FIGURE 11.3 Loyalty Needs Both Attitude and Behaviour

		BEHAVIOUR: STRONG	BEHAVIOUR: WEAK
ATTITUDE	STRONG	Loyalty	Latent Loyalty
	WEAK	Spurious Loyalty	No Loyalty

SOURCE: Adapted from Dick, Alan S., and Kunal Basu. "Customer Loyalty: Toward an Integrated Conceptual Framework." *Journal of the Academy of Marketing Science* 22, no. 2 (1994): 101.

WINDOW ON RESEARCH

How Important Is Customer Loyalty Online?

In studies on online retailing by Bain & Company/Mainspring, it was found that customer loyalty, measured as repeat purchases and referrals, is the key to profitability for online businesses. The studies covered three categories—apparel, groceries, and electronics—with over 2,000 online customers. Customers were found to be profitable for online retailers only if the retailer could retain the customer for a minimum of 12 months, with at least four visits from the customer to the site in this 12-month period. The study showed that the behaviour of loyal online customers is very similar to that of loyal offline customers. Online customers who are loyal spend more, refer more people, and make purchases in more categories from the same retailer. For example, by the third year of their relationship with an online apparel retailer, repeat customers spent 67 percent more than they did in the first six months. Over three years, referrals from online grocery customers purchased an additional 75 percent of the original shopper's purchase value. Specific findings from the research include:

- Online retailers lose money on one-time shoppers—Online grocers can break even only if they retain a customer for 18 months.
- Repeat purchasers spend more over time—Customers spent 23 percent more in months 31–36 of their relationship than in the first six months at online grocers.
- Referrals obtained through positive word of mouth is the best way for online retailers to get new customers—After the first purchase, an apparel shopper had referred three people to the site, and after 10 purchases, the shopper had referred at least seven people. For consumer electronics, the average customer had referred 13 people after 10 purchases.
- Retailers need to treat customers as "assets," not "transactions"—Online retailers can expect loyalty from customers only if they make efforts to provide value and convenience to customers and earn their trust.
- Finally, as in the offline world, it is extremely important for online retailers to measure customer satisfaction and retention parameters on a regular basis. This will help the online retailer segment customers according to their shopping habits, identify the factors that are important to each segment, and develop strategies that cater uniquely to each segment.

Reichheld and Schefter from Bain & Company state that "Price does not rule the web, trust does." When customers trust an online vendor, they are willing to share personal information in return for customized advertising, promotions, and products from the retailer. This, in turn, increases trust and strengthens loyalty. Having surveyed re-purchase patterns at leading websites, they found that the five primary determinants of loyalty are quality customer support, on-time delivery, compelling product presentations, convenient and reasonably priced shipping and handling, and clear and trustworthy privacy policies.

Venkatesh Shankar, Amy K. Smith, and Arvind Rangaswamy compared customer satisfaction and loyalty in online and offline environments. They focus on attitudinal loyalty, since it signifies re-purchase based on commitment and an internal predisposition to the brand/organization. With the travel industry as the context (lodging sector—data on customers who used online and offline media to make hotel reservations), they show that customer satisfaction for a service chosen online is the same as when it is chosen offline. However, loyalty to a service provider is higher when the service is chosen offline. They propose that certain characteristics of the online medium may be responsible for this difference in loyalty. As the customer considers fewer options from a smaller consideration set, through regular use of bookmarks, information on these options is more frequently reinforced than in the offline context.

Online chat groups and communities can also create an "envelope" that restricts the influence of competitive brands. As the customer's online experience becomes more and more positive, some of this positive feeling rubs off to the online medium itself, strengthening the medium's role in loyalty creation. It follows from the study that in order to keep customers loyal, online service providers need to improve their service quality, offer a good online experience, and invest in loyalty-building initiatives.

Several e-merchants are trying to lure new customers through online e-coupons. (One example is E-coupons: **http://www.e-coupons.com.**) An e-coupon reduces search costs for consumers in terms of sifting through newspapers and other print media. Since the customer goes through an active process of identifying and printing the e-coupon, it is also more likely that he or she will redeem this coupon, as against other coupons that are usually available to the customer. It has been found that e-coupons are most popular among grocery shoppers. Other categories that show a high redemption of e-coupons are toys, books, and music.

SOURCE: Adapted from Pastore, Michael. "Customer Loyalty: Key To E-commerce Profitability." March 30, 2000. http://cyberatlas.internet.com/markets/retailing/article/0,,6061_331431,00; Reichheld, Frederick F., and Phil Schefter. "E-Loyalty: Your Secret Weapon on the Web." *Harvard Business Review* (July–August 2000):105–113; Shankar, Venkatesh, Amy K. Smith, and Arvind Rangaswamy. "Customer Satisfaction and Loyalty in Online and Offline Environments." eBRC Working paper (October 2000). http://www.ebrc.psu.edu/pubs; Allen, Darren. "Earning Customer Loyalty." *eMarketer*, November 22, 2000. http://www.emarketer.com/etopics/articles/20001122_ loyalty.html; Fortin, David R. "Clipping Coupons in Cyberspace: A Proposed Model of Behaviour for Deal-Prone Consumers." *Psychology & Marketing* 17, no. 6 (June 2000): 515–534.

Richard Oliver has developed a framework (Figure 11.4) to specify four different levels of customer loyalty. The vertical dimension in the framework reflects the "degree of individual fortitude"—the degree to which the customer is able to resist offers/advances from the brand's competition, a result of the customer's own commitment to the brand. At the low end of the "individual fortitude" continuum, the customer only has brand-related information, while at the high end, the customer builds a defensive shield against the brand's competition.

The horizontal dimension refers to low and high phases of community and social support. At the low end, the community and social support is persuasive but passive in nature, while at the high end, it serves to proactively promote loyalty. Thus a 2 × 2 grid is formed across the two dimensions as shown in Figure 11.4. At high levels of individual fortitude and community and social support, customer loyalty is highest. Conversely, at the low levels of both dimensions, customer loyalty is weakest, since it stems only from product superiority. This is the traditional view of loyalty.

As the customer moves from low to high fortitude (and low social support), the customer becomes more committed to the brand, and brand re-purchase is based on his or her own "determined self-isolation." In terms of relationships, this state is equivalent to "love for the brand." The low-fortitude, high-social support cell is labeled "village envelopment," where

FIGURE 11.4 A Framework for Brand Loyalty

		COMMUNITY AND SOCIAL SUPPORT	
		HIGH	LOW
INDIVIDUAL FORTITUDE	HIGH	Immersed Self-Identity	Determined Self-Isolation
	LOW	Village Envelopment	Basic Product Superiority

SOURCE: Oliver, Richard L. "Whence Consumer Loyalty." *Journal of Marketing* 63, special issue (1999): 33–44. Reprinted with permission of American Marketing Association.

the customer is nurtured and proactively encouraged to use selected brands without his or her own active commitment to the brand. Some examples of villages or communities are website chat rooms, senior citizen organizations, card clubs, where attention from group members makes the customer want to be a part of the community.

The customer experiences a state of "immersed self-identity" at high levels of individual fortitude and social support—the highest form of loyalty in the framework. Here, the customer proactively seeks the social environment for the brand, since it not only supports the customer's self-concept, but also reinforces it through the social system. Some examples of this highest state of loyalty are found in religious institutions, fan clubs, alumni organizations, and the Harley Davidson H.O.G. (Harley Owners Group) club, where the customer associates with the product and affiliates with the social setting, since it is highly reinforcing and supportive of the same.[17]

CUSTOMER LOYALTY TO STORES

Store loyalty A customer's predominant patronage of a store, based on a favourable attitude.

The concept of store loyalty is analogous to that of brand loyalty. Following the definition of customer loyalty presented earlier, **store loyalty** is a customer's predominant patronage of a store, based on a favourable attitude. That is, the customer shops at the store more than at any other store for a type of merchandise and has a more favourable attitude toward that store. Like brand loyalty, store loyalty can be measured by customer agreement with pertinent statements, such as those shown in Table 11.3.

TABLE 11.3 Illustrative Measures of Store Loyalty

These statements may be rated on a five-point scale (where 1 means Strongly Disagree and 5 means Strongly Agree); stronger agreement shows higher loyalty.

1. I like this store very much.
2. For this group of products, I have a favourite store.
3. When buying (product), I always shop this store first.
4. In the past three months, a majority of my shopping trips have been to this store.
5. I prefer to shop at this store even if another store advertises some deal.
6. I usually divide my shopping among two or three stores.

NOTE: Item 6 needs to be reverse-scored so that strong disagreement indicates store loyalty.

LO 5 A MODEL OF STORE LOYALTY

Retailers want customers not only to visit their store but also to visit it again and again. They want to know how to earn their customers' loyalty, i.e., they want to know what makes a customer loyal to a store. Customers' store loyalty depends on two sets of factors: the "what" factor and the "how" factor. The "what" factor refers to what products the customer gets at the store—these are what he or she goes to the store for in the first place, and are what he or she might walk out of the store with. The "how" factor refers to the process entailed in customers' acquisition of those products.

The "What" Factor

The things for which a customer goes into a store include a mix of merchandise quality, assortment, price value, and store brands.

Merchandise Quality

By merchandise quality, we mean the quality of the products the store carries and offers. Stores differ vastly on this element, with merchandise ranging from shoddy to medium to premium quality. The merchandise quality is generally controlled by the brand names the store decides to carry. The store could carry well-reputed, high-quality brands, or it could carry lower-quality brands. It is intuitively obvious that the better the merchandise quality of a store, the more likely the customers are to develop store loyalty toward that store.

Assortment

A store's **assortment** is the number of different items the store carries. This includes the number of diverse product categories (e.g., appliances versus food), product varieties (e.g., in the produce section, whether the store carries products like tropical fruits and exotic vegetables), and the number of brands for the same product categories (e.g., for yogurt: Danone, Yoplait, etc.), and the size and colour varieties.

Assortment
The number of different items a store carries.

Although assortment will influence a customer's patronage, customers do not necessarily want a vast, unlimited assortment that could create shopper confusion. Instead, they want the store to carry their preferred brand and a few other related major brands so that they can compare both initially, when their brand preference is still fluid, and later, from time to time, when they want to compare leading brands. For example, a regular buyer of Danone yogurt may see an advertisement for Yoplait and may want to check it out in the store. If the regularly visited store did not carry Yoplait, this is likely to negatively affect the customer's perception of the store as an adequate store.

Within the preferred brand, customers also want availability of different sizes and colours. For example, customers would want to be able to buy, on different occasions, Danone yogurt with strawberries, prunes, cherries, or plain vanilla without having to visit another store.

In many product categories, such as in clothing, cosmetics, perfumes, jewellery, music CDs, and books, customers intrinsically desire variety. For these product categories, they value a large assortment of styles or content.

For services, too, the concept of assortment applies. Service providers who offer a bundle of related, rather than limited, services are likely to be preferred by customers. For example, in business services, an accounting firm that provides account audit services, cost-containment consulting, and tax advice is likely to be preferred over the one that offers audit services only.

Both in business and household customer markets, customers like to do **one-stop shopping,** buying all of their requirements of related products in one place or from one source. Stores like The Real Canadian Superstore attract customers by offering an assortment of product categories far greater than a typical supermarket (such as Safeway), and yet at lower prices. Loblaw's has 68 Real Canadian Superstores across Western Canada, and they continue to grow. The Real Canadian Superstore has maintained and expanded its one-stop-shopping experience for its customers. Loblaw's stores provide a wide, growing, and successful range of products to meet the everyday household needs of Canadian consumers. They have also introduced "convenience" departments in their newest stores, including housewares, bed-&-bath, electronics, apparel, footwear, baby, toys, books and magazines, jewellery, flowers, DrugStore pharmacy, optical centre, walk-in medical centre, and a digital photo centre. In addition, President's Choice (PC) Financial Services offer core banking, a popular MasterCard®, PC Financial auto, home, travel, and pet insurance, as well as the PC points loyalty program.

One-stop shopping (OSS)
The practice of acquiring all related products from one supplier.

For business products, stores such as Staples and Grand & Toy offer one-stop shopping for wide-ranging items such as paper supplies, fax and phone machines, computers, and furniture, as well as, at Staples, services such as photocopying and printing. For business services, FedEx Kinko's offers a complete range of document-preparation services.

Price Value

Customers seek low prices for the goods they buy. This is the appeal of deep discounters such as Costco. However, customers do not always, or even often, seek low-price merchandise; rather, they seek the lowest or near-lowest price, but, still, only for the quality of merchandise they desire. In addition, customers do not always bother to ensure that the price they are getting is the lowest possible; they want to feel confident only that the price is comparably low, and that if there is a lower price elsewhere, it is negligibly lower. The important point to note is that customers seek a generally low price for a given quality of merchandise. Wal-Mart and Dollarama are good examples of offering customers a low price.

Store Brands

Yet another attraction for the customer is store brands, the brands that carry a store label and are available exclusively at that store chain. Store brands add to the assortment the store presents the customer for comparison. One of these comparisons is, of course, on price vis-à-vis the national brands. Since store brands are considerably lower in price, the availability of store brands becomes one avenue for customers to maximize their price value from the store. In addition, store brands could be unique, either in value, performance, or features available, by definition, only at the specific store chain. This exclusive availability is yet another source of customers' loyal patronage. (For more on the role of store brands, see the Window on Research.)

In a recent survey, the Loblaw's President's Choice brand was ranked second as the best managed brand. Launched in 1984, the aim of the first President's Choice (PC) products was to offer better value to Canadian consumers. Today, the brand has expanded beyond a price-point focus to offer quality and health-focused alternatives to consumers. *PC Blue Menu* is aimed at the growing demands of health-conscious consumers, *PC Organics* was introduced as a result of consumer demand for organic foods, and *PC Mini Chefs* extends the range of President's Choice products to provide parents with a healthy option for their children as well. President's Choice has now expanded its product offerings, as mentioned earlier.[18]

The "How" Factor

Store loyalty also depends on how favourable the shopping experience is in a particular store. This "how" factor includes ease of merchandise selection, in-store information and assistance, convenience, problem resolution, and personalization.

Ease of Merchandise Selection

A store's merchandise selection ease refers to how easily and effortlessly customers can select products. This depends on several features: layout of aisles and shelf displays, shelf tags, product information cards, and signage. Merchandise should be arranged for easy access and for easy inter-brand comparisons. According to some reports, until recently, customers complained about the tall shelves in Toys "R" Us stores; customers, especially short and elderly customers, found it difficult to reach the merchandise for inspection. Similarly, correct price and brand shelf tags should allow easy evaluation, and comparable size and quality brands (including store brands) should be placed side by side for easy comparison. Store signage should be visible from throughout the store to help customers locate the aisles and shelf facings. Finally, items should not be out of stock. These actions make it easy for the customer to make his or her product selection efficiently and effortlessly. This ease, in turn, positively influences a customer's decision to patronize the store regularly.

In-Store Information and Assistance

By in-store information and assistance, we mean the availability of credible information about the merchandise and salesperson assistance in shopping. Merchandise selection ease provides efficiency in the self-selection of items, and most stores in the Western world are organized for self-selection. But beyond self-selection, customers sometimes need information and assistance from salespersons (for example, to see a product demonstration). If customers find that salespersons are not easily available, or if they are not knowledgeable or fair and impartial in their advice, that detracts from customers' buying efficiency or effectiveness. On the other hand, the availability of salespersons who are knowledgeable, credible, and trustworthy makes the store attractive for customers to patronize.

Convenience

Customers also want convenience, or ease in getting to the store and getting out of it once the merchandise selection is completed. This translates into ease of reaching the store location, parking availability, and quick checkout.

Location has always been a critical factor in a store's success. Generally, a supermarket attracts customers from up to an 8 km radius, and a department store or a mall from up to a 25 km radius. The location, therefore, basically determines who will choose to shop there regularly. Convenient parking is also a consideration in store preference, particularly for older consumers. Once a customer has completed his or her product selection, nothing is more important to the customer than to be able to check out and go home as soon as possible. Quick checkouts, therefore, become another important component of convenience. All else being equal, customers like to patronize stores that offer convenience on several levels.

Problem Resolution

When they need problem resolution, or remedy for mistakes or oversights, customers want this service to be easy and hassle-free. The most typical problems are the need to return or exchange merchandise. Stores with a liberal return policy that allows customers to return unused merchandise within a reasonable time, or that will repair or replace the faulty merchandise within a reasonable time, even beyond the warranty period, are likely to earn customers' repeat patronage.

Personalization

By personalization, we mean positive employee behaviour toward customers. Customers expect store employees to be pleasant and courteous in their interaction, and eager to help customers during their shopping. Stores differ greatly on this dimension. Those that hire employees with poor interpersonal skills and low aptitude for socialization with customers are likely to earn less loyalty from their customers.

WINDOW ON RESEARCH

Determinants of Store Brand Acceptance

What leads customers to buy store brands? This question was investigated by Paul S. Richardson, Arun K. Jain, and Alan Dick. They surveyed a sample of 582 grocery shoppers about their acceptance and purchase of store brands in 28 product categories (e.g., bacon, soups, juices, frozen vegetables, paper towels, and laundry detergents). Their findings were the following:

- Among the demographic characteristics, family size and income were correlated with store (private) brand-buying behaviour, but education level and age were *not* related. Larger households were more likely to buy private brands, as were lower-income households.
- Among beliefs and psychological variables, shoppers' familiarity with store brands, perceived value for money, perceived quality differential between national and store brands, and perceived risk affected store-brand buying. Shoppers who were familiar with store brands and who believed that store brands give you good value for the money were more likely to buy store brands, but if they perceived risk of poor quality (a perception that was aided by lack of familiarity), then they were less likely to buy store brands.
- The personal trait of intolerance for ambiguity (i.e., discomfort in uncertain situations) acted against private-brand acceptance.

Another study of 1,000 grocery shoppers in the United Kingdom by Ogenyi Ejye Omar has shed some light on this question. Generally, national food brands were perceived as superior to store brands in terms of quality, packaging, consistency, and image, but were perceived as lower as to good value for money. The store-brand shopper had slightly less formal education, was young, likely to be a female between 18 and 24 years of age, had at least one or two children living at home, had a larger family, had lower socioeconomic status, lived mainly in rented accommodations, and tended to be thriftier and more adventurous. The store-brand shopper shops frequently and longer, ostensibly striving for the best price and value for money. In contrast, national-brand shoppers prided themselves on shopping for food quality, good product packaging, and good product design and appearance.

SOURCES: Adapted from Richardson, Paul S., Arun K. Jain, and Alan Dick. "Household Store Brand Proneness: A Framework." *Journal of Retailing* 72, no. 2 (1996): 159–85; Omar, Ogenyi Ejye. "Grocery Purchase Behaviour for National and Own-Label Brands." *Service Industries Journal* 16, no. 1 (January 1996): 58–66. http://www.luc.edu and at http://www.buffalo.edu.

LO 6 STORE CHOICE

In the previous section, we discussed the factors that contribute to store loyalty. But how do customers decide which grocery store to shop at? Do they shop there regularly or occasionally? Do they shop there exclusively, or is it just one of the several grocery stores that they shop at? Why do they shop there rather than at other stores? Are there other stores in the area? Are they less convenient? More expensive? Less friendly? Or what? And what about the clothing store, the hardware store, or the appliance store? Do they have a favourite store in each of these categories?

These questions are important to any store owner. Owners want to get you to shop at their stores, again and again, in preference over other competing stores; they want you, in other words, to become a loyal customer. Therefore, they need to understand customers' shopping behaviour, how customers decide where to shop, as well as the factors that influence customers' store loyalty.

HOW CUSTOMERS SHOP

A typical customer generally has the option of three or four general merchandise stores to shop at; for supermarket items, the choice may even extend to ten stores. How does the customer choose the store to shop at? The number one factor in store choice is location; this was also the conclusion of a survey of about 10,000 supermarket shoppers conducted by *Consumer Reports*. But location is a relative criterion, not an absolute one. That is, customers do not always go to the nearest store, even though they want to minimize their travel distance. Sometimes, they will go to a distant store for better quality, selection, or price. Merchandise quality and price were the second and third criteria in the *Consumer Reports* study. In actuality, customers do not choose a store on the basis of a single factor, nor do they always value various factors in a specific priority order. Rather, a dynamic *interplay* of factors influences their choice.[19]

To understand this dynamic interplay, let us consider the supermarket-shopping behaviour of a family we shall call the Nobel family. The Nobels live in a suburb of a Canadian metropolis, near two supermarkets: Sobeys, 3 kms to the south, and Safeway, 2 kms to the north. (Both are big supermarket chains with stores in a number of Canadian cities.) The nearest convenience stores are a Mac's gas station at a main-road crossing about 1 kilometre to the northeast and a 7-Eleven at about the same distance but slightly off the main road.

The Nobels rarely shop at the convenience store except for gas. Their most frequent gas station is Mac's, where they occasionally buy milk when they run out of it and it is not convenient to visit the supermarket. They never shop at 7-Eleven. They divide their main food shopping between Safeway and Sobeys, shopping more often at Sobeys because it is on Mrs. Nobel's way to work. They shop at Safeway every week or so to take advantage of price specials. They visit Sobeys about once a week for a major shopping trip when they buy the bulk of the weekly requirements, and once a week for a filler trip to buy only a few items. In some weeks, they split the major shopping between Sobeys and Safeway to take advantage of price deals at each store.

The Nobels also shop for food at a few other stores. About 2 kms beyond Safeway is a new store, The Real Canadian Superstore, which is a *supercentre*, a store that sells food as well as apparel and hard goods (e.g., small appliances, electronics). Although it is farther, the Nobels shop there once every two to three weeks; this would be their major shopping trip, and they typically spend substantially more there than at Sobeys. There is also a Sam's Club (about 8 kms west) and Costco, a warehouse store about 10 kms west, but the Nobels never shop at either. Even though the Nobels visit the nearby mall (about 1 km from the Costco store), they never consider food shopping and mall shopping as a single trip. Finally, about 16 kms to the northeast, there is Tropicana, a store that features exotic vegetables and international food items. The Nobels shop there about every two months because they enjoy the merchandise variety. They consider the trip an excursion, a combination of purchasing and the excitement of browsing through the exotic products.

The Interplay of Decision Criteria

Although no two families are alike in their food shopping (and shopping for other products), the Nobel family illustrates the sort of interplay of factors that influences a customer's store choice:

- *Distance* is an important consideration, but it is not always measured from home or in kilometres; rather, it is measured by convenience, such as whether it is on the way to work, and on or off the main road or main commuting route. Moreover, small differences in distances are ignored so that a slightly farther store may be chosen on occasion, even without any other advantage. In fact, Weber's Law and the related concept of just noticeable difference (JND), seen in Chapter 4 to explain price perceptions, apply to store distances as well: some stores that are only slightly farther than the nearest may not even be perceived as being farther (particularly if they are not on the same linear path). Moreover, even among the distance differences that are perceived, some small differences might be considered negligible as tradeoffs with other store features.

- If two or more stores are equally convenient from a distance standpoint, then other factors (quality, assortment, and price) influence the store choice. If these other factors are significantly inferior at the nearest store, then a distant, less convenient store is likely to be chosen for regular shopping. The most convenient store may continue to be chosen, however, for filler trips.
- A typical customer does not limit food shopping to just one store. Rather, customers have a repertoire of stores, shopping at one store most frequently and regularly. For example, an average North American household makes an average of 2.2 visits per week to a supermarket. However, for a majority of households (more than 80 percent), only one visit is made to their most preferred supermarket. Thus, a majority of households rely on more than one food store for their food needs.[20]
- If there are stores that specialize in quality, assortment, or price deals, these stores are likely to be included in the repertoire of stores. They will be visited despite the locational disadvantage, but on a special occasion rather than a regular basis.

The most important point is that customers have a *repertoire* (i.e., assortment) of stores. This concept is analogous to the consideration set, or preference set, discussed in Chapter 8. Customers have consideration sets and preference sets not only for brands but also for stores. They limit their shopping to these stores. The choice of a specific store from the repertoire is based on the exigencies of the specific situation. For example, is this an emergency, a major shopping trip, or a filler trip? Is one of the stores in the repertoire running a price special?

As shown in the flow chart of the decision process in Figure 11.5, a store decision begins, but often does not end, with distance considerations. (The flow chart is an attempt to assemble a reasonable description of the process as inferred from a number of unrelated studies, existing marketing literature, and the authors' own customer observations and intuitive reflections.[21] To understand the store choice process for a particular clientele, marketers and researchers must conduct specific studies in their trading area.)

Yet another way of looking at the store choice decision is in terms of the total costs of shopping, both fixed and variable. A shopper is likely to visit the store with the lowest total shopping costs. The fixed costs for the customer are travel distance, shopper's inherent preference for a store, and historic store loyalty; the variable cost is dependent on the customer's shopping list—the products and the respective quantities to be purchased. Bell, Ho, and Tang suggest that the concept of "basket-size threshold" can be used to measure the relative competitiveness of a given pair of stores. Depending on the level of fixed and variable costs associated with a store, a threshold level for the customer's basket size can be determined, which can help him or her decide which store is best to shop at. For large basket sizes, stores with high fixed costs and low variable costs would be preferrable since the fixed costs are distributed among a large number of items.[22]

FIGURE 11.5 A Flow Chart of Customers' Store Choice Decision Process

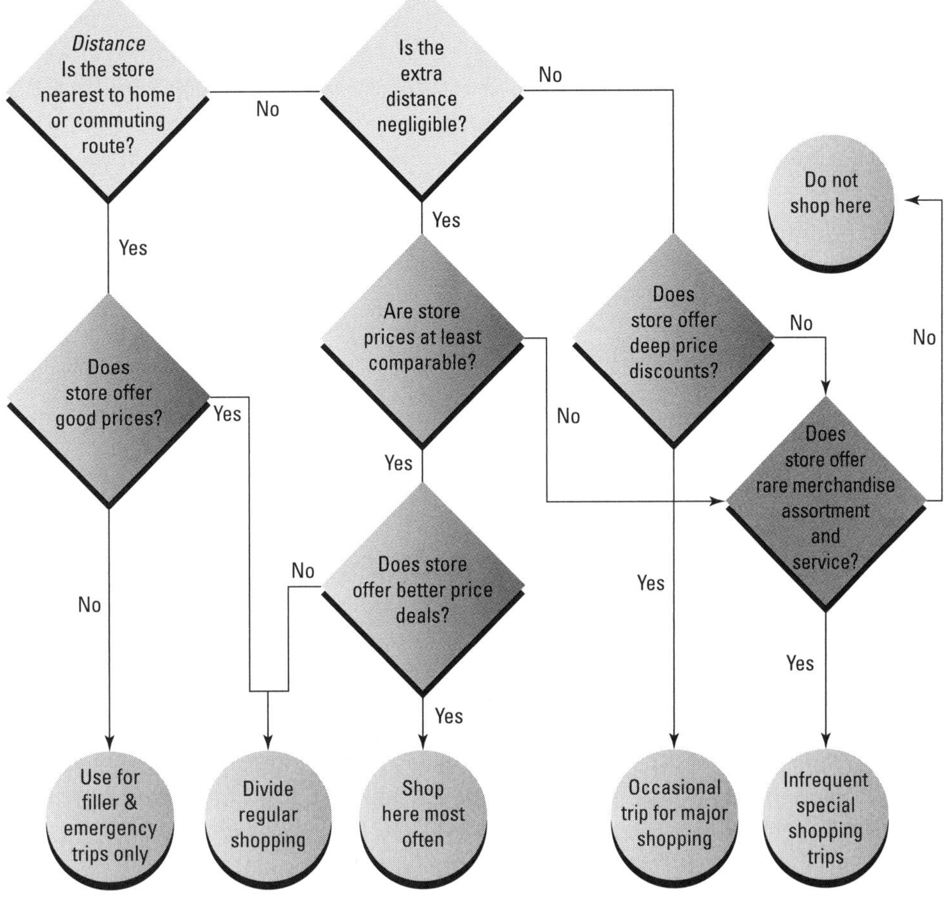

Choices Based on Nonlocational Criteria

The previous description mainly contrasts location and nonlocation as choice criteria. How do customers choose among the other factors—namely, quality, assortment, and price? The answer is twofold. First, as in the case of the Nobel family, if the store offers a substantial advantage with regard to any one of these factors, it may be included in the repertoire. If different stores offer one each of these advantages, they all may be included in the repertoire, although for occasional shopping only.

Second, if all the stores offering price or quality or assortment were conveniently located, convenient enough for the customer to make each a regularly shopped store, customers might select the store with the advantage they value the most. While some customers may patronize each type of these stores to regularly take advantage of each of these three factors, most customers would value one advantage more than others and choose the store with that advantage as their regular store. This last point is important in understanding how stores differentiate themselves. They differentiate themselves first on price, assortment, or merchandise quality. These serve as the basis of the first tier of store classification: Supermarkets tend to offer medium levels of merchandise and assortment at moderate prices, at levels considered acceptable by the mass market. Some supermarkets, such as Super C, and supercentres, such as The Real Canadian Superstore, feature low prices more than do other supermarkets. Warehouse stores offer limited selection but very attractive prices. Specialty stores, such as Les 5 Saisons in Montreal, focus on fine merchandise selection. Some supermarkets, such as Longo's in Toronto, make fresh produce their stores' special focus. Such differentiation strategies work by a process of customer **self-selection**—customers self-select themselves to be the customers of the store that offers the advantage they seek.[23]

Self-selection The idea that customers self-select themselves to be the customers of the firm that offers the advantage they seek.

Three other factors also play a role: (1) service—the courtesy and helpfulness of store personnel; (2) in-store display—the ease of finding the merchandise; and (3) atmospherics—the pleasantness of the ambiance (e.g., the lighting, the appearance, the music, and in general, the cheeriness or the gloominess of the store). These factors are generally used, however, as second-tier factors; that is, they help in choosing the store from among those that offer similar price, assortment, and quality. When these first-tier factors are equalized, customers are likely then to choose a store that offers one or all three of the second-tier advantages.

PLANNED, UNPLANNED, AND IMPULSE BUYING

Once a customer selects and visits a store, the marketer's next concerns are whether he or she buys something and what he or she buys.

All products that customers buy in the store can be classified as planned or unplanned purchases. **Planned purchases** are those that the customer had planned to buy before entering the store. **Unplanned purchases** are those the customer did not intend to buy before entering the store. The customer need not have specifically decided not to buy those products; the customer may have simply not thought about those products.

Planned purchases The purchases that a customer had planned to buy before entering the store.

Unplanned purchases Purchases that a customer did not intend to buy before entering the store.

Unplanned purchases can be of three types:

1. **Restocking unplanned purchases** are purchases of items the shopper had not thought about buying at the time but has been using regularly. He or she buys it because of an in-store display or special deal, knowing that the item will be needed in the future.
2. **Evaluated new unplanned purchases** are those items the customer needs but that had not been recognized prior to this purchase occasion. These may either be products not already in use by the customer (e.g., a cellular phone) or products in use already and not yet in need of replacement. The customer simply decides to buy additional units to expand their collection (e.g., wardrobe, one more TV set in the house) or to get extra features in newer units (e.g., high-definition television).
3. **Impulse purchases** are the extreme kind of unplanned purchase: spontaneous and completely unpremeditated. The customer buys in response to feeling a sudden urge to buy something. These purchases are made quickly and without an evaluation of need.[24]

Restocking unplanned purchases Purchase of items that the shopper had not thought about buying at the time but uses regularly.

Evaluated new unplanned purchases Purchases of items for which the need had not been recognized prior to the purchase occasion.

Impulse purchases The implementation of previously unplanned purchases, with purchase decisions made on the spur of the moment.

The best way to study planned buying is to observe the use of shopping lists. According to a Gallup study, about 55 percent of supermarket shoppers use a shopping list. However, the use of shopping lists does not rule out unplanned buying. One reason is that the use of unplanned buying depends on how exactly an item is written down on the shopping list. A person may write only the general item type (e.g., entrée), a specific product category (e.g., frozen pasta), or a specific brand (e.g., McCain). Thus, there can be degrees of unplanned buying. Second, even when the product or brand is specified, customers may deviate from the shopping list, buying a different brand or product from the one on the shopping list. Finally, customers may buy additional items not on the shopping list. For example, the same Gallup study found that an average shopping-list user had planned to buy 10.5 items, on the average, but ended up buying 16.

Unplanned purchases can occur for several reasons. The planned item may be out of stock and may be replaced by another item. Or a substitute item may be on sale. In addition, the store may be featuring an item not on the list, and the customer may realize he or she forgot to write it down, or may judge it as being needed in the future. Thus, a good price deal might induce customers to **forward buy** an item for future consumption.

Forward buying
A practice wherein customers buy an item for future consumption.

Customers may make mental rather than physical paper lists; a researcher might count these customers as list nonusers making unplanned purchases, whereas, in fact, they are merely buying items on their mental lists. Still, the use of a shopping list does signify greater use of planning compared to unplanned purchases. A study in New Zealand found that grocery shoppers who had come to the store with a shopping list bought, on average, seven fewer items and spent $13.13 less than shoppers who did not bring a list.[25]

In-Store Factors

Whether the purchase is planned or not, several in-store factors influence exactly what is bought or not bought. In-store factors refer to those characteristics of the store, customer, or situation that affect the customer's decision process inside the store. These include knowledge of the store, time pressure, the shopper's companion, special store promotions, atmospherics, and customer mood.

Generally, customers shop at stores about which they are knowledgeable in terms of merchandise display and store procedures. Customers like to shop at stores where they feel in control; familiarity with the store gives them that feeling. This encourages **exploratory shopping,** or browsing after collecting the items on the shopping list, in contrast with being in unfamiliar stores, where they would feel disoriented about where items are.

Exploratory shopping
Just browsing after collecting the items on the shopping list.

Time pressure is the second in-store factor. Customers hassled with time pressure tend to limit their purchases to pre-listed items. The effect is compounded if the customer is under time pressure and is also shopping in a new store where prior store knowledge is absent.[26]

Shopping companions also influence the purchases. More than half of customers shop with a companion.[27] Often children accompany parents on shopping trips, and they make new requests inside the store, many of which parents will accede to. If other companions, such as friends, are themselves under time pressure, they limit exploratory shopping and, consequently, unplanned purchasing. Special store promotions play a significant role in inducing unplanned purchases. Some customers find special promotions simply irresistible, and take advantage of the special deal either for forward buying or for making an impulse purchase of a new item.

Atmospherics, the physical setting of the store, can make a store either a pleasure to linger in or a drag that one wants to be done with quickly. Atmospherics include colours, lighting, cleanliness, even fragrances or smells, and, of course, background music. One study showed that when the background music tempo was slow, customers spent more time in the store and, on an average, spent more money.[28]

Atmospherics
The physical setting of the store that influences customer behaviour.

A customer's pleasant mood can induce exploratory shopping and a desire to reward oneself by buying unplanned items. Unpleasant moods limit customer attention to the task at hand, namely buying the planned items. Customers bring moods into the store, but moods are also created or altered by store atmospherics.[29]

NON-FOOD SHOPPING

While many factors previously described above apply to non-food shopping as well, the selection process for a non-food store is somewhat different because of the infrequent nature of purchase. While a customer shops in a food store about weekly or even more often, the shopping for non-food items may be once every few months (e.g., clothing), once a year, or even less often (e.g., appliances).

Since non-food shopping is generally more high-involvement shopping, distance and convenience take a back seat, up to a point. Suppose you wanted to buy some furniture; say, a sofa. You are likely to be willing to drive 5 to 10 km, and even 20 km if you thought the store might offer something of great value. Significant factors in deciding on the store are expected merchandise (quality and selection) and price levels, customer service, store image, and special advertised promotions.

By merchandise and price levels and by customer service, non-food stores differentiate themselves (just as food stores do) from their competitors, and customers decide which stores meet their level of needs. For example, among furniture stores, some sell country-style furniture, some colonial style, and some contemporary American or contemporary European; customers would readily eliminate some stores on that basis. Regarding price levels, some stores are priced very upscale, and they would intimidate customers seeking economy-priced furniture. On the other hand, low-priced furniture stores would not interest upscale clientele.

Store image
The sum total of perceptions customers have about a store.

Store image, the sum total of perceptions customers have about the store, is determined by these merchandise, service, and price factors; it is also determined by atmospherics, advertising, and store personnel. Store image determines the kind of clientele a store will attract, but the clientele also feed back into store image. Finally, the sale promotions of the day exert a major influence in the store's inclusion in the customer's list of stores to visit.

SHOPPING MOTIVES

So far we have described shopping purely as a purchasing activity. That is, we shop so we can buy what we want; if we did not want to buy anything, we would not go shopping. But from personal experience, we know that is not always true. We often go shopping even when we don't really have anything particular in mind to buy. In common parlance, this activity is called window shopping. A more accurate term would be **store visiting**—the practice of visiting various stores and shopping centres without necessarily planning to buy anything.

Store visiting
The practice of visiting various stores and shopping centres without necessarily having any plans to buy anything.

Shopping motives
The reasons customers have for visiting stores.

If customers don't necessarily have any plans to buy, why would they visit a store? What, in other words, are customers' **shopping motives** or reasons to visit a store? When not expressly shopping to buy something, customers may be motivated to visit a store for one or more of the following reasons:[30]

- *Recreation*—Visiting a store can be fun. Many stores are set up to provide a sensory experience. The colorful display of clothing in specialty clothing stores such as Benneton, the rock video blasting, the strong aromas in the Starbucks coffee shop, and even the hustle and bustle of people walking, chatting, browsing: all of these can be very stimulating to the senses. Many customers, therefore, visit stores as a means of recreation when they have nothing better to do at home.[31]

- *Socialization*—Visiting stores also offers opportunity for social interaction with other people, both acquaintances and strangers, and with store personnel themselves. Some stores even become hangouts for singles who want to meet others with similar tastes, such as customers with literary interests at bookstores.

- *Seeking Status*—Store employees often attend to customers very courteously, addressing them with terms of respect, and respond to their information and assistance needs, thus giving those customers a definite sense of social status.
- *Self-Gratification*—In contrast to the other motives, this one does require some actual purchasing. But the goal of purchasing might be not so much the utility of the product purchased, but rather the sense of reward that can come from spending money. This can occur both when a person is feeling depressed, or alternatively, when the person feels he or she deserves a reward.
- *Information*—Visiting stores is a good source of information about what is new in the market and what is fashionable. Some customers have a strong interest in particular product categories, and they like to stay well informed about these. Market mavens, described in Chapter 5, often visit stores to satisfy this motive.

Shopping motives can also be classified as utilitarian or hedonic in nature. As discussed, the customer experiences utilitarian shopping value when he or she gets the desired product on a shopping trip with the least effort, while hedonic value is obtained from the fun and pleasure associated with the buying process. In a comparison of overall shopping value (utilitarian and hedonic) of a typical North American and Russian shopping experience, Griffin, Babin, and Modianos found that North American shoppers report higher levels of utilitarian shopping value compared to Russian shoppers. However, Russian and North American shoppers report comparable levels of hedonic value. They found that Russian shoppers report comparable levels of hedonic value even in the face of poor service and unpleasant shopping experiences because they make relative judgments based on their own shopping experiences and expectations, rather than on absolute information about the shopping experiences in external environments as in North America.[32]

ONE-STOP SHOPPING

LO 7

Suppliers who offer a variety of products may want their customers to engage in one-stop shopping (OSS), the practice of acquiring all related products from one supplier. This supplier may be a manufacturer, a service company, or a reseller. The phrase "related products" refers obviously to an arbitrary set of products. To some customers, it may mean all products of a particular type (e.g., all appliances or all clothing); to others, these product categories may be broader (e.g., all household durable goods). Customers may also construe related products to mean products pertaining to a category of needs: for example, all of one's health-care needs, or all financial products, such as checking account, savings account, credit card, debit card, mortgage, and investments. Often, the customer's view of what products are related is shaped by an observed instance of one-stop availability. For example, until banking became available inside supermarkets, customers may not have thought of banking services as belonging to the "basket" of supermarket goods.

Customer Motivations for Seeking OSS

Customers seek one-stop shopping (OSS) because of its potential to provide convenience, cost savings, and integrated products. Customers today are experiencing increased time pressure. They value OSS because it saves time by not having to acquire related products from different suppliers or stores. Buying related products from different suppliers will also add to the cost of buying. For household customers, it may be the cost of transportation to different stores and the cost of baby-sitting services if adults like to leave their children home when shopping. For business customers, the increased employee time needed for multiple-stop shopping translates directly into labour costs. Secondly, suppliers of OSS save on costs of doing business (just as customers do), and they might be able to pass on a part of these cost savings to customers.

The third benefit of OSS to customers is that it helps them obtain better-integrated product groups. For example, when customers obtain all of their financial services from an OSS supplier, there is better coordination between various financial products, and the customer can move funds from one portfolio to another. Business customers of computer software can be offered more integrated software suites if they buy them from the same supplier.

A superb example of one-stop shopping is Wal-Mart, which carries apparel, general merchandise, and packaged food products. Even though food is less profitable than general merchandise or apparel, Wal-Mart carries it because it offers customers one-stop shopping convenience. In its supercentres, Wal-Mart's big pull for customers is that it carries approximately 6,000 different items, from food (produce, bakery, deli, frozen foods, meat) to toothpaste to treadmills under one very big roof. Wal-Mart's experience demonstrates that the lure of one-stop shopping brings in new customers, or it brings in current customers more often.[33]

Risks of OSS

On the flip side, one-stop shopping has some potential perceived risks. Customers may not want to put all their eggs in one basket. Customers may believe, rightly, that they can lower the risk by diversifying their suppliers. For example, in financial services, apportioning one's investments among two or three brokers may seem to offer better protection against bad investment decisions. Business customers of advertising agencies might perceive the risk that the creative work will not be creative enough if handled by a single agency; hiring multiple agencies for portions of work is seen as a way to diffuse this risk. A second risk is that the customer's fate is tied to a single supplier. If the supplier goes out of business, for example, the customer's business could suffer.

Implications For Marketers

For marketers, OSS gives rise to some imperatives. First, due to increasing customer demand for time and cost savings, customer preference for OSS is going to increase. Marketers who don't constantly expand the product portfolio to offer OSS are at risk. What is critical is to find out, by constant customer research, just what products are considered appropriate candidates for OSS. Another implication is that OSS offerings should be value-based. In other words, OSS should offer better value to customers, in time and/or cost savings, than what the customer can obtain from buying the bundled products individually.

Finally, OSS suppliers should study the risks customers perceive in OSS buying, and should endeavour to reduce these risk perceptions. They should design OSS bundles with reduced risks (for example, by dealing in diversified financial portfolios, or by hiring diverse creative talent in advertising). Then they should communicate how the company minimizes potential risks.

CUSTOMER LOYALTY TO PRODUCTS AND STORES AND THE THREE CUSTOMER ROLES

In this section, we discuss the relevance of various concepts covered in the chapter to the three customer roles: user, payer, and buyer. Some concepts are relevant to the market value that users seek; others are relevant to payers; and still others capture the buyer role. Table 11.4 presents an overview.

The first concept is brand loyalty. We defined it in two ways: behavioural and attitudinal. The former relates to the buyer role, as it stems from the buyer's consistent purchase of the same brand. The latter, the attitudinal brand loyalty, reflects the user's preference for the brand based on a favourable attitude. Next, we presented a model of brand loyalty, describing factors that promote or, alternatively, detract from brand loyalty. Of the factors that promote loyalty, brand-performance fit, as well as social and emotional identification, is a user value. When users find a brand that offers these values, they want the reinforcement of rewards these values reflect. Habit and history are relevant to both user and buyer roles. Users get conditioned to the brand and its specific features, and seek it as a conditioned response. Buyers want to routinize their purchases, and buying based on history or habit helps achieve this routinization.

The factors that act against brand loyalty are the attraction of alternatives, which comprises brand parity, competitors' promotional activities, and the customer's variety-seeking drive, product involvement, and price sensitivity. Brand parity reflects user indifference to brand choice. Competitors' promotional activity is directed the most at the payer role. Variety seeking is primarily the user desire to inject some variety into use experience, but buyers too may tire of dealing with the same brand seller and may seek an alternative. Product involvement means that users care about what they use. Finally, price sensitivity is most relevant to the payer role; when customers are price sensitive, the payer role dominates in brand decision.

The next concept is brand equity, which has five components: performance, social image, value, trustworthiness, and identification. The first two components are most relevant to the user role. If a brand scores well on these two components, the user is pleased; accordingly, the payer is willing to pay for these superior user values. The third component, value, as defined here, refers to the ratio of outcome to input (i.e., how much reward the customer gets, and at what cost). Therefore, in the computation of value, the user value and the payer value are both taken into account. With trustworthiness, users can use and enjoy a product without fear of failed performance. It also gives buyers relief from the fear of being taken advantage of. Finally, identification is a user value. When products give superior scores on all five components, they satisfy the needs and desires of all three roles. Accordingly, then, that brand's equity is high.

We then discussed a model of store loyalty. Here, the "what" factors of merchandise quality and assortment appeal to the user role; users want to maximize these factors. Price value appeals most to payers. And store brands also appeal to payers as a means of cost reduction; for users, they imply a burden to evaluate the store brand and ensure that it has good quality. The "how" factors (merchandise selection ease, in-store assistance, convenience, problem resolution, and personalization) all appeal to the buyer role. It is as buyers that customers often seek these factors in the store to which they choose to be loyal.

In explaining how customers make their store choice, we described three decision criteria: distance/convenience of location, price, and merchandise quality and assortment. These three criteria are of relevance, respectively, to the buyer, payer, and user roles. When a store is chosen despite the greater distance, the buyer is giving up convenience for the sake of either the payer (i.e., to get better prices) or the user (i.e., to get better merchandise), or both.

TABLE 11.4 Customer Loyalty to Products and Stores and the Three Customer Roles

Concept	User	Payer	Buyer
BRAND LOYALTY			
Behavioural			• Reflects buyer's sale consistent behaviour
Attitudinal	• Reflects user preference		
A MODEL OF BRAND LOYALTY DETERMINANTS			
Brand-performance fit	• User value		
Social/emotional identification	• User value		
Habit and history	• User conditioning to product/source		• Buyer routinizes brand decision
Attraction of alternatives			
Brand parity	• Reflects user indifference		
Competitor promotions		• Most appealing to payer	
Variety seeking	• Users may seek variety in product/use		• Buyers may desire variety in sellers they deal with
Product involvement	• Users care about the brand		
Price sensibility		• Payer role dominates when customers are price sensitive	
BRAND EQUITY			
Performance Social image	• Most relevant to user roles	• Payers willing to pay for these superior user values	
Value	• User values are compared with payer value		
Trustworthiness	• Users can enjoy the product with assurance		• Trust of brand maker most valuable to buyers who may be accountable for this decision
Identification	• Users feel an attachment to the brand		
STORE LOYALTY			
"What" factors Merchandise quality Assortment	• Users want to maximize these factors		
Price value		• Payers most interested	
Store brands	• Users want to ensure quality	• Payers want to minimize costs	
"How" factors Merchandise selection ease In-store assistance Convenience Problem-resolution Personalization			• Buyers seek these benefits in a store
STORE CHOICE			
Distance/convenience			• Of concern to buyer
Price		• Of concern to payer	
Merchandise quality and assortment	• User influence		
UNPLANNED AND IMPULSE PURCHASES			
Exploratory shopping	• Can be driven by user role seeking new items		• Buyers may try to minimize future task
In-store promotions		• Most relevant to payer role	
Atmospherics Knowledge of the store Time pressure Purchase companion			• Buyer is influenced the most by these factors

Finally we discussed unplanned and impulse buying, and six factors that encourage or suppress them: namely, exploratory shopping, in-store promotions, atmospherics, knowledge of the store, time pressure, and shopping companion. Exploratory shopping may be driven by the user role, in that the user may be trying to explore what else might be worth buying. The buyer may also be trying to explore what else is in the store so that, by buying it now, he or she may minimize the future buying task. In-store promotions are targeted to the payer role. Finally, the last four factors influence the buyer role. Thus, any of the three customer roles may drive a particular unplanned or impulse purchase.

SUMMARY

LO 1

We began this chapter with a description of brand loyalty. We defined behavioural brand loyalty as consistent purchase of the same brand, and attitudinal brand loyalty as high liking of the brand. Combining these two concepts, brand loyalty is the consistent re-purchase of the same brand based on favourable attitude toward it.

LO 2, 3

We then presented a model of brand loyalty, accounting for factors that induce a customer to become brand loyal, as well as those that deter a customer from doing so. Among the former are three factors: perceived brand performance, social and emotional identification with the brand, and habit and history of brand usage. The deterring factor is the attraction of the alternative brands, which, in turn, consists of market factors, such as brand parity and competitive promotions, and customer factors, such as variety seeking, price/promotion sensitivity, and low product involvement.

LO 4

Following this, we presented a related concept, namely brand equity and its two views. From the investors' viewpoint, it is a brand's financial worth; from the customers' point of view, it is the perceived relative superiority of a brand name. The rest of the discussion focused on the customer-based brand equity, which was described as having five components: performance, social image, value, trustworthiness, and identification. Brand equity is highest when the brand scores well on all five components.

LO 5

In the second part of the chapter, we discussed customers' store choice and loyalty behaviour. We described the concept of store loyalty, which refers to a customer's predominant patronage of a store based on a favourable attitude. We presented a model of store loyalty comprised of "what" factors and "how" factors. The former refer to the products the customer gets at the store, whereas the latter are the processes entailed in shopping at that store. The "what" factors include merchandise quality, assortment, price value, and availability of store brands. The "how" factors include the ease of finding merchandise; availability of in-store information and assistance; convenience of location, parking, and checkout procedures; the quality of problem resolution (e.g., ease of obtaining refunds and exchanges); and personalization (i.e., employee behaviour).

LO 6

We then discussed the fact that customers choose stores based on location and distance as their first criteria, but these criteria are tempered by consideration of other factors: quality, assortment, and price. These factors lead customers to form a repertoire of stores at which they usually shop. We presented a flow-chart model of how customers form this repertoire and then distribute their shopping over this repertoire.

Once the store is chosen, product choice begins. Customers do not always buy just what they had planned to buy. Rather, unplanned and impulse purchases also occur. We described these types of purchases. Several in-store factors play a role in a customer's shopping experience and the extent to which unplanned and impulse purchases might occur; these factors include knowledge of the store, time pressure, special store promotions, store atmospherics, customer mood, and whether there is a shopping companion.

Customers generally shop to make a purchase. Often, however, other motives also exist. These include recreation, socialization, status seeking, self-gratification (i.e., rewarding oneself by spending some money), and acquiring information.

LO 7 An important development in customers' shopping behaviour is the concept of one-stop shopping (OSS). This refers to the practice of acquiring all related products from the same supplier or store. Customer motivations for seeking OSS include convenience, cost savings, and integrated products (a range of products that coordinated well, e.g., buying all the computer network components from the same supplier). These benefits are balanced by consideration of the risks in OSS, which is, after all, dependence on a single source. We suggested that OSS is an important opportunity for marketers. Marketers need to find out, through constant customer research, just what products customers consider appropriate for OSS. And then marketers should develop OSS offerings that give customers some added value over the alternative of customers buying those products from individual sources.

In the final section, we revisited the various concepts described in the chapter, identifying their relevance to the three customer roles. We pointed out that consideration of the three customer roles helps a marketer identify the link between specific product and store loyalty-building tools and the role-specific market values that customers seek.

KEY TERMS

Assortment 411
Atmospherics 419
Attitudinal Brand Loyalty 399
Attraction of Alternatives 402
Behavioural Brand Loyalty 398
Brand Equity 405
Brand Loyalty 399
Brand Parity 402
Brand Valuation 404
Competitive Promotional Activity 402
Customer Loyalty 407
Evaluated New Unplanned Purchases 418
Exploratory Shopping 419
Forward Buy 419
Impulse Purchases 418
One-Stop Shopping (OSS) 411
Planned Purchases 418
Restocking Unplanned Purchases 418
Self-Selection 418
Shopping Motives 420
Store Image 420
Store Loyalty 410
Store Visiting 420
Unplanned Purchases 418

DISCUSSION QUESTIONS AND EXERCISES

1. Identify any five brands to which you are loyal. Discuss why you are loyal to those brands, using the explanations offered in this chapter.
2. As a store manager, you just read the model of store loyalty described in this chapter. You are excited because you believe you have found the key to making your customers loyal to your store. Briefly outline your action plan.
3. You just read the section on brand equity discussed in this chapter. As a brand manager of (1) a consumer packaged-goods company or (2) a home insurance company, you make it your goal to strengthen your customer-based brand equity considerably over the next five years. Outline your plan of action.
4. Interview five household customers to understand their store-choice process for supermarkets. Create a flow chart of their store-selection process similar to the flow chart shown in the chapter. Identify how different customers differ in their store choice and discern if there might also be a common underlying overall pattern.
5. Interview two customers who do not buy store brands and two who do. Synthesize your interviews to describe customers, perceptions of store brands, and what explains whether or not customers would consider any store brands. Relate the underlying reasons for both types of customers to components of brand equity (treating store as a brand).

APPENDIX

Customer Satisfaction and Loyalty to Brands—Insights from International Markets

Europe

A survey of English adults by BMRB International shows that 61 percent of the U.K.'s most affluent shoppers agree on their philosophy of brand loyalty: "when they find a brand they like, they stay with it." However, an alarming finding is that 50 percent of the respondents do not believe that brands are better than own-label. Own-label brands have claimed 31 percent of the U.K.'s grocery sales according to Datamonitor. The trend in the U.K. is to create brand loyalty through coupons.

Japan

The Japanese are strong brand loyals. The older Japanese customers' reliance on brand names dates to their formative years during the Second World War and the years of post-war poverty when goods were scarce and brand names provided the customers with safety and dependability in a product. The younger Japanese customer is status- and fashion-conscious, and brand names cater to this consciousness. The Japanese consumer's hierarchical concern with brands can be seen in the way the various Suntory brands have occupied different positions in society. In the early 1960s, the best-selling Suntory was a light whiskey called Red; a few years later, Kaku was priced higher. The most premium brand was called Old. Later on, priced even higher for senior executives, came Suntory Reserve. When a Japanese salaryman selects a Suntory brand, he does so solely according to his position in the company. Suntory Old dominates the Japanese market in the middle level, and Reserve is what one drinks when one reaches high management.

Mexico

NAFTA (the North American Free Trade Agreement), enacted in January 1994, has created a regional trading block within North America, and it has benefited North American firms by fostering rapid growth in the Mexican market. NAFTA is slowly reshaping Mexico's infrastructure and economic environment, yet North American firms have to tackle several brand-management issues to succeed in the Mexican market. Given the low purchasing power of the Mexican consumer, price is more important to him or her than quality. Yet quality considerations are not completely discarded. The Mexican consumer favours generic products over branded products in canned foods due to the price advantage, but not in categories such as personal care. This is because the consumer lacks the confidence in the performance of generic personal-care items compared to the branded products. Thus, private labels or generic brands could be used to penetrate the mass market in some categories. Small package sizes, persuasive advertising, focus on warranty, value, and country-of-origin could all help reduce price-sensitivity. Also, to sell in Mexico, firms must understand and follow Mexican labelling requirements, which are continually changing, and the ambiguity in law makes compliance difficult. Distribution in Mexico is dominated by family-owned and -operated stores, and firms need to understand the importance of personal relationships and trust in Mexican business. Finally, distribution patterns and consumer behaviour seem to differ considerably across the country, and regional variations in strategy would be essential to succeed in the Mexican market.

China

A survey of Chinese consumers in 20 cities shows a preference for well-known brands in the food and beverage categories. Seventy-eight percent of consumers continually purchase the top three brands of instant noodles, while 57 percent of consumers buy the leading three brands of MSG. The top three brands of toilet bowl cleaner and washing machine detergent are continually purchased by 75 percent and 65 percent of consumers, respectively. However, for certain foods and daily products, such as soy sauce and some detergents, brands are almost all local, with few major national brands. Zhang Zhongliang, general-secretary of the China Economic Prediction Centre, predicts that in China, the hot products for consumer purchase in the coming years will be: renovated household appliances such as DVDs; convenience foods such as instant noodles and prepared frozen foods; IT products that facilitate communication, including PCs, pagers, and mobile phones; relaxation and recreation products that improve health; educational products; and consumer products associated with home remodelling.

Russia

Results of the first Russian survey on customer satisfaction conducted by the Stockholm School of Economics provide information on consumer loyalty patterns in several sectors, such as food, clothes, and telecommunications. The European Customer Satisfaction Index (ECSI) was calculated for brands in the different categories. The food market survey included commonly used products, such as beer, sausage, and yogurt. Consumers indicate high satisfaction levels with imported products in each of these categories, sometimes more than the local brands, yet there is more loyalty to the local brands, primarily because they are cheaper than the imported brands. The researchers divided the clothes sector on the basis of producers, and found that among central department stores, local markets, local supermarkets, boutiques, and other stores, consumers are least satisfied with the local markets, but are most loyal to them, primarily because of the price factor. Boutiques are highest in satisfaction ratings and follow second in loyalty. The telecommunications market was divided into two kinds of providers: wire communications providers and mobile telecommunications providers. It was found that sub-sector local providers have room for improvement in their services, as they are at a much lower level of satisfaction than foreign ones.

SOURCE: Adapted from Palumbo, Fred, and Paul Herbig. "The Multicultural Context of Brand Loyalty." *European Journal of Innovation Management* 3, no. 3 (2000). http://www.emerald-library.com; Ghosh, Amit K. "Brand Management in Post-NAFTA Mexico." *Journal of Product & Brand Management* 7, no. 2 (2000). http://www.emerald-library.com; Yelkur, Rama. "Consumer Perceptions of Generic Products: A Mexican Study." *The Journal of Product & Brand Management* 9, no. 7 (2000). http://www.emerald-library.com; "Survey Of Consumer Behaviour In China." *ChinaOnline*, November1999. http://www.chinaonline.com/industry/consumer/NewsArchive/Secure/1999/november/B9111715-SS.asp; Agasieva, Janna. "Statistical Research on Consumer Behaviour in the Northwest Region of Russia." BISNIS, 1999. http://www.bisnis.doc.gov/bisnis/country/.

NOTES

1 John Gray, "Treasure or Trash?," *Canadian Business*, June 7–20, 2004, 27; John Gray and Luba Krekhovetsky, "King of the Kruller," *Canadian Business*, June 7–20, 2004, 45; Rebecca Harris, "Down–Home Smarts," *Marketing*, Feb. 7, 2005, 15.

2 Embert Vaandering, "Hey, Big Spender: How Canadian Tire Scored Big with a Campaign That Put Its Unique Promotional Currency at the Heart of Its Integrated In-Store and Online Campaign," *Marketing*, Jan. 14, 2002, 8; Timothy Woolstencroft and Jeannette Hanna, "The Keys to Success," *Marketing*, June 20, 2005, 44.

3 Holloway, Andy, "The Customer is King," *Canadian Business*, July 18–Aug.14, 2005, 62.

4 Dan M. Tratensek, "Hand and Power Tools: Consumers, Professionals Show Increasing Brand Loyalty," *Do-It-Yourself Retailing*, June 1, 1999; Melanie Wells, "Cult Brands," *Forbes*, April 16, 2001.

5 "The Power of Private Label: A Review of Growth Trends Around the World, 2005," ACNielsen, http://www2.acnielsen.com/news/20050927.shtml.

6 Jacob Jacoby and Robert W. Chestnut, *Brand Loyalty Measurement and Management* (New York: John Wiley & Sons, 1978), 2.

7 Alan S. Dick and Kunal Basu, "Customer Loyalty: Toward an Integrated Conceptual Framework," *Journal of the Academy of Marketing Science* 22, no. 2 (1994): 101.

8 Susan Fournier, "Consumers and Their Brands: Developing Relationship Theory in Consumer Research," *Journal of Consumer Research* 24 (March 1998): 343–74.

9 Sharon Beatty and Lynn Kahle, "The Involvement-Commitment Model: Theory and Implications," *Journal of Business Research* 6, no. 30 (1996): 149–68.

10 Banwari Mittal, "An Integrated Framework for Relating Diverse Consumer Characteristics to Supermarket Coupon Redemption," *Journal of Marketing Research* 31 (November 1994): 533–44.

11 David A. Aaker, *Managing Brand Equity* (New York: The Free Press, 1991).

12 http://www.brandfinance.com/pdfs/Canadasmostvaluablebrands2005.pdf; John Gray, "What's in a brand?," *Canadian Business*, Dec. 26–Jan. 15, 2006, 73.

13 Kevin L. Keller, "Conceptualizing, Measuring, and Managing Customer-Based Brand Equity," *Journal of Marketing* 57 (January 1993): 1–22.

14 Walfried Lassar, Banwari Mittal, and Arun Sharma, "Measuring Customer-Based Brand Equity," *Journal of Consumer Marketing* 12, no. 4 (1995): 11–19.

15 C. B. Bhattacharya, Hayagreeva Rao, and Mary Ann Glynn, "Understanding the Bond of Identification: An Investigation of Its Correlates Among Art Museum Members," *Journal of Marketing* 59, no. 4 (October 1995): 46–57.

16 Kevin L. Keller, Wagner A. Kamakura, and G. J. Russell, "Measuring Customer Perceptions of Brand Quality with Scanner Data: Implications for Brand Equity," *Report Number 91–122* (Cambridge, MA: Marketing Science Institute); Pierre Francois and Douglas MacLachlan, "Ecological Validation of Alternative Customer-Based Brand Strength Measures," *International Journal of Research in Marketing* 12 (1995): 322; R. Kenneth Teas and Terry H. Grapentine, "Demystifying Brand Equity," *Marketing Research* 8, no. 2 (Summer 1996): 25–29.

17 Richard L. Oliver, "Whence Consumer Loyalty," *Journal of Marketing* 63, special issue (1999): 33–44.

18 "The Power of Private Label: A Review of Growth Trends Around the World," ACNielsen, http://www2.acnielsen.com/news/20050927.shtml.

19 Barbara E. Kahn and Leigh McAlister, *Grocery Revolution: The New Focus on the Consumer* (Reading, MA: Addison-Wesley, 1996).

20 *Ibid.*, p. 96.

21 Michel Laroche, Mark Cleveland, and Elizabeth Browne, "Exploring Age-related Differences in Information Acquisition for a Gift Purchase," *Journal of Economic Psychology* 25 (2004): 61–95; Easwer S. Iyer, "Unplanned Purchasing: Knowledge of Shopping Environment and Time Pressure," *Journal of Retailing* 65 (Spring 1989): 40–57.

22 David R. Bell, Teck-Hua Ho, and Christopher S. Tang, "Determining Where to Shop: Fixed and Variable Costs of Shopping," *Journal of Marketing Research* 25 (August 1998): 352–69.

23 Art Thomas and Ron Gardland, "Supermarket Shopping Lists," *International Journal of Retail and Distribution Management* 21, no. 2 (1993): 8–14.

24 Rook, "The Buying Impulse."

25 Thomas and Gardland, "Supermarket Shopping Lists."

26 C. Whan Park, Easwer S. Iyer, and Daniel C. Smith, "The Effects of Situational Factors on In-Store Grocery Behaviour: The Role of Store Environment and Time Available for Shopping," *Journal of Consumer Research* 15 (March 1989): 422–33; Mark Cleveland, Barry J. Babin, Michel Laroche, Philippa Ward, and Jasmin Bergeron, "Information Search Patterns for a Christmas Gift Purchase: A Cross-National Examination of Gender Differences," *Journal of Consumer Behaviour* 3, no. 1 (September 2003): 20–47.

27 Quoted in Kahn and McAlister, 123.

28 Ronald E. Milliman, "Using Background Music to Affect the Behaviour of Supermarket Shoppers," *Journal of Marketing* 46, no. 3 (1982): 86–91.

29 Robert J. Donovan, John R. Rossiter, Gilian Marcoolyn, and Andrew Nesdale, "Store Atmosphere and Purchasing Behaviour," *Journal of Retailing* 70, no. 3 (1994): 283–94. Marie-Odile Richard, "Modeling The Impact of Internet Atmospherics on Surfer Behaviour," *Journal of Business Research* 58, no. 12 (1994): 1632–1642.

30 Danny Bellenger and Pradeep K. Korgaonkar, "Profiling the Recreational Shopper," *Journal of Retailing* 56, no. 3 (1980): 77–92; Barry J. Babin, William R. Darden, and Mitch Griffin, "Work and/or Fun: Measuring Hedonic and Utilitarian Shopping Value," *Journal of Consumer Research* 20 (March 1994): 644–56.

31 Peter N. Bloch, Nancy M. Ridgway, and Scott A. Dawson, "Shopping Mall as a Consumer Habitat," *Journal of Retailing* 70, no. 1 (1994): 23–42; Michel Laroche, Lefa Teng, Richard Michon, and Jean-Charles Chebat, "Incorporating Service Quality into Consumer Mall Shopping Decision Making: A Comparison Between English and French Canadian Consumers," *Journal of Services Marketing* 19, no. 3 (2005): 157–163.

32 Mitch Griffin, Barry J. Babin, and Doan Modianos, "Shopping Values of Russian Consumers: The Impact of Habituation in a Developing Economy," *Journal of Retailing* 76, no. 1 (2000): 33–52.

33 Based on a report in *Chicago Tribune*, June 23, 1996, Business Section, 1.

CHAPTER 12

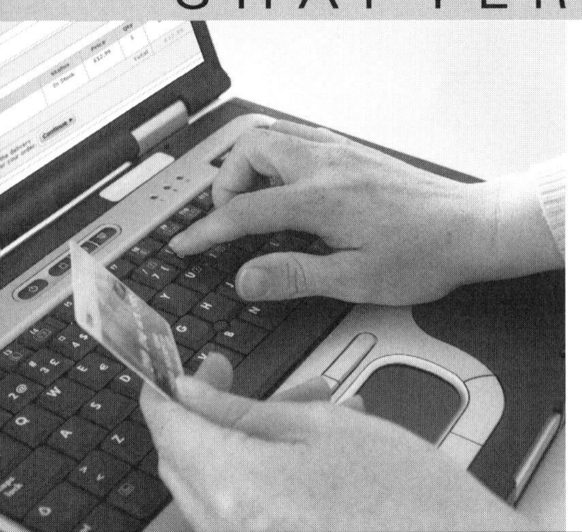

Online Customer Behaviour

LEARNING OBJECTIVES

After reading this chapter you should be able to:

LO 1 Understand the characteristics of the Internet and e-commerce.

LO 2 Describe the online B2C customer.

LO 3 Identify the products customers buy online.

LO 4 Explain the three pre-purchase stages of the online decision-making model.

LO 5 Explain the characteristics of the purchase stages of the online decision-making model.

LO 6 Explain the characteristics of the post-purchase stage of the online decision-making model.

Creating an Amazon Online Shopping Experience

If there is a company synonymous with the Internet, it is Amazon.com. Over the last few years, this Seattle-based company has diversified from being only a bookseller to being a huge seller of a large selection of other products, such as music CDs, cookware, toys and games, and tools and hardware. Its revenues have also grown, from $147 million in 1997 to $8.5 billion in 2005. When Jeff Bezos, founder of Amazon.com, was vice president at D.E. Shaw, a Wall Street investment bank, he read a statistic that the Internet was growing at the rate of 2,300 percent. This encouraged him to enter the unchartered territory of e-commerce.

Bezos's vision comprised primarily two elements: first, to build the world's most customer-centric company; and second, to set up a place where customers could buy books and more. To this end, he first tried to understand how the medium of the Internet could be best used to develop a customer-centric company. Early on, he realized the potential of the Internet in developing relationships with customers through an understanding of customer preferences and their actual purchase behaviour. Amazon used this feature of the medium to its best advantage in order to provide customers with personalized recommendations, thus building loyalty for the Amazon brand. Its main aim was to deliver the values of convenience, large selection, reliable service and delivery, and low prices to customers, all in one place. In line with his vision, Bezos also wanted Amazon to move from being the "world's biggest online bookstore to becoming the world's biggest store," a place where a customer could buy *anything*. Amazon's vision struck a chord with customers, visible in the growth of its customer base. During the 2004 holiday season, its tenth, Amazon set a single-day record with more than 2.8 million units ordered, or 32 items per second, worldwide.

Why did Amazon get into the books business online? Books represent one of the few product categories suitable for online selling. First, it has a large number of items: there are more than 3 million different titles available and active in print worldwide. Second, a book is informational in nature and, therefore, can be previewed online with sample chapters, table of contents, editorial reviews, and customer reviews. Third, it is a low-value and, hence, a low-risk item; and finally, it is easy to ship. With this clear value proposition, Amazon has dominated the book market. Amazon is best known for the compelling shopping experience it provides to its customers. Some of the innovations that it has pioneered are:

1. *One-click shopping*—Amazon realized that customers want an online ordering process that is simple, and wherein each new transaction with the retailer does not require them to enter personal information again and again. Hence, the company introduced one-click shopping. It retains in its database all relevant customer information, thereby speeding up the ordering process.
2. *Product reviews*—Customers can read product reviews on the Amazon website and can also see other customers' ratings of these reviews.
3. *Purchase circles*—The company groups items sent to particular zip and postal codes, and items ordered from each domain name. This data is aggregated, and bestseller lists of items popular with specific customer groups are generated, called Purchase Circle lists, and posted online.
4. *E-mail alerts*—Amazon sends e-mails to customers about products available from their favorite author or musician.
5. *Recommendations*—Amazon uses different personalization techniques, including "collaborative filtering" (explained later in the chapter) to suggest different products to its customers. It greets customers by name every time they log in, and recommends books based on their earlier purchases, their preferences, and the preferences of other customers who have bought items similar to the customer's purchase.
6. *Wish list*—Every customer can create a wish list of items on the site, and friends and acquaintances can view the wish list to order gifts.
7. *The page you made*—Amazon found that customers often wanted to revisit a portion of the site that they had visited a moment ago, and there was no way to do this except using the "back" button on the browser. So they found a way to create a special page for each customer with those portions of the site that the customer has recently viewed. Now the customer only needs to visit this page to learn immediately what she or he viewed a few clicks ago.

Then, in its attempt to get a greater share of the customer's overall shopping basket, Amazon made forays into several other categories, such as music, DVDs/videos, toys, electronics, home improvement, software, jewellery, clothing, and more. So, it has indeed become more than an online bookstore.

Amazon represents the face of e-commerce. It has brought the best of the Internet to customers, for which it has been amply rewarded with a large customer base and loyalty. At the same time, it also has experienced withdrawal from customers when it deviated from what made it successful in the first place. Most retailers on the Internet, including Amazon, now realize that the Internet is a tough place to survive, and the savvy customer who buys on the Internet is even tougher to please.[1]

In every chapter of this book, we have addressed issues related to online customer behaviour. This chapter focuses specifically on emerging buying behaviour, both of individual and institutional customers, in the online world. (See Figure 12.1 for conceptual framework.) The chapter begins with a brief history of the Internet and e-commerce, and then elaborates on the activities in the three main stages of online customer behaviour: pre-purchase, purchase, and post-purchase. A section on business-to-business (B2B) business models and e-procurement is presented next, and the chapter closes with a harbinger of the trends in online customer behaviour.

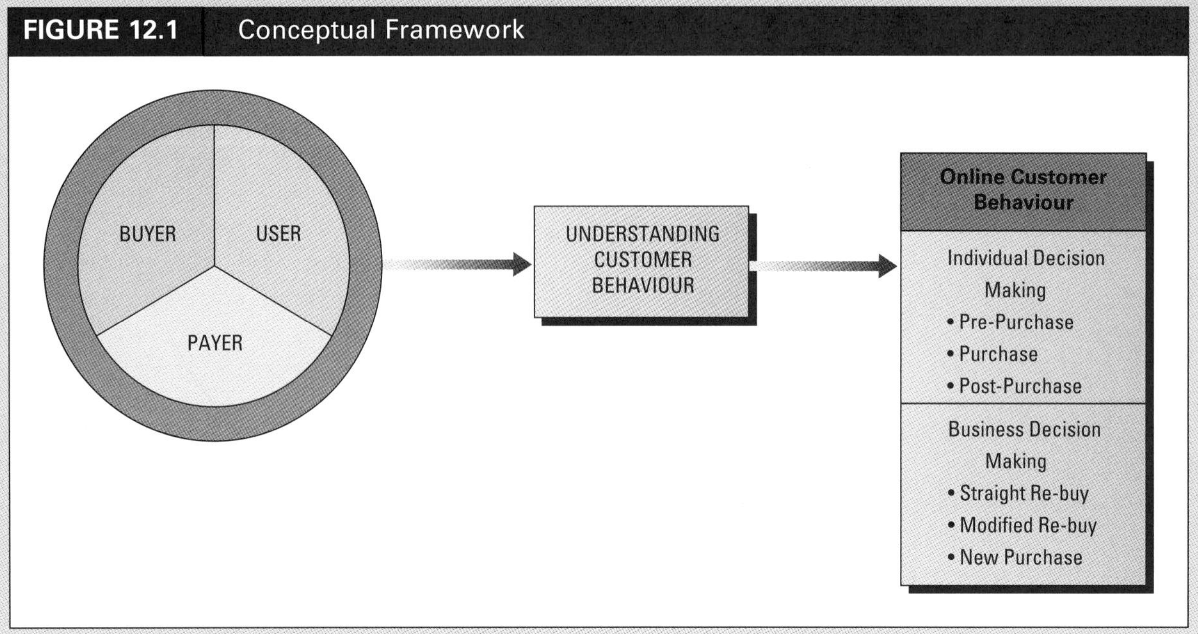

THE INTERNET AND E-COMMERCE: A BRIEF HISTORY

History of the Internet and the World Wide Web

Let us briefly visit where it all started—the history of the development of the Internet and the World Wide Web. The Internet is a large system of interconnected networks. It originated in the 1960s when the U.S. Department of Defense, in preparing for the possible effects of a nuclear attack, commissioned the development of networks that could operate independently, without central control. The network model was used to connect four computers in 1969—one each at the University of California at Los Angeles, SRI International, the University of California at Santa Barbara, and the University of Utah—laying the foundation for the first network, called the ARPANET. Many computers were connected to this network over the years, and several applications, such as e-mail, FTP (file transfer protocol), and Telnet were developed to send and receive messages and files across computers on the network. Several other networks, such as the BITNET, CSNET, and USENET, came into existence in the later years.

The early 1980s saw an explosion in personal computer use, with powerful, affordable computers in the market. Soon there was a need for a public network across which businesses could interact for commercial transactions. In 1986, the NSFNET was developed with funding from the National Science Foundation (NSF), and it functions as the backbone communication service for the Internet today. By 1995, the Internet was substantially privatized, and the operation of main Internet connections was taken over by a group of privately owned companies. Since then, the Internet has been opened to business activity, and this has fueled its growth.

The World Wide Web, according to Tim Berners-Lee, the inventor of the hypertext system, is an "abstract space of information." The Web exists because of programs that communicate between computers on the Internet. The Web made the Internet useful for commercial use by making it simple to organize and retrieve information.[2] According to International Data Corp. (IDC) projections (**http://www.idc.com**), the number of people using the Internet is expected to exceed 1 billion sometime in 2007. That means more than 16 percent of the world's population is talking, learning, and buying on the Internet.

The Appendix in Chapter 3 details the status of the Internet information infrastructure in different regions of the world. The Window on Practice shows the impact of the Internet and the World Wide Web on a small village in rural India.

E-Commerce in Canada

The Internet has fundamentally reshaped the way businesses and consumers communicate, interact, and transact in Canada and around the world. Today, e-commerce is taken for granted. Despite the dot-com bust in 2000, there is no denying the fact that e-commerce is big and is here to stay. Canadian household e-commerce spending grew from $417 million in 1999 to $3 billion in 2003. Statistics Canada and a report by eMarketer forecasts that by 2008, Canadians will spend $8.3 billion online.[3] In the United States, online sales in 2004 reached US$141 billion, and are expected to rise to US$316 billion by 2010, accounting for about 12 percent of all retail sales from about 7 percent in 2004.[4]

The Statistics Canada 2004 Survey of Electronic Commerce and Technology indicated that the online sales by Canadian companies and governments grew substantially for the fifth consecutive year in 2004, although e-commerce still accounted for less than 1 percent of total operating revenues for private businesses. Combined private and public sector online sales increased 50 percent to $28 billion. Online sales by private firms increased 45 percent to $26 billion, while those by the public sector more than doubled to $2 billion. Sales to households accounted for less than 24 percent of the value of online sales by large firms. Small firms, those with fewer than 20 employees, reported that 41 percent of the value of their online sales was to households. Among Canadian companies, the use and complexity of their websites continue to increase. In 2004, 37 percent of Canadian firms had a website, a steady growth from 34 percent in 2003 and 32 percent in 2002. These websites have also developed in capability, as firms now offer more features than ever.[5]

According to the annual revenue survey commissioned by the Interactive Advertising Bureau of Canada (IAB) (**http://www.iabcanada.com**), online advertising revenues will exceed $800 million dollars in 2007, about 43 percent more than the 2005 figure.

Characteristics of the Internet that Aid E-Commerce

LO 1

The launch of the Netscape browser in 1994 kick-started the e-commerce revolution. The technology barrier was broken, and anyone could get on to the Internet and use it for commerce without being a technology geek. The Internet was also amenable to commerce because of a few very salient characteristics. Peterson, Balasubramanian, and Bronnenberg list the special characteristics of the Internet as follows:

1. The ability to inexpensively store vast amounts of information at different virtual locations
2. The availability of powerful and inexpensive means of searching, organizing, and disseminating such information

WINDOW ON PRACTICE

Impact of Internet in Rural India

Rosy opens her PC, logs on to Yahoo! chat, and types a message: "Madhu, are you there?" Comes the reply: "Yes, what's the matter?" "Can you tell me where I can find information on colleges that offer diploma courses in automobile engineering?" "Give me a few minutes. I'll find out and send you an e-mail." Five minutes later she opens her e-mail and finds a few URLs relevant to her query. Common enough scenario, right? Happens between friends all the time. Easiest way to get information is using the Internet and a little help from your friends. Except that Rosy lives in a small village in the state of Tamil Nadu in India called Padinettamkudi, about 22 miles from the nearest big city, Madurai.

Padinettamkudi has about 1,000 people, has no public telephones nor a road leading to the village, and the local school offers classes only up to the eighth grade. A few months ago, most people in Padinettamkudi had not even seen a PC, much less used one. And today, in this little village, Rosy is one of the many stakeholders in a mission to make Internet a part of the reality of every individual in rural India. She is a village Internet kiosk operator, managing a kiosk in her village, set up for her with the assistance of n-Logue, a rural Internet service provider, incubated by the TeNeT Group of IIT—Madras, a premier educational institution in Chennai. Using the services n-Logue enables for her, she is able to bring the benefits of the Internet to the people of Padinettamkudi. The kiosk equipment cost Rs. 51,500 (about $1,260) and was bought by a local retailer with a loan from a bank. He appointed Rosy to run the kiosk for him for a fixed salary and a percentage of the profits.

With Rosy's help, people in Padinettamkudi are using the Internet to connect to the outside world for a variety of their needs. They are contacting the government for birth, income, community, and pension certificates, and to send complaints about various problems in the village. They are contacting hospitals requesting information on symptoms of cataracts, and sending pictures of the affected eye so that doctors may suggest the next course of action for the patients. Rosy has been trained to take pictures of cataract-affected eyes by personnel from the Aravind Eye Hospital. She can also conduct a similar preliminary test for myopia in young children and then set up appointments for them at an eye hospital to correct the problem. Experts at the Tamil Nadu Agricultural College and Research Institute answer queries from farmers on crops, and livestock-related queries are sent to the Tamil Nadu Association for Veterinary and Animal Sciences. A local software company has provided the kiosk with software—free of charge—to promote adult literacy, and Rosy helps adults learn how to read and write.

The more common uses of the Internet also abound in Padinettamkudi: looking up horoscopes, sending e-mails to children abroad, watching movies, booking bus and train tickets, searching for jobs, and so on. Rosy has announced a movie show for 7 p.m. and rented a DVD from a video library. A couple of women and children await the show eagerly. Soon, it's show time! As Rosy presses the Play button, the little room is filled with the sounds of a popular Tamil movie song. "Gemini, Gemini, Gemini, Gemini…" and the audience watches the small screen with rapt attention!

SOURCE: Adapted from Alexander, Elizabeth. "A Day in the Life of a Village Kiosk Operator." 2002. http://www.n-logue.com/. Reprinted with permission of the author.

3. Interactivity and the ability to provide information on demand
4. The ability to provide perceptual experiences that are far superior to a printed catalogue, although not as rich as personal inspection
5. The ability to serve as a transaction medium
6. The ability to serve as a physical distribution medium for certain goods (e.g., software)
7. Relatively low entry and establishment costs for retailers.[6]

These characteristics of the Internet as a marketing channel have changed the way customers shop for products. The Internet has eased the time and place constraints that are imposed by traditional retailing. Further, the vast availability of information, the ease with which it can be searched, and the comparison aids available to evaluate the information have resulted in an informed consumer. Armed with such information, the customer is able to exercise a lot more power in a buying decision today, both offline and online. For example, today there are few consumers who purchase a car without obtaining information on the invoice price of the car on the Web. Knowing the invoice price makes it easy for the customer to bargain for prices with the dealer. At the same time, the Internet is also increasing revenues for marketers by allowing them to personalize their products and marketing communications for customers. It is also driving down costs for marketers through the use of Web self-service channels at the consumer end, and through e-procurement and market research at the supplier end.

Today's World Wide Web is still only an approximation of the capabilities and functionality that can be expected in the next five to ten years. As communication bandwidths rise with the increase of broadband connections, and as customer terminals (i.e., Internet access devices) becomes more powerful, sophisticated, easier to use, affordable, and portable, it will be possible to exchange an enormous range of services on the Web at nominal cost.[7]

WHO IS THE ONLINE B2C CUSTOMER IN CANADA?[8]

LO 2

Internet Use

The Canadian Internet Project 2004 survey revealed that nearly three out of every four Canadians use the Internet (72 percent), and home is the most common location for Internet access. More men (75 percent) than women (69 percent) access the Internet. In the United States, the gender gap is even smaller: 77 percent are male and 75 percent are females (2003 figures). According to surveys conducted in 14 countries in the UCLA World Internet Project and released January 14, 2004 (**http://www.ccp.ucla.edu**), the gender gap in Internet use was as high as 20 percent in Italy (men, 42 percent; women, 22 percent) to as low as 2 percent in Taiwan (where 25 percent of men are Internet users, compared to 23 percent of women). It is reasonable to conclude that the gender gap shrinks with time and rate of Internet penetration. The larger gaps appear in those countries where Internet use is in the early stages of diffusion.

Canadians spend an average of approximately 13.5 hours per week online and, overall, men are online more hours in an average week than are women (14.7 versus 12.2 hours per week). However, as mentioned in Chapter 2, women are "seekers" online, meaning they go online for a specific reason, while men tend to be "surfers" or "browsers." It follows that women spend relatively less lime on the Internet compared to men and are light users. However, women have been found to be loyal to the sites they visit.

More English-speaking (74 percent) than French-speaking (66 percent) Canadians are online. English-speaking Canadians spent on average 14 hours per week, whereas French-speaking Canadians spent 11 hours. Furthermore, among Quebec residents, those who are French-speaking are significantly less likely to be online than those who are English-speaking (66 percent versus 75 percent). Although there exists a slight divide when considering language group and Internet access in Canada, perhaps it is most important to note that more than two out of three respondents in each language group are active users of the Internet.

Seventy-seven percent of those online predominantly use English, while 16 percent use French as their primary language; 2 percent reported using a combination of the two. The balance of Internet users indicated they use another language while online.

Internet use is highest in Alberta, Ontario, and British Columbia. In each of these provinces, more than three out of four individuals are online. The lowest level of Internet use, albeit only slightly less than the rest of Canada, is found in the Atlantic region. It is noteworthy that, in all areas of Canada studied, a majority of citizens is online.

Figure 12.2 provides a breakdown of Internet users by both gender and age group. The only statistically significant differences were found in the 65+ age bracket. Within this age group, men are more likely than women to be online (41 percent versus 24 percent). Overall, the highest proportion of Internet users is in the youngest age category. Of those in the 18–24 age range, comprising 15 percent of the population, 90 percent are online. The lowest proportion of users is in the oldest age category, those in the 65+ age group (7 percent of the population); only 31 percent are online. The largest age group on the Internet is the 35–44 age group, comprising 24 percent of the total online population, followed by the 25–34 (22 percent), the 45–54 (20 percent), and the 55–64 (12 percent).

Overall, there is a strong negative correlation between Internet use and age. This pattern is the same for both English-speaking and French-speaking Canadians. The majority of Internet users fall into the 18–44 age range. It is this group that tends to be the target for Internet marketing and new applications and services. It seems likely, however, that user-friendly services aimed at older Canadians might emerge as an important niche market, especially given the relative affluence of the "baby boom" generation. Given that the population in Western countries is growing older, and given that they have the purchasing power, it makes sense for websites to target older consumers and pay special attention to customer service as a differentiator. As it becomes difficult for seniors to engage in recreational and social activities outside the home, they are looking to the Internet as a substitute outlet. Marketers need to understand this motivation when seniors are online, and provide them with a compelling retail experience.[9]

As one might expect, there is a positive relationship between household income and Internet use. The proportion of the population that uses the Internet increases with level of income: the higher the income, the more likely a person is to be online. In the less than $40,000 income quartile, 57 percent of individuals use the Internet, whereas in the fourth income quartile (annual household income of $80,000+), 91 percent use the Internet. Likewise, the likelihood of being online increases with the level of education a person has achieved. More than 80 percent of Canadians who attended college or university use the Internet, compared to less than 35 percent who did not graduate from high school.

LO 3 E-Commerce Use

More than half of Canadian Internet users (52 percent) report having ordered or purchased products online. As with other Internet services, English-speaking Canadians tend to be earlier adopters than French-speaking Canadians. Whereas some 55 percent of English-speaking Canadians have bought something online, only 43 percent of French-speaking Canadians have done so. In addition, there are significant differences by geographic area. Residents of B.C. (63 percent) and Alberta (60 percent) are above the national average, while those of the Prairie region (44 percent) and Quebec (46 percent) are below. Men (58 percent) are more

FIGURE 12.2 Internet Use Across Both Gender and Age Groups

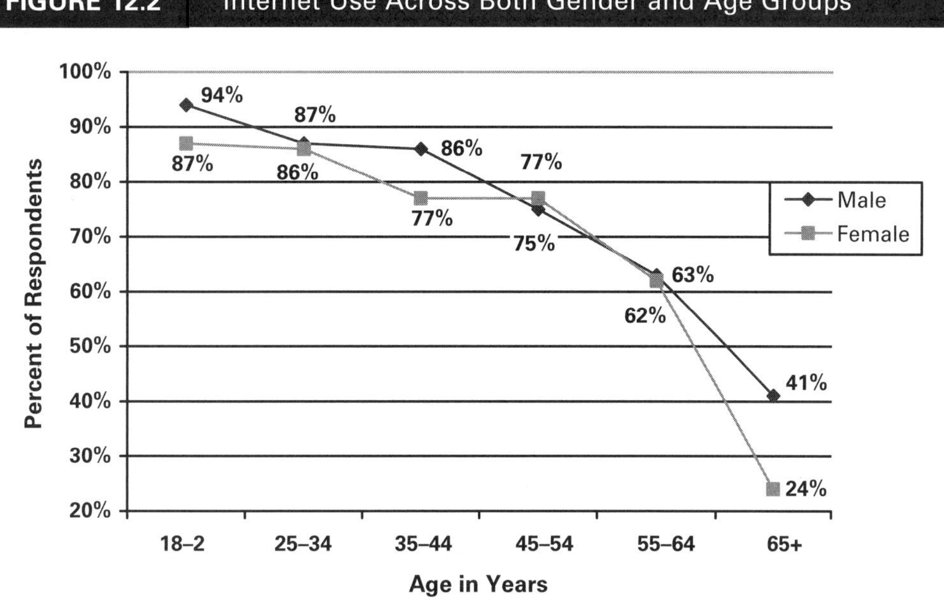

SOURCE: Canadian Internet Project, 2004. http://www.cipic.ca.

likely than women (46 percent) to have made a purchase online. Age, on the other hand, is not a decisive factor, although those 55 years of age and older are somewhat less likely to have made a purchase than are those in other age groups.

Not surprisingly, using the Internet for commerce is positively related to household income (the strongest relationship). Some 70 percent of Internet users with an annual household income of $80,000 or more have made a purchase, compared to just 42 percent of those with income below $40,000. The proportions for education are similar: roughly 58 percent of university and college graduates have shopped online, while only 32 percent of those who have not completed high school have done so.

Experience online and time spent online are also strong predictors of participation in online commerce. More than two-thirds of experienced users—those who have been online for seven years or more—have made an Internet purchase, compared to 39 percent of those who have been online less than five years. Heavy users of the Internet are more than twice as likely as light users to have made a purchase online.

Having access to the Internet at home is also an important predictor. Whereas 91 percent of users with home access had made a purchase, only 69 percent of Internet users without home access had ever done so.

In short, household income, education, and access to and general comfort with the Internet are the best predictors of who is likely to shop online. As online shopping services develop, these gaps are likely to diminish. Figure 12.3 shows the kinds of products that respondents reported having purchased on the Internet in the previous three months. Books were the items most commonly purchased, followed by electronic goods (combining computers, CDs, software, and other items), travel arrangements, and clothes.

PRODUCTS CUSTOMERS BUY ONLINE

In order to understand the buying behaviour of Internet customers, it is first necessary to understand what products are suitable or not suitable for e-commerce. One factor that makes products more or less suitable for online commerce is what Rashi Glazer has called "an '**information intensiveness continuum,**' signifying the levels of various types of information associated with products." At one end are traditional products that are information-independent, and, at the other end, information about the products is itself extremely important (see Table 12.1). Products become more and more amenable to e-commerce as their information intensiveness increases.[10]

Information intensiveness continuum Signifies the levels of various types of information associated with products, with traditional goods and services that are information-independent at one end and information-dependent products at the other end.

Another factor is two types of goods: **search goods** and **experience goods.** Search goods are products whose features can be objectively assessed before the purchase; in contrast, experience goods need to be personally experienced to judge their quality. Accordingly, the Internet makes it easier for customers to engage in an online transaction for search goods. However, for experience goods, information alone may not be sufficient for the consumer to purchase it on the Internet unless the customer has already experienced the product.

Search goods Products whose features can be objectively assessed before the purchase.

Experience goods Products that need to be personally experienced to judge their quality.

FIGURE 12.3 Products Purchased on the Internet

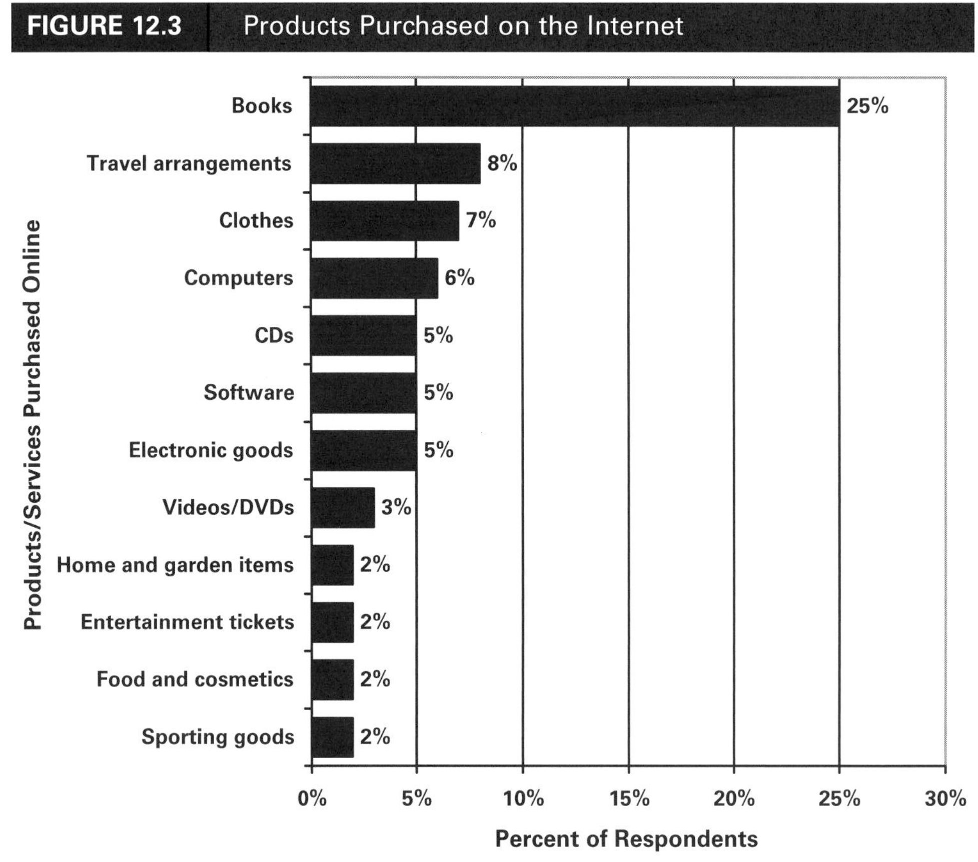

SOURCE: Canadian Internet Project, 2004. http://www.cipic.ca.

TABLE 12.1 The Information Intensiveness Continuum

INFORMATION INTENSIVENESS		
Continuum	**Details**	**Examples**
Information independent	Information exchanged by firm with customers in transactions has no bearing on product features.	Traditional goods, standardized services
Information is critical to marketing effort.	Information is not part of the product itself, but is critical in providing a solution to the customer's problem.	Information associated with selling effort in industrial buying situations
Information helps provide customized offerings.	Information collected through customer feedback and other sources is processed to develop customized products at individual or segment level.	"Custom built" computers, bicycles, and products in high-technology industries
Information is part of the offering, but is secondary to the main product.	Information is collected for the secondary product in the bundle and it is of help to market the primary product, but the secondary product is not marketable by itself.	Electronic inventory system to sell hospital supplies
Information about the product is a marketable product itself.	Information is used to "initially" market the product, but later becomes an independently marketable product that adds to company revenues and profits.	FedEx tracking services, airline reservation systems

SOURCE: Adapted from Glazer, Rashi. "Marketing in an Information-Intensive Environment: Strategic Implications of Knowledge as an Asset." In *Internet Marketing*, edited by Sheth, Eshghi, and Krishnan, 37–39. Orlando, FL: Harcourt Inc, pp. 31–61.

Peterson, Balasubramanian, and Bronnenberg suggest three additional factors: **cost and frequency of purchase, value proposition,** and **degree of differentiation.** Regarding the first factor, goods vary from low-cost, frequently purchased goods to high-cost, infrequently purchased goods. The more frequently purchased and low cost the product is, the less suitable it is for Internet-related marketing. As for the second factor, products vary according to their value proposition; that is, whether they are tangible and physical or intangible and service-related. Intangible and service-related goods, especially if they are digital in nature, have an advantage on the Internet. The third factor is the degree to which a product is differentiable. The higher the degree of differentiation possible for a product, the more suitable it is for the Internet. This is because the vast amount of information available on the Internet makes it very easy for consumers to compare prices, leading to extreme price competition for goods and services that are not differentiable from their competitors.[11]

ONLINE DECISION MAKING: PRE-PURCHASE STAGE

LO 4

The Internet affects customer decision-making behaviour in all three stages: pre-purchase, purchase, and post-purchase. Let us discuss each in turn. Marketers have always been interested in the way customers search for information, the sources they use, and the mental processes that aid and detract from their search process. They also have studied how customers evaluate the information collected to make a decision on the product to purchase among competing alternatives. The task of deciding from among alternatives is vastly complicated by the options that are available to the online shopper.

Problem Recognition

Customer problem recognition is triggered by internal or external stimuli. Its occurrence due to internal stimuli is similar for online and offline customers. The occurrence due to external stimuli may, however, differ. For instance, the sight of a computer may act as a stimulus to go online and browse the Internet. The customer could also be motivated to go online by offline advertising, on television, for example, where an Internet company could advertise an online product offering. The Internet may also serve as an external stimulus for problem recognition, primarily through banner advertising while the customer is browsing the Internet. The customer may not have recognized a need, but exposure to the solution-product would make the customer realize a latent deprivation. For a health-conscious customer, for example, information on dietary requirements obtained during exploratory browsing of the Internet could stimulate problem recognition.

Advertising on the Internet is used to generate primary as well as secondary demand. The customer becomes educated about what a new product will do and how it can solve a problem. It is hoped that this will generate secondary demand. For instance, the customer might click on a banner advertisement to find out how to lose weight and manage a diet. When the customer clicks on the banner, they are taken to a generic website where marketers of exercising equipment, diet foods, and nutritional supplements have pop-up advertising. This is an example of how the Internet can generate primary and then secondary demand. Comparison sites are another source of secondary demand generation. Comparison sites not only give the customer increased confidence by reducing the risk of purchasing from unknown websites, but they also offer the customer the opportunity to switch brands.

Information Search

Once the need has been recognized, customers search for information about various alternate ways of solving the problem. Although traditionally customers have been restricted to a fairly narrow evoked set of brands, this has now expanded greatly due to the easy availability of information on the Internet.

As discussed earlier, the most conspicuous characteristic of the 21st-century customer is time pressure. The advent of technology, including mobile computing devices, permits the "always-on-the-go" customer to make well-informed purchase decisions via the Internet. As a result, consumers are using the Internet in large numbers and in almost all categories for information search. The Multi-Channel Retail Report 2001 conducted by J.C. Williams Group and Bizrate.com found that the Internet is the most effective pre-purchase influencer among all channels: store, catalogue, and online channels.[12]

A Maritz Research survey among 25,000 buyers of new cars and trucks in each of the three years found that in 2002, 77 percent of first-time car buyers who used the Internet visited vehicle manufacturer websites at some point in their shopping experience, and 65 percent obtained vehicle pricing and product information online. Increases from 2000 occurred in both of these categories, as did the number of first-time buyers who visited a car dealer's website (44 percent in 2000 to 56 percent in 2002) and those who requested or obtained a price quote online (22 percent in 2000 to 34 percent in 2002).[13] Customers are, thus, still not comfortable about making a complex decision such as the purchase of the car directly on the Internet.

In the real-estate category, it is more difficult to complete every aspect of the transaction online compared to the purchase of a car. The closing and the attendant paperwork cannot be done online yet. Furthermore, since only a real estate agent has access to all the information in the MLS system, most people end up using a broker. An Ipsos Reid survey conducted in June 2004 found that 36 percent of those who looked at real estate listings online visited a property they found on the Web. Fourteen percent contacted an agent from an online listing, and 11 percent said they submitted an offer on an online listing.[14]

Apart from the website, an important source of information for customers on the Internet is word of mouth, or its online equivalents: online discussions, chat rooms, and community discussions. Sites such as epinions.com consolidate buyer feedback and provide customer reviews for products to aid others in making a purchase decision. The reviewers are actually compensated based on how useful their reviews are rated by readers. A study by Bickart and Schindler shows that consumers who gathered information from online discussions (Internet forums or bulletin boards) reported greater interest in the product topic than did those consumers who acquired information from the marketer-generated sources (such as corporate Web pages).[15]

In some areas, online groups have gone beyond influencing other customers. For example, health is an area that is widely researched on the Internet. The CIP showed that more than half of Internet users searched for medical information online. Online patient groups are becoming a big force in the health sector. Take, for example, the clinical trials by Novartis AG in 2000 for a new drug called Gleevec for leukemia patients. Patients who were on the first trials for the drug used their own Internet support groups to lobby with Novartis to speed up production of the drug and expedite approval from the Food and Drug Administration.[16]

Recommendation systems exert another type of interpersonal influence and mass customization on the Internet. Currently these systems fall into two classes that use different types of information sources to provide recommendations. The first system is **collaborative filtering**—"prediction of a person's preferences as a weighted sum of other people's preferences." Correlations are calculated between common sets of products bought by groups of people over a period of time, and these correlations are used to calculate weights. Amazon.com uses this process of collaborative filtering to recommend new books to customers. However, when the site does not have enough customers, these recommendations are made based on common products bought by a few customers who may not be representative of the group. In order to overcome this problem, researchers suggest that websites could create "pseudo-users" or "bots" and combine them with real customers in a collaborative filtering system. The other drawback of the system is that to make the recommendation, it does not incorporate the customer's own preferences with regard to product attributes. The second system used by websites for recommendations is **content-based filtering.** Here, the recommendations are based on consumer preferences for product attributes. It follows that when customers do not provide a reasonable amount of information with regard to their preferences, the content-based filtering system will not be able to make relevant recommendations. Ideally, recommendation systems should incorporate five different kinds of information to provide exact recommendations: a person's expressed preferences, the preferences of other customers, expert evaluations, item characteristics, and individual characteristics.[17]

Collaborative filtering
A computer program that allows the prediction of a person's preferences as a weighted sum of other people's similar preferences.

Content-based filtering
A recommendation for websites based on consumer preferences for product attributes.

From the above discussion, it is evident that the democratization of information leading to low-cost information search is one of the most significant outcomes of the Internet revolution, and information search is one of the first uses that is put to the Internet.

Finally, research shows that customers are more likely to express search and purchase intentions via the Internet when they have a positive attitude toward Internet shopping in general. A greater number of purchasing experiences on the Internet also resulted in higher search and purchase intentions via the Internet. Perceived behavioural control in terms of access to the Internet, the skills to navigate the Internet, time, etc., were also significantly related to intention to search on the Internet. Marketers can use this data to encourage people to search on the Internet, specifically by creating an image of risk-free shopping on the Internet, providing rewarding Internet shopping experiences, and offering easy-to-navigate sites. The study also found that intention to search via the Internet was the strongest predictor leading to purchase intent in an online pre-purchase intentions model. This shows that search and purchase may not be independent processes, especially for search goods, and it is important for online retailers to make it extremely simple and pleasurable for customers to use their websites to do searches that may lead to purchases via the Web.[18]

Evaluation of Alternatives

As is evident from this section, the Internet has paved the way for an informed customer. But the customer is also a "cognitive miser." It is difficult for customers to make decisions when they are inundated with information. Given that the Internet has increased the amount of information available, it has also developed methods for customers to make the best use of the information available.

Shopbots
Internet tools that allow comparison by price and product features, and across retailers.

Electronic recommendation agents called **shopbots** or **smart bots** make it easier for consumers to reduce their search costs and also to improve the quality of their shopping decisions. Häubl and Trifts define an electronic recommendation agent as "a software tool that (1) calibrates a model of the preference of a consumer based on his or her input information and (2) uses this model to make personalized product recommendations (in the form of a sorted list) in a decision task based on its understanding of the consumer's preference structure."[19] Shopbots allow comparison by price and product features, and across retailers. Some examples of shopbots are **shoptoit.ca** in Canada and **mySimon.com** and **Shopper.com** in the United States, which compare products, prices, and stores across several categories such as books, clothing, electronics, software, jewellery, and health and beauty. Analyzing customer behaviour with shopbots, Brynjolfsson and Smith show that, although price is an important determinant in the purchase decision of shopbot customers, retailer brand name is also considered an important dimension in the decision-making process. Customers are found to use the brand name to make judgments about the retailer on issues like delivery time. Hence, to ensure a positive brand image, websites should endeavour to provide customers a positive online retail experience in terms of ease of use, delivery services, privacy policies, and return policies. However, shopbot customers are very sensitive to how price is allocated among item cost, shipping costs, and taxes; hence, retailers may need to find innovative ways to reduce shipping costs for shopbot customers.[20]

In Chapter 8, we saw that customers use two categories of choice models, compensatory and non-compensatory, to select one of the alternatives available to them. In a compensatory model, the customer chooses by considering all of the attributes of a product and mentally trading off the perceived weaknesses of one alternative for its perceived strengths. Given the large amount of information available on the Web on a large number of alternatives, it is difficult for customers to evaluate the alternatives using a compensatory model. Even at the shopbots discussed above, the customer is more than likely to use a non-compensatory model to deal with the information deluge.

There are several non-compensatory models: conjunctive, disjunctive, lexicographic, and elimination by aspects. The customer can use any of these models to select an alternative. The conjunctive and disjunctive models seem best suited for the choice process on the Internet. In the conjunctive model, the customer sets a minimum cutoff on all salient attributes and examines only those alternatives that meet the minimum cutoff on each attribute. For example, customers can compare different brands of digital cameras at sites such as **dpreview.com** by specifying their preferences on different criteria such as price, resolution, digital zoom, manual focus, and built-in flash. The site then provides a table in which different brands of cameras that meet the customer'scriteria are compared side by side. This table makes it easy for the customer to evaluate the alternatives and make a choice. Customers can also use the disjunctive non-compensatory model to make a choice. This model entails a tradeoff between aspects of choice alternatives to arrive at the chosen brand/product.

In the B2B sector, the Internet can provide tremendous cost savings in searching for buyers and suppliers, and making price and product comparisons. Especially with regard to small purchases, search costs can be high relative to the value of the product. Alf Sherk, the founder of e-chemicals, claims: "When you are dealing with one- or two-drum quantities, the cost of comparison shopping can be more than the cost of the product."[21] Shopbots are already in use in B2B commerce for purchase of non-strategic items. For example, NexTag is a hybrid search agent that uses a combination of shopbot and Web auction, and allows users to negotiate directly with merchants over product prices, configurations, and options. NexTag's Business eXchange also provides companies with a forum to reach a deal on a wide range of products.[22]

As the Internet grows into a medium that is widely used for commerce, there is one difference that marketers can envisage between the online and the offline mediums. They realize that the information they provide to customers at the website and the information they collect about the customers shopping at the website are as valuable as, or are even more valuable than, the products that they sell online. Marketers find that information given to customers online keeps them coming back to the site, thereby building interest in and loyalty to the brand. The Window on Practice example of Robin Hood Flour shows how a company has used the online medium to develop and sustain loyalty for a product as generic as flour. Furthermore, the information collected at the site on each customer visit makes it easy for the marketer to personalize its marketing pitches, promotions, and products to the customer.

WINDOW ON **PRACTICE**

Robin Hood Flour

Flour may be one of those products that one cannot really imagine being sold or bought online. Most people consider it a commodity, available in stores across the country and relatively cheap—clearly, a "low-involvement" product. The beginnings of the Robin Hood brand of flour date back to 1909 in Moose Jaw, Saskatchewan. Today, the brand is a trusted household name available in grocery stores throughout the country. Who'd have thought a flour brand could create a vibrant online community of moms chatting about everything from recipes and parenting to even the brand's latest ad efforts? Robin Hood has done just that, with The Robin Hood Baker's Forum (**http://www.robinhood.ca**), launched in February 2001 in English and French. The primary objective of the website is definitely *not* "sales" of flour. The site has hundreds of searchable recipes and a baker's forum for exchanging baking tips, creating an online recipe box, and e-mailing recipes to friends. There is also a list of frequently asked questions and a list of fall fairs in Canada.

(continued)

The site also features a section on baking with kids. When the brand launched its "Elizabeth and Andrew" campaign in the fall of 2005, the forum lit up with members talking about how much they loved the new animated spokeskids. The three 30-second, fully computed animated spots feature two children named Elizabeth and Andrew who are being interviewed in a documentary-style show about why they enjoy baking with their mom. The graphic creates a visually engaging commercial that immediately raises interest in the viewer. (One user was so intrigued she asked what networks they're running on, as she hadn't seen them yet.) A thriving online community not only fosters consumer engagement with the brand, but also provides valuable feedback. Robin Hood can collect customer data when bakers sign onto the site and then mail them coupons or new recipes.

SOURCE: Bourdeau, Annette. "Brilliant! Online Communities." *Strategy*, January 2006, 8; "Robin Hood Cooks the Web." *Marketing*, March 5, 2001, 1.

LO 5 ONLINE DECISION MAKING: PURCHASE STAGE

Once customers have evaluated the alternatives available for purchase, they are faced with two options. Using the information garnered from the Internet, they can visit a brick-and-mortar store and buy the product, or they can make the purchase on the Internet itself. The online marketer is trying to make the purchase process more attractive to customers through personalization. The customers are, however, plagued by concerns of privacy of information submitted to retailers and security of credit-card transactions on the Net.

Personalization

Online retailer Lands' End found personalization to be the answer for customer returns caused by the problem of "poor fitting clothes." To tackle one of the top reasons for returns on its site, it set up a utility on its website that allows customers to order custom-made chinos. A general description of the customer's hip shape, thigh shape, and some specific measurements are sent to a joint creator software company called Archetype Solutions. This company uses algorithms to create an appropriate clothing pattern based on the measurements, which is then electronically transmitted to the custom manufacturer. Thus, both the customer and the Lands' End site benefit from personalization—the customer gets clothes to size, and the site has low returns.[23] As seen in Chapter 2, it is now possible for marketers to mass-customize products because of flexible manufacturing technology in the production stage and computer capabilities in managing customer-specific preferences. Customers will, thus, be able to routinely offer direct input into the making of the product, a process called **co-production.** Also, by linking directly into production systems, customers will engage in self-service, self-design, and self-ordering and provisioning.

Co-production
A situation wherein customers routinely provide direct input into the making of a product.

This concept of mass customization and personalization is not just restricted to tailoring the product. In the online marketplace, personalization in the decision-making process begins with recognizing the customer by name when she or he visits the website. This can be followed by a personalized page for the customer, presenting only products of interest to that customer (developed through an analysis of preferences stated by the customer). Customers can be apprised of promotions and deals for products of their choice and interest using data from their previous purchases and their stated preferences as a guide. Amazon.com, discussed at the beginning of the chapter, is a case in point. The possibilities are endless, and websites are doing all they can to ensure customer loyalty.

As Don Peppers and Martha Rogers put it, the key is to "identify" your customers, "differentiate" between them on their needs and their value to the firm, "interact" with them, and finally, "customize" your company's response to the customers based on their needs. Personalization is "customizing some feature of a product so that the customer enjoys more convenience, lower cost, or some other benefit."[24] Canada Post's Picture Postage™ stamps service (**http://www.picturepostage.ca**) is a good example of B2C personalization. On their website, consumers can submit a digital picture and edit the picture to fit the frame of their choice and then order their stamps.

Wind and Rangaswamy define another concept called "**customerization,**" which they find to be an improvement over one-to-one marketing and personalization. They state that customerization is a strategy that is under the "control of customers" as opposed to personalization and one-to-one marketing, which are usually under the "control of the marketer." Under the customerization strategy, the customer is involved in designing the product and supplies, with just a reasonable amount of prior information needed for a "build-to-order" production process designed to develop a product to best fit his or her needs. B2B customers also get a higher advantage of direct links to the production and supply systems of their suppliers. The same trend toward customerization is seen in all B2B markets and exchanges on the Internet, such as Chemdex, e-Steel, etc.[25]

Customerization
Under the customerization strategy, the customer is involved in designing the product and supplies, with just a reasonable amount of prior information needed for a "build-to-order" production process designed to develop a product to best fit his or her needs.

At the next level, companies also can use the data available to tailor prices for different customer segments in the online world, as is the case in the offline world. Dell has implemented a successful customized pricing mechanism through its premier-pages program. Dell has also developed customized websites for each of its corporate customers with the models that have been approved by the customer purchase department. The site is also customized with the price that has been negotiated for each corporate customer depending on the volumes bought by the customer. The system also takes into account the purchasing process and billing procedures specific to each customer.

Buy.com has incorporated a semblance of dynamic pricing (a pricing system of nonfixed pricing that varies the price in real time across customers) on its website. It uses dynamic pricing software that has bots, which search for price changes that have occurred at competitor sites and recommend changes in prices of products at Buy.com. This is verified by a person at Buy.com, and this pricing process ensures that the website has the lowest prices for consumer electronics and computer hardware and software on the Web. However, the company's ability to tailor prices is tempered by customer acceptance. As mentioned in the Window on Practice in Chapter 7, Amazon faced irate customers when it instituted a dynamic pricing strategy on its site without informing its customers.

Over a period of time, it is also important to note that customers are not going to take the trouble of switching from site to site for a few dollars. Eric Johnson and his colleagues found that just 10 percent of the households that shopped for a book online visited more than one site during a shopping trip, and just 20 percent of such households looking for compact disks shopped around. However, 80 percent of airline ticket shoppers visited at least two sites.[26] Customers tend to stay with sites that they are already familiar with in terms of navigation and purchase experiences. To most customers, it seems a waste of time to go through this whole process at another site just to save a few dollars. In another study, Johnson and others found that on an average, the customer spent 400 seconds (about 6⅔ minutes) at the Amazon site on his or her first visit, which dropped to less than 200 seconds (about 3⅓ minutes) on his or her fifth visit to the site. If the median income for Web users is estimated at $53,000, the study states that the customer saves $1.44 for the 200 seconds saved in time that comes from site familiarity. In fact, Erik Brynjolfsson found that online shoppers who use shopbots to compare prices also tend to patronize sites they are familiar with, although the items are available a few dollars cheaper on another site. He calculated the price advantage of an already-visited retailer over a new retailer at $2.49 for the same item.[27]

Online Purchase: Privacy Concerns

There is a growing concern among customers about the amount of personal information collected on the Internet and how it is used. Results from the CIP survey indicated that privacy on the Internet is an important concern for Canadians. Almost half of all respondents said they would be extremely concerned if asked to provide personal information to obtain a product over the Internet. English speakers, women, and older Internet users were all more concerned about privacy than were other groups. Users from households with annual incomes over $80,000, heavy users, and very experienced users were slightly less likely than other groups to be concerned about privacy issues. Security fears are an important factor that might inhibit the growth of online commerce and, possibly, the development of other Internet services.

Apart from the overt method of collecting data on customers through forms at the website, online businesses also constantly plant electronic "cookies" onto the customer's computer that enable them to get different kinds of data about the customer. The World Wide Web Consortium has developed a standard called the "Platform for Privacy Preferences Project" (P3P) over the last several years, and Microsoft's newest version of Internet Explorer browser, 6.0, comes equipped with P3P. This standard makes it possible for the customer to find out which website is sending cookies, what kind of information the cookie gathers, and who is going to see this information. The P3P also has an automatic blocking device with which the customer can prevent cookies from residing on the hard drives of their computers. P3P allows the customer to decide which cookies to block and which ones to allow access to. This allows them to keep those cookies that help sites recognize the customer, remember passwords, and store other preferences about the site. At the same time, the customer can block those cookies that collect personal information to transmit to their respective websites.[28]

Companies are using authentication technology, filters, audit controls, custom-tailored software, professional consulting services, and permission-based content technology to ensure the privacy of customer data. As seen in Chapter 2, online users are protected by the federal *Personal Information Protection and Electronic Documents Act,* which regulates how personal information (included that collected in Internet transactions) can be used. The *Canadian Code of Practice for Consumer Protection in Electronic Commerce* provides a voluntary code so that business can better serve online consumers. Its ten principles form the basis for the Model Code for the Protection of Personal Information (see Chapter 2). Third-party entities have also emerged online to provide legitimacy and trustworthiness to websites. For example, the Canadian Marketing Association (CMA) has introduced codes of ethics and standards for privacy and special guidelines for marketing to children and teenagers. Seals of approval from organizations such as the Better Business Bureau (**BBBonline**) and **WebTrust** (from the Canadian Institute of Chartered Accountants), confirm adequate privacy compliance.

As privacy concerns increase, customers are more likely to (a) provide incomplete information to websites, (b) notify ISPs about unsolicited mail, (c) request removal from mailing lists, and (d) "flame" online entities sending unsolicited e-mail. They are also unlikely to register at websites that request information, and likely to decrease purchase behaviour at those sites.[29] An interesting finding is that consumers' attitudes toward direct marketing indirectly affect purchase decisions on the Internet through their level of concern for privacy. When consumers have a positive attitude toward direct marketing, their concern for privacy is lower, and the lower the concern for privacy, the higher is their catalogue shopping experience. The study showed that the greater the consumer's catalogue shopping experience, the greater is his or her purchase intention for products on the Internet. Consumers' privacy concerns are also lower when they have more control over the personal information they provide to websites.[30]

Security Concerns in Online Purchase

After privacy, the second most important reason that customers do not complete a purchase online is online credit card payment security. After surveying 8,500 adults, ages 18 and over, in 16 different countries, research firm Ipsos-Reid reports that potential online credit-card fraud was cited as a "major" concern by 46 percent of adults and a "moderate" concern by 26 percent. This concern with security was found to vary by country: In France, 63 percent of respondents considered security a major concern, while only 15 percent of respondents cited it as a major concern in China. About 47 percent of people in the United States and 54 percent in Canada considered online credit fraud as a "major" concern.[31]

A survey conducted in May 2005 by the firm Pollara among 1250 B.C. and Ontario residents observed that 45 percent of B.C. residents and 41 percent of those surveyed in Ontario don't feel safe from threats such as hackers and identity theft while shopping online. In fact, four in 10 Canadians feel "unsafe" when shopping online, and nearly one in four when banking online.[32] There are also gender-based differences in the perceptions of risk related to credit-card misuse, fraudulent sites, and loss of privacy associated with online purchasing. Research shows that women perceive a higher level of risk in online purchasing than men, even after controlling for differences in their Internet usage. Yet, women are more willing than men to buy online when a site is recommended by a friend.[33]

One of the methods by which websites tackle security is to force customers to log in with a username and password. Technology is making it easy for customers to keep track of passwords at several sites. Customers can take advantage of a new device called U.are.U Personal, which can recognize their fingerprint and can then be set up for identification purposes at several of their frequently visited websites. Once it is set up, a touch of the finger can log the customer into the site, and there is no way anyone else can hack this information. Apart from this, companies also rely on encryption of data, such as credit-card information, to ensure transaction security. The Secure Sockets Layer (SSL) and Secure HyperText Transfer Protocol (S-HTTP) are two protocols used by companies to provide secure information transfer through the Internet.

Trust in Online Purchase

The final solution to security and privacy problems for online retailers would be to engender trust in their brands. A study of 299 consumers across 12 countries in three broad regions of the world (North America, Western Europe, and Latin and South America) showed that the three important factors that affect customers' online purchase intention and loyalty are site quality, affect, and trust. The trustworthiness of the site has a positive impact on both purchase intention and loyalty. It follows that websites need to engender trust by providing such things as service guarantees, privacy policies, third-party credentials of credibility, and customer testimonials.[34]

Urban, Sultan, and Qualls state that "Web trust is built in a three-stage cumulative process that establishes (1) trust in the Internet and the specific web site, (2) trust in the information displayed, and (3) trust in delivery fulfillment and service." They suggest that websites could use software-enabled virtual advisors in the form of personal shopping consultants. These virtual advisors could interact with customers to understand their needs and provide them with suggestions to fulfill those needs. They developed a site called Truck Town for truck and sport-utility vehicle buyers featuring a virtual auto mechanic, and they asked 280 Boston-area respondents who had purchased a truck within the previous 18 months to evaluate the site. They found that more than 75 percent of Truck Town's visitors said that they trusted these virtual advisors more than the dealer from whom they last purchased a vehicle. They conclude that "trust will soon be the currency of the Internet," and virtual advisors can be a cost-effective method to build trust in websites.[35]

In the area of delivery fulfillment, shoppers mention shipping or delivery charges as one of the important reasons for abandoning a virtual shopping cart, according to research firm Jupiter Media Metrix. Since shipping charges are a crucial element of the cost for an online retailer, Jupiter suggests that retailers should give related information about shipping charges to customers long before they reach the last stage of their purchasing process. Standardizing shipping rates according to weight (as for Canada Post) would also make customers more comfortable about the charges, since they are familiar with the system. After e-tailer **1-800-flowers.com** allowed customers to preview potential shipping charges along with shipping charge options, the number of delivery-related calls dropped from 100 a day to nearly zero. Other retailers such as Sears and Best Buy are allowing customers to purchase online and then pick up the item at the nearest Sears or Best Buy brick-and-mortar outlet, eliminating shipping charges altogether.[36]

Converting Browsers into Customers

Last but not least, a challenge for online retailers is to devise strategies to convert online browsers into customers. Wendy W. Moe and Peter S. Fader have built an online buyer-conversion model to determine when browsers will turn into buyers. They state that a customer might require a number of visits to the website before deciding to purchase from the site. They classify the visits as:

1. *Directed purchase visits*—The customer visits the site to purchase a product.
2. *Search-and-deliberation visits*—The customer is searching for information, considering different options, and intending to purchase in the future.
3. *Hedonic-browsing visits*—The customer is browsing on the Net for pleasure and recreation.
4. *Knowledge-building visits*—The customer is scanning the market, and any information gathered in this process could impact future purchases.

Moe and Fader's model analyzes visit and purchase data for a customer to predict the exact visit that will lead to a purchase. Websites can use these models to provide customers with the right cues to induce purchase. For example, when the website knows that a particular customer is likely to purchase on his or her third visit to the site, he can be routed to a faster server on that visit so that his purchase experience is quick and convenient. On the other hand, customers who need an incentive to purchase can be targeted with promotions. Several e-tailers have started directing frequent buyers to faster servers to enhance their experience on the site. Online retailers need to track customer response to these tactics to help customers convert from browsers to purchasers.[37]

ONLINE DECISION MAKING: POST-PURCHASE STAGE

LO 6

Satisfaction and Loyalty

The problems that consumers encounter with retail websites include:

- long upload sessions
- difficulty getting their credit cards accepted
- never receiving an item that was paid for
- no phone number listed for contact
- slow response time
- and lack of coordination between different parts of the company.[38]

With services like the Better Business Bureau (**http://www.bbbonline.org**) and PlanetFeedback (**http://www.planetfeedback.com**), it is much easier for customers to get their grievances addressed. This puts added pressure on marketers, since the impact of dissatisfied customers is also magnified through the medium of the Internet (higher reach).

Customer service has received a major boost from the widespread adoption of the Internet. In fact, Web-based self-service is a boon to customers and companies alike. Customers are able to take care of minor repetitive issues such as address changes, tracking a package, or looking at the status of a submitted application, without having to call the company and waste time. At the same time, companies realize that allowing customers to handle these issues by themselves not only saves them a packet, but also helps them keep a customer better satisfied. This feeling comes from the control that the customer feels over the whole process. Web self-service can be primarily segmented into content based and transaction based services.

1. *Content-based services*—Most of these customer inquiries are general in nature and require static information. Site FAQs are a great way to handle these queries.
2. *Transaction-based services*—These services require dynamic information. Customers want to place orders, fill out applications, make payments, keep track of their purchases, etc. Each of these transactions requires individualized information to be retrieved from back-end databases and supplied to the customer when there is a specific request.[39]

Yet, it is important that companies not assume that the Internet is a self-service channel. All customers do not have the same level of comfort with the Internet, and even if they are extremely Internet-savvy, they are not always willing to do most of the job when it comes to purchasing a computer or buying airline tickets. "Co-production" is a good alternative since it focuses on "customer service" and not "self-service." In this model, customers state their preferences once, and the company helps reduce the customer's consideration set by generating a set of alternatives that closely match the customer's preferences. The focus is on providing the customer with the right choice, as opposed to many choices or not enough choices. Companies like Dell are already using the model. Dell completes all the back-end processes such as grouping products by customer segments and displaying in-stock items, while allowing customers to configure their own PCs and check their order status online. It has also developed custom web pages for all its corporate customers that display only those configurations that have been preapproved by the company and the negotiated prices for the configurations.[40]

Finally, as mentioned in the Window on Research in Chapter 11, customer loyalty is the key driver of profitability for online businesses. Loyalty by customers is manifested in two ways: by repeat purchases at a site, and by referring customers to the site. Research shows that a website cannot expect to break even without at least four repeat visits from a customer in a period of twelve months. Further, referrals represent the best form of new customers since the site does not have to spend a single penny to get them to the site, and they provide revenues and refer more people if they have a satisfying shopping experience. Hence, the key to success in online retailing is to foster loyalty among its customers.

Tackling Returns

One of the most annoying parts of the online purchase process is tackling returns. Customers appreciate the convenience of purchasing online, but they also hate the thought of having to ship the product back to the company if it is not to their satisfaction. Some companies such as Best Buy have solved this problem by integrating the brick-and-mortar operations of the company with the online arm. Customers who have purchased online and are not satisfied with their purchase can return the product at the nearest brick-and-mortar outlet.

CUSTOMER BEHAVIOUR IN BUSINESS-TO-BUSINESS (B2B) COMMERCE

B2B commerce is much larger than B2C. As reported in the Statistics Canada Survey of Electronic Commerce and Technology 2004, sales from business to business in Canada amounted to $20 billion, which represented about 75 percent of total e-commerce by private firms, up from 68 percent the year before. Sales from one business to another are still concentrated in large, private sector companies. In 2004, these large firms accounted for 63 percent of business-to-business sales. For the fourth consecutive year, the wholesale trade sector accounted for the largest value of e-commerce sales. Wholesalers sold just over $6 billion worth of goods online last year, nearly one-quarter of total private sector e-commerce. We believe that the purchasing function will see two strategic shifts in the future, and these strategic shifts underlie the basis of B2B commerce.

Global sourcing—The Internet is the answer to **global sourcing** that businesses have been waiting for. It overcomes the limitations of geography and provides the key catalyst required for B2B commerce, bringing together suppliers and buyers on a common platform across the world with a transparency on price (Does price vary by geographic region or by size of customer, and am I getting the market price?), availability (Where can I find the product I need?), suppliers (Are there several suppliers of the same product?), and products (Is there a substitute or alternate product available on the market?).

Relationship orientation—Business buying behaviour is both operationally and strategically complex. Suppliers and buyers would like to tap into the "self-help" model associated with the Internet to make business-to-business transactions transparent and efficient, but simple buy-sell transactions will not be the end goal. Suppliers would like to learn of their buyers' demand function so that they can adjust their production schedules and inventory holdings and lower their order-processing costs. In turn, buyers would be interested in uniform pricing, finding alternative sources of supply, and better control over their procurement processes. These preferences will lead both buyers and sellers to seek a relationship orientation.

VALUE CREATION IN B2B MARKETPLACES[41]

B2B marketplaces create customer value in at least four ways. First, they expand everyone's market reach. For example, in the United States, half of the gross domestic product comes from fragmented industries such as electronic components, health care, and life sciences. B2B marketplaces help buyers and suppliers in these industries meet at a common platform. Chemdex maintains a register of 2,200 suppliers and more than 26,000 users of life sciences materials.

Second, B2B marketplaces generate lower prices for buyers. In a survey of companies using B2B marketplaces for procurement, half reported paying lower prices after they used the B2B marketplace. FreeMarkets (a B2B exchange company) says that its customers have experienced savings of 7 to 10 percent for commodities and 7 to 25 percent for custom purchases. Buyers are able to get lower prices because they reach more suppliers through the marketplace or, sometimes, more efficient suppliers. Other elements working to their advantage are price competition among suppliers and access to excess-inventory stocks at really low prices.

Third, B2B marketplaces cut the cost of the buyers' operations. Most B2B marketplaces are trying to provide their customers with value-added services that usually need to be taken care of at the buyer end. The e-Steel B2B exchange, with more than 2,200 buyers and sellers, automates the entire transaction process and takes care of order tracking, inventory management, and reordering processes that generate significant cost savings for buyers. Among companies that have begun online procurement, 56 percent cited greater efficiency and improved speed and accuracy in procurement as a result of B2B exchanges.

Finally, these marketplaces identify industry best practices. Some e-marketplaces have developed distinctive, high-value-added content.

Sell-side business models
Online exchange sites run by a single supplier or distributor seeking buyers.

Buy-side business models
Buying organizations using Internet-based technologies to buy from contracted suppliers.

E-procurement
The process of using a buy-side operating model.

Exchanges
Websites run by a third party to bring buyers and sellers together vertically within an industry sector, or horizontally across industry sectors.

B2B BUSINESS OPERATING MODELS[42]

How do B2B customers find suppliers and vice versa? This depends on how B2B exchange operations are set up. They can be classified into four types: (1) sell-side models, (2) buy-side models, (3) marketplaces and exchanges, and (4) auctions and reverse auctions.

The **sell-side business models** are "online exchange sites run by a single supplier or distributor seeking buyers." Companies such as Cisco (**http://www.cisco.com**) and Dell (**http://www.dell.com**) are the best examples of this model; they have set up personalized Web pages for their business customers. The **buy-side business models** involve a "buying organization using Internet-based technologies to buy from contracted suppliers." This process is called **e-procurement.** For example, General Electric (**http://www.ge.com**) uses a buy-side website for its procurement function. The third form of B2B models are the **neutral marketplaces** and **exchanges,** "web sites run by a third party to bring buyers and sellers together vertically within an industry sector or horizontally across industry sectors." Chemconnect (**http://www.chemconnect.com**) is an example of a vertical exchange for the chemical industry. Finally, the last B2B business model is auctions and reverse auctions which involve "a structured electronic market for bidding for products by buyers (auctions) or sellers (reverse auctions)." **Carbid.ca** and **FreeMarkets Online** are examples of auctions and reverse auctions, respectively.

Which B2B business model would a B2B customer use? That depends on the type of purchase need or buyclass. The buyclass could be straight re-buy, a modified re-buy, or a new task procurement need.

Straight Re-Buy

Straight re-buy
A product that has been purchased before, and needs to be re-purchased without any modifications.

A B2B Internet-based business model is most beneficial in a **straight re-buy** purchase occasion for several reasons. First, decision making is generally autonomous for straight re-buys. Second, the transaction costs of procurement are high, particularly in view of a low value of each transaction. Third, product requirements are clear and prespecified. Since competitive brands are relatively undifferentiated, the buyers of straight re-buys have tremendous power over sellers, and if the prices are non-standardized, the Internet helps in driving down prices. Typically, the buyers have the option of following types of B2B marketplaces: the catalogue hub, buyer aggregator, market exchange, and liquid exchange.

Catalogue Hub—This is a sell-side website featuring an online catalogue, encompassing a large number of product manufacturers/suppliers, and guaranteeing that a listed product is available at a fixed price. For example, Cambridgesoft's site **ChemACX.com** is an online catalogue site featuring more than 200,000 products from over 210 chemical suppliers. This model is best suited when the search costs for buyers are high, time is critical in purchasing, and price volatility is relatively low. **Sciquest.com** and **PlasticsNet.com** are two other catalogue hubs.

Buyer Aggregator—This is a buy-side online site that combines demand within and across buying enterprises to transact as a buyer group. Because it represents a large demand aggregated from a multitude of buyers, it is able to gain an advantageous low price from suppliers, thus benefiting the buyers. This model was pioneered by **Accompany.com.** In the U.K., demand aggregators such as Purchase Pooling Solutions, Inc. (**http://www.transitpool.com**) provide procurement savings for public-sector customer entities.

Market Exchange—Online market exchange sites bring together buyers and sellers, such as ChemConnect's World Chemical Exchange, and New View Technologies™ (**newview.com**). The pricing mechanism can be a simple offer/buy, offer/negotiated buy, or an auction offer/bid approach. Some major companies such as General Electric, Siemens, and Shell are now using for their entire straight re-buy procurement private exchanges that link the company and its chosen suppliers.

Liquid Exchange—Finally, straight re-buy customers in some product categories can also use the liquid exchange model—"a model where buyers and sellers bid and ask for the products in real time, and prices are transparent and purchases are guaranteed via a constant supply that generates the market's liquidity." For example, **HoustonStreet.com** is a liquid exchange for physical crude oil and refined products.

Modified Re-Buy

In case of a modified re-buy, the complexity is increased by the introduction of new specifications. There is a higher degree of interaction between the three roles. Therefore, the seller will have to be able to manage increasingly complex conflict resolution issues. This is obviously far more challenging to manage via the Internet. Typically, reverse auctions are the B2B model adopted under the modified re-buy purchase occasion.

Reverse Auctions—A reverse auction involves one buyer (usually large) and multiple sellers. In a reverse auction format, the buyer presents his need, and multiple sellers bid prices to meet this need. The seller who quotes the lowest price at closing is offered the bid. An example of a reverse auction market is FreeMarkets™ (**http://www.freemarkets.com**), which helps large buyers like GM, Quaker Oats, and Deere & Co. drive down their procurement costs.

New Purchase

When the customer is considering a new purchase situation, there is extensive interaction between the three roles. Payers have to juggle money, including raiding new capital, while buyers may need to go through an extensive process of identifying new suppliers. There is considerable uncertainty about the design/performance requirements of the product. Hence, the buyer seeks information extensively, is far more concerned with finding the right solution, and relies on the technical expertise of the seller. In this scenario, it is extremely difficult to market or sell on the Internet. The challenge of satisfying all three parties becomes considerably greater over such an impersonal medium where the level of human interaction is low. A business trading community B2B model provides the specialized information that the buyer will need; auctions are more often used for one-time and unique purchases.

Business Trading Community—A concept pioneered by **VerticalNet.com,** a business trading community is a site that acts as an "essential, comprehensive source of information and dialogue for a particular vertical market." VerticalNet's communities contain product information and enable B2B exchanges of information, supplementing existing trade shows and trade association activities. Another website, **Buzzsaw.com,** in the building design and construction industry, allows building owners, architects, engineers, contractors, suppliers, and manufacturers to share information and manage building projects more efficiently.

Auction—In this model, the price of an item is determined dynamically by bids submitted for the item over a period of time. This model is based solely on price, and is best used when the items being traded are unique in nature, there is high price volatility, buyers and/or sellers are fragmented, and time is less critical in purchasing. CARbid.ca (**http://www.carbid.ca**), which conducts B2B auctions of used cars, and **Liquidation.com** are auction models.

Learning New Behaviours in the B2B Marketplace

According to International Data Corp. (IDC), B2B exchanges are predicted to reach US$8 billion by 2007 as online sourcing and procurement becomes more standardized and widely expected.[43] Both buyers and sellers have to adapt to a new set of marketplace rules to obtain the highest efficiency from online exchanges.

Buyers need to realize that B2B exchanges are more than just "simple order matching." In order to reap significant benefits from B2B exchanges, they will need to adopt a "relationship approach" and invest time and effort in acquiring/building capabilities, implementing new technologies, and changing the organization.

Firms participating in exchanges also need to realize that the nature of their participation in exchanges is dependent not just on their IT capabilities but also on their own reasons for joining the exchange. They should join a marketplace exchange not just to establish an image of being technologically savvy in the market, but also to achieve specific goals of efficiency. The firm will need to re-engineer its business processes to participate in the exchange, and this will require building IT capabilities.[44]

Sellers will have to focus on specialization as they search for comparative advantage in the B2B commerce arena. As of the spring of 2000, the *Economist* estimated that there were about 750 online marketplaces in the United States, and most analysts estimate that that number will continue to rise. But they also predict that three companies in each segment will end up with 70 percent of the market share in technology markets, and, hence, the market will consolidate at around 2,000 to 3,000 exchanges in total. The ones that will remain will have the following characteristics: (1) they will have focused on specialization; (2) they will offer the customer end-to-end solutions, beginning with deep information content for (and related to) the transaction and the facilitation of the transaction; and (3) they will provide all the support services for the transaction by connecting not only with buyers and sellers but also with different entities at every step of the supply chain.

Private exchanges are also becoming popular because public market exchanges have not been able to live up to their expectations. Fifteen percent of the world's largest companies already have private exchanges according to Jupiter Research, mainly because they provide the ability to centrally manage procurement across many business units; integrate with back-end systems; link production, inventory, warehouse, and order-management systems; are more secure; and can limit participants to suppliers whom the company knows and trusts.

FUTURE TECHNOLOGY AND THE INTERNET CUSTOMER

Two developments in technology will offer new opportunities for the Internet customer: **mobile commerce** and **telematics.**

Mobile commerce
The buying and selling of products with the aid of mobile phones.

Telematics
The wave of the future whereby one's car, refrigerator, television, and medicine cabinets would be Internet-ready.

Mobile Commerce

An aid to the anytime/anywhere purchasing and consumption need is the mobile phone. By the end of 2005, the number of mobile subscribers had reached over 2 billion, and a market study by Portio Research predicts that by the end of 2009, half of the world's population will be using mobile phones. Africa now boasts the fastest growth rate in the world, with a forecast of 265 million new mobile subscribers over the next six years.[45] As handset penetration increases, Nokia predicts that consumers will begin to use their phone to connect to the Internet more than personal computers. Wireless Internet services can be made more personalized for customers compared to any other means of communication. First, mobile telephones are usually with customers and are switched on most of the time. Second, wireless network operators using a GSM (global system for mobile communication) standard would be able to uniquely identify a user and be able to send him or her personalized communication. Finally, the operator is able to pinpoint the user's location exactly, thus presenting the user with an array of new applications.

Telematics

In the next ten years, customers can expect the car, the refrigerator, the television, and the medicine cabinet in their bathroom to be Internet-ready, thus presenting thousands of opportunities for service from marketers. The car could keep track of the date when it is to be serviced next, and the refrigerator could automatically order items that fall below a particular stock level. Interactive television could make it easy for customers to order through the television, and the medicine cabinet could supplement discussions with the pharmacist and the doctor. As an example, the ubiquitous Internet could help GM convert a car into a "communications intermediary." The gas companies would be interested in knowing how much gas is left in the tank, mechanics would want to know when the car is due for its next service, and restaurants and retailers would be interested in knowing the area in which the car is cruising.

The concept of the ubiquitous Internet could apply to any other place where the customer is physically present: shopping malls, airport lounges, parking garages, etc. At all these locations, marketers could provide customers with mobile devices that help the customer by providing him or her with information relevant to their needs, and at the same time, capture information for marketers.

ONLINE CUSTOMER BEHAVIOUR AND THE THREE CUSTOMER ROLES

In this section, we pull together all the various concepts covered in the chapter and illustrate their relevance to the three customer roles, with emphasis on what marketers can do to influence and manage online customer behaviour. (See Table 12.2.) In the case of individual decision making, by definition, the user and buyer roles are combined in the same person. Often the same individual also plays the payer role. Therefore, the customer has more control over what to buy and is less likely to indulge in impulse purchases. The three roles come into play in the online decision-making process: problem recognition, information search, alternative evaluation, choice or purchase, and the post-choice experience.

Recognizing a problem or deprivation through internal stimuli is similar for an online and offline customer. Although problem recognition has been considered the domain of the user role, the other two roles can also be the source of problem recognition. For instance, from the payer perspective, the perception that online purchases may cost less than offline purchases may act as an impetus to browse the Internet for bargains. The key issue is how to demonstrate price value for online products. For example, airlines suggest a 10 percent reduction in tickets if you buy online as opposed to purchasing tickets through travel agents or call centres. Likewise, buyers, when exposed to banner ads on the Internet, may feel that current vendors do not provide convenient or satisfactory service.

TABLE 12.2 Individual and Business Online Decision Making and the Three Customer Roles

Concepts	User	Payer	Buyer
	INDIVIDUAL CUSTOMER ONLINE DECISIONS: UNIQUE ASPECTS		
Problem recognition	• Users are most frequent problem recognizers. • Offline advertising media creates pull demand for website.	• Realization that online prices are more competitive than offline can act as a stimuli for problem recognition.	• Buyer dissatisfaction with current options and well-targeted banner advertising can provide an impetus to seek change.
Information Search	• Users can seek pertinent information from other users via Internet forums; managing word-of-mouth is therefore critical.	• Payer seeks price comparisons, which is extensively available on the Internet. • Marketers should also promote economics of online shopping.	•This is critical to the buyer. • Information is extensively available on the Internet. • Marketers must ensure that the website is easy to navigate with neither too much or too little information.

(continued)

			• The low switching costs enable buyers to move to another website quickly.
Evaluation of alternatives	• User values are most important. • Marketers should try to understand the online profile of the customer and provide products accordingly.	• Payers will seek to maximize price value through comparison. • Transparency of all costs will be beneficial to the marketer and the payer.	• A compensatory choice model to aid selection is generally not suitable in an Internet environment. Instead Web pages provide the option for the buyer to use a conjunctive or disjunctive model.
Purchase	• The user role is less important in this aspect.	• The key issue is how to demonstrate price value for online products. • Prior experiences and comparable prices are key. • Marketers should make price simple and transparent and state all additional charges upfront.	• Marketers should address buyer concerns about trust, security, and privacy when purchasing over the Internet. • The buyer is also concerned about the ease of use of the website.
Post-purchase	• Experience is determined largely by user role. • Similar to the offline market, marketers can provide stimuli to convince the customers that they have made the right choice, thereby increasing satisfaction and developing loyalty.		• The Internet largely facilitates dissemination of word-of-mouth. • The promise of anonymity ensures that a nonaggressive buyer can also express opinions freely. • The extent of salience in the dissatisfaction and the degree of attribution to the marketer may, however, impact the tendency for the buyer to complain.
	BUSINESS CUSTOMER ONLINE DECISIONS: UNIQUE ASPECTS		
Straight re-buy buyclass	• User role is limited due to the standard product specifications.	• Payer is seeking price advantages via the Internet. • Reduction in transaction costs is an incentive to use catalogue hub, buyer aggregator, market exchange, or liquid exchange models.	• The buyer is seeking to routinize and automate the process as much as possible and therefore prefers to use Internet exchanges as much as possible.
Modified re-buy class	• User is more involved as new specifications have to be defined.	• Payer involvement also increases as an acceptable price level has to be determined.	• Buyer role interacts to a great extent with user and payer; increased supplier involvement is also sought.
New purchase buyclass	• User is very involved in the process as a completely new set of specifications is defined. • Supplier input is key.	• Extensive pricing search is undertaken by the payer role to understand and determine an acceptable price level.	• Buyer role is very complex as there is extensive interaction with user and payer departments as well as with suppliers who are also seen as playing consultant roles. • Selling over the Internet is very challenging in this scenario.

In the information search stage, ample product information is readily available, enabling users to evaluate a product's benefits more thoroughly. The payer can compare prices across a wide variety of vendors, and the buyer finds it easy to collect all the information. Buyers who enjoy browsing help the user role identify new solutions, whereas those who are comparison shoppers help the payer find the best value. Although traditionally the customers have been restricted to a fairly narrow consideration set of brands, this has now expanded greatly due to the ease of accessing information on the Internet. Even an uninvolved buyer can provide extensive information to the user role, due to the minimal search effort required.

In the alternative evaluation stage, the user values are the overriding criteria. Marketers find that information given to customers online keeps them coming back to the site, thereby building interest and loyalty toward the brand and increasing the probability of positive user evaluation. Given the large number of options available to the buyer, a compensatory choice model to aid selection is generally not suitable in an Internet environment. Instead, Web pages provide the customer with the option of using a conjunctive or a disjunctive model.

In the purchase stage, the buyer and payer values become the most important. The payer needs to know what the additional charges are (shipping, taxes, etc.). Often, high shipping costs are a deterrent to purchase. The buyer seeks ease of use and navigation when looking at a website. If it is difficult to navigate and there is either inadequate information or too much of it, the switching costs are low enough to make the buyer move to another website immediately.

In the post-purchase stage, the buyer may experience buyer's remorse, while the user evaluates the usage experience. The Internet has opened forums to disseminate positive or negative word of mouth by the buyer, even for a less aggressive buyer role.

In the business-buying scenario, role specialization is far more pronounced than it is for household customers, which increases the complexity of online business-to-business marketing, depending on the buyclass occasion. The buyclass affects all three roles.

In a straight re-buy situation, a B2B Internet-based business model is most beneficial. Decision making is more autonomous when compared to other models and the website does not have appeal to all three roles; typically, the buyer will be the only point of interaction. In this scenario, the buyer has tremendous power, and if prices are nonstandardized, the Internet helps to drive down prices. Typically, the catalogue hub, buyer aggregator, market exchange, and liquid auction models are used to satisfy this procurement need.

In the case of a modified re-buy situation, the complexity is increased by the new specifications that are introduced. There is a higher degree of interaction between the three roles, and reverse auction is a suitable B2B model for the modified re-buy purchase occasion.

When the customer organization is attempting to undertake a new purchase occasion, there is extensive interaction between the three roles. Payers have to raise new capital, and buyers seek information extensively from suppliers to meet the new design/performance requirements. A business trading community B2B model provides the specialized information that the buyer will need, while auctions are more often used for one-time and unique purchases.

SUMMARY

LO 1 We began this chapter by discussing the Internet's potential. Predictions for e-commerce revenues as well as for the number of people going online indicate that e-commerce is big and is here to stay. Furthermore, the Internet has certain characteristics, including the ability to inexpensively store vast amounts of information at different virtual locations; the availability of powerful and inexpensive means of searching, organizing, and disseminating such information; interactivity; the ability to provide information on demand; the ability to provide perceptual experiences that are far superior to a printed catalogue, although not as rich as personal inspection; and the ability to serve as a transaction medium and a physical distribution medium for certain goods (for example, software). From a retailer's perspective, the relatively low entry and establishment costs make this an attractive marketing and sales medium.

LO 2 We then described the individual customer's decision-making process online. In the problem recognition phase, the Internet is used as an external stimulus. Advertising on the Internet is used to generate primary as well as secondary demand. When the customer moves to the information search stage, the easy availability of information on the Internet has greatly expanded the customer's traditionally narrow evoked set of brands. As a result of this accessible information and increasing time pressures, consumers are using the Internet in large numbers and in almost all categories of information search. When the individual moves into the evaluation-of-alternatives phase, while the Internet has increased the amount of information available to customers, it has also developed methods for customers to best make use of the information available to them. In this context, electronic recommendation agents called "smart bots" or "shopbots" make it easier for consumers to reduce their search costs and also improve the quality of their shopping decisions. In the choice stage, we discussed personalization as well as the challenges of privacy and security concerns that customers have while transacting over the Internet. Finally, under post-purchase behaviour, we discussed ways that the Internet can be used to increase satisfaction and develop loyalty after the purchase of the product.

LO 3 We then discussed the implications of conducting B2B transactions over the Internet. We stated our belief that the purchasing function will see two strategic shifts in the future: global sourcing and relationship orientation, which underlie the basis of B2B commerce, directly impacting the business decision-making process. We then discussed how B2B marketplaces create value by expanding everyone's market reach; generating lower prices for buyers; cutting the cost of the buyer's process; and identifying and disseminating industry-wide best practices.

LO 4 B2B e-commerce business models are very simply listed in four categories as sell-side models, buy-side models, marketplaces and exchanges, and auctions and reverse auctions. The sell-side business models usually pertain to a single supplier or distributor, seeking buyers using the Internet. The buy-side business models involve a buying organization using Internet-based technologies to buy from contracted suppliers. This process is called e-procurement.

LO 5 The B2B business model that is typically selected will vary, depending upon the type of purchase need or buyclass. The buyclass could be a straight re-buy, a modified re-buy, or a new task procurement need. A straight re-buy occasion uses the catalogue hub, buyer aggregator, market exchange or liquid exchange models, while a modified re-buy occasion demands the use of reverse auctions. A new task purchase occasion uses a business trading community or an auction model.

To best derive value from the Internet, buyers have to develop a relationship approach to doing business, and focus on partnering with supplies. Sellers have to focus on specialization as they search for comparative advantages in the B2B commerce arena. Finally, firms participating in exchanges must realize that their nature of participation in exchanges is not just dependent on their IT capabilities, but also on their own motivations to join the exchange, which in turn impacts their degree of efficiency in operations. **LO 6**

KEY TERMS

Buy-Side Business Models 453
Collaborative Filtering 443
Content-Based Filtering 443
Co-Production 446
Customerization 447
E-Procurement 453
Exchanges 453
Experience Goods 440
Global Sourcing 452
Information Intensiveness Continuum 440
Mobile Commerce 456
Neutral Marketplaces 453
Recommendation Systems 443
Search Goods 440
Sell-Side Business Models 453
Shopbots 444
Smart Bots 444
Straight Re-Buy 454
Telematics 456

DISCUSSION QUESTIONS AND EXERCISES

1. The chapter outlines the characteristics of products that lend themselves better to sale on the Internet. Interview three consumers regarding whether or not they would feel comfortable buying each of the following products, and compare and analyze their reasons vis-à-vis the product characteristics:
   a. Online advice on personal health issues
   b. A private brand of pasta sauce
   c. Milk from your local grocer delivered within one hour of ordering online under a one-year binding contract at a price current in that store on the day of ordering, with a two-gallon minimum and a 50-cent per-delivery charge

   Also comment on what kinds of consumers might find these online product offerings to be attractive.
2. The chapter discusses various steps in consumer decision making and the Internet's ability and limitations in taking the consumer through these steps. Discuss these for the following situations:
   a. A consumer deciding which anti-virus program to buy online
   b. A consumer choosing an MBA program to enroll in
   c. A consumer who is unfamiliar with Europe leasing an apartment in Paris for one year
3. You market one of the following products to business customers: (a) office furniture, (b) lubricating oil for machine tools, or (c) scrap leather collected from shoe factories. Review all online alternatives described in the book and identify which options the prospective customers of each of these products are most likely to use. Explain your answer.
4. Select two companies—a consumer-goods company and an industrial-goods company—that have in place an e-procurement program, and interview the director of each

program. Identify the hurdles in bringing more of their procurement online, i.e., expanding the scope of e-procurement.

5. You are the marketing director of a large company with both online and offline presence. A renowned consumer advocate (who is also the president of a consumer privacy group) has written a letter to your president, expressing concern about the tracking of website visitors using cookies and other tools. The writer acknowledges that this practice is common to all websites, but still asks that you stop this practice altogether. Write a letter to the consumer advocate outlining the advantages of such consumer online-behaviour tracking to consumers themselves and how your company uses that information to deliver these advantages while at the same time ensuring no negative effects on the consumers who visits your website.

NOTES

1 Adapted from Sandeep Krishnamurthy, "The Amazon.com Case," in *E-Commerce Management: Text and Cases,* South-Western College Publishing, krishnamurthy.swcollege.com, (2002), ISBN: 0324152523.

2 "A Brief History of the Internet and Related Networks," http://www.isoc.org/Internet/history/cerf.html; Gary P. Schneider and James T. Perry, *Electronic Commerce* (Toronto: Thomson Learning), 14–20.

3 Statistics Canada: The Daily, April 20, 2005 *Survey of Electronic Commerce and Technology (SECT) 2004.*

4 Jennifer LeClaire, "The Evolution of E-Commerce," *E-Commerce Times,* July 2, 2005, http://www.ecommercetimes.com/story/40249.html.

5 Electronic Commerce and Technology, *The Daily,* April 20, 2005, Statistics Canada.

6 Robert A. Peterson, Sridhar Balasubramanian, and Bart J.Bronnenberg, "Exploring the Implications of the Internet for Consumer Marketing" in *Internet Marketing,* eds. Sheth, Eshghi, and Krishnan, 120–47 (Orlando, FL: Harcourt Inc., 2001)

7 Jagdish N. Sheth and Rajendra S. Sisodia, "Consumer Behaviour in the Future," in *Internet Marketing,* eds. Sheth, Eshghi, and Krishnan, 72–90 (Orlando, FL: Harcourt Inc., 2001)

8 Canada Online! A comparative analysis of Internet users in Canada and the world: Behaviour, Attitudes and Trends 2004, October 2005, Canadian Internet Project, http://www.cipic.ca. The Canadian Internet Project is a research initiative funded by the Canadian Media Reserach Consortium, under the direction of Professor Charles Zamaria (Ryerson University) and Dr. Fred Fletcher (York University) in partnership with the following parties: Bell Canada, the Government of Canada, Telefilm Canada and the Ontario Media Development Corporation.

9 Donna Hoffman, Tom Novak, and Ann E. Schlosser, "The Evolution of the Digital Divide: How Gaps in Internet Access May Impact Electronic Commerce," *Journal of Computer Mediated Communication* 5 no. 3 (March 2000), http://www.ascusc.org/jcmc/vol5/issue3/hoffman.html.

10 Rashi Glazer, "Marketing in an Information-Intensive Environment: Strategic Implications of Knowledge as an Asset," in *Internet Marketing,* eds. Sheth, Eshghi, and Krishnan, 31–61 (Orlando, FL: Harcourt Inc., 2001)

11 Robert A. Peterson, Sridhar Balasubramanian, and Bart J. Bronnenberg, "Exploring the Implications of the Internet for Consumer Marketing," in *Internet Marketing,* eds. Sheth, Eshghi, and Krishnan, 120–47 (Orlando, FL: Harcourt Inc., 2001)

12 Michael Pastore, "Multichannel Shoppers Key to Retail Success," October 11, 2001, http://ecommerce.internet.com/news/insights/trends/article/0,3371,10417_902101,00.html.

13 Survey: Consumers Trust Dealers and the Internet, Bodyshop, November 2003, vol. 23, iss. 6.

14 Jim Adair, "Canada's Public MLS Site Comes Under Fire," http://Realtytimes.com.

15 Barbara Bickart and Robert Schindler, "Internet Forums as Influential Sources of Consumer Information," *Advances in Consumer Research* 28 (2001): 135, http://www.vancouver.wsu.edu/acr/home.htm.

16 Laura Landro, "The Best Way to Get Reliable Health Information," *The Wall Street Journal,* November 12, 2001.

17 Asim Ansari, Skander Essegaier, and Rajeev Kohli, "Internet Recommendation Systems," *Journal of Marketing Research* 37 (August 2000): 363–75; Mary Kwak, "Web Sites Learn to Make Smarter Suggestions," *Sloan Management Review* 42, no. 4 (Summer 2001): 17.

18 Soyeon Shim, Mary Ann Eastlick, Sherry L. Lotz, and Patricia Warrington, "An Online Prepurchase Intentions Model," *Journal of Retailing* 77 no. 3 (Fall 2001): 397–416; Marie-Odile Richard and Ramdas Chandra, "A Model of Consumer Web Navigational Behavior: Conceptual Development and Application," *Journal of Business Research* 58, no. 8 (August 2005): 1019–1029.

19 Gerald Häubl and Valerie Trifts, "Consumer Decision Making in Online Shopping Environments: The Effects of Interactive Decision Aids," *Marketing Science* 19, no. 1 (2000): 4–21.

20 Eric Brynjolfsson and Michael D. Smith, "The Great Equalizer? Consumer Choice Behaviour at Internet Shopbots," *MIT Sloan School of Management,* July 2000, http://ebusiness.mit.edu/papers/tge.

21 Kevin Jones, "Ecommerce Liposuction: Key to Stealth Strategy," *Forbes ASAP,* June 4, 1999.

22 John Edwards, "Is That Your Best Offer?" November 1, 2000, http://www.cio.com/archive/110100_et.html.

23 "Front End," *Information Week,* November 12, 2001, 17.

24 Don Peppers and Martha Rogers, *The One-to-One Manager* (New York: Doubleday, 1999).

25 Jerry Wind and Arvind Rangaswamy, "Customerization: The Next Revolution in Mass Customization," *Journal of Interactive Marketing* 15, no. 1 (Winter 2001): 13–32.

26 Eric J. Johnson, Steven Bellman, and Gerald L. Lohse, "Cognitive Lock-In and the Power Law of Practice," March 12, 2002, http://www.cebiz.org/downloads/power_law_lockin.pdf; Eric J. Johnson, Wendy W. Moe, Peter S. Fader, Steven Bellman, and Gerald L. Lohse, "On the Depth and Dynamics of Online Search Behaviour," July 2002, http://www.cebiz.org/downloads/power_law_lockin.pdf.

27 Erik Brynjolfsson and Michael D. Smith, "The Great Equalizer? Consumer Choice at Internet Shopbots," MIT Working paper, http://July 2000, ebusiness.mit.edu/papers/tge.

28 Bill Richards, "Following the Crumbs—The Rise of I-Commerce," Supplement to *The Wall Street Journal,* October 29, 2001.

29 K. B. Sheehan and M. G. Hoy, "Flaming, Complaining, Abstaining: How Online Users Respond to Privacy Concerns," *Journal of Advertising* 28, no. 3, 37–52.

30 Joseph E. Phelps, Giles D'Souza, and Glen J. Nowak, "Antecedents and Consequences of Consumer Privacy Concerns: An Empirical Investigation," *Journal of Interactive Marketing* 15, no. 4 (Autumn 2001): 2–17.

31 "Online Fraud: Though Victim Percentage is Low, Fear is High," *Estats-Enews,* http://www.emarketer.com, June 29, 2001.

32 McLean, Dan, "Fate of e-Commerce is Anything but Secure," *Computer World Canada,* November 11, 2005.

33 Ellen Garbarino and Michal Strahilevitz, "Gender Differences in the Risk Perceptions and Effectiveness of Risk Reducers in Online Purchasing," *Advances in Consumer Research* 28 (2001): 99.

34 Patrick D. Lynch, Robert J. Kent, and Srini S. Srinivasan, "The Global Internet Shopper: Evidence from Shopping Tasks in Twelve Countries," *Journal of Advertising Research,* May–June 2001, 15–23.

35 Glen L. Urban, Fareena Sultan, and William J. Qualls, "Placing Trust at the Center of Your Internet Strategy," *Sloan Management Review* 42, no. 1 (Fall 2000): 39–48.

36 Ellen Neuborne, "Break It to Them Quickly," *Business Week e.biz,* October 29, 2001, p. Eb 10.

37 Wendy W. Moe and Peter S. Fader, "Which Visits Lead to Purchases? Dynamic Conversion Behaviour at E-commerce Sites," Working paper discussed in Mitch Betts, "Turning Browsers to Buyers," *Sloan Management Review* 42, no. 2 (Winter 2001): 8–9.

38 Michael Silverstein, Nina Abdelmessih, and Peter Stanger, Winning the Online Consumer 2.0—Converting Traffic into Profitable Relationships, BCG Report, 2/25/2001, http://www.bcg.com/publications/files/022101_Winning_online_consumer_ report_summary.

39 Bill Chambers, Gail Donnelly, and Joshua Shehab, "Web Self-Service: A Good Buy," *Information Week,* August 13, 2001, 39–42.

40 Youngme Moon and Frances X. Frei, "Exploding the Self-Service Myth," *Harvard Business Review* (May–June 2000): 26–27.

41 Ryan Kerrigan, Eric V. Roegner, Dennis D. Swinford, and Craig C. Zawada, "B2-Basics," The McKinsey Quarterly 1 (2001), http://www.mckinseyquarterly.com.

42 The section on B2B commerce has been adapted from several research reports—E-commerce B2B report, 2000, http://www.emarketer.com; Andy Blackburn, Hal Sirkin, and Jim Andrew, The B2B Opportunity: Creating Advantage through E-Marketplaces, October 2000, http://www.bcg.com/publications—browse by E-commerce; Coming into Focus: Using the Lens of Economic Value to clarify the Impact of B2B e-Marketplaces, CAPS Research and Mckinsey and Company, September 2000, http://www.mckinsey.com/features/caps_white_paper/featured%20paper.html; Charles Phillips and Mary Meeker, The B2B Internet Report—Collaborative Commerce, Morgan Stanley Dean Witter, April 2000; Building the B2B Foundation—Positioning Net Market Makers for Success, ATKearney 2000, http://www.atkearney.com/main.taf?site=1&a=5&b=3&c=1&d=4.

43 Quoted in Dan Blacharski, E-commerce Trades and B2B Exchanges, 05/04/2005, http://www.itworld.com/nl/it_insights/05042005/.

44 Rajdeep Grewal, James M. Comer, and Raj Mehta, "An Investigation into the Antecedents of Organizational Participation in Business-to-Business Electronic Markets," *Journal of Marketing* 65 (July 2001): 17–33.

45 http://www.portioresearch.com/opinion3_convergent.html.

CHAPTER 13

Creating Market Values for the Customer

LEARNING OBJECTIVES

After reading this chapter you should be able to:

LO 1 Understand the concept of value delivery.

LO 2 Explain how to create market value for users (performance, social, emotional).

LO 3 Explain how to create market value for payers (price, credit).

LO 4 Explain how to create market value for buyers (service, convenience, personalization).

LO 5 Explain how to measure value delivery.

Wanted: VALUE

> Value, not money, is the basic currency of all human interaction. When we meet someone, we often try to quickly assess how long it would be worth our while to talk to that person. If an incoming phone call shows up on our caller ID, we promptly decide if we would gain anything by taking the call at that time. If we get 10 letters in the mail, we look through them and then choose to open only those that we expect to contain some information of value to us. This is even truer for marketplace exchanges. The only reason the customers are even in the marketplace is that they are looking for something of value. The business that can deliver them that value, and deliver more of it than its competitors, gains the customer's patronage.
>
> (*ValueSpace*, 2001, 3–4)[1]

What underlies some companies' ability to offer outstanding value? How can other marketers create market values for their customers? Examples of value innovation abound: Barnes and Nobles bookstores are like large theatres, complete with coffee shop and music room; British Airways offers showers in the arrival lounge; Harry Rosen's sales associates use data from the client information system to alert customers about when a shipment of one of their favorite brands arrives (see the Window on Practice); and L.L. Bean will gladly refund merchandise returned anytime during its lifetime, no questions asked.

We begin this chapter by discussing the two dimensions of value delivery: effectiveness and efficiency. Following that, we present specific management tools that would enable firms to deliver market values to customers. These tools are specific to individual values that the firm might wish to pursue. We also discuss the ethical issues specific to each of these values from a consumer's standpoint. The next section deals with a measurement strategy. Our discussion dwells first on a method of determining customer values; it then suggests measurement statements to assess how well various value-delivery tools are doing their job, from the customer's viewpoint. In the final section, we return to the opening theme of the book, namely, customer orientation and the firm's ultimate goal of keeping customers happy. We conclude by suggesting a measurement tool that tells the firm just how happy its customers are.

LO 1 ➧ VALUE DELIVERY

Value delivery A firm fulfills a customer's need or want.

As defined in Chapter 1, value is what customers seek in products and suppliers.[2] It stems from a product's potential to satisfy the customer's need or want. The fulfillment of a customer's need or want is called **value delivery**.

WINDOW ON **PRACTICE**

Value in Service Delivery at Harry Rosen

On February 4, 1954, Harry Rosen and his brother Lou opened a menswear store in Toronto's Cabbagetown, with only $500. Since then, Harry Rosen has become a major menswear retailer, with 35 percent of the Canadian market for high-end men's clothing, 16 stores across Canada, 600 associates, and more than $150 million in sales. Harry Rosen has become a major brand its innovative approach to menswear. Harry Rosen's designers have developed a portfolio of prestigious brands. Their progressive stores and advertising, along with great service quality, play an important role in their success. Commitment to service value by a superior staff, as well as the use of technology, selection, and presentation, give Harry Rosen a strong competitive advantage. The brand connotes a service promise, which has been used as a marketing and sales strategy to communicate its value proposition. In his co-authored book *Ask Harry!: The Harry Rosen Story*, Harry Rosen says: "We don't perceive ourselves as being in the clothing business. We don't just sell suits and sport jackets. It's a relationship-based business. My business is to get to know you, to have you build a relationship with one of my highly trained associates. I want to be your clothier for life. The whole key to our business is loyal clients. I strongly believe we have a corporate culture that has a love of quality and a love of clients. And building customer relationships is a managed process."

With a comprehensive customer information system, Harry Rosen's "one client at a time" service level can be maintained while dealing with many customers. Technology allows Harry Rosen to build personal information that associates use regularly to develop relationships with customers. "We want to know about them—not just their sizes, but where they work, their family structure, their lifestyle and so on—all so we can advise them," says Rosen. For example, the information system is used to profile clients and inform them of special store events, or when a delivery of one of their favorite brands is made. Harry Rosen is reaching out to its customer base through phone calls, e-mails, its quarterly e-mail newsletter, and its bi-annual catalogue. Its strategy is to convert prospects into customers and develop a life-long relationship with frequent clients. Rosen has won numerous marketing awards, and he is also known for his commitment to community; community service is viewed as an integral part of his career.

SOURCES: Adapted from "Canada's 50 Best Managed Companies." http://www.canadas50best.com/en/. BuildingtheBest/QuotesFromBook/Chapter5.htm; Sasvari, Joanne. "Everybody Loves Harry: The Menswear Giant Celebrates 50 Years in Business." *Calgary Herald*, February 24, 2004, D1. http://www.harryrosen.com; Ryan, Thomas J. "All-Star Salute Harry Rosen Inc. - Nominated by GERS Retail Systems." December 1, 2005. http://www.apparelmag.com/ articles/dec/dec05_8.shtml.

DIMENSIONS OF VALUE DELIVERY

Value delivery has two dimensions: effectiveness and efficiency. **Effectiveness** is the ability of the product to meet the customer's needs and wants. **Efficiency** is minimal cost to the customer, measured in money, time, and physical effort, to receive that value. The less a product costs, the more efficient it is from the customer's point of view.

Effectiveness
How well a product meets the customer's needs and wants.

Efficiency
How little it costs the customer in money, time, and physical effort to receive the value he or she seeks.

If a marketer's offering fulfills a customer's needs and wants very well, and if in obtaining and using that offering, the customer has to expend as few resources (time, money, and physical effort) as possible, then both efficiency and effectiveness are being simultaneously harnessed to achieve the *best value* for the customer (see Figure 13.1). There are many examples of companies offering both effectiveness and efficiency in delivering customer value. For example, the Toyota Camry is a high-quality car sold at a relatively low price. Mass merchandise catalogue companies such as L.L. Bean offer customers better-known, branded products (effectiveness) with the convenience of shopping from home (efficiency).

In the business-to-business service markets, Federal Express offers a value via both effectiveness and efficiency. It offers effectiveness by satisfying customer need for on-time, guaranteed delivery of time-sensitive documents and packages. On the efficiency side, it conserves the customer's time and effort resources via its pickup service and via offering customers computer software so they may process the shipping themselves. However, its price value is no better than its competitors'. Business firms also offer efficiency value to customers by providing access via the Internet and thereby minimizing customer effort in interacting with the firm.

Firms that offer electronic document delivery, such as a database or an article from a journal, offer both effectiveness and efficiency; having the information on an electronic medium allows customers to use that information more effectively, for example, via word search, cutting and pasting, moving the text around, or enhancing the graphs and photos. Also the customer effort is minimized (i.e., it saves the effort of getting it by mail or going to the library).

TOOLS FOR CREATING CUSTOMER VALUES

To offer various values to the customer, marketers need to incorporate certain attributes and elements into their offerings. For example, to offer convenience as a value, marketers have to incorporate certain time- and effort-saving mechanisms into the product or into the manner in which customers can purchase that product. As seen in Chapter 1, different types of value are sought by the user, payer, and buyer roles. Users seek performance value and social and emotional values. Payers want price value and credit and financing values. Buyers desire

FIGURE 13.1 Dimensions of Value Delivery

Effectiveness (Need/want fulfillment)		Efficiency (Resource conservation): Poor	Efficiency (Resource conservation): Good
	Good	Effectiveness value	Best value
	Poor	Poor value	Efficiency value

service value and convenience and personalization values. Offering each of these market values requires certain marketing tools, summarized in Table 13.1 and described in the following sections.

TABLE 13.1 Tools for Creating Market Values

User Values	**Performance** • Quality improvement • Innovations • Mass customization • Warranties and guarantees	**Social** • Price exclusivity • Limited availability • Social image ads • Exclusive offerings	**Emotional** • Emotional communications
Payer Values	**Price** • Low price from lower margins • Low price from increased productivity (achieved through economies of scale, modernized plant, automation, business process reengineering)	**Credit** • Acceptance of credit cards • Offering of own credit card • Deferred payment	**Financing** • Leasing • Customized financing
Buyer Values	**Service** • Product display and demonstration • Knowledgeable salespersons • Responsiveness. • User support and maintenance service	**Convenience** • Convenient point-of-access • Automated transaction recording	**Personalization** • Personal attention and courtesy • Interpersonal relationships

LO 2 CREATING MARKET VALUES FOR USERS

The user is primarily concerned that the product performs as desired and that its use delivers social and emotional benefits.

PERFORMANCE VALUE

The user obtains the universal value of performance when the product delivers its physical performance better than competing alternatives do, and when the product performs that way consistently, without failure. A vivid example of what's meant by performance value is 3M Worldwide's double-coated tape, used to bond two surfaces. As reported in *ValueSpace*, one application of this tape is sheet metal bonding in the body of a truck. The current methods for bonding are riveting or welding. 3M is working toward replacing the rivets with double-coated tapes. The adhesive tape will eliminate any air gaps that inevitably remain between any two riveted surfaces and will give a seamless joint. This would mean a good moisture seal and no vibration noise. And, of course, the bonding would be as strong as possible. Moreover, using adhesive tape instead of rivets or welding would save on production costs as it takes much less time and skill to apply a bonding tape than to apply rivets or welds.

Physical performance stems from the physical composition of the product. As such, it is directly linked to product attributes and to product quality. More specifically, firms can offer superior performance value by adopting four tools: quality improvement, product innovation, mass customization, and warranties and guarantees.

Quality Improvement

Companies can offer better performance value by building quality into their products. Many firms aim for zero defects, eliminating product failures completely. The automobile industry is an illustrative case. As late as the early 1980s, the North American automobile industry offered cars that, with few exceptions, broke down frequently. Japanese cars became the choice of many consumers simply because they were more reliable. In the late 1980s to early 1990s, the North American car industry turned to building quality into their cars and, consequently, regained some of the lost market share. In fact, Saturn was created by General Motors simply to build a quality car company from scratch—free from the legacy of poor quality with which its parent company, in the eyes of many consumers, has been afflicted.

In the services industry, firms can improve the quality of their offerings by hiring well-qualified service staff and then by continually training and retraining them.[3] For an example of a service firm committed to zero defects, see the Window on Practice.

An absence of quality in products can be a major ethical concern, in both the consumer and business markets. Take the case of the tread separation in the Firestone/Bridgestone ATX tires on the Ford Explorer in late 2001 that resulted in several hundred injuries, including the deaths of at least 46 people in North America. Most troubling in this case is the fact both Ford and Firestone may have known of these quality defects since 1993, but they remained quiet

WINDOW ON **PRACTICE**

FedEx Quality Improvement Program

Quality has been a top priority at Federal Express right from the outset. It achieved, for example, 99 percent levels of reliability on its on-time delivery. Yet FedEx was not satisfied, for it realized that a 99 percent on-time delivery would still leave a lot of customers (those affected by the 1 percent error rate) irate. So it began a program of zero failures, counting errors in absolute numbers rather than as percentages. The company developed a Service Quality Index (SQI), computed daily, based on errors in 12 different delivery events weighed by the seriousness of the error that was reflective of the amount of aggravation caused to customers. For example, missing a promised delivery date generated five points, compared to one point when a customer requested that an invoice be adjusted. If *everything* went wrong, the SQI daily score would be 40 million. In 1988, when the program was established, the estimated SQI score was 152,000 points per day. The company set its first goal at holding to this level (which actually implied a 20 percent improvement, given forecasted growth in package volume of 20 percent). FedEx's employees surpassed this goal, with an actual 1989 SQI score of 133,000 points. Accordingly, the company's profit goals were reached, too. This level of attention to detail in its quality program has enabled FedEx to offer its customers unparalleled performance value.

SOURCE: Adapted from Lovelock, Christopher H. "Federal Express Quality Improvement Program." In *Marketing Challenges: Cases & Exercise*. 3rd ed. edited by Christopher H. Lovelock and Charles B. Weinberg, Case 44. (New York: McGraw Hill, 1993) 545–558. http://www.federalexpress.com.

about it, until they finally had no choice but to recall millions of these tires. Similarly, in the case of machinery, it is important that the machines are absolutely safe to use; otherwise, they endanger the lives of several people working on them in factories.

Product Innovation

Firms can also increase the performance value of their offerings by designing new features in products. Consider DVDs that enable slow-motion viewing, automobiles equipped with antilock braking devices, aqua-tread tires that do not slip on wet pavement, detergents that clean in cold water, and hotels that offer in-room fax service. Today we take them for granted, but when they first appeared, each added to the performance value derived by the user. Current examples of innovations are automobiles equipped with navigation devices (an electronic map that shows where you are and gives directions to your desired destinations), a great value to rental-car customers driving in unfamiliar cities; computers that convert voice into written text; software that allows manipulation of photographic images; many Internet-based information sources; and new antidepressant medications.

Companies that focus on innovation have a culture of innovation. One of the most innovative companies in America is 3M. To foster its climate of innovation, 3M is reported to have instituted the following work rules: (1) 25 percent of each division's revenue should come from products that did not exist five years ago; and (2) researchers are encouraged to spend up to 15 percent of their resources on unassigned projects of personal interest. Other innovative companies are Microsoft and Intel, where products are being constantly upgraded to newer versions every 18 months or so.

Innovative companies also spend more on R&D. PIMS (Profit Impact of Marketing Strategies) is a program of data gathering and analysis that analyzes about 3,800 business units on about 200 pieces of data to identify strategy factors that determine business profitability. An analysis of firms in the PIMS database found that R&D investment leads to more sales from new products (see Figure 13.2). Furthermore, the proportion of sales from new products was positively correlated with the gains in market share[4] (see Figure 13.3).

FIGURE 13.2 R&D Leads to More Sales from New Products

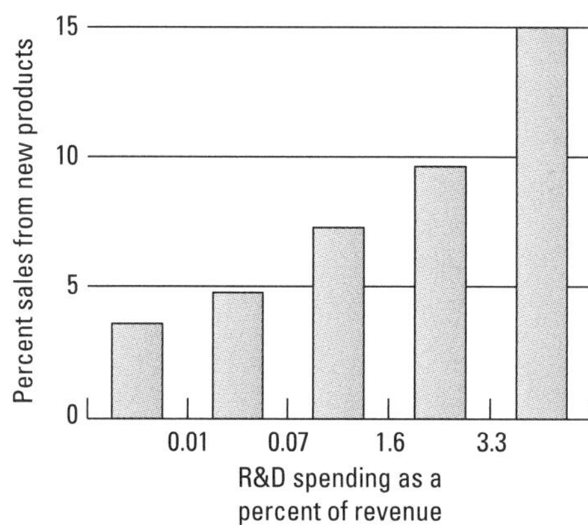

SOURCE: Reprinted with the permission of The Free Press, a Division of Simon & Schuster Adult Publishing Group, from MANAGING CUSTOMER VALUE: Creating Quality and Service That Customers Can See, by Bradley T. Gale, pp. 202–203. Copyright © 1994 by Bradley T. Gale.

FIGURE 13.3 New Product Activity Leads to Gains in Market Share

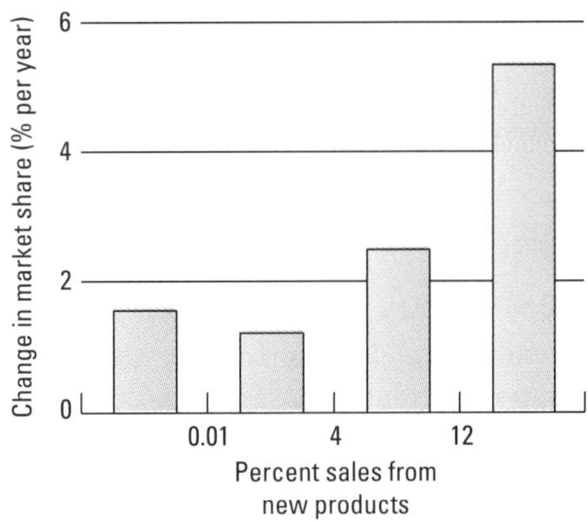

SOURCE: Reprinted with the permission of The Free Press, a Division of Simon & Schuster Adult Publishing Group, from MANAGING CUSTOMER VALUE: Creating Quality and Service That Customers Can See, by Bradley T. Gale, 202–203. Copyright © 1994 by Bradley T. Gale.

Innovations are the lifeline of a company, yet innovations that result in unneccessary obsolescence, are non-migratory in nature, or do not create value for the customer are really not innovations in an ethical sense.

Another ethical issue with regard to innovations arises when certain products are introduced in developing countries as innovations. Nestlé came under fire for its aggressive marketing of powdered baby formula in developing countries. Its marketing messages suggested that the powdered baby formula was better for the baby compared to mother's milk. Nestlé has also launched a brand of bottled water called "Pure Life" in Pakistan and Brazil, which raises the ethical issue of selling water in countries where an estimated 1 billion people lack access to basic water services.[5]

Product innovations in certain categories, like alcoholic beverages, can also be risky. In a test marketing exercise of St. Ides Freeze & Squeeze, a Slurpee-style "Special Brew" with 6 percent alcohol, the product was placed alongside children's frozen snacks and Italian ices in stores. This prompted children to ask for the product, and so parents purchased it for them, assuming that the product was good for children since it was in the aisle for child products. The test marketing created a stir against marketers who are trying to use such products to train children to be future drinkers.[6]

Mass Customization

The third tool for improved performance value is **mass customization,** the offer of customized products to individual customers without raising the price due to customization.[7] Motorola, for example, offers 20 million varieties of pagers, and assembles them after it receives the customer order from one of its salespersons in the field who transmits the order from a laptop. Similarly, Hewlett-Packard offers customized products to its business customers. This is made possible mainly by producing the product in modules and then assembling the product from these modules as the last step in the supply chain, such as at the distributor warehouse.

Mass customization
Tailoring the product to the customer's specific needs, without sacrificing the speed or cost efficiencies of conventional mass production methods.

The first customers to benefit from mass customization were organizations because their orders tend to be relatively large. However, advances in automation and information processing have enabled mass customization to meet the needs of consumers. As detailed in the Window on Practice, Levi Strauss will even customize a single pair of jeans.

The ethical question in the case of mass customization concerns whether too much variety is good or bad for the consumer. And is lack of standardization necessarily a bad thing?

Warranties and Guarantees

To alleviate customer apprehensions of possible product failures, companies also offer warranties or guarantees. Whereas warranties offer certain insurance by the manufacturer that specific product features will perform as promised, guarantees are offered by the stores that sell the product. Sears, for example, offers a satisfaction guarantee that gives customers the opportunity to return a product if they are not satisfied with it. L.L. Bean offers a lifetime warranty that you can return its merchandise if it proves unsatisfactory, no matter how long ago you bought it. In business-to-business markets, companies such as Caterpillar and Boeing are well known for offering outstanding warranties.

One service company that offers unmatched performance value is the Miami-based Bugs Burger Bug Killer (BBBK), which provides a zero-defect exterminating service. This zero-defect performance is backed by, and reflected in, its extraordinary performance guarantee. Customers don't pay a dime unless they are satisfied that the company has successfully destroyed all pests and breeding and nesting places. Should defects be found later, the company refunds the previous 12 months' service fee and pays for service by a competing firm for one year. Should a guest in a hotel or restaurant serviced by BBBK find a bug, the company would pay for the guest's meal or room and offer a free gift for a future meal or room. The

WINDOW ON **PRACTICE**

Blue Jeans for You Alone

If you walk into the Original Levi's Store in Cincinnati, Ohio, you will be greeted by a sales clerk with a measuring tape in hand and a personal computer (PC) on a nearby desk. He will take your measurements, feed the data into a computer, make final adjustments to the blueprint of a pair of jeans that pops up on the PC screen, push the transmit key, give you a receipt for the $40 you paid, and send you home. Forty-eight hours later, the jeans arrive at your home, delivered by FedEx! The jeans must fit you like a glove or you can return them for a full refund.

This is how it works: The PC in the retail store transmits the data to the Levi's factory in Tennessee. There, the data is received directly by a robotic tailor who cuts a bolt of denim precisely to the customer's measurements. Usually, the jeans are shipped back to the store in three weeks, but for a small extra charge, customers have the option of receiving them within 48 hours. The service is a blessing to women, many of whom have difficulty finding jeans that fit them. When the service for women's jeans was first introduced in the store, sales went up by 300 percent compared with the same period the previous year.

SOURCE: Adapted from Rifkin, Glenn. "Digital Blue Jeans Pour Data and Legs into Customized Fit." *New York Times*, November 8, 1994, A1, D8. http://www.levi.com.

company charges about four times the market rate, and customers who value performance and quality happily pay it.[8]

Sometimes, warranties and guarantees from manufacturers provide customers with immeasurable security; however, when there is a problem, the manufacturer gets out of its commitments using the fine print on the warrantee or guarantee—a cause of ethical concern.

SOCIAL AND EMOTIONAL VALUES

The personal values that satisfy customers' wants are the social and emotional values. These are neither engineered in the product nor delivered via better service. Rather, they are created by association with other desirable objects, persons, situations, or symbols.

Social values are derived from the association of a product with one or more social groups in society. These groups may be defined on the basis of demographic, socioeconomic, or cultural-ethnic characteristics, and tend to be defined in the customer's mind as either a positive or negative stereotype. For example, the stereotype of a rich person driving a Porsche may be perceived to be a positive stereotype by some and a negative stereotype by others.

Marketers offer social and emotional value through

- prestige pricing,
- limited availability,
- social-image-based marketing communications that focus on association with desired persons or objects or symbols,
- new exclusive offerings,
- and emotional communications.

Prestige Pricing

Pricing a product high enough so that only a few customers can afford it ensures that the product will be sold in limited target markets. Ubiquitous availability and universal use of a product detract from its exclusivity. High price itself leads to prestige, which is further fueled by limited penetration in the mass market. Marketers seeking to offer customers this value would not then seek to simultaneously offer price value. High-priced cars such as Lotus, Rolls Royce, and Lamborghini; watches such as Rolex and Concorde; and pens such as Mont Blanc all give their owners social prestige.

At the same time, when price is used as an indication of quality, it sometimes leads to irrational buying and conspicuous consumption. Sometimes children and consumers who really cannot afford prestige prices become targets of prestige pricing. Children are driven by peer group pressure to purchase high-priced products, and the poor use prestige pricing as their insurance against the risk of product failure.

Limited Availability

Related to exclusive pricing is the strategy of limited availability. Many products are offered in limited editions and quantities and, for this reason, acquire social value for their owners. Examples include the Cobra limited edition of Ford Mustang; First Day postage stamps, which are bought by customers on the first day of issue; and rare pieces of art, such as original paintings by Rembrandt or Van Gogh.

Limited editions of products are sought by customers not just for their real value but also for their possession value, and this is a cause of ethical concern. It creates extra transaction costs for the customers as they search harder for the product, and it also creates artificial demand and inflated prices. Web sites such as eBay thrive in the trade of such collectibles.

Social-Image-Based Marketing Communications

Much of the social and emotional value stems from marketing communications that associate the product with certain social symbols and feelings. Thus, Nike athletic shoes are depicted as suited to the serious athlete while AirWalk is for the young and trendy. Elizabeth Taylor's Passion perfume is for the successful, mature woman, while Tommy Boy or Tommy Girl colognes are for teenagers and adolescents.

These communications stem not only from advertising but also from other elements of the marketing mix. Thus, a product design could convey a sleek, modern image or traditionalism; it could be gaudy or subtle, signifying poor or refined taste. Price also communicates social exclusivity. Place has social image associated with it, such as a location in a business district or in a run-down strip mall. Moreover, social observations on the street about who is using a product also communicate its social value. Loss-leader pricing is one specific approach within the lower-margin strategy category. Stores typically offer a few selected items at a very low price, sometimes below cost, to attract customers. They take a loss on these items in the hope of making more profit on other items that the customers buy.

The most important drawback of social-image-based marketing communications is that it leads to consumerism and materialism. It is manifested in the chronic purchasing of new goods and services without a thought for whether these products are actually needed.

Such marketing communication in the fashion and beauty industry has also created the image of the "perfect woman." Millions of women around the world go on diets to conform to this image, leading to eating disorders such as anorexia and bulimia. Furthermore, some reality TV shows have created a greater public awareness of cosmetic surgery. In 2004, more than 1.7 million surgical cosmetic procedures were performed in the United States. (See http://www.plasticsurgery.org.) Increasing numbers of Canadians are also turning to cosmetic surgery. According to surveys conducted by Medicard Inc. and the University of Toronto in 2002 and 2003, there were over 302,000 surgical and non-surgical cosmetics enhancements performed in Canada in 2003, an increase of about 25 percent from 2002. Surgical procedures increased from 86,207 in 2002 to 100,569 in 2003. The most popular procedures were liposuction, breast augmentation, and facelifts.[9] Even some children's toys, such as the Barbie and Ken dolls, have been criticized for beginning the indoctrination for such images in childhood itself.

New Exclusive Offerings

The fourth avenue for delivering social and emotional value is expanded product offerings that already possess social or emotional value for a segment of customers. For example, Budget Rental Car Company was the first one to recognize the opportunity and to offer luxury cars, like the Lincoln. Today, Budget is the only company that offers Jaguars, a car that connotes a great social value to many consumers.

Emotional Communications

Many of the tools that create social value also create emotional value. The feeling of exclusivity of ownership, for example, gives some people an emotional uplift. But a more direct way to engender emotional value is the use of **emotional communications**—communications that evoke some emotional experience in the viewer or reader. Valentine's Day gifts such as flowers, candy, and diamond jewellery are sold as symbols of love, and much of the emotional symbolism is communicated to customers by specialized communications. **Social cause marketing** programs that promote social causes, such as race unity, arouse strong emotional bonds of identification among many viewers. For example, Benetton uses very vivid images of social causes, such as race harmony and AIDS research, to establish such an emotional bond with its target customers, who generally can be characterized as global youth: broad-minded youth with an awareness of global issues.

Emotional communications Communications that evoke some emotional experience in the viewer or reader.

Social cause marketing Marketing programs that promote social causes.

One legendary commercial that is the epitome of emotional advertising is from the Coca-Cola Company. In the ad, a child offers a bottle of Coke to Mean Joe Greene, a football star. After initially declining, the football player finally accepts the Coke at the child's insistence. The child watches his hero gulping the beverage; the football star is so moved by the child's gesture, and perhaps so delighted by the thirst-quenching beverage, that he tosses his jersey to the grateful child. This advertisement was so successful in generating the desired emotions in viewers that it was used worldwide.

Use of children in emotional communication to sell products has long been criticized as unhealthy. Another example of emotional advertising that seems quite opportunistic is advertising the "hope," "wish," and "longing" for babies to the vulnerable group of infertile or desperate couples. As Dr. Kathleen Nolan, a bioethicist at the Hastings Institute, says cautiously, "It seems wrong to play upon the pain of infertility in order to sell fertility services."[10]

CREATING MARKET VALUES FOR PAYERS

LO 3

The types of value most important to payers involve low cost and ease of making payments. Thus, marketers' tools to create value for payers include keeping the cost of the purchase and use of the product low, and offering services that are helpful to payers.

Price Value

The price value represents the relative affordability of the product to the customer. It is the degree of economic sacrifice the customer has to make to purchase the product.

As seen in Chapter 1, affordability is a function of buying power and prices. Buying power depends on the buyer's disposable income. Price comprises both the initial purchase price and the cost of maintaining the product usage-ready, or the cost of using the product. The concept of lifetime cost or life-cycle costing captures these two components. Marketers of initially high-price items need to draw customer attention to the life-cycle cost of their offerings.

Take a refrigerator, for example. The cost of electricity and maintenance over the 12 years it is likely to last is estimated to be as much as 65 to 70 percent of the total cost of using the product. In other words, the initial cost is only approximately 30 percent of the total cost. With such a product, affordability goes beyond the initial cost and must include the cost of upkeep and maintenance over the product's life. One way in which companies are sensitizing customers to this notion of life-cycle costing is by attaching energy guide tags to the front of appliances in stores.

While affordability is a characteristic of the customer (which the marketer cannot alter), price is an element of the marketing mix, and the marketer can do something about it. Companies that want to differentiate themselves on this value are constantly striving to offer the product at a lower price. To reduce price, companies can opt for two approaches: (1) accepting lower margins, and/or (2) reducing production costs by improving productivity.

The AMA Code of Ethics recognizes that the ethical issues in pricing arise from marketers engaging in price fixing, practicing predatory pricing, and not disclosing the full price associated with any purchase.

Low Price from Lower Margins

Lower-margin approach
Selling at a low-profit margin in order to attract customers.

The **lower-margin approach** consists of selling at a low-profit margin to attract customers. Many firms use this approach, cutting their prices below the competitors' price to attract the competitors' customers. Long-distance phone companies that are not the market-share leaders (e.g., Sprint) have used price as a competitive weapon to take share away from the market leader. Similarly, smaller airlines, such as CanJet and Southwest Airlines, offer extremely low fares. These companies offer limited schedules; the national airlines attempt to match fares on the routes these smaller airlines operate.

The lower-margin approach is often the outcome of a *strategic insight*. That is, some companies simply figure out the right formula that enables them to offer the required price value. Budget Rental Car Company performed an analysis of its costs and car-usage pattern and figured out that it can profitably offer unlimited mileage, a practice the company then pioneered. Likewise, Texas Instruments decided to sell its electronic calculators with a low-price strategy because it foresaw the potential drop in production costs that would result from the experience learning curve.[11]

Some companies, like Value Village, use tactics that not only appeal to the payer but encourage repeat business and reinforce the image of the company as an ethical firm. Value Village is a large for-profit thrift store chain, and one of its core values is to provide benefits for the community through charity alliances. Under a unique business model, the company partners with local nonprofit organizations by purchasing and reselling donated items. The nonprofit partners collect and deliver donated goods to Value Village, who pays them a bulk rate for the items regardless of whether or not those items ever make it to the sales floor. Value Village staff then sorts through the donations and selects the highest-quality reusable items. These items are value priced and displayed in their stores according to style, use, size and colour. Value Village (Savers) has more than 120 charity partners throughout Canada, the United States, and Australia. More than $100 million is paid annually to nonprofit partners. As up to half of all donations are unsuitable for sale, over 220 million pounds of clothing, shoes, toys, and other items are shipped to developing nations each year. More items are going to people who need them, and are staying out of landfills. Customers feel good about being part of this effort, and so the strategy is beneficial to the business.[12]

Low Price from Increased Productivity

Increased-productivity approach
An approach in which a firm strives for a lower cost of production by raising productivity.

The second enabler of lower price is the **increased-productivity approach**, in which a firm strives for a lower cost of production. Higher productivity makes individual firms or whole industries more competitive by enabling them to offer better economic value to the customer. A case in point is Compaq, which had been losing in sales and market share for years. In 1992, following a major restructuring effort designed to sharply hike productivity, it was able to cut prices, offering customers good economic value on its computer products, which were already known to be high in performance value. By 1994, the company's revenues had doubled, making it Number 1 in the PC business with a 12-percent market share. More important, despite a price cut, its profits increased fourfold.[13] More recently, both Dell and Gateway computers have successfully expanded the consumer PC market with very clever commercials and lower prices through economies of scale.

To lower production costs, companies can choose from among several strategies. They can develop economies of scale, use modernized plants that operate more efficiently, automate processes, and use business process re-engineering.

Economies of Scale

Economies of scale occur when larger volume leads to lower per-unit costs. This happens both because larger production units may run more efficiently and because they distribute fixed-cost overheads over a larger number of product units. High-volume firms can also negotiate more favourable prices from their suppliers, which then reduces their cost of production or of acquisition of resalable items. Wal-Mart, for example, is able to negotiate long-term contracts with its suppliers on favourable terms because of the size of its purchases.

One of the key findings of the PIMS study referred to earlier also confirms the role of the economies of scale. It found that market share and profitability are strongly related. The reason is that the larger shareholders produce and operate on a larger scale and, thus, obtain a lower cost due to economies of scale. This reduced cost allows them both a higher margin and a capability to offer better price value to customers.[14]

Modernized Plant

Outdated plant and equipment run inefficiently, and any modernization of plant reduces production costs. The casebook *Marketing Challenges* describes a company in Vancouver that produced skylights, whose modernized plant gave it a 20 percent cost advantage over Columbia Plastics, a manufacturer of skylights in Seattle. This cost advantage gave the Vancouver firm the ability to offer better economic value to Columbia's customers, stealing substantial business from the latter.[15]

Furthermore, the adoption of better substitute technologies may enable better cost structures. Thus, the use of plastic and fiberglass as a substitute for metal components in such wide-ranging products as automobiles, chemical tanks, plumbing piping, boats, and rocket combustion chambers has enabled various pioneering companies to differentiate themselves by offering their customers better price value.

Automation

Many companies have reduced costs through automation, which is the use of technology and machines to substitute, partly or wholly, for the human labour that would otherwise be required to perform a task. Automation may simply make an employee's work more efficient, or it may remove the need for an employee to personally attend to the customer.

An important change in the retail industry is the replacement of bar codes with "smart labels" using RFID. This technology permits the storage of detailed information about individual products and allows that information to be looked up as needed via the Internet. Until recently, it was viewed as being too expensive and too limited in functionality for many commercial applications. However, advances in technology have both reduced the cost of individual system components and provided increased capabilities. Unlike traditional bar codes,

RFID tags can hold much more information about products. They can be read-only or writeable, recording additional information to the genealogy of each RFID tag. Generation 2 RFID technology allows for several tags within one pallet to be traced, keeping an accurate record of mixed goods.[16]

RFID tags are used in aviation, from baggage handling to parts and inventory management. RFID will create value for airline travellers in terms of faster passport checks and passenger identification, faster check-in and baggage handling processes, less lost luggage, and fewer complaints. Air Canada is using RFID tags for real-time tracking of catering equipment to improve utilization and reduce loss and/or theft.

Meanwhile, Wal-Mart, the world's largest retailer, has adopted RFID in a big way in North America. By January 2007, Wal-Mart will have more than 600 suppliers shipping cases and pallets of products with RFID tags to more than 1,000 locations that can receive tagged products and merchandise. Wal-Mart reports that using RFID has reduced stock-outs by 16 percent, and that when an item is out of stock, if it was tagged with RFID, it was replenished and put on the shelf three times faster than it normally would. RFID will help keep prices low and improve service, while providing better in-stock selection for customers, and will also help for product returns, recalls and warranties, and to fight counterfeits. According to International Data Corporation, investment in RFID will reach nearly $1.3 billion in 2008, up from the current level of $91.5 million.[17]

The Window on Practice presents an overview of a Canadian initiative to encourage the use of RFID among food producers, manufacturers, distributors, and retailers.

While RFID technology offers numerous benefits, certain characteristics of the technology also raise a number of privacy concerns. For example, the small size of the tags and the

WINDOW ON **PRACTICE**

Food for Thought: RFID

RFIDs, the information-laden chips as small as a pinhead, will soon be tracking food shipments from the farm to the grocery checkout counter. A new Canadian RFID Centre opened in September 2005 in Markham, Ontario. There, Canadian food producers, manufacturers, distributors, and retailers can see first-hand how RFID technology can improve every aspect of their industry, from asset tracking to safety. The centre features a working scale model of grocery distribution, with shipping pallets, coolers, freezers, and a retailer's receiving warehouse. At the centre, companies can discover how this technology can work for them. This is the first facility of its kind using generation-two RFID technology that allows tags to go through a range of realistic environments, right down to sub-zero freezers. "There is a lot of interest in perishable product tracking now—food traceability," said S. Verma, RFID practice leader for IBM Canada at the Centre. "Companies may soon be embracing the technology whether they like it or not—and the pressure will be coming from two sources." The federal and Quebec governments are working to establish standards for the traceability of certain food products. Quebec's requirements are scheduled to come on stream in 2006, while Ottawa's are due in 2008.

While RFID is more of a backroom application, consumers may find store shelves better stocked, and it will also help with product recalls and produce freshness.

SOURCES: Makris, Steve. "Product Tracking RFID Technology Comes of Age in Canada Marketplace." *The Edmonton Journal*, September 24, 2005; Christmas, Brian. "It's Wednesday. Do You Know Where Your Goods Are?" *The Globe and Mail*, November 2, 2005.

ability to uniquely identify an object pose potential threats to individual privacy. In this respect, the ten principles of the CSA Standard, attached as schedule I of the *Personal Information Protection and Electronic Documents Act*, provide the basis for a privacy management framework that can be applied to RFID technology.[18]

Examples of the automation of the encounter with the customer include the use of ATMs, voice mail in companies, and automatic checkout on the TV screen in many hotels. Also, electronic commerce is the latest attempt to automate customer information services and sales transactions. Business websites offer information, searchable by the user, based on his or her specific information needs. Because users self-navigate, it saves company costs over a human agent providing information. Not only do these procedures reduce a company's cost of serving its customers, but sometimes they also save customers time and hassle and, thus, offer convenience value.

A report shows that there are some banks that charge a customer for ATM services without being completely transparent about the issue. This results in small charges on customers' accounts, which may or may not come to their notice. Similarly, customers are quite happy about the e-ticketing option offered by airlines, but they are not too happy about the fact that most airlines are going to charge them a $10 fee if they ask for a paper ticket. It feels like automation is leading to a charge for the basic services that a customer takes for granted.

Business Process Re-Engineering

The objective of business process re-engineering is to design entire business processes (e.g., order-fulfillment process, equipment-installation process, new-product-development process) to make them more efficient. Re-engineering differs from simple quality upgrade or continuous improvement. Rather than merely improving it, **re-engineering** redesigns a process, starting with a blank slate. The objective is to reduce the **cycle time** (the total time it takes for the entire production and/or delivery task to be completed), the amount of labour input, and the component and processing costs.[19]

Re-engineering The redesign of business processes to make them more efficient.

Cycle time The total time it takes for the entire production and/or delivery task to be completed.

For example, with the emergence of the Internet, Canada Post faced a massive overhaul in its operations. The public perceived Canada Post as outdated and inefficient, and customer satisfaction was low. The Window on Practice briefly outlines the re-engineering at Canada Post.

WINDOW ON **PRACTICE**

Re-Engineering at Canada Post

Canada Post (**www.canadapost.ca**) delivers 37 million pieces of mail each day to more than 31 million Canadians located at almost 14 million addresses and over 1 million Canadian businesses from coast to coast. Its more than 55,000 employees and 7,000 postal outlets—the largest retail network in Canada—are a trusted presence in communities across the country, as they have been for more than 150 years.

At the end of the 20th century, Canada Post was facing a rapidly changing marketplace. Fierce competition for its traditional markets from new Internet technologies posed a significant threat to the existing operations. The evolution and growing acceptance of these new technologies was driving the rapid expansion of e-commerce and shaping customer demands for greater speed, flexibility, and information. Considering that 50 percent of Canada Post's revenue and more than 50 percent of its gross margins were based on letter mail, it meant letter mail erosion would have a negative impact on the revenue base of the

(continued)

crown corporation. Canada Post realized then that it had to move quickly if it wanted to expand its national mail franchise into a universal electronic service for Canadians. And so, in 1999, Canada Post was the first postal administration in the world to adopt electronic delivery (ePost) to replace its legacy systems with a single enterprise system. This would provide integration and standardization, address long-standing inefficiencies, and essentially change the way the public corporation did business.

In 2001, the corporate website was overhauled. Now, consumers can access the self-service Online Business Centre to track packages and calculate rates and purchase products, while commercial customers can place orders and create shipping documents online using Electronic Shipping Tools. In 2002, it rolled out new bar codes, handheld devices that capture customer signatures, more accurate sizing of parcels, and a centralized database. Customers are now able to find out what is happening to their mail at every stage of delivery.

In 2003, Canada Post extended its delivery services to evening and Saturday in 21 major urban centres for **chapters.indigo.ca** customers in response to evolving consumer demands. In its largest special delivery effort to date, Canada Post delivered more than 70,000 copies of "Harry Potter and the Order of the Phoenix" to Canadians on Saturday, June 21, the book's release date. Canada Post "delivered the magic" to online shoppers who had pre-ordered the book on Amazon.ca or chapters.indigo.ca by June 17. Delivering the magic on a Saturday is just one way Canada Post is evolving to meet the changing needs of its customers in the electronic age who are demanding the convenience of flexible delivery times, including Saturday.

Canada Post offers one of the lowest postal rates in the industrialized nations while still making a profit. In 2004, Canada Post's revenues reached $6.7 billion, continuing its record of profitability since 1995. Canada Post also has a global agenda. It has created InnovaPost to offer IT services to other postal agencies around the world.

Canada Post continues to address the challenges brought on by rapid technological changes by investing in new products. As a world leader in the provision of innovative physical and electronic delivery solutions, Canada Post creates value for its customers and new ways to communicate.

SOURCES: "Canada Post Delivered the Magic to Amazon.ca and Chapters.Indigo.ca Customers." *Canada NewsWire*, June 23, 2003, 1; Himmelsbach, Vawn. "Canada Post Stamps Out Letter Mail Erosion with SAP." *Technology in Government*, September 2004. http://www.canadapost.ca.

Credit and Financing Values

Payers seek credit and financing values because those values improve affordability by creating deferred payments or providing credit. Specifically, credit value is delivered in several ways:

- Sellers may accept credit cards issued by third parties or banks.
- Sellers may issue their own credit cards or give credit by other instruments. For example, a small store might give a credit voucher that the customer signs as proof of having received credit.
- Sellers may allow a delayed or deferred payment, such as in the 90-days-same-as-cash options used by many vendors.

Offering credit was a pioneering strategy adopted by Sears, which, on top of its promise of satisfaction guaranteed, always offered financing arrangements that enabled customers to charge their purchases. Sears were offering credit cards to customers long before any other major retailer did.

Financing goes beyond simple credit, and involves specific payment schedules designed for a customer or for a group of customers. Leasing is one such system of financing. Another means is customized financing, offered by many companies, especially to business customers buying capital equipment. Nortel Networks, which manufactures telephone equipment such as switches, cable, and transmission equipment, has partnered with Key Equipment Finance

(KEF) to offer financing features that enables customers without the necessary capital to quickly modernize their telephone networks.

Leasing not only helps as a mechanism to defer large cash outlay but also may offer tax advantages to both individuals and companies. Some companies have leasing subsidiaries or divisions. One of these, GE Capital Canada (**www.gecapitalcanada.com**), offers customers affordable options to finance their purchases. Business customers of manufacturing equipment also find leasing an attractive option. In addition to the financing value received from leasing, customers also receive enhanced performance value: leasing avoids technological obsolescence, which is an important concern in purchases of computers and telecommunications equipment.[20]

Financing is possible for both services and products, both consumables and durables. For example, dental-care costs may add up to thousands of dollars, which becomes a significant burden on customers lacking dental insurance. Recognizing an opportunity, some dentists have begun to accept credit cards or installment payments from patients. By doing this, dentists provide a financing value and make themselves more attractive than their fellow dentists who do not offer financing.

Ethical issues abound in credit and financing. Customers are lured by the "no annual fee," "pre-approved" credit cards and then are charged massive interest for the balances they run up on the card. One wonders whether it is ethical for financial institutions to lure a minimum-wage earner or a college student in this manner. In the lending sector, the Home Ownership and Equity Protection Act came into place to guard homeowners against unscrupulous lenders. These lenders targeted elderly homeowners with lending schemes that involved giving them home-secured loans with high interest rates or high closing fees and impossible repayment terms. More often than not, these homeowners would not be able to meet the repayment terms, and the lenders were able to foreclose on the house. Customers need to be wary of scams in credit and financing as they look to satisfying these values from marketers.

CREATING MARKET VALUES FOR BUYERS

LO 4

In general, buyers are looking for good service before and after they make their selections. In addition, they want their purchases to be convenient, not too time-consuming, and in a time and place that fits their schedule.

SERVICE VALUE

Whereas the performance value is built into the product by the manufacturer or the service designer (the economists call this **form utility**), the service value is created by the distribution system. Customers receive service value during pre-purchase and post-purchase phases of product acquisition.

Form utility
Whereby performance value is built into the product by the manufacturer or the service designer.

Pre-Purchase Service

During pre-purchase, a buyer needs product information and help in assessing the fit between customer needs/wants and what the product delivers. Marketers in general, but retailers in particular, are expected to offer these values, and retailers who offer them in a superior way can differentiate themselves from their competitors. Marketers can offer this value by having the product on display or ready for demonstration and/or for trial use, and by hiring knowledgeable and responsive salespersons who can answer customer questions.

Product on Display or Demonstration

Although a number of alternative forms of *non*-store retailing (e.g., telemarketing) have come into existence, retail stores continue to have their appeal, foremost because of their merchandise-on-display utility. For some customers, there is nothing like being able to walk into a store and see, touch, and feel the merchandise. Stores that showcase their wares better (for example, with life-size models, reality-enhancing props, and attractive lighting) would have an edge, other things being equal, over their poorly merchandised competitors. Industrial distributors offer similar value by offering the product for demonstration. Trade shows are an effective means of displaying product developments, as are fashion shows for clothing. Even catalogue marketers recognize the service value of product displays, so they use high-resolution photographs of goods in their catalogues.

Another tool marketers can use to offer service value is having the product available in trial sizes. In supermarkets, new food items are offered as taste samples. A test drive of a car offers similar service value. Various kinds of subscriptions and memberships, offered free for the first month, are instances of service value to the purchase-decision maker. Similarly, shoe stores offer the customer an opportunity to take the shoes home, try them for a week or a month indoors, and return them if they do not fit; this too offers service value to the customer. This service value in product trial is unavailable to you when you are a tourist in a foreign country; as a tourist you will generally not consider buying products that you want to have the option of returning later if they do not fit.

Several of these free subscriptions and memberships play on the premise that once the customer tries the product, he may not take the trouble to return it after 30 days or cancel the membership afterward. Sometimes, even when the customer wants to cancel the same, the marketer makes it very difficult for the customer to quit, causing dissatisfaction for the buyer.

Knowledgeable Salespersons

The second resource that marketers can use and offer to customers is product knowledge. Retail store salespersons and other salespersons vary greatly in the degree of competence and product knowledge they possess. Salespersons at a discount store tend to be substantially less knowledgeable about their products than those at a specialty store. Professional photographers, for example, would prefer to patronize specialty camera shops than discount stores; likewise, those who play any game seriously (rather than leisurely) would prefer to shop at specialty sporting-goods stores.

Professional, knowledgeable salespersons help not only by offering better product knowledge but also by assisting the customer in choosing a product that would better fit the customer's needs and wants. Clothiers with personal service, for example, would help the customer choose the right suit; such personalized advice is simply unavailable at large department stores. Likewise, a computer company's salesperson helps the customer figure out which equipment and options would meet his or her needs better. Insurance salespersons can distinguish themselves by taking the time to assess a customer's needs and recommending an insurance product accordingly. Financial asset managers, stock brokers, and other bank officers can likewise distinguish themselves from their competitors by offering up-to-date information and advice about their products.

Yet, there are salespeople who provide the customer with selective information and betray the buyer's confidence in this resource. Such tactics might help the marketer sell the product the first time, but when the buyer realizes the fraud, she or he is likely to boycott the marketer for good.

Service in the Post-Purchase Phase

Generally known as after-sales service or after-sales product support, service in the post-purchase phase refers to all the assistance a marketer can provide to maintain the product use-ready. This service value accrues inasmuch as it enables the user to derive the maximum utility from the product. Two specific avenues are available to marketers for this service: product-use advice and product maintenance. The Window on Research describes the process of "after-marketing"—marketing efforts directed at the customer after s/he has made the purchase.

WINDOW ON RESEARCH

After-Marketing

Whether or not customers are satisfied with the outcome of a purchase decision, the customer relationship can benefit from after-marketing. After-marketing refers to the marketing efforts directed at the customer after she or he has made the purchase. The goals of after-marketing are to ensure customer satisfaction and to maintain the relationship. Terry Vavra, who coined the term *after-marketing,* defines it as the process of providing continued satisfaction and reinforcement to individuals or organizations that are past or current customers. Customers must be identified, acknowledged, communicated with, audited for satisfaction, and responded to. The goal of after-marketing is to build lasting relationships with all customers.

Relationship marketing or retaining customers becomes important in markets that are saturated (i.e., overall demand is not growing) and where major competitors have achieved parity on the core product. According to one study, 65 percent of the average company's business comes from current satisfied customers. Says Philip Kotler, "Smart marketers try to build long-term, trusting, 'win-win' relationships with customers, distributors, dealers, and suppliers."

Retaining customers requires marketers to exhibit care and concern for them after they've made a purchase. It includes:

- promoting activities and efforts to keep customers satisfied, even after the purchase,
- doing everything possible to ensure re-purchase,
- constant measurement of sustained customer satisfaction,
- letting customers know they are cared for.

The first step in the after-marketing process is maintaining a customer information file. Without customer records containing the customer's contact address as well as a history of previous interactions and transactions, it is not possible to engage the customer in an after-marketing program, much less build a relationship. For example, a car dealer who sells the customer a car would need to save the customer information from the sales documents; moreover, it would help if the information is stored on an electronic medium so that it is accessible to the car service personnel who are responsible for after-marketing.

The second step is the identification of possible customer contact points and specifying them on a time line that also spells out the purpose and content of each contact (i.e., the firm prepares a blueprint of customer contact points). In the automobile dealer example, the service shop would prepare a blueprint for each recent car buyer, identifying when the dealer service should contact the customer and for what purpose.

The next step is the analysis of informal customer feedback. Customers would, from time to time, offer comments on their experience with the product and advise on what the company might do differently. It is very important for a marketer to analyze and use this feedback. However, rather than just depend on informal feedback, the firm should conduct satisfaction surveys from time to time. The firm should respond to specific customer concerns voiced in formal surveys or informal feedback. The firm

(continued)

should also have in place a program of periodic communication with its customers. This can be in the form of a periodic mailing, such as a newsletter, or a periodic callback just to inquire if the product is performing to the customer's satisfaction. Beyond such communications, the marketer should consider hosting special events that will bring the customer closer to the marketer and give an opportunity for the marketer to listen to the customer. Some customers will inevitably switch to an alternative marketer/supplier; the marketer should learn from losing a customer. This can be done by an exit interview (i.e., asking the customer to share his or her reasons for switching to a competitor).

Additionally, the marketer may examine customer records to identify, for the switching customers as a group, any special characteristics or circumstances that motivate switching customers to change their suppliers. These steps will bolster a marketer's after-marketing efforts, whose goal is to bring customers into a long-term relationship with the firm.

SOURCES: Adapted from Vavra, Terry G. *Aftermarketing: How to Keep Customers for Life through Relationship Marketing.* 2nd ed. (Chicago: Irwin Professional Publishers, 1996); Kotler, Philip. *Marketing Management* (Upper Saddle River, NJ: Prentice Hall, 1997), 12.

Product-Use Advice and Support

Consumers often need assistance in using the product, and marketers who offer this assistance differentiate themselves from their competitors. Thus, companies have toll-free technical assistance lines, especially for technical products such as personal computers. In 1993, General Electric commissioned a state-of-the-art customer advice facility it calls the Customer Answer Centre. The service representatives who answer customer questions on its toll-free phone lines are equipped with online product information as well as an instant display of customer records. This helps them resolve customer problems efficiently and affectively. The centre receives about 2 million calls a year, and the company has experienced a significant increase in customer satisfaction since the centre began.

Note that the quality of user advice is a user value, but ease of obtaining it is a buyer value. For example, if user support is not part of the original seller's offering, then the buyer has to procure it from elsewhere. Thus, service value for the buyer is obtained when user support and maintenance support are available to the buyer along with the original item's purchase.

Product Maintenance

Perhaps the most significant service value accrues from the product maintenance service that the marketer offers a customer. If a car breaks down, the customer wants it repaired quickly and without any inconvenience. It is for this reason that Lexus, for example, gives the customer a loaner car during a repair period.

Product downtime can be immensely consequential in business products, such as computers, copiers, and communication networks. Xerox realized the importance of minimizing the downtime on its office equipment and set up an infrastructure—an army of 12,000 service reps—so that its service reps could reach any customer's location within North America within 30 minutes. This outstanding service value (along with the performance value of its improved equipment) made Xerox the preferred supplier for many new customers. The company experienced its greatest growth rate of the past ten years.

In the service industries, the core product itself is service (e.g., haircutting for a hair salon, access to special channel broadcasts for cable TV companies). How good this core product is constitutes the performance value. The manner in which this core product is delivered constitutes service value in our values framework.

Gearing a firm to deliver superior service value to customers is actually what differentiates a manufacturing-driven company from a marketing-driven company. Generally, manufacturers are concerned with producing the right products in the right quantities at the right time and at the right cost. They see marketers as having little understanding of their role in the corporation. In a manufacturing-driven company, everything is done to ensure low costs and a smooth production process. Simple products, narrow product lines, and high-volume production are the goals of a manufacturing-driven firm. In contrast, a marketing-driven firm will be more concerned with satisfying customers' needs.[21] The importance placed on service value forces companies to move from a manufacturing-driven to a marketing-driven mentality.

CONVENIENCE VALUE AND PERSONALIZATION VALUE

As seen in Chapter 1, convenience and personalization values accrue from being able to obtain a product in a hassle-free and socially pleasant exchange with delivery personnel. Similar to the social and emotional values, it represents an influence on the customer's wants. It is something that is preferred, not needed.

Convenient Point of Access

To deliver convenience value, firms can provide convenient points of access. They can locate the distribution and retail facilities conveniently, and keep them open 24 hours. Banks now have branch locations inside supermarkets, and many banks offer Saturday and Sunday banking services. Domino's distinguished itself by offering convenience value through home delivery of pizzas, a pioneering practice that made a significant dent in market leader Pizza Hut's market share. Ultimately, to remain competitive, Pizza Hut had to offer home delivery as well. Supermarkets offer this value by ensuring short checkout lines and by delivering the groceries to a customer's car or even their homes. Some clothiers will alter a suit, press it, and deliver it to a customer's home. Companies such as Staples will deliver office products over a minimum purchase price to a customer's home. Many fast-food restaurant chains, such as Tim Hortons, McDonald's, and Burger King, have increased their sales by going beyond their free-standing traditional store design and opening small-scale service counters at diverse locations such as university campuses, corporate cafeterias, shopping malls, and airports, and, in the case of Tim Hortons, even within gas stations.

Some companies sell in the customer's home or office. Banking by phone, computer, and Internet are examples of such a convenience. This service is valued so much by a segment of British customers that one British bank works exclusively on a banking-by-phone basis.

Automated Transaction Recording

Automation is a significant means of offering convenience. This sometimes takes the form of convenient access, as at ATMs for banking; telephone-based automated response systems, such as the ones used by banks; document shipping companies such as FedEx; and the customer service departments of many companies. They also offer convenience by automating the transaction so it is not held up by the unavailability of service employees. Selected supermarkets are testing a device that the customer uses to scan each item as she or he places it in the shopping cart; this would eliminate altogether the need for checkout lines. Similarly, many gas stations are equipped with a credit-card reader right at the pump. This pay-at-the-pump feature is a source of great convenience value, especially to customers with small children in the car, who may be apprehensive about leaving the car unattended.

The advantage for marketers in e-commerce is the fact that there is an automated recording of all the data at the site that is visited by the consumer. This data relates both to personal information with regard to the consumer and to transaction information. The data is of great value to the marketer, but there is is an ethical concern about the use of the information to send unsolicited offers to customers, spam their mail, and sell the data to other parties who also then target these consumers.

Interpersonal Relationship

As seen in Chapter 1, personalization value accrues from sales and service employees treating customers with personal attention and courtesy. This avenue of offering service value is especially important in service businesses. A car rental agent, hotel registration clerk, airline ticket agent, or a waiter or waitress who shows courtesy in dealing with the customer is offering a service value, and this can be an important differential advantage for service firms. Likewise, insurance agents, doctors, and even hairstylists should get to know their clients personally. And if customers communicate with the company via e-mails, the company response should not look like a form letter; rather, it should show care for the customer as an individual. In business markets, interpersonal relationships matter even more. To deliver personalization value, companies need to engage in frequent, personalized communications. And designated account reps as well as senior executives should make frequent client visits. The purpose of these visits should be not only to discuss task-related issues but also to build and maintain a personal relationship with clients.

The Window on Practice presents examples of customer value drivers employed by some of *Fortune* magazine's Most Admired Companies.

WINDOW ON **PRACTICE**

Customer Value Delivery Excellence of the World's Most Admired Companies

Performance Value from Quality Obsession at Caterpillar

Caterpillar Inc. measures its product quality by defect rate, which is any failure in machine operations. It tracks these defects by the age of the machine in three brackets: VEHR—very early hour failure, registered within the first 21 hours of operation; DRF1—Dealer Repair Frequency One, registered during 22 to 200 hours of operations; and DRF2—registered during 201 to 1,000 hours of operations. Such close tracking is part of its vigorous Continuous Quality Improvement (CQI) programs.

For a glimpse of the vigour and power of its CQI programs, let us briefly look at its CQI project for the paint job on its tractors. While some might think of paint on a heavy machine as a merely cosmetic feature, Caterpillar recognized that the quality of the paint job (good or poor) is the first thing a customer notices. And, indeed, customers noted and complained about paint defects such as poor coverage, runs and sags, embedded dirt, and uneven gloss or finish. So the paint line team in the Track-Type Tractor (TTT) division set up a CQI project. The team identified and implemented improvements in equipment, processes, and worker tasks. The result? Within 20 months after the project started, the CQI team virtually eliminated all paint defects. And Caterpillar counts, mind you, any slight unevenness in finish on any square inch of the tractor surface as a defect. And customer response? Complaints about paint on the machines declined from 113 in 1990 to 7 in June 1995, and to *zero* since then!

Performance Value Theory from Innovation at 3M

Is there room for product innovations in basic products such as roof granules? It would be unlike 3M if it did not innovate, no matter how established the product category. So the company's roofing granules division has developed a very innovative type of granule for special applications. It is the algae block copper roofing granule system. If you drive in Florida, you will notice a black streak on the rooftops there. For a long time it was believed to be fungi that develops in humid climates. 3M researched this problem and found that it is not fungi; rather, it is an organism that, to protect itself from the sun's rays, secretes a black-brown-reddish pigment. It is this pigment that gives the roof shingles their undesirable streak. So 3M set out to find a solution. With experimentation, its scientists discovered that copper is toxic to the organism. The new granule system, therefore, first coats the granules with a layer of soluble copper (cuprous oxide) prior to applying the ceramic and colour layers. This is done with a highly sophisticated proprietary process, but the process is also expensive, raising the cost of these granules to about $800 per ton (as compared to $80 per ton for ordinary granules). Fortunately, copper granules need be used only in a 10 percent mix with regular granules, thus bringing this delightful innovation within affordable price range.

Performance Value for Product Customization at UPS

A second avenue is custom-designing a shipping service specific to a client. Yes, indeed, the company has the capability to put into place a custom-designed package-movement operation either as a one-time or an ongoing operation. Case in point: A few years ago, a music company was launching a new CD featuring an anthology of previously published Beatles songs. The company's plan was to introduce the CD on Sunday night network TV and have the CDs in the stores the next morning. Secrecy was the company's top concern—and for fear of leaks, it would not even deliver the product to UPS before that Friday. UPS agreed to take on this special task. The client delivered the packages on Friday evening in armoured vehicles. From that point, UPS assumed control and "staged" the product movement to meet both security and on-time delivery requirements to music stores all over the country. The special network UPS put together for this music company is testimony to the company's customization capability.

Price Value through Increased Productivity at Rosenbluth

Rosenbluth International (RI) has also constantly sought to reduce its operational costs. It has done so by two means: automation of the reservation processes and low-cost location of its centralized services. One clear example of automation is its E-Res® system. E-Res® is an agentless system useable by clients themselves on their desktop/laptop computer; it includes and automatically applies the client's travel policy constraints. U.S. giant retailer Wal-Mart is a recent RI client, where travelers use the E-Res® system when they can, and the company estimates that it will save 10 percent of its $30 million air travel budget!

To reduce its operating costs, RI was the first travel agency to create a centralized reservation centre in 1980, called IntelliCenters. Where would you think these centres are located? At its headquarters in Philadelphia? In some other metropolis? Near its major client clusters? No. They are located in rural North Dakota, Delaware, and Allentown, Pennsylvania, because the labour costs are low in those areas. If clients use these centres rather than customer service centres (CSC) or dedicated offices, they can save 30 to 40 percent per ticket in booking costs. That is a tremendous value price.

Service Value through User Support at Fossil

What value retailers seek most is good profit margins on products with good performance. Fossil's scientific inventory management at the retail level is a source of higher margin for the retailer since his or her inventory costs are significantly reduced. Fossil acts almost like a partner in managing the retailer's inventory. The average watch inventory turnover in department stores is 4 percent; that is, 4 percent of the inventory moves every week. Fossil makes its inventory move 5 percent so that the retailer has to carry only 20 weeks' inventory instead of the usual 25 weeks. And the company aims to make 65 percent of the watch lines move at this speed. The other 35 percent are newer styles, not yet established. Recall that five times a year, the company introduces new styles. Fossil claims that, by its initial margin and by enabling lower inventory costs, its watches are one of the most profitable product lines for its department store merchants.

(continued)

Personalization Value at XBS

A manufacturing company makes sewing machines, and the machines come packed with an owner's manual. The current practice is to print it in bulk and enclose it with the product being shipped to retailers. This practice is slated to change for many of the businesses. In the digital age, the manual can be stored and distributed digitally, and then printed by the dealer at the time of the product sale. The manual can even be customized for a specific model and/or for a specific customer. Now, as a supplier of this outsourced service, XBS can simply take over the current (traditional) manual printing service and run it more efficiently, or it can print more model-specific manuals in smaller quantities. Better still, it can distribute the manual to the retailer in a digital form for the retailer to customize it, incorporating value-added after-market services the dealership might offer, and print it on a "just in time" basis. This is, in fact, what it does for a number of clients.

Suppose XBS runs your company's mailroom services, and you want a certain category of mail distributed much earlier than currently delivered or even feasible. XBS can do it. One of its financial services clients, for example, wanted the mortgage applications distributed by 9 a.m. instead of the current delivery by 11 a.m. (Doing so would shorten the entire loan-approval cycle by one full day.) So XBS redesigned the whole document process for mortgage applications. It created a special return envelope that could be identified by sight, contracted with FedEx Corporation for a special 8:30 a.m. delivery of that envelope, and assigned an associate to deliver the envelope to the designated mortgage processing officer by 9 a.m.

Thus, from initial service configuration for a new customer site to sub-process redesign on an ongoing site, XBS offers customization to enhance its total performance valuespace for its clients.

SOURCE: Mittal, Banwari, and Jagdish N. Sheth. *Valuespace: Winning the Battle for Market Leadership, Lessons From the World's Most Admired Companies* (McGraw Hill, 2001).

LO 5 ⮞ MEASURING VALUE DELIVERY

With so many tools available for delivering customer values, marketers must ensure that their organization is delivering the values their target markets most desire, and that customers are aware it is doing so. The most effective way to do this is with the basics of marketing management: (1) find out what customers want, (2) organize to deliver those values, and (3) measure how well, in customer perceptions, those values have been delivered.

To identify the specific benefits and processes customers want on each of the six values, the marketer would conduct customer research. A blueprint for conducting this research is presented in the Window on Research.

That model focuses on value assessment related to product use. We can also apply this type of evaluation to the purchase and payment situations. In keeping with the three customer roles, a complete assessment should include customer values in using, paying for, and buying the product.

Once the values are identified, an organization has to organize efforts and strategies to deliver these values. This may require substantial investments in equipment, technology, and human resources. The principal action strategies have already been described in the chapter.

As these strategies are implemented, they need to be appraised to determine whether implementation is progressing as planned and whether the strategies are effective. One means of appraisal is internal audits, in which a cross-functional team of managers rate the various processes. For example, for re-engineering the process (which helps deliver price value), managers should assess the degree to which the re-engineering project has been implemented, as well as the extent to which re-engineering has improved productivity and lowered costs.

Some of these processes are not visible to customers, so customer input cannot be used to assess progress; for example, the re-engineering process itself is not visible to customers, nor are customers concerned about *how* a firm manages to deliver specific values. For these internal

WINDOW ON RESEARCH

Process for Determining Customer Value

A customer has certain goals and purposes when using a product. Robert B. Woodruff defines *customer value* as the customer's perceived preference for and evaluation of those product attributes, attribute performances, and consequences of use that facilitate (or block) the achievement of those goals and purposes. Thus, customer value includes customer perceptions at three levels:

1. *Attribute performance*—Whether the product has the desired attributes and attribute performances.
2. *Attribute consequences*—Whether using the product has the desired consequences.
3. *Goals pertinent to attribute consequences*—Whether the consequences of using the product help the customer meet his or her goals.

If using the product meets each of these desires, the result is satisfaction in that area.

To measure a customer's overall satisfaction with the received value, the marketer would assess satisfaction at all three levels. For example, for Healthy Choice frozen entrées, attribute performance might be that fat content is low; a related consequence could be that it will keep blood-cholesterol levels low. The customer goal would be staying healthy. To assess customer value for Healthy Choice, then, marketers would have to assess how well the brand meets the performance, consequences, and goals levels.

How can managers use this process to form a strategy to enhance customer value? As shown in Figure 13.4, the marketer conducts research to learn which values at the three levels (performance, consequence, and goals) customers desire. Further research, combining customer interviews with management intuition, would then narrow the list to the most important of those values. Further surveys would assess the firm's delivery of those important values—how well the firm is satisfying those values. The final step is not a measurement but a diagnostic analysis: managers must identify causes of the value-delivery gap and possible corrective actions. All these steps should be informed by a futuristic perspective: what are the customers likely to value in the future?

SOURCE: Adapted from Woodruff, Robert B. "Customer Value: The Next Source for Competitive Advantage." *Journal of the Academy of Marketing Science* 25, no. 2 (1997): 139–153. http://www.healthychoice.com.

FIGURE 13.4 A Process for Determining Customer Value

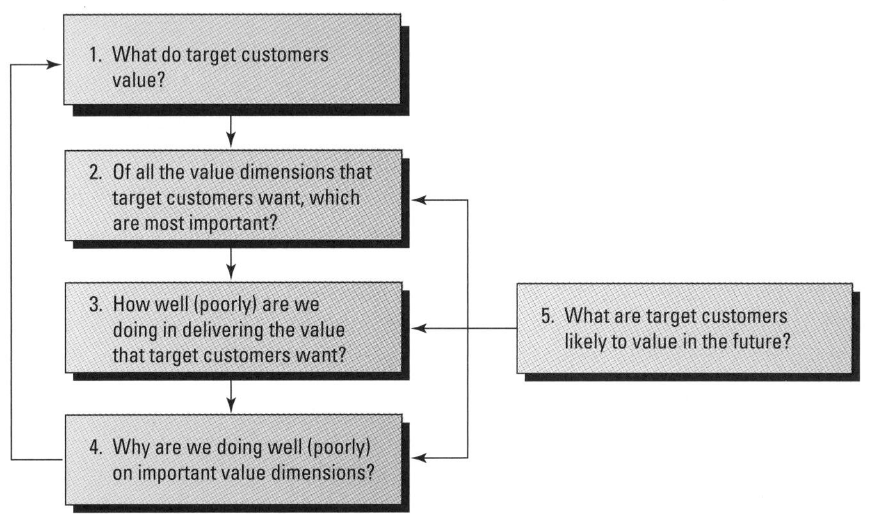

processes, management's own assessment is the only option. However, the outcome of these processes, as delivered to customers, is visible to customers and, indeed, experienced by them as six market values. Therefore, marketers should solicit customer appraisal of these experiences.

To do this, marketers should assess the firm's success, both in satisfying the six values and in using value-creation tools in a way that customers experience and appreciate. They can make both assessments by asking customers to rate statements about the product and the firm. Thus, to measure success in satisfying the six values, the marketer can use statements such as the ones given in Chapter 1. For example, to measure the performance value of a Saab automobile, customers can be asked to rate their degree of agreement with the statement "My Saab gives me good gas mileage"; to measure the price value, they can rate the statement "This brand at this price is a good bargain."

Marketers can also measure how well the various tools are delivering specific values they were purported to deliver, and whether the firm has been able to improve value delivery over the years. Marketers can do this by having customers rate statements such as those in Figure 13.5. These statements are illustrative and may not all apply to every company. Some are especially suitable for business-to-business customers, and others are general but may still need adaptation to specific product situations. As a marketer, you would use them as a basis for thinking about how they apply to individual situations, and for researching their utility in improving your firm's ability to deliver customer values.

Fulfilling the Business Purpose by Delivering Customer Value

Research into value-delivery processes helps marketers focus on what should be their fundamental business purpose: to make the customer happy.

FIGURE 13.5 Sample Questions for Measuring Customer Perceptions of Value Delivery Processes

User Values	Disagree Strongly 1	Disagree 2	Agree 3	Agree Strongly 4	Don't Know DK
PERFORMANCE VALUE PROCESSES					
QUALITY IMPROVEMENT					
The quality of this firm's products is superb.	□	□	□	□	□
The quality of this firm's products has improved continuously over the last several years.	□	□	□	□	□
INNOVATION					
The firm has consistently introduced breakthrough designs and new technologies in its products.	□	□	□	□	□
The firm's current products represent significant advances over its earlier versions of a few years ago.	□	□	□	□	□
The firm's products are one step ahead of what the competition offers.	□	□	□	□	□

CUSTOMIZATION

The firm is able to offer me individually customized products.	☐	☐	☐	☐	☐
The firm's products are available in a large variety and with options so that I can have the kind of product I like.	☐	☐	☐	☐	☐
I can purchase a custom-made product from this firm without sacrificing timeliness.	☐	☐	☐	☐	☐

WARRANTIES AND GUARANTEES

The firm offers one of the best warranties in the industry.	☐	☐	☐	☐	☐
The firm truly follows a no-questions-asked full-refund policy.	☐	☐	☐	☐	☐

SOCIAL VALUE

PRICE EXCLUSIVITY

The firm prices the product high enough to maintain its exclusivity.	☐	☐	☐	☐	☐
The product's price gives me a special satisfaction of possessing an exclusive, not-too-common product.	☐	☐	☐	☐	☐

LIMIT AVAILABILITY

The firm makes its products available too narrowly.	☐	☐	☐	☐	☐
I like the fact that the product's distribution is restricted.	☐	☐	☐	☐	☐

SOCIAL IMAGE ADS

Advertisements for the product show the product in association with people and images that I find appealing.	☐	☐	☐	☐	☐

EXCLUSIVE OFFERINGS

Over time, the firm has extended its product line to include other prestigious brands.	☐	☐	☐	☐	☐

EMOTIONAL VALUE

EMOTIONAL COMMUNICATIONS

I can personally identify with the social causes that the firm promotes in its communications.	☐	☐	☐	☐	☐
When I view the firm's advertisements, I can visualize the wonderful emotional experience I will have when I use the product.	☐	☐	☐	☐	☐

Payer Values

PRICE VALUE

Over time, this firm has consistently offered me better price value for its products.	☐	☐	☐	☐	☐
Compared with three years ago, the firm is offering me better products without raising the prices.	☐	☐	☐	☐	☐
I think that the firm cares about reducing my costs without sacrificing what I get from its products.*	☐	☐	☐	☐	☐

CREDIT

The firm offers liberal credit terms.	☐	☐	☐	☐	☐
The firm offers interest-free deferred-payment plans.	☐	☐	☐	☐	☐

FINANCING

The special financing plan the firm offers suits my needs very well.	☐	☐	☐	☐	☐
Over the years, the firm has customized its financing options for my needs.	☐	☐	☐	☐	☐

(continued)

Buyer Values	Disagree Strongly 1	Disagree 2	Agree 3	Agree Strongly 4	Don't Know DK
SERVICE VALUE					
GENERAL					
Over time, the firm has made it increasingly easy for me to do business with it.	☐	☐	☐	☐	☐
PRODUCT DISPLAY					
The firm makes it easy for me to inspect the product and see it working before deciding to buy it.	☐	☐	☐	☐	☐
KNOWLEDGEABLE SALESPERSONS					
This firm's employees seem to have been well screened and well trained for their jobs, and I find them very knowledgeable about their products.	☐	☐	☐	☐	☐
USER SUPPORT					
If users of this product need help in operating or using the product, they can easily receive advice from the firm.	☐	☐	☐	☐	☐
MAINTENANCE SUPPORT					
It is easy to obtain the required maintenance to keep the product always ready for use.	☐	☐	☐	☐	☐
RESPONSIVENESS					
The firm handles complaints in a friendly manner and tries to do whatever it takes to win a customer over.	☐	☐	☐	☐	☐
CONVENIENCE					
POINTS OF ACCESS					
I find the firm's products conveniently located.	☐	☐	☐	☐	☐
I can access the firm anytime, from anywhere I like.	☐	☐	☐	☐	☐
Over the past few years, the firm has considerably expanded the ways I can obtain its products.	☐	☐	☐	☐	☐
AUTOMATED TRANSACTION RECORDING					
Employees who record the transaction seem to be well equipped with the technology to complete my transaction efficiently.	☐	☐	☐	☐	☐
The firm has the systems and technology in place that makes it very easy for me to obtain its products.	☐	☐	☐	☐	☐
This firm seems to have organized its various departments, operations, and procedures to maximize customer convenience.	☐	☐	☐	☐	☐
I find it very convenient to complete the transactions with this firm using its self-service technology.	☐	☐	☐	☐	☐
PERSONALIZATION					
PERSONAL ATTENTION					
The firm's employees are very polite, courteous, and pleasant.	☐	☐	☐	☐	☐
The firm's employees and managers consider no other activity more important than to attend to a customer like myself.	☐	☐	☐	☐	☐
The firm's employees seem to show an understanding of my perspective and treat me as a person, so that I feel very happy dealing with them.	☐	☐	☐	☐	☐

*These items may be especially useful for business customers.

Addressing that issue returns us to the theme with which we started the book. Most marketers don't have the luxury of being customers for the products that they market. Hence, by applying the concepts in this book, managers learn about customers and their behaviour with respect to the various market values they seek. The tools we presented in this chapter are supposed to deliver those values. The ultimate goal of implementing these value-delivery tools is to make the customer happy.

As seen in Chapter 1, the purpose of a business is to satisfy a customer. In this context, General Electric Company's vision of itself is worth reading.

> Customers are ... the lifeblood of a company. Customers' vision of their needs and the company's view become identical, and every effort of every man and woman in the company is focused on satisfying those needs.[22]

We would rephrase GE's assertion slightly: *Happy* customers are the lifeblood of a company. Therefore, a firm must do everything feasible to make and keep its customers happy—so happy, in fact, that customers delight in doing business with the firm.[23] They take pride in the company's existence and in its actions; rather than just draw on its resources, they are eager to support it. Establishing such relationships of mutual support and nurturance is the ultimate goal of customer orientation.

That customers would support such a relationship for a long time in the future is the *final customer judgment* for which companies should strive. Figure 13.6 presents an instrument to assess this final judgment by asking customers to rate a set of statements. The total of each customer's ratings is his or her judgment, conveniently scored as an index anchored at zero and 100, with 100 being the perfect score. Companies falling below this score should strive to bridge the gap.

Companies and organizations must never underestimate the mandate to become customer oriented. As the authors argue in *ValueSpace*, companies that invent new customer value possess certain traits. They observe customers close-up. They dig customer need to its essential core. And they keep their eyes on a singular target: creating far-reaching new ValueSpace for the customer. These traits indeed lead a business to mold its own self-concept in the customer's image:

> This reinvention of oneself as a corporate being, this customer-centred adoption of a new self-identity, the constant contemplation of the customer's desires—this is what it takes to invent unparalleled ValueSpace for the customer. This is what it takes to win the battle for market leadership. This is what it takes to thrive.
>
> —*ValueSpace, 2001, 250*[24]

The customer behaviour concepts and applications presented in this book can help solicit important customer-value orientation.

FIGURE 13.6 Assessment of the Customer's Final Judgment

Please rate the following statements on a 0–10 scale where 0 means you disagree entirely, and 10 means you agree wholeheartedly.

- The firm understands my needs and preferences well.
- I can trust the firm not to take advantage of me as a customer.
- The firm values and shows its appreciation for my business.
- The firm takes specific actions to keep me as a customer.
- I can identify myself with the firm's products and its actions.
- The firm can count on me as its supporter.
- I enjoy dealing with the employees of this firm.
- I love this firm's products.
- I love to do business with this firm.
- I expect to continue my relationship with this firm for a long time.

SUMMARY

LO 1 In this chapter we presented various strategies and tools that businesses can employ to offer each of the six values to customers. For the universal, performance value, companies need to focus on programs of quality improvement, R&D to create innovations in products, mass customization, and warranties and guarantees. To differentiate themselves on service value, firms need to become more responsive in their dealings with customers. They need to offer better service during the pre-purchase and post-purchase phases. Superior service value depends on employee competence, knowledgeability, courtesy, and responsiveness. These employee traits can be managed by careful selection and training and retraining. Service value also requires an infrastructure capable of handling product repair or maintenance service without much downtime. Finally, price value can be offered by lower-margin or higher-productivity strategies. Firms can improve productivity by automation and process re-engineering.

LO 2, 3, 4 The three personal values, too, require certain strategies and tools. For social and emotional values, a marketer needs to manage its marketing communications. All of its communications need to be strategically directed to create a focused social image and associations. Quality, price, and distribution exclusivity can be harnessed to give a product a social image of prestige. Situations and settings (i.e., ambiance) can be used to create mood and emotional association. The convenience value can be enhanced by increasing the points of access (e.g., by strategic location of product delivery, and by easy, 24-hour access to a firm's employees). Another way to offer convenience value is by automating the recording of the transaction. Finally, firms can differentiate themselves on financing value by offering easy payment terms, low financing rates, and leasing arrangements.

Firms should attempt to differentiate themselves by exceeding on more than one type of customer value. Of course, what exactly will constitute value to a specific customer in a specific product or market situation needs to be constantly researched. Customer-driven companies are constantly listening to the voice of the customer and are continually striving to offer better value to their customers. LO 5

KEY TERMS

Cycle Time 479
Effectiveness 467
Efficiency 467
Emotional Communications 475
Form Utility 481
Increased-Productivity Approach 476
Lower-Margin Approach 476
Mass Customization 471
Re-engineering 479
Social Cause Marketing 475
Value Delivery 466

DISCUSSION QUESTIONS AND EXERCISES

1. Consider your own role as a customer of the following companies: (a) your supermarket, (b) your post office, (c) your dentist, and (d) the mail catalogue company you occasionally buy clothing from. For each of the company's products, reflect on your own needs, wants, and preferences when doing business. Identify what each company could do to offer you better marketing values, illustrating your answer for each specific market value you might desire.
2. Assume that you are the marketing director for a large chain of hotels. How will you ensure that you are delivering superior market values to your customers? Write your company president a memo outlining your plan of action to substantially enhance the market values your hotel chain is currently delivering to its customers. Now do the same exercise assuming that you are a house insurance agency. Consider all three roles.
3. Review Figure 13.5, Sample Questions for Measuring Customer Perceptions of Value Delivery Processes. The measures in the questionnaire are generic, and they may need adaptation (and wording change) for specific companies or product categories. Adapt these measures and design a questionnaire for use by (a) a bank, (b) a supermarket, and (c) a company selling office furniture and supplies to small home offices. *Note:* To ensure that the questionnaire makes sense, answer it yourself as a customer of these companies.
4. Is it possible to measure the usefulness of a company's various actions in delivering value to customers? What approaches are there for this purpose? Briefly explain each approach relating it to specific values.

NOTES

1 Banwari Mittal and Jagdish N. Sheth, *ValueSpace, Winning the Battle for the Market Leadership, Lesson from the World's Most Admired Companies* (McGraw Hill, 2001).

2 Robert B. Woodruff, "Customer Value: The Next Source of Competitive Advantage," *Journal of the Academy of Marketing Science* 25, no. 2 (Spring 1997): 139–53; Stanley F. Slater, "Developing a

Customer Value-Based Theory of the Firm," *Journal of the Academy of Marketing Science* 25, no. 2 (Spring 1997): 162–67.

3 Robert Jacobson and David A. Aaker, "The Strategic Role of Product Quality," *Journal of Marketing* 51 (October 1987): 31–44.

4 Michael Schrage, "Few Try to Imitate 3M's Successes," *Boston Globe*, October 11, 1992, 2.

5 Ernest Beck, "Populist Perrier? Nestle Pitches Bottled Water To World's Poor," *The Wall Street Journal*, June 18, 1999.

6 http://web4.insite2.gale.com/insite2/session/122/987/14641402w4/InSite2?Cmd=top&Code=&Dbav=CCDB_CHLT_CMGZ_CPNL_CBF_CBF_PRM,1997.

7 B. Joseph Pine II, Bart Victor, and Andrew C. Boynton, "Making Mass Customization Work," *Harvest Business Review*, September/October 1993.

8 Tom Richman, "Getting the Bugs Out," *Inc.* (June 1984): 61–64; Christopher W.L. Hart, "The Power of Unconditional Service Guarantees," *Harvard Business Review* (July–August 1988): 54–62.

9 http://www.medicard.com/canadian_stats.php.

10 Ellen Goodman, "The Ethics of Marketing Babies," *The Boston Globe*, April 13, 1989.

11 George S. Day and David B. Montgomery, "Diagnosing the Experience Curve," *Journal of Marketing* (Spring 1983): 44–83.

12 http://www.savers.com/charity.

13 "Productivity to the Rescue," *Business Week*, October 5, 1995, 134–36.

14 Robert D. Buzzell and Robert T. Gale, *The PIMS Principle Linking Strategy to Performance* (New York: The Free Press, 1987); R.G. Wakerly, "PIMS: A Tool for Developing Strategy," *Long-Range Planning*, June 1984, 92–97.

15 Christopher H. Lovelock and Charles B. Weinberg, "Columbia Plastics Division of Fraser Industries, Inc.," in *Marketing Challenges: Cases and Exercises* (McGraw Hill, 1993).

16 Office of the Privacy Commissioner of Canada, Fact Sheet, RFID Technology, http://www.privcom.gc.ca/fs-fi/02_05_d_28_e.asp.

17 Beyond Compliance: RFID Creates Value for SMBs, http://www.ibm.com/businesscenter/smb/ca/en/newsletterarticle/gcl_xmlid/36402/nav_id/index; Brian Christmas, "It's Wednesday. Do You Know Where Your Goods Are?" *The Globe and Mail*, November 2, 2005; "Wal-Mart to Expand RFID: Next January, 1000 Stores Will Be Able to Receive Tagged Products," *Knight Ridder Tribune Business News*, March 2, 2006, 1.

18 Office of the Privacy Commissioner of Canada, Fact Sheet, RFID Technology, http://www.privcom.gc.ca/fs-fi/02_05_d_28_e.asp.

19 William Wrennall, "Productivity: Reengineering for Competitiveness," *Industrial Engineering* 26, no. 12 (December 1994): 12 (3).

20 "Equipment Leasing Is a Wise Investment," *The Office* 118, no. 2 (August 1993): 18 (3).

21 Philip Kotler, *Marketing Management: Analysis, Planning, Implementation, and Control* 7e, (New York: Prentice-Hall, 1991): 701.

22 General Electric, *1990 Annual Report.*

23 Richard L. Oliver, Roland T. Rust, and Sajeev Varki, "Customer Delight: Foundations, Findings, and Managerial Insight," *Journal of Retailing* 73, no. 3 (1997): 311–36.

24 Banwari Mittal and Jagdish N. Sheth, *ValueSpace, Winning the Battle for the Market Leadership, Lesson from the World's Most Admired Companies* (McGraw Hill, 2001).

Glossary

A

Acculturation The process of learning a new culture.

Actual self A person's self-image of who he or she is.

Addressability A feature of a database wherein each customer's address is known in order to enable a marketer to address marketing communications individually on a one-on-one basis.

Adoption (of an innovation) Customer acceptance of an innovation for continued use.

Advocate sources Communication sources that have a vested point of view to advocate or promote.

Affect The feelings a person has toward an object or the emotions that object evokes for the person.

Affective choice mode (ACM) A decision mode wherein affect or liking for the brand results in a choice based not on attribute information, but on holistic judgments.

Affordability The possession of adequate economic resources needed to buy and use a product.

Aggressive personality A person who values personal accomplishment over friendship and seeks power and admiration from others.

Annual purchasing agreements Agreements made by government agencies with specific suppliers, which allow the governmental entity to purchase small items routinely.

Approach/avoidance motivation The human desire to attain a goal-object and to avoid an object of negative outcomes.

Arousal-seeking motive The drive to maintain the organism's stimulation at an optimal level.

Assimilation and contrast Information within the acceptance range is assimilated and accepted; information outside of this range is contrasted and rejected.

Assortment The number of different items a store carries.

Asymmetrical power One party has more power over the other.

Atmospherics The physical setting of the store that influences customer behaviour.

Atomistic family unit A person living alone.

Attitude hierarchy The sequence in which the three components of attitude—cognition, affect, conation—occur.

Attitude Learned predisposition to respond to an object or class of objects in a consistently favourable or unfavourable way.

Attitude molding Forming a new attitude or changing a preexisting attitude.

Attitude persistence After initial attitudes are formed through exposure to ads, the extent to which these initial attitudes persist over time until the actual purchase decision is made.

Attitude strength The degree of commitment one feels toward a cognition, feeling, or action.

Attitude valence The favourableness and unfavourableness of attitudes, i.e., of thoughts, feelings, and actions about an object.

Attitudinal brand loyalty A customer's consistent re-purchase of a brand due to his or her preference for it.

Attraction of alternatives How attractive a customer finds alternative brands to be.

Attribution motivation The innate human need to assign causes to events and behaviours.

Attributions Inferences that people draw about the causes of events and behaviours.

Authoritarian families Families where parents exercise strict authority over children; children learn to obey their elders in all matters.

Autonomous decisions Decisions that are made independently by the decision maker.

Autonomy One's power to control his or her own life.

Awareness set Brands that a customer is aware of.

B

Bargaining A method of conflict resolution, based on distributive justice for all, wherein the dissenting members negotiate a give and take.

Behavioural brand loyalty A customer's consistent re-purchase of a brand.

Behavioural compatibility The degree to which an innovation requires no change in existing behaviour.

Behaviourally anchored scales Measurement scales that use descriptions of specific behaviours, to which the respondents express their reactions.

Behaviourism theory The theory that a person develops a pattern of behavioural responses because of the rewards and punishments offered by his or her environment.

Beliefs Expectations that connect an object to an attribute or quality.

Biological determinism The belief that human behaviour is determined by biological factors such as genetics and DNA.

Borrowing power The anticipated level of income of a person (lifetime disposable income and asset accumulated through savings); a primary indicator, in addition to income and wealth, of a customer's economic condition.

Brand belief A thought about a specific property or quality associated with a brand.

Brand equity The enhancement in the perceived utility and desirability that a brand name confers on a product.

Brand loyalty A customer's commitment to buy and use a given brand repeatedly.

Brand parity The concept of how similar and mutually substitutable the brands are.

Brand valuation The financial worth of a brand name.

Business A licensed entity engaged in the business of making, buying, or selling products for profit or nonprofit objectives.

Business cycle A cycle of boom and recession experienced by the business world and caused by fluctuations in the economic environment.

Business markets Customers who buy products for use in the organizations they work for.

Buyclass Type of purchase need, in terms of its newness.

Buyer A person who participates in the procurement of the product.

Buyers' remorse The regret customers feel after buying a product because they are unsure if buying it was wise.

Buying centre All the members of a customer firm who play some role in the purchase decision.

Buy-side business models A buying organization using Internet-based technologies to buy from contracted suppliers.

Buy-to-browse ratios The proportion of customers who come to browse on the internet concluding the browsing by buying.

C

Central processing route Message content is attended to and scrutinized actively and thoughtfully.

Change agent A person or organization that brings about a planned social change.

Change targets People whose behaviour change agents attempt to alter.

Changing demographics Change in characteristics such as age, income, and geographic location of customers in a given market.

Classical conditioning The process in which a person learns an association between two stimuli due to their constant appearance as a pair.

Climate A component of the geophysical market environment, consisting of temperature, wind, humidity, and rainfall in an area that affects consumers' needs for food, clothing, and shelter.

Cocooning The habit of staying at home rather than going out.

Cognition A thought about an object.

Cognitive consistency The principle that a person desires consistency among all his or her beliefs or thoughts.

Cognitive dissonance A tension between two opposite thoughts, typically manifested after a customer has bought something but is uncertain whether a correct choice was made.

Cognitive learning The acquisition of new information from written or oral communication.

Collaborative filtering A computer program that allows the prediction of a person's preferences as a weighted sum of other people's similar preferences.

Commitment An enduring desire to continue a relationship, and to work to ensure its continuance.

Communicability The extent to which an innovation is socially visible, or the ease of communicating information about it in social groups.

Compensatory model A decision rule and process wherein a customer makes a choice by considering all of the attributes and benefits of a product and mentally trading off the alternative's perceived weakness on one or more attributes for its perceived strength on other attributes.

Competitive promotional activity Special price deals available on competing brands.

Complexity The amount of effort required to comprehend and manage the product during its acquisition.

Complexity of an innovation The difficulty in comprehending an innovation.

Compliance Steering customer behaviour by government regulation.

Compliant A personality trait with which a person acts in an agreeable manner to earn the acceptance and friendship of others.

Compulsive buying A chronic tendency to purchase products far in excess of one's needs and resources.

Compulsive consumption An uncontrolled and obsessive consumption of a product likely to ultimately cause harm to the consumer or others.

Conation The action a person wants to take toward an object.

Concept-oriented families Families that are concerned with the growth of independent thinking and individuality in children.

Concurrent protocols A record of respondent thoughts at the time of decision making.

Conditioned stimulus (CS) A stimulus to which a new response needs to be conditioned.

Conjunctive model A decision-making procedure wherein the customer examines all the alternatives in a set of attributes or evaluative criteria in order to identify an alternative that would meet minimum cutoff levels for each attribute.

Consideration set All the brands in a product category that a customer will consider assessing for purchase.

Consumer Another term for "customer," but in a household market.

Consumer behaviour odyssey A qualitative research project undertaken in the late 1980s in the United States that involved personal visits by an interdisciplinary team of academic consumer researchers to a variety of consumer sites.

Consumer socialization The acquisition of the knowledge, preferences, and skills to function in the marketplace.

Content-based filtering A recommendation for websites based on consumer preferences for product attributes.

Convenience sampling A method wherein a group of customers are recruited based on convenient availability.

Convenience value A saving in the amount of time and effort needed to acquire the product.

Co-production A situation wherein customers routinely provide direct input into the making of a product.

Corporate image The public perception of a corporation as a whole.

Corrective advertising Advertising whose message includes a correction of a previous deception.

Country-of-origin effects Bias in customer perceptions of products due to the country in which they are made.

Credit value Freedom from having to exchange cash at the time of purchase or from becoming liable for immediate payment.

Culture Everything a person learns and shares with members of a society, including ideas, norms, morals, values, knowledge, skills, technology, tools, material objects, and behaviour.

Customer A person or an organizational unit that plays a role in the consummation of a transaction with an organization.

Customer behaviour Mental and physical activities undertaken by customers that result in decisions and actions to pay for, buy, and use products.

Customer conversion ratio Proportion of website visitors who end up making a purchase.

Customer culture A culture that incorporates customer satisfaction as an integral part of the corporate mission and plans.

Customer decisions Decisions customers make in the marketplace as buyers, payers, and users.

Customer equity (goodwill) Customer support for a supplier's well-being.

Customer expectations Customers' economic outlook about the near future; this outlook shapes their spending.

Customer loyalty A customer's commitment to a brand, store, or supplier, based on a strong favourable attitude, and manifested in consistent re-patronage.

Customer militancy The behaviour of frustrated and dissatisfied customers entailing the taking of the law into their own hands.

Customer orientation Gaining a thorough understanding of customers' needs and wants, and using them as the basis for all of the firm's plans and actions in order to create satisfied customers.

Customer problem Any state of deprivation or discomfort or wanting (whether physical or psychological) felt by a person.

Customer satisfaction A positive feeling ensuing from a successful outcome of a market transaction.

Customer visits A research program wherein a marketing firm's managers visit customer firms to interview buyers as well as users of their product and to observe their product in use.

Customerization Under this strategy, the customer is involved in designing the product and supplies, with just a reasonable amount of prior information needed for a "build-to-order" production process designed to develop a product to best fit his or her needs.

Customization Receiving the product in a manner tailor-made to an individual customer's circumstances.

Customized data Data that is collected at the behest of a small group of pre-identified customers, and made available only to sponsoring companies.

Cycle time The total time it takes for the entire production and/or delivery task to be completed.

D

Deceptive advertising Advertising that has the capacity to deceive a considerable segment of the public.

Deep involvement A customer's extreme and ongoing interest in a product.

Democratic justice A family norm in which each family member is given a voice in family decisions.

Democratic families Families where every family member has an equal voice and self-expression, autonomy, and mature behaviour are encouraged among the children.

Demographics Easily verified, objective characteristics of a group of customers.

Descriptive beliefs An association in the customer mind that links an object or person to a quality or outcome.

Detached personality A person who is independent minded, entertains no obligations, and admits little social influence on personal choices.

Diagnosticity The ability to diagnose why certain attitudes are the way they are.

Diffusion process The spreading of an innovation's acceptance and use throughout a population.

Discretionary expenditures The purchase of goods and services to make life physically or psychologically more comfortable beyond sustenance.

Disguised-nonstructured technique A questionnaire design wherein the research purpose is not apparent to the customer, nor are the response categories provided.

Disguised-structured technique A questionnaire design wherein the real intent of the question is disguised, but the response categories are provided.

Disintermediation A practice in which the customer is able to transact directly with a firm without any intermediaries.

Disjunctive model A decision-making procedure that entails tradeoffs between aspects of choice alternatives.

Door-in-the-face strategy A strategy of eliciting a behaviour by first making a large request whose refusal is followed by a small request.

Drive An internal state of tension that produces actions purported to reduce that tension.

E

Ecological design A strategy of influencing behaviour by the design elements of the physical facility surrounding the customer.

Ecology Natural resources and the balance and interdependence among vegetation, animals, and humans.

Economy The state of a nation with respect to levels of employment, wages, inflation, interest rates, currency exchange rates, and aggregate household savings and disposable income.

Effectiveness How well a product meets the customer's needs and wants.

Efficiency How little it costs the customer in money, time, and physical effort to receive the value he or she seeks.

Ego The conscious mediator between the id and the superego.

Ego-defense function An attitude that is held to protect a person's ego.

Electronic data interchange (EDI) A computer-based link between a supplier and its business customer that transmits customer inventory data to the supplier and automates the reordering and shipping of the depleted product.

Elimination by aspects (EBA) A decision-making procedure wherein the customer examines all alternatives one attribute at a time in the ranked-order sequence with minimum cutoff attribute values.

Emotional communications Communications that evoke some emotional experience in the viewer or reader.

Emotional hierarchy of attitude A sequence of attitude components in which a person first feels an emotion toward an object, then acts on it, and then becomes knowledgeable about it.

Emotional value The enjoyment and emotional satisfaction users obtain from products.

Emotions The consciousness of the occurrence of some physiological arousal, followed by a behavioural response along with the appraised meaning of both.

Enculturation The process of learning one's own culture.

Enduring involvement The degree of interest a customer feels in a product on an ongoing basis.

Environmental marketing Marketing of products in a manner that attempts to minimize the damage to the environment.

Environmentally conscious A customer who actively seeks out products with minimal impact on the environment.

E-procurement A buying organization that uses Internet-based technologies to buy from contracted suppliers.

Evaluated new unplanned purchases Purchases of items for which the need had not been recognized prior to the purchase occasion.

Evaluative beliefs An association in the customer mind that links an object to personal likes or dislikes, preferences, and perceptions.

Evaluative consistency A process wherein the missing attribute is assumed in order to conform to the overall evaluation of the brand.

Evoked set Brands in a product category that the customer remembers at the time of decision making.

Exchanges Websites run by a third party to bring buyers and sellers together vertically within an industry sector or horizontally across industry sectors.

Expectations Prior beliefs about what something will possess or offer.

Experience goods Products that need to be personally experienced to judge their quality.

Experiential consumption The use of a product in which the process of use itself offers value.

Experiment A research method in which respondents are placed in a controlled situation, and then their response is observed or recorded.

Expertise Possessing knowledge about the innovation that is not yet common knowledge.

Exploratory shopping Just browsing around after collecting the planned items on the shopping list.

Extended problem solving (EPS) A product selection strategy wherein the customer engages in an extensive information search and prolonged deliberation in order to minimize the risk of a wrong choice.

External attributions Assigning the cause of someone's behaviour to situational demands or environmental constraints that were beyond the control of the individual.

External stimuli Marketplace information that causes problem recognition.

F

Family A group of persons related by blood and/or marriage.

Family life cycle concept The different stages a family goes through—starting from the time a person is young and single, to the time when he or she becomes a single solitary survivor.

Family relationship The degree of mutual respect and trust between parents and adult offspring, and the harmony of their relations and communication.

Festinger's Dissonance Theory Theory that two cognitions are in dissonance (i.e., in conflict): the cognition that the decision has been made and the cognition that the decision may not have been the best choice.

Financial well-being Financial products such as financial planning, wills and trusts, mutual funds and stocks, etc., acquire new significance in the lives of aging customers.

Financing value Offering the terms of payment more affordably by distributing the liability over an extended period of time.

Fishbein model Psychologist Martin Fishbein's formulation that attitude toward an object is the sum of the consequences of that object, weighted by the evaluation of those consequences.

Fishbein's extended model of behavioural intention Psychologist Martin Fishbein's formulation that a person's intent to engage in a behaviour is the weighted sum of his or her own attitude toward that behaviour, and others' expectations about he or she performing that behaviour.

Focus groups A research method wherein a small group of customers participate in a group discussion, steered by a moderator, on specified issues.

Foot-in-the-door strategy A strategy of eliciting a behaviour by first asking for a small favour whose acceptance is followed by a larger request.

Forced irrelevance An external environmental factor that renders prior solutions irrelevant.

Form utility Whereby performance value is built into the product by the manufacturer or the service designer.

Forward buying A practice wherein customers buy an item for future consumption.

G

Gender-role orientation The degree to which specific behaviours and norms are linked to a person's gender rather than being shared across genders.

Generation 'X' Persons born in the United States between 1965 and 1975.

Geographic redistribution Refers to the shift in population density from one region of a nation or world to another.

Geographical variation Different patterns of consumption in different regions.

Global sourcing A purchasing function that overcomes the limitations of geography and seeks suppliers all over.

Global warming The progressive warming of Earth's climate due to an increase in hydrocarbons in the atmosphere resulting from increased industrialization.

Goal-object Something in the external world whose acquisition will reduce the tension experienced by an organism.

Government Legal entities empowered to organize and govern a city, state, or nation.

Government policy A market context factor comprising monetary/fiscal policy and public policy.

Green consumer A customer concerned about the deteriorating environment and willing to modify his or her customer behaviour to save the environment.

Group traits Common biogenic categories such as race, gender, and age.

Groups Two or more persons sharing a common purpose.

H

Habit A learned sequence of responses to a previously encountered stimulus.

Habitual purchasing Simply repeating previous purchases.

Hedonic consumption The use of products for the sake of intrinsic enjoyment rather than to solve some problem in the physical environment.

Heider's balance theory The principle that a person will modify some of his or her beliefs to make them balanced or congruent with the rest of his or her beliefs.

Heuristics Quick rules of thumb and shortcuts used to make decisions.

Household A consumption unit of one or more persons, identified by a common location with an address.

Household markets Customers who buy products for their personal use.

I

Id A division of the human psyche that refers to the basic source of inner energy directed at avoiding pain and obtaining pleasure; it represents the unconscious drives and urges.

Ideal self A person's self-image of who he or she would like to be.

Ignorance paradox The tendency of less knowledgeable customers to seek less information rather than more.

Imitative behaviour The adoption of the behaviour of those whom a person admires or considers successful.

Imitators Those who adopt an innovation after observing others who have adopted it.

Importance of purchase How important a purchase is in the customer's life.

Impulse purchase The implementation of previously unplanned purchases, with purchase decisions made on the spur of the moment.

Increased productivity approach An approach in which a firm strives for a lower cost of production by raising productivity.

Index of consumer confidence A nationally tracked measure of economic pessimism/optimism felt by customers in Canada.

Individual traits Unique biogenic and psychogenic aspects of the individual customer.

Inference making Reaching a judgment about an object based on incomplete information.

Information board A table of information in which the cells contain the information about the extent to which the brand specified in the corresponding row contains the attribute specified in the corresponding column.

Information content The information contained in the stimulus that moves the perceptual process beyond sensation or stimulus selection toward organization and interpretation.

Information intensiveness continuum Signifies the levels of various types of information associated with products, with traditional products that are information-independent at one end and information-dependent products at the other end.

Information overload Customers are exposed to so much information that they are unable to process it to make a decision.

Information processing mode (IPM) A decision mode wherein the customer acquires, evaluates, and integrates information about brand attributes to arrive at an overall brand evaluation.

Information processing research A class of research whose focus is on studying the information customers process for reaching a decision.

Innovation A good, a service, or an idea that a customer perceives as new.

Innovators Customers who are the first ones to adopt an innovation.

Instant gratification The desire for an immediate satisfaction of a need or want.

Instant marketing Being ready to offer without delay a product when the customer wants it.

Institutions Relatively permanent groups with a pervasive and universal presence in a society, such as schools, religions, and the family.

Instrumental conditioning The learning of a response because it is instrumental to obtaining some reward.

Instrumentality of market values Products being instrumental in fulfilling needs or wants of customers.

Interattribute inference A process wherein the customer infers the value of one attribute based on another attribute.

Intergenerational influence (IGI) Influence of family members and the transmission of values, attitudes, and behaviours from one generation to another.

Internal attributions Ascribing the cause of someone's behaviour to personal dispositions, traits, abilities, or motivations and feelings.

Internal stimuli Perceived states of physical or psychological discomfort that cause problem recognition.

Interpretation A step in the perception process in which meaning is attached to the stimulus.

Interpretative research A method of research in which a researcher observes a group of consumers in their natural setting, and interprets their behaviour based on an extensive understanding of the social and cultural characteristics of that setting.

Involvement The degree of personal relevance of an object or a product to a customer.

J

Joint decisions Decisions wherein more than one decision maker participates.

Just noticeable difference (j.n.d.) The magnitude of change necessary for the change to be noticed.

K

Knowledge function The degree to which an object adds to a person's knowledge.

L

Laddering A research technique to identify means-end linkages.

Lead users Innovative users of a product who use it in ways that suggest how the product should be modified for better utility.

Learning Any change in the content of long-term memory.

Learning hierarchy A sequence of attitude components wherein a person thinks first, feels next, and acts last.

Level of adaptation The level at which a person develops adequate familiarity with a stimulus so that the stimulation is perceived as normal or average.

Lexicographic model A decision model wherein the available alternatives are compared in sequence by the rank-ordered attributes.

Life status change Major events in a customer's life that change his or her status or personal context.

Lifestyle retail brands Brands sold in retail stores that are sought by customers principally for symbolic value and meaning for their lifestyles.

Lifestyles The way a person lives.

Lifetime value The cumulative value a firm can obtain from a customer over his or her lifetime.

Limited problem solving (LPS) A product selection strategy wherein the customer invests a limited amount of time and energy in searching and evaluating alternative solutions.

Lower-margin approach Selling at a low-profit margin in order to attract customers.

Low-involvement attitude hierarchy A sequence of attitude components in a person's acquisition of attitude toward objects that are of low salience or importance.

M

Market mavens Individuals who possess information about markets and disseminate it to other customers.

Market orientation *See* Customer orientation.

Market values The benefits (tangible or intangible) a customer receives from a product.

Marketer sources Communication sources that act on behalf of the marketer of the product itself.

Marketing concept A firm focuses on making what the customer wants.

Marketing myopia A narrow vision wherein a firm views itself in limited, product-centered ways—as makers and sellers of products it produces and sells.

Maslow's hierarchy of needs Psychologist Abraham Maslow's theory that human needs and wants exist in a hierarchy so that higher-level needs are dormant until lower-level needs are satisfied.

Mass customization Tailoring the product to the customer's specific needs, without sacrificing the speed or cost efficiencies of conventional mass production methods.

Materialism The importance a consumer attaches to material possessions.

Maturation A self-perceived obsolescence of prior preferences.

Means-end chains Linkages between the product's physical features and customers' fundamental needs and values.

Mental budgeting The idea that customers mentally set aside budgets for product categories.

Mobile commerce The buying and selling of products with the aid of mobile phones.

Modelling The learning of a response by observing others.

Modified re-buy A purchase item that is similar to the previously purchased item, but entails some changes either in design/performance specifications or in the supply environment.

Moods Short-lived and less intensely felt emotions.

Motivation The state of drive or arousal that impels behaviour toward a goal-object.

Motivation research (MR) A research method directed at discovering the conscious or subconscious reasons that motivate a person's behaviour.

Multiattribute models of attitude A rule that suggests that overall attitude is formed on the basis of component beliefs about the object, weighted by the evaluation of those beliefs.

Mutual goals Those goals that require each exchange partner's cooperation and by whose achievement each partner profits.

N

National culture The culture prevalent in a nation.

Nature Biological factors; the premise that a person's genetic makeup determines human behaviour, such as emotions, sexual preference, tribalism, love of status, notions of beauty, sociability, creativity, and morality.

Necessary expenditures The purchase of products needed for minimal sustenance.

Need An unsatisfactory physical condition of the customer that leads him or her to take action to remedy that condition.

Need for cognition The human need for information and for understanding the world around us.

Negative cue An inference-making strategy wherein the customer simply treats the missing information as a negative cue, which then affects the overall judgment negatively.

Neglectful families Families having parents who remain distant from their children and neglect them.

Negligent consumer behaviour Customer behaviour that puts oneself or others at risk, or that would, in the long run, impose heavy costs on society.

Neo-Rich Persons who have recently become affluent.

Network A group of firms that deal with each other on a preferential basis.

Neutral marketplaces *See* Exchanges.

New task A purchase item new to the buying organization.

Nondisguised-nonstructured technique A technique in which the purpose of the study is not disguised; however, the customer response categories are not predetermined.

Nondisguised-structured technique A technique that makes the research purpose obvious and seeks responses along prespecified response categories.

Non-family household A household that does not contain a family.

Non-marketer sources Communication sources that are independent of marketer influence.

Normative beliefs invoke moral and ethical judgments in relation to someone's acts.

Norm of reciprocity An expectation that an act of favour or concession toward someone must be returned by a comparable act of favour.

Nuclear family unit A family comprising a married couple with children.

Nurture The familial and social environment; the premise that behaviour is determined by a person's upbringing, family life, parental values, peer group influences, school, and religious group.

O

Odd pricing The setting of prices just below the next round number.

One-stop shopping (OSS) The practice of acquiring all related products from one supplier.

Opinion leadership The giving of information and advice that is accepted by the recipient of the opinion.

Optimal level of stimulation The level at which balance is reached so that the person is neither bored nor overwhelmed by new experience.

Organization A process of stimulus categorization in which the sensed stimulus is matched with similar object categories in one's memory.

Other-brand averaging A process wherein the missing attribute value is assumed to be an average of its values across all other brands.

Outsourcing Procuring products that were once produced by the customer him/herself.

P

Partner-specific investments Investments that one party makes on processes dedicated to the other party.

Passive consumers Persons who are not consuming the product themselves but who, as bystanders, are being negatively affected by the consumption of others.

Payer A person who pays or finances the purchase.

Perceived justice Customers' perception that they were treated fairly during the conflict resolution process, and that the outcome itself was fair.

Perceived risk The degree of potential loss (i.e., amount at stake) in the event that a wrong choice is made.

Perceived risk of an innovation The uncertainty that the innovation might cause an unanticipated harm.

Perception The process by which an individual selects, organizes, and interprets the information received from his or her environment.

Perceptual and preference mapping An analytical technique for obtaining a visual map in a multi-dimensional space that shows consumer perceptions of similarity among and preference for various product alternatives.

Perceptual distortion In interpreting a stimulus, a person's prior beliefs interfere and distort the meaning to conform to those beliefs.

Perceptual threshold The minimum level or magnitude at which a stimulus begins to be sensed.

Performance risk The probability that the product may not perform as expected or desired, or that there may be physical side effects or unwanted consequences.

Performance value The quality of the physical outcome of using a product.

Peripheral processing route A message is interpreted cursorily by attending to its form rather than its content.

Permissive families Families wherein children are given relative independence in conducting their own affairs, especially in their adolescent years.

Personal safety The safety of one's own person from crime or harmful consumption.

Personal values Those that satisfy the *wants* of the customer.

Personality trait A consistent, characteristic way of behaving.

Persuasion A rational method of conflict resolution wherein some members persuade others by demonstrating how the other person's position will lead to a sub-optimal outcome.

Phased decision strategy A two-stage decision procedure wherein the alternatives are first eliminated, and then the remaining alternatives are compared for a final choice.

Planned purchases The purchases that a customer had planned to buy before entering the store.

Planned social change Active intervention by an agency with a conscious policy objective to bring about a change in some social or consumption behaviour among the members of a population.

Politicking A conflict resolution method wherein members form partisan coalitions and then "manage" the decision with behind-the-scenes maneuvering.

Popular culture The culture of the masses in a nation, with norms, rituals, and values that have a mass appeal.

Power dependence The relative dependence of one party on the other because of the resources the other party possesses.

Price value A fair price and other financial costs incurred when acquiring the product.

Pricing proposal A proposal made by a supplier to government, using a specific government form, certifying current cost and pricing data for each line item.

Primary demand Demand for the product category itself.

Primary emotions Basic human emotions that humans have acquired based on the evolutionary process.

Problem recognition A realization by the customer that he or she needs to purchase something to get back to the normal state of comfort—physically and psychologically.

Problem routinization Defining a decision problem so that no new decisions need to be made.

Problem solving A rational approach to conflict resolution wherein participants search for more information, and deliberate on the new information.

Process-induced affect Affect (i.e., feelings) that is generated when a customer processes information about a product.

Processing by attributes (PBA) The process of assessing brands wherein all the available brands are compared simultaneously for one attribute at a time.

Processing by brands (PBB) The process of assessing one brand entirely before moving on to the second brand.

Product A term that indicates either a good or a service, or both.

Proprietary data Data collected by private business firms that are in the business of collecting and marketing information of interest to a class of clients.

Protocols Customers' verbatim responses to certain information-processing tasks, often elicited by asking the respondent to speak his or her task-related thoughts aloud.

Psychographics Characteristics of individuals that describe them in terms of their psychological and behavioural makeup.

Psychology of complication The customer desire to redefine a problem so that decisions have to be made anew.

Purchase-decision involvement The degree of concern and caring that customers feel in a purchase decision.

Purposive behaviour The expending of energy to attain some goal-object.

Q

Qualitative research A method of gathering data wherein the respondent answers questions in his or her own words rather than being limited to preassigned response categories.

Quality cue A piece of information that can be used for making inferences about the quality of a product.

Quality of life A person's living condition measured by the absence of crime, traffic congestion, and pollution, and the opportunity for education, recreation, and general well-being.

Quantitative research A research method wherein a person's answers are obtained on a numerical scale.

R

Reciprocity The customer practice of buying from a supplier because he or she (the supplier) in turn buys something else from the customer.

Recreational needs A person's need for entertainment and recreation.

Re-engineering The redesign of business processes to make them more efficient.

Reference groups Persons, groups, and institutions that we look up to for guidance for our own behaviour and values.

Reference price The price customers expect to pay for a product.

Regional economic integration The realignment of nations into region-based economic blocs, such as the European Free Trade Association (EFTA).

Regional marketing The practice of adapting the marketing program according to customer diversity from one region to another.

Relationship-based buying The customer practice of limiting his or her choice to a single supplier.

Relative advantage The superiority of an innovation compared to the current product it will replace.

Request for proposal (RFP) A method of government procurement adopted for products that are new, complex, or entail large sums of money, and where negotiations are deemed necessary.

Restocking unplanned purchases Purchase of items that the shopper had not thought about buying at the time but uses regularly.

Retrospective protocols Respondents' reports of their thought processes about a decision made in the past.

Role formalness The degree to which interactions between the supplier and customer are limited to the formal roles of the parties.

Role specialization Dividing the customer roles (user, payer, and buyer) among individuals or groups.

Roommate families Families whose members structure their time, location, and activities independently of one another and with minimal sharing.

Rosenberg model Psychologist Milton Rosenberg's formulation that attitude toward an object is a function of the extent to which the object is instrumental in obtaining various values, weighted by the relative importance of those values.

Rote memorization The rehearsal of information until it gets firmly lodged in the long-term memory.

Routine problem solving (RPS) A product selection strategy wherein the customer considers no new information, and instead simply repeats previously made choices.

S

Satisficing The customer's (or decision maker's) acceptance of an alternative that he or she finds satisfying, rather than an arduous search for the most optimal alternative.

Schachter's two-factor theory Psychologist Stanley Schachter's theory that the experience of emotion depends on two factors: autonomic arousal and its cognitive interpretation.

Search goods Products whose features can be objectively assessed before the purchase.

Search strategy The pattern of information acquisition by customers to solve their decision problems.

Secondary demand Demand for a specific brand of product.

Secondary research An examination of secondary data to answer the questions that are of interest to the marketer.

Selective demand Demand for a specific brand of product.

Self-concept A person's image of oneself—who he or she is.

Self-perception theory The idea that people often infer their attitude by observing their own behaviour—thus making attitude an inference from behaviour rather than a cause of it.

Self-selection The idea that customers self-select themselves to be the customers of the firm that offers the advantage they seek.

Selling concept The firm focuses on persuading the customer to buy what it makes and offers.

Sell-side business models Online exchange sites run by a single supplier or distributor seeking buyers.

Sensation A step in the perception process in which the person attends to an object or an event in his or her environment with one or more of the five senses.

Sensory A stimulus characteristic that stimulates any of the five senses.

Service value The assistance customers seek in buying a product.

Shopbots Internet tools that allow comparison by price and product features, and across retailers.

Shopping motives The reasons customers have for visiting stores.

Simulation A research method wherein real-world conditions are created in a laboratory to study the behaviour of customers.

Single-source data The organization of both purchase incidence and consumer characteristics data in a single integrated record.

Situational involvement The degree of a person's interest in a specific situation or on a specific occasion.

Smart Bots *See* Shopbots.

Smart products Products that can communicate their "functioning status" to an outside agent or receive communication from an outside agent in order to adapt their function within predefined limits.

Social cause marketing Marketing programs that promote social causes.

Social class The relative standing of members of a society reflecting a status hierarchy.

Social marketing The application of the principles and tools of marketing for planned social change.

Social orientation families Families that are more concerned with maintaining discipline among children than promoting independent thinking.

Social risk The probability that a customer's significant others may not approve of the innovation adoption.

Social value The benefit of a product directed at satisfying a person's desire to gain social approval or admiration.

Stimulus Any object or event that a person perceives in his or her environment.

Store image The sum total of perceptions customers have about a store.

Store loyalty A customer's predominant patronage of a store, based on a favourable attitude.

Store visiting The practice of visiting various stores and shopping centres without necessarily having any plans to buy anything.

Straight re-buy A product that has been purchased before, and needs to be re-purchased without any modifications.

Subculture The culture of a group within the larger society.

Subjective norms A person's perception about what others expect from him or her.

Superego The moral side of the psyche, which reflects societal ideals.

Supplier-customer partnering Establishing a partnership-like relationship with one's supplier or with one's customer.

Switching costs Costs a customer would have to incur if he or she switched suppliers.

Syncratic decisions Decisions in which each family member plays an equal role.

Syndicated data Data that is of interest to a potentially large number of users, regularly collected by standardized procedures and made commercially available to all interested marketers.

Systematic search A comprehensive search and evaluation of alternatives.

T

Techno-consumers Consumers who derive consumption satisfaction merely from having been to a high-culture place.

Technology The use of machines and devices to facilitate a practical task.

Technophiles Customers who are deeply interested in technology.

Technophobes Customers who fear new technology.

Telematics The wave of the future whereby one's car, refrigerator, television, and medicine cabinets would be Internet-ready.

Test marketing A research method of testing a marketing mix on a limited market as a precursor to deciding whether to implement that mix in the entire market.

Thematic apperception test (TAT) A series of ambiguous pictures shown to respondents who are then asked to describe the story of which the picture is a part.

Time shift A period when nonwork-related activities may be pursued.

Time shortage The lack of free time.

Tolerance for ambiguity The degree to which a person remains free from anxiety in the face of uncertainty and lack of complete information.

Topography The terrain, altitude, and soil conditions of a location on Earth where customers buy and use a product.

Trait theory of personality The view of a person as a composite of several personality traits.

Transaction-specific investments (TSIs) Any special equipment or technology or human resources that need to be dedicated to meeting the needs of a particular customer/supplier partner.

Trialability The extent to which it is possible to try out an innovation on a small scale.

Trust A willingness to rely on the ability, integrity, and motivation of the other party to act in the best interests of the trusting party.

Trustworthiness The perceived benevolence and dependability of the opinion giver.

U

Unconditioned stimulus (UCS) A stimulus toward which a person already has a pre-existing specific response.

Universal values Product benefits that satisfy the *needs* of the customer.

Unplanned purchases Purchases that a customer did not intend to buy before entering the store.

Usage segmentation Segmenting the market based on the brand, product, and quantity customers use.

User A person who actually consumes or uses the product or receives the benefits of the service.

Utilitarian function An object's degree of usefulness.

V

Value compatibility The degree to which an innovation is free from contradicting a person's deeply held values.

Value delivery A firm fulfills a customer's need or want.

Value synergy Each value enhances the utility of another value.

Value-expressed function The degree to which an object helps express a customers' personal values and tastes.

Values The end states of life; the goals one lives for.

Values and lifestyles (VALS) A well-known psychographic segmentation scheme, widely in use, based on customer responses to a set of questions on their values and lifestyles.

Verbatim The recording of respondent answers exactly in their own words.

Verifiable benefit An advertising claim that can be verified by independent scientific tests.

Virtual reality An interactive, immersive, computer-generated 3D visual and sound display of stimuli and situations representative of their real (physical) versions.

Visual image profile A research technique to elicit the nonverbal response of customers by presenting them with visual images of human emotions to identify their own emotional experiences.

Voluntary simplicity A tendency to simplify life and adopt economic behaviours of low consumption and ecological responsibility.

W

Want An unsatisfactory psychological/social condition of the customer that leads him or her to take action to remedy that condition.

Weber's Law Named after the German Scientist Ernst Weber, the law states that the larger the base quantity, the larger the magnitude of change needed for being noticed.

Word association A research technique wherein the respondent is asked to state what associations are invoked by the presentation of each word in a set.

Z

Zaltman metaphor elicitation technique (ZMET) Consumer researcher Gerald Zaltman's patented research technique to help respondents identify and report the rich imagery they hold as a result of their experience in the consumption of a product.

Photo Credits

p. 2, © Jose Luise Pelaez, Inc.; p. 38, © WizData, Inc.; p. 96, © Losevsky Pavel; p. 126, © Stephen Coburn; p. 158, © PhotoCreate; p. 200, © 2007 JupiterImages and its Licensors. All Rights Reserved.; p. 233, © Serdar Yagci; p. 278, © Supirjono Suharjoto; p. 320, © Losevsky Pavel; p. 369, © 2007 JupiterImages and its Licensors. All Rights Reserved.; p. 396, © 2007 JupiterImages and its Licensors. All Rights Reserved.; p. 432, © Ingvald Kaldhussater; p. 465, © 2007 JupiterImages and its Licensors. All Rights Reserved.

Window on Research/Window on Practice Boxes: © PhotoAlto/SuperStock

Company Index

Name Index

Subject Index